FINAL CUT PRO 2024 GUIDE FOR BEGINNERS

BREIGITA STARTARE

Copyright © 2024 Breigita Startare
All rights reserved.

INTRODUCTION

In a world where video has become the dominant medium for storytelling, creativity, and communication, the ability to craft compelling narratives through visual media has never been more accessible—or more essential. At the heart of this revolution lies the power of video editing software, and for those seeking to harness their creative vision, few tools are as robust, versatile, and celebrated as Final Cut Pro.

For anyone stepping into the world of video editing, the journey often begins with a mix of excitement and intimidation. The possibilities feel endless, but so do the questions: How do I get started? What tools do I use? How do I make my ideas come to life on the screen? This is where the right guidance can make all the difference. Mastering Final Cut Pro is not just about learning how to click buttons or apply effects; it's about understanding the artistry and precision behind creating videos that resonate, inspire, and captivate audiences.

Final Cut Pro has long been recognized as a standard-bearer in the editing world, known for its seamless balance between professional-grade features and user-friendly design. It is equally cherished by indie filmmakers, YouTube creators, and seasoned professionals alike. Yet, as with any powerful tool, unlocking its full potential requires a foundation of knowledge and a willingness to experiment. This guide is designed to provide that foundation and offer a structured, approachable path to becoming proficient in video editing, no matter your starting point.

The beauty of Final Cut Pro lies in its intuitive interface and sophisticated capabilities, which cater to both beginners and experienced editors. From managing raw footage to delivering polished, professional-grade projects, the software encompasses every stage of the editing process. What sets it apart is its ability to grow with the user. Whether you're embarking on your first project or fine-tuning advanced techniques like multicam editing and color grading, this tool adapts to your creative needs and ambitions.

For beginners, the most daunting part of video editing is often the first step—opening the software and confronting the myriad of tools, panels, and options that seem to stretch endlessly. But this sense of overwhelm is short-lived once you grasp the basics. Through practice, you'll discover that the tools are not as complex as they initially appear, and each feature has been thoughtfully designed to streamline the editing process. The key is learning how to navigate the software effectively and understand what each function offers.

At its core, video editing is about storytelling. It's about taking raw footage and transforming it into a cohesive narrative or artistic expression. Final Cut Pro provides all the tools necessary to shape your vision, from organizing your media to crafting seamless transitions, fine-tuning audio, and applying cinematic effects. However, learning to wield these tools effectively is a journey, one that begins with mastering the essentials and gradually building confidence in more advanced techniques.

An essential part of becoming a skilled editor is understanding the workflow—how to approach a project from start to finish in a way that maximizes efficiency without stifling creativity. This begins with proper project setup, ensuring your footage and files are organized, and progresses to using the editing tools with precision. Along the way, you'll learn to employ creative enhancements like titles, effects, and transitions, as well as technical adjustments such as audio correction and color grading. Each step adds a layer of professionalism to your work and brings your vision closer to life.

Final Cut Pro also stands out for its emphasis on accessibility and flexibility. While it is loaded with professional-grade features, its layout and functionality are designed to be approachable for beginners. The software's keyboard shortcuts, drag-and-drop interface, and streamlined workflows are all geared toward helping users edit efficiently and intuitively. For those new to editing, these features reduce the learning curve, allowing you to focus on developing your creative skills rather than wrestling with technology.

As you gain confidence, you'll find yourself exploring Final Cut Pro's more advanced capabilities. Tools like multicam editing, audition clips, and precision trimming elevate your editing prowess, enabling you to handle complex projects with ease. The software's audio and color correction tools open new dimensions for crafting immersive, polished videos, while its integration with other platforms and applications ensures compatibility in diverse production environments. Whether you're creating content for personal enjoyment, professional endeavors, or social media, the flexibility of Final Cut Pro ensures that your work can meet the demands of any audience.

Video editing is as much about technical expertise as it is about creativity. The ability to see beyond the footage in front of you—to envision the final product and understand the steps to achieve it—is what separates a casual editor from a skilled creator. This guide is designed to help you develop both aspects. You'll not only learn the mechanics of Final Cut Pro but also cultivate the mindset and problem-solving skills necessary to navigate challenges and bring your creative ideas to fruition.

As the industry evolves, so too does the software, and Final Cut Pro remains at the forefront of innovation. Its support for immersive 360° video, seamless export options, and powerful tools for integrating with other applications reflect its commitment to empowering creators. Whether you're working on a passion project, a professional assignment, or experimenting with new formats, Final Cut Pro is equipped to meet the challenge.

This introduction to video editing is more than a technical tutorial; it's an invitation to explore a world of possibilities. The ability to edit videos is a skill that opens doors to storytelling, professional opportunities, and creative expression. The journey may feel overwhelming at first, but with practice and the right guidance, the tools become second nature, and the process becomes a rewarding outlet for your vision.

The chapters ahead are structured to take you step by step, breaking down the software's features into digestible, practical lessons. Along the way, you'll find tips, shortcuts, and insights to help you work smarter and more creatively. By the end of this guide, you'll not only feel comfortable navigating Final Cut Pro but also confident in your ability to produce videos that reflect your unique voice and vision.

For beginners, the key to success lies in persistence and curiosity. The more you explore, the more you'll discover, and the more confident you'll become. Final Cut Pro is a tool of boundless potential, and this guide aims to equip you with the knowledge and inspiration to make the most of it. As you embark on this journey, remember that every professional editor was once a beginner, and every masterpiece starts with a single frame.

CONTENTS

INTRODUCTION iii
CONTENTS vii

Chapter 1: Introducing to Final Cut Pro 1
Chapter 2: Keyboard shortcuts in Final Cut Pro 31
Chapter 3: Navigating the Basics of Final Cut Pro 33
Chapter 4: Setting Up Your First Project 45
Chapter 5: Exploring the Interface Layout 54
Chapter 6: Fundamental Editing Techniques 73
Chapter 7: Organizing Footage with Keywords 80
Chapter 8: Managing Clips: Selection, Ratings, and Search Tools 101
Chapter 9: Enhancing Projects with Titles and Effects 116
Chapter 10: Precision Editing with Trimming Tools 129
Chapter 11: Advanced Techniques - Multicam, Replacements, and Auditions 156
Chapter 12: Crafting Audio for Professional Results 178
Chapter 13: Fine-Tuning with Color Correction and Grading 220
Chapter 14: Adjusting Video Properties and Effects 246
Chapter 15: Seamless Transitions and Creative Retime Edits 282
Chapter 16: Preparing and Exporting Your Final Video 295
Chapter 17: Integrating with Other Applications and Platforms 313
Chapter 18: Editing Immersive 360° Videos 352
Chapter 19: Troubleshooting and Problem Solving 367

Conclusion 391

CHAPTER 1: INTRODUCING TO FINAL CUT PRO

I. WHAT IS FINAL CUT PRO?

Overview of Final Cut Pro

Final Cut Pro is a professional-grade video editing software developed by Apple Inc. It is renowned for its intuitive interface, powerful features, and seamless integration with Apple's ecosystem. Designed for everyone from beginners to seasoned professionals, Final Cut Pro allows users to create stunning videos, whether for personal projects, professional productions, or creative experiments.

Originally introduced in 1999, Final Cut Pro has evolved into a sophisticated non-linear editing (NLE) platform, offering tools for editing, color correction, audio design, and more. Its hallmark lies in its ability to combine advanced capabilities with user-friendly design, making it a go-to choice for filmmakers, YouTubers, and content creators alike.

Final Cut Pro's appeal extends beyond professionals, thanks to its streamlined workflow and ease of use. Whether you're crafting cinematic masterpieces or quick social media clips, Final Cut Pro empowers you to bring your vision to life.

Key Features and Capabilities

Final Cut Pro stands out in the crowded video editing software landscape because of its robust features and capabilities. Here are some of the most noteworthy:

1. **Magnetic Timeline**

    The Magnetic Timeline is a revolutionary editing feature that eliminates gaps and sync issues. It allows clips to snap together automatically, ensuring a seamless editing process. You can group clips, rearrange sequences, and experiment with layouts without worrying about disrupting the timeline structure.

2. **Optimized Performance** Final Cut Pro is optimized for macOS, leveraging the power of Apple Silicon chips. It delivers blazing-fast performance, even when working with high-resolution 4K or 8K footage. Background rendering ensures smoother playback and editing without delays.

3. **Advanced Color Grading** The software offers an intuitive color grading toolset, including color wheels, curves, and HDR support. Editors can achieve precise control over brightness, saturation, and hue, elevating the visual quality of their projects.

4. **Multicam Editing** Multicam editing in Final Cut Pro allows you to sync and edit footage from multiple cameras simultaneously. This feature is especially useful for interviews, live events, and productions requiring multiple perspectives.

5. **Motion Graphics and Effects** Final Cut Pro integrates seamlessly with Apple's Motion software, enabling users to create and apply custom motion graphics, titles, and transitions. The library of built-in effects and templates makes it easy to add polish to your videos.

6. **360° Video Editing** For creators working with immersive content, Final Cut Pro supports 360° video editing. It allows you to view and edit spherical videos in a VR headset or on-screen, providing tools to enhance and transform your footage.

7. **Audio Editing and Integration** The software includes advanced audio editing features like noise reduction, equalization, and surround sound mixing. You can also sync audio automatically with video clips, saving time and ensuring high-quality results.

8. **Seamless Collaboration** Final Cut Pro makes collaboration easier by supporting XML workflows and sharing options. Editors can work on shared

libraries or export projects for use in other post-production software.

9. **Export and Delivery Options** The program supports a wide range of output formats, including ProRes and H.264. Whether you need files for cinema, streaming platforms, or social media, Final Cut Pro offers tailored export settings.

Comparison with Other Video Editing Tools

While Final Cut Pro is an exceptional tool, it exists in a competitive field alongside Adobe Premiere Pro, DaVinci Resolve, and iMovie. Here's how it compares:

1. **Final Cut Pro vs. Adobe Premiere Pro**

    - **Performance**: Final Cut Pro is optimized for macOS, delivering superior speed and stability on Apple hardware. Premiere Pro, while powerful, can be resource-intensive and less stable on macOS.

    - **Subscription vs. Purchase**: Final Cut Pro requires a one-time purchase, making it more cost-effective in the long run. Premiere Pro operates on a subscription-based model, which may appeal to users needing Adobe's Creative Cloud suite.

    - **Interface**: Premiere Pro offers a traditional NLE interface, while Final Cut Pro's Magnetic Timeline simplifies editing for newer users.

2. **Final Cut Pro vs. DaVinci Resolve**

    - **Color Grading**: While Final Cut Pro provides robust color tools, DaVinci Resolve is widely regarded as the industry standard for color grading.

    - **Ease of Use**: Final Cut Pro is more accessible to beginners, whereas DaVinci Resolve has a steeper learning curve.

    - **Cost**: DaVinci Resolve offers a free version with limited features, but the paid version, Resolve Studio, competes directly with Final Cut Pro's pricing.

3. **Final Cut Pro vs. iMovie**

    - **Features**: Final Cut Pro offers professional-grade features absent in iMovie, such as multicam editing, advanced color grading, and motion graphics.

- **Target Audience**: iMovie caters to casual users and beginners, while Final Cut Pro is designed for serious enthusiasts and professionals.
- **Learning Curve**: While iMovie is simpler, Final Cut Pro provides scalability for those looking to advance their skills.

Final Cut Pro is a versatile and powerful video editing tool that caters to a wide range of users, from beginners to professionals. Its unique combination of ease of use, advanced features, and seamless integration with the Apple ecosystem makes it a standout choice for creators. Whether you're exploring video editing for the first time or looking to upgrade your workflow, Final Cut Pro offers the tools and capabilities needed to bring your creative vision to life.

II. THE EVOLUTION OF FINAL CUT PRO

A Brief History of Final Cut Pro

Final Cut Pro, often referred to as FCP, is a cornerstone in the world of video editing. Its journey began in the late 1990s when Macromedia developed the initial concept for a non-linear editing (NLE) software. Apple acquired the software in 1998, envisioning a cutting-edge tool that could transform video editing on its macOS platform. The first version, **Final Cut Pro 1.0**, was released in 1999, revolutionizing the video editing industry with its professional-grade features at an accessible price point.

From its inception, Final Cut Pro was designed to cater to both amateur and professional filmmakers, a market gap left by more complex and expensive alternatives like Avid Media Composer. Its intuitive interface, coupled with powerful editing tools, quickly gained popularity among video editors, independent filmmakers, and even Hollywood productions.

One of the most significant shifts in Final Cut Pro's history came in 2011 with the release of **Final Cut Pro X**. This update was a complete overhaul of the software, built from the ground up to leverage modern macOS technology. While the redesign initially received mixed reviews, it eventually became the standard for Apple's video editing suite, praised for its speed, innovative features, and streamlined workflows.

Key Milestones in Its Development

The evolution of Final Cut Pro is marked by several key milestones that highlight its growth and adaptability to the ever-changing demands of video editing:

1. **1999: The Birth of Final Cut Pro 1.0**

   Apple introduced Final Cut Pro as a professional editing tool at an affordable price. It quickly gained traction, becoming a go-to choice for independent filmmakers and small production studios.

2. **2002: Gaining Industry Recognition**

   Final Cut Pro won its first Emmy Award for Technical Excellence, cementing its status as a serious competitor to established industry giants.

3. **2005: Adoption in Major Productions**

   Final Cut Pro was used in the editing of the Academy Award-winning film *Cold Mountain*, marking its acceptance in Hollywood and high-budget projects.

4. **2007: Transition to Intel Macs**

   With the release of Final Cut Pro 6, Apple optimized the software for Intel-based Macs, significantly improving performance and enabling features like ProRes, a high-quality codec for post-production.

5. **2011: The Controversial Launch of Final Cut Pro X**

   Final Cut Pro X introduced a radical redesign, including the Magnetic Timeline, a modernized 64-bit architecture, and improved speed. However, the removal of several legacy features led to backlash from professional editors. Over time, updates reintroduced many of these features, winning back users.

6. **2016: Embracing 360° Video and VR**

   Final Cut Pro became one of the first mainstream NLEs to support 360° video editing, demonstrating Apple's commitment to emerging technologies like virtual reality (VR).

7. **2020: Optimized for Apple Silicon**

   The release of Apple's M1 chip brought unparalleled speed and performance enhancements to Final Cut Pro, enabling real-time editing of 8K video and faster rendering times.

8. **2024: Final Cut Pro 2024**

With the latest release, Final Cut Pro 2024 introduces groundbreaking features, including AI-driven editing tools, expanded cloud collaboration, and deeper integration with Apple's ecosystem. These updates aim to redefine professional video editing by merging innovation with simplicity.

Transition to Final Cut Pro 2024

The leap to **Final Cut Pro 2024** is a defining moment in the software's evolution, reflecting advancements in technology and shifts in user needs. This iteration focuses on harnessing the power of artificial intelligence, cloud computing, and Apple's cutting-edge hardware.

1. **AI-Driven Editing Tools**

    Final Cut Pro 2024 introduces AI-powered features to streamline repetitive tasks and enhance creativity. Tools like automatic scene detection, smart cropping, and AI-generated transitions help editors work faster without compromising quality.

2. **Cloud Collaboration**

    Recognizing the need for remote workflows, Final Cut Pro 2024 expands its cloud collaboration features. Editors can now work on shared projects in real time, whether they are across the room or across the globe. This feature integrates seamlessly with iCloud, ensuring secure storage and version tracking.

3. **Performance on Apple Silicon**

    Building on the success of M1 and M2 chips, Final Cut Pro 2024 is optimized for Apple's next-generation hardware. It leverages advanced GPUs for real-time rendering, supports HDR workflows, and handles 8K and 16K footage with ease, making it a powerhouse for demanding projects.

4. **User-Centric Interface Enhancements**

    The interface in Final Cut Pro 2024 has been refined to balance power and simplicity. Customizable workspaces, context-sensitive tools, and improved search functions make it more accessible for beginners while remaining robust for professionals.

5. **Integration with the Apple Ecosystem**

    True to its roots, Final Cut Pro 2024 deepens its integration with Apple's ecosystem. Features like AirDrop for projects, Handoff between iPad and Mac, and seamless transitions between Motion and Logic Pro enhance productivity and convenience.

6. **Emphasis on Sustainability**

   In alignment with Apple's sustainability goals, Final Cut Pro 2024 introduces energy-efficient rendering processes and reduced carbon footprints during export workflows. This commitment aligns with the growing demand for eco-conscious production tools.

The evolution of Final Cut Pro exemplifies Apple's dedication to innovation and excellence in video editing. From its early days as a disruptor in the industry to its current status as a leader in professional editing, Final Cut Pro has consistently adapted to technological advancements and user demands. With the release of Final Cut Pro 2024, the software sets a new standard in video editing by combining AI, cloud capabilities, and performance optimization. As it continues to grow, Final Cut Pro remains a vital tool for creators, pushing the boundaries of what is possible in video production.

III. SUBSCRIPTION AND PRICING

Understanding the pricing structure of Final Cut Pro is essential for determining whether it fits your budget and needs as a video editor. Apple's approach to pricing has evolved over the years, balancing value with accessibility for a wide range of users, from casual hobbyists to seasoned professionals. This section will delve into the key aspects of Final Cut Pro's pricing, including its one-time purchase model, subscription alternatives, and available discounts.

Final Cut Pro Pricing Overview

Final Cut Pro is widely recognized for offering professional-grade video editing tools at a competitive price. Unlike many of its competitors, which operate on a subscription-based model, Final Cut Pro follows a one-time purchase structure.

The current price for Final Cut Pro is **$299.99**, which provides lifetime access to the software, including updates. This pricing model has positioned Final Cut Pro as an attractive option for users looking to avoid the recurring costs associated with subscription-based software like Adobe Premiere Pro. Moreover, once you purchase Final Cut Pro, you can install it on multiple Macs associated with the same Apple ID, making it a cost-effective solution for teams or individuals with multiple devices.

Key features included in the one-time purchase:

- Access to all tools and features, with no limitations.
- Compatibility with Apple's latest hardware and macOS updates.
- Regular software updates at no additional cost.

Subscription vs. One-Time Purchase Options

The debate between subscription-based software and one-time purchase models is significant in the video editing industry. Each option has its advantages, and the choice depends on the user's priorities, budget, and editing needs.

One-Time Purchase Advantages

Final Cut Pro's one-time purchase model offers several benefits:

1. **Cost-Effectiveness:** Over the long term, paying $299.99 upfront is often cheaper than an ongoing subscription.
2. **No Recurring Payments:** Users do not need to worry about monthly or yearly fees.
3. **Lifetime Updates:** Unlike some competitors, Final Cut Pro includes updates without requiring additional purchases.

Subscription-Based Alternatives

While Final Cut Pro does not currently offer a subscription model, it competes directly with Adobe Premiere Pro, which operates on a subscription basis as part of Adobe Creative Cloud. Premiere Pro's pricing starts at **$20.99/month** for individuals, totaling over $250 annually. For access to the full Creative Cloud suite, the cost increases to **$54.99/month** or over $600 per year.

Key Benefits of Subscription-Based Models:

- Access to a broad suite of tools and apps.
- Easier for short-term projects or users who prefer lower upfront costs.
- Continuous updates as part of the subscription plan.

Why Final Cut Pro Stands Out

Final Cut Pro's pricing model appeals to users who prefer to avoid recurring payments and have consistent access to a professional editing suite without worrying about losing features if they cancel their subscription. It's particularly attractive for independent creators, small businesses, and educators seeking a predictable investment.

Discounts and Educational Pricing

Apple recognizes the needs of students, educators, and institutions, offering significant discounts on Final Cut Pro as part of its educational pricing program. This initiative is designed to make professional tools more accessible to the next generation of creators.

Educational Discount Bundle

For eligible students and educators, Final Cut Pro is available as part of the **Pro Apps Bundle for Education**. Priced at **$199.99**, this bundle includes:

- Final Cut Pro
- Motion (a motion graphics and animation tool)
- Compressor (an encoding and delivery tool)
- Logic Pro (a professional audio editing suite)
- MainStage (a live performance tool for musicians)

This bundle offers incredible value, providing all five professional applications for less than the standalone cost of Final Cut Pro.

Eligibility Requirements:

- Must be a student enrolled in a degree-granting institution or an educator at a K-12 or higher education institution.
- Proof of eligibility, such as a valid student ID, may be required.

Free Trial

For users hesitant to make a purchase, Apple provides a **90-day free trial** of Final Cut Pro. This trial includes full access to the software, enabling users to explore its features and determine whether it meets their needs before committing to the purchase.

Periodic Discounts

While Final Cut Pro's one-time price rarely changes, Apple occasionally offers promotional discounts or bundles, particularly around major product launches or events like Back to School sales. Monitoring these promotions can provide additional savings.

Long-Term Value of Final Cut Pro

Final Cut Pro's pricing model is designed with long-term value in mind. While the initial investment may seem higher compared to subscription-based competitors, the absence of recurring fees and the inclusion of free updates make it a cost-effective solution over time.

For example:

- Over five years, the cost of Final Cut Pro remains $299.99.
- By contrast, Adobe Premiere Pro's subscription cost (at $20.99/month) amounts to over $1,250 in the same period.

This substantial cost difference highlights the value Final Cut Pro offers to users seeking a professional-grade tool without the burden of ongoing expenses.

Final Cut Pro's subscription and pricing model reflects Apple's commitment to delivering professional video editing tools at a competitive and accessible price point. The one-time purchase structure, combined with options like the educational bundle and free trial, ensures that creators of all levels have the opportunity to experience its powerful features. Whether you're a student, an independent creator, or a seasoned professional, Final Cut Pro offers exceptional value, making it a leading choice in the world of video editing software.

IV. CREATING AN ACCOUNT AND LOGGING IN

To start using Final Cut Pro, you'll need an Apple ID, which serves as your gateway to downloading the software, managing your subscription (if applicable), and accessing updates. In this section, we'll cover the essential steps to set up an Apple ID, link it to Final Cut Pro, and handle your account effectively.

Setting Up an Apple ID

Your Apple ID is a unique account used across Apple's ecosystem, including the App Store, iCloud, and Final Cut Pro. If you don't already have one, creating an Apple ID is a straightforward process:

1. **Visit Apple's Website or Open the App Store**
    - On your Mac, open the App Store or navigate to Apple ID Account in your browser.
    - Alternatively, you can create an Apple ID during the initial setup of your Mac or iPhone.

2. **Fill in Your Details**
    - Provide basic information such as your name, email address, and a secure password.
    - Choose security questions and answers to protect your account.

3. **Verify Your Email Address**
    - Apple will send a verification code to the email address you provided. Enter this code to activate your account.

4. **Enable Two-Factor Authentication (Optional)**
    - For added security, enable two-factor authentication. This step ensures only you can access your account, even if someone knows your password.
    - To activate, go to **System Preferences > Apple ID > Password & Security** and follow the prompts.

5. **Complete Your Profile**
    - Add billing information if you plan to purchase Final Cut Pro or other apps. You can use a credit card, PayPal, or Apple Gift Card balance.

Your Apple ID is now ready, granting you access to Apple's services, including downloading Final Cut Pro.

Linking Your Account to Final Cut Pro

Once your Apple ID is set up, linking it to Final Cut Pro is the next step. This ensures that your license is associated with your Apple account, allowing you to download, update, and reinstall the software as needed.

1. **Purchase or Download Final Cut Pro**
    - Open the **App Store** on your Mac.

- Search for "Final Cut Pro" in the search bar.
- Click the **Buy** or **Download** button. You'll be prompted to sign in with your Apple ID to complete the purchase or download.

2. **Verify Ownership**
   - After purchase, Final Cut Pro is linked to your Apple ID.
   - This linkage ensures that updates and reinstallations are free as long as you use the same Apple ID.

3. **Check Licensing Status**
   - To confirm that Final Cut Pro is associated with your account, go to the App Store, click on your profile picture, and check your purchased apps.

4. **Syncing Across Devices**
   - If you own multiple Macs, you can install Final Cut Pro on all of them using the same Apple ID. Open the App Store on each device, sign in, and download the app from your purchase history.

Logging In and Managing Your Subscription

Logging into Final Cut Pro is simple, as the app uses your Apple ID credentials for authentication. Here's how to log in and manage your account effectively:

1. **Logging In**
   - Once Final Cut Pro is downloaded and installed, launch the application.
   - If prompted, enter your Apple ID and password to authenticate your access.
   - You may also need to sign in when downloading updates or accessing shared libraries via iCloud.

2. **Managing Your Account**
   - To manage your Apple ID settings or subscription, open **System Preferences** on your Mac and click **Apple ID**.
   - Here, you can view account details, update your payment method, and

check storage usage if you're using iCloud with your Final Cut Pro projects.

3. **Subscription-Free Model**
   - Final Cut Pro operates on a one-time purchase model, meaning there's no recurring subscription to manage.
   - If you purchased Final Cut Pro as part of the Pro Apps Bundle for Education, your account will also reflect ownership of related apps like Motion and Compressor.

4. **iCloud Integration for Projects**
   - Linking your Apple ID to iCloud allows you to store Final Cut Pro libraries and media files in the cloud.
   - To enable this feature, go to **System Preferences > Apple ID > iCloud**, and ensure "iCloud Drive" is checked. Then, in Final Cut Pro, set your library location to iCloud.

5. **Troubleshooting Login Issues**
   - If you encounter problems signing in, ensure your Apple ID and password are correct. Reset your password if necessary via Apple's Account Recovery.
   - For issues related to app purchases, contact Apple Support or check your purchase history in the App Store.

Tips for Managing Your Final Cut Pro Account

- **Backup Your Credentials:** Save your Apple ID login information securely to avoid losing access to your account.

- **Use iCloud for Collaboration:** If you're working with a team, iCloud can be a powerful tool for sharing libraries and collaborating in real time.

- **Stay Updated:** Regularly update Final Cut Pro to access the latest features and security enhancements. Updates are free for all users with a valid Apple ID linked to the purchase.

- **Monitor Device Limitations:** While you can install Final Cut Pro on multiple Macs, ensure that all devices are signed in with the same Apple ID.

Creating an account, linking it to Final Cut Pro, and logging in are essential steps in getting started with this powerful video editing software. Apple's seamless integration of the Apple ID ensures that you can easily purchase, manage, and update Final Cut Pro across devices. By following these steps, you'll not only gain access to one of the industry's most advanced editing tools but also enjoy the benefits of a secure and user-friendly account management system.

V. INSTALLATION AND INITIAL SETUP

Getting started with Final Cut Pro begins with downloading, installing, and optimizing the software for your Mac. This guide walks you through the entire process, from verifying system compatibility to fine-tuning preferences for the best performance.

How to Download and Install Final Cut Pro

Installing Final Cut Pro is a straightforward process, thanks to its availability through the Mac App Store. Here's a step-by-step guide:

1. **Purchase or Access the App Store**
    - Open the **App Store** on your Mac.
    - Search for "Final Cut Pro" using the search bar.

2. **Purchase or Download**
    - If you're buying Final Cut Pro for the first time, click the **Buy** button. You'll need to sign in with your Apple ID and confirm payment. The price is $299.99 unless you are eligible for an educational bundle discount.
    - If you already own the software, simply click the **Download** button to install it on your current Mac.

3. **Start the Installation**
    - Once the download begins, it may take some time depending on your internet speed. The app is large, so ensure you have a stable connection.
    - Final Cut Pro will automatically install itself after the download is complete. You can find it in the **Applications** folder or the Launchpad.

4. **Activate Final Cut Pro**
   - Launch the app for the first time. It may prompt you to sign in with your Apple ID to verify the purchase. Enter your credentials to activate the software.

5. **Update to the Latest Version**
   - After installation, check for updates to ensure you have the latest features and performance enhancements. Open the App Store, go to your profile, and look for updates under purchased apps.

System Requirements and Compatibility

Before installing Final Cut Pro, it's crucial to confirm that your Mac meets the system requirements to ensure smooth performance.

1. **Hardware Requirements**
   - **Processor**: Final Cut Pro runs optimally on Macs with an Apple Silicon chip (M1 or M2). It also works on Intel-based Macs with at least a quad-core processor.
   - **Memory**: A minimum of **8GB RAM** is required, but **16GB or more** is recommended for 4K editing and complex projects.
   - **Graphics**: Final Cut Pro requires a GPU that supports Metal for accelerated rendering.
   - **Storage**: At least **4GB of available disk space** for installation. Additional space is needed for media and project files.

2. **Software Requirements**
   - **Operating System**: Final Cut Pro 2024 requires macOS **Monterey (12.5)** or later. Updating to the latest macOS version is recommended to leverage performance improvements.

3. **Additional Considerations**
   - For 360° video editing and advanced features, ensure your Mac has the hardware capacity to handle intensive tasks.
   - Check your external devices like storage drives and cameras for compatibility with Final Cut Pro.

4. **Testing System Performance**
   - Run a benchmark test after installation to gauge how your Mac handles high-resolution editing. Use sample projects to test rendering times and playback quality.

Setting Up Preferences for Optimal Performance

After installing Final Cut Pro, configuring your preferences can significantly enhance your editing experience. This step ensures the software is tailored to your workflow and maximizes your Mac's performance.

1. **Set Up Project Libraries and Locations**
   - Open Final Cut Pro and create a new project library.
   - Choose a storage location for your library that has ample space and fast read/write speeds, such as an external SSD. This minimizes lag and reduces strain on your system's internal storage.

2. **Adjust Playback Settings**
   - Navigate to **Preferences > Playback** and configure settings based on your workflow:
     - Enable **Better Performance** for smoother playback during editing, especially with high-resolution footage.
     - Use **High Quality** mode for final previews and exports.

3. **Optimize Rendering and Background Tasks**
   - Go to **Preferences > Playback** and adjust rendering settings:
     - Enable **Background Rendering** to save time by automatically rendering while you edit.
     - Set the render format to **ProRes 422** for a balance between quality and file size.
     - Reduce the interval for rendering to prevent large processing queues.

4. **Customize Keyboard Shortcuts**
   - Access **Final Cut Pro > Commands > Customize** to set up shortcuts

that align with your editing style. This customization improves efficiency and speeds up repetitive tasks.

5. **Configure Import Settings**
    - Navigate to **Preferences > Import** to manage how media is handled:
        - Enable **Create Optimized Media** for smoother editing with large files.
        - Use **Leave Files in Place** if you want to reference original files without copying them into the library.

6. **Set Color Correction Defaults**
    - For advanced users, configure default settings for color grading and HDR workflows under **Preferences > Color**. This ensures consistency across projects.

7. **Fine-Tune Audio Preferences**
    - Adjust audio settings under **Preferences > Audio**:
        - Enable automatic synchronization for audio and video clips.
        - Set your default output device to external speakers or headphones for precise sound monitoring.

8. **Enable iCloud Sync for Libraries**
    - If you use multiple Macs or collaborate with others, enable iCloud syncing for your project libraries. This feature ensures that changes are updated across all devices.

9. **Test Performance Settings**
    - Start a small project to test your preferences. Monitor playback quality, rendering times, and system resource usage to identify any necessary adjustments.

Pro Tips for Optimal Setup

- **Use External Storage**: For large projects, an external SSD is ideal for fast data transfer and freeing up internal storage.
- **Maximize GPU Usage**: If your Mac has a discrete GPU, ensure it's fully

utilized by checking **Activity Monitor** during editing.

- **Monitor Thermal Performance**: Use tools like Macs Fan Control to prevent overheating during extended editing sessions.
- **Regular Maintenance**: Clear cache files and optimize your library regularly to keep Final Cut Pro running efficiently.

Installing and setting up Final Cut Pro is a straightforward process that becomes even more rewarding with the right optimizations. By ensuring your system meets compatibility requirements and configuring the software's preferences, you'll set yourself up for a seamless editing experience. Whether you're editing home videos or professional productions, these steps provide a strong foundation for creative success.

VI. SMART STUDY TECHNIQUES FOR FINAL CUT PRO

Learning Final Cut Pro can seem daunting at first, but with the right strategies, you can quickly become proficient in this powerful video editing software. Smart study techniques, combined with the wealth of resources available, can significantly accelerate your learning journey. This guide outlines effective methods to learn Final Cut Pro, including leveraging tutorials, using the help menu and forums, and practicing with sample projects and templates.

Learning Resources: Tutorials, Guides, and Courses

A structured approach to learning Final Cut Pro begins with utilizing the wealth of tutorials, guides, and online courses available. These resources cater to a wide range of skill levels, from beginners to advanced editors.

1. **Official Apple Tutorials and Documentation**
    - Apple provides a comprehensive user guide and tutorial videos on its website. These resources are free and cover every aspect of Final Cut Pro, from basic editing to advanced features like multicam editing and color grading.
    - Explore Apple's Final Cut Pro Support Page to access official guides and documentation.

2. **YouTube Tutorials**
    - YouTube is an excellent platform for learning Final Cut Pro through video tutorials. Many creators offer step-by-step instructions on

specific tasks, such as adding transitions, working with audio, or color grading.

- Popular channels like Peter McKinnon, Justin Odisho, and Ripple Training specialize in Final Cut Pro content and frequently share beginner-friendly videos.

3. **Online Courses**

    - Platforms like Udemy, Skillshare, and LinkedIn Learning offer structured Final Cut Pro courses. These courses often provide lifetime access to lessons and allow you to learn at your own pace.

    - Examples include:
        - *Final Cut Pro X: Beginner to Intermediate* on Udemy.
        - *Video Editing in Final Cut Pro* on Skillshare.

4. **Books and eBooks**

    - Books like *Apple Pro Training Series: Final Cut Pro X 10.4* by Brendan Boykin provide in-depth knowledge and are great for those who prefer text-based learning.

    - Many of these books include practical exercises and downloadable media files.

5. **Workshops and Webinars**

    - Look for live workshops or webinars conducted by professional editors or training centers. These sessions often include interactive elements, enabling you to ask questions and receive real-time feedback.

Leveraging the Help Menu and Community Forums

Final Cut Pro includes built-in tools and access to online communities that can provide instant assistance and foster collaborative learning.

1. **Help Menu**

    - The built-in **Help Menu** in Final Cut Pro is an invaluable resource. Access it by clicking **Help** in the top menu bar and selecting **Final Cut Pro Help**.

    - Features include:

- Search functionality for specific topics.
- Detailed explanations of features, tools, and workflows.
- Step-by-step instructions for common tasks.

2. **Apple's Support Communities**
    - Apple hosts an official Final Cut Pro Support Community where users can post questions and share knowledge.
    - This forum is a goldmine for troubleshooting, tips, and exploring advanced techniques.

3. **Third-Party Forums and Communities**
    - Join forums like **Creative COW**, **Reddit's r/FinalCutPro**, or **VideoHelp** to interact with a broader community of editors.
    - These platforms are great for discovering creative solutions, exploring plugin recommendations, and networking with other users.

4. **Social Media Groups**
    - Platforms like Facebook and LinkedIn host groups dedicated to Final Cut Pro enthusiasts and professionals. These groups often share tutorials, case studies, and discussions about the latest updates.

5. **FAQ Sections and Troubleshooting Guides**
    - Frequently check Apple's FAQ section or community-sourced troubleshooting guides to resolve technical issues or understand specific features better.

Practicing with Sample Projects and Templates

Hands-on practice is one of the most effective ways to learn Final Cut Pro. Using sample projects and templates allows you to experiment with features, tools, and workflows without the pressure of creating from scratch.

1. **Download Sample Projects**
    - Apple and third-party training resources often provide sample project files. These files come with preloaded media and organized timelines, allowing you to practice editing, color correction, and transitions.

- Explore the Apple Pro Training Series, which includes downloadable sample projects aligned with their lessons.

2. **Explore Built-In Templates**
    - Final Cut Pro includes built-in templates for titles, transitions, and effects. Experimenting with these tools helps you understand how to enhance the visual and aesthetic quality of your videos.
    - Access templates via the **Titles and Generators Sidebar** in the Final Cut Pro interface.

3. **Create Your Own Practice Projects**
    - Import free stock footage and audio from websites like Pexels, Unsplash, or Freesound. Use these assets to experiment with different editing techniques and tools.
    - Try recreating a scene from your favorite movie or YouTube video to hone your skills.

4. **Experiment with Tools and Effects**
    - Dedicate time to learning individual features, such as color grading, keyframing, or audio editing. Create mini-projects focused on each tool to master them step by step.
    - Use the Magnetic Timeline to practice arranging clips and adjusting transitions seamlessly.

5. **Save and Analyze Your Work**
    - After completing a practice project, review your work critically to identify areas for improvement.
    - Compare your edits to professional examples and make adjustments to refine your techniques.

Pro Tips for Effective Learning

- **Set Achievable Goals**: Focus on mastering one feature or tool at a time instead of overwhelming yourself with the entire software.
- **Track Your Progress**: Keep a journal or document noting what you've learned and what areas you want to improve.

- **Seek Feedback**: Share your work with peers, instructors, or online communities for constructive criticism.
- **Stay Updated**: Keep an eye on updates and new features introduced in Final Cut Pro, as they may streamline your workflow or introduce exciting possibilities.

By combining tutorials, community resources, and hands-on practice, you can learn Final Cut Pro efficiently and effectively. Utilize structured learning materials to build foundational skills, explore community forums for collaborative problem-solving, and practice with sample projects to solidify your knowledge. With consistent effort and the right tools, mastering Final Cut Pro becomes a rewarding and achievable goal.

VII. THE RIGHT MINDSET FOR LEARNING FINAL CUT PRO

Learning Final Cut Pro requires more than just technical knowledge; it demands the right mindset. Success in mastering this powerful video editing tool hinges on your approach to learning, your patience and creativity, your dedication to continuous improvement, and your ability to stay updated with its ever-evolving features. Here's how to cultivate the mindset needed for a successful Final Cut Pro journey.

Developing Patience and Creativity

Patience and creativity are foundational traits for video editors, especially those learning a complex software like Final Cut Pro.

1. **Patience is Key**
    - **Mastering the Learning Curve**: Final Cut Pro's interface, tools, and features may seem overwhelming at first, but it's essential to embrace the learning process. Break down your learning into manageable chunks, focusing on one tool or technique at a time.
    - **Repetition Builds Proficiency**: Editing requires trial and error. Whether it's trimming a clip, syncing audio, or applying effects, don't be discouraged by mistakes. Each error teaches you what works and what doesn't.
    - **Setting Realistic Expectations**: Understand that it takes time to become proficient. Celebrate small victories, such as successfully using the Magnetic Timeline or mastering a new effect.

2. **Unleashing Creativity**
    - **Think Like a Storyteller**: Editing isn't just about cutting footage; it's about crafting a narrative. Ask yourself how each cut, transition, or effect serves the story you're telling.
    - **Experiment Fearlessly**: Final Cut Pro offers a wealth of tools, effects, and features. Dedicate time to exploring them. Experiment with color grading, transitions, and motion graphics without fear of making mistakes.
    - **Draw Inspiration from Others**: Watch professional videos, movies, or YouTube creators who use Final Cut Pro. Analyze their editing choices and try to replicate techniques to build your own creative toolkit.
3. **Balance Patience and Creativity**
    - Patience and creativity go hand in hand. Patience allows you to learn the technical aspects, while creativity inspires you to use those skills to produce something unique and compelling.

Building a Habit of Continuous Improvement

To master Final Cut Pro, you need to cultivate a mindset of ongoing growth. Video editing is an art and skill that evolves over time, and committing to continuous improvement will ensure you stay ahead.

1. **Set Specific Goals**
    - Define what you want to achieve with Final Cut Pro, whether it's creating professional videos, enhancing personal projects, or learning for fun.
    - Break your goals into smaller milestones, like mastering the basics of the timeline, learning color correction, or improving audio editing skills.
2. **Practice Regularly**
    - Consistent practice is the key to improvement. Set aside time each week to work on small projects or explore specific tools.
    - Use practice sessions to refine your workflow and discover shortcuts that save time.
3. **Seek Feedback**

- Share your work with peers, instructors, or online communities for constructive criticism. Fresh perspectives can provide valuable insights into areas you might overlook.
- Learn to accept feedback with an open mind and use it to grow.

4. **Learn from Mistakes**
    - Mistakes are inevitable, but they're also opportunities to learn. Whether it's an improperly rendered file or a mismatched audio track, analyzing and fixing errors will deepen your understanding of the software.

5. **Stay Curious**
    - Push your boundaries by experimenting with features you haven't used before. If you've mastered basic editing, try multicam editing or work on a 360° video.
    - Explore third-party plugins and integrations to expand Final Cut Pro's capabilities.

Staying Updated with New Features

Final Cut Pro is constantly evolving, with Apple regularly introducing updates that enhance performance and add new features. Staying informed about these changes ensures you can leverage the latest tools and workflows.

1. **Monitor Software Updates**
    - Check for updates regularly in the **App Store**. Apple's updates often include new features, bug fixes, and optimizations that improve performance.
    - Review the release notes for each update to understand what's new and how it impacts your projects.

2. **Follow Official Channels**
    - Visit Apple's Final Cut Pro Support Page to stay informed about updates, tutorials, and tips.
    - Subscribe to Apple's newsletters or social media channels for announcements about new features or webinars.

3. **Engage with the Community**

- Join forums like Apple's support community, Reddit's r/FinalCutPro, or Facebook groups where professionals and enthusiasts discuss updates. These platforms are great for learning how others are using new features in their projects.

4. **Take Online Courses on New Features**
    - After a significant update, many online course providers and YouTubers release tutorials explaining how to use new tools effectively. Investing time in these courses ensures you stay at the forefront of the software's capabilities.

5. **Experiment with New Tools**
    - When new features are introduced, test them in your projects. For example, if Apple adds AI-driven editing tools, explore how they can speed up your workflow or improve your results.

6. **Keep Documentation Handy**
    - Bookmark the official Final Cut Pro documentation for quick reference when exploring new features. Apple often provides detailed guides on how to implement updates effectively.

Pro Tips for Maintaining the Right Mindset

- **Celebrate Progress**: Reflect on how much you've learned and achieved over time to stay motivated.

- **Find a Mentor or Community**: Connect with experienced editors who can guide you and inspire your growth.

- **Stay Open to Change**: As the software evolves, be willing to adapt your workflow to incorporate new tools and techniques.

The right mindset for learning Final Cut Pro combines patience, creativity, and a commitment to continuous growth. By setting clear goals, embracing challenges, and staying updated with new features, you can transform from a beginner to a skilled editor. Remember, learning Final Cut Pro is not just about mastering the software; it's about cultivating an attitude of curiosity, persistence, and innovation that will serve you well in all your creative endeavors.

VIII. FUTURE APPLICATIONS OF FINAL CUT PRO

Final Cut Pro is more than just a video editing tool—it's a gateway to exciting career opportunities, personal creative expression, and relevance in today's rapidly evolving digital landscape. As the demand for high-quality video content continues to grow across industries, mastering Final Cut Pro opens doors to a wide range of possibilities. This section explores how Final Cut Pro can shape future careers, enhance personal projects, and help users stay competitive in the digital-first world.

Expanding Career Opportunities in Video Editing

The rise of video as a dominant form of communication and entertainment has made video editing a highly sought-after skill. From film production to corporate marketing, the applications of Final Cut Pro are vast, offering professionals the tools they need to succeed.

1. **Breaking into the Film and Television Industry**
   - Final Cut Pro has been used in several high-profile film productions and TV shows, proving its capability in professional environments.
   - Mastery of Final Cut Pro enables aspiring editors to work on commercials, documentaries, music videos, and even feature films. The software's tools for color grading, audio mixing, and multicam editing are particularly valued in cinematic projects.

2. **Opportunities in Digital Marketing and Social Media**
   - Businesses increasingly rely on video content for marketing campaigns, social media engagement, and brand storytelling.
   - Proficiency in Final Cut Pro allows editors to create polished videos tailored to platforms like Instagram, YouTube, and TikTok, making it a critical skill for marketing agencies and freelancers.

3. **Freelance and Remote Editing Roles**
   - With the growth of remote work, freelance video editors are in high demand. Platforms like Upwork, Fiverr, and Behance are full of opportunities for Final Cut Pro users to work with clients worldwide.
   - The software's seamless iCloud integration enables remote collaboration on projects, giving freelancers an edge.

4. **Specialized Roles in Niche Industries**
    - Niche sectors such as wedding videography, sports editing, and educational content production require skilled editors who can craft compelling narratives.
    - Final Cut Pro's user-friendly tools and advanced features allow editors to excel in these specialized fields.

5. **Teaching and Mentoring**
    - Experienced Final Cut Pro users can expand their careers by teaching video editing to others. Whether through workshops, online courses, or private lessons, sharing expertise can be both rewarding and lucrative.

Enhancing Personal Projects and Content Creation

Final Cut Pro isn't just for professionals—it's also a powerful tool for hobbyists, content creators, and anyone with a creative vision. Whether you're documenting family memories or building a personal brand, the software empowers you to produce high-quality videos.

1. **Creating Engaging Social Media Content**
    - Platforms like YouTube, Instagram, and TikTok thrive on visually stunning content. Final Cut Pro's tools for effects, transitions, and titles make it easy to create eye-catching videos that stand out.
    - The ability to export videos in various aspect ratios ensures compatibility with different social media platforms.

2. **Building a Personal Brand**
    - For influencers and entrepreneurs, video content is key to establishing a strong online presence. Final Cut Pro's professional-grade tools allow creators to produce polished videos that reflect their brand identity.
    - Features like color correction and audio enhancements ensure high production quality, even for beginners.

3. **Documenting Family and Life Events**
    - Final Cut Pro can transform home videos into cinematic keepsakes.

- Whether editing wedding footage, birthday celebrations, or travel diaries, the software helps create memories that last a lifetime.
  - Its intuitive interface and drag-and-drop functionality make it accessible for those new to video editing.

4. **Learning Through Personal Projects**
   - Working on personal projects is one of the best ways to learn Final Cut Pro. Experimenting with transitions, effects, and audio can help users build confidence and creativity.
   - Personal projects also serve as a portfolio for aspiring editors looking to showcase their skills to potential clients or employers.

5. **Expanding into Emerging Media**
   - Final Cut Pro supports 360° video editing, opening opportunities for users interested in creating immersive content for virtual reality (VR) or augmented reality (AR) applications.
   - As these technologies grow in popularity, personal projects in 360° video can lead to exciting opportunities in gaming, training, and virtual experiences.

Staying Relevant in a Digital-First World

In today's digital-first landscape, video content dominates communication, marketing, and entertainment. To remain relevant, it's crucial to adapt to trends and leverage tools like Final Cut Pro to meet the evolving demands of audiences and industries.

1. **Keeping Up with Content Trends**
   - Short-form videos, live streaming, and interactive media are shaping the future of digital content. Final Cut Pro's robust editing tools allow creators to adapt their workflows to these formats effortlessly.
   - Its support for high-resolution editing, including 4K and 8K, ensures content remains crisp and visually appealing on any platform.

2. **Harnessing AI and Automation**
   - Final Cut Pro integrates AI-powered features, such as smart cropping and scene detection, which streamline editing processes and save

time. Staying updated with these tools ensures you remain competitive as the industry embraces automation.

3. **Adapting to Cross-Platform Integration**
    - As content creators work across multiple platforms, the ability to export and format videos efficiently is critical. Final Cut Pro's advanced export settings and compatibility with Apple's ecosystem make it ideal for producing versatile content.

4. **Investing in Continuous Learning**
    - The software is regularly updated with new features and capabilities. Staying current with these updates ensures you can leverage the latest tools to create innovative projects.
    - Joining online communities, attending webinars, and following industry trends help editors stay ahead of the curve.

5. **Sustainability in Digital Content**
    - As environmental consciousness grows, Final Cut Pro's efficient rendering and exporting processes align with sustainable content production practices, appealing to eco-minded creators and businesses.

Final Cut Pro opens doors to a wealth of future applications, from expanding career opportunities to enhancing personal creativity and maintaining relevance in a fast-paced digital world. Whether you're aiming to break into professional editing, create compelling personal projects, or stay ahead of industry trends, the software equips you with the tools to succeed. By embracing its capabilities and continually honing your skills, you can turn your passion for video editing into a dynamic and rewarding journey.

CHAPTER 2: KEYBOARD SHORTCUTS IN FINAL CUT PRO

Keyboard Shortcuts in Final Cut Pro

Mastering keyboard shortcuts in Final Cut Pro is an essential step for any editor aiming to increase speed, efficiency, and productivity. These shortcuts allow you to navigate the software, perform edits, and manage your workflow with ease. Below is an overview of key categories and examples of shortcuts to help you get started:

Navigation and Playback

- **Play/Pause: Spacebar**
- **Move Playhead to Start: Home**
- **Move Playhead to End: End**
- **Jump Forward/Backward by Frames: Arrow keys**
- **Toggle Full Screen Viewer: Command + Shift + F**

Basic Editing

- **Blade Tool: B**
- **Select Tool: A**
- **Zoom In/Out Timeline: Command + + / Command + -**
- **Undo: Command + Z**
- **Redo: Command + Shift + Z**

Clip Management

- **Insert Clip: W**
- **Overwrite Clip: D**
- **Connect Clip: Q**
- **Trim Start/End to Playhead: Option + [/ Option +]**
- **Toggle Skimming: S**

Timeline and Project Organization

- **Create New Project**: Command + N
- **New Event**: Option + N
- **Expand Audio/Video**: Control + S
- **Toggle Snap to Grid**: N
- **Zoom to Fit Timeline**: Shift + Z

Effects and Color

- **Open Effects Browser**: Command + 5
- **Open Color Inspector**: Command + 6
- **Apply Default Transition**: Command + T
- **Render All Effects**: Control + R

Workflow Optimization

- **Duplicate Clip**: Command + D
- **Open Preferences**: Command + ,
- **Quick Export**: Command + E
- **Toggle Magnetic Timeline**: Command + Option + W

Customizing Shortcuts

You can also customize your shortcuts:

1. Go to **Final Cut Pro > Commands > Customize**.
2. Assign specific keys to frequently used commands for a tailored workflow.

By incorporating these shortcuts into your editing routine, you'll save time and achieve smoother creative flow while working in Final Cut Pro.

CHAPTER 3: NAVIGATING THE BASICS OF FINAL CUT PRO

ABOUT FINAL CUT PRO 2024

Final Cut Pro is professional video editing software made by Apple. It used to have an "**X**" in the name, but Apple took it out. Customers who want more video editing tools than iMovie has to offer can get what they want from it. Besides that, it can meet the needs of pros who are really into making movies. Final Cut Pro 2024 is different from other video editing software because it is made with the user in mind. Its easy-to-use design makes it simple for newbies to start, and its advanced features meet the needs of professional editors. Final Cut Pro 2024 is truly the best software in its class. It works perfectly with other Apple products and has great speed.

Also, people who like to make their own movies will love it. There are many built-in effects and tools in Final Cut Pro that can help you make your movies look great. Plus, sites like YouTube and Vimeo make it easy to share your final work. The powerful video editing tools in Final Cut Pro are one of its best features. No matter if you're working with 4K, 8K, or even VR footage, Final Cut Pro 2024 makes it easy to edit and change your videos precisely. It has a lot of editing tools and effects that make it easy to improve your footage, add cool visual effects, and make transitions that look natural. Another cool thing about Final Cut Pro is that it works well with iPhones, iPads, and other Apple goods. Thus, it is simple to add movies from your iPhone to Final Cut Pro so that you can edit them.

FINAL CUT PRO - MAIN FEATURES

People also choose this program because it supports a huge number of formats. DV, HDV, and many other types of files can be uploaded and edited. Besides that, it can play movies from 2K up to 8K without slowing down. iMovie for iOS and iPadOS lets you bring in material. If you want to edit several clips at once, make sure they can be used together, and then click the button that goes with each one. In addition, you can edit an infinite number of tracks, mix video from various cameras, and create 360-degree footage in Pro. As for the tools, you can start with simple ripple, roll, and slide options and work your way up to more complex ones. It is thought to be one of the best editing programs for Macs. You will be happy to see that there are many transitions, audio and video effects, color correction tools, sliders, curves, and generators for this video editor.

TERRIFIC FEATURES IN THE UPDATED VERSION

The best thing about the newest version is that it works with new Macs that are running **Apple Silicon M1** for video editing. You can now also look for and download a user manual and have media instantly transcoded when you copy or merge a project. **Smart Conform** is an-other important feature that uses AI machine learning to crop widescreen material so that it is easy to watch on phones and social media sites. This is similar to the auto-reframe tool in Adobe Premiere Pro. I think that the newest changes to proxy files are particularly helpful for people who work as video editors and often do their jobs from home.

Another benefit is that 3602 footage can be stabilized, and you have more ways to work with the RED RAW and Canon Cinema RAW Light files. The inspector panel and the audio crossovers were also improved by the makers. You can edit 3D object movements and use the stroke filter in the companion app, FCPX Motion. The compressor can add camera LUTs and creative LUTs. Most people were looking forward to the **Sidecar** feature in macOS Catalina. It adds a second screen to an iPad. Also, the color masks and range separation tools have been updated so that you can now use them to check the quality of HDR movies. The Color Inspector's HSL settings (Hue, Saturation, and Lumi-nosity) help you choose colors more correctly.

NEWBIE-FRIENDLY INTERFACE

As long as you know how to use Apple products, Final Cut Pro will be very easy for you. The layout looks like other apps made by the same company. Every choice is easy to understand, and the tools are all set up in a way that makes sense. It takes a while to get around the tabs, but the next time you need it, you'll have no trouble finding the required option without any problems. The process of editing videos is also very easy to understand. However, because the program has so many tools and features, you should take the time to try them out and understand their effects. The new and better timeline index seems very useful in this case. Now, all you have to do to change the layout of the timeline is drag and drop audio parts. Professional filmmakers also like that Multicam editing is available and that different video tracks can be changed. You don't have to worry that your project will be lost if your computer is slow or something else goes wrong because it has an auto-save feature. There is safety in every frame.

EXTENSIVE SIVE LIBRARY

During the editing process in Final Cut Pro, media files are shown as icons, not just any icons. They are animated icons! Not only can you cut the video using the timeline or a different window (as you would in most other tools), but you can also use the file's icon. This gives these moving icons more use. You can make the button bigger to cut the video more accurately if the file isn't too long.

Top-Notch Color Correction Tools

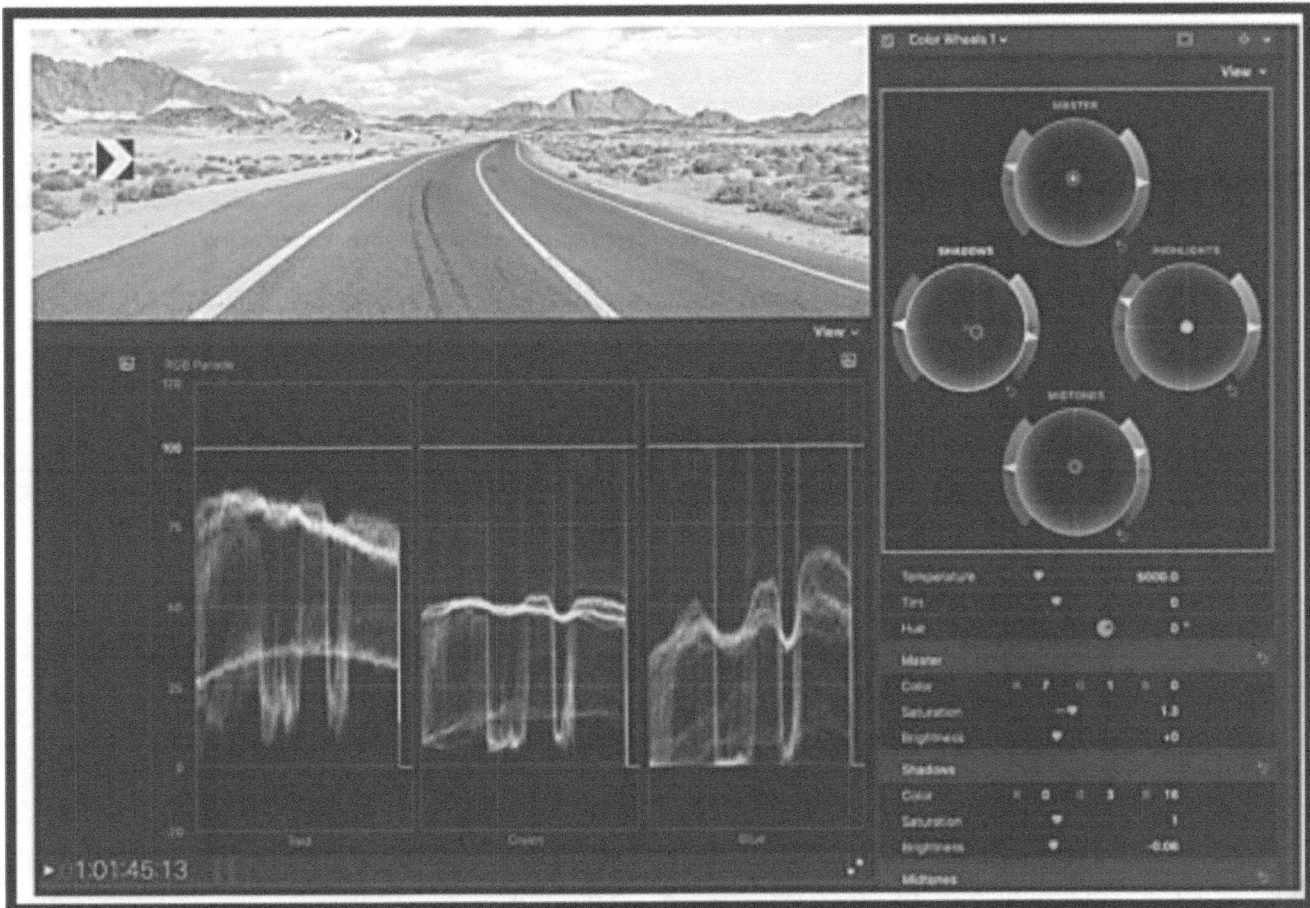

Color grading is important in many fields, not just photos. Without color correction, even the most beautiful times won't look as interest-ing as you think they will. That's why you should always take the time to pro-edit your footage's color.

Adjustablecolor wheels. The most potent color adjustment tool in Final Cut Pro is likely this one. It has four wheels that let you change the color, intensity, and brightness of the whole picture, or just the highlights, shadows, and glares. Sliders in the tool let you change the temperature, tint, and hue of the movie as a whole. Two curvy sliders are on each wheel. The one on the left controls the saturation, and the one on the right controls the brightness. You can choose the tone you want by turning the wheel in the middle.

Precise color curves. Color Curves is a simpler tool that does the same things that Photoshop and Lightroom do with related tools. It lets you quickly make the color changes you need without having to fiddle with a bunch of buttons.

Cinematic Mode Function for iPhone 13 Users

People who make movies with their iPhone 13 will love this mode. It lets you start recording, pulling focus, or even tracking focus on your phone as soon as you turn it on. This sounds really cool, but Final Cut Pro can do a lot more than that. In fact, users can change the f-stop on their macOS computers manually, just like they can with a regular camera. Here, though, you can make all of the changes right in the editing suite. The blurriness of the background will get worse if you lower the number, and better if you raise it. Changing it over time will change how strong the effect is. Of course, the automatic product might not be perfect, since even the smartest programs aren't always better than human eyes. You can rely on this mode, though, if you're not picky about how you edit backgrounds.

Object Tracking Option

The truth is that most people who edit movies on a daily basis have used object tracking at least once. It's not a new idea. It's either built into most non-linear video producers or can be bought as a separate tool that you can add to the program. I think the people who worked on FCP did the right thing by making this tool available throughout the program. This way, more people will be able to learn it and use it for their projects. I like how easy it is to use Object Tracker in this version of Final Cut Pro. Anyone can figure out how to get the most out of it. To find Object Tracker, go to the tab of the Inspector. After that, add a new tracker, change its size, and put it where you want it. Finally, click "**Analyze**" in the sample window and wait a few seconds while FCP does the rest. It's very easy to connect an element or text box to the counter. You only need to know exactly where the buttons and options are.

Straightforward Multicamera Video Editing

When recording from more than one camera, this program's ability to edit from more than one camera comes in very handy. The process of video editing isn't particularly difficult, but it can be tricky to time the various clips. It's one thing if the video was recorded with a professional camera that supports timecode or has gear that automatically syncs it. When you have to edit video images from multiple cameras that were shot in various forms or with various settings, the situation is very different. Usually, you timethe clips by sound if that's the case. Most of the time, you have to do it manually, but some video editors have third-party tools that make it easier. In our case, you don't need to run any extra apps because Final Cut Pro already has the features you need. The software instantly checks all the audio tracks and makes sure they are in sync with all the videos from all the cams.

Agile Background Rendering

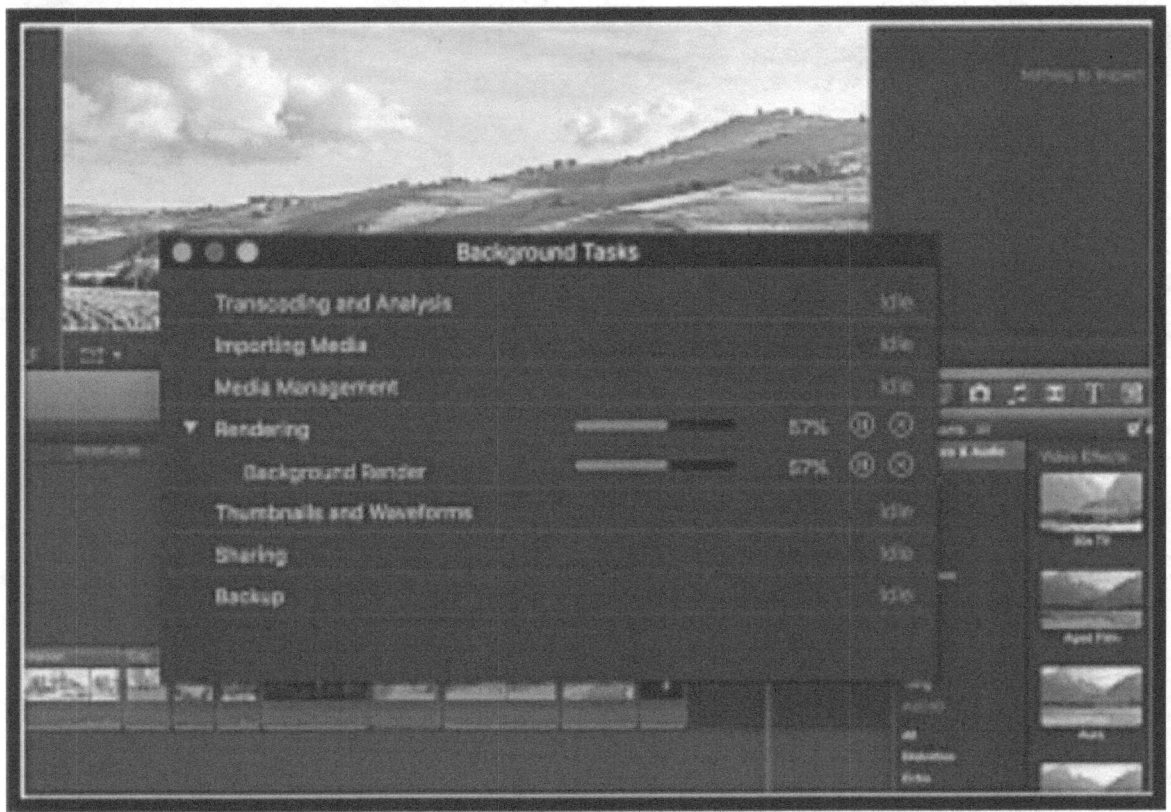

The background rendering tool in Final Cut Pro lets you see how edited clips will look before you actually edit them. What good things does it do? The best thing about it is that all of your changes are made instantly, so your computer doesn't have to work too hard. The renderer stops whenever you make a new edit and only restarts when you're finished. With this technology, you can watch a demo of your edited movies right away and in high definition. But Apple's developers made a big mistake when they thought about the biggest benefit of background rendering. All the produced files need to be saved on the HDD so that you can preview them. This means that you can quickly run out of disc space, and there's no way to change or limit the cache size for this feature.

Clear 360° Video Editing

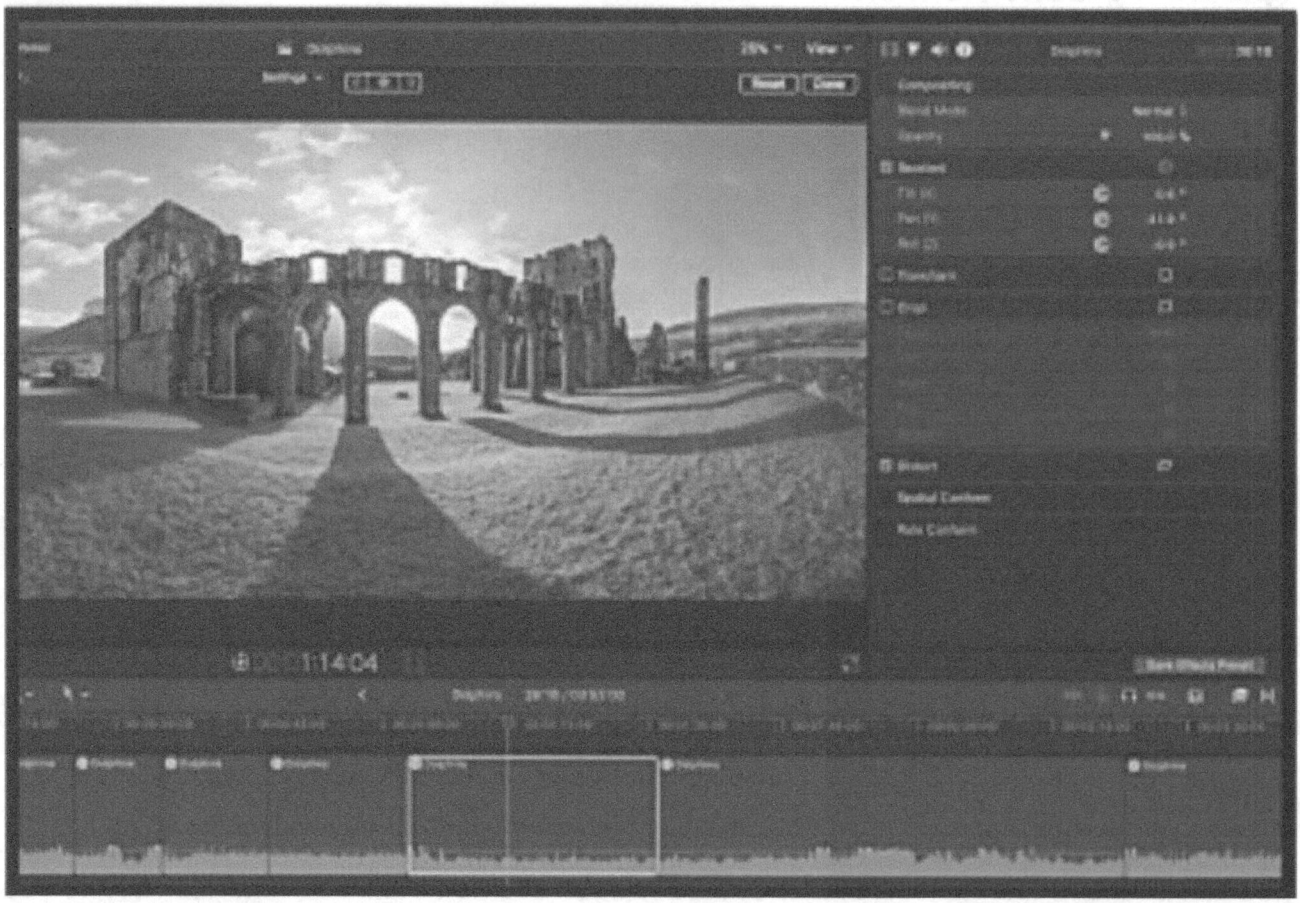

When you use Final Cut Pro, it's easy to edit 360° movies for VR or panoramic clips for Facebook, YouTube, and other sites. The software works with almost all formats, up to and including 4K and 8K, and has a number of useful tools, such as a horizontal leveling tool, the ability to change the viewer's start ing perspective, and a Patch tool. With the exception of 360° video, it works similarly to Adobe Con-tent-Aware Fill and can magically get rid of items like tools or street signs based on the context. The Patch tool in this 360° video editing software works well on features that are hard to understand, like grass and fancy floors. My MacBook almost crashed though from all the heavy processing that went into editing videos.

Cutting-Edge Sound Editing Options

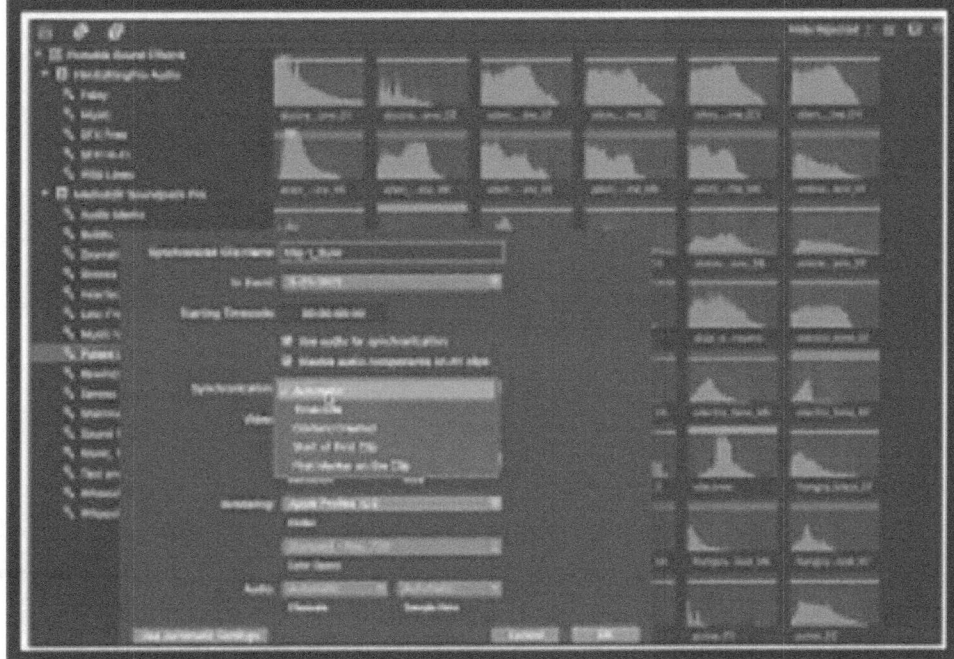

You can edit sounds in Final Cut Pro, which is another great thing about this program. It can get rid of annoying sounds like humming and beeping on its own, or you can change the settings yourself. Final Cut Pro comes with over 1300 free sound effects and a number of tools, making it one of the best video makers for YouTube. One cool trick you can useis to join different audio tracks together. For example, if you're usinga DSLR camera to record HD video and another device to record sound at the sametime, the Match Audio tool will line up both audio sources.

Lots of Transition Effects

It has more than 120 video effects. Blur, distortion, stylization, and colorization are the effects that people use the most. You can also search for an effect by name, which is very helpful because there are so many of them. A simple set of keys can be used to apply the most common transition, which is cross dissolve. It's usually very easy to add transitions because you don't have to make a second line on the timeline; you just add the effect between the clips you need in one step.

Final Cut Pro - Technical Specifications

Minimum System Requirements

- At least macOS 13. 5
- 8GB of RAM (16GB is suggested for third-party plug-ins and effects)
- Metal-capable graphics card (only for Intel-based Macs)
- 5.8GB of free space on the hard drive
- Some features need a Mac with Apple silicon. Some features require internet access; fees may apply. To make Blu-ray discs, you need a Blu-ray recorder.

CHAPTER 4: SETTING UP YOUR FIRST PROJECT

Setting Up Your Workspace

There are fixed desk setups in Final Cut Pro that tell you where and how big the browser, viewer, inspector, and timeline should be, as well as other important parts of the program. You can make and save new workspace plans if none of the ones that are already there work for you. It's easy to share your customized workspace setup with other people after you've saved it. You can add extra areas like the timeline index, the event viewer, the comparison viewer, and the audio meters when you make your own plans.

Choose a workspace Layout

- In Final Cut Pro, go to **Window** > **Workspaces** and pick a layout from the list.

Save custom workspace layouts

1. Put the parts of the main window in Final Cut Pro in the order you want them.
2. Go to **Window** > **Workspaces** > "**Save Workspace as**."
3. Give the new layout a name, then click Save.

The new arrangement has been added to the list of workspaces.

Tip: To save a change to a custom layout that's already been made, make the change and then go to **Window** > **Workspaces** > **Update [name] Workspace.**

Arrange the main window in Final Cut Pro for Mac

The browser, viewer, timeline, sidebar, and inspector are the main parts of the Final Cut Pro window. You can change the size, show, and hide these places to fit your working style and the job at hand, even on different screens. There are also standard workspace setups that come with Final Cut Pro, and you can make your own and save them.

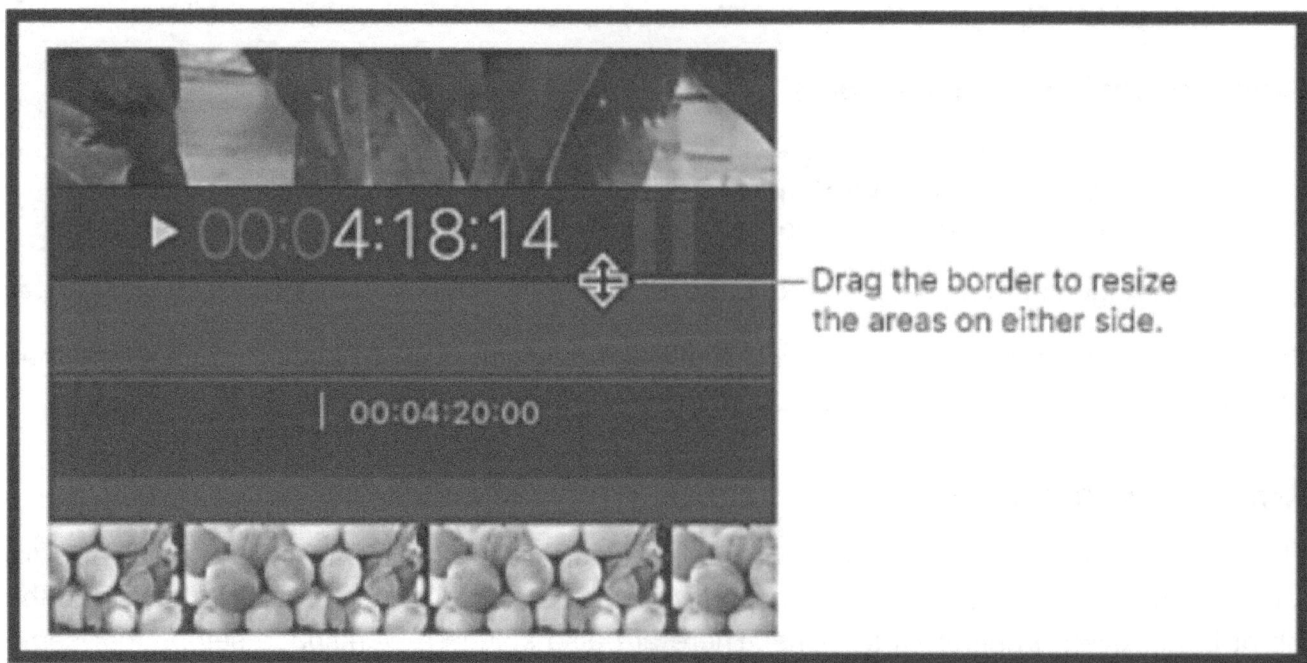

Resize areas of the Window

You can move the line between two parts of the Final Cut Pro window. One spot gets bigger while the other gets smaller as you pull.

Drag the border to resize the areas on either side.

The bottom of the browser and viewer work together as a single border when both are shown.

Resizing one change the size of the other as well.

Show or Hide the Sidebar

To choose different kinds of media, the sidebar on the left of the browser has three panes: the Libraries sidebar, the Photos, Videos, and Audio sidebar, and the Titles and Generators sidebar. When you click on an item in the sidebar, like an event with clips or a group with sound effects or 3D titles, the browser shows you what that item contains. Any of the sidebars can be shown or hidden.

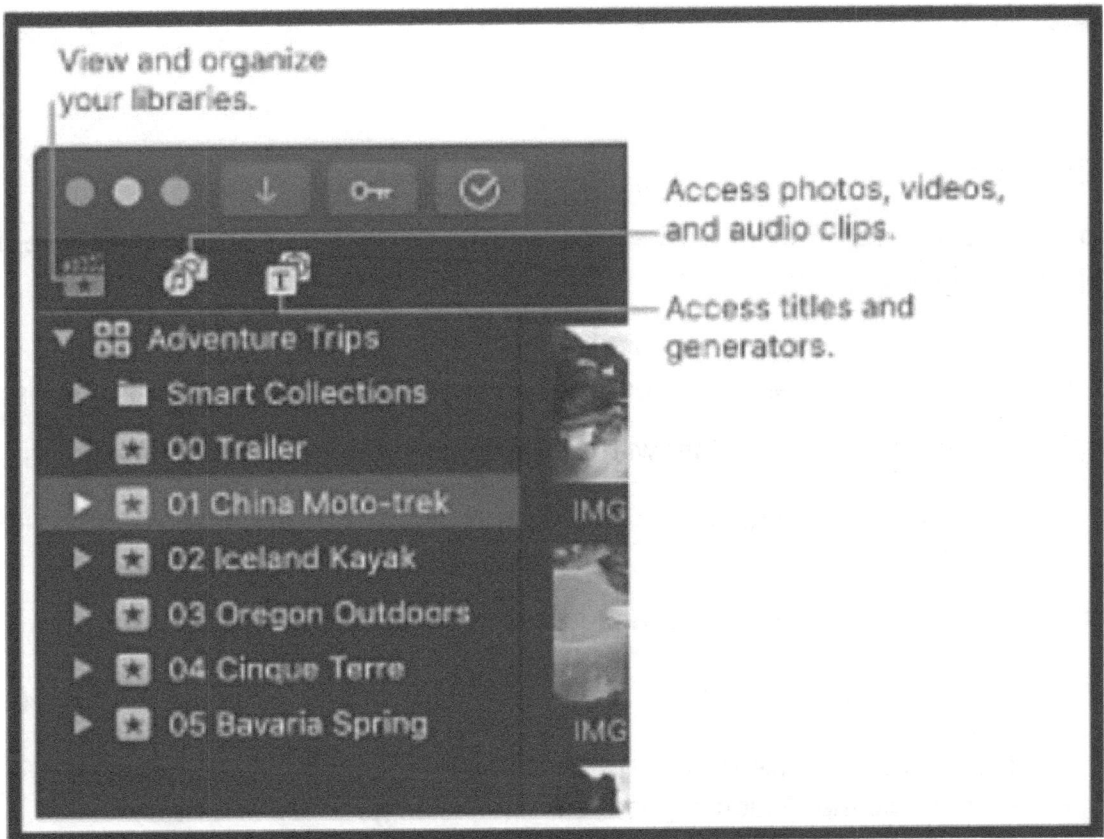

Do any of these things in Final Cut Pro:

- *Show the Libraries sidebar*: In the top left area of Final Cut Pro, click the **Libraries** button. You can also press **Command-1** or go to **Window > Go To > Libraries.**
- Show the Photos, Videos, and Audio sidebar: Click the Photos, Videos, and Audio button in the upper left area, or go to **Win-dow > Go To> Photos, Videos, and Audio**, or press **Shift-Command-1.**
- *Show the Titles and Generators sidebar*: To show the Titles and Generators tab, click the button in the upper left area that says **"Titles and Gene rators"** or go to **"Window"** and select **"Go To."** You can also press **Option-Command-1.**
- *Show or hide the sidebar*: Press **Command-Grave-Accent** (`) or choose **Window > Show in Workspace> Sidebar** to show or hide the sidebar. You can also hide the sidebar by clicking the button for the sidebar that's currently shown (the button is highlighted).

Share Custom workspace layouts

It is simple to move personalized workspace layouts to another computer or give them to coworkers and friends.

1. Save a unique workspace layout in Final Cut Pro.
2. Click on **Window**, then **Workspaces**, and finally Open **Workspace Folder** in Finder.

In the Finder, the Workspaces folder with all the setups you made yourself appears.

3. Pick out the custom layout files you want to share in the Finder. Then, go to **File > Compress.**

Note: Compressing the files stops any changes to unique layouts during transit.

4. Email or use another easy way to send the final ZIP file (with the extension .zip) to your friend or coworker.
5. Double-click the ZIP file on the Mac that you want to receive to open it.
6. Press and hold the Option key in the Finder, then go to **Go > Library.**
7. In the Library folder, drag the custom layout files to this spot:

/Users/username/ Library/Application Support/Final Cut Pro/ Workspaces/

Customizing the Interface

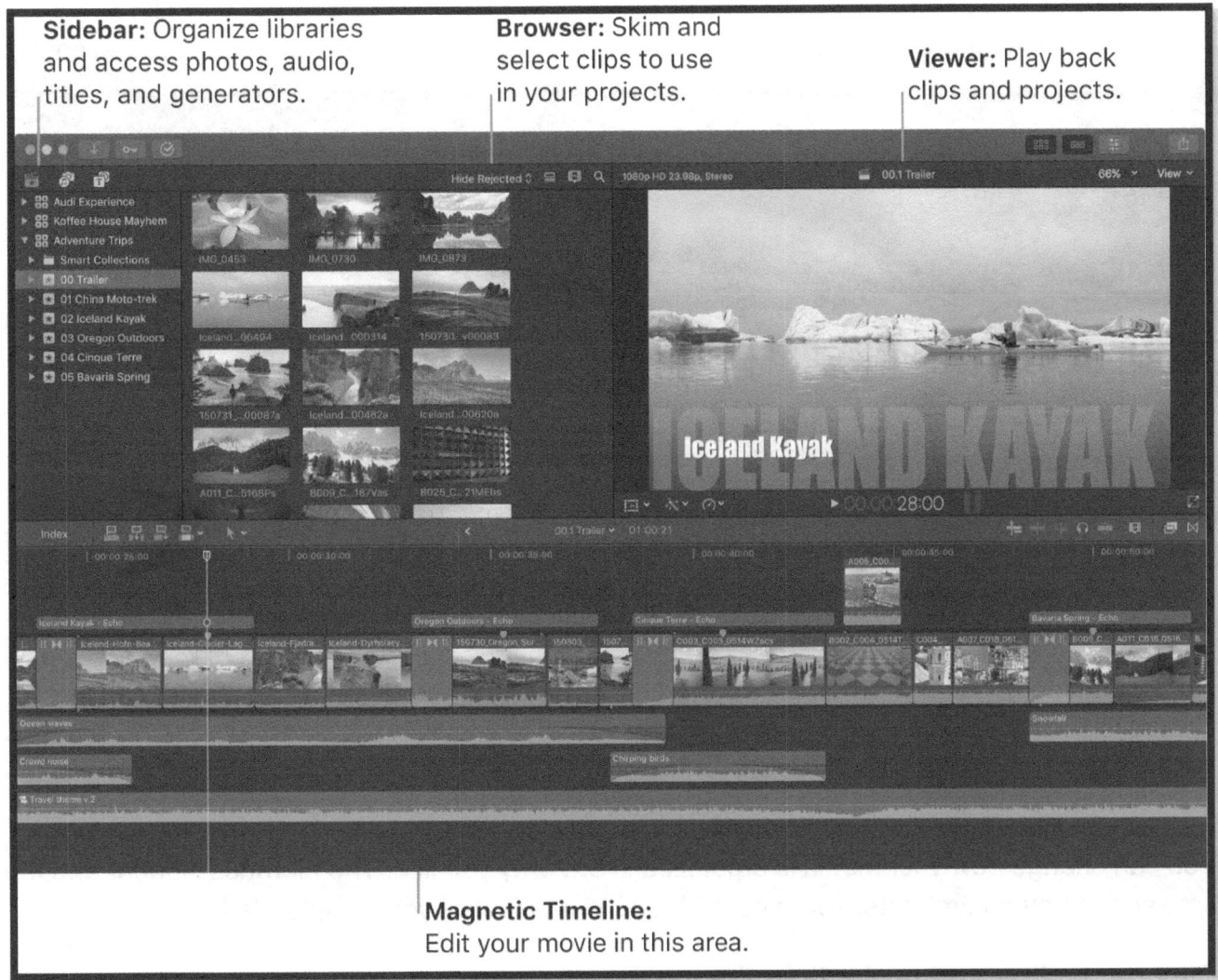

Organize media in the Libraries sidebar and the browser

The media you imported can be found in events in your library. (An event is like a box that holds projects and clips.). In a library, when you choose an event, its clips and projects show up in the browser on the right.

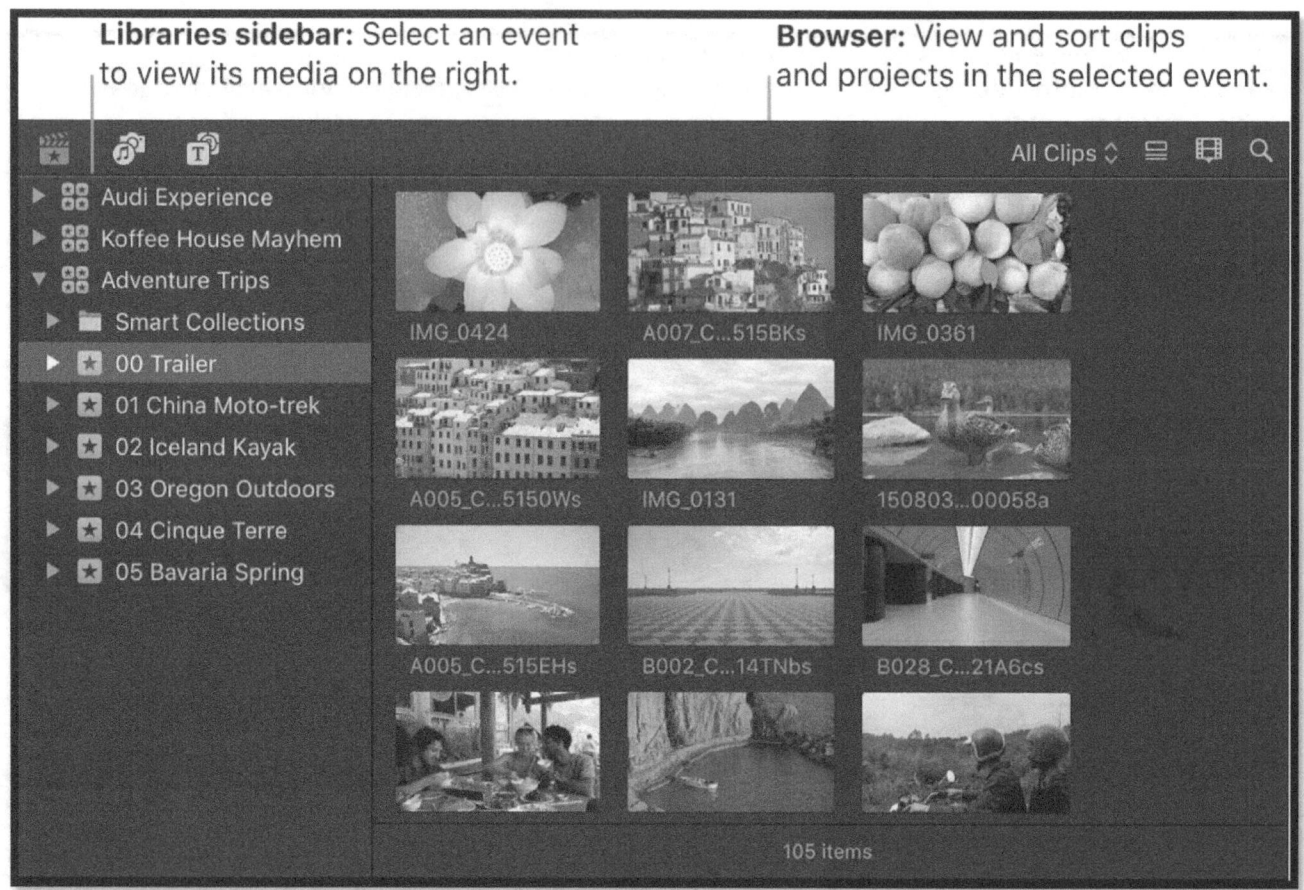

You can change how your media is organized in any way you like. The Libraries sidebar and the browser let you control, rate, sort, and add tags to media that you've uploaded.

Play back clips and projects in the viewer

This is where you watch your videos, like clips and projects with a quality of 6K or higher. You can play back events, projects, or single clips on a second screen or in full screen. You can show two clips at once in the event viewer, which is a different video screen that can be put next to the main viewer. One clip can be from the browser and the other from the timeline.

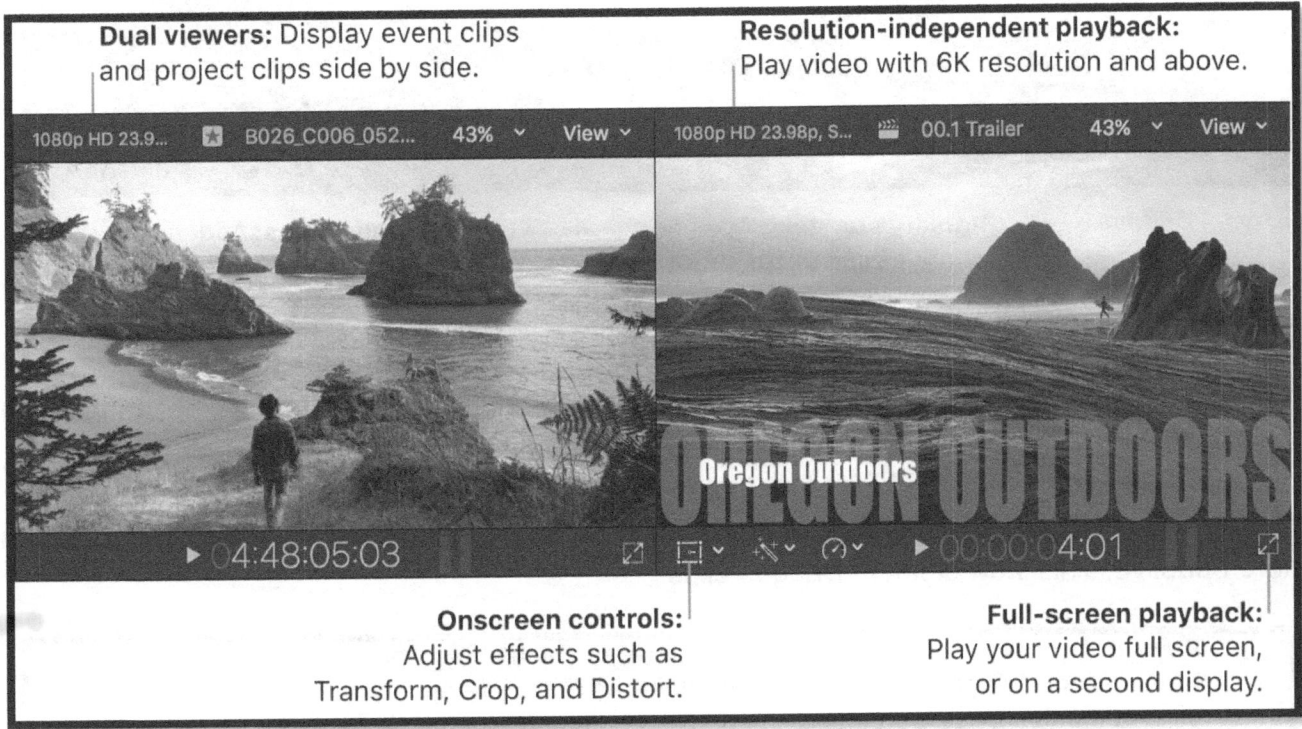

You can also change the settings for a lot of different effects and transitions by moving the buttons that appear on top of the video in the player.

Edit your project in the Magnetic Timeline

You make your movie by adding and arranging clips and making all of your changes on the timeline, which is at the bottom of the Final Cut Pro window. When you drag clips into place on the timeline, they "magnetically" move to fit. Moving clips around will make the clips around them close up to fill the empty space. You can store all the information you need for your final movie in a project. This includes the selections you made when editing and links to all the source clips and events.

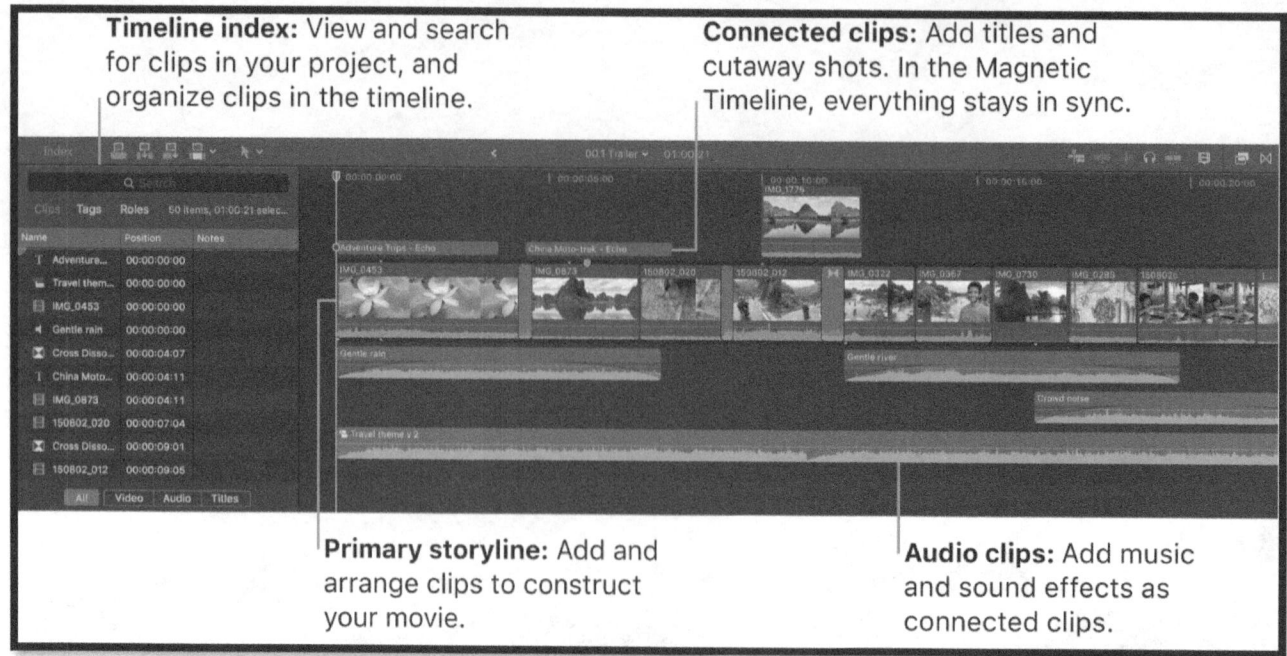

With a click, you can put clips into audio lanes, which are different layers in the timeline that can be seen clearly. This is done based on their roles. Because roles tell you what kind of clip it is, each audio lane only has one kind of sound. One audio lane might have song clips and another might have sound effects, for instance. Pro offers reference points that make editing simpler and more effective. This view clearly arranges clips.

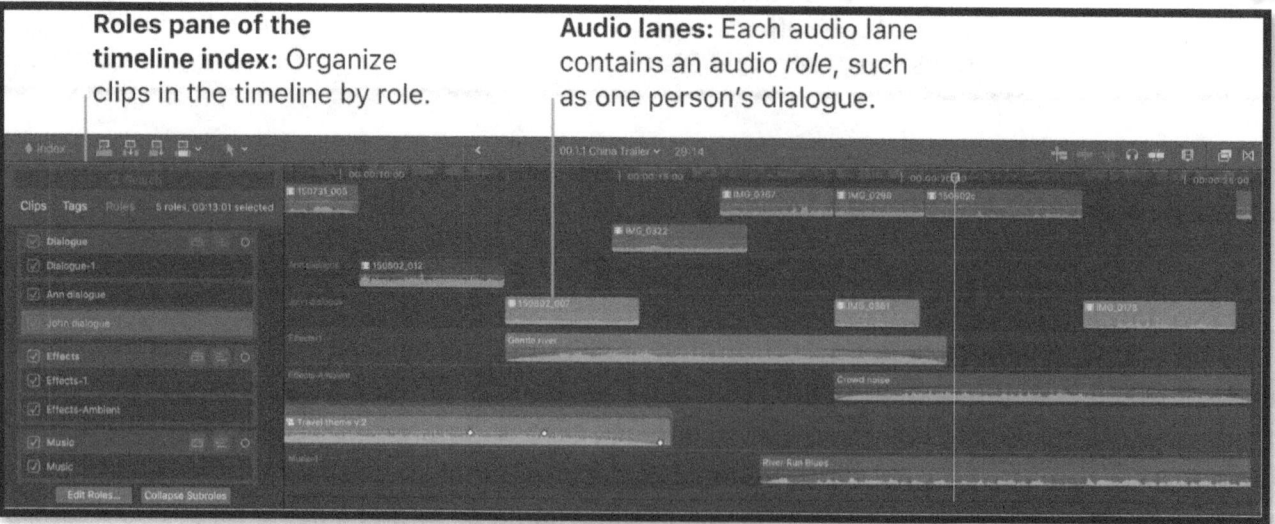

Configuring Preferences

A setting changes how a certain feature in Final cut pro works. You can always turn off or on most settings. Here is a list of all the settings for Final Cut Pro.

Open Final Cut Pro Settings

- If you want to open the settings pane for Final Cut Pro, go to **Final Cut Pro > Settings** or press Command-Comma. Then, click a button at the top of the window.

Note: In the Final Cut Pro menu, "Settings" shows up as "Preferences" on computers running macOS Monterey or older.

Copy Final Cut Pro settings between computers

It is possible to copy Final Cut Pro settings to another Mac that also has Final Cut Pro loaded. This way, both computers will have the same settings.

1. **Go to the following place to find the Final Cut Pro settings file:**

/Users/ username/ Library/Preferences/com.apple.FinalCut.plist

2. On the other Mac, copy the settings file to the same spot.

If you have to, delete any previous versions of the file that are stored there.

Reset Final Cut Pro settings

You can return Final Cut Pro's settings to the way they were when you first got it.

- Open Final Cut Pro and press Option-Command at the same time.

Final Cut Pro erases all of your settings and putsa file on your PC called VideoAppDiagnostics-FinalCut that stores a copy of your old settings.

CHAPTER 5: EXPLORING THE INTERFACE LAYOUT

Exploring the Interface Layout

You can see the main window in FCP in this image. I have a few sources open in the browser on the left, and you can see some media clips there. In the Timeline, you can see a music video I worked on, and in the Viewer, you can see a shot from a drone. As you can see, the Audio Meters are open in the bottom right corner, and the Color Wheels are shown in the Inspector in the top right corner.

You can change a lot about the layout. You can pick which panes to see and how much space they take up. There are also some floating win-dows, but let's start with the most important ones.

Overview

You will work in a single window for most of your time in FCP. The editing process is mostly a single-window experience, though addi-tional windows will be shown to change settings, import media, and export. There are several panes inside this single window. You can change the size of each pane by dragging its sides, and you can change its contents using menus and dropdowns. (Press Command-0 to re-turn your area to its original state if it looks very different from these pictures.)

First, take a look at the image's upper left corner:

You can find, sort, tag, and pick your videos in this area, which is called the Browser. You can find pictures, music, and sound effects there, as well as title and background themes that have already been made. This is where you find things that you want to add to your edit. **The Viewer is where you watch videos and is at the center of everything. Here's a picture of it:**

This could be a clip from the browser you're looking at or a frame from your current timeline. It could also show more like video scopes to check the color or angles in a multicam clip or extraoptions for titles or effects.

The Timeline is at the bottom of the screen. Your current edit, as you can see here:

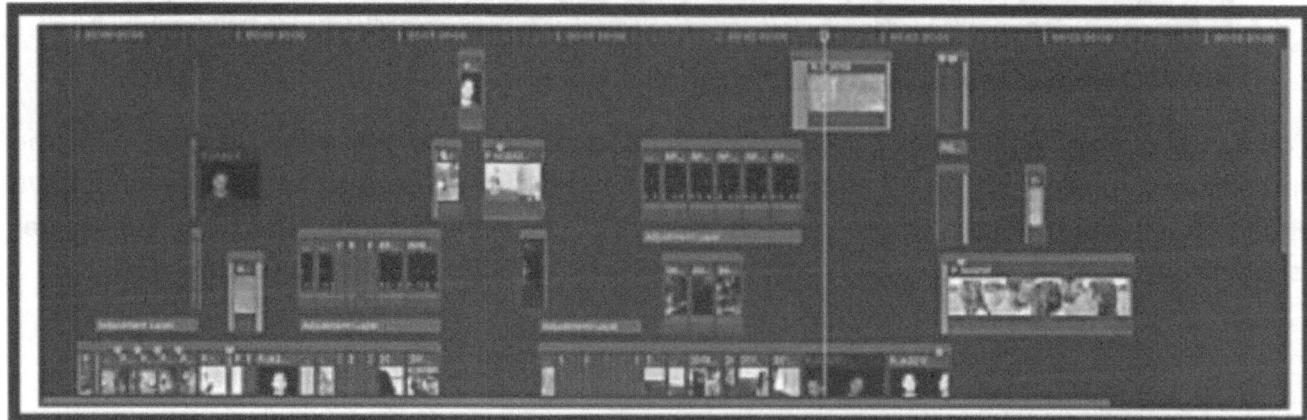

This is where clips are put in order, moved around, and put above or below other clips. You can trim, roll, slip, and slide your edits there. You can also swap clips, change speeds, set markers, and do a lot more. The "magic" takes place there.

The Inspector is to the right of the screen. It's where you can change many features, as

shown below:

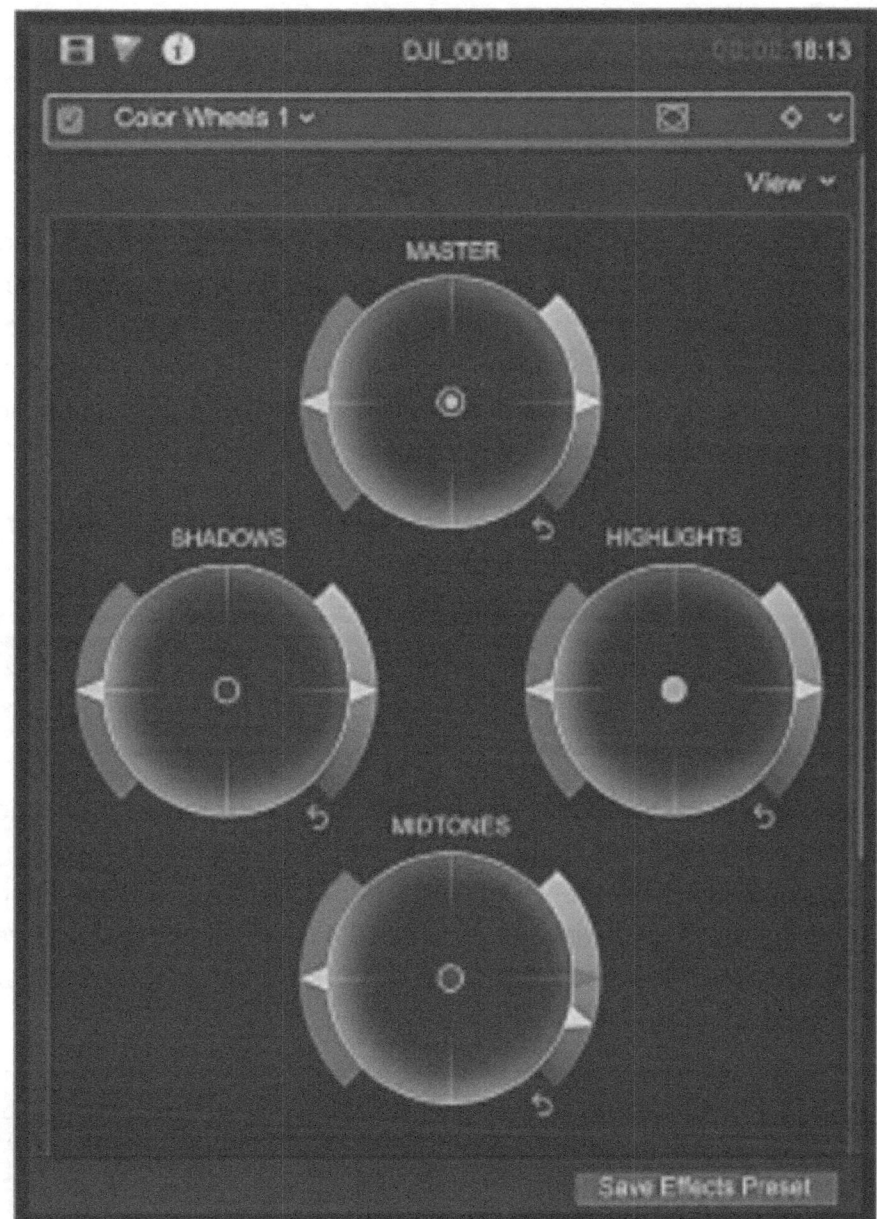

Usually, you'd use this to change the color, size, level, or video effects you've applied to one or more clips in the timeline. But you'll probably use this earlier in the process as well, to look at or change a clip's features in the Browser and do other things as well. Now that we know the basics, let's look at some of the more specific parts of the interface in more detail.

In the central bar

In the centre of the screen, at the top of the **Timeline** panel, is a bar with several icons and a few words. On the left, you'll see this:

The first thing you'll see is the word **"Index,"** which starts theTimeline Index and lets you move around and change how your timeline is shown. There are then four editing buttons below the timeline that let you copy video from the browser above. If you move your mouse over these buttons, a short cut key will appear. You can press that key instead of clicking on the button, which is often faster. To the right of these buttons is a pop-up window called Tools that shows an arrow right now. These tools do make things easier.

There is a title and a menu in the middle of the screen, next to a length or timecode that is surrounded by two arrows and looks like this:

With the arrows, you can jump to other recent Projects or step backout of stacked things like Compound Clips. The name and time code tells you which Project you're working on and where the playhead is, respectively. The menu lets you duplicate your current Project, change its settings, and do other things. This is new in version 10.4.9. The following picture shows that as you move to the right, some tog- gle buttons are lit up blue when they're on and white when they're off.

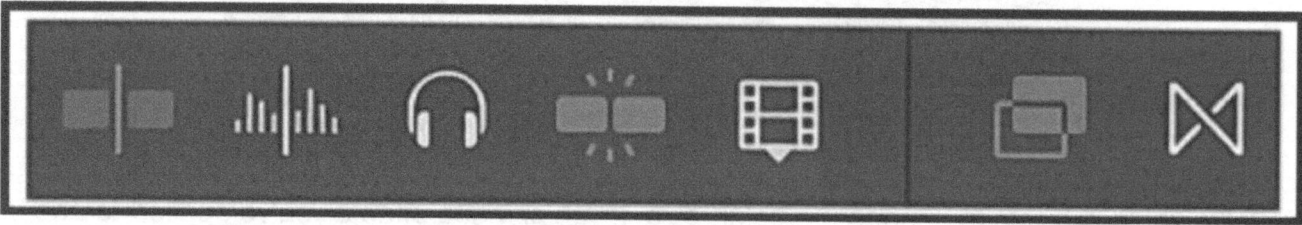

The first four are **Skimming, Audio Skimming, Solo**, and **Snapping**. These let you tweak some of the more specific partsof timeline edit-ing. Next is a filmstrip button that takes you to the **Clip Appearance** menu. This is where you can change how the timeline looks, such as how far in you have zoomed in, how much space is given to audio and video, how tall the clips are, and so on.

The clip appearance icon to the right of the Browser looks a lot like this one. When you open **Video Scopes**, the icon looks a little different. You can expect this button to give you relevant display options no matter where you find it. When you click on the **Effects** and **Transitions** buttons to the far right of the main gray bar, an extra browser will appear or disappear. This gives you access to a variety of ways to change how a clip sounds, looks, or changes during an edit. And that's the central bar.

In the Browser

There are buttons and menus on the left and right sides of the Back up in the Browser.

The first icon on the left is **Libraries**, which is where your footage is stored. The second icon takes you to **Photos and Audio**, and the third icon shows **Titles** (for text) and **Generators** (for backgrounds and filler material). In each of these places, there is a sidebar on the left with higher-level groups and material on the right. If you click on the item you're currently looking at one more time, you can hide or show the sidebar. Moving from one area to the next, you'll notice a different selection of buttons and options for the **Libraries, Photos and Audio**, and **Titles and Generators** sections. Most of the time, these let you find and change the picture you're looking at.

In the Viewer pane

In the image below, you can see the Viewer pane, which has a lot of useful details and controls:

In the upper left corner, you can see the playback's resolution and frame rate. In the upper middle corner, you can see its name. There are two menus in the upper right corner. The first one, Size, lets you change how big the video is on the screen; it's usually set to fit to the Space Available. The View menu, on the other hand, lets you add extra panes and layers and change the playback settings. There is three drop-down menu in the bottom left corner of the Viewer that give you access to on-screen settings that you can change in the Viewer.

The first offers Transform, Crop, and Distort: to resize, rotate, crop, and stretch the video directly. The drop-down menu that follows has a selection of color correction and audio enhancement. The third button allows you to retime video in a variety of ways, including speeding up, slowing down, stopping time, and changing speed over time. There is a play/pause button in the bottom middle of the Viewer, to the left of a small lgroup of numbers and icons. This button also shows if looping is on. The next part is a timecode screen that shows what hour, minute, second, and frame the clip or sequence is currently playing back at. There are small Audio Meters to the right of the time-code, and if you click on this small button, a much bigger one will appear down the right side of the timeline. Finally, there is an icon in the bottom right corner of the Viewer that lets you play videos on full screen. (To get out of this mode, press Escape.)

Other important windows and controls

You'll find the normal round "traffic light" window settings at the very top of the main window, just below the left most Mac menu bar:

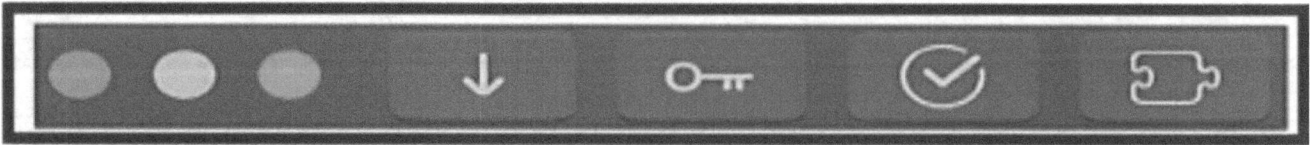

When you press the green button, you go into full screen mode. This is good if you want to focus on one app at a time, but not so great if you want to see more than one at once. It also hides the settings for the traffic lights, but you can move your mouse to the top of the screen to see them or press Escape to leave. The traffic lights have three (or maybe four) buttons next to them. Each of these buttons opens a new window. They handle importing videos, making and applying keywords, and showing the progress of tasks running in the background. If you have loaded any workflow extensions, you'l lsee a fourth button that lets you access them. These let outside developers connect to FCP so that more complicated processes can be used. The menu bar makes it easy to get to some other important apps. To open the Settings/ Preferences window, go to **Final Cut Pro > Settings** (or Preferences on an older version of macOS). This is where you can **change some im-portant settings about warnings, background processing, and other things, as shown below:**

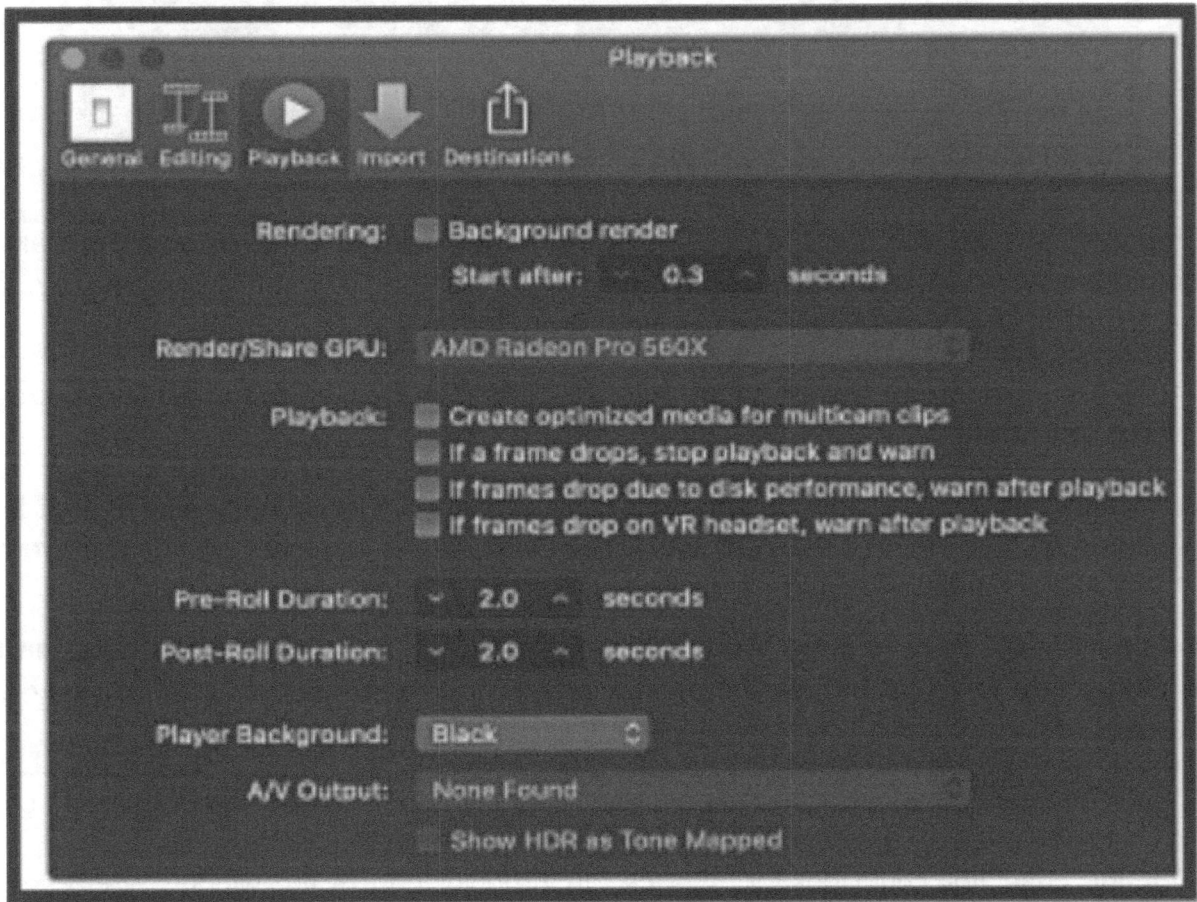

The Command Editor can be foundby going to Final Cut Pro > Commands > Customize. This is where you can find and set up keyboard shortcuts, as shown below:

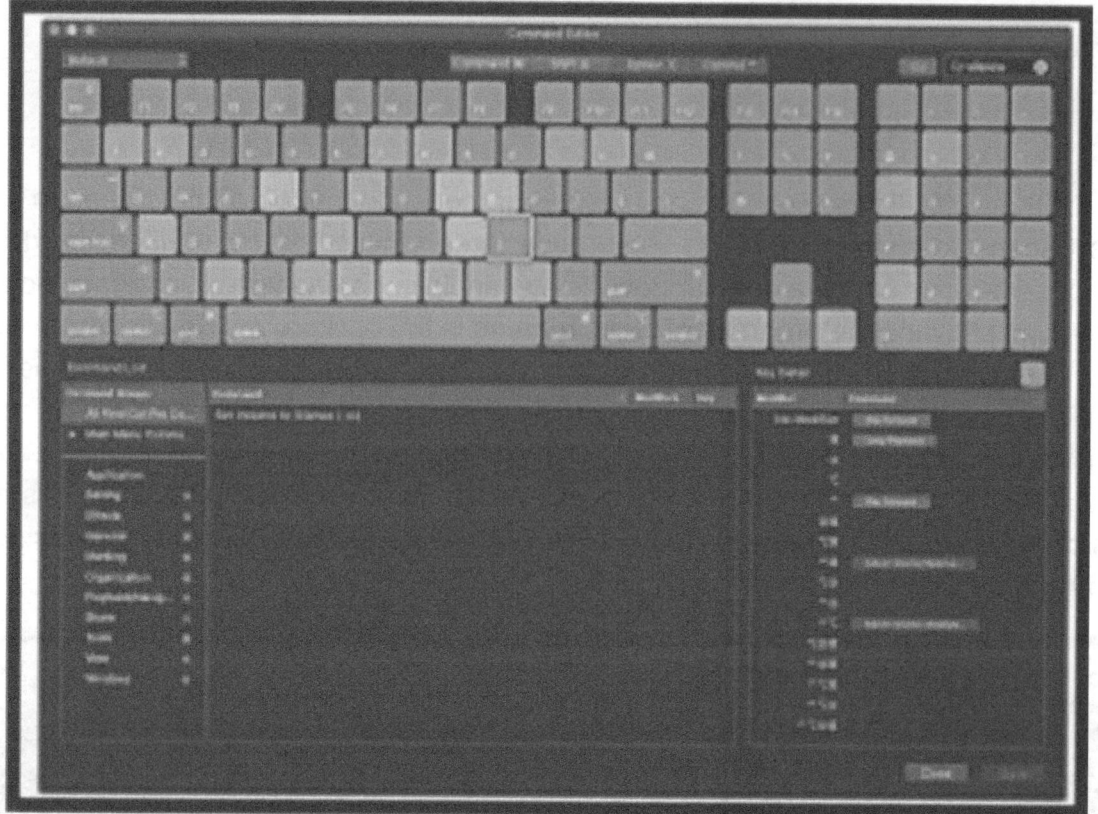

It is important to note that modifier keys like **Command, Option, Control,** and **Shift** are not needed to make shortcuts, but they can be used if you want to. To put this another way, the **0** key could be linked to a command just like **Shift-0** or **Option-0**.

Now that you know about the modifier keys, you can use the Command Editor window to find these shortcuts:

- To find a shortcut, all you have to do is click on a key on the onscreen keyboard. In the bottom-right corner of the window, you'll see what actions that key maps to when you use any mix of modifier keys.

This helps when you're looking around the program and need to find the function that goes with a key you just hit. Here area few more steps you need to take to make new shortcuts:

1. To make a shortcut, type the command into the search box in the upper right corner to see a list of commands that match at the bottom of the window:
- In this case, you could look for "**silence**." In the lower part of the window, you'll see the single command "**Set Volume to Silence (-∞).**"
2. Next, click on the modifier keys you want to use above the keyboard and then drag the command to the key you want to use it with. You can also typethe shortcut key in stead. The above **Silence** command works great with the number zero.
3. If this is your first time making a shortcut, make a copy of the command set and name it something different. The menu in the upper left corner of this moving window lets you pick command sets, which are groups of shortcuts, import, export, and control them.

4. Finally, check the computer display or the list below it to make sure that the command has been given.
5. Press **Save** and **Close** when you're done.

Creating a Library

In FCP, everything you do is saved in a **Library**. Video and audio clips, your modified projects, photos, songs you've used, and everything elselive in **events**. **Events** are stored in libraries. At its most basic, this can be an easy process, but there are times when you may want to take a more complicated route.

Creating and naming a Library

1. Go to **File > New > Library.**
2. Give your Library a name that makes sense and fits the whole job it does.

Deciding where to store media

If you've ever changed this option, it will have been changed for any new Libraries as well, so it's worth checking.

Media files are saved inside a Library by default. Here is a simple pro process to do it:

1. Click once on the browser's Library name.

2. To find **Library Properties**, go to the **Inspector** box on the right side of the screen.

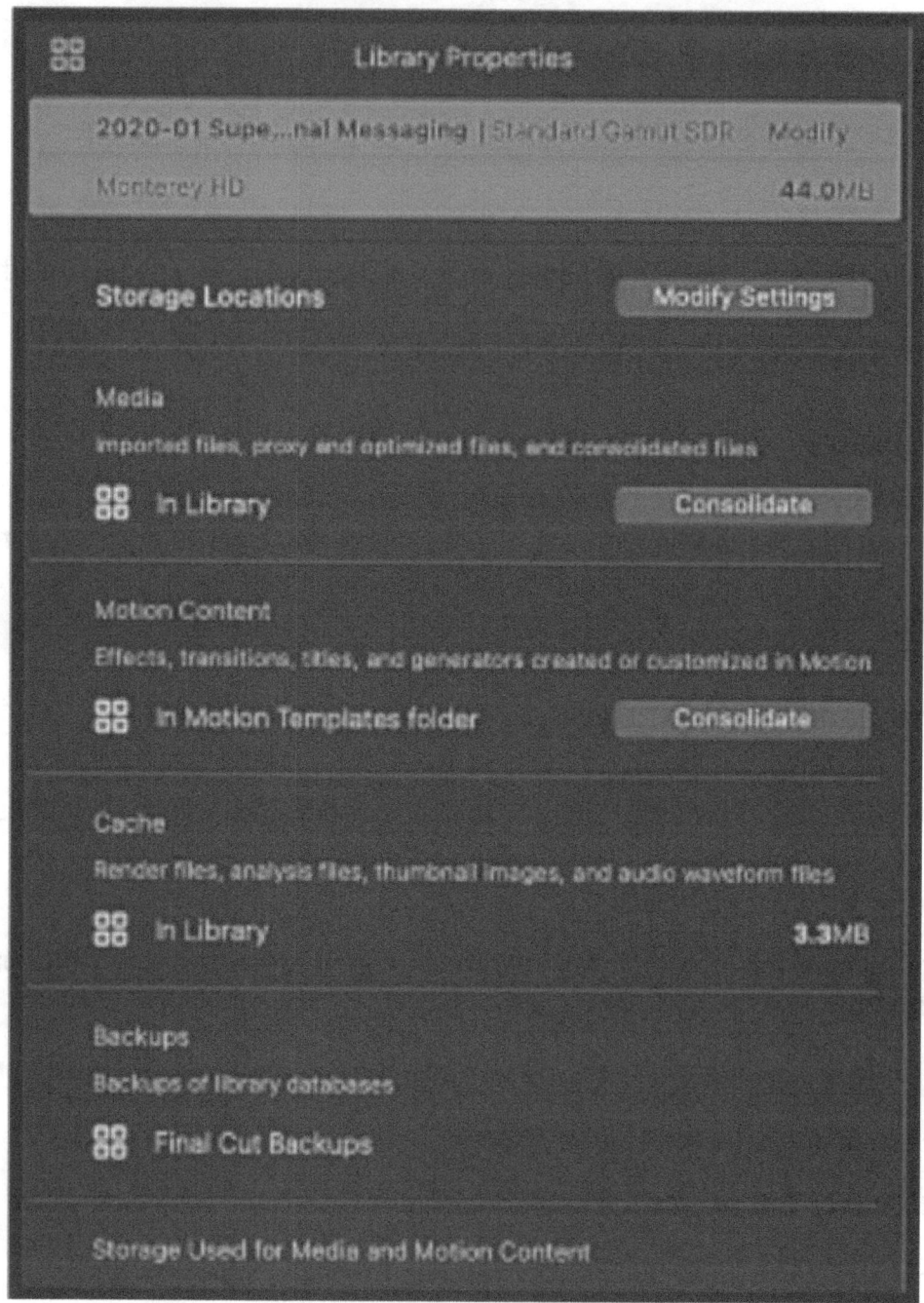

3. Next to **Storage Locations** at the top of these settings, click on the **Modify Settings** button (not **Modify**).

4. **A sheet will slide down from the main window's top:**

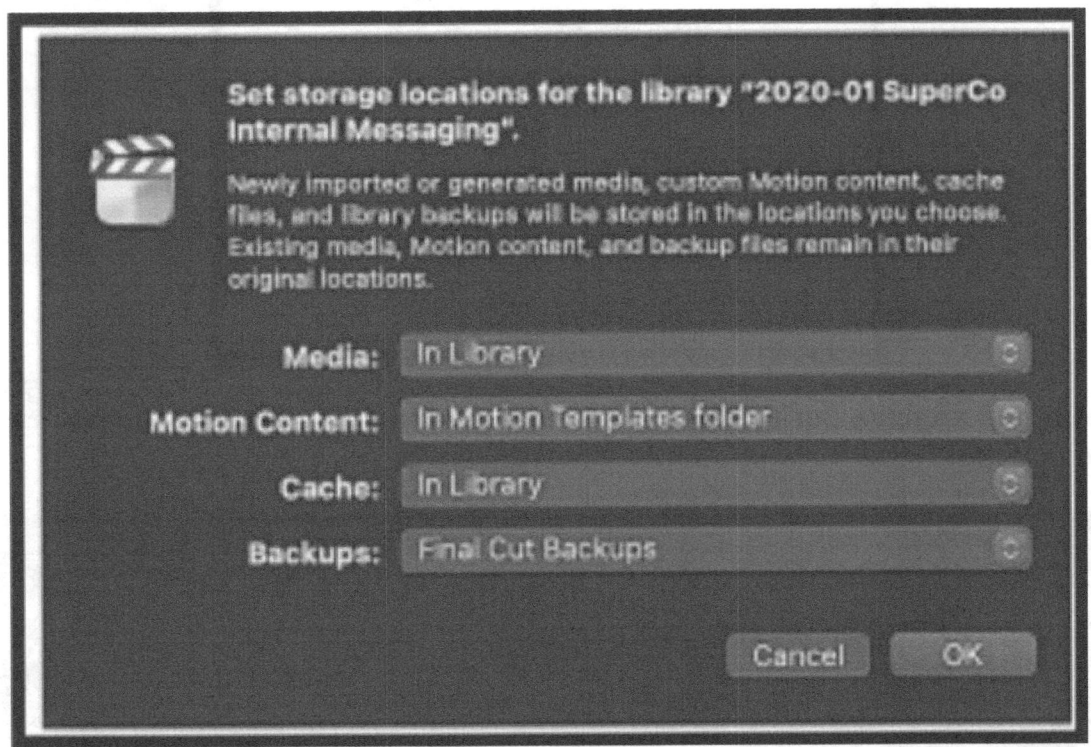

5. The "**In Library**" option should be chosen for **Media**, but the menu will also let you pick an external folder from any linked drive.

I strongly advise new editors to go with the "**in Library**" option, which you can think of as "**self-contained**." It's incredibly easy to move around, almost fool proof, and dead simple. The library on an external drive can be openedon any other Mac with FCP without any prob-lems because of missing media. You can use more complicated shared processes if you store your media in an area outside of a Library, but it can also be a pain. First, you can now move both the media and the Library that doesn't have any media in it. You have to move both of these if you want to move to a different Mac. You may also need to sync your media on the second Mac. If you change any of these storage places, you will need to remember that the settings for any new Libraries you make will be different. Also, media that is already in the Li-brary will not be moved instantly to a newplace. **If you have media in the Library, it is usually best to do a Consolidate process to keep it all together:**

1. To choose the Library, click on its icon in the Browser.
2. It's safer to click on a Library's icon, but clicking on its name normally works too. If a Library is already chosen, a second click on its name will change its name.
3. Go to **File > Consolidate Library Media...**

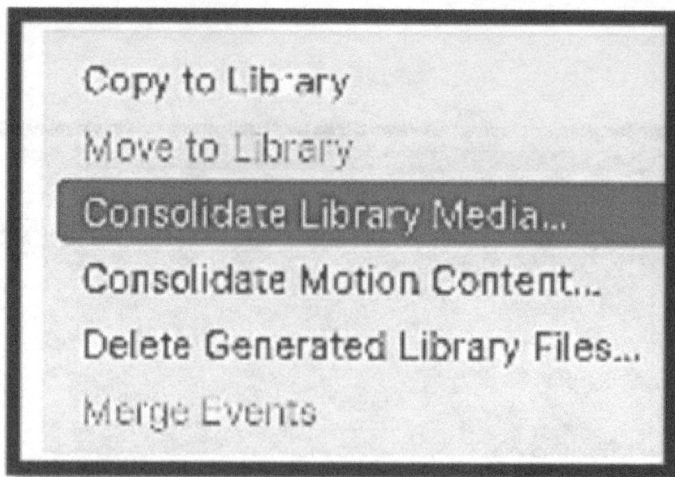

A new text box appears during the Consolidate process to ask what kinds of media you wants to include:

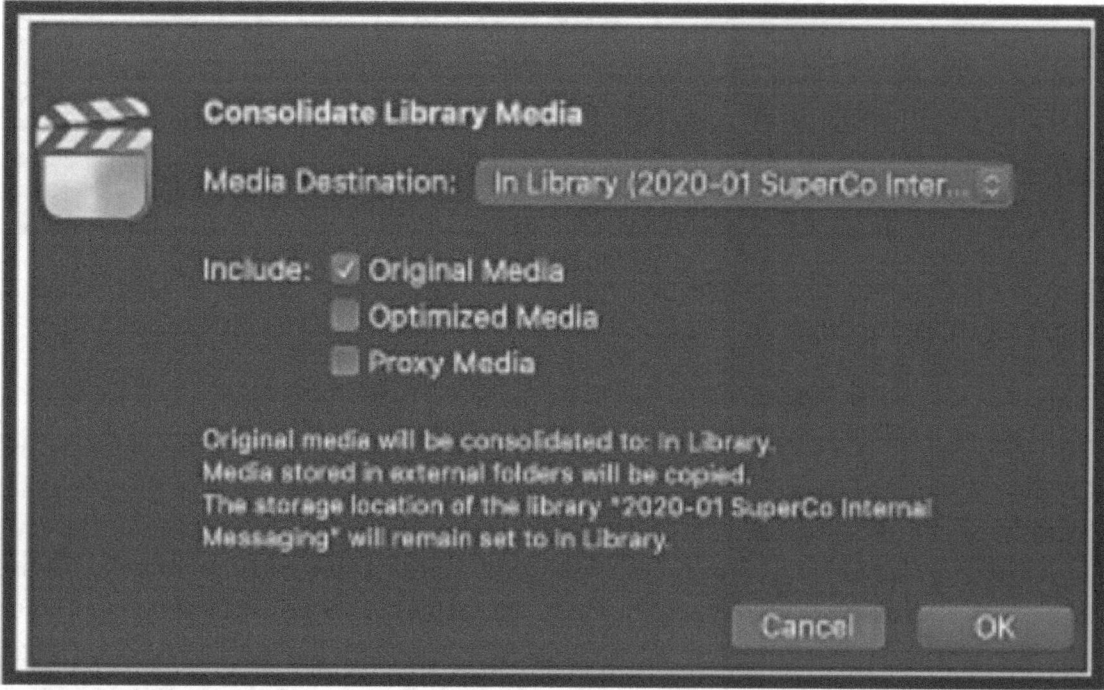

The quickest method is to check the media types you want to use and then let FCP do the rest. Keep in mind that FCP willoffer to make new media types for you if you try to combine ones that don't already exist. Do more than just check the boxes! You'll still want to copy these types of media if you've used them.

Importing Media Files

You can bring your files into Final Cut Pro in two main ways. The first way is to click and drag items from the Finder into the Events that go with them. These cond method involves starting an import window and making selections from there. Let's talk about these ways in more depth.

Click-and-drag method

- Drag the proper footage into the empty Events area in the upper left corner of your Final Cut Pro screen by opening your assets folders in Finder.
- Audio files go into the Audio Event, raw footage intothe Raw Footage Event, and so on. All of your valuables will be made visible as you do this.

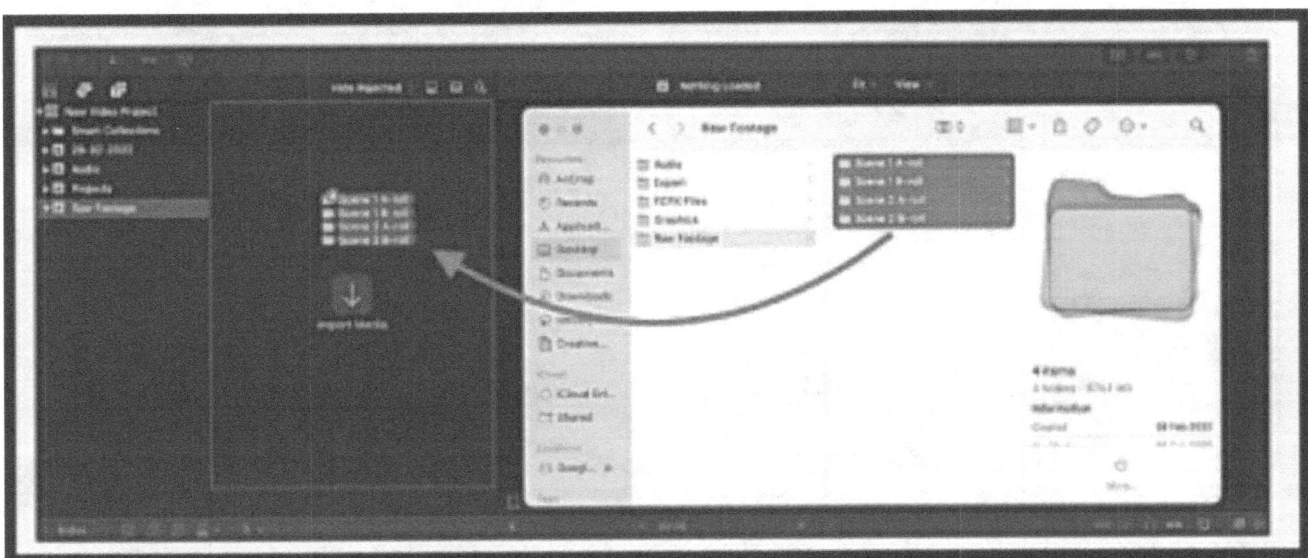

As shown above, if you dragged in more than one organized folder, the assets inside them are given searching terms to keep the orig-inal structure (see below).

Import window method

You can click the Import Media option in an **Event** or use the File menu **(File > Import > Media)** if you don't like clicking and dragging. Usually, clicking and dragging will work, but if you use either of these options instead, youhave more control over other import settings, so we'll also look at those.

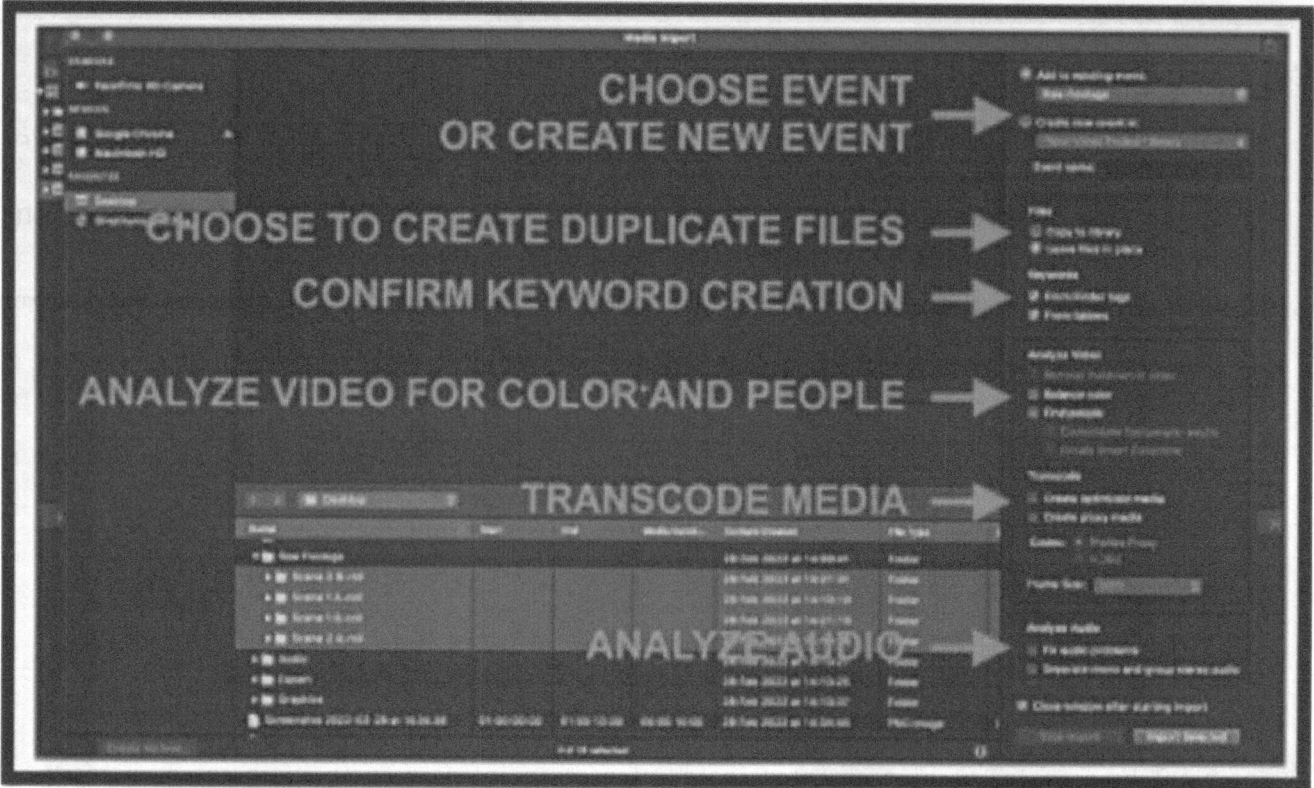

You can choose which Event the chosen clips should go into at the top right of the import window.

Below that, you can choose to make copies of all the files that are being import ed. If my footage is already organized at source, I would leave this box blank because it will take up a lot of drive room. As you go down, you can choose if you want keywords to be made in a way that matches the layout of your folders. Then, you can choose to review downloaded videos aut omatically to even out the colors and find people to search for in your **Smart Col-lections Event**. You can choose to make optimal or alternative media second from the bottom. Depending on the format of your video, this could make your edit go much faster in the long run by making versions of your files that work better in Final Cut Pro X. It might not be necessary for smaller tasks, though. Finally, you can choose to conduct an audio analysis on the assets that are being loaded, just like the video analysis option. I prefer to have direct control over these changes, so I leave it and the video analysis options ignored.

- Click **Import Selected** after making your selections.

Supported File Formats

Video Formats

- Apple Animation codec
- Apple Intermediate codec
- Apple ProRes (all versions)
- Apple ProRes RAW and Apple ProRes RAW HQ
- AVCHD (including AVCCAM, AVCHD Lite, and NXCAM)
- AVC-ULTRA (including AVC-LongG, AVC-Intra Class 50/100/200/ 4:4:4, and AVC-Intra LT)

- Canon Cinema RAW Light (requires the camera manufacturer's plug-in software)
- DV (including DVCAM, DVCPRO, and DVCPR050)
- DVCPROHD
- H.264
- HDV
- HEVC
- iFrame
- Motion JPEG (OpenDML only)
- MPEG IMX(D-10)
- QuickTime formats
- REDCODE RAW (R3D) (requires the camera manufacturer's plug-in software)
- Uncompressed 8-bit 4:2:2
- Uncompressed 10-bit 4:2:2
- XAVC (including XAVC-S)
- XDCAM HD/EX/HD422
- XF-AVC
- XF-HEVC

Audio Formats

- AAC
- AIFF
- BWF
- CAF
- MP3
- MP4
- RF64
- WAV

Still-Image Formats

- BMP
- GIF
- HEIF
- JPEG
- PNG
- PSD (static and layered)
- RAW
- TGA
- TIFF

Container Formats

- 3GP
- AVI
- MOV (QuickTime)
- MP4

- MTS/M2TS
- MXF

Importing from Cameras and Devices

Using camera archives

The **Import** window opens up another way to work, which isn't necessary for most people but is worth thinking about when working with certain cameras. In the bottom left area of the **Import** window, there is a button that says "**Create Archive**" when an SD card is added or a camera is directly linked. There is a window where you can choose where to save a perfect copy of the media card's file format when you click this. It's clear that this takes up a lot of room, and if you already have another backup plan, it may not be necessary. But if your camera saves to separate files and you load them with drag-and-drop, you probably won't need camera backups. Still, they do make it possible to **re-import** lost media, which can be useful sometimes.

Reimporting media

You might find yourself in a strange situation if you stop an import or an import fails because of a crash or a media drive being removed. Clips might be present, but the real media is still on the camera or SD card. There should be a small camera icon in the bottom left corner of the clip to let you know that this has happened.

That's a big warning: if you remove that card or camera, the picture will showered

"Missing Camera" icon and message, andyou won't be able to use the clip:

Do these things to get over this problem:

1. Hook up the camera or SD card that has the media on it.
2. Click on **File**, then **Import**, and then **Reimport from Camera/Archive.**

The camera is still available most of the time, and this process is easy. You will lose the clip, though, if the media has been erased. Be sure that you've loaded the cards safely and backed them up twice before you delete them. Camera archives are a good way to back up the original media, but I like to back up my whole main media drive to another local drive and have my whole system backed up automatically on-line. **File > Relink Files** is the command you'll need to reconnect any external media that you may have lost.

Importing from iMovie or FCP for iPad

People who are moving up from iMovie to FCP will be happy to know that it"s pretty easy to move their edits over. On your iPhone or iPad, the Pro service operates as follows:

1. Startup iMovie and tap the Project you want to move once.
2. Click the **Share** button at the bottom, then click **Options, Project,** and **Done.**
3. Pick a way to get the Project to your Mac, like using AirDrop.

If your Mac and iOS device are connected to the same Wi-Fi net work and AirDrop is open in the Finder on your Mac, this is the most user-friendly option for sending files.

4. With the Project now on your Mac, go to **File > Import> iMovie iOS** Projects and find the. **iMovieMobile** file and click on **Import**. (This file will be in **Downloads** if you used AirDrop.)

Now a new Event will be made, and all of your media clips and a Project will be in it.

It's even easier to switch from iMovie to FCP on the same Mac:

1. Pick the Event with the clips and Project that you want to move to FCP.
2. Go to **File > Send Event to Final Cut Pro.**

Now there is a new Event in a new Library. When you're done with a job in FCP for iPad and want to move it to your Mac:

1. Choose your Project from the list of **All Projects** on the sidebar.
2. Tap **Share** in the upper right corner and pick **Final Cut Pro for iPad Project**.
3. Make sure **Include All Media** is chosen on the sheet that comes up, and then press **Export**.
4. Send the project to your Mac by airdrop.

CHAPTER 6: FUNDAMENTAL EDITING TECHNIQUES

Creating a New Project

In Final Cut Pro, you have to make a project before you can make a movie. The project keeps track of the media you use and the choices you make when editing.

These things happen when you make a new Final Cut Pro project:

- Give the project a name.
- Specify where the project is stored in the event.

Most of the time, you store projects in events that also hold the media that was used to make the project. If you drag media into the time-line from the Finder or from the Photos, Videos, and Audio tab, it will be put in the same event as the project. If you want to, you can also set the project's starting timecode and its video, audio, and render features. You add clips from an event in the library to your project after you've made it.

Note: If you're working on a project and haven't added media to Final Cut Pro yet, you should do so.

1. In Final Cut Pro's Libraries sidebar, choose the event where you want to make the project and press "**Next**."
2. Select **File > New > Project** (or press **Command-N**).

Tip: You don't have to enter the project settings manually; the video features of a certain clip can be used to instantly make a project. Right-click on a clip in the browser and select "New Project." Type in a name for the project and click "OK."

3. In the new window, in the Name box, type a name for the project.
4. Click the "**In Event**" menu and pick a different event if you want to save the project in a different event than the one you chose.
5. The timecode for your project should start at avalue other than 00:00:00:00. Type a value in the Starting Timecode field to change this.

Note: This is where you can start a new project if the regular setting sare shown. Just click OK. You can add a clip to the new (empty) project timeline. If the properties of the clip match a built-in standard, Final Cut Pro changes the properties of the project to match the properties of the clip.

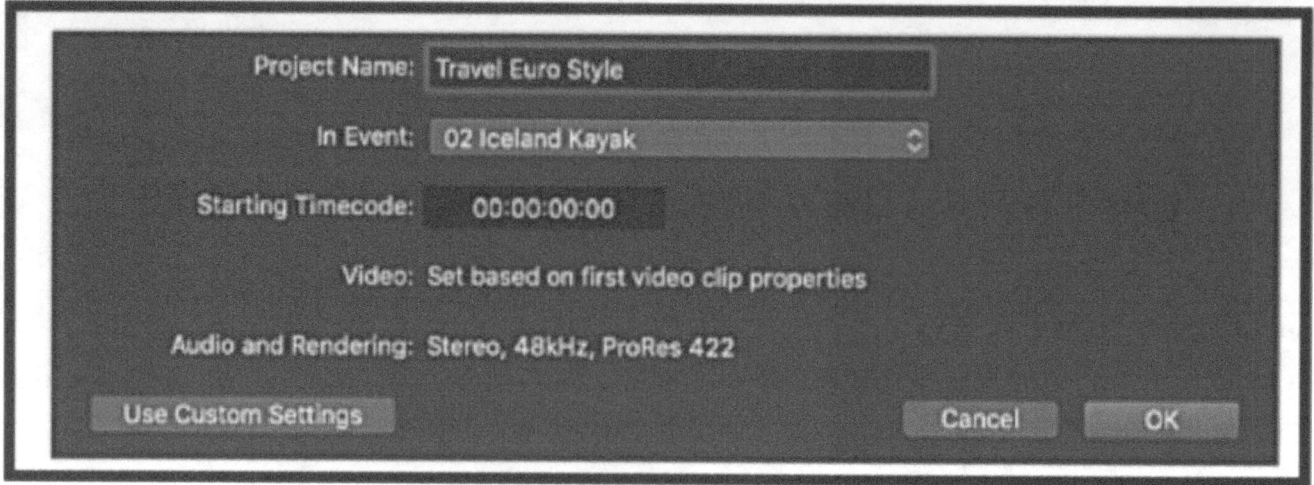

6. Click **Use Custom Settings** if you want to change the project settings even more.

Note: By default, Final Cut Pro shows the automatic settings. However, it remembers the settings you last used, so you may not need to do this step.

7. Use the pop-up options in the custom settings view to change any setting about the videoor audio of the project.
8. Click the OK button.

The browser shows the new project with the name you chose in step 4. You can now edit your project in other ways, like adding titles, spe-cial effects, background music, sound effects, and more. You can also add clips from the browser.

Setting Project Properties

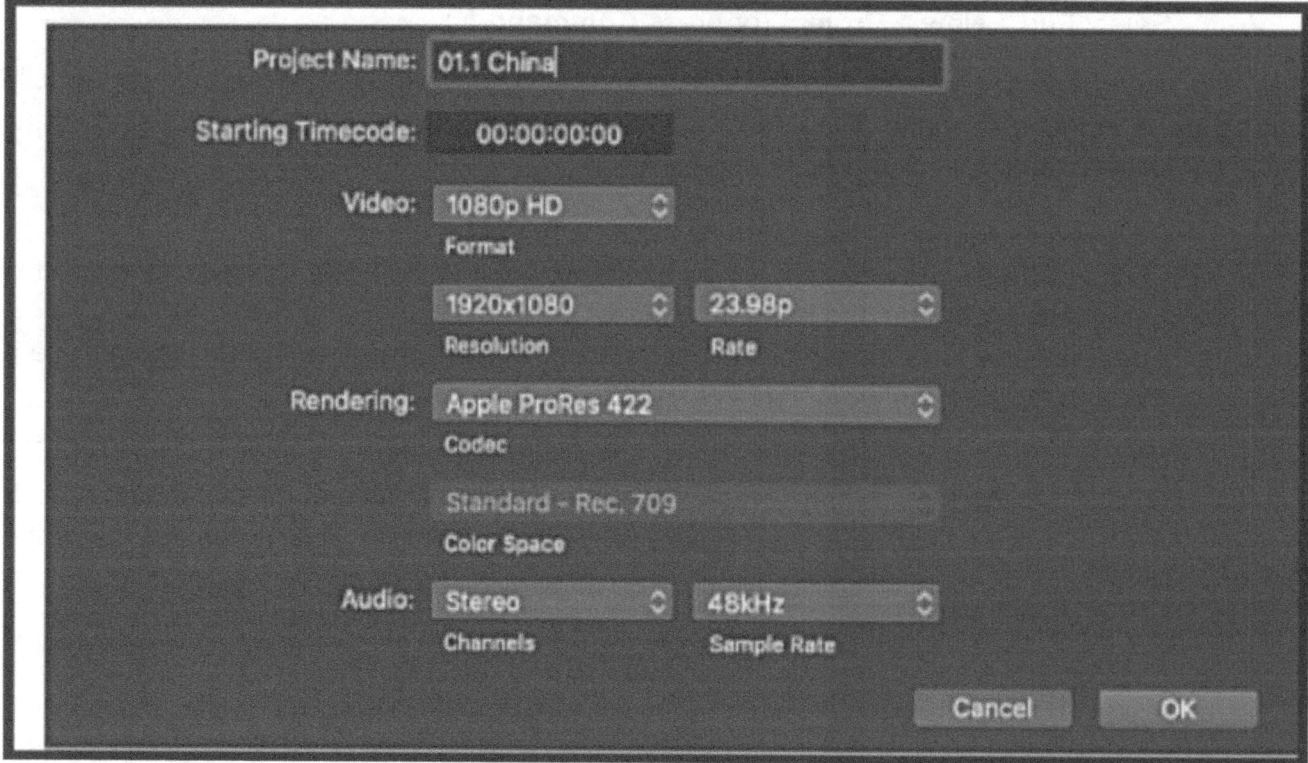

Project Name

- Project Name: Type a name for the project here.

Starting Timecode

- *Starting Timecode*: Type a number if you want the timecode to begin at a different time than 00:00:00:00

Video

- Format: The video format is a way of recording the video. You can also choose an aspect ratio.

Note: The Projection Type pop-up menu shows up when you choose 360° from the Format pop-up menu.

- **Resolution**: Pick the video's frame size. The format determines the frame sizes that can be used. In the Format pop-up box, choose Custom to enter any frame size you want.
- **Rate**: Pick the number of frames per second (fps).

Note: Keep in mind that you can't change the frame rate of a project that already exists unless the timeline is empty.

Rendering

- *Codec*: Pick the codec that will be used for background rendering in your project.
- *Color Space*: Pick the color spacefor your project, like the color space of the render files for your project. You should pick a color space that matches the one you plan to export for final delivery. This menu shows wide-gamut settings when the Library Properties inspector's color processing setting is set to Wide Gamut HOR. The rendering color space is picked for you based on other settings for standard formats. If you choose NTSCSD as the video file, for example, the color space will be set to Standard - Rec. 601 (NTSC).

Note: This setting also controls the color space of images sent to video scopes, the color space used to find colors that aren't in the right range, the color space of files shared with the Export File share option, and the color space of images that shows up on your computer screen.

Audio

- **Channels**: The audiocan be presented as stereo or multiple surround sound, depending on the channel setting.
- **Sample Rate**: Pick the audio sample rate for your project. The sample rate is how many times a sound is measured per second. Higher-quality audio and bigger file sizes result from a higher sample rate pro, while lower sample rates result in lower-quality audio and smaller file sizes. The source material you're working with and the final location of your audio will determine the sample rate you select.

Templates

Making library structure templates is a quick and easy way to save time and makes use of them in any future libraries.

Creating templates

Setting up a new library and selecting the right order for events, groups, Keyword and Smart Collections will let you save templates for later use. Following that, you save the empty library some where you will remember. Right-click on the empty library in the Finder and choose "**Duplicate**." This will make a copy of the format you want to use next time.

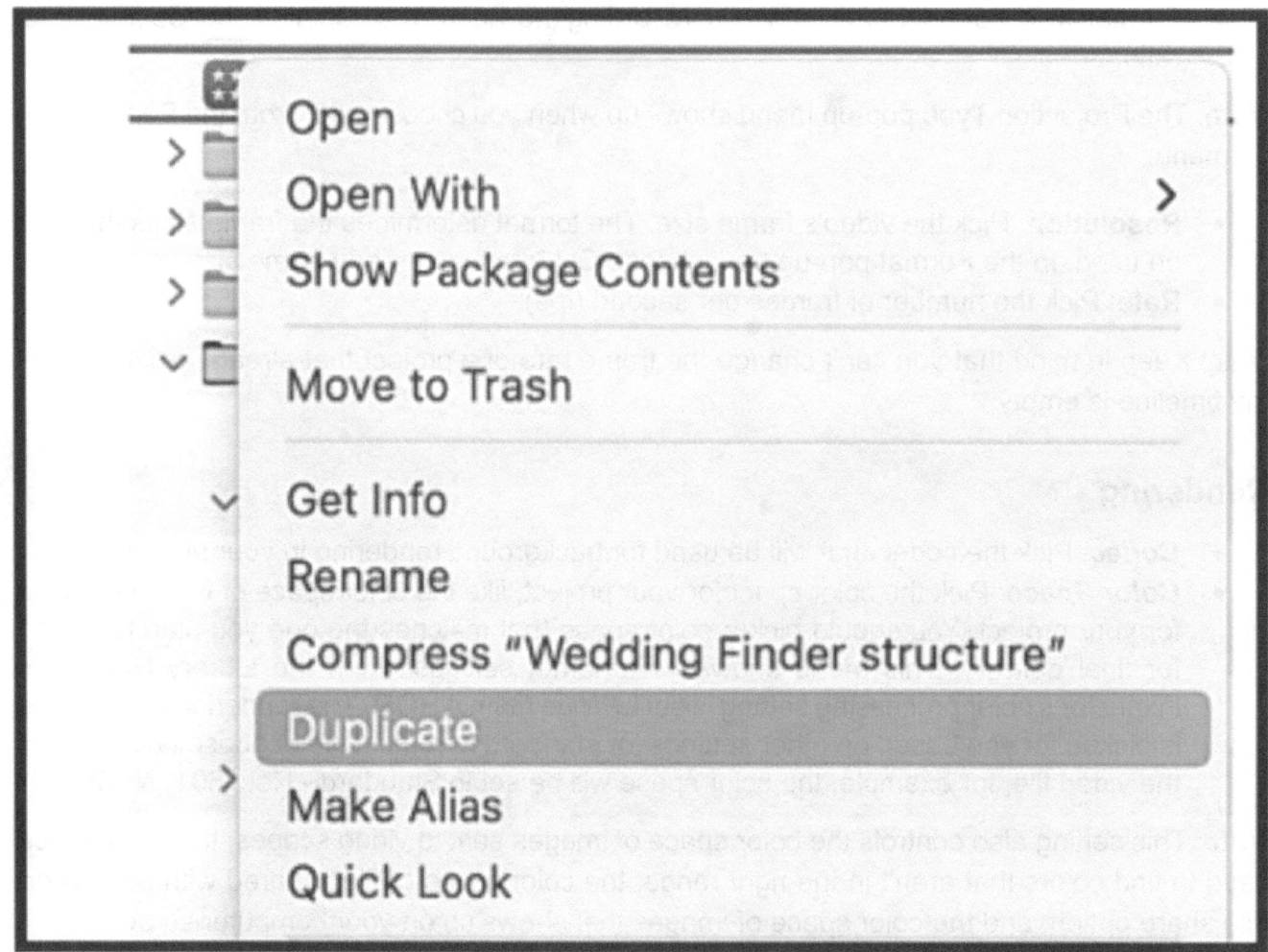

If there isn't any media in the template yet, it duplicates right away. You would have to wait a while if you wanted to duplicate a working library that has media in it. Choose the library that was duplicated, give it a name, and then double-click it to open the template in Final Cut Pro. This is a great way to organize camera footage shot onyour favorite cameras in Final Cut Pro intoSmart Collections. The camera footage will be added to the relevant Smart Collection automatically as soon as it is imported. You can change the way Final Cut Pro is organized to fit your editing style or styles if you need to do different kinds of editing. This is where the idea of themes comes from. You should put all of your media into different groups, but how do you quickly find a certain clip if you forget which collection it's in? This is even more important forSmart Collections, which store media without you having to do anything.

Insert clips in Final Cut Pro for Mac

When you use an insert edit, you move all the clips after the placement point later in the timeline to make room for the new clip. There are no lost clips in your project. When you edit an insert clip, the project gets longer by the length of the clip that was added.

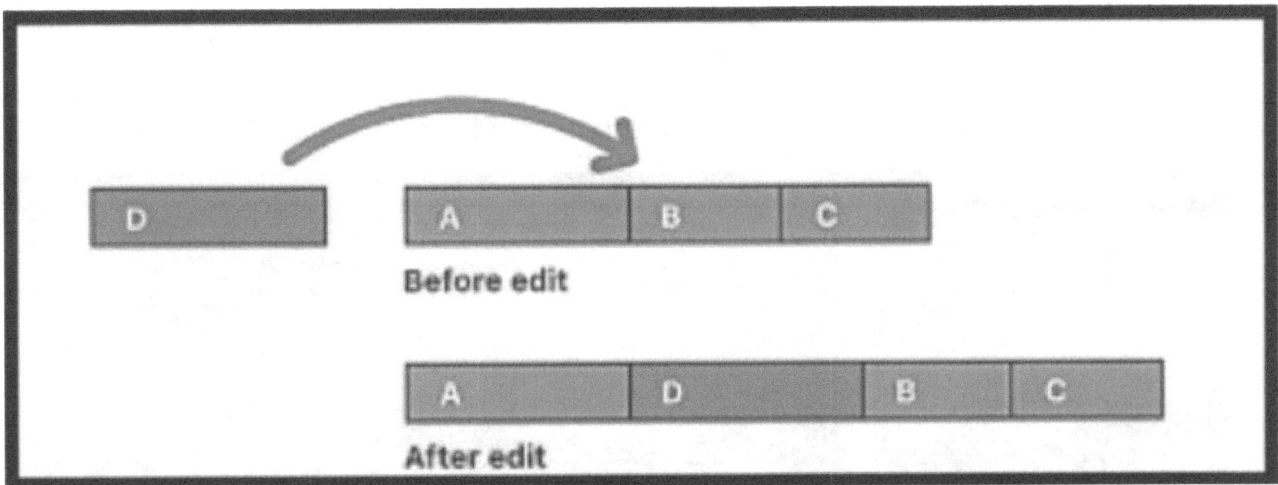

When you want to add a new shot to the beginning or middle of your project, you can use insert edits. You can also use an insert edit to switch between the action in a current clip and the action in a new clip that was just added. After the inserted clip, the action in the first clip starts up again.

Insert browers clips in the timeline

1. In Final Cut Pro, go to the browser and choose one or more clips.
2. Move the playhead to the spot in the main storyline or a chosen storyline (or make a range selection) where you want to add the clip.
3. Pick one of these things to do:
   - You can press W or go to Edit > Insert.

Note: The edit will happen at the skimmer point if you use the keyboard shortcut and the skimmer is in the timeline.

   - In the upper left part of the timeline, click the "Insert" button.

The clip shows up in the timeline, and all the clips that came after it are moved ahead. The clips are put in at the playhead point if the skimmer is not present. You can cut an existing timeline clip at the insertion point when you do an insert edit. The second half of the clip is moved to the end of the newly inserted clip, along with the rest of the footage to the right of the insertion point.

Drag-and-Drop Clips

If you want to add clips between other clips in Final Cut Pro, you can drag them to the timeline. The Libraries, Photos, Videos, and Audio, or Titles and Generators sidebars can be used to showclips in the browser. You can then drag them to the timeline. You can also drag clips straight from the Finder to the timeline to add them.

- In the timeline, drag the clip you want to add to an edit point (aspace between two clips).

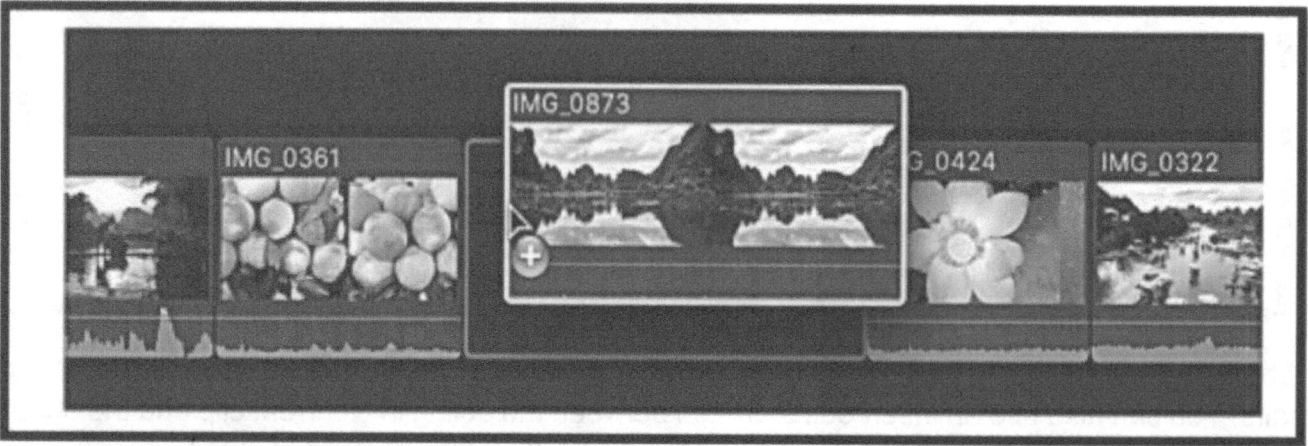

When you add the clip to the timeline, all the clips that come after it are moved to the right.

Overwrite clips in Final Cut Pro for Mac

When you do an overwrite edit, oneor more source clips replace any clips in the main storyline or a chosen storyline, beginning at the playhead or skimmer position or a range selection start point. The length of your project stays the same because no clip items are rippled forward.

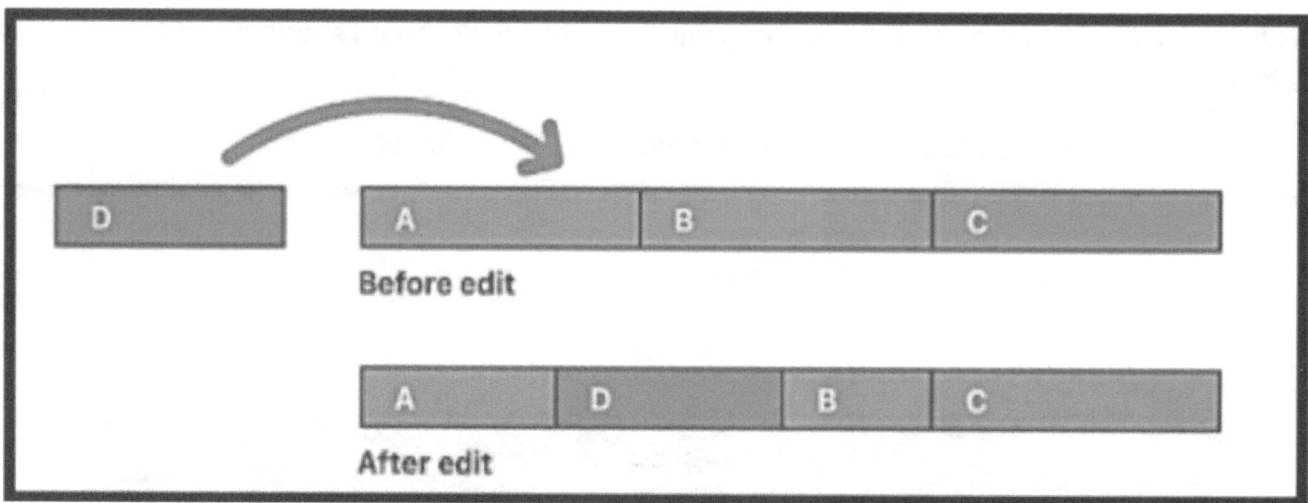

It is not the same as replacing media to overwrite it. Overwriting only works with range selections, not whole clips, and it's not limited by the edges of clips. When you want to change media for a certain amount of time instead of replacing specific shots, use an overwrite edit. **Note**: You can also make overwrite edits with three-point editing.

1. In Final Cut Pro, go to the browser and choose one or more clips.

The clips show up in the timeline in the order that you chose them if you choose more than one.

2. In the main storyline or a chosen plotline, do one of the following to set where you want the replace clip to begin in the timeline:
- Put the playhead in place.
- Pick an area in the timeline that includes one or more clips.

Note: The overwrite command doesn't affect timeline selections that are whole clips. There is no need to choose a range in the timeline because the overwrite clip starts where the playhead or skimmer is.

3. Press the D key or go to **Edit > Overwrite.**

The original clip is part of the main plot and overwrites any other clips that are playing at the same time.

Note: The edit will happen at the skimmer point if you use the keyboard shortcut and the skimmer is in the timeline.

Press **Shift-D** to replace the playhead back so that the end point of the overwrite clip, not its beginning point, is lined up with the spot you want to change.

CHAPTER 7: ORGANIZING FOOTAGE WITH KEYWORDS

Reviewing your media

You probably already know that the **spacebar** plays and pauses music, but there's more to pro-media review than that. Skimming is very important, and the Viewer has a lot of small options as well. First, let's talk about why you shouldn't click so much.

Skimming is awesome

When making the shift to FCP, clicking is likely the first habit most editors will need to break. You don't have to click on a clip before play-ing it back. In fact, clicking on a clip can lead to problems if you accidentally drag it and change the selection. Instead, move your mouse over the filmstrip of a clip right before a cert ain time and press the spacebar.

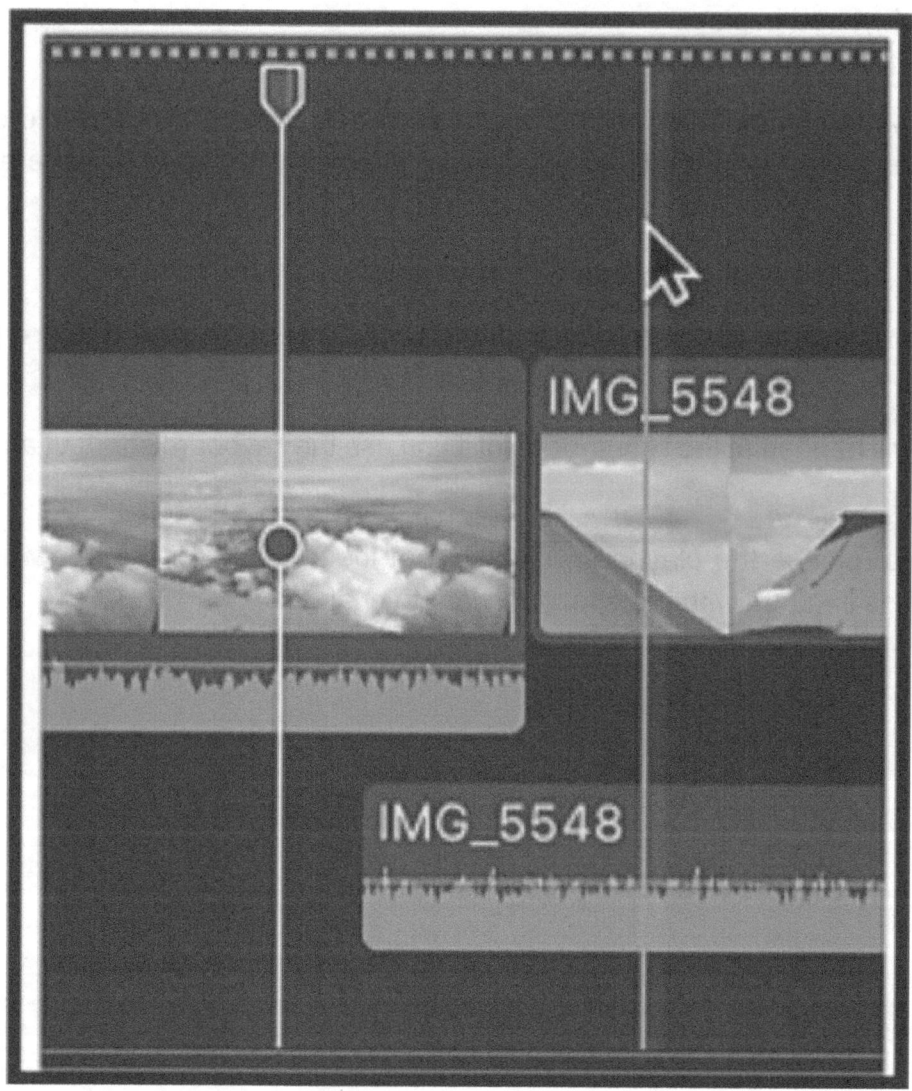

The Playhead and the Skimmer are the two ways that FCP can show where you are in time. The Browser will show the following when you move your mouse over a clip's filmstrip:

- The **Playhead** is a white line with an arrow at the very top. It can be positioned with a click and stays put even if the mouse cursor goes to another spot.
- The **Skimmer** is a red line that moves with the mouse and can only be seen when the mouse is over a clip.
- This button in the middle of the menu or the S shortcut can turn the **Skimmer** on or off (blue means on):

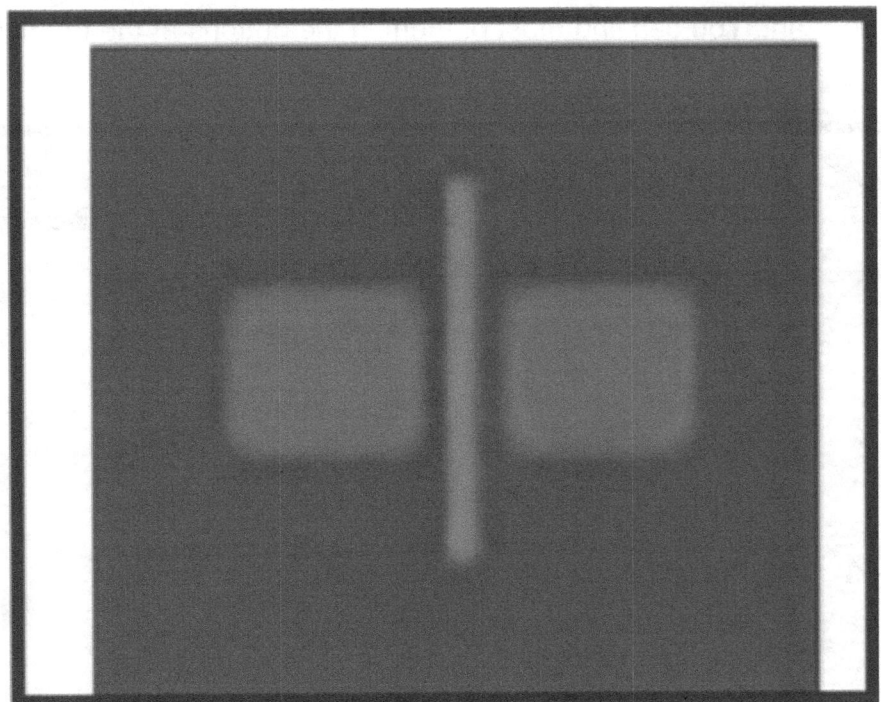

- The **Skimmer** is more important than the **Playhead** if it's there.

Most people find the Skimmer very useful because it lets you move through clips as quickly as you can drag your finger over its filmstrip. The thumbnail that the cursor is currently over will change to reflect the exact frame that the cursor is over. In the Viewer, you will also be able to see the full size of the frame. If you don't like skimming, just press S to turn it off. If you only have an issue with the audio, you can turn it off by pressing the next button or **Shift+ S**:

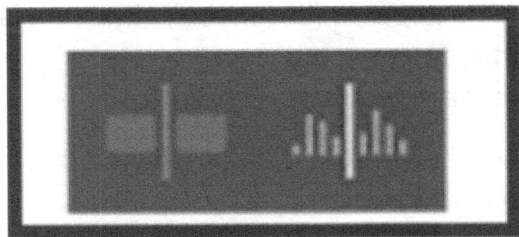

The Skimmer is also a great way to learn common shortcuts because if you have to click on a button to do something, the Skimmer will go away and your mouse will leave the current pane. In order to set the Playhead position, you will need to click if you don't want to learn shortcuts. Your eyes will probably be on the Viewer as you skim and click to move the Playhead, so it's time to take a closer look.

Exploring the Viewer

The Skimmer and the Playhead can both change a thumbnail in the filmstrip of a clip, but the Viewer is bigger and easier to see. Several options are available for showing video, but for now, only a few are important. You can find most of them in the buttons at the top right of the Viewer pane.

You can change the size of the video in the first menu, and you can do these things quickly by using shortcuts. To target the Viewer, click it once, then do the following:

- Press **Command + plus** to zoom in (this is really the equals key).
- Press **Command + minus** to zoom out
- Press **Shift + Z** to make the video fit the screen

This last option is persistent, so when you've chosen **Fit**, you can resize the Viewer by dragging its edges, and the video will resize to match:

Most of the time, this **Fit** view is the best way to make the video as big as possible. However, you might want to view it at **100%** to see all the frames you shot. One interesting thing about a 5K iMac is how few pixels a Full HD 1080p picture takes up. You can change the video level and show or hide graphics in the second **View** menu.

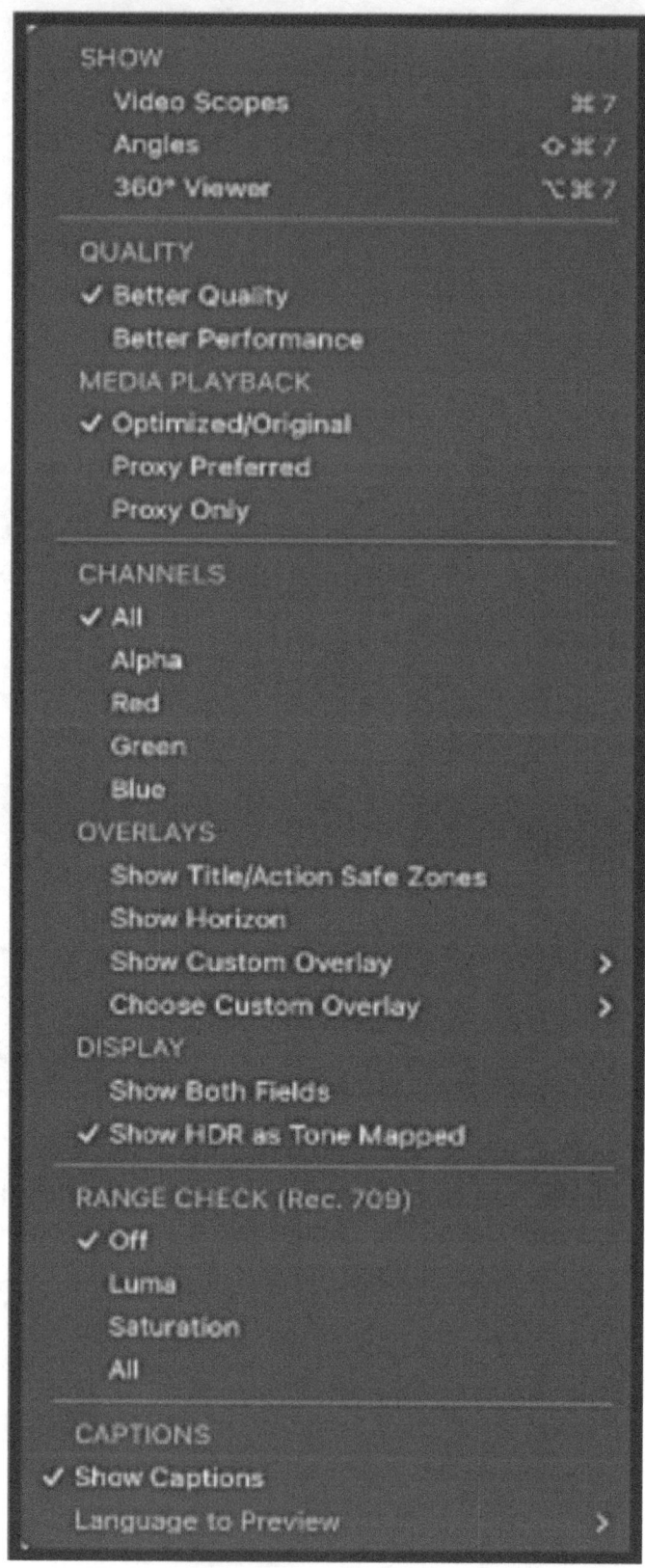

Keep in mind that the button in the upper right area can be used to turn on a second display. The menu next to the button can then be used to choose what goes on that display. If you connect a second screen and don't set it to mirror the first one, this button and menu will only show up:

You can choose the Viewer right away, leaving the first screen with only the Browser and the Inspector (if you need it). Some editors like to use a vertical screen for the Browser instead, which also works. In addition to these second display options, you can also set one device to only show raw video.

A/V Output

You can put the Viewer on a second screen and use the button in the bottom right corner to go into fullscreen mode. But there's another way to show video in fullscreen. You can pick an external device for A/V output in **Final Cut Pro > Settings/Preferences** under **Playback**. This is the last option from the list at the bottom. Any 4K, UHD, or 1080p TV that is attached via HDMI should also work. Third-party external connections also work.

NOTE: This is not a Viewer, so there are no quality or layer options. This is a raw video output feed instead, meant for a high-quality dedi-cated output, which could be a second or even a third dedicated display.

This is the pane in **Settings/Preferences** that has **A/V Output:**

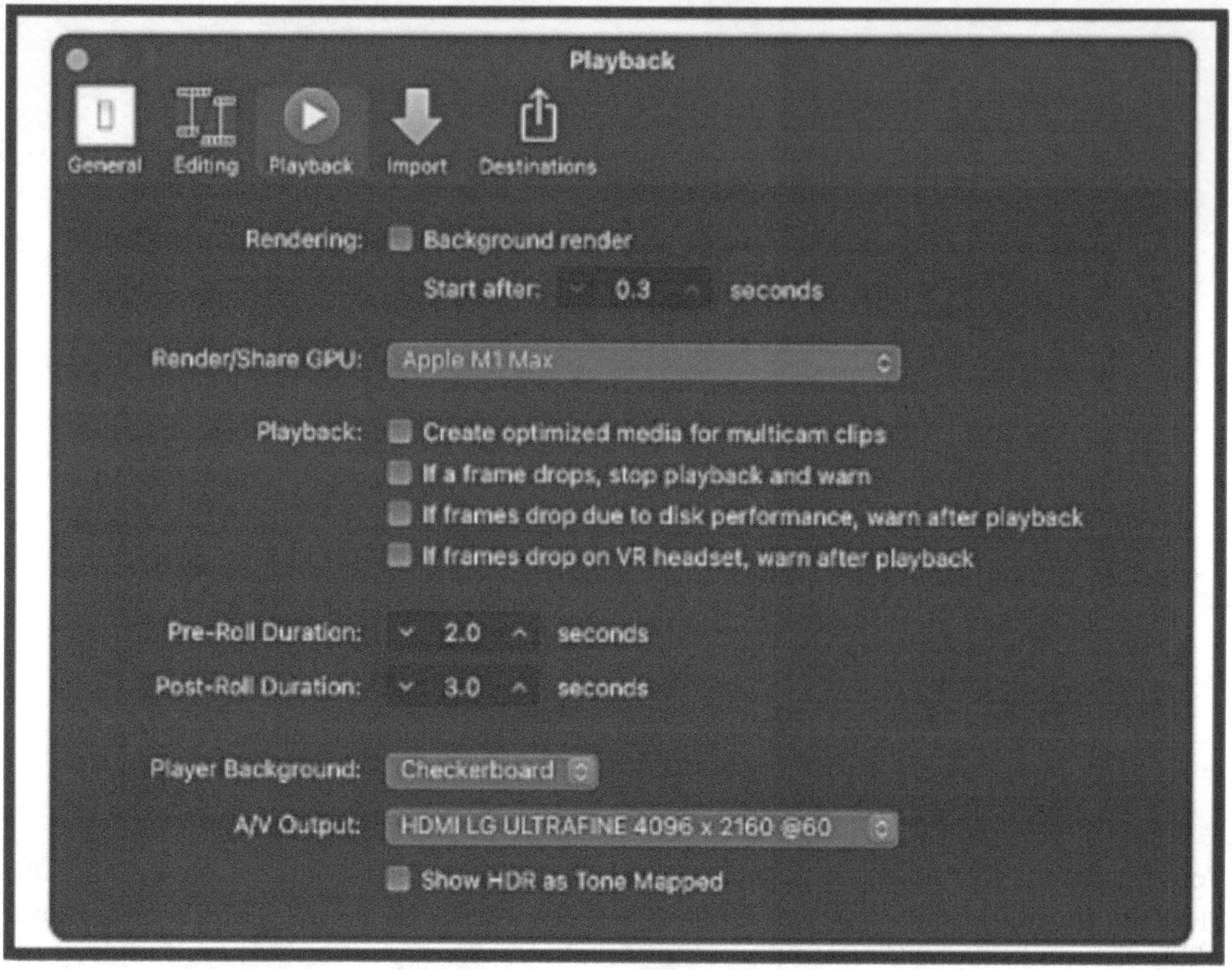

After setting up, you need to turn on **A/V Output** by going to **Window > A/V Output**. If you had the **Viewer** on the same second display as the **A/V Output** before, it will now move back to the main screen before the second display is taken over by a fullscreen output. This looks great, but computers that aren't very fast may have trouble with it. Also, there will still be a normal Viewer on the main screen that shows the normal settings and layers.

Browser view options

The two buttons in the top right area of the Browser are the same as the ones in the **Import** window. On the left is a drop-down menu for **Clip Filtering** and on the right is a search sign.

There is a Filmstrip/List button in the top right corner, just like in the Import window:

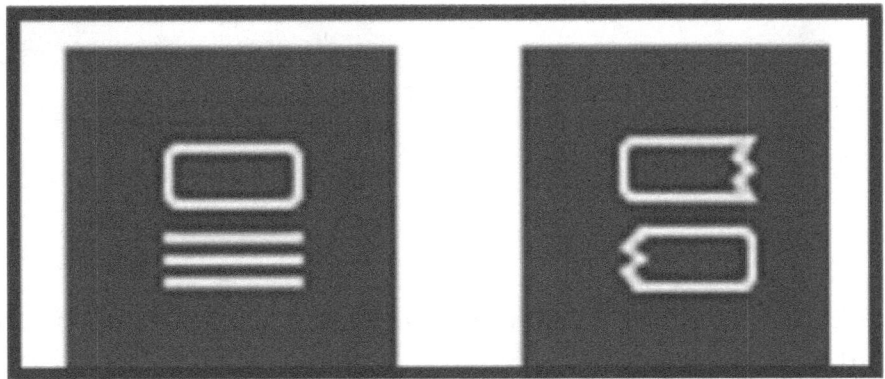

The icon indicates *not the current state, but what you'll switch to if you click on it:*

- **List** view is best for A-roll that is visually repeated, like conversations, where the pictures won't tell you much.
- **Filmstrip** view is great for B-roll and other things you can quickly look over.

You'll switch between these views a lot because each one is useful in some situations.

List view

This is a good use for List view, with a little blurring on the filmstrip to protect privacy:

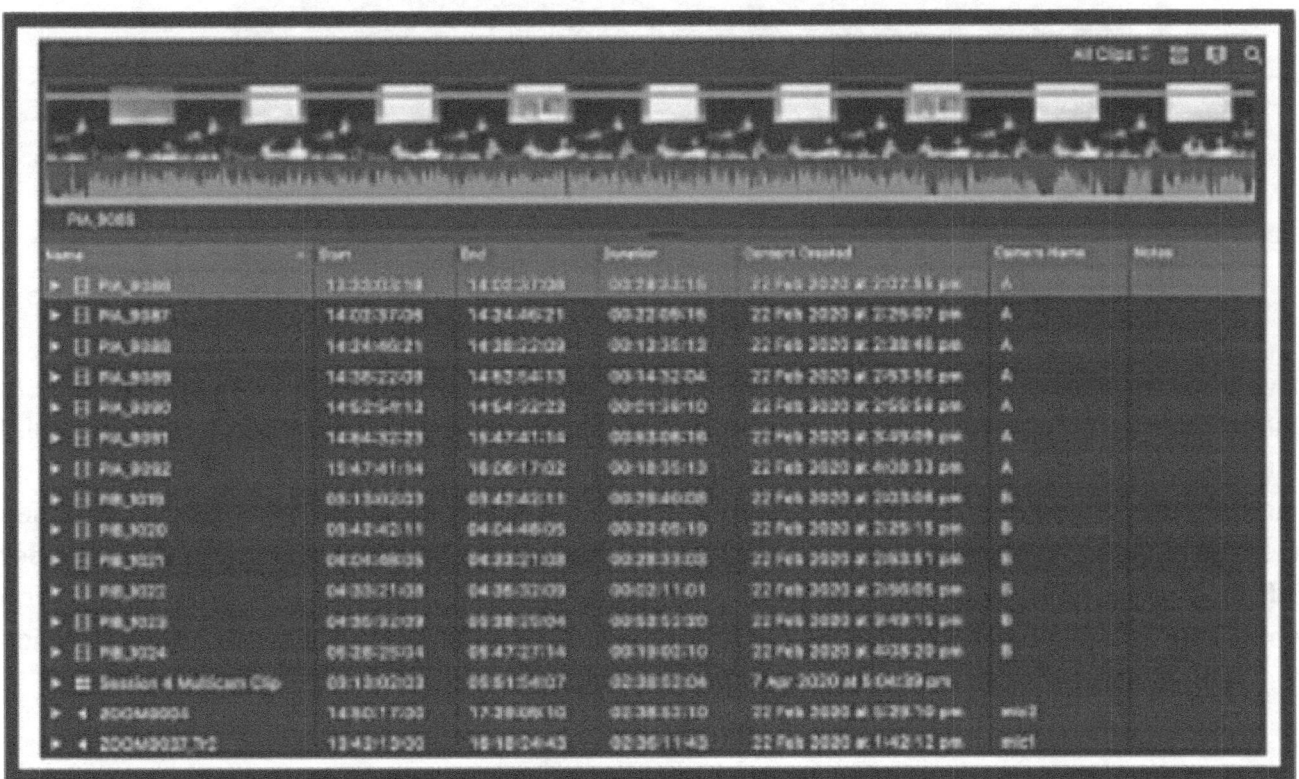

There are many ways to use the column headers at the top:

- Click on the column header to sort by that column.
- To reverse a column's sort, click on the currently selected column header. To change the size of a column, drag the column header's edge.

- Drag the column headers to the left or right of other column headers to change the order of the columns.
- To show or hide a column, right-click on its name and pick one of the options that follow:

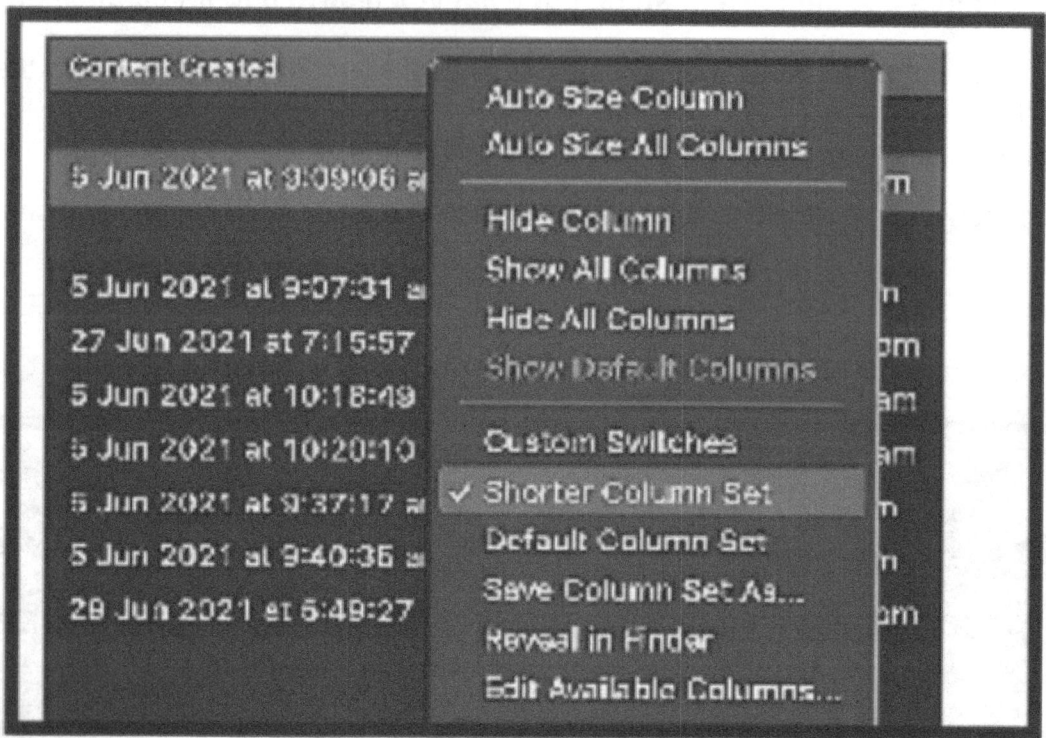

If your camera starts every clip at 0:00:00:00, the **Start** and **End** columns might not be very useful. But if your camera can use a **Time of Day** timecode, these columns are more useful. I usually sort my clips by **Name, Date Created,** or **Duration**, but that's just the beginning. You can do much more complicated things with this. You can also pick which information properties to show in these fields, not just the ones that are shown by default. To get to the **Column Set Editor**, choose **Edit Available Columns**... From there, you can turn on or off any feature you want. The view can be changed using the drop-down menu at the top right of the Browser, which also lets you sort with, hide, show, and rearrange columns.

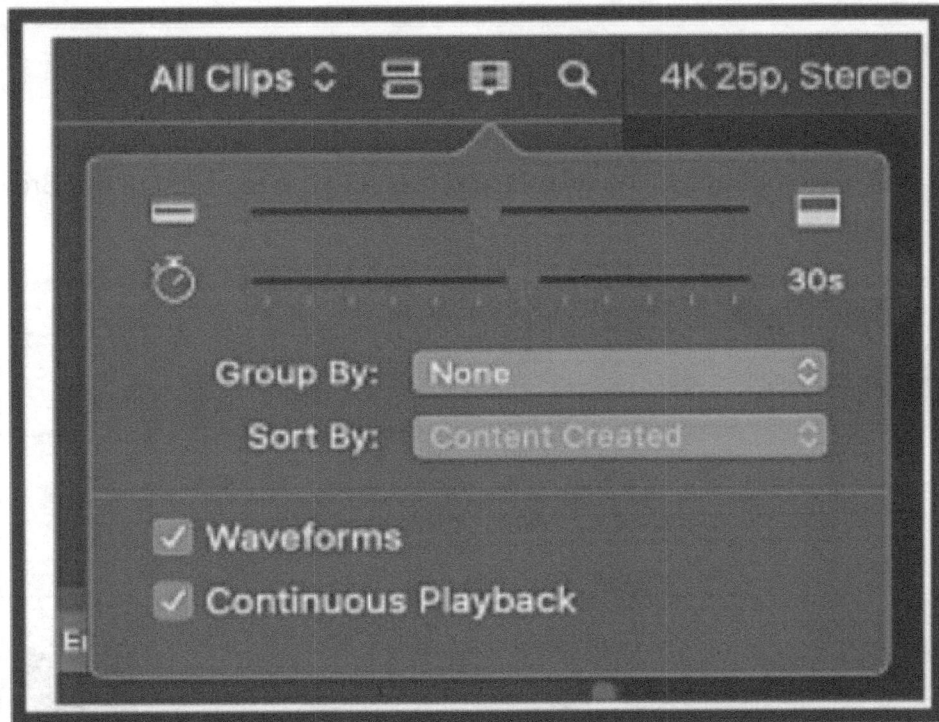

Filmstrip view

In Filmstrip view, you can see this type of footage best. It has a lot of B-roll and visual shots. You can see right away if the shot is static or moving, and you know exactly what's in it:

Filmstrip view has more options in the drop-down menu at the top right of the Browser because there are no columns:

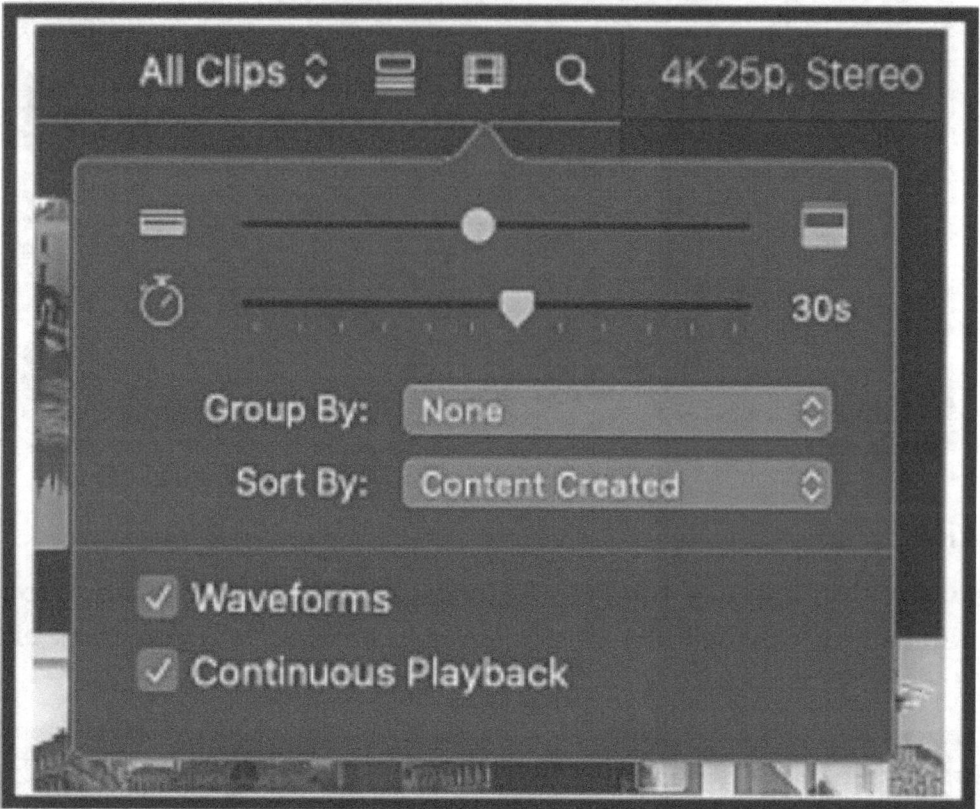

Playback shortcuts

The **spacebar** (play/pause) is an easy-to-hit shortcut that works well as a first step. That's not all you need to know, though. You'll also need to know how to use a few more keys. If you want to watch a lot of video, you may need to play it back very quickly. On the other hand, you might want to play it back much slower when you need to be very clear about which frame you want. That and more are coming up soon.

Basic shortcuts

The three keys you should really drive home are J, K, and L:

- **L** plays forward.
- **K** pauses.
- **J** plays backward:

Your most important shortcuts today will probably be these keys, which you can use in the Viewer, the Timeline, and even QuickTime Player. You can use these with either your left or right hand, and with a mouse or trackpad. **For easy access, make sure to leave your three fingers on these keys. There's more, though:**

- Press **J** or **L** over and over to double the speed of playing in that direction: 2x speed, 4x speed, 8x speed, and so on.
- To go to 1 x speed in the opposite direction right away, press the opposing playback key.

You can use these popular editing keys to play at four times the regular speed by pressing **L** three times or **J** two times. **This is a quick way to look overvideo or at least get a general idea of it. K also has some tricks, which are these:**

- To move one frame forward, hold down **K** and then press **L**.
- To move one frame backward, hold down **K** and tap **J** at the same time.
- To play in slow motion with slowed-down audio, press **K** and then **J** or **L**.

Also, the horizontal arrow keys are important:

- → moves forward one frame.
- ← moves back one frame.
- **Shift +** → moves forward 10 frames.
- **Shift +** ← moves back 10 frames.

Examining metadata

There are a lot of fields by default in **List** view, but they don't show everything that can be stored in a file. You can now see this info and may be change it in either the Inspector or the **List** view of the Browser, though it takes some work.

Metadata in List view

Metadata, which is data from the camera that is connected to media files, can be pretty dull and technical. It's something that a program should handle, not you. You might not care too much about each clip's codec or color profile. Still, some of this information can help you make smart decisions by finding files that have certain traits.

Many people use the default fields in the List view to find the most useful information. You can sortfiles by any of these factors to find specific ones:

- **Duration**: If you need a clip that is long enough to fill in a certain-sized gapin your edit.
- **File Type**: If you want to separate audio, video, and stills.
- **Video Frame Rate**: You can use Video Frame Rate to find high-frame-rate footage and frame-rate mismatches.
- **Frame Size**: Frame Size lets you zoom in
- **Codecs**: Codecs lets you find footage that might be harder to work with directly.
- **Camera Name**: Useful when setting up multicams
- **Shot/ Scene/ Reel**: This is used to organize clips from longer shoots.

Right-clicking on a column title and selecting **Edit Available Columns** lets you add more columns if you want to.

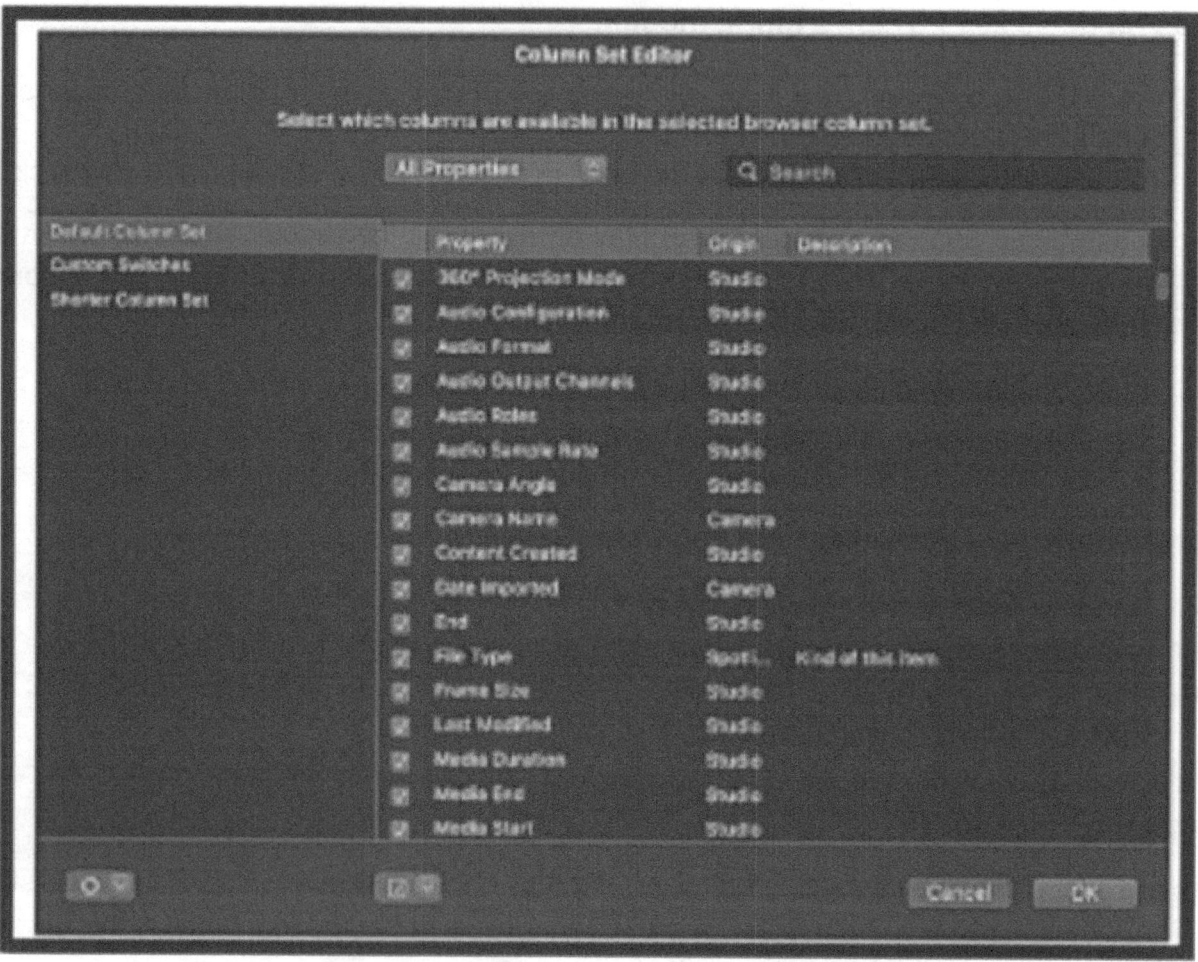

It might seem hard to understand this long conversation, but it's not. First, look at one of the features in the long column on the right, like **Anamorphic Override**. The usual set can't be changed, so you might be asked to make a new one. If so, name it **Extended Video Properties**. Choose your new **Column Set** from the list on the left, and then add any features you want to be able to change. The menu at the top of the window lets you quickly jump to a certain type of information, like **Video Properties or Camera Properties**. You could also go back to **All Properties** and search using the field in the upper right corner:

Click the marked **X** sign to clear the search field before going on. It's important to remember that any columns you already chose will be part of your new **Column Set**. To see the properties that were included, click twice at the top of the (unlabeled) checked column, which is to the left of the **Property** column. You can now select any of the default features that you don't want to be part of this set. You can still include them if you want to, but you can also turn them off one at a time in **List** view. Finally, there are two choices at the bottom of this screen. You can make new Column Sets, copy or delete old ones, using the "cog" menu on the left. Use with care: the "checkbox" menu in the middle bottom lets you quickly check or uncheck all the features that can be seen. If a property is editable, like **Notes** or **Anamorphic Override**, you can change it right in the Browser after applying this message. You'll now see columns for all the properties you chose. You can click once to sort by any column and then click again to un do the sort. If you right-click on any column title, you can choose which columns to show or hide. Screens aren't big enough to show all the information you might want to see, which is a bad thing about this new power. The Inspector may be a better option if you want to see a lot of information about a file all at once.

Metadata in the Inspector

The Inspector gives you a smaller view of the metadata features of a single file and has a number of pre-set metadata views that make it easy to quickly find specific categories. **For the planning process, here's how to make the most of your workspace:**

1. If you can still see the Timeline, press the middle button in the upper right corner of the main window to hide it:

2. Open the **Inspector** and click on the **Info** tab button at the top:

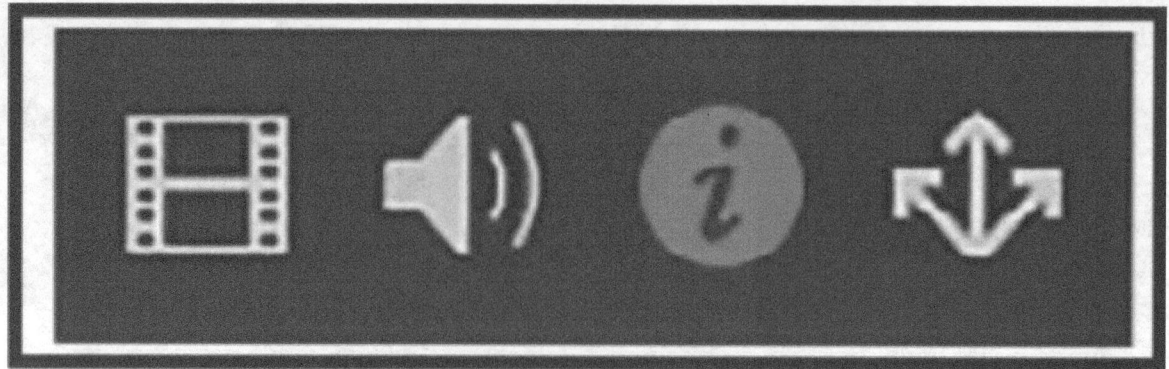

3. The metadata menu will probably say **basic or general** in the bottom left part of the **Inspector** pane.

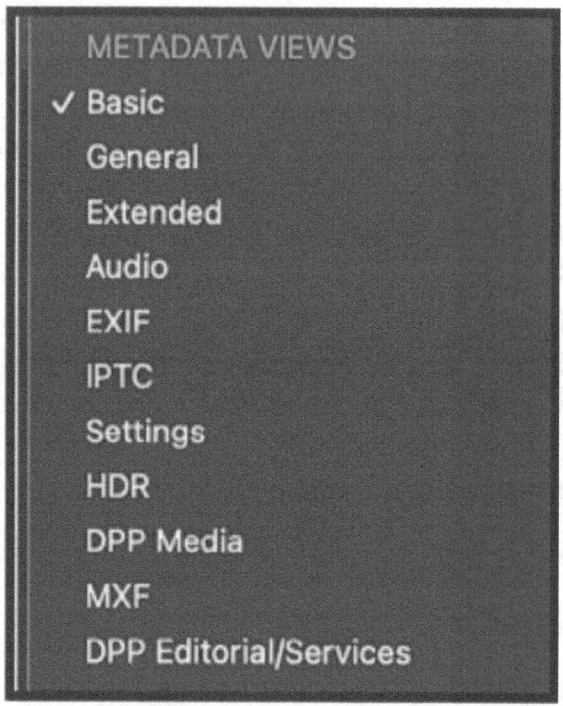

This menu lets you choose which information fields to show in the Inspector. And FCP won't be able to read all the datain every type of file. No recording device will write data to every field. You can choose any of the other metadata views to look at other data that is there, or you can use **Edit Metadata View**... from the same menu to make your own collection. If you still can't find what you need, **Add Custom Meta- data Field** lets you make brand-new metadata fields...

Understanding and applying Keywords

To start using Keywords, all you have to do is come up with a simple one- or two-word description of each of your clips. This will help you find them again later. Focusing on what's in the shot, like water, trees, sky, people, or animals, is a popular trick. Another approach could be to focus on how the shots will be used, such as **A-roll and B-roll, introductory shots, and conclusion shots**. Maybe a close-up, medium-length, or long-length shot would help. There are lots of different methods that might work in different editing scenes and at different stages of the process. Yes, Keywords are information, but they're not as technical and more about the content of the shot. They're kept in the Library instead of on the media files themselves. It will help you a lot to plan ahead for the Keywords that will work best for each job before we get into the details. First, th ink of categories, which are ways you might want to look for things. Next, think of Keywords that fit into each group.

Here are some examples of categories andthe keywords that go with them:

- **Shot content: hands, buildings, water, trees, grass, people, animals, boats, planes, or paper**...The kind of footage you're working with does make a big difference in this.
- **Location: interior, exterior, stage, set, park, hall, office, parking lot, backlot, desert, lake, or field. Script-based: reel, scene, shot, take, or circled.**
- **Focal length: extreme close up, close up, medium, headand shoulders, long, tele, or over the shoulder.**
- **Planned usage: A-roll, B-roll, introduction,** or **conclusion.**
- **Rights: royalty-free, royalty-paid, original, archival,** or **stock.**
- **Legal permissions: release signed, location release signed, parental release signed,** or **release not required.**
- **People:one person, two people,** or **group shot.**
- **Selected shots: best, good, worst,** or **check continuity.**

Even better, you don't have to use all of these methods for every job. If you're editing a video of your familyon vacation, you might only need a list of topic keywords. For a trip to Venice, my content Keywords included **accademia, canals, crowds, family, gondolas, piazza san marco, rooftops, streets, walking,** and **water CU (closeup).**

Applying Keywords to clips

It's time to add Keywords to your clips once you have a rough plan. Here's how to do it:

1. Find the **Key** button in the upper left corner of the screen and press it to open the **Keywords** window:

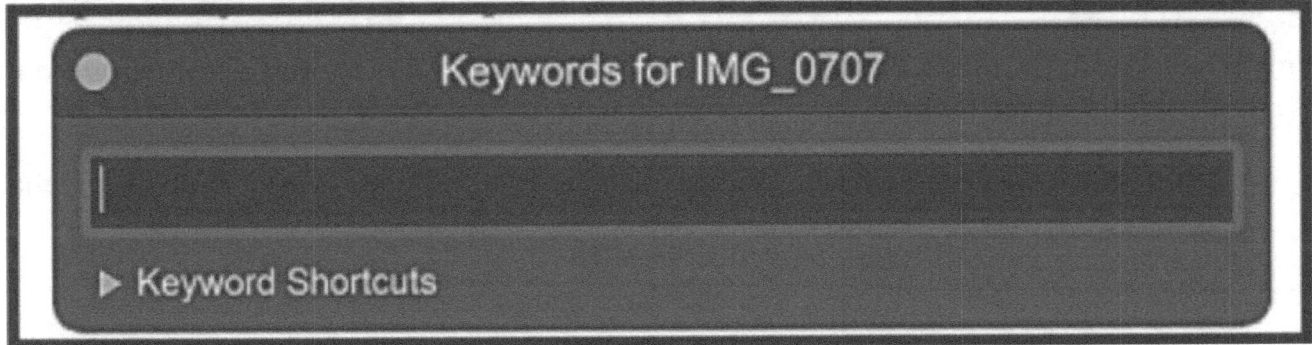

If you haven't used this window before, it will just show a blank line. This window can grow to show Keyword Shortcuts. Okay, that's fine for now.

2. To choose the first clip in your **Event**, click on it.
3. Type the first keyword that best describes this clipin the **Keywords** window. Then, press the **tab, comma,** or **return** key to finish the keyword:

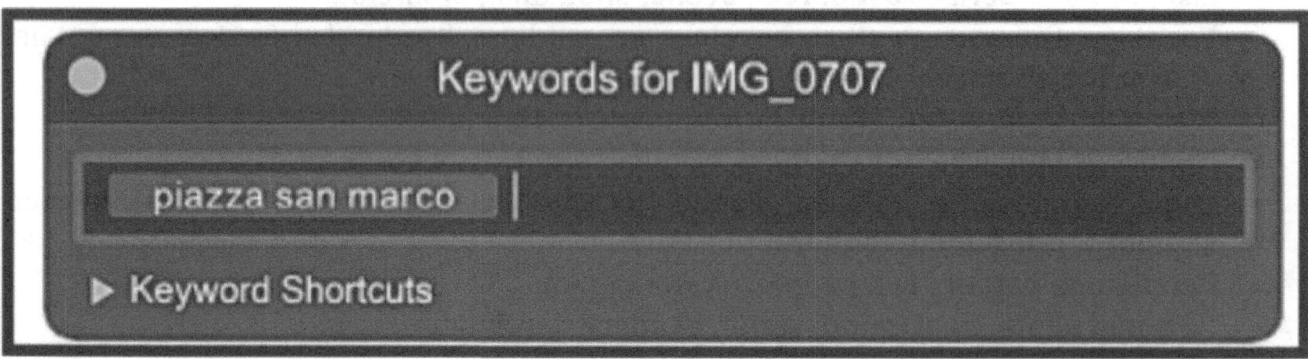

4. Do this process again to add a second Keyword if you can think of one that fits. This is what you'll see:

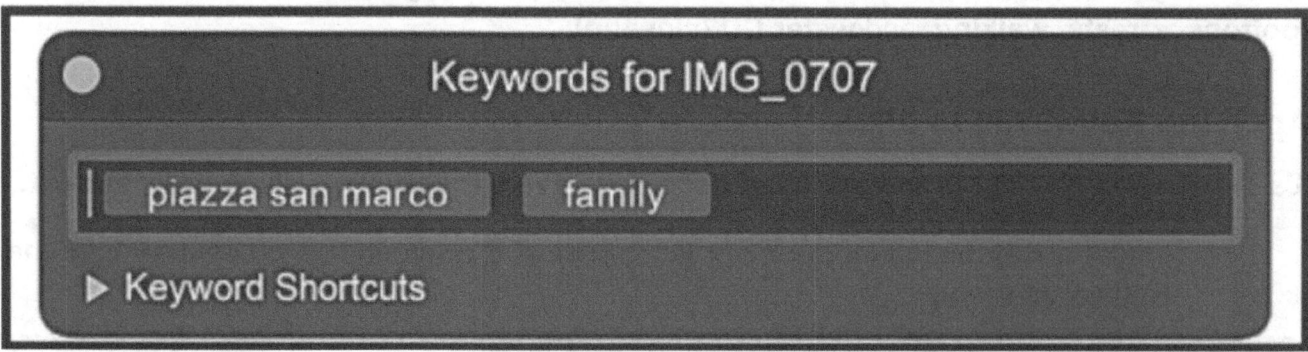

You"ll have instantly made a couple of Keyword Shortcuts after adding a few Keywords. Do these things to see them:

- If you want to see the shortcuts, click the triangle to the left of **Keyword Shortcuts** at the bottom of the **Keywords** window.

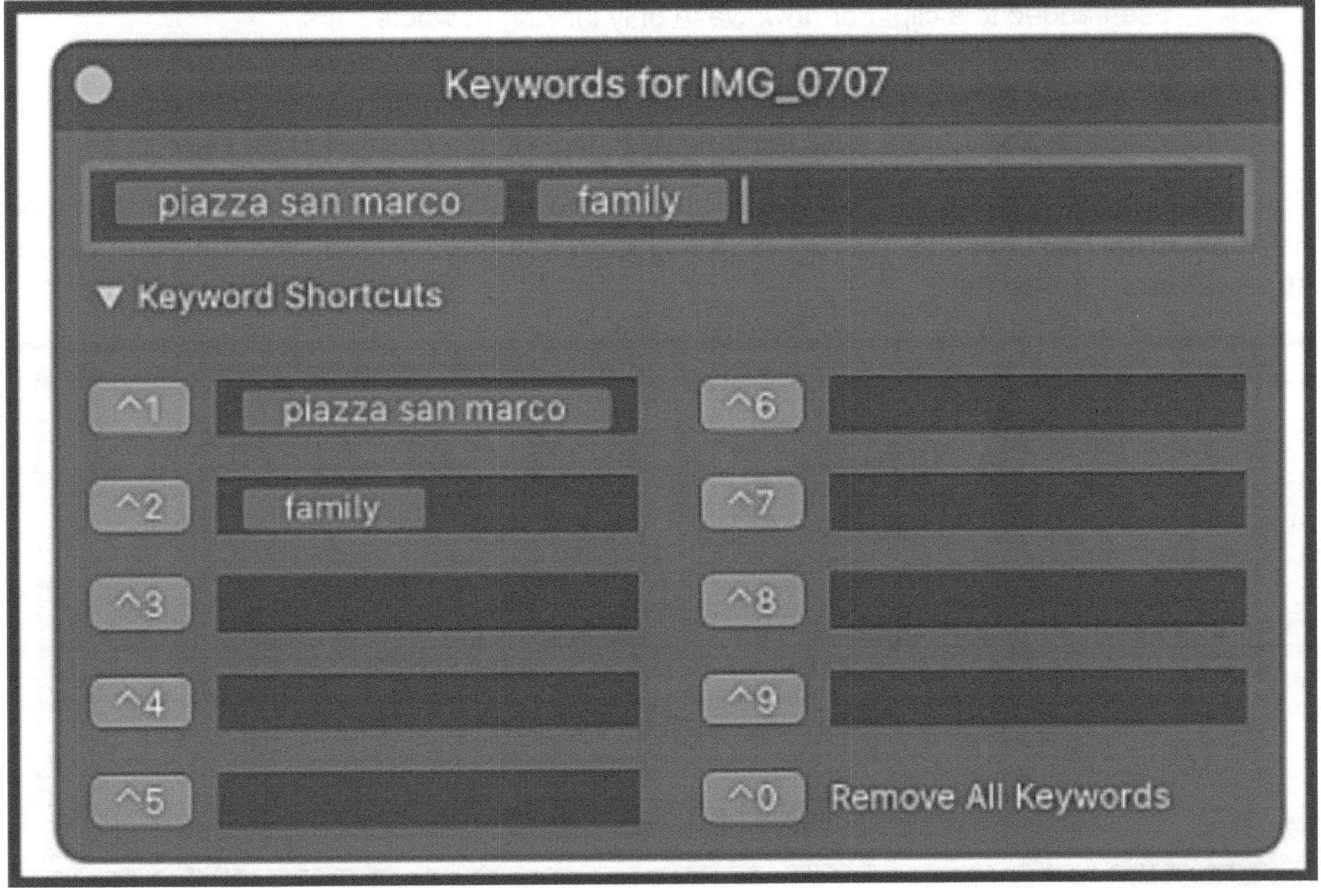

- Every Keyword you use is also added to the permanent shortcut fields below. To access these fields, press the key and any number from **^1 to ^9**. Since these are saved, you may see other shortcuts here if Keywords were added to any Library on this Mac before now.

NOTE: You can edit those shortcut boxes by clicking and typing directly, but changing shortcuts won't change the present clip. No matter what Keywords are in the shortcut boxes, they are still shown at the top of the window for the present clip.

- Press to move to the next clip and type new Keywords.
- Once you start typing the first few letters ofa Keyword, it will offer to auto complete it. You can accept the idea by pressing the **comma, tab,** or **return** key, or you can keep typing.
- To usecurrent Keywords, press the shortcut keys. If you would rather, you can also click on the button next to the shortcut field.

A **Keyword Collection** will be added to your Event for every new Keyword that is made. Each one holds all the clips that are tagged with that Keyword. To see all of those clips at once, just click **on a Keyword Collection. It's not as clear that Keyword Collections can also be used to give Key words, like this:**

1. To see all the Keyword Collections for an Event, click the disclosure triangle to the left of the Event name.
2. Drag a clip into a Keyword Collection that's already there to use that Keyword on that clip.

3. There are three things you can do if you want to know exactly which keywords have been added to a clip. For now, we're only looking at whole clips.
   - Open the **Keywords** box and look at the top line:
   - Select **View > Browser > Skimmer Info (^Y)** and move your mouse over the clip.
   - To see more about a clip, click the triangle to the left of its name in **List** view.

You may also notice that clips that have Keywords show a blue line across the bottom of their **tiny film strip. The blue line means that a Keyword has been added, and the other colors show different properties:**

You can find the **Clip Filtering** menu at the top of the Browser. It will probably say **"All Clips"** or **"Hide Rejected." This menu changes the clips that are shown and hides the ones that don't meet the following conditions:**

1. Select **No Ratings or Keywords** from the **Clip Filtering** menu:

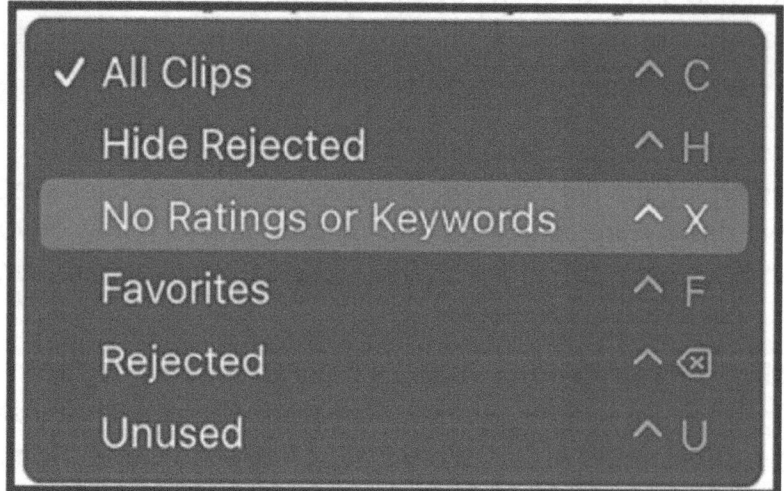

2. From the **Clip Filtering** menu, choose **All Clips** to see everything again.

If you want to add more Keywords to some of your clips, you will need to go through the steps again. It's easy to add more keywords to the **Keywords** window, use **Keyword Shortcuts**, or add clips to Keyword Collections by dragging them.

Here's one last way to add Keywords very quickly:

1. Click on the background in the browser to make sure that noclips are chosen.
2. Move your mouse over the clip you want to add a Keyword to, but don't click on it!
3. Press a Keyword shortcut to add the Keyword(s) that match to that clip.
4. Go through the process again, hoveringover each clip, and then hitting a Keyword shortcut.

Searching with Keywords

Here is where you will use the keywords you've already used to make it easy to find clips. You'll also learn how to go even further. But first, the easy, important, and magical part. As you can see, when you apply a Keyword (like "**gondolas**") to a clip, you also add it to a matched **Keyword Collection**. This collection holds all the clips that share the same Keyword without actually changing them. The clip can be seen in the Keyword Collection, the Event where it was imported, and any other Keyword Collections you've added to clips that have the same clip.

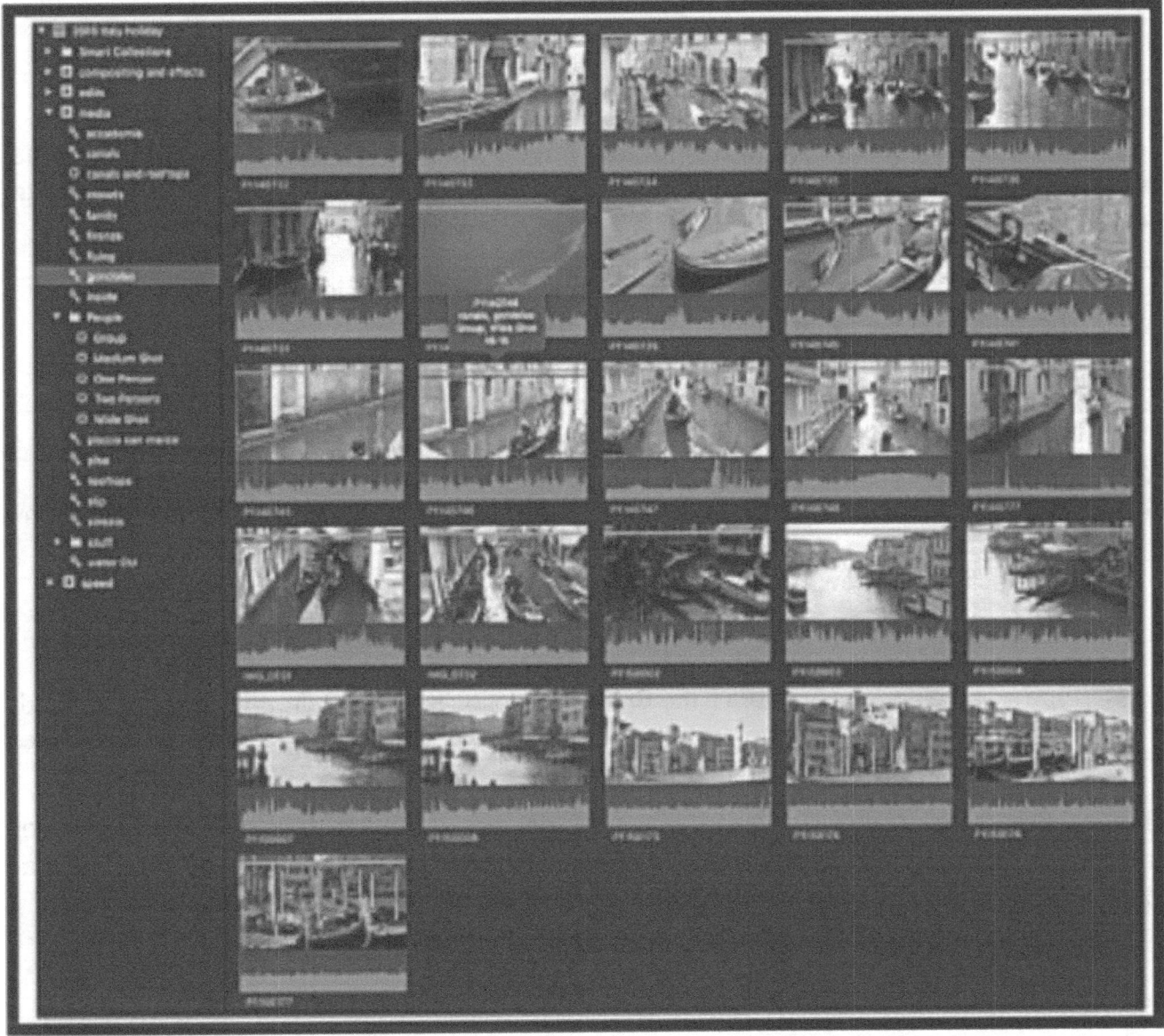

Keyword Collections can group together similar clips just like files or bins can. The difference is that the same clip can show in more than one Keyword Collection - for example, **water** and **gondolas** could be added to the same clip. In the editing process, this makes it much eas-ier to find clips. Using more than one Keyword on a singleclip makes it easier to find. This is different from bins or files, which lock a clip away in one place and can make it harder to find.

Even better, it's simple to mix the items of different Keyword Collections:

- To choose a Keyword Collection, click on it. Then, on the right, you'll see the clips that have that Keyword.
- Press the Command key and click on a second Keyword Collection to see clips that use that Keyword as well.

This makes it easy to search for more than one thing, like **rooftops** OR **canals**. But what if you want a shot that includes both **rooftops** and **canals**?

However, that's also pretty simple and needs a different approach:

- Click on the magnifying glass in the browser's upper right corner to bring up a search field.

You could put in this space to find clips that have a word or phrase in their name, notes, keywords, or other places, but we're not going to do that. We'll instead do the things below.

- To the right of the newsearch box, click on the small window icon.
- This brings up the **Filter** window, which is very powerful:
- Press the Plus button in the upper right corner of the Filter window and pick Keywords:
- Using the settings in the Keywords area, uncheck all of your Keywords. Then, check only two of them, like this.
- Change "**Include Any**" to "**Include All**" to turn "OR" into "AND,"
- From now on, only clips that have both of those keywords will show up in the view below it:
- Finally, click the "**New Smart Collection**" button at the bottom of the **Filter** window.

A Smart Collection is like a saved search in that it only shows clips that meet certain criteria.

- Type a name and press return if the Smart Collection's name is already chosen and ready to edit. (If you clicked some where else and lost the selection, click once on it and then press return to start renaming it.)

The new Smart Collection will show up in your Event along with the Keyword Collections. You can choose to view its clips at any time. For clips to fit into a Smart Collection, you can't just drag them in, but you can add keywords or notes to make them match the search criteria. Additionally, you can edit those parameters by double-clicking a Smart Collection.

CHAPTER 8: MANAGING CLIPS: SELECTION, RATINGS, AND SEARCH TOOLS

Selecting part of a clip

Some things can go wrong with the selection process, so make sure you're working with clips that haven't already been partially cho-sen. Then, carefully follow these steps:

1. Change the view to **Filmstrip** instead of **List**. We'll use **Filmstrip** view for this, but these steps can also bedone in **List** view.
2. Type **Command-A** and then **Option-X** after clicking on one of your clips.
3. This will get rid of any selections in your clips, which makes the next step easier. It's now simple to pick out a part of a clip by clicking and dragging.
4. Click on an empty patch of screen in a clip, then drag to adifferent spot in the same clip and let go.

There is an "**In**" **point** where you click and an "**Out**" **point** where you let go. This makes this part of the clip your selection. In this case, you'll be pullingfrom the **Out** point and letting goon the **In** point when you drag backward to the left:

It will remember the last In and Out point you set on a clip until you set a new one. This stays true even if you click on the background in between clips. The selection, however, can be altered:

- Begin out side of the present selection and drag a new one from In to Out.

You can also change the current selection with the mouse:

- Drag the edges of the selection to move the "In" and "Out" points:

But two shortcut keys are much easier to remember and use to move or place a selection. Put the playhead where you want it, skip over a clip, or just start playback, and then do these things:

- Press "I" to set an "In" point where the skimmer or playhead is right now.
- Press O to set an Out point where the skimmer or playhead is right now.

You can move through a clip with the I and O shortcuts, which are faster than trying to grab the edge of a selection and drag it to the right place. You can also use the keyboard, mouse, or keypad to do this. If you tap I or O again, the old In and Out points are changed, and you can change your mind as many times as you want. You can even press I or O while the video is playing. With **JKL's** multiple playback speeds, you'll be able to quickly mark the right part of a clip.

The steps you might take to mark a clip with a false start are shown below:

1. Press the **spacebar** to begin playback after making a selection.
2. Tap "I" to set a new "In" point after a short time:

3. If you tap "I" again after a few seconds, you'll clear the last "In" point and set a new one:
4. To set an Out point, play the clip for a few more seconds and then tap O.

Sometimes you'll want to delete the whole selection or delete selections from several clips at once, like we did at the beginning of this process.

The following steps should be taken if you want to start over after making selection ranges on one or more clips:

- Press ⌥ **X** to remove a selection from all the clips that are currently chosen.

Even though it's faster to tap **I** or **O**, you should always press ⌥ **X** first to clear the old selection before dragging and releasing to make a new one. Most of the time, you'll drag the old selection instead if you don't. This problem shows up more often in List view, where clicking to choose a full clip lasts longer.

NOTE: You can make more than one In and Out point on a single clip. Still, if you want to choose a different range for a single clip, hold down **Command** and drag on its icon.

Finally, let's say a fewwords about how selections stay in place. As you may already know, clicking on a clip chooses the whole thing and makes a yellow circle around it. There is an "In" point at the beginning and an "Out" point at the end. It's helpful to pick a whole clip like this if you want to add a Keyword to it or use it in an edit. However, clicking next to the clip's filmstrip in the List view doesn't get rid of the selection. So, if you pick part of a clip, clicking on it again doesn't get rid of it in either Filmstrip or List view. You should use **Option key+ X, I, or O** to pick what you want instead of dragging the edges of a current selection, which is slow and painful. Also, get used to not clicking for no reason, especially in List view.

Rating as a Favourite

Not only will I show you how to rate parts of clips as "good," but I'll also give you some tips on how to work with our own content. You'll have a "wow" moment when you see this part of the process in action as you learn FCP, so don' t skip it. This is easy stuff that packs a punch. Aselection is temporary, so if you've chosen the "good" part of a clip, you should mark it as a Favorite so that you can remember it and find it more easily in the future.

One key is all it takes to do this:

- To mark the selection as a **Favorite**, press **F**.

A Favorite is shown on the image as a green line above the blue Keyword line. Yes, you can make a different part of the same clip a Favorite. Just follow the same steps as before:

1. Press "**I**" to set an "**In**" **point** where the skimmer or playhead is now.
2. Press **O** to set an **Out point** where the skimmer or playhead is right now.
3. Select the selection and press **F** to mark as **Favorite**:

The best thing is to have a selection selected when you press F. The full current clip will be marked as a Favorite if no selection is open, which isn't always useful. Undo (Command-Z) is usually the fastest way, but you can also remove a Favorite by unrating it:

- Press **U** to remove **Favorites** from the selection.

Now all you have to do is make everything you like a Favorite. If you have a longer clip, like an interview or longer B-roll, you should look through it for material that might be useful. This is how it will go:

1. Move your mouse to the beginning of a clip and press the **space bar** to begin playing.
2. Should nothing interesting happen, presses **L** a few times to speed things up until something that might be interesting does happen?
3. If you want to skip back to the beginningof the possibly interesting part, press **J**. Then, press **L** to play forward and **I** to mark an In point.
4. Watch the video and listen to it as it plays back.
5. If you like this part, press **O** at the end and then **F** to make it a Favorite.
6. If it's bad, don't save it as a favorite. Instead, playit forward, if you have to.
7. Do this process again; hitting **I** to set a newIn point when the next thing that might be interesting begins, and then **O** and **F** when that interesting thing ends.
8. Press to go to the next clip when the current one is over. The **Continuous Playback** option will make this happen on its own.

There are a lot of good ways to mark something as Favo rite. For interviews, I like to use the keyboard more, with one hand on the **J, K, L, I, and O** keys and the other on the **F** key. I'll do a lot of quick **JKL** moves to get to the right In point before pressing **I**. At the Out poin t, I'll keep a close eye on things and press **O**. After some practice, you'll be able to guess the In and Out points by looking at the audio pattern and noticing where words begin and stop. You don't have to stop the video; just press **I** and **O** while it plays, and **F** before pressing **I** again to turn the selection back on.

I usually like to use the mouse to scan visual B-roll. I quickly move my right hand over the video and click and drag to pick things. My left-hand rests on **F** to make notes as I go. Of course, the Browser's Filmstrip view is a good way to get a feel for what's in a clip, so you'll know where to put the In and Out points before you start. When you're in your own Library, go ahead and make several parts of different clipsyour favorites right now. You may do this process quickly or more slowly. It will take longer to make properly marked Favorites at first, but they will need fewer changes in the future. I like to take my time with conversations and don't tighten up my B-roll edits too much. It will depend on the edit and how long it takes you to pick your Favorites. But **do use them. Selections don't have to be perfect, but the more work you do now, the less you'll have to do later:**

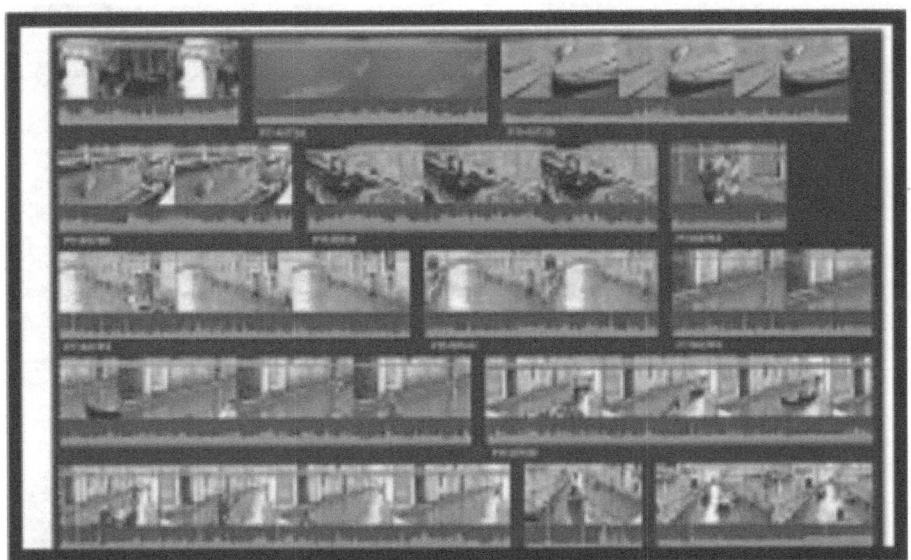

You've drawn some green lines, which is a good start. However, I promised you a "wow" moment, and now it's here.

Showing only the Favorites

The last selection on each clip will still be highlighted in yellow, and your clips will now be surrounded by green Favorite lines. You can click on a clip's green line to change the selection back to one of your favorites, which can be useful. But this isn't the best time to use that trick. Instead, look at the top of the Browser for the **Clip Filtering** menu we talked about earlier, which should show **All Clips**.

- You can press **Control-F** or choose **Favorites** from this menu.

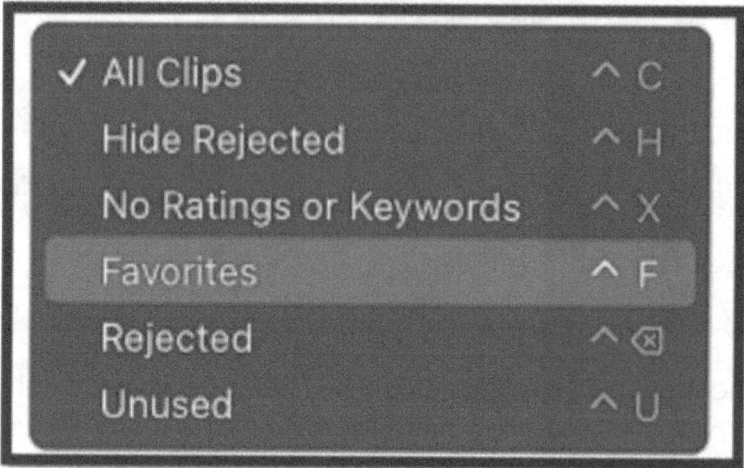

You can only see your Favorites right now; everything else is hidden. Take a moment to really understand that. You can just ignore every-thing you don't care about, which is very helpful. You'll see two different clips with the same name if you mark two parts of the same clip. You can still use keywords. If you choose a **Keyword Collection** in the **Clip Filtering** menu while **Favorites** is on, you'll see the best clips in that area.

It's also true in Smart Collections:

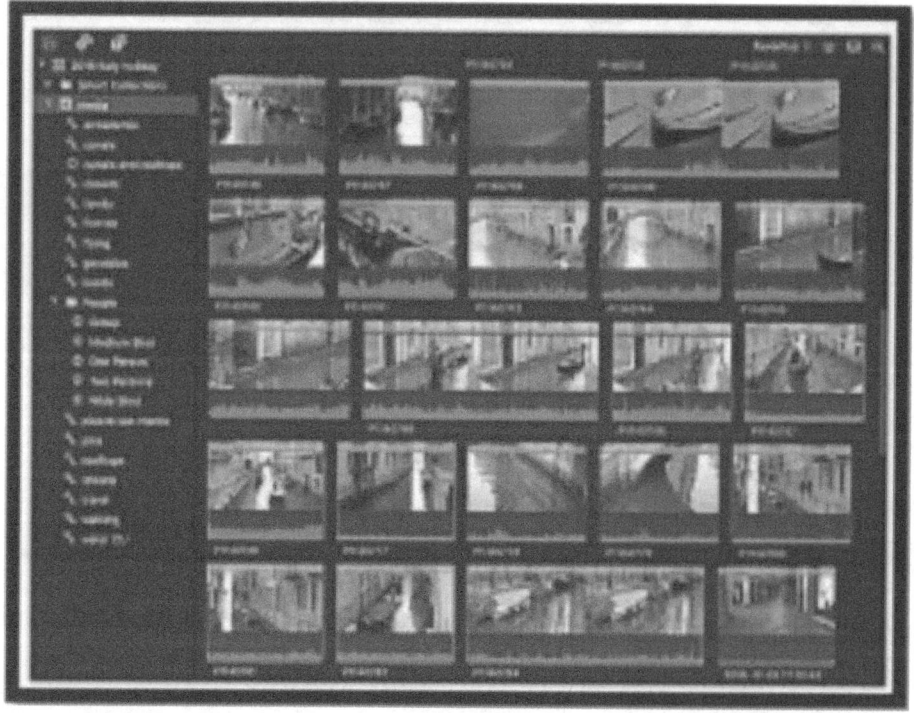

You can still see the less good parts of your clips if you need to. From the **Clip Filtering** menu, choose **All Clips**. You can picture the whole edit from the clips you see here. All you have to do is put them in the right order. This list of the best clips will make it easy to find the right ones if you don't get them the first time.

Rating as Rejected

The Favorite parts and the rest are the twolevels of "good" so far. What about the "bad" parts? This lesson will teach you how to Reject, which is the other end ofthe rating process. **You're telling the computer that the selection is bad or useless when you mark a part of a clip as Rejected instead of as Favorite. Also, the work flow is very similar:**

1. Use the keyboard or mouse to mark the clip's "in" and "out" points.
2. Mark that selection as **Rejected** by pressing the **delete** key, not the forward delete key.

When you open the Browser and choose **"All Clips,"** a red line willappear on that part of the clip. They can't be both Favorit e and Rejected at the same time; it has to be either one or the other. You can unrate a certain area with **U**, just like you can with Favorites.

The **Clip Filtering** box has another option that might work well here: **Hide Rejected**. You won't see any red lines in this mode because they are completely covered. Also, clips with rejected parts in the middle will be split into two or more different pieces. You can use Rejected.

labeling on clip parts instead of or along with favorites if you'd like. Because you no longer need to see the clapper board at the beginning and end of a clip, some editors like to reject it. Another use is to reject short gaps between questions in long interview clips so that each question can be its own clip. For me, I don't use Reject very often because I like using Favorites more. You could, however, reject and use **Hide rejected** as a happy medium if you'd rather not limit your view to only favorites:

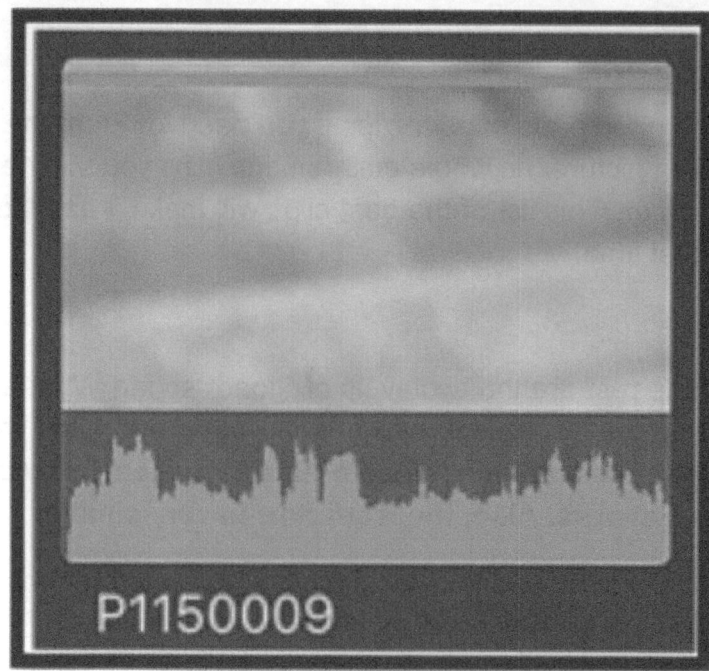

One last thing about the really bad video: You shouldn't just delete the whole clip if you find one that is completely useless, like if you accidentally hit the record button. Press **Command-Delete** instead to get rid of it, and the clip will be gone for good.

Even though hard drive space isn't expensive, you shouldn't waste it:

Storing additional information

It's useful to be able to rate a clip part as good or bad, but what if you want to add more detailed notes about it? This can be done in a number of ways, and while it's an option, it's a good idea for bigger productions. Selective Keywords? Sure. Making changes to clip names or making notes? Of course. Adding Markers to Keep Track of Time? Done.

Selective Keywords

Adding keywords to specific parts of clips instead of whole clips is one way to do this. Keywords **can have very long names, and some key words may also be used for the same thing.**

The method is easy to guess:

1. Use the keyboard or mouse to mark the clip's **"in"** and **"out"** points.
2. To use a keyword, go to the **Keywords** box.

I think this is a good way to work with longer, more complicated clips, but not so much with shorter ones. Personally, I like to use Keywords ords on whole clips, and that, along with a more specific favorite, is often all you need. If you want to organize things even more precisely, you can add keywords to ranges. This is most likely to bedone if your operators prefer longer continuous shots, possibly with multiple takes in a single clip. **Selective Keywords** can also be used to group together similar ideas from several clips, like conversations with different people about similar issues. Like always, you can use favorites, but you can also add a keyword to a certain area to keep track of the subject being talked about. Once all the interviews have been handled, the parts of each interview that are linked will be put together in a set of keyword collections.

Notes

You can put any amount of text in the **Notes** field, which is in the **List** view of the browser and the **Info** tab of the inspector. It's possible to add these notes to a single clip or even to a favorite rite **inside a clip. They could be for VFX artists, the director, or anything else. Here's how to add a note to a single clip:**

- Select a clip or a **favorite** by clicking on it. Then, click again in the empty **Notes** field and type your note:

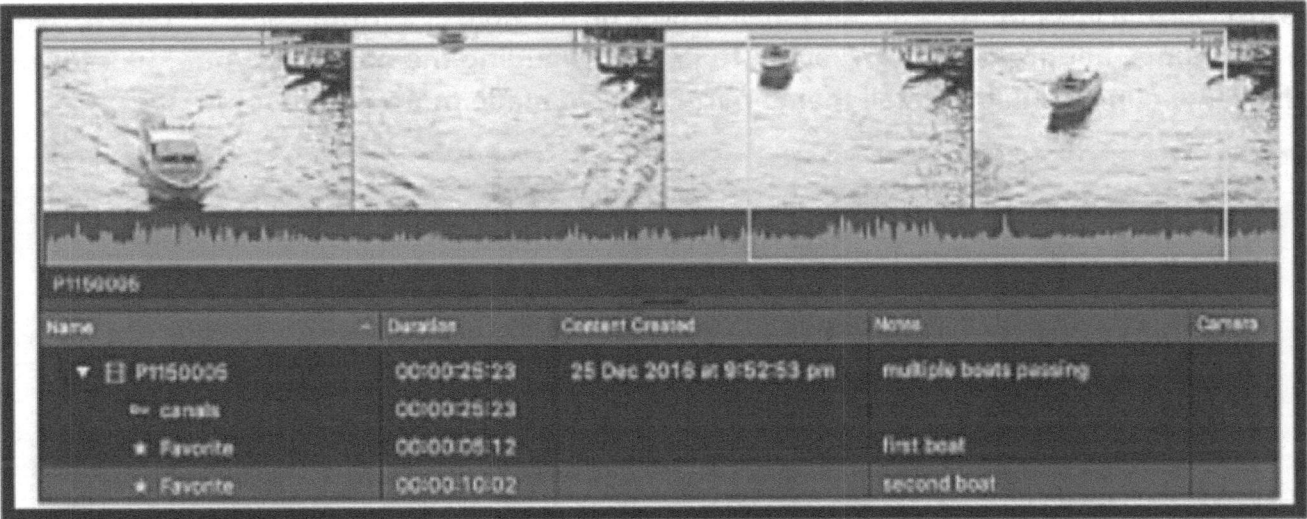

You could also do the following for one or more clips:

1. Choose one or more clips from the browser.
2. Start up the **Inspector** and go to the **Info** tab.
3. Use the button in the bottom left area to switch to the **Basic**, **General**, or **Extended** metadata view.
4. In the **Notes** field, write a note:

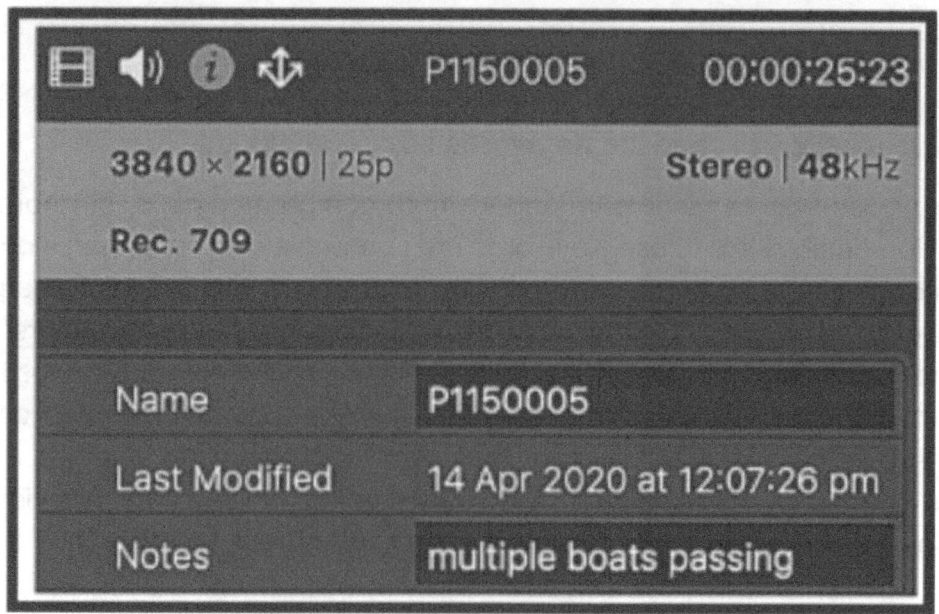

An inspector can only add a note to a whole clip; it can't be added to a favorite part of a clip. Adding general-purpose writing is possible in other ways as well, but notes are a handy way to do it.

Names

Clip names can also hold information. I usually suggest that the original media name be used as the clip name, but some editors like to change the names of clips to include general text. Changing the name of a favorite range is probably a better idea. At the moment, each favorite is just called a favorite. To change the name, click on the word **"Favorite,"** press **"Return,"** type a **new name, and press "Return" again to finish. Changing the names of your favorites on the same clip will help you tell them apart if you've made more than one:**

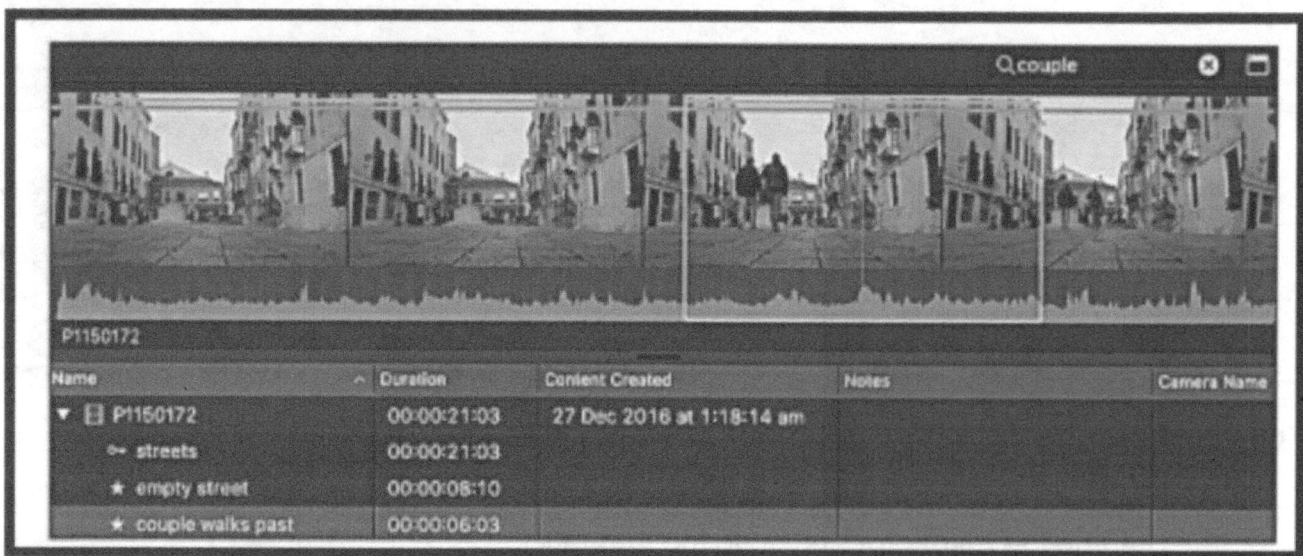

Now we'll talk about the last way, **Markers**, which let us write a long note in one place instead of across a range.

Markers

For more detailed notes, add a **Marker**. A Marker is linked to a frame instead of a range, but its name can be long and useful. **Also, you can make different kinds of Markers that do different things. Do the following things to make a marker:**

1. Move the mouse over or click on a frame in the clip.
2. Press **Option-M** to create a marker and edit its name.
3. **Pick a name for the new Marker:**

If you do not want to name a marker, pressing **M** is enough. If you don't move the mouse between pressing **M** and **P**, you could also press **M** twice to make it and then edit it. Why make a **Marker?** **For one good reason, a marker is easy to see in any browser view, but notes and favorite names can only be seen in the list view when the triangle that hides a clip is open:**

You can click on a marker to see its name in the **Skimmer Info** (to ggle with **Control-Y** if you don't see it) above your mouse. If **Snapping** is turned on, it will be easy to hit Markers as you skim. You **can always press N to turn on or off snapping, which is a tool that will be used more frequently during the editing process:**

Advanced searches

To begin a fairly large job, you can click on a keyword collection, then look at the favorites, and then scan the clips visually to find the one you remember. Although organizing text is necessary for staying calm during a big job.

1. Click the magnifying glass in the browser's upper-right area to bring up a search field.
2. **Type a word that goes with any clipboard notes field name, as well as a name you've given to a favorite range or marker, into the search field:**

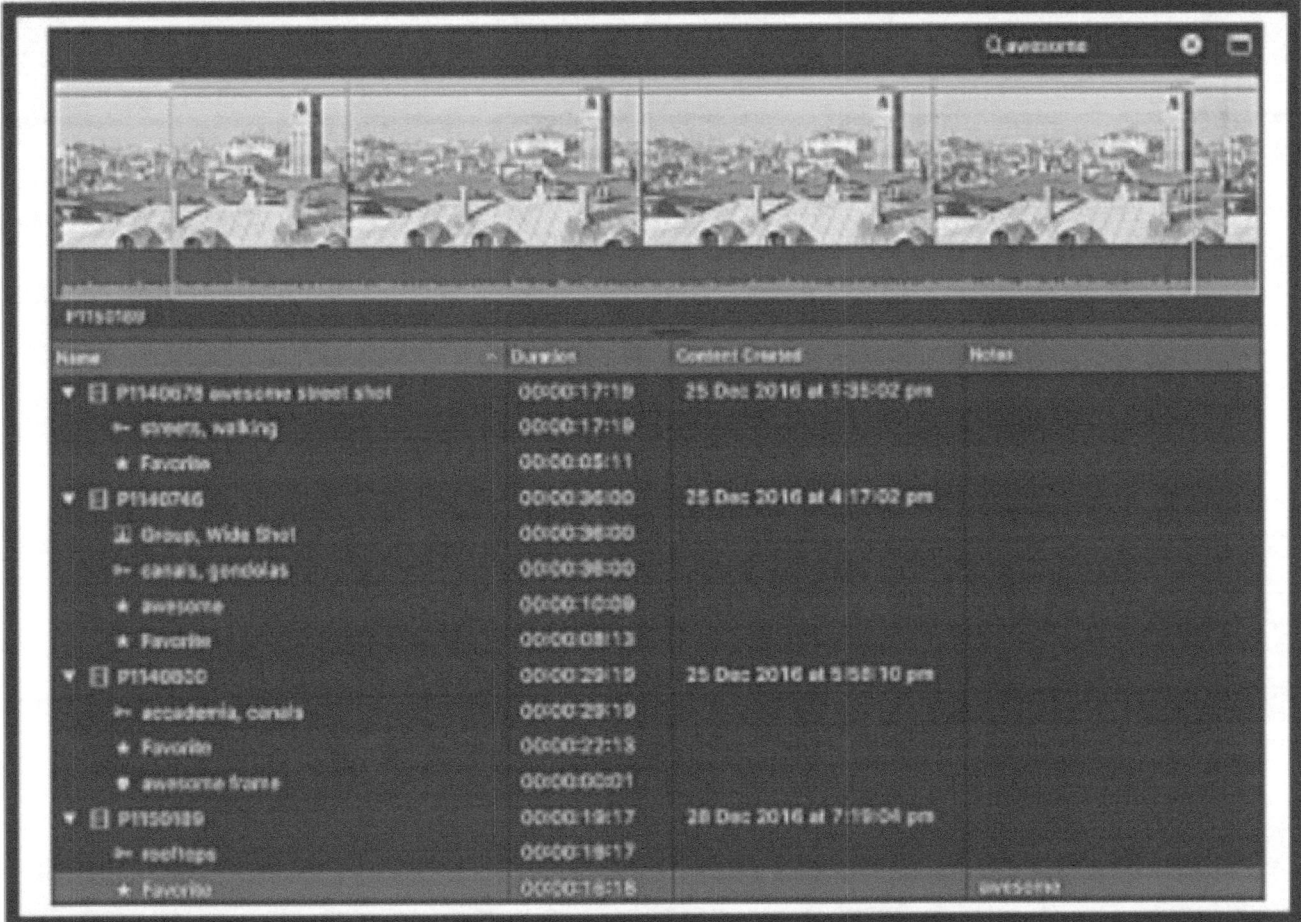

You will only see clips that use that word somewhere in the current view, which could be a **Keyword collection or a smart collection.** What matters is not which field the word is stored in:

- Click on the little window button to the right of the new search box.

The **Filter** window will now show up, and the word you picked will already be in the text field. There is a choice right before the name that lets you choose which clips to exclude with the word **"Does Not Include."** You can narrow down your search even more by adding **Favorite** or **Rejected**:

- Select **Ratings** from the drop-down menu in the upper right part of the **Filter** window.

You now have the option to only show favorites or rejected clips. Since **"All"** is in the upper left corner, the Rating and the words you looked for work together to narrow down the results and show fewer clips.

Even though that's generally what you want, you could pick **Any** instead of **All** if you only want to see clips that meet either text or rating requirements. Then, clips will show up that meet at least one of the requirements. That would be good if you wanted to expand your selection, but we want to make it even smaller, so leave **All** in the top-left box and then:

- Add people to the search by pressing the plus sign (+) and picking the one-shot type.

I'm looking at clips of one person who has the word **"awesome"** in the are Favorites:

Like before, you can save this search as a **Smart Collection** to look at it later. You might see more things in this **Smart Collection** in the future if you keep adding keywords, text, and reviews.

You can narrow your search by the following, including those we've already talked about:

- **Text**, such as names, notes, markers, and more
- **Ratings**, including places that were favorites and rejected
- **The media type**, such as **stills, video with sound, video only, or audio-only**
- **Type**, to find various special clip types, such as multicam and synchronized
- **"Used Media"** lets lets you see if a clip has been used in the current timeline. This is helpful when you're looking for something new.
- **Keywords**, to include or leave out clips that have certain keywords
- **People**, including or excluding certain types of people or amounts of people
- **Format Info**, which lets you lookat a number of technical file properties
- **Media representation**: this lets you find clips that are original, optimized, proxy, or Proxy, or that are missing.
- **Date**: To search a creation or import date that is on, before, or after a specific date, as well as in a recent timespan, such as the last week
- **"Roles," which let you include or leave out clips with certain roles:**

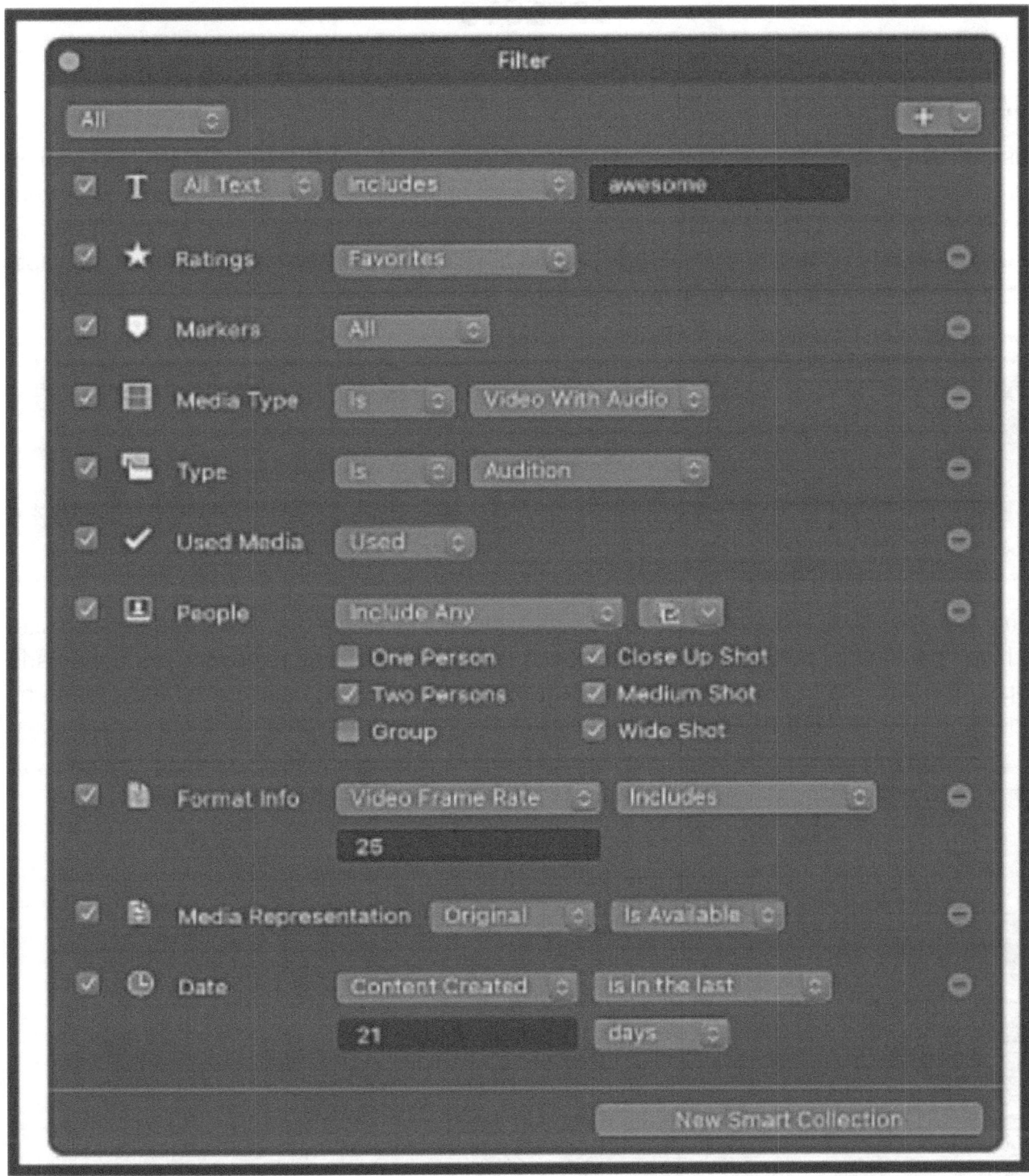

That's a pretty long list, and you might never need all the power it gives you. But an open **Smart Collection** is a great way to find a shot if you're working on a bigger project and the director asks to see the best different takes of a certain line of conversation. For the best results, make sure you tag your clips correctly.

CHAPTER 9: ENHANCING PROJECTS WITH TITLES AND EFFECTS

WHAT ARE TITLES?

Titles are dynamic regular templates that you just need to fill in with text. Some titles are just plain text boxes, while others have spaces for small animations that you can also add to your video. The button for **Titles** and **Generators** is above the media browser. This is because when you add titles and generators to a project in the timeline, Final Cut Pro treats them like clips. Next to the browser's title bar, third from the left, is the **Title** button:

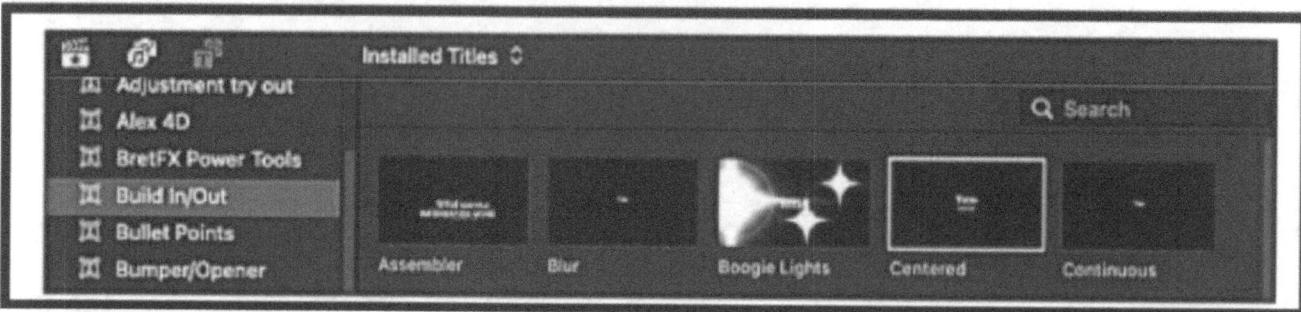

A Final Cut Pro title is like a box that you can fill with text. A simple title, like the **Centered** title, which you can find in the **Build In/Out** section of the title browser, does nothing more than add a clip to the timeline so you can put your text in the middle. You can turn off the motion by unchecking **Build In and Build Out** in the inspector:

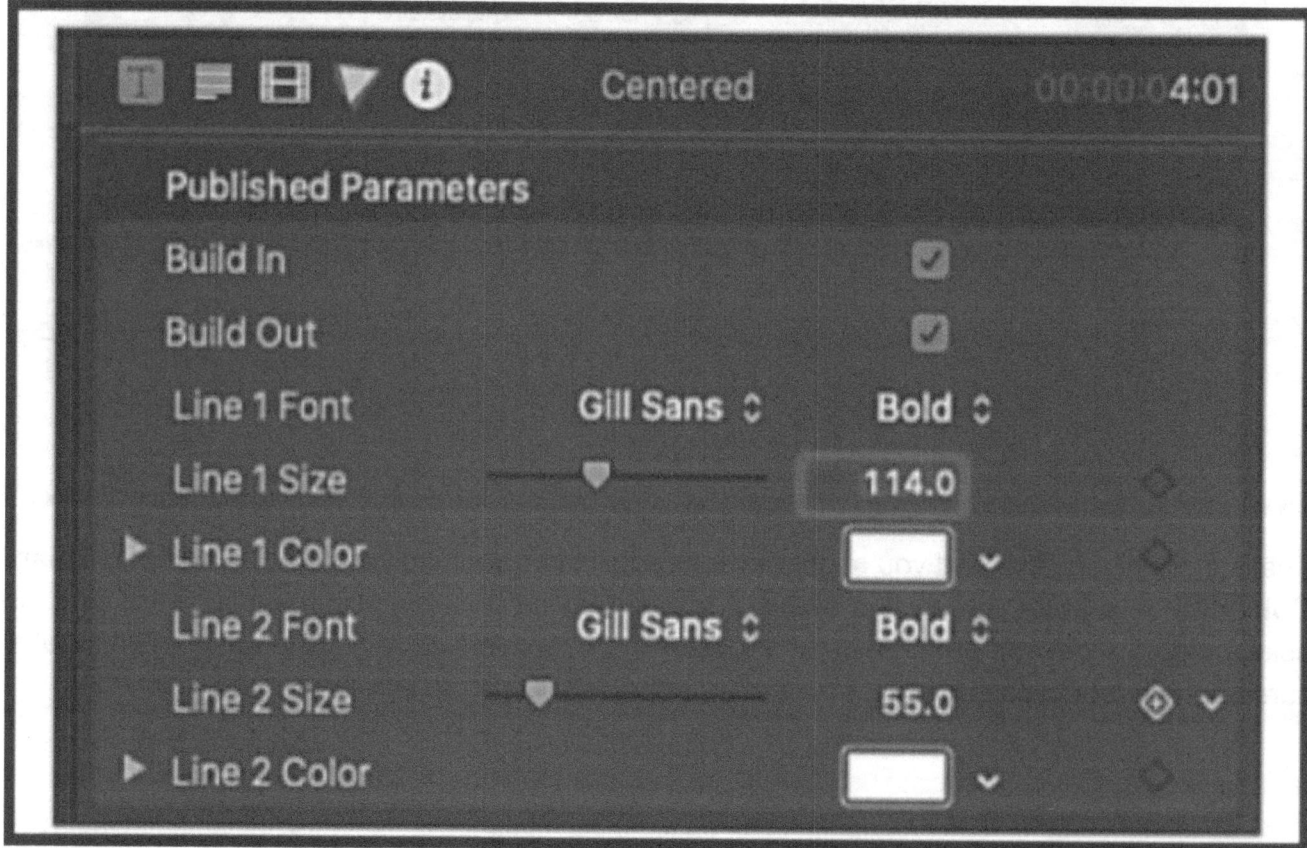

If you put your mouse over the **Title** picture in the browser, you can see a sample of the animation. As you drag the mouse, the animation will show up in the viewer. When you open a title, it will already have a font chosen for you. This is about as simple as it gets: the **Centered** title. All titles will include different amounts of animation or options. You can change their settings or use them. The animated boxes that hold text in Final Cut Pro titles were made in Apple's Motion app.

Animated titles

Openers are titles that have a lot of animation. They help you make an introduction quickly and give your video a more professional look than a simple opening title. These starters can range in length from a few seconds to a few minutes, and they will typically have drop zones where you can add your own media.

Drop zones

Titles, generators, and even effects can all have drop zones! They look dangerous, but they're just what they say they are: a spot to put your media. There are, however, different ways to add media and move it around in different drop zones. Some drop zone creators are more skilled at creating them than others.

If you follow the rules for drop zones, they will be easy to use. The following picture shows the Drop Zone for the inspector:

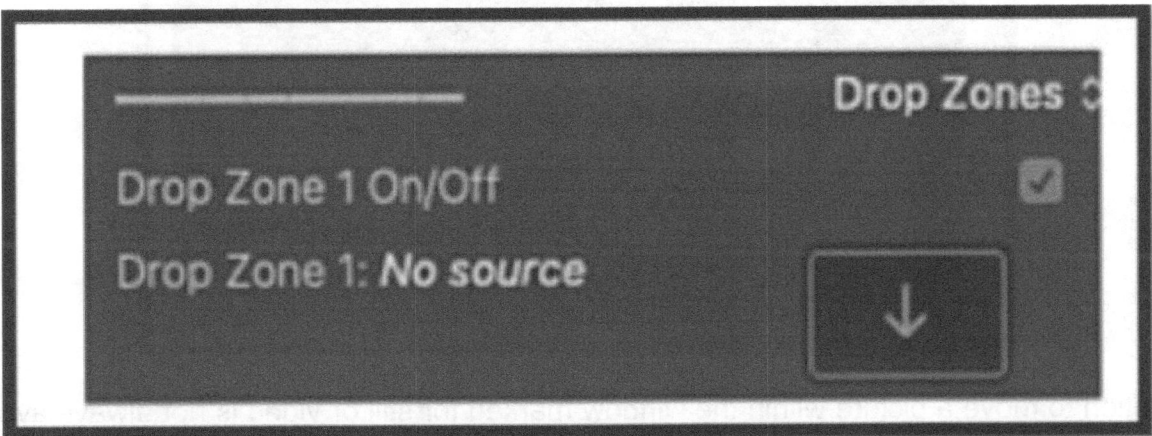

To use the drop zone, you click on it. You should now be able to see the media you want to put in the drop zone. The drop zone will not work if you open another part of Final Cut Proto and see the media. Simply remember to make sure the media is visible before clicking in the inspector's drop zone. In addition to the timeline, you can use clips from the media browser. The drop zone can take both pictures and videos. If you use video, though, keep in mind that it needs to last longer than the motion that the drop zone shows. For example, if the drop zone animation lasts 5 seconds, the video in the drop zone must also last 5 seconds. Once the title animation starts, if the video is too short, it will freeze before the animation is over. It's important to make sure you click on the video at a time that gives it enough time to play, even if the video is longer than the animation. In the drop zone, the video starts playing at the point where you click. Under some titles, there will be options that let you turn off the drop zone.

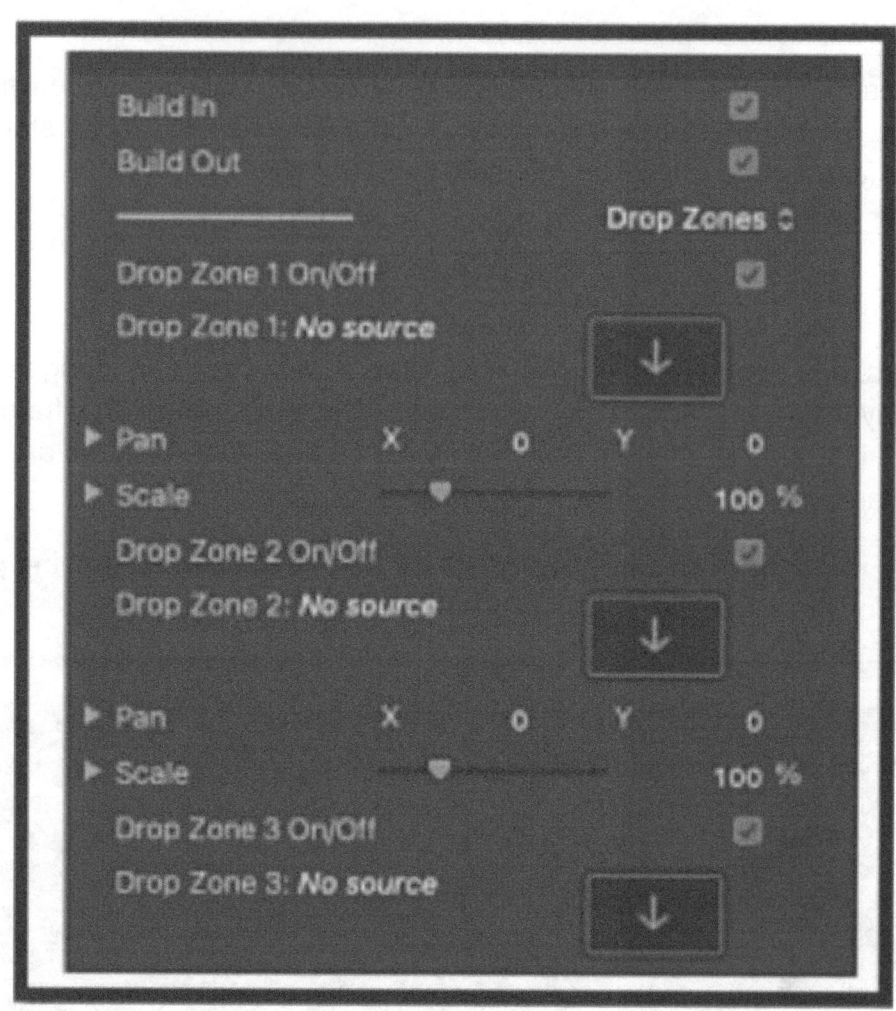

The option to move a picture within the window marked for still or video is not always available to makers of animations with drop zones. But most of the time, there will be buttons in the inspector that let you change the X (horizontal) and Y (vertical) positions. If adding a picture to the dropzone doesn't let you move it, you might be able to change where it is by changing the X (horizontal) and Y (vertical) dimensions in the inspector.

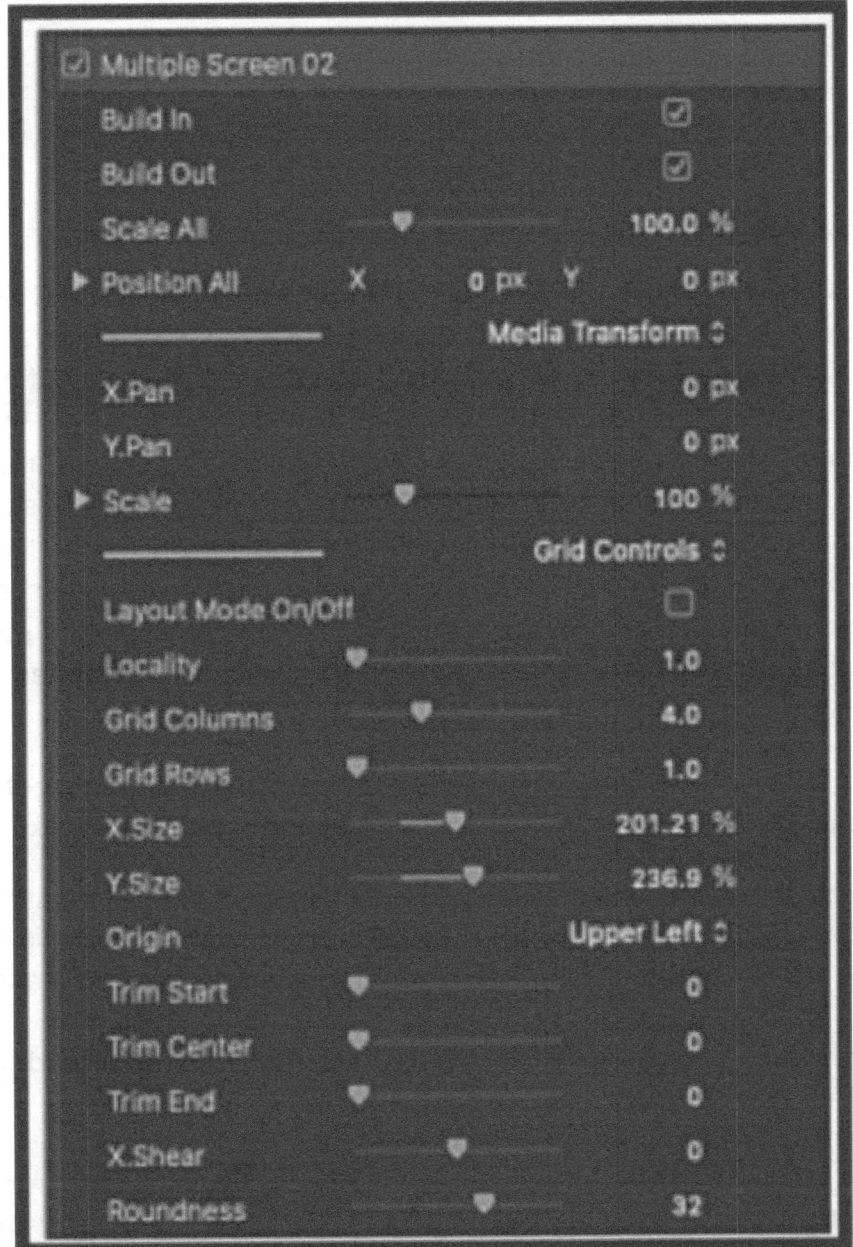

Other titles allow you to drag the picture into the viewer in addition to positioning it using the tools in the inspector. It does the same thing in a different way. I believe that the only way you will get used to dropping zones in animations is to play around with each one for awhile after you buy it. This takes away from some of the point of buying an effect in the first place, which was to quickly add something extra to the edit without having to spend time making it yourself. Of course, adding drop zones isn't the only thing that animation titles do. There are effects that make it look like you spent a lot of time making the video better. In most title animations, there will be a set num-ber of writing boxes. Just delete the words from fields you don't need. You can add some of the easy-moving titles that come with Final Cut Pro if you need more text areas. You can add a simple title as a linked clip above the animated title to do this. This works because the background of simple titles is clear, letting the main title in the track below show through. You can make a combination clip of the different effects if you want to use these titles together as a theme for other videos.

Adding text to a title

First, you should know that font and text are two different words that you should not use for the same thing. There are many things that make up text, like the size, color, and style. Text is made up of more than just the font, which is just a style. There are clear rules about how to use text in videos. This is because text in videos is not the same as text on paper, even though we usually treat them the same. A video doesn't have as much details as words on a page. These tiny squares make text in video, even 4K video, look bad. You can also read words on a written page for as long as you need to figure it out. You decide how long the words need to be looked at in order for your brain to understand them. The video has a smaller quality and some pixels. It also plays for a set amount of time, and you can't change it unless you stop the screen or go back and read it again. It means you have to figure out the text quickly, unlike printed text, which stays there until you're done.

It's important to show the writing properly because if people don't get to read it, the information is lost. The list below will help you figure out how to put text in a title:

- The text in a video should stay on screen for as long as it needs to, but not so long that it gets boring. The editor should be able to read it out loud twice while it's on the screen.
- Make sure the text is big enough to read, not in italics or script, and not angled or horizontal.
- The font size for HD video might be smaller than for SD video, and it might be even smaller for 4K.
- You can read sans serif fonts better than serif fonts.
- Pick a color for the text that stands out from the background.
- Text that is light should go on dark backgrounds, and text that is dark should go on light backgrounds.
- Don't use backgrounds with lots of designer texture.
- When writing important things, don't use fancy styles.
- Use an outline around text that you want to warn people about.
- To broadcast or stream, use the **Broadcast Safe effect**.
- When you stream, use **Title Safe Zone** lines.

When the **T** tab at the top is blue, you type the text in the inspector. When the Text tab is selected, which means the text is marked in white in the viewer, most titles will also let you change the text.

Click on the button with the horizontal lines on the left. This is the **Text** tab.

You can make all kinds of changes to text, even 3D text, when the **Text** tab is chosen.

Elements

When you add elements to Final Cut Pro, it turns into a simple image's designer.

Counting

The **Number, Currency, Percent, Scientific, Spell Out, Binary, and Hexadecimal** options for counting up or down are provided by **Count-ing**, one of the most useful generators, and these can be changed in the inspector. It can be helpful to show clients how long a certain scene lasts.

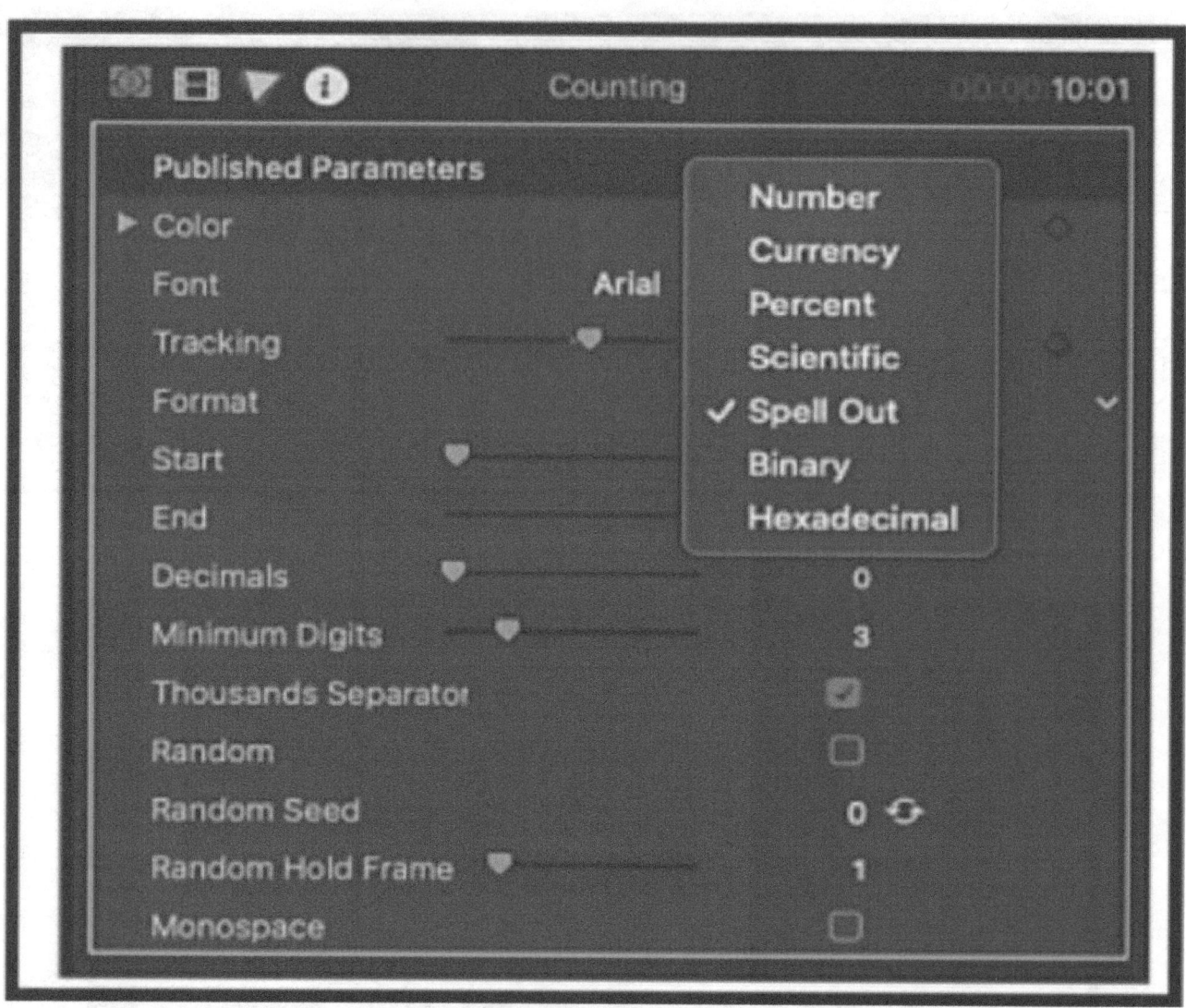

Placeholders

Placeholders are great for making a rough edit because they give you a place in the timeline to put clips that you are still waiting to get.

Shapes

You can make 12 different forms with shapes, which gives you some basic visual editing skills.

You can change a shape's size, color, edge, and drop shadow:

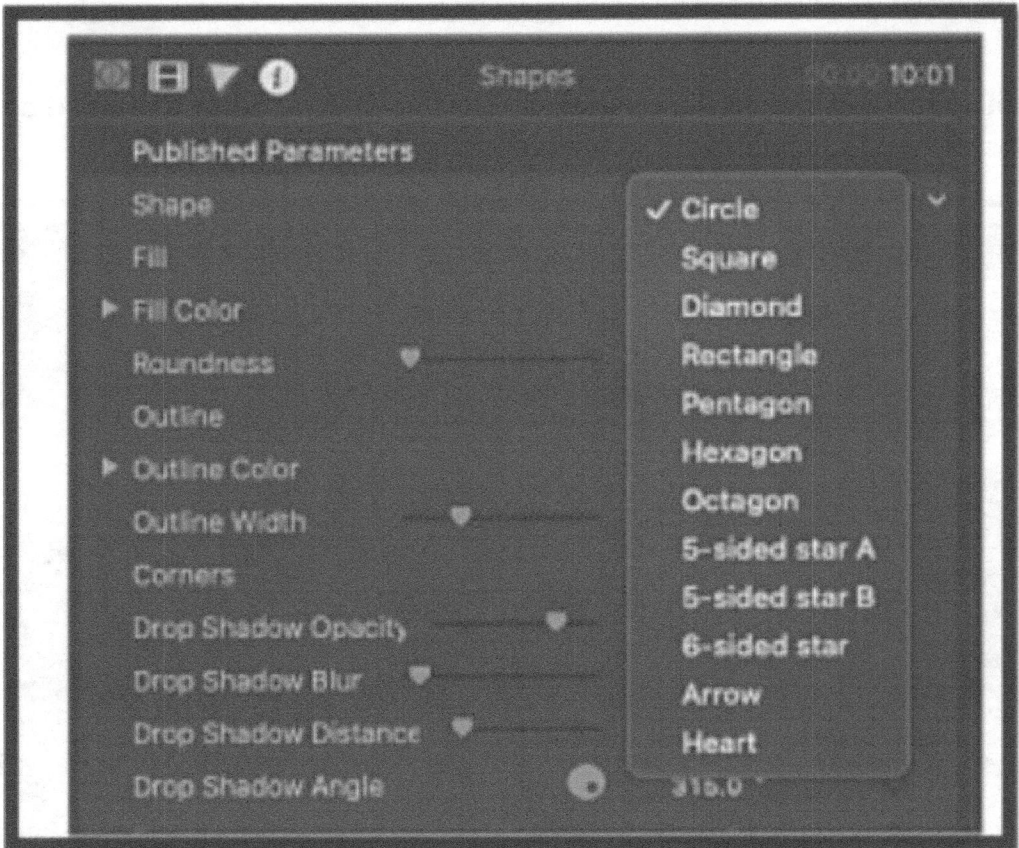

From the elements group, timecode is the final piece I will talk about.

Timecode

Always add a timecode to a draft before giving it to a client so that they can find the exact spot where they want to make changes. This timecode tells you where in the timeline the timecode generator is added. You can move the title around on the screen and change it.

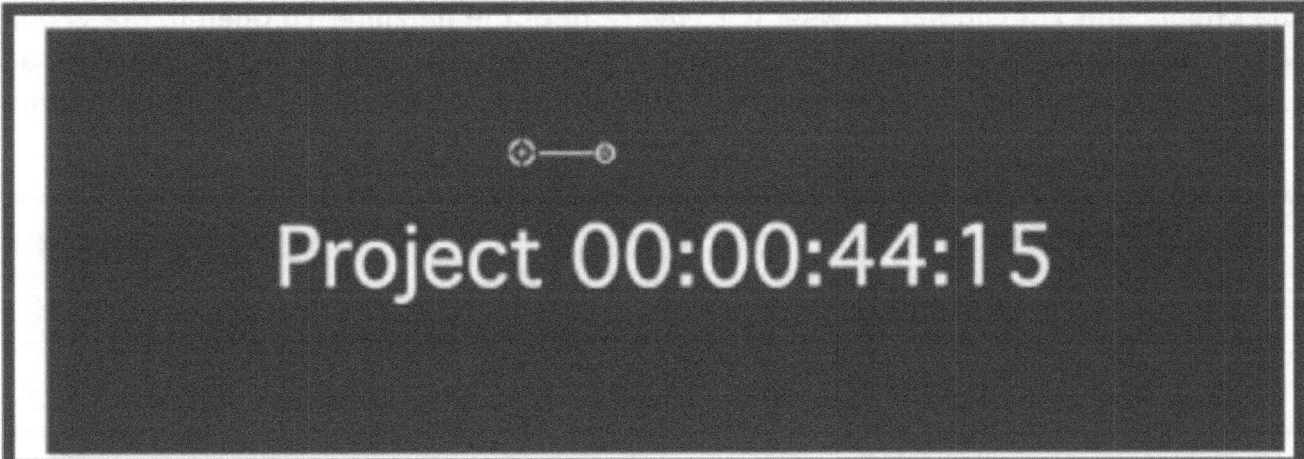

Solids and textures

There is a clear background in a clip that you can color with solids. The color should be a title. When there is no alpha background, the bright white background is used below brands or still pictures. Since they aren't full-screen, the bright white fills in the black spaces on both sides of the image after it. Textures are like patterns, but they are made of one solid color. There are 12 styles of textures, each with its own set of options:

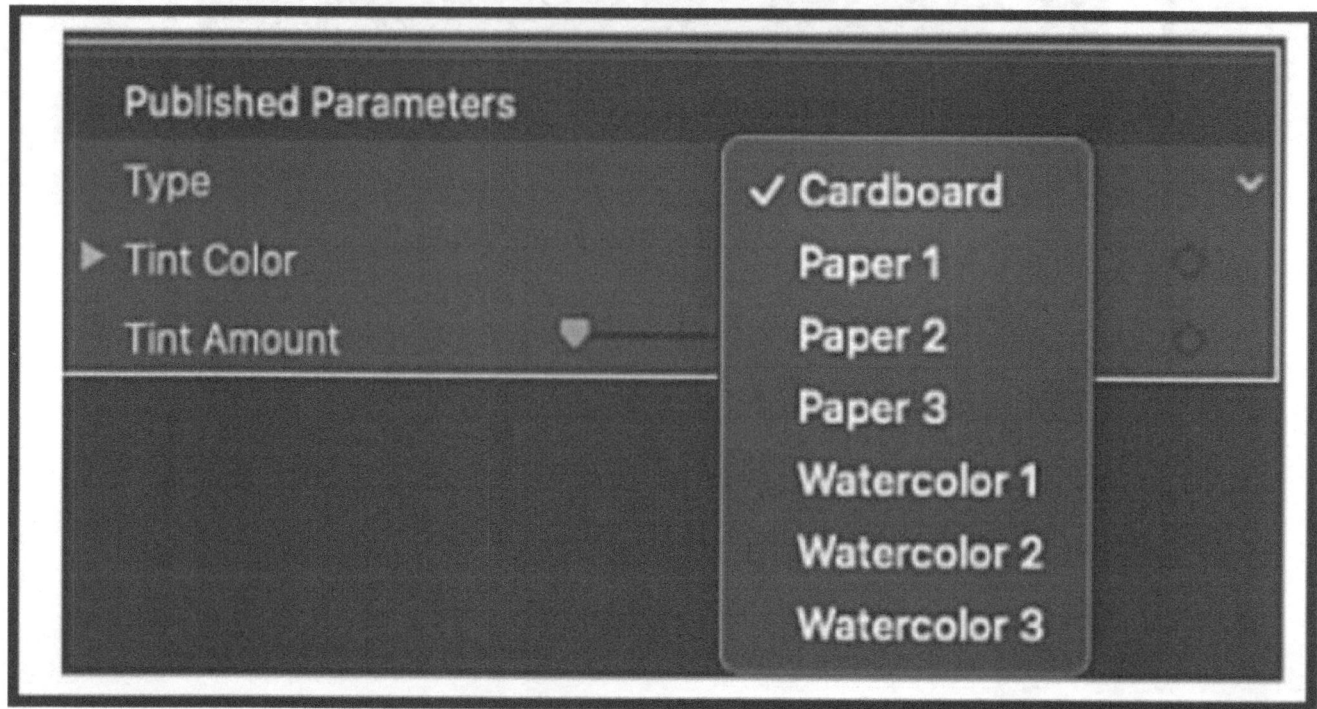

While effects are add-ons that change how your video looks, generators are short videos that play in your video. Some effects, like the Keyer effect, can totally change your video, allowing you to work with a green screen.

What are the effects?

The Effects and Transitions browser is to the right of the timeline. To open it, press one of the two buttons in the upper right corner of the menu bar. The browser can show all effects and transitions that are installed, or it can only show those that are in certain projects:

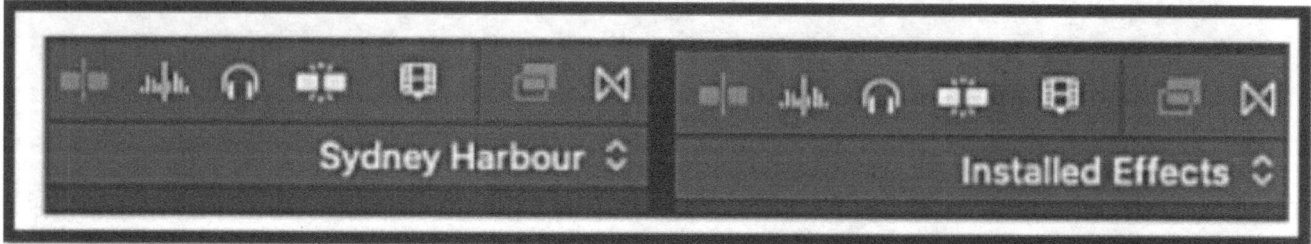

There are both video and audio effects in the browser when effects are picked. To look for the different titles for effects, go to the bottom of the browser and click on "All" in the sidebar:

When you move your mouse over an effect in the browser, an image of the effect will show you how it will look in the clip that is currently chosen in the timeline. After that, the effect is moved into the clip in the timeline. If you first choose the timeline clip and then double-click the effect in the browser, you can also add it. In the inspector, where you can see the effect settings for **Show/Hide**, changes are made. The box lets you turn the effect on or off. You can change a value **and add keyframes when you reveal the chevron.**

To get rid of the look, make sure the yellow outline is visible, and then press the Delete key:

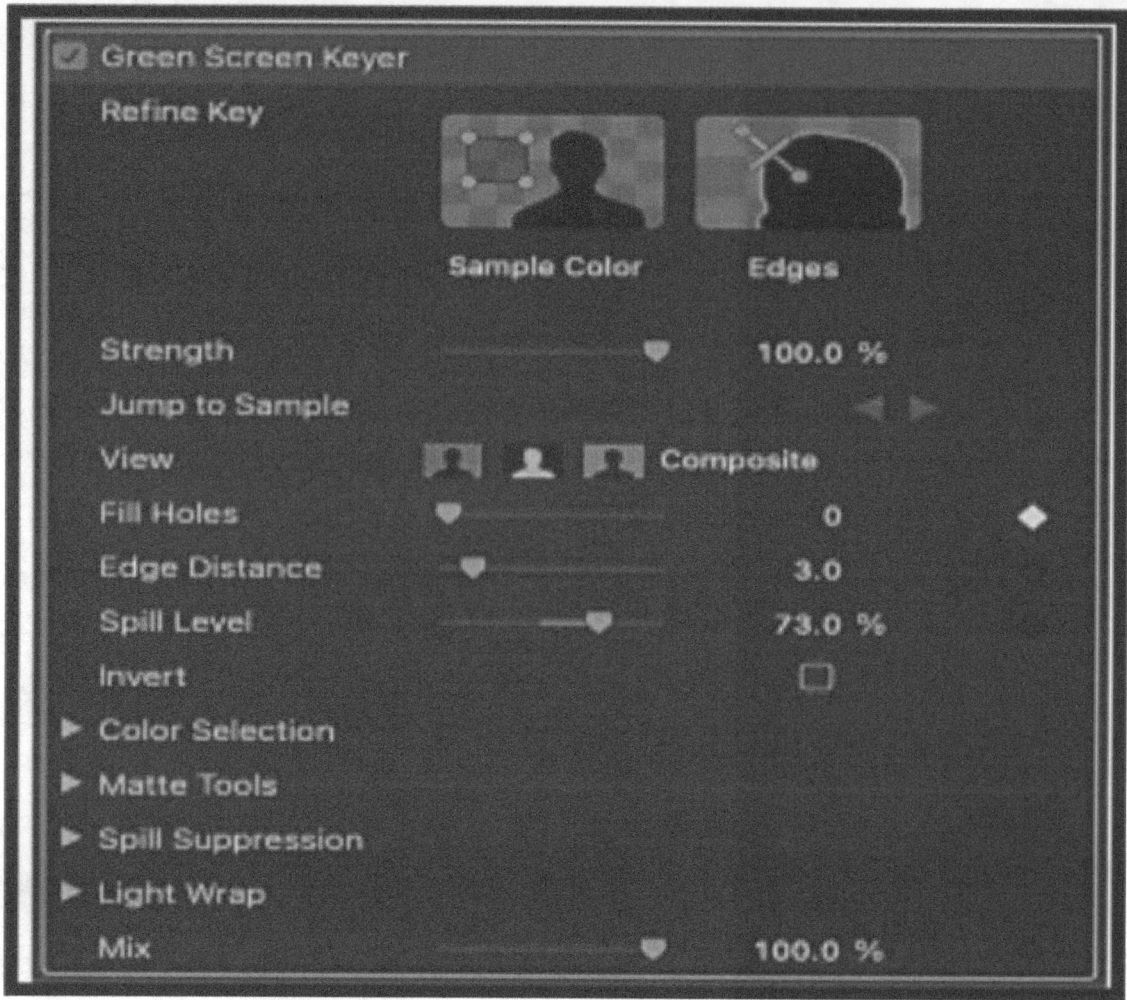

Some effects can change the shape of clips in the timeline, but most effects just change the color.

Effects categories

There are two main types of effects, with most of them having to do with color and the different shades of it. **Comic Looks, Color Presets, and Looks** are the usual subheadings. In a way, other effects are like generators in that they include acts. **Keyer**, which makes a green screen, **Sharpen**, and **Masks** are some of these. One part of a plug-in is an effect, which is used in a selected clip in the timeline.

What are transitions?

Transitions are typically used sparingly in business settings. People often say, "Just because you can doesn't mean you should." When you first start editing videos, it's easy to think that adding transitions at every edit point will make them more interesting. Not a good thought. The idea comes from the thought that every time you edit, you can see a jump to the next clip. This is because you were too close to the edit. If you are new to editing, I think you should take a break and watch the saved movie on a different screen after at least a few hours. Don't pay attention to the cuts; watch the movie as a whole. You need to smooth out the edit places if the straight cuts are making things sound bad. There's a chance that transitions will be used in that. You will learn that a transition effect is not necessary to go from one scene to the next as you become more professional at editing. A few thin gs are only done by pros. This is the first step in the process. The camera operator will film events that lead into the next scene. As an editor, you will sometimes be given a clip with a scene that ends quickly and doesn't have anything to do with the next clip. Finding a spot in the clip where the next scene will flow naturally without breaking the narrative flow is your choice. If you can't make the flow from one scene to the next work, you might want to add a transition. There are a few different effects that can be used to hide the jump cut. A cutout of a skyline moving quickly is often used as a transition in a play. A different common practice is to add a scene that has nothing to do with the main theme of the video. That result, which moves quickly, shows that time has passed. You can get the same effect with a longer fade-to-black if you don't have the right film. For talks or conversation scenes where the subject changes, use a shorter fade-to-black (but not too short, or it will be too sudden). It's possible for viewers to become so used to seeing a fade-to-black that they only see the fade and not the cut.

Two categories of transition

There are two types of transitions: those that hide the cut, like the ones we've already talked about, and those that make the cut stand out as a new start or change in the story in the video. Try out all the cool swirls and wipes that come with the plug-in packs you bought if this last type of transition is necessary. If the transitions that come with Final Cut Pro are all you have, look **through the subheadings for Movements, Objects, and Wipes in the sidebar of the Transitions browser:**

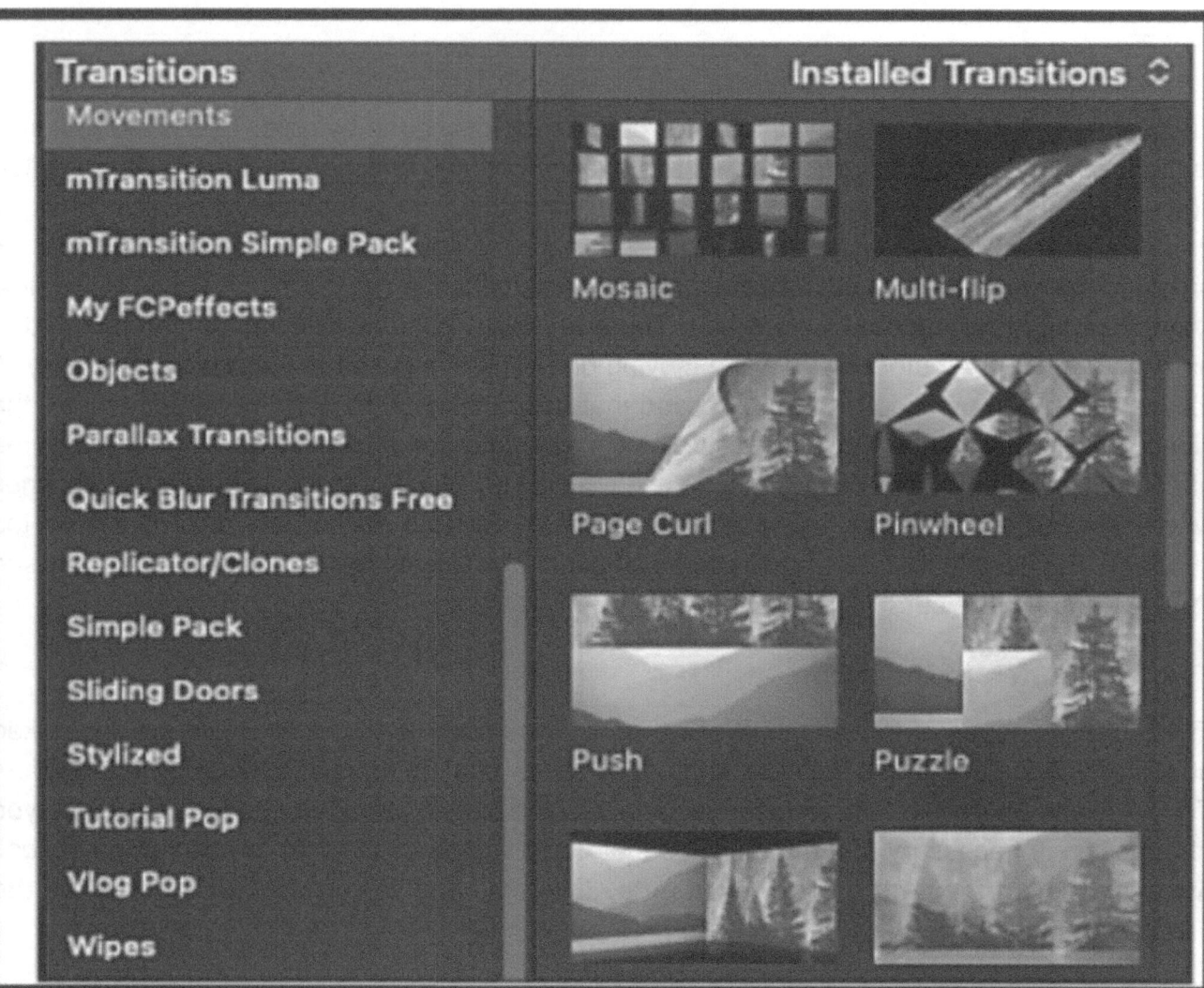

CHAPTER 10: PRECISION EDITING WITH TRIMMING TOOLS

A quick word on the best ways to switch between tools before we start. You'll be switching between the regular **Select** tool (A) and the **Trim** tool (T), which is located in the regular edit menu, to make the majority of these changes. Press the keys!

The following image shows the tool menu:

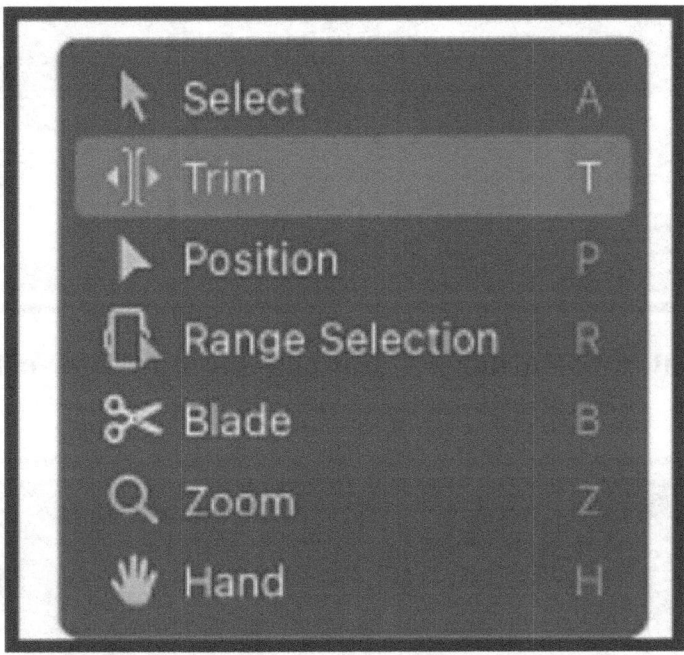

Keys can be used as a permanent or temporary switch, just like all other tool shortcuts:

- If you want to stay in the **Trim** tool until you change to another one, just press and let go of the **T** key.
- Hold down the **T** key to briefly switch to the **Trim** tool. Do your trimming work, and then let go of the **T** key.

If you choose the "temporary" option, the tool you chose before will still be chosen when you let go of the key. All of the tool shortcuts work with this method. For now, we'll start with the regular **Select** tool. Press the **A** to switch to it, and we'll talk briefly about trimming before moving on to rolling. For now, use regular clips instead of multicam clips to move things along. This is because editing works differently with multicams.

Rolling an edit

A regular trim changes either the "In" or "Out" point on a clip. A **roll edit**, on the other hand, changes both the "Out" point and the "In" point on two clips at the same time, by the same amount of time. In the primary Storyline, it works best with two clips that are next to each other. But it can also work with two clips in a connected Storyline or even with two clips that are linked but don't have a gap between them. Why do you want to do that? Because it lets you change the length of one clip for another without changing the timeline. The first clip gets longer, the second clip gets shorter, and none of the other clips move. Let's quickly go over how a regular trim works, because this is important.

Understanding a regular trim edit

Take a look at this timeline before a regular one-point trim action (using the Select tool) with a single Out point chosen to see how regular trims affect edits:

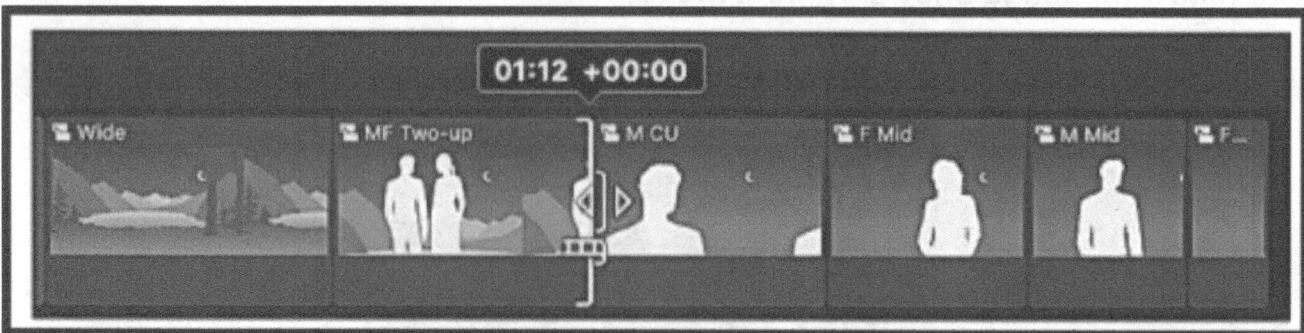

Now that the Out point is being moved, you can see how later clips are being pushed down the timeline:

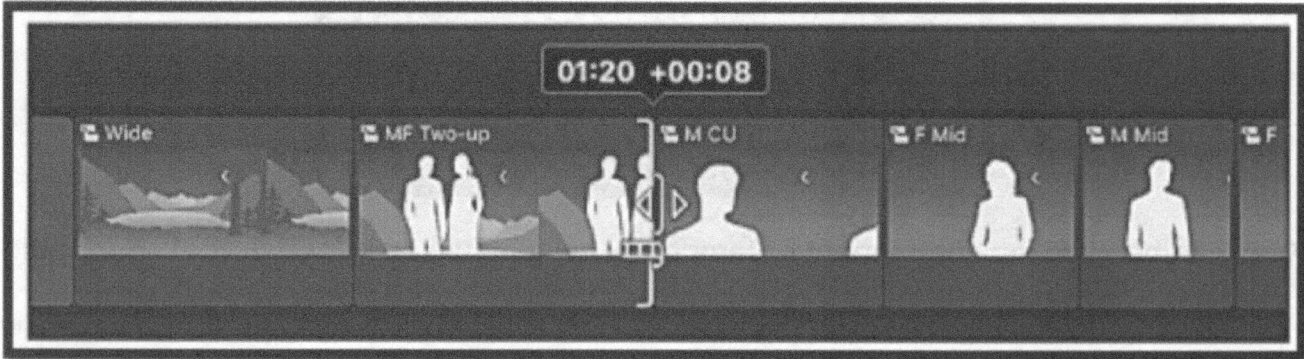

The previous clip would have moved forward to fill the gap if the "In" point gap if the In point had been chosen instead, as shown in the next image:

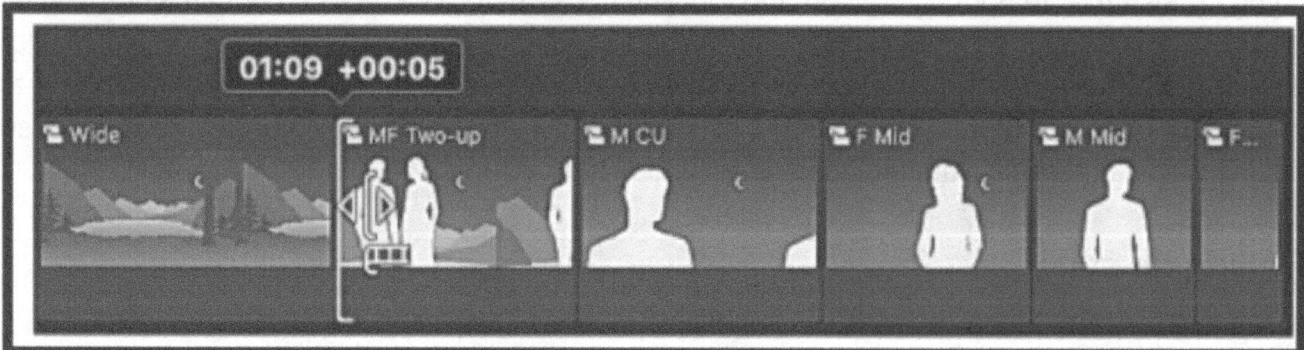

Even though you've already done both of these things a few times, feel free to practice if you're not sure. The two-up display will show up in the **Viewer** while you do this, but only one side will change. That's because you're only changing one edit point. After you understand, keep reading.

Performing a Roll Edit

Since changing one point isn't always enough, let's try changing two points with a roll edit:

1. Press **T** to get to the **Trim** tool.
2. **Place your mouse over the space between two clips to see this cursor:**

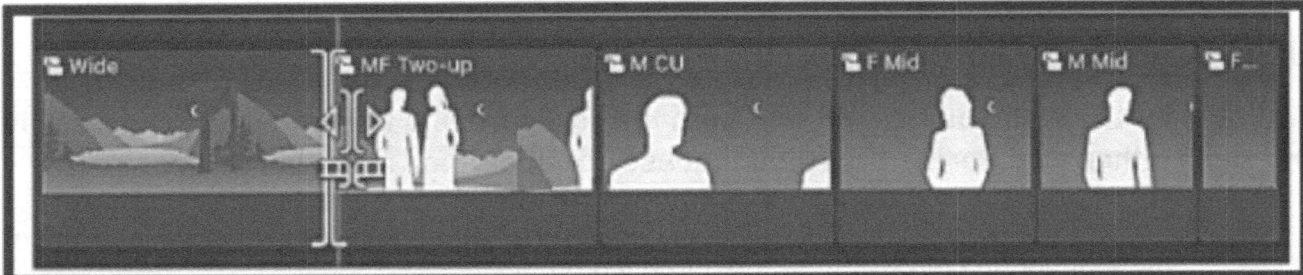

The normal trimming cursor has one In or Out sign and one filmstrip. The roll cursor, on the other hand, has two filmstrips, an out point and a nearby In point. This means that two edit points will be changed.

3. **To make a roll edit, click and drag left or right:**

This time, both frames will be shown in the two-up display in the **Viewer**. Other things you'll notice are that the timeline stays the same length and that none of the other clips change. Because of this, the roll function is very useful when you are almost finished editing and don't want to change anything else. As you might guess, you can only roll a clip as far as the media will let you. You'll see a red clip edge that stops you from moving if you drag all the way to the beginning or end of a clip.

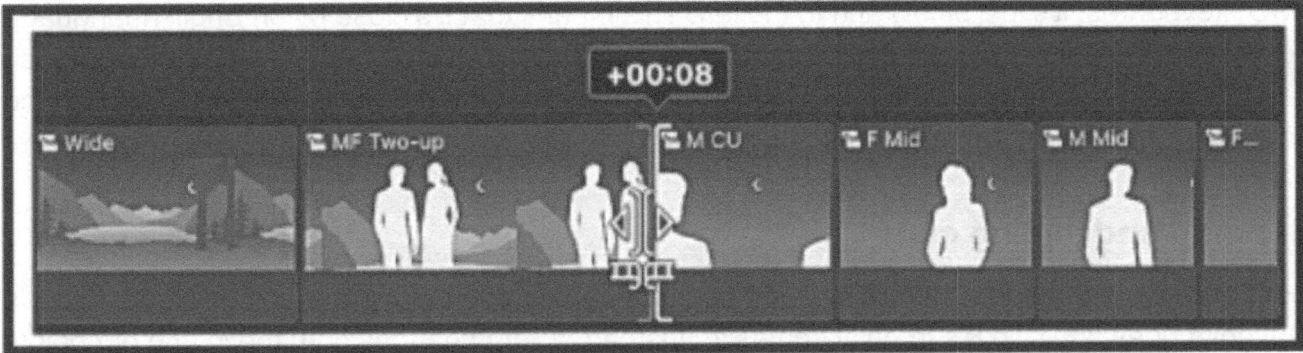

You probably won't have any trouble starting the roll operation, but you can still do a normal one-point trim operation with the **Trim** tool - you just need to be more precise about where you put the mouse. Moving closer to the middle of two edits makes the cursor change to show a two-point roll. If you move a little farther to either side, the cursor will change back to show a normal one-point trim. As always, a quick **Command-Z** will fix anything that goes wrong. Most of the time, I just press **A** to switch to the **Select** tool instead of having to fiddle with the **Trim** tool to find the right spot for a one-point trim.

Using keyboard shortcuts to roll

As you might expect, you can roll with both the keyboard and the mouse. The process is the same either way. Here is a method that uses both of them at the same time:

1. Press **T** to bring up the **Trim** tool, and then move your mouse over two clips, just above the Out and In points that are next to each other.
2. Click the edit button while the **Roll** cursor is visible to select both points at once.
3. To move both points one frame to the left, press the **comma** key. To move both points one frame to the right, press the **period** key.
4. To move both points 10 frames to the left, press **Shift-comma**. To move both points 10 frames to the right, press **Shift-period**.

It's easy to make small changes to an edit with these shortcuts. A few frames can make a huge difference in a scene. After you make changes, don't forget to check your work by pressing **Play around Edit (Shift)** or ?. We'll change the video and audio together for now, but we'll soon separate them.

If you really don't like using a mouse, you don't have to select anything at all.

- **or apostrophe (')** goes to the first frame of the next clip;
- **or semicolon (;)** goes to the first frame of the previous clip;
- **[** selects the out point of the clip to the left of the playhead.
- **]** selects the in point of the clip to the right of the playhead.

You will need one more key to choose two points for a Roll edit.

- \ Picks both out and in points around the playhead

On Australian and North American (ANSI) keyboards, the key is to the right of [and]. On UK (ISO) keyboards, it's just below and to the left. This means that it's close by on English-language keyboards and some international keyboards as well. Either a hybrid mouse/keyboard approach or a keyboard-only approach is fine. If you'd rather hover with the mouse and then switch to the keyboard, make sure **Snapping** (N) is turned on.

Slipping and sliding clips

Both of these operations change two edit points, but they don't move the points where Clip A's Out point goes and Clip B's In point comes in. Instead, a **Slip** changes both the in and out points on the same clip, as shown below.

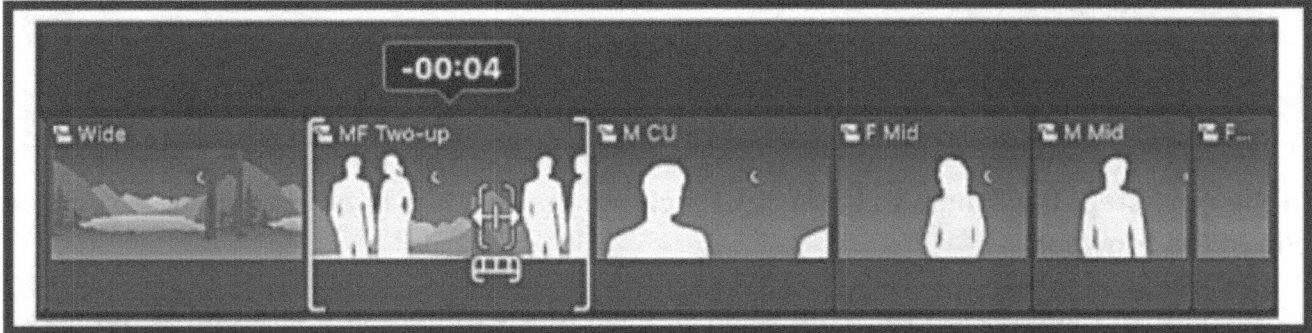

Less often used, the slide operation changes the out point before a clip and the in point after a clip:

Without some good examples, that probably won't make a lot of sense, so let's look at some extra ones.

Using a slip edit

Adding a clip that moves will help you follow along since this is easier to do than to explain. Here, I've added a shot of a boat moving from left to right to the timeline. The boat is fully in the frame at the beginning of the shot, but it's out of the frame to the right by the end.

If you're using your own media, make sure you only use a small part of a clip, ideally a third of the way through. Select a timeline clip and press **Shift-F** to **Reveal in Browser** to see the original browser clip. (That's a match frame move, if you know what it is.) You can see the whole source clip selected in the browser. If you have **View > Browser > Used Media Ranges** turned on, you can also see an orange line below the part of the clip that is being used, which looks like this:

In the next step, it will help to know how a clip in the timeline is connected to its source clip in the browser.

To make a slip edit, select the Trim tool (T), click in the middle of a clip that is not close to the left or right edges, and drag it sideways:

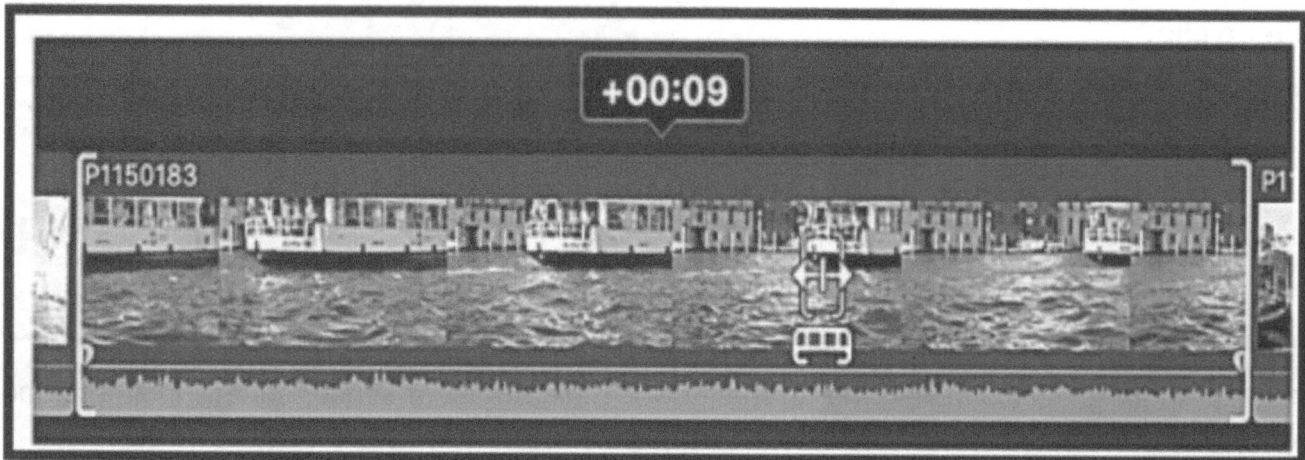

This works naturally because the film strips are moving. To use an earlier part of the clip, drag to the right. To use a later part of the clip, drag to the left. The filmstrip thumbnails will show you what's going on, and as you drag, the **Viewer** will show you the new In point and Out point of the clip. This is where I dragged to the left to use the last part of the clip. That's why the shot **ends after the boat has left the frame. It starts with the boat about to leave the frame and ends after it has left the frame. The viewer looks like this while I hold down the mouse button:**

Once you let go of the mouse, you can see that the orange line is now further along in the clip in the browser:

What would happen if I used the Trim tool to move the clip to the right? I'd Slip the clip earlier and eventually run out of media, as you can see:

The left-hand filmtrip tells me that I'm at the beginning of the clip and have no more media to use. That's also clear to me from the red clip edge in the timeline, as shown:

When you let go of the mouse, the browser tells the same story:

It's easy to see the connection here. A clip on the timeline is like a window that lets you see a part of its source clip. With Slip, you can grab the whole source clip and move it back and forth to see a different part of it. Rolling and one-point ripple-trim change the edges of this "**window**," but **Slip** doesn't. You only use a different part of the timeline clip, but it stays the same length. It might help to see another useful example. So, let's say you need to use a 4-second shot of a group of kids standing still.

You chose an interesting part in the middle of the shot. The client does notice, though, that one of the kids makes a rude move near the end of the shot. This could be fixed by selecting the **Trim** tool and dragging it to the right. This would move the gesture past the out point and into the beginning of the clip. To slip, you'll need more media. As you might expect, dragging with the **Trim** tool won't work if you want to use a whole source clip on the timeline. There is no extra media to show or hide, so both clip edges will be red. Sorry, I didn't start recording a few seconds earlier in the last clip; it would have been helpful to catch the boat coming into and leaving the frame. Options are popular among editors. OK. You can now slip and roll. There is one more thing you can do with the **Trim** tool.

Using a slide edit

A slide edit is like a Roll with a clip in the middle. The dragged clip goes to the left or right when you press Slide. However, the clip you're pulling only changes in time; its contents stay the same. As if the two clips were moving next to each other, the out point of the first clip and the in point **of the second clip are both changed. The middle clip is moved around in the timeline, but everything else stays the same. How do you do it, then? How to do it:**

- To make a slide edit, pick the **Trim** tool (T), hold down the **Option** key, and click in the middle of a clip that isn't close to the left or right sides. Then, drag the clip to the side.

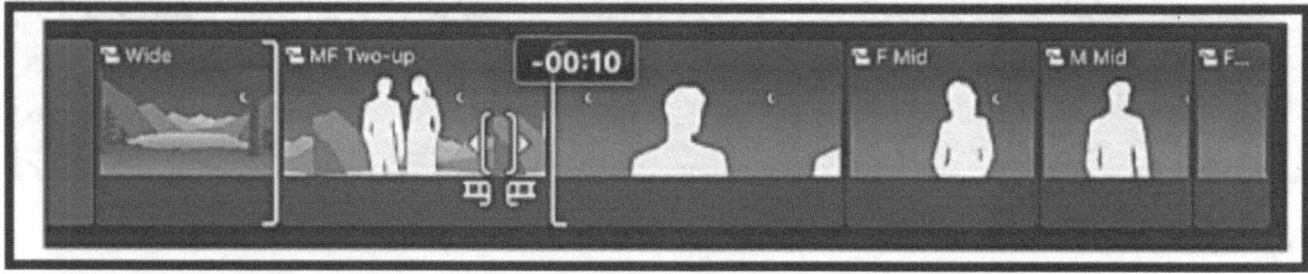

When I **option-drag** the second clip, the wide clip before it and the close-up clip after it are changed in a slide operation. This isn't some-thing that many editors do very often because it's so similar to something they do all the time with linked clips. The same thing would happen if you moved the active clip left or right if it were above the other clips in this case. This would happen if the active clip was a connected clip instead of a Storyline clip.

This is how it would look:

In fact, I don't slide very often because I know I'll need to shift a clip around in order to get it just right. But if you do slide, the **Viewer** will show a two-up screen, just like when you roll or slip. It doesn't show two-up when you move a clip that is connected. Slide is also a good choice because it keeps your timeline simple by reducing the number of vertical clips. One or two layers of connected clips aren't a problem, but a simple edit is easier to understand at a glance, and you don't need as much screen room to see your whole timeline. As with Roll and Slip, there is no two-up display that lets you use the **comma** and **period** keys to move things around. As you know, there is no keyboard shortcut that can get a clip ready for a slip or slide nudging action. So **you'll need to use the mouse at some time. First, press T to switch to the Trim tool. Then, do the following to get ready for a slip or slide on the keyboard:**

- **Click** in the middle of a clip to get ready for a slip move.
- **Option-click** in the middle of a clip to get ready to slide.

After that, you can use the **comma** and **period** keys to slip or slide by 1 or 10 frames, with or without the **Shift** key.

Softening audio with split edits (J- and L-cuts)

Back in the rough-cut stage, the goal was to make an edit sound good and then use a B-roll to hide it. Even though that's still a great way to work, **split audio edits** let you trim the video and audio parts of a clip at different times. This lets you hear a person before you see them (**J-cut**) or after you see them (**L-cut**). It's important to note that cutting the audio and video separately makes the edit less harsh, and it's not simple to do with easier editing software. **Your changes will be better if you use this method, even if the client doesn't understand why. An image of this can be seen here:**

Expanding and collapsing audio

In FCP, a clip can have audio, video, or both. Unlike most other **non-linear editing systems (NLEs)**, it treats these as one clip. It's not easy to send something out of time because the audio and video will always match up. The audio and video tracks get stuck together at first but are easy to separate in a standard process. Some new FCP users might think that removing the audio component completely is a good way to get the same effect. It's not, though. Detach audio only when you have a good reason to. As you can see, the **Detach Audio** command is in the **Clip** menu. However, it's not always the best choice because it makes it too easy to move a clip's audio out of time. If the disconnected clip came from the main storyline, you're left with a video clip and a connected audio clip. That's fine, but moving a connected clip is a breeze. If the disconnected clip was a connected clip, things would be even worse. You now have two different clips related to the same Pri-mary Storyline clip, and you'll need to remember to pick, move, and edit them every time. ugh all around.

Instead, to briefly split the audio part of a clip, do the following:

- Select **Clip > Expand Audio**, or double-click on the audio waveform of a clip in the timeline.

When you do this, the audio part of a clip (the pattern you can see) jumps down from the video. **The video and audio edges will be lined up the first time you open a clip, but you can now edit each one separately by trimming or rolling. The keys to easing cuts are trimming and rolling. A longer version of an audio clip can be seen here:**

First, let's look at an example of how to make a J-cut in real life. You need to get a shot of someone talking on camera, like in an interview or a show. Do these things:

1. Look for a clip of someone talking, pick out the part where they're talking, and add it to the main storyline, as shown in the image below.

2. Look for a B-roll clip that's a good way to start the first shot.

An appropriate B-roll could include a shot of that person going or talking to someone else, or it could be about what they're talking about.

3. Put the B-roll video clip in front of the talking video clip in the main storyline.

4. To make the audio of the speech clip bigger, double-click on its waveform.

You might want to drag the speech clip's audio point to the left to make it longer and fit under the first clip. Unfortunately, this only makes the clip's audio start earlier. Since you already picked the right audio, this would add noise, quiet, or extra speech to the beginning of the clip that you don't want. Proceed as follows instead.

5. Move the speech clip's video point to the right to make it start later.

It does what you want. The audio now starts under the first B-roll clip, so you can hear the person before you see them. When you zoom in for more information, you can see:

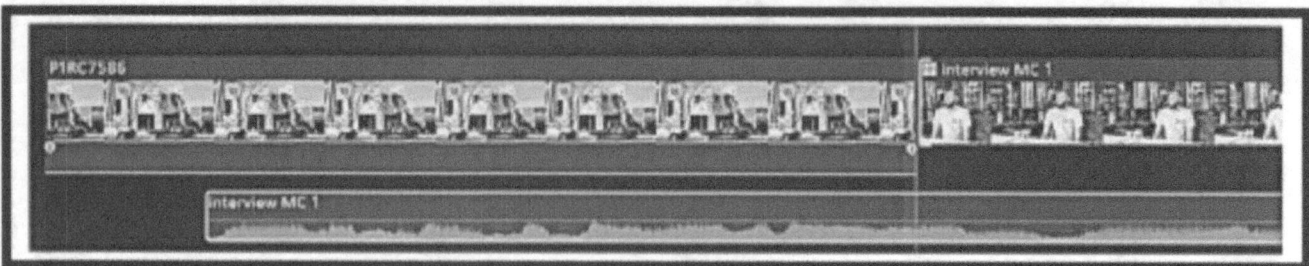

This is similar to linking the B-roll clip above the main storyline in a technical sense, but it is much easier to handle in real life. The edit is based on the main story, and most of the time, you want clips of people talking to drive the edit. When you expand audio in this way, you can put the right clips in charge while still being able to finetune the transitions between them. This is a good way to do it, as shown, if you want the audio of a clip to go beyond the usual clip boundaries.

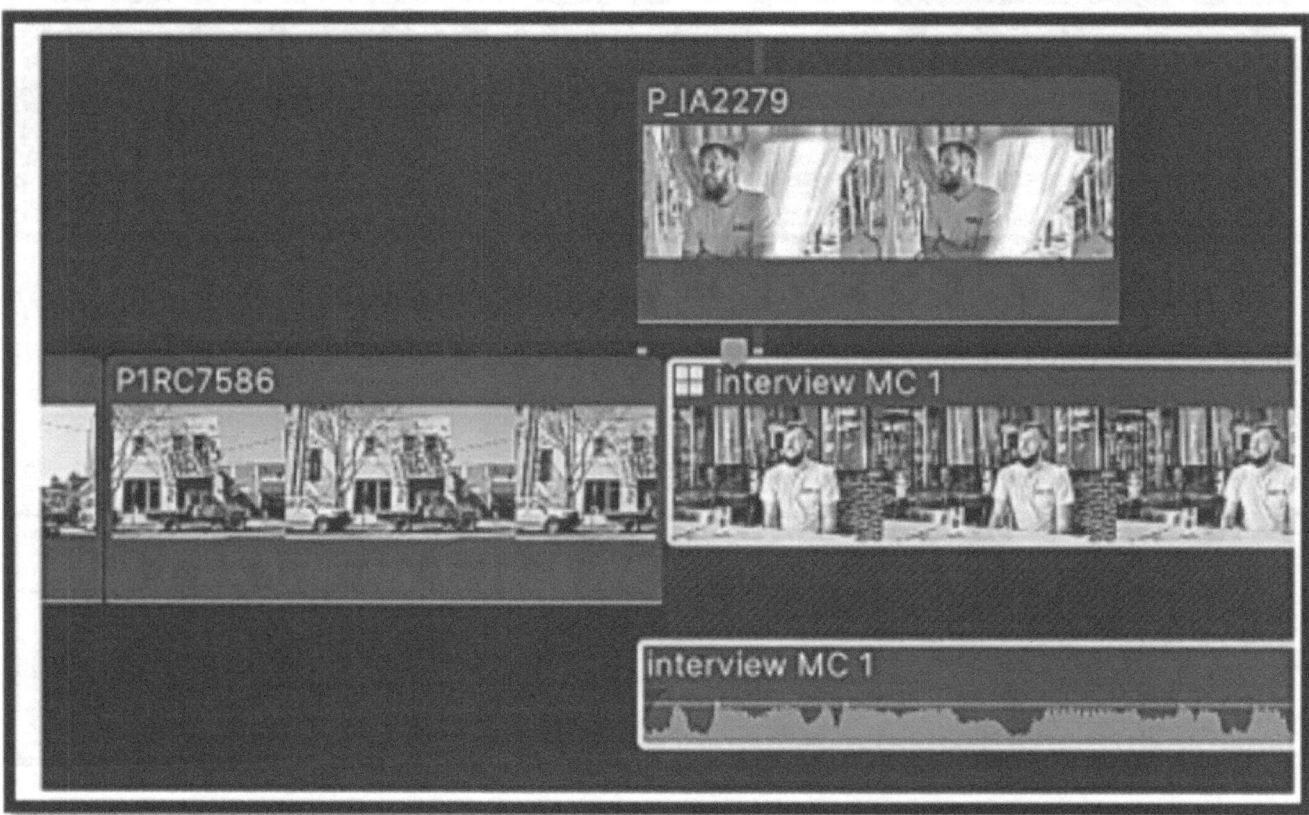

You would expand the audio, then move the "Out" point of a "talking" clip to the left so that a B-roll clip can sit on top of the audio from the first clip. This is similar to an L-cut, but done backwards. This method isn't used very often, but it's still useful, as shown in the image below:

There is a tool called "Collapse Audio" that lets you visually put back together larger audio parts. Proceed as follows to use this:

- In the timeline, double-click on the audio waveform of a clip or go to **Clip > Coll Audio.**

Keep in mind that collapsing audio doesn't change the way anything sounds, but it might look different. If a clip's audio doesn't cross with the video that goes with it, it will be hidden when the clip is collapsed. Here's an example of audio that was expanded and began and ended before the video.

This is what the audio looked like after it collapsed:

It's possible not to see collapsed audio, but it can still be heard. That's why I usually leave it stretched if the length has been changed. This means that if you change the video part of a clip, the expanded audio will stay the same length. However, if you trim the clip's unified start or end points after it has been flattened, any gaps that its audio start and end points had when it was expanded will still be there. Some of the time, this will let you hear a different part of the clip, which might not be a problem. Select the whole timeline (**Command-A**) and press the shortcut (**Control-S**) to do **Clip > Expand Audio** for all clips at once. This will help you figure out where the audio is and make everything bigger. If you want to make things easier, press the **Control-S** shortcut again to collapse all the audio clips. (There are more tr icks you can use to separate audio clips into their individual parts). Expanding audio lets you do more than just J-cuts and L-cuts; it also lets you make audio breaks between two clips, making it the most flexible way.

Overlapping audio edit points

If you want to run two clips of different people together or only toplay part of a clip of someone talking, you should probably cross the audio of the two clips a little. There might be a drop-in sound when the background noise goes away if there is a space between the two clips, but this won't happen if they meet. Of course, it's not always easy to edit clips, and you'll run into a lot of different problems in differ-ent jobs.

Take a look at this image:

To smooth out the edges of words, you may need to overlap two edits at the same time. This is especially true if you need to pull out good words that were said next to bad words. You should find this process pretty easy if you've already cut out a few extra words (like "um" or "ah") from someone's speech to make a shorter soundbite. A new feature in 10.4.9 makes it even easier:

1. Use the **Range Selection** tool to pick out the part of a clip that you don't want.
2. Press "**Delete**" to get rid of it.
3. Click on both clips at the same time, then press **Option-T** (or go to **Modify > Adjust Audio Fades > Crossfade**) to add a **Crossfade**.

Now the **fade handles** on the clip are working, and the two clips overlap for a length of time that **you set in Settings/Preferences under Editing. You can play it back to see if it sounds good. If you want, you can change the results with a more manual method from there**:

1. Make the audio bigger on each of the audio waveforms.
2. Trim the audio parts so that they only have the parts you want to use.
3. Trim the video parts to change how the audio clips overlap and the timing.
4. Put a B-roll cutaway above the jump cut to hide it.

You shouldn't lie, but you shouldn't be afraid to make a speaker sound better or more professional, either. You can make as many changes as you want; the cut away will hide all of them. This kind of editing happens a lot.

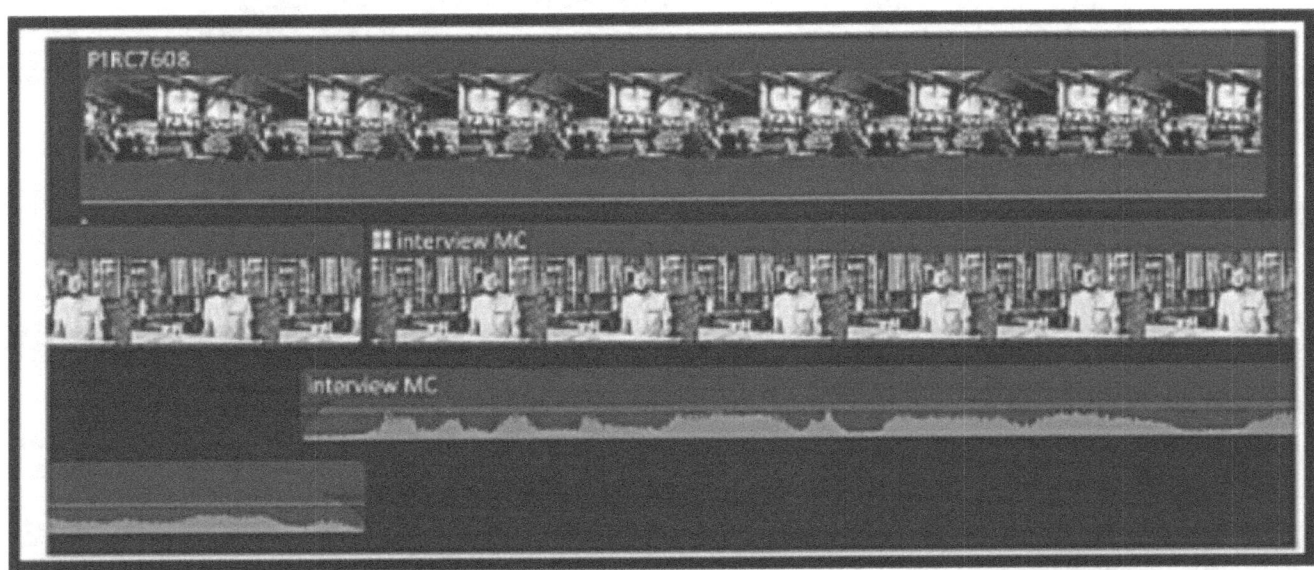

You can get to and change those built-in fade handles on any audio clip, with or without a **Crossfade**. How? Keep reading.

Fading audio edits

You can see that adding a **Crossfade** makes the fade handles on a clip visible. However, the fade handles on every audio edge are the same. They are an important part of making audio changes sound smooth because they let you fade that sound in or out. A smooth transition from one music track to another can be achieved with the help of audio fades.

To get to the fade handles for a clip:

1. Move your mouse over the left or right edge of an audio waveform until you see a teardrop.

When you move your mouse over this teardrop, you will see a pointer with two black arrows going left and right, as shown:

2. Click on the teardrop and drag it towards the middle of the clip until you get the length you want. If the clip's edge changes, undo it and try again.

Almost every time you edit audio, you should use fades to make sure that each clip starts and ends with silence. You might hear a click or a pop when an audio clip cuts in the middle of a noise. In **Final Cut Pro**, go to **Commands > Customize** and press **Option-Command-K** to add shortcuts to the following instructions that are normally hidden. This makes adding audio fades easy.

- **Apply audio fades.**
- **Remove audio Fades**

- **Toggle Audio Fade In**
- **Toggle Audio Fade Out**

These commands use the default length of the **Audio Fade**. You can change this length as well as the **Crossfade** length in the **Editing pane** of **Settings/ Preferences**. You can set either or both of these to a very short time if you want to, as shown here:

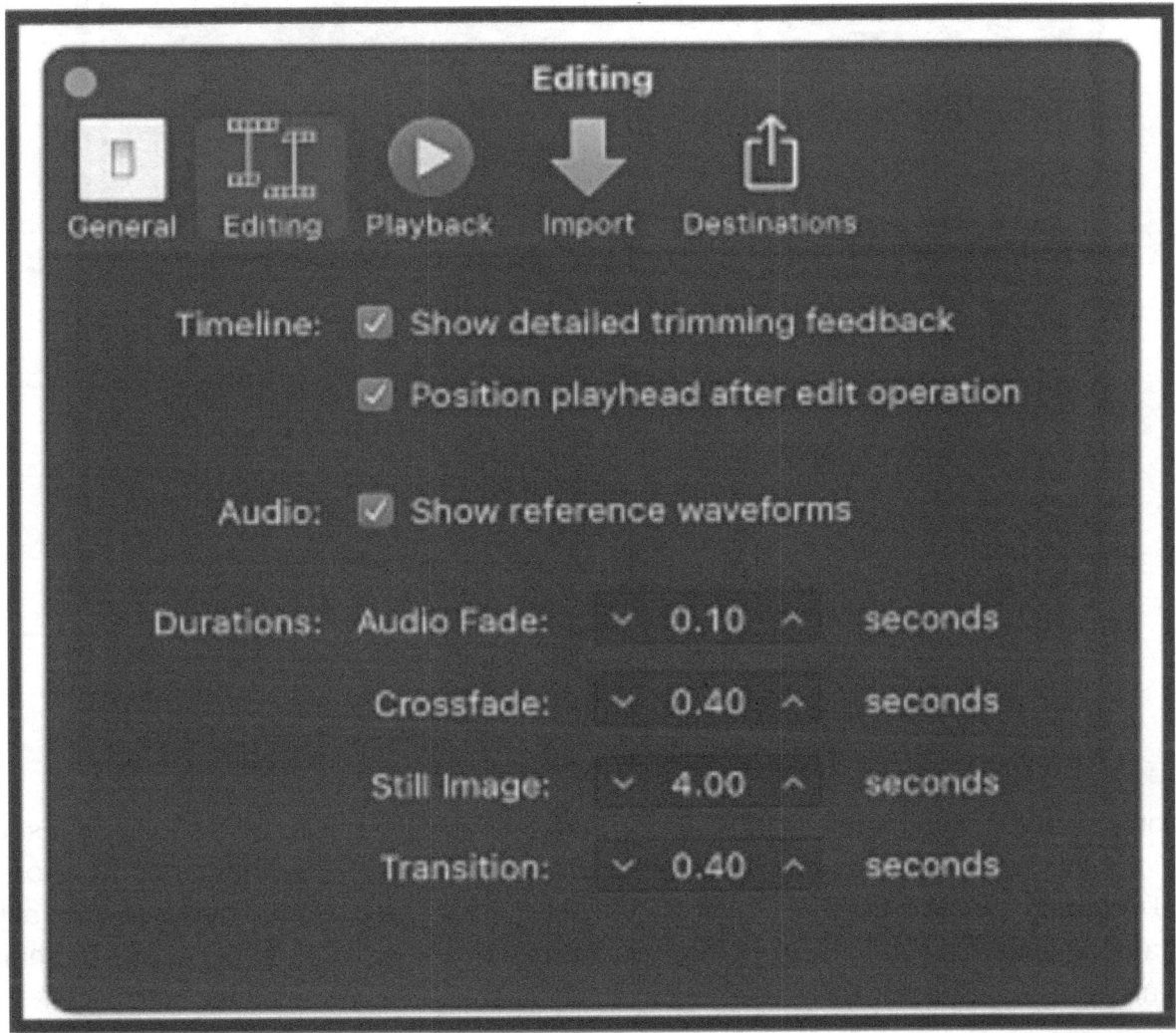

Crossfade clips have the same handles, but the edges of a normal clip will be set to **+3dB** and **Crossfade** clips will have the **S-curve** fade style. If you right-click on the handle, you can pick your own style:

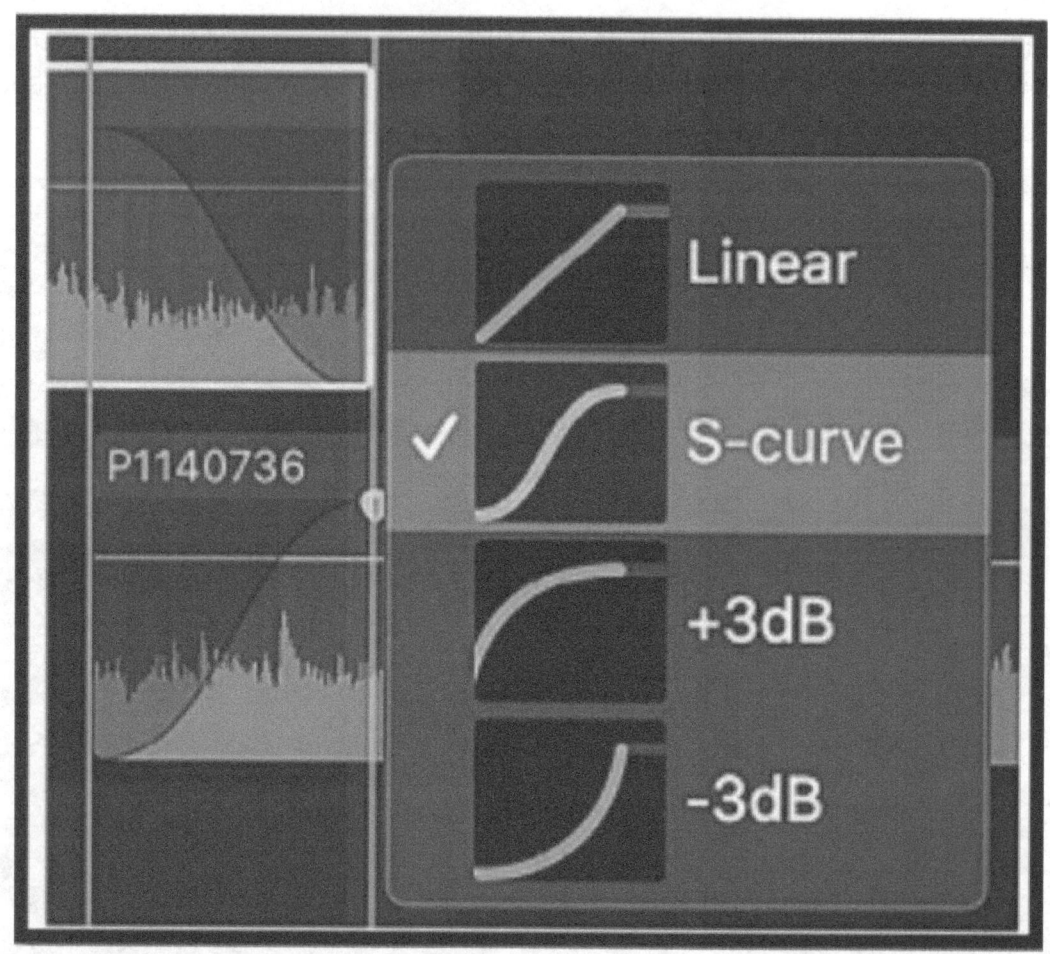

How long should a fade handle last? The only rule that always applies is "as long as it sounds good," but this really depends on the situation. As a general rule, keep fades pretty short. But when I'm mixing two clips together, I just make sure there's some overlap between the tracks to avoid an odd pause. If you think of yourself as a visual editor, don't be afraid to try your hand at audio as well.

This is how a fade-in should look:

Try something different: add some foley effects (post-production sounds like footsteps or gunshots) and mood from the **Sound Effects** library, and play it over and over until you're satisfied. You'll notice that sound effects are shown in a different color because they play a different role.

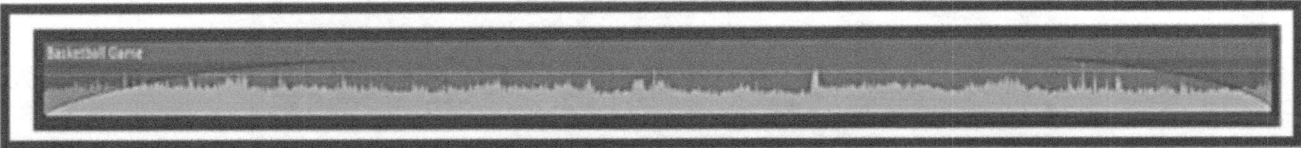

It gets easier to hide the beginning or end of any one part the more of them you have in the mix. Remember to change the relative volume of clips by moving the volume line up and down.

Fading music for beat-matching

For example, music can benefit from a slightly different approach, such as fades that can be short or long. Sometimes you need to quickly change the speed, and other times you'll need a **pretty hard cut that goes straight into the next scene with a bang that can be seen and heard. An easy trick to use if you need to play a short piece of music again:**

1. Add the connected audio clip to a storyline.
2. To make a duplicate, **option-drag** it inside the storyline.
3. Trim off the beginning of the second clip at the "In" point to get to a similar-sounding part of the music, as shown in the image below:

4. Double-click the audio waveforms on both clips to **Expand audio.**

The next sneaky trick works even though the clips don't show anything.

5. To see the beats, use the timeline's appearance menu (it looks like a film strip) to make the waves bigger, like this:

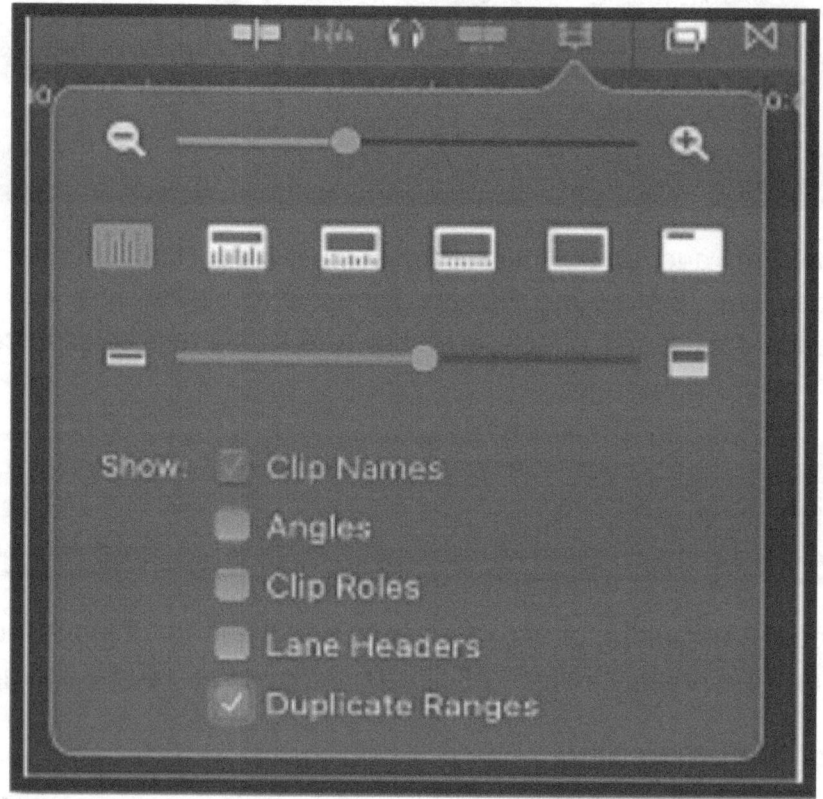

The slider at the top controls the zoom level; the second set of icons determines what is shown in each clip's filmstrip (select the leftmost icon to only see audio waveforms); and the slider below the icons determines the height of the clip. After that, do this.

6. **Cut the length of one or both of the video edges so that the peaks of the two audio tracks that play in order meet, as shown:**

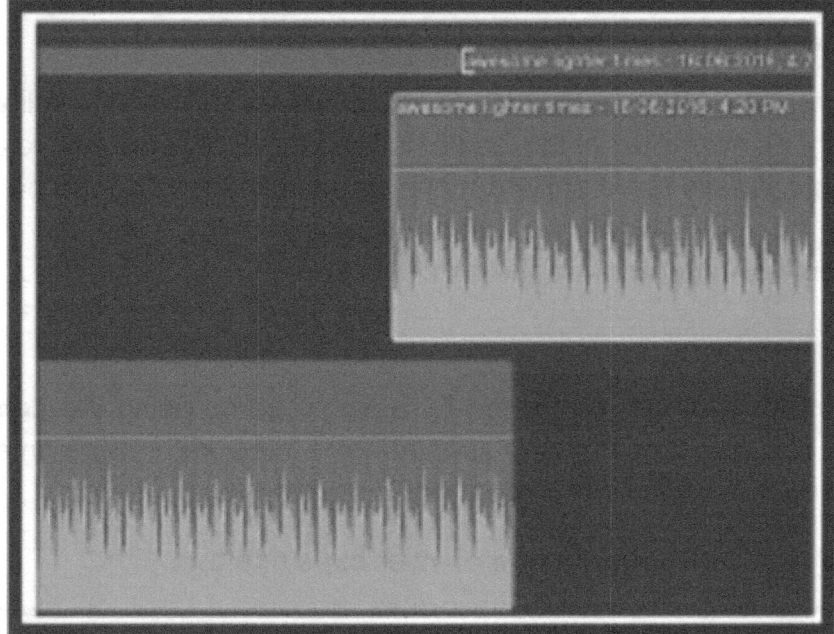

7. Zoom in and change the audio edges by trimming off any extraneous audio.
8. Until the beats in the waves match up perfectly, use the **Trim** tool to slip the second audio clip.

When you slip audio in a storyline clip or any audio in a loosely linked clip, keep in mind that the audio will move by subframes. This is much smaller than a frame, so you have fine control over how the beats match, as you can see here:

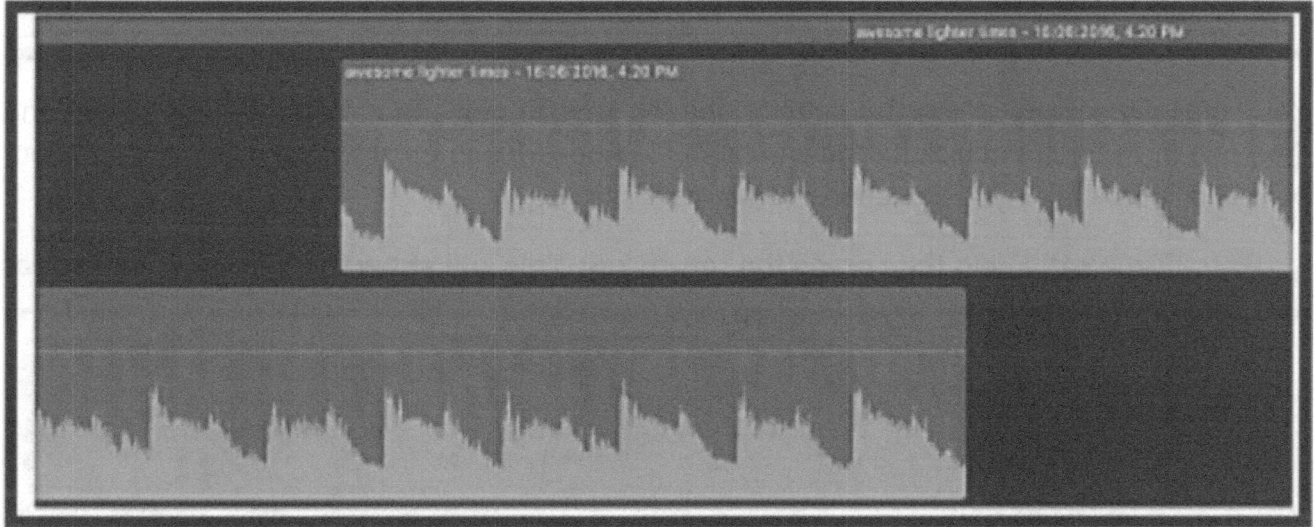

9. **Add fades to transition between the two tracks, as shown here:**

Multiple music clips can be beat-matched pretty easily in this way, and this approach is much more flexible than just fading one clip out and another clip in. Sound effects don't need as much work because they can usually stand on their own. Just make sure you use only the part of the effect you need (they can be quite long) and fade it out when you're done with it. The mouse, the **comma**, and the **period** moving shortcuts can be used to trim both audio and video in any way. However, they move by a full frame. Use the **option-comma** and **option-pe-riod** keys on the keyboard to make audio segments Slip changes. If you want to go faster, add the **shift key**.

Editing numerically and with the precision editor

Since editing is more of a skill than a science, not every editor or writer will want to be exact. Sometimes, though, it's helpful to set the length of a clip (or all of your clips) to a certain number. For example, if a client asks for "a second more on that clip," it's great to be able to do it with just one click and four quick words (**+, 1, period**, and **return**). You'll learn how to edit with numbers, set the time exactly, and use the precision editor to get a better look.

Trimming using numbers

A chosen edit point (or clip) can be moved by a single frame using the **comma** and **period** shortcuts, but you can also move by any amount using **plus** and **minus** timecodes. Here are some steps that show how to answer a client who asks for "a second more.".

1. **Choose an "Out" point on one of your clips like this:**

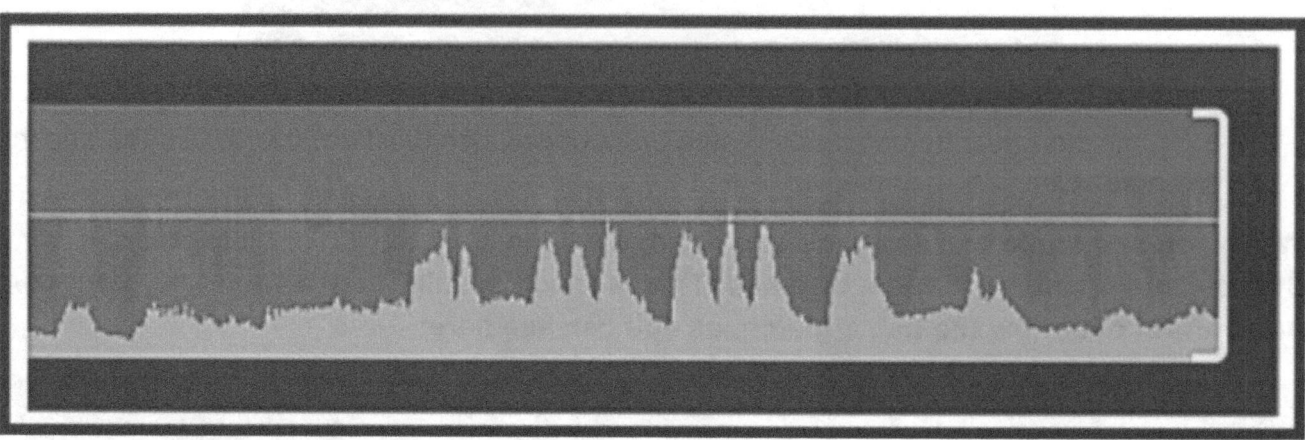

You could either click on the Out point or use the keys to move the playhead to that point and then use the shortcut to pick it. You can use [to choose the in point, while] will choose the out point. For a Roll ed it, you can choose both with \

2. **Type +100, and then press the return key. This will show the following timecode:**

You use a plus sign to move to the right and a minus sign to move to the left. Depending on how many characters you type, the time-code entry is read in different ways.

- It's called "**frames**" if you put one or two numbers.
- The first two numbers you enter are seconds, and the last two are frames if you enter three or four digits.
- If you enter five or six digits, the first two are minutes, the next two are seconds, and the last two are frames.
- A period (.) is the same as two zeros, or "00."

- If you put a number that is greater than the available units, like 80 frames or 65 seconds, the extra amount is changed to the next unit.

You can see the output being calculated as you type in the timecode displayed below the viewer. Here are some examples:

- **+215** = Move the chosen edit point to the right by 2 seconds and 15 frames.
- **+265** = Move the chosen edit point 4 seconds and 15 frames to the right (in a 25-FPS timeline, 2 seconds and 65 frames equal 4 seconds and 15 frames).
- **-50** = Move the chosen edit point 50 frames to the left (based on frame rate, this could be just over or just under 2 seconds).
- **-2.** = In any framerate, -2 means to move the chosen edit point two seconds to the left.
- **+5..** = move the chosen edit point to the right by 5 minutes.

You can either add or take away time from a clip, depending on which edit point you choose. When you move in points to the left or out points to the right, the clip gets longer. When you rolledit, one clip gets longer while another gets shorter, so choose the edit point(s) how-ever you want and then type away. Take a look at this:

It's the same process to move a clip instead of an edit, but be careful. Moving a Primary Storyline clip with numbers will do a slide action, taking time from one clip and giving it to the other side. Connected clips can move easily, but not Primary Storyline clips.

If you want to move anything, you can use this basic approach to precision:

1. Use the **Select** tool to pick out an edit point on one of your clips. The **Trim** tool can be used to pick out two edit points, or you can choose to select the whole clip.
2. Type + or -, then a timecode, and finally press **"return."**

There are also ways to use numbers to set the duration of a clip.

Setting the clip duration

What if your client says they want a clip that is "exactly 4 seconds" long instead of "a second longer"? It's simple, but you can't just use **plus** or **minus**. **Change Duration** is the command, but you'll use **Ctrl-D**. To set the length of time, do these things:

1. Pick out one or more clips.
2. **Press Ctrl-D, then type a timecode (without pressing Ctrl), and finally press return. This will cause the following time-code to show up:**

Keep in mind that you only need to hold down Ctrl while pressing D, and you'll need to press return at the end of each one.

- **Ctrl-D4**: Make the clip you've chosen last for 4 seconds, an absolute change.
- **Ctrl-D+2**: Make the clip you've chosen two seconds longer, which is a relative change.
- **Ctrl-D1** makes the clip you've chosen one frame long, which is useful for time-lapses or animation routines.

Take a look at this image:

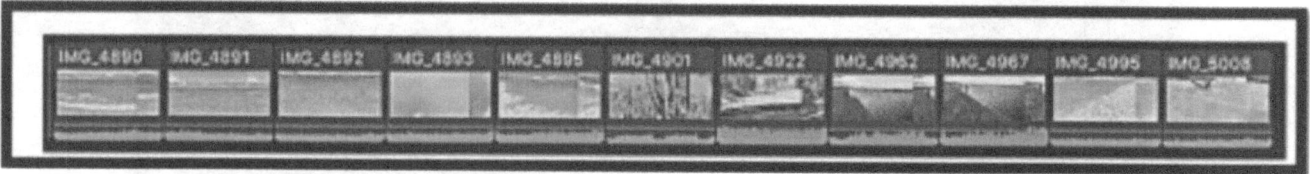

Also, if you pick all the clips at once, you can quickly fill a timeline with movies or stills of a certain length by doing the following:

1. Press **E** to to add something to the **Timeline**.
2. Click on the **Timeline**.
3. Press **Command-A** to pick out all of the clips at once.
4. Press **Control-D3** to make all of the clips 3 seconds long.
5. As shown in the image below, press **Command-T** to add the default **Dissolve** transition between all of these clips:

Moving to a specific timecode

Another similar process is needed to jump to a certain timecode on the timeline. You'll need to use the **Move Playhead Position** command before entering the timecode. The short cut **is Ctrl-P**, and you should instantly type in a timecode in seconds and frames after it. If this is something you do a lot, you might want to give this command a different key. In **Final Cut Pro > Commands > Customize**, the top-right search field in Final Cut Pro lets you look for "**move playhead.**" Then, **you can drag that command to any key that isn't being used. If your keyboard is enlarged, the clear key is unused, right next to all those useful number keys. If you give it, you'll see this:**

You'd want to jump to a certain timecode if someone gave you a paper edit with changes marked with times. If you're not going to use **To Do Markers** to keep track of changes, make sure you always work from the end of a change list to the beginning. If you don't, the first ripple edit you make will void later timecodes. Finally, if you need to look at the timecode often, try turning on two moving windows that you can resize: **Window > Source Timecode and Window > Project Timecode**. In a completely different setting called Precision Edit, there is one last useful way to edit exactly.

Using the precision editor

This separate editing mode offers a way to focus on a single edit at a time, see how much more media is available for the current edit, and make edits and Roll ed is in both old and new ways. Just double-click on an edit in your timeline to go into this mode. To leave, press the **Escape** key. The timeline is now split in half, and in the middle of the screen is a line of gray boxes that show primary storyline edits. One edit at a time is shown, with older clips at the top and newer clips at the bottom. You can click on edits in your timeline or use the following keyboard shortcuts to move between them: **semicolon** or to go back; **apostrophe** or to go forward.

Take a look at this image:

A roll edit is made by dragging on the gray boxes in the middle of the current point. In this mode, you can see what you'll be showing because you can see the film strips for the empty parts of the previous and next clips, as shown:

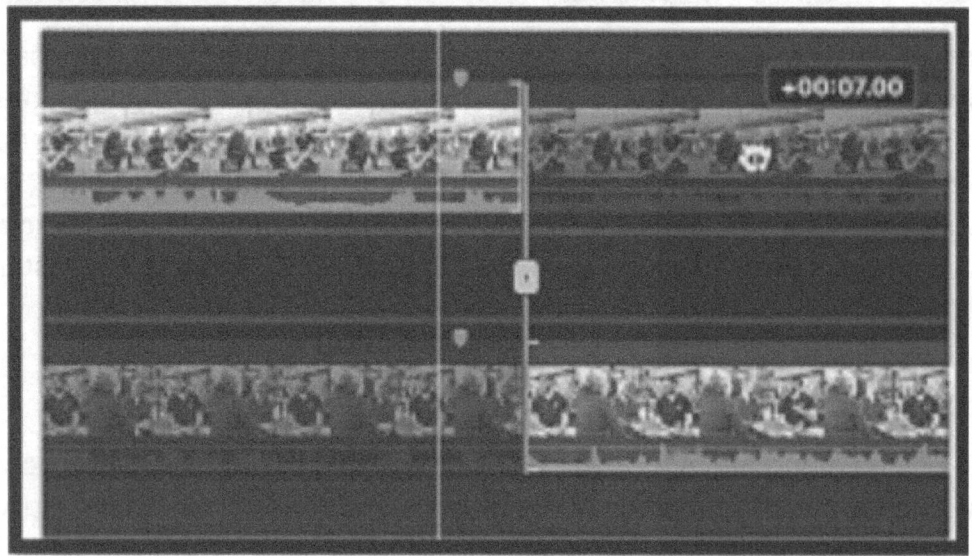

For a normal trim, move the mouse up to get to an out point or down to get to an In point, then click and drag it left or right. There are two less clear ways to trim: drag on either side of the upper or lower filmstrip to move the in or out point, or click on the filmstrip to make that point the new in or out point. And all the nudging (**comma/period**), edge-selecting (**[,]**, or ****), **Trim Start, Trim End**, and **Play Around Edit** (**Option**-[, **Option** -], and **Shift-/**) shortcuts work here too. Have a look:

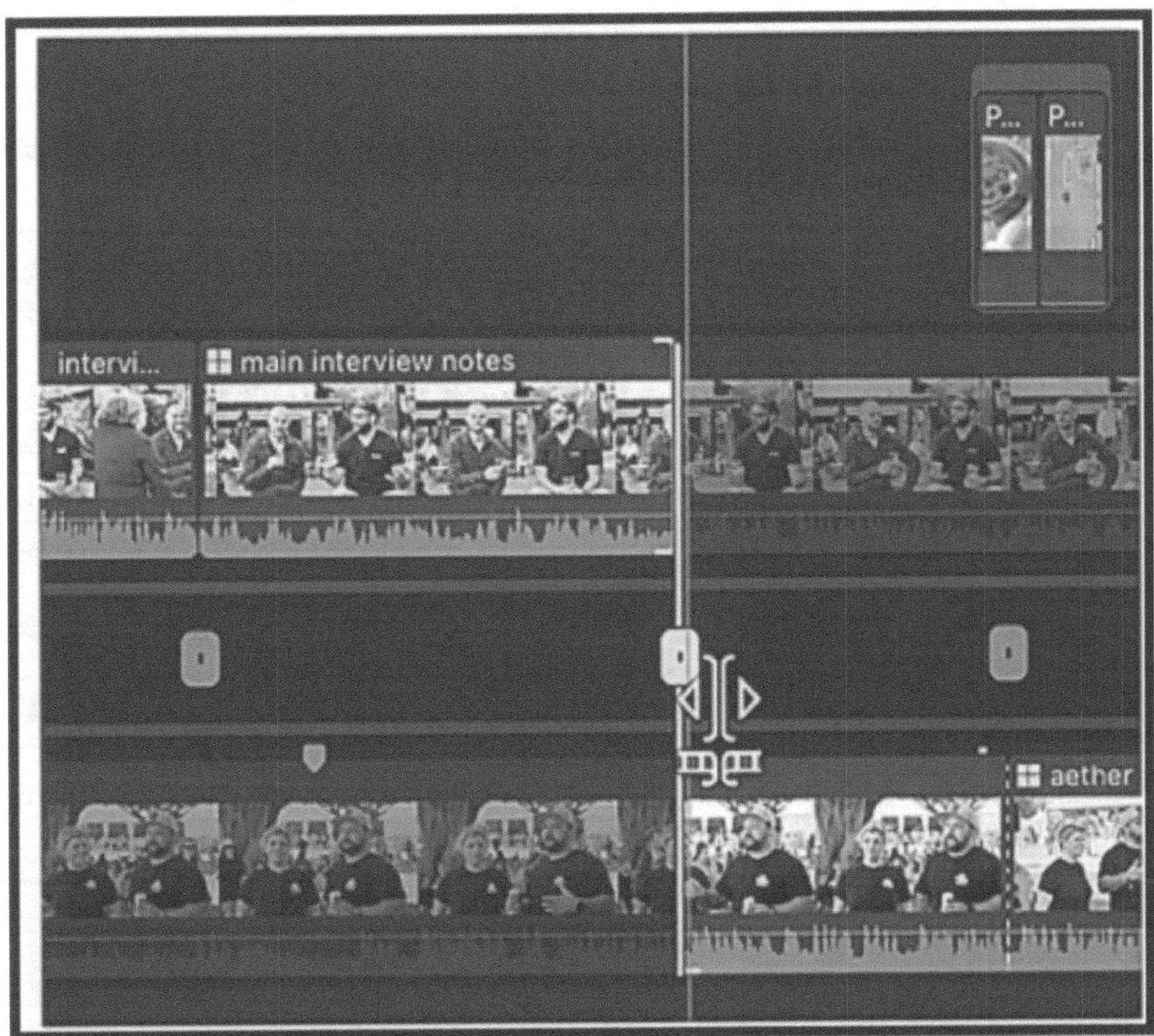

Some people never use this mode, but it's a great way to see every edit in your timeline. This is also a great way to show a client that you're making good decisions when you're going over an edit with them and they want to know which media they can't see. Still, don't use it if you don't like it.

CHAPTER 11: ADVANCED TECHNIQUES - MULTICAM, REPLACEMENTS, AND AUDITIONS

Understanding Multicam footage

A Multicam Clip syncs up several viewsat the same time. You can pick at any time which view and sound you want to hear when you are editing a Multicam Clip:

You can play the clip continuously to see what was recorded, or you can cut out parts you don't want:

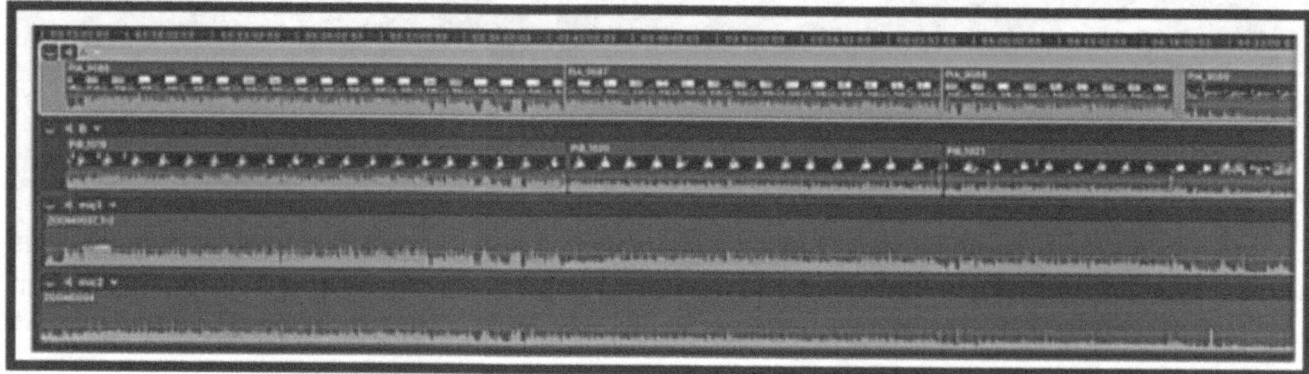

Multicam Clips are usually made with video from several cameras and audio recorders that are all working at the same time, but that's not the only way to get Multicam footage. Multiple shots taken one after the other (in the same place or in different places) can be synced as separate Multicam views when a singer lip-syncs to a recorded audio track.

You could also sync up a videoof the presenter giving a presentation with a copy of the presentation on the screen. In order for the audio to sync with the clips, all you need to do is make sure that each camera is recording audio. Move some Multicam footage into the project and sync it up now if you haven't already. You can practice with any two cameras, even phones. However, it will be easier if you can use matched cameras with matched settings. Record some words on all of your devices, and th at's all that really needs to be said.

Here are the steps you should have already taken once youhave the video:

1. Bring in your source clips.
2. Use the **Angle Editor** to make a Multicam Clip and check the sync.

NOTE: The **Angle Editor** is the on ly tool youneed to make changes inside the Multicam. You can use it to sync properly, change the color or position of an entire clip, or change the angles. All you have to do to edit the finished clip is drag the whole Multicam Clip into a normal Project and cut it there.

Now that your Multicam Clips are ready to be edited, it's easy to begin:

1. Choose a Multicam Clip from the **Browser** tab and choose most of it. Mark the In and Out points as normal.
2. Open a project or make one, then add your Multicam Clip to the timeline with the letter **E**.

For Multicam Clips to work best, pick the best audio channel and then show the **Angle Viewer**, which shows all of your angles along with the main **Viewer**. First, let's pick the best audio.

Preparing to edit with the Angle Viewer

Multicam editing typically requires one good audio source and several video sources. Anything else that was audio had already done its job by helping to sync up the video, so it wasn't really useless. First, though, we can pick out the right audio track. **Now let's begin**:

1. Right-click the Multicam Clip on the Timeline. After that, pick **Active Audio Angle** and then the right track's name:

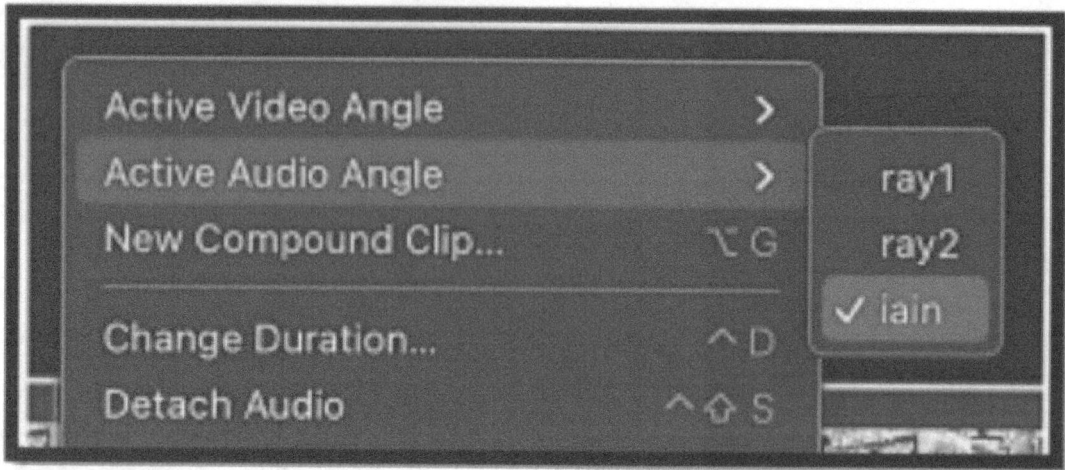

This should be easy if youhave named your angles properly, but if not, you"ll have to listen to find the best one.

2. Press **Shift-Command-7** to bring up the **Angle Viewer**:

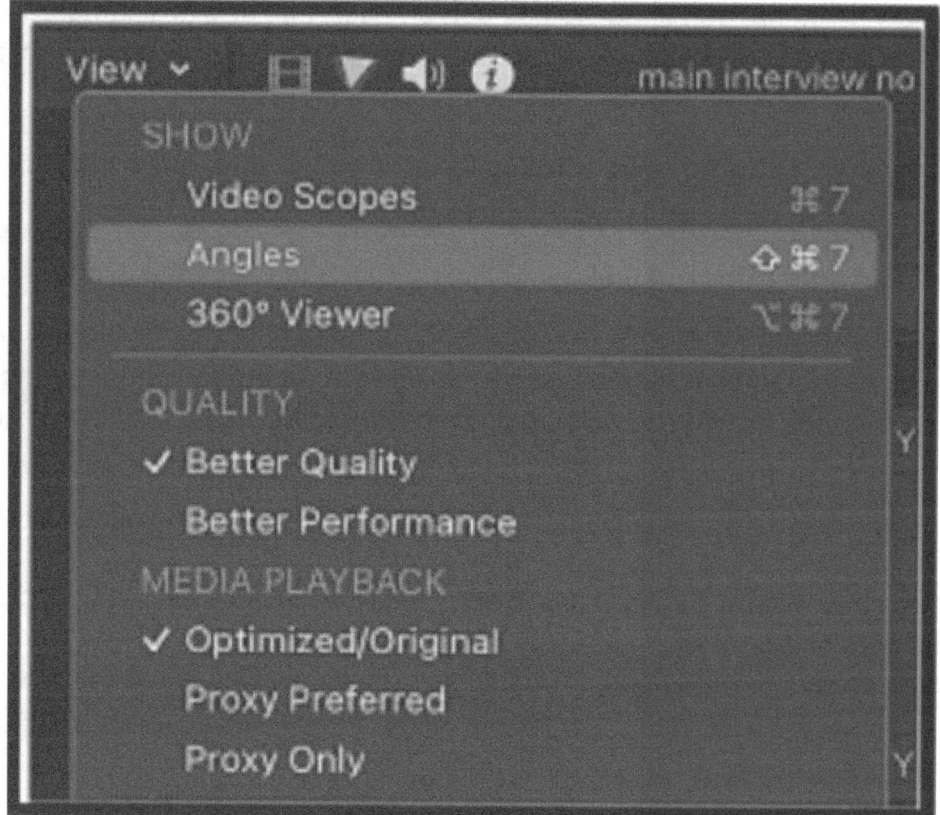

There is also a **View** menu item called **Angles** that has this command. It now splits into two, four, nine, or sixteen angles to the left of the main Viewer. The more angles you show here, the more likely it is that you'll have problems. Going to the **Settings** menu will let you change how many angles you can see at once.

3. From the **Settings** menu in the upper right corner of the **Angle Viewer**, pick either **2 or 4 angles:**

Most of the time, you only need to show video angles. That means that two video angles and an audio-only angle would be enough. I can only see four of the five angles in this Multicam right now. The buttons in the middle of the bottom of the Angle Viewer let me switch to a different set of four angles.

But the top left option is the most important one.

4. Click on the second of the three buttons in the **Angle Viewer's** upper left corner:

When this switch is turned on and off, changing angles will only change the video angle. The audio will stay on the angle you chose when you right-clicked and picked an audio angle earlier. You can change the audio angle (or both the audio and video angle) if you want to, but it will depend on how many good audio sources you have. Which audio is the best?

- The mic that sounds best wins whether you're asking one person or no one at all.

- Change to the best audio source(s) for each person as they talk if you're asking two people.

NOTE: It's also possible to hear multiple audio angles at once.

Switching angles

After setting up everything, it's time to try live editing, as if you were a vision mixer at a live event. To start playback, move your mouse over the beginning of your Project's Timeline and press the **spacebar. Then, while it plays, do one of these things:**

- To cut and switch to a new angle, click inside the **Angle Viewer**.
- Press the **1, 2, 3, ..., 9** keys to cut and move to that angle:

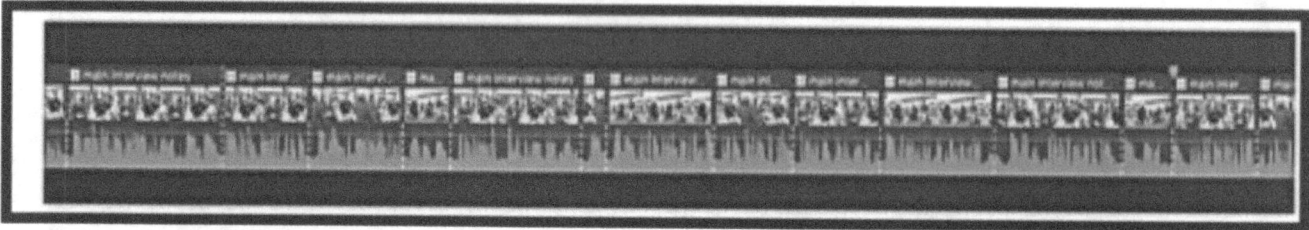

If you want to change the position, you can pause, rewind, or play faster. No need to work in real-time. If you want to skip to a different point, just press a number key. For most simple Multicams, there are two video views, so you'll have to press 1, 2, 1, 2 a lot. A through edit, which looks like a straight white line through the clip, shows you where each cut you make is. You'll learn that there are different ways to make edits as you gain experience.

You may change angles for a number of reasons, such as:

- **There's no choice**: either the camera was hidden or it wasn't recording at that time.
- **Variety**: This current angle has been on screen for too long.
- **Content**: This is the best way to show this piece of information.
- **Editing**: cutting from one angle to another can hide a jump cut.

In addition, there are certain things to think about when making an edit:

- In a pause between words, which also makes it possible to reduce pauses.
- Right where your subject blinks, which makes a natural point to edit.
- To draw attention to something to make it stand out right before an important point.

Now that you've chosen your first angles, it's time to clean it up.

Replacing and editing existing angles

It's great if the cuts are in the right places. You can add a cut-in mistake, pick it with a click, and then press **delete** to get rid of it. A **Roll** edit will do the trick if you only need to move the cut. You don't have to switch to the **Trim** tool. When used with Multicam Clips, the **Select** tool will do a **Roll** edit on its own:

What if you need to take some of the clip off? There are several options here:

- **To make a simple one-point ripple trim edit, select the Trim tool (T), move to the edge of the clip, and then click and drag:**

- **Use the Range Selection tool(R) to pick out and delete a section of the clip:**

- If you cut out a part of a Multicam Clip, the changes around it will no longer be "through" edits and will not have a white line next to them:

And finally, what if you just picked the wrong angle for a part of the clip? You don't have to make any new cuts to change any angles that are already there. **Either of these things should be done while playing or hovering:**

- If you want to change the clip to a different angle, **option-click** in the **Angle Viewer**.
- To change the position of the current clip, press **Option 1, Option 2, Option 3, ... Up to Option 9.**

I always use the keys because clicking is too slow, and that's the only way to work while I'm moving my mouse over the Timeline. There is one more important option here, though.

Editing inside a Multicam angle

Multicam video often has long records, which lets you make changes to a full angle at once. If you want to change everything about a Multicam an gleat once, go ahead and do this:

1. In order to get to the **Angle Editor**, double-click on a Multicam Clip.
2. Ad just the audio volume, for instance, to a specific angle.
3. Click once on the left-pointing arrow to the left of the center bar to return to your Project:

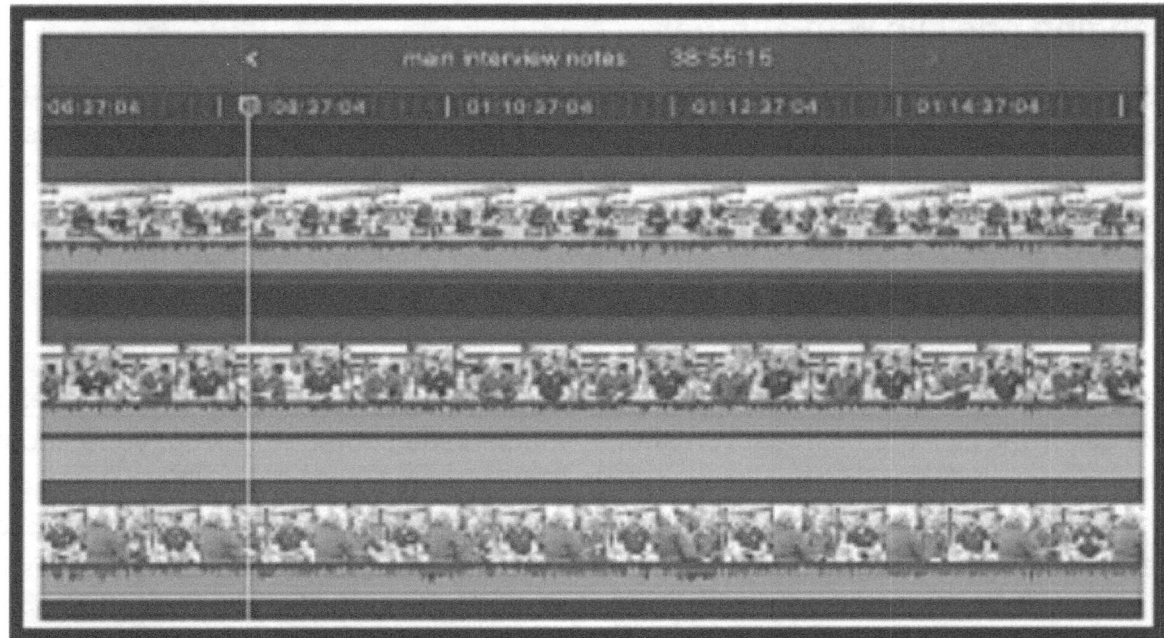

This action changes every instance of that position with the Multicam Clip in the Timeline. It's **the best way to make changes that affect the whole project. Don't forget to check the icons in the upper left corner of each view to see which one you can see and which one you can hear:**

When you're making changes to the way things look in the Inspector, click on the TV icon to the left of an angle's name to make sure you're seeing the angle you chose. There are different views that you can hear and see at the same time. When making basic changes like color, audio, and cropping, it's best to do them in the Multicam angles instead of at the Timeline level. It's easier to make color corrections that look good when the **Angle Viewer** shows you all the angles at once. It won't take long to match up all the angles. In general, it will be a lot easier and more reliable, and you won't have to deal with problems that come up when audio plug-ins act differently on short clips than on long ones. If you make some basic changes at the multicam level, you can still make more changes at the timeline level; both will work.

Exchanging one clip with another

Multicam angles are nice to have, but you have more options than you might think even if you don't have them. If you like one reaction shot more than another, it doesn't matter if that response was to those exact words at that exact time it can be from any take as long as no one's lips are seen moving wrong. You're essentially locked into the matched audiofor that shot if you can see lips moving to words you can't hear or see lips not moving when you can hear they should.

NOTE

You'll see that reaction shots are often "cheated" in this way once you know about it. Most of the time, the editor will pick the best reaction shot. If you can see someone talking, you'll know that the words they're saying are probably not quite in syncor, worse, are from a different part of their conversation. For much less work, youcan switch out one B-roll sh ot for another, and a client may have good reasons why a shot youlike isn't good at all. A smart editor always has other clips to choose from. Here are two ways to try out a different clip. The easy, short-term way is different from the better, longer-lasting way.

Showing or hiding a clip

One simple trick you might use every day is toggling a clip on and off. For example, you might want to try out a new quiet B-roll shot to replace an old one. In simple terms, you do the following:

1. Choose a different B-roll shot in your browser that you might use instead. (This should be easy if you usea "b-roll" keyword and Favorites.)
2. In your Timeline, move your mouse over the beginning of the B-roll shot you want to change.
3. To put the new clip on top of the old one, press the **Q** key.
4. **Play the whole thing through:**

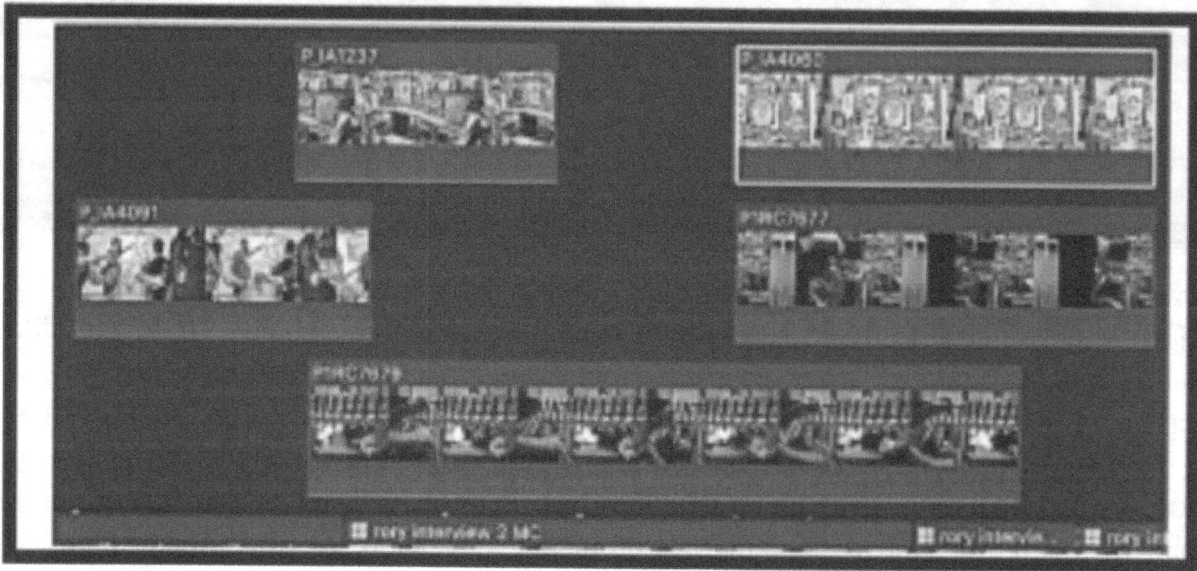

It's risky because what if the top clip is a frame short and you see it pop through? Placing one clip on top of another will hide it, but it won't remove any audio. To keep everyone safe, you should hide the clip you don't need. Press **V** to turn a clip on or off, both visually and loudly. Clips that have been hidden are grayed out and darker. You can turn off clips again by pressing **V** again, and they can still take up space in both the main plot and any other stories.

5. Press **V** to turn the clip you've chosen on and off.
6. Play through the part again:

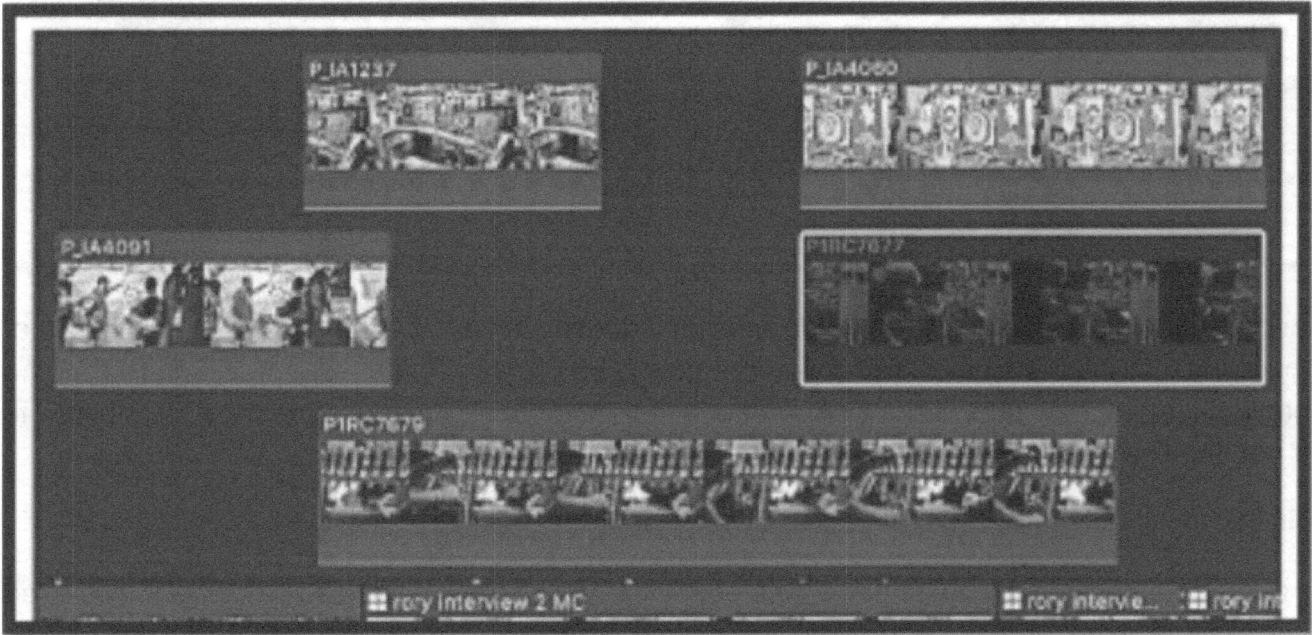

Once you've made your decision, you can either delete the clip you don't like or hide the other option and give your client the final say. Do the following to go back to the first B-roll choice:

1. To hide the top clip, pickit out and press **V**.
2. To see the bottom clip, pick it out and press **V**.

The nice thing about this method is that it's clear; there's a clear visual reminder in the Timeline that there's a stopped clip at acer- tain point, and this alone can prompt you (or your client) to look again:

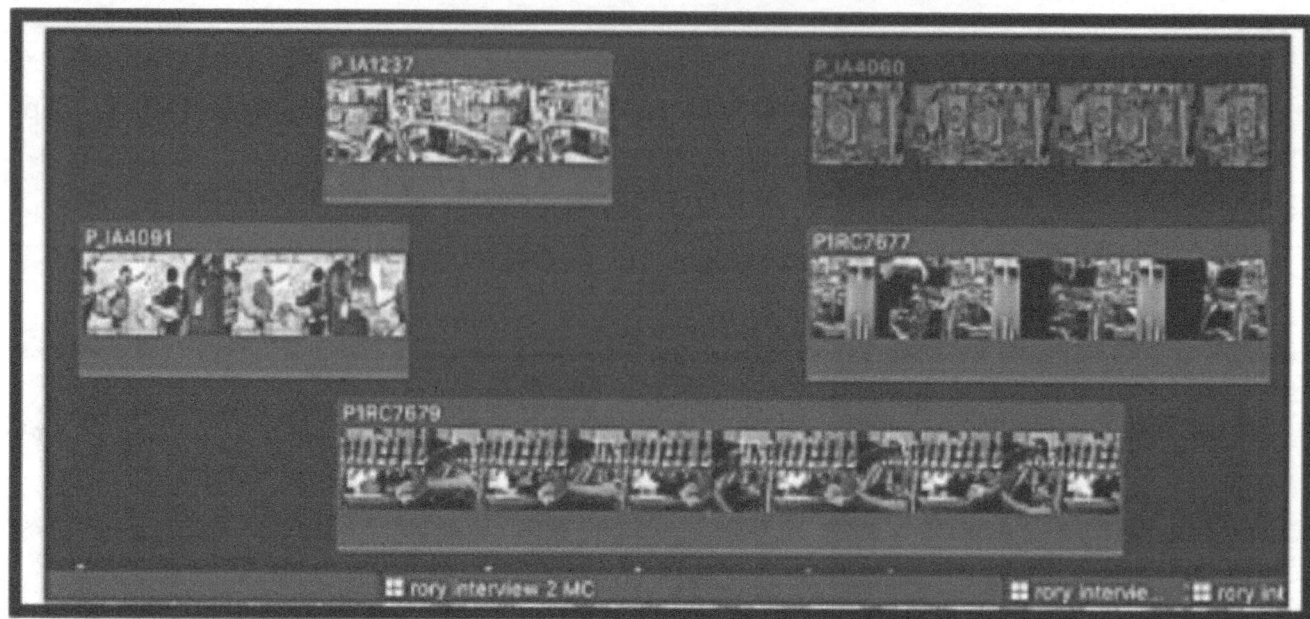

Because a blocked B-roll clip works on its own, it doesn't have to be the same length or begin at the same point as any other clip. If you put new clips on top of older clips, make sure that the beginningof the new clips starts exactly at or just before the beginning of the older clips below it. If not, the final result will have a flash frame of the lower clip.

NOTE

Another method is to move different clips below the main storyline instead of above it. I've used this to store extra clips close to where they came from while leaving the top area empty. I also turn these clips off to make them less noticeable. It's easy to make the final choice: just leave the new clip visible above and, if you want, turn off the old clip below. You could just delete the old clip if you're sure you don't need it and it won't change anything else in your Timeline.\

Deleting a clip from a Primary or related Storyline could cause problems if it's connected to and separate from other clips:

- If the deleted clip is on the main storyline and is linked to other clips, those linked clips could also be deleted.
- If you delete a clip from a Storyline that is linked to it, other clips in that Storyline may move.
- Other clips might move if the new clipis longer than the delete one.

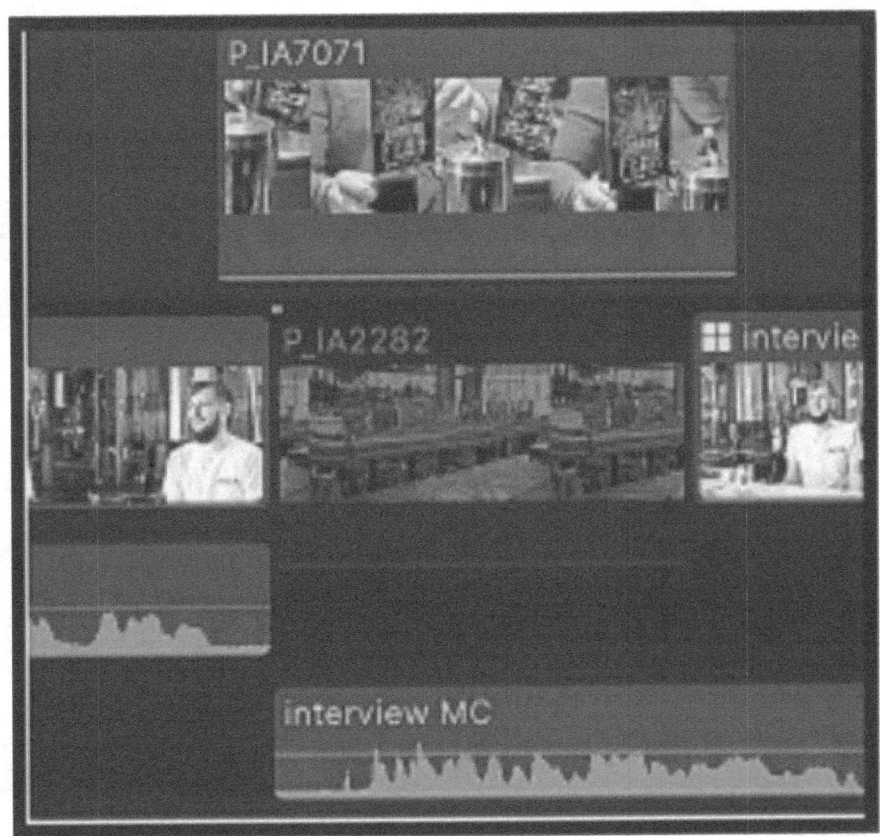

You might want to try these two other ways to get rid of a clip from the main story if you want to avoid these problems:

- Press and hold **Shift** and **delete** to get rid of a clip and leave a space where it used to be.
- To overwrite a clip in the Primary Storyline with a connected clip, select the connected clip and choose "**Overwrite to the Primary Storyline**."

You should be careful because leaving an old clip in place, even though it can be seen, or removing it can havebad results if you're not careful. You should use a different, more lasting method to switch from one clip to another, even if you just use changing display as a quick check. This is called **replacing**.

Replacing clips

This method simply substitutes oneclip for another without giving your client any options. You use this when you've made up your mind, that is when you know one shot needs to go and you have the other one ready.

You can change a clip in a number of ways, but here's an easy one:

1. In your browser, find a different source clip that you want to use instead:

2. There is a drop-down menu next to the edit buttons on the left side of the main gray bar. Select Video Only from that menu:

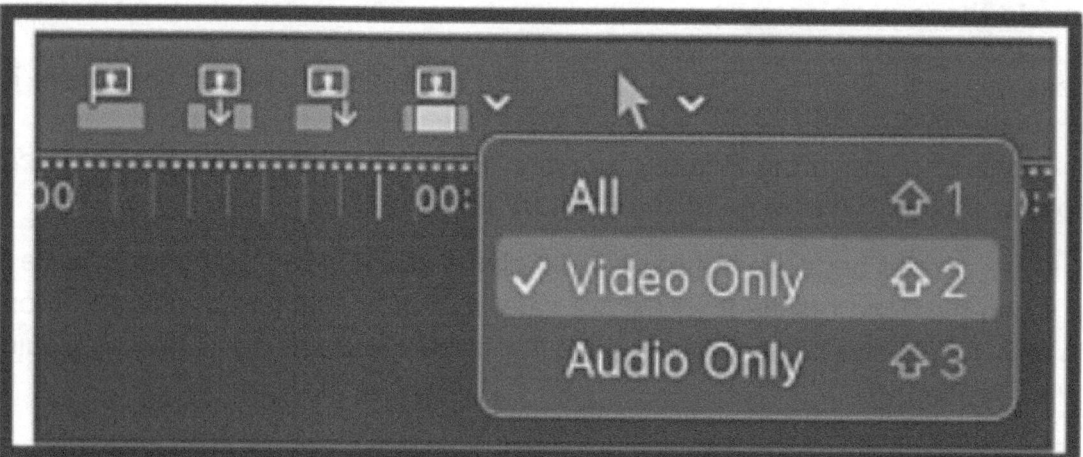

Although you can change clips with or without audio, we don't want audio in this case. To include audio instead, simply skip this step or set the choice next to the edit buttons to All.

3. Hold down the mouse button and drag the selection right onto the clip in your Timeline that you want to replace.

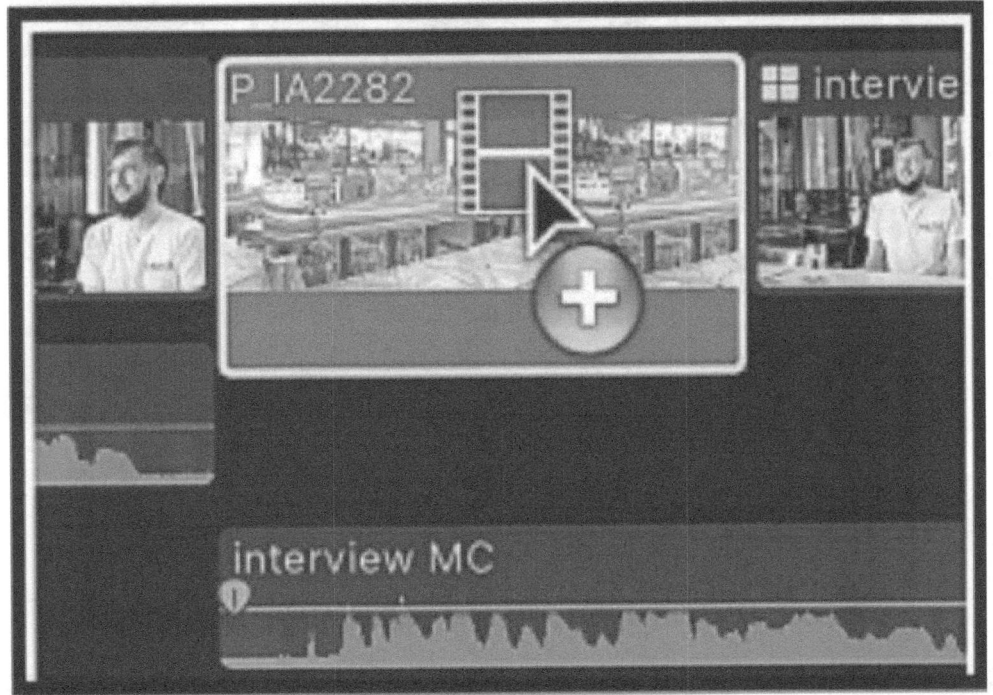

After you do this, the clip you dragged to the Timeline will light up and turn white. This lets you know that a menu with new options is about to show up.

4. **When the clip turns white, let goof the mouse button and choose Replace from the menu that comes up:**

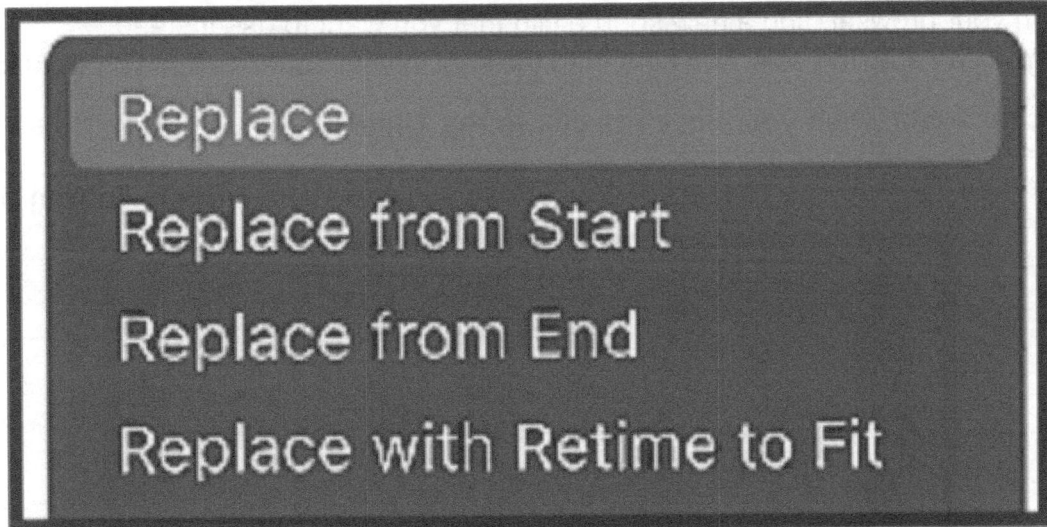

The new clip will now be put in place of the old one.

NOTE

You can use the keyboard to replace it instead of waiting for the menu to show up. Just select boththe source (**Browser**) and destination (**Timeline**) clips and press **Shift-R**. This probably won't make anyone upset when you trade one linked B-roll clip for another. You won't mind if the new clip is a little longer or shorter; nothing will be thrown out of time because clips that are linked are separate. There is no need to delete anything when replacing a clip in the main story. Everything is fine, right? Not quite the audio below has a break:

You can't be sure that the source and destination clips are the same length, so using the **Replace** command could make your Primary Storyline (or a linked Storyline) wave, which could change how clips are synced further down the Timeline. This is especially important if you added music and synced it with your existing edit. Changing the length of any clip could throw the music out of time. **So, if you need to replace clips in a Timeline that is almost finished, you might want to use Replace from Start instead of Replace. It's almost as easy to use:**

1. In your browser, find a new source clip that you want to use instead.
2. You can drag the selection right onto the shot in your Timeline that you want to replace.

It will light up again when you move the clip to the Timeline.

3. When the menu comes up, let goof the mouse and choose **Replace from Start**:

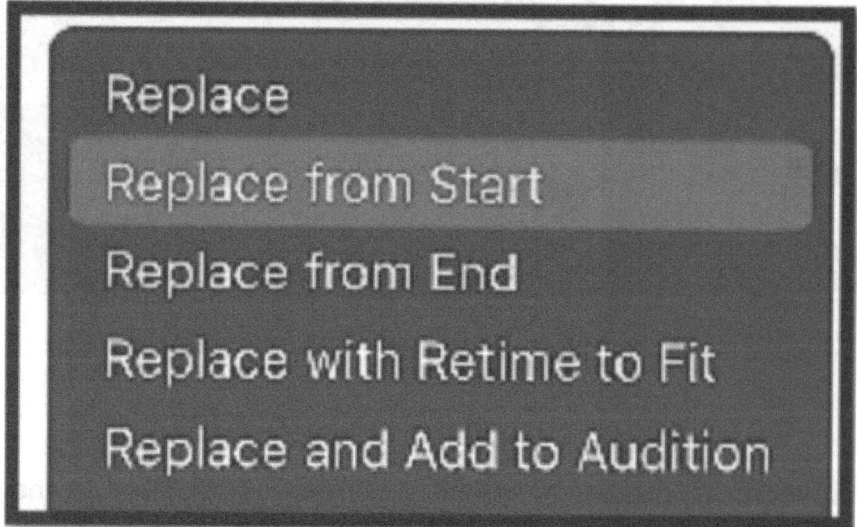

If you have both clips chosen, the key is **Option-R**, and the result is generally more like what you want. When you do a regular **Replace**, the In and Out points you chose in the Browser are both taken into account. If the source clip is longer or shorter than the destination clip, the length of the destination clips changes. The Timeline clip keeps the same length, though, when

Replace from Start is used. This is similar to a three-point edit with an In and Outpoint on the Timeline:

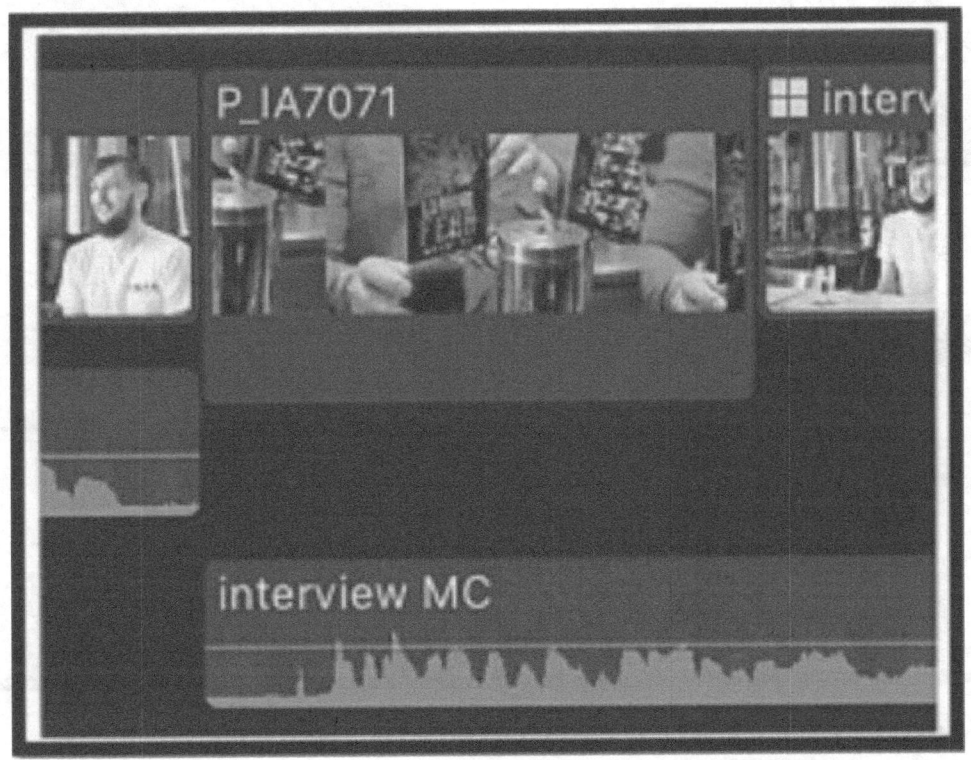

How? It doesn't matter what the Out point of the source clip is; the Out pointon the source clip is set by the length of the destination clip in the Timeline. **If there isn'tenough media, you'll be warned because replacing it would lead to a ripple edit:**

When the length of the Timeline clip is more important than the length of the source clip, I'll use **Replace from Start. Replace** is fine for the early stages of the process, but I don't want to mess up anything when a Timeline is almost done. There is also a third option called **Re-place from End**. This option skips the source clip's "In" point and starts from the "Out" point, going backward until it finds enough media to fill in the gap. This is like back timing when joining or overwriting, and you use it when you need a clip to end at a certain point, like when a control panel light goes on or a smile or look happens. It doesn't come with a shortcut key for **Replace from End,** but you could add one by assigning it something like **Option-Shift -R**.

Creating and using Auditions

The happy medium between fully replacing one clip with another and putting a stopped clip on top of another is called an audition. With **Auditions**, you can replace any clip at any time with one of several differen t"picks." You could use them to give a client a choice of different B-roll options, different ways to tell the mainstory or even different ways to treat titles or effects.

The best way to use Auditions is a lotlike replacing:

1. Pick out a new source clip in your browser that youmight be able to use instead.
2. You can drag the selection right onto the shot in your Timeline that youwant to change.

The video clip youadded to theTimeline will turn on.

3. When the choice comes up, let go of the left mouse button and choose **Replace and Add to Audition.**

Shift-Y is the shortcut for these actions if you'd rather use keys. It doesn't matter which way you use **Replace and Add to Audition**; the new clip will replace the old one in the Timeline. It will put the clips below into a Storyline if the length of the new clip is different from the length of the old clip.

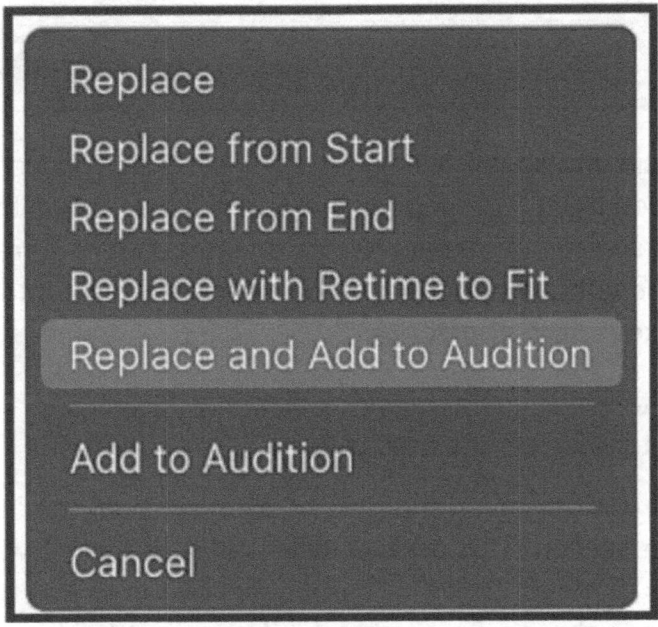

As of now, it works the same way as **Replace**. But if you look at the clip in the Timeline, there's a small spot light icon in the upper left corner. When you click on this button, a pop-up window will appear with al lthe other options that can be changed in the clip. These are the **picks** within an **Audition**.

Yes, you can do this again and again, adding as many picks as you want to the same **Audition** clip and switching between them. The pop-up Audition window shows the currently chosen pick with a star and the others with dots. It also shows an imageof the currently chosen pick above and the other picks to the left and/or right. **You can click on thumbnails to pick a new pick, and you can also use keyboard shortcuts:**

- **Control-Option-** to switch to the previous pick.
- **Control-Option-** to switch to the next pick.

Add to Audition is an extra command that can be found in both the in-Timeline pop-up menu and the **Clip > Audition** section. This adds a new choice to the list without changing the one that's already there. You can also click the "**Duplicate**" button to add a new pick that is based on the one that is currently chosen. This is helpful if you want to show options like a bigger or narrower form of a clip, two different color correction methods, or one slipped to show a different part of the same piece of media. You should learn how to color fix, add video effects, and add audio effects before you go back to duplicating. **Clip > Audition > Duplicate** from Original is another command that you canuse if youwant to get fancy. It duplicates from the first choice in the list. Press "**Done**" to close the **Audition** window when you're done.

Also, you can make Auditions in a different way than the Timeline: in the Browser. Do the following if you can't choose which group of clips is best:

1. To choose a "good" area in each of your possible clips in the **Browser**, click and dragor press **I** and **O**.

2. To add more clips to your selection, hold down the **Command** key and click on each one.
3. If you want to make a new Audition clip in the **Browser** window, choose **Clip > Audition > Create (Command-Y)**.

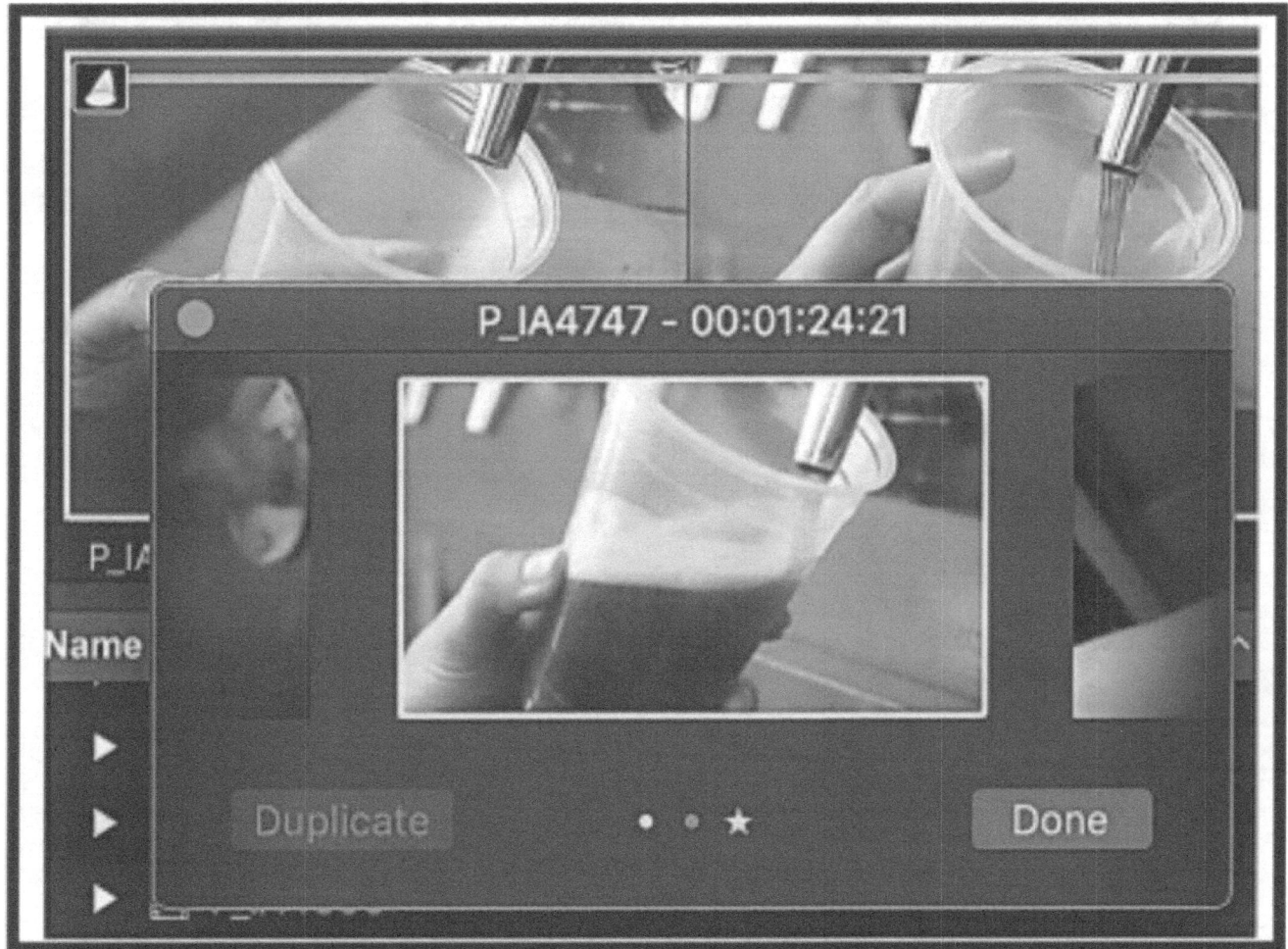

All of the other clips are there as picks when this Audition clip is added to a Timeline. This is a clean way to show the client different options if you know they will want to see them. Anyway, here are some interesting facts about Auditions that you should remember if you choose to use them. They do have pros and cons. Firstly, **the length of each clip within an Audition is remembered**. When you change the length of an Audition pick and then switch to a different pick, the duration will change to match the length of the new clip. Remember this if you don't want your Timeline to move. This is helpful if you want to copy an Audition to compare long and short versions of the same clip. Secondly, **anything connected to an Audition clip on the Primary Storyline is actually connected to the current Audition pick**. This in-cludes any clips that are connected and even how long those clips are connected for. If you change the pick in the Audition, everything that islinked to the old pick will go away and be replaced by everything that **is linked to the new pick. Really helpful if you need to quickly switch between groups of sound effects that are linked to a clip. Here's what we need to do**:

1. Take a clip from the Main Storyline that you like and add one or more sound effects to it.
2. To copy the clip, select it and then go to **Clip > Audition> Duplicate** as Audition.

3. Get rid of any clips that are linked to the Audition, and then add one or more new sound effects.
4. If you switch between the Audition picks, all the sound effects that go with them will also change.

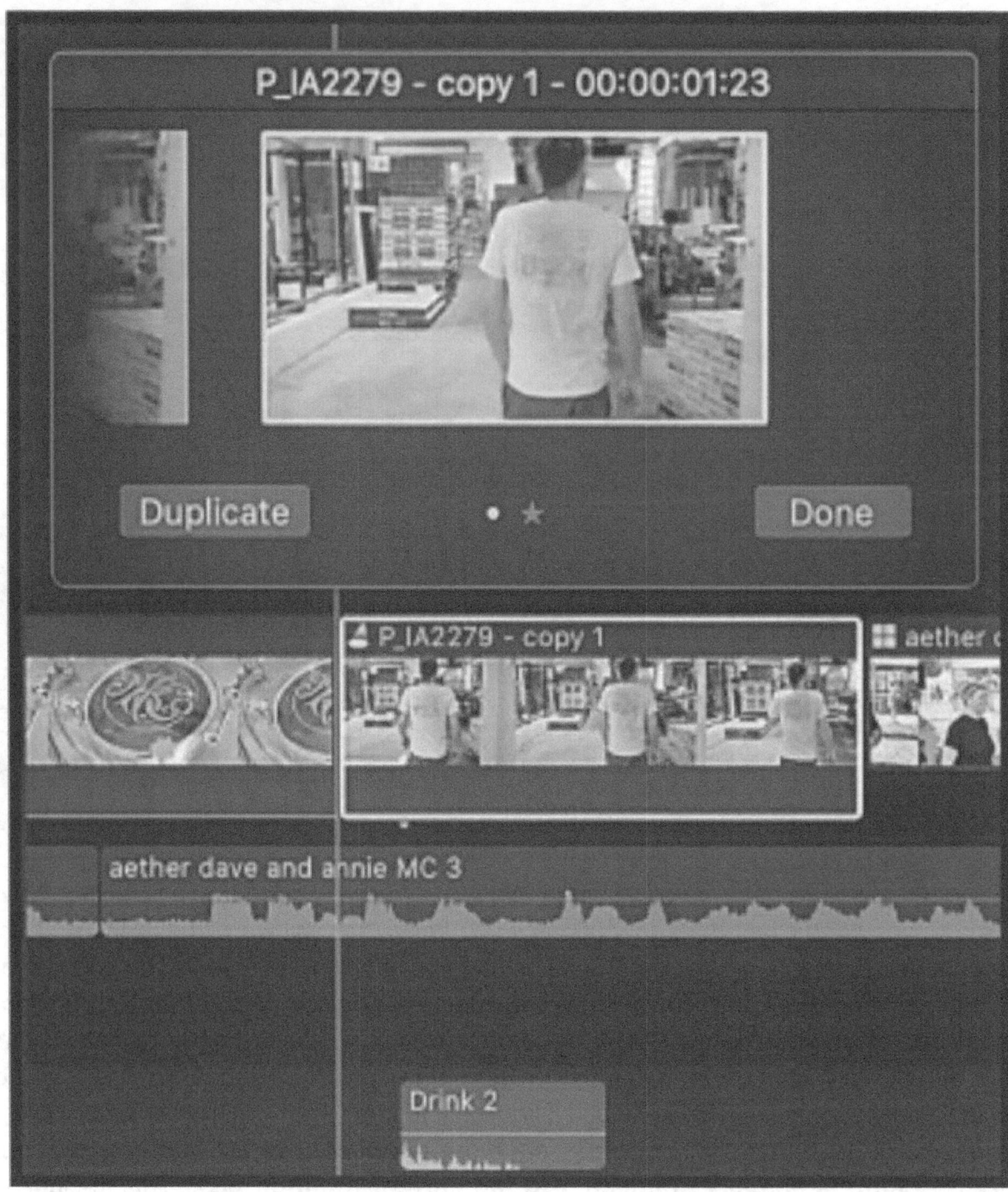

Even though this is helpful, be careful when trimming anything that's linked to an Audition clip, because if the Audition pick changes, you might lose your changes. Keep things safe by going to **Clip > Audition > Finalize Audition**. This will lock in the current pick and get rid of the special Audition state. Thirdly, **there's no command to replace an Audition from the start or end. Because of this, to add a new clip the same length as the old one, you'll need to**:

1. In your Timeline, choose the destination clip.
2. Press **Control-D** and note its duration.

3. Pick out a new source clip in your browser that you might be able to use instead.
4. Press **Control-D** and type in the duration you just wrote down and then press **return**.
5. Tap **Shift-Y** to **Replace and Add to Audition**.

Even though this takes a little more work, it's a great way to give a client options with the same lengths of time each. One last thing: you can't add a Multicam clip to an Audition. Because of how they interact with the Magnetic Timeline and connections, auditions can be very useful but also add some complexity. If you want to use Auditions but don't want all of this complexity, you could use them as connected clips instead, where changes you make in the Audition won't affect anything else. Just make sure you finish them when you're sure of your choices. You could also not use them at all and spend more time finding the right clips in the Browser or use **V** to turn Timeline clips on and off instead.

CHAPTER 12: CRAFTING AUDIO FOR PROFESSIONAL RESULTS

We'll start by recording an original audio to make sure you have some suitable material to work with. We'll move on to audio changes now that we have those new voiceover clips. You'll learn more complicated ways to animate (or automate) volume over time as you go from simple volume settings. You will learn how to fix audio problems like background hiss and hum, change the volume in small steps, and add more complex audio effects like compression, advanced equalization (EQ), and special effects. Lastly, you'll learn the cool things that Roles can do when they're paired with compound clips.

Recording and editing a voiceover

You can use any microphone you have on hand to record and edit a video with the built-in **Record Voiceover** tool. It's possible to get a voice over early or late in the process, even though we're adding narration to an edit that was already done. Postponing the official Voiceover recording until the edit is almost final, however, allows for last-minute script changes or a lack of voice talent. Stay flexible. AA high-quality microphone will need to be set up in a good environment for audio recording and connected to a high-quality audio interface in order to get a recording that is suitable for the final output. For short recordings, you can use your Mac's built-in microphone. But if you want to do professional work, you might need to buy some extra gear, like a high-end USB microphone or an XLR microphone with an external interface device. A lot of audio recorders, including ones made by Zoom, can also be used as external interfaces. A good way to work is to record a temporary scratch audio track yourself based on the first draft of the script. This is because timing is much easier with a voiceover than without one. To make the **video match the draft voiceover, you can edit it and even suggest changes if the script doesn't quite match the video:**

You can replace your draft voiceover in the edit after the voiceover artist receives the final script and sends you the pro audio files. You might do the final voiceover for other projects, even if it's added very late in the process, like at this point. It doesn't matter what you choose. To begin, press **Option-Command-8** or choose **Window > Record Voiceover**:

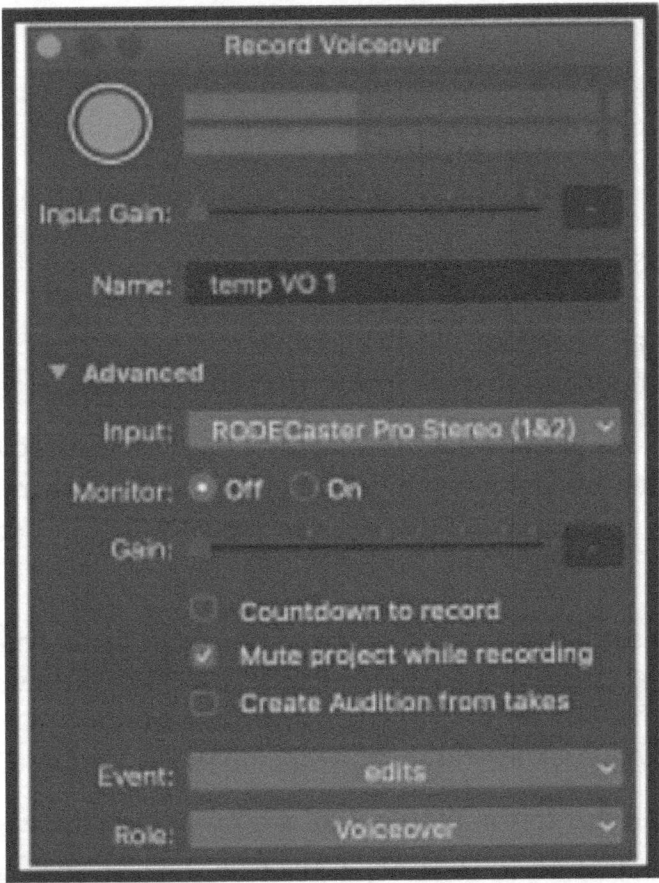

If you click the big red button, it will add a new recording to the timeline at the point where the Playhead or Skimmer is right now. If you click it again, it will stop. This list of options mostly speaks for itself:

- **Name**: This is the name that will be given to the new voiceover clip.
- **Input**: The camera and channel(s) that are being used for recording. Please keep in mind that the "Stereo" option shown is usually from a mono microphone.
- **Monitor**: When this option is turned on, you can listen to the recording through the device you are currently using. If you don't want feedback, you should only use this with headphones on.
- **Gain**: Gain is a virtual volume knob that some devices have. The interface shown in the previous image has hardware volume controls instead of virtual ones, which is why the slider is grayed out.
- **Countdown to record**: If this option is turned on, there will be a visual and audible countdown before the recording starts.
- **Mute project while recording**: If this option is chosen, the current timeline will be quiet while the recording is going on. It's important if you're not using headphones.
- **Create Audition from Takes**: This feature combines several recordings that are at the same point in the timeline into a single audition clip. This is helpful if you record more than one take, since each take will be saved as a separate audition pick in the same clip.
- **Event**: The library event where the recording files will be kept.
- **Role**: This is the audio role that will be given to the recordings. If you want to treat voiceovers differently, use **dialogue** or make a special role or sub-role for them.

First, you should put together a few clips in the timeline that could have a voiceover added to them. It's fine to have a more complicated timeline with clips that are connected to each other.

A narrator would help with anything. Now that you have that, here are the easy steps:

1. From the **Input** menu, open **Record Voiceover** and picture the built-in microphone or a different microphone that is attached.
2. When you speak, make sure the level meters move and aren't too loud (going up to the red on the right) or too quiet (goingdown to the green on the left).

NOTE: Better audio devices will catch less noise at a lower level. Because of this, recordings made with better equipment can be made much louder without also increasing noise. If you plan to use these recordings in your final delivery, you should buy good equipment and get your environment ready.

3. You can add a single sentence by clicking on a spot in the timeline.
4. First, press the circle-shaped red button. Then, talk a few words into the built-in microphone. After a short pause, say a few more words.
5. To stop recording, click the red button that looks like a square.

Your recording has been put to the timeline as a connected clip, as you can see:

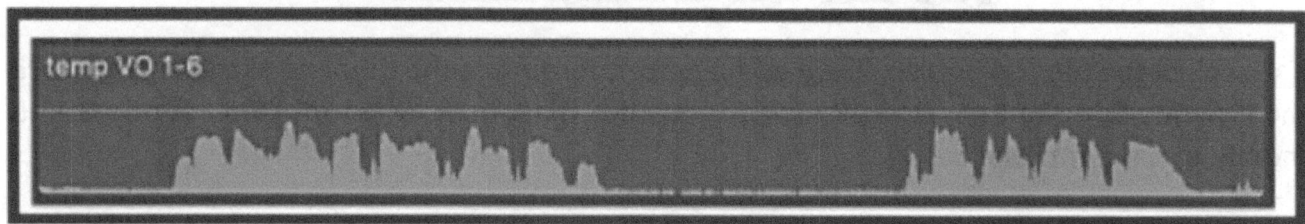

You would end up with two separate clips, but the second one would be in the wrong place if you used the Range Selection tool to pick out and delete the part of the clip you didn't want.

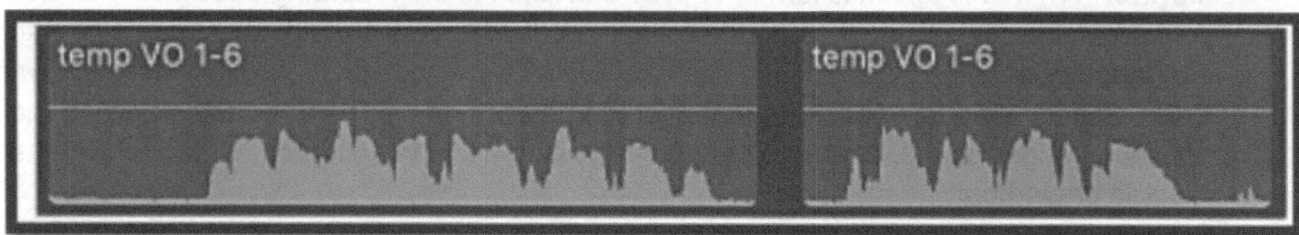

Instead, finish it first while the voiceover is still chosen:

1. If you want to put the audio clip inside a storyline, press **Command-G**.
2. To get to the **Range Selection** tool, press **R**. Then, pick out the pause you don't want and press **delete**.

As you get rid of the useless pause, you'll see that the space between the two good parts is filled:

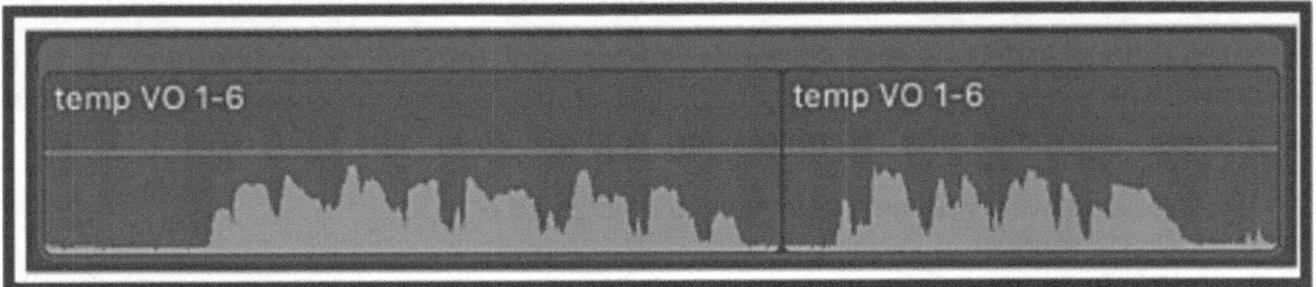

If there's any kind of problem that you can hear around the edit, do these things:

1. Click on the two clips and press the **Option-T** key to add a **Crossfade**.
2. If you double-click on the waveform, you can make one or both parts of the edit bigger.
3. If you need to, you can drag the fade handles to make the ends of the two clips fade together.
4. Right-click on each fade handle to change the type of fade if you need to.
5. To match the two audio waveforms, trim the video component on one or both sides if necessary.

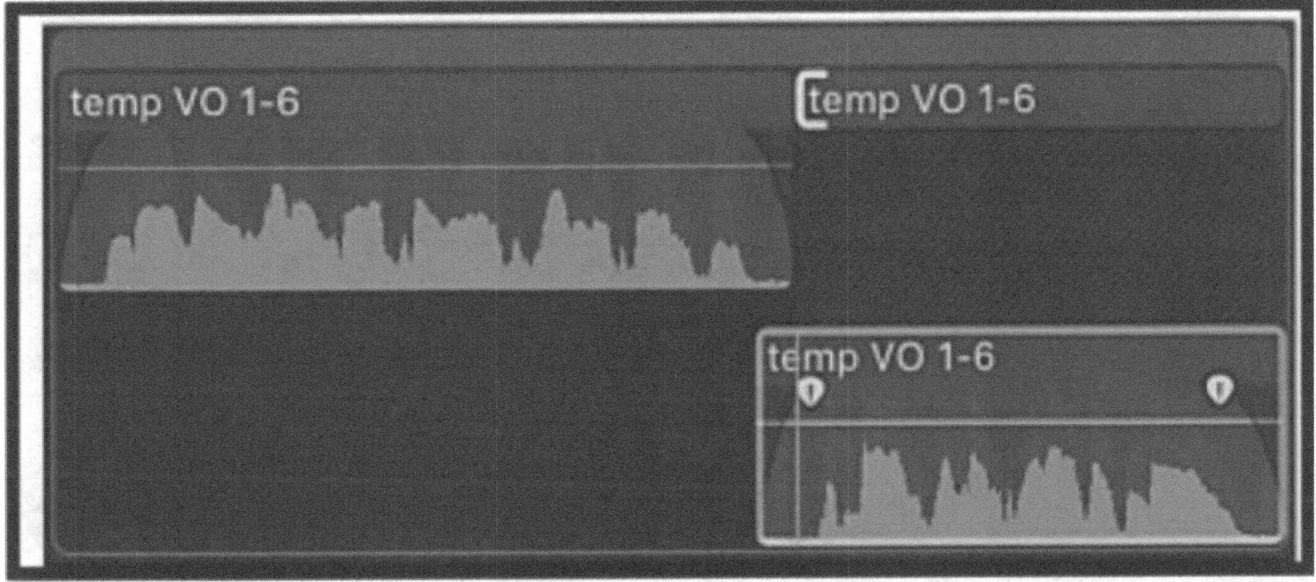

This kind of short recording could be erased and made again, but storylines are a great way to clean up longer recordings. When reading a full script, one of my best tricks is to cough out loud every time I make a mistake and then repeat the word or phrase that I mispronounced before moving on. **In the finished waveform, this makes it easy to see the mistakes. I can also use Range Selection to pick out the bad parts and hit delete without even listening to them again:**

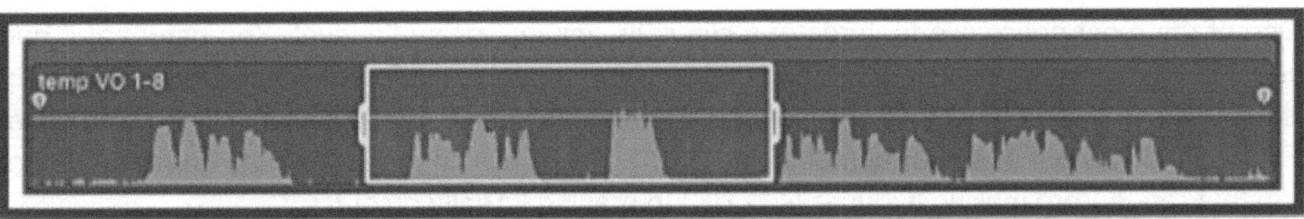

Even professionals make mistakes, and plots are sometimes changed after the speech recording is done. In order to steal a piece of audio (a word, a phrase, or a few seconds of room tone) from **one place and put it somewhere else, it may occasionally be necessary to cut up professional voiceovers. The rough work is as you'd expect:**

1. Pick out what you need from the source clip and copy it.
2. Paste it where you want it.
3. **Blade** the destination to make an entry point, and then drag the new audio piece to that spot.
4. This will let you remove part of the original recording.
5. **Trim**, expand the audio, and change the fades to finish the job after **crossfading** with **Option-T.**

You can connect the new clip to the existing ones if all you need to do is add content. But if you'd rather fill in the blanks as you work, a Storyline (either linked or primary) is very helpful. **Locations have their own sound, so don't forget to add room tone back if you take out some words and need to add a pause:**

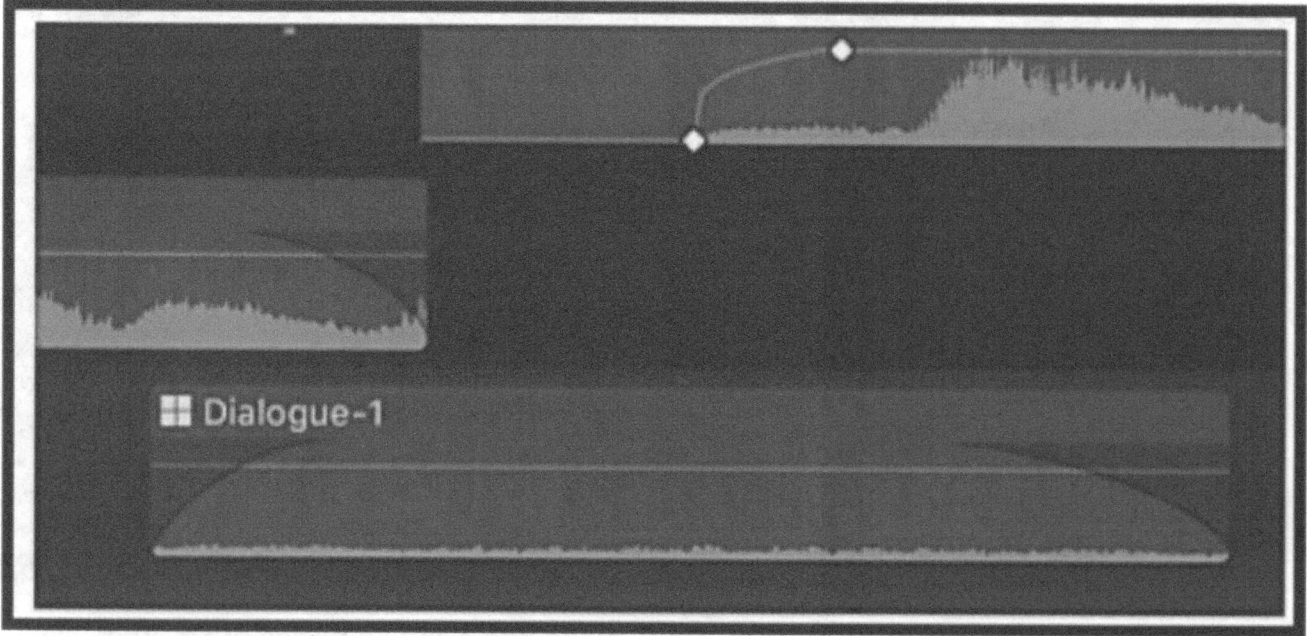

You should be used to the editing part by now; cutting clips up should be easy for you. Aside from that, you've probably also moved the sound levels of the audio files around a bit while changing them. After that, you'll learn how to make even more changes.

Adjusting volume levels

One of the most noticeable features of a clip is its volume, or audio level. You can hear it and see it in the browser, the inspector, and the timeline, though in different ways. Decibels, or **dB**, is the unit of measurement for audio volume. There is no such thing as a silent clip on a timeline. Every clip starts out at a neutral (not silent!) **0 dB**. There are changes that can be made to that clip that range from making it louder **(+12 dB)** to making it really quiet **(-∞)**:

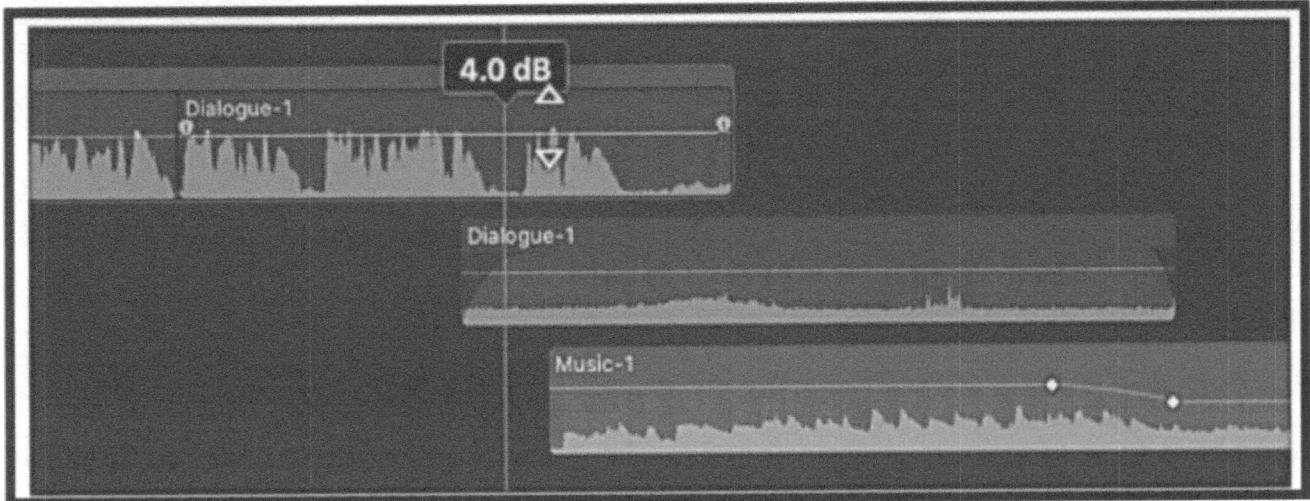

It's very different when you play back a timeline. The absolute number, which is also recorded in decibels and can be seen in the **Audio Meters (Shift-Commandd-8),** is the sum of all the sounds that are playing at the same time. With the previous high indicated by thin lines on the meters **and numbers at the top of each channel, these moving meters display the overall audio at any given time:**

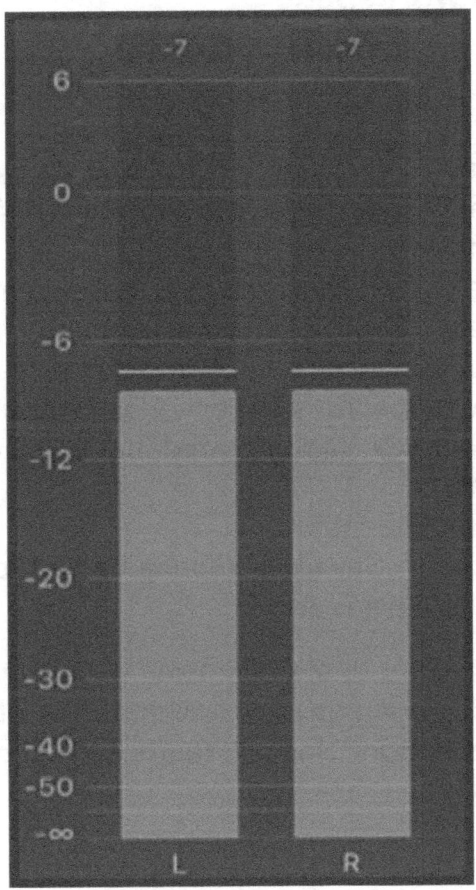

The output value should always be negative, and the level of that value should change based on what you want to send. The old rules for TV delivery said that the average level should be about **-12 dB** and the loudest sounds should be at **-6 dB**. That mostly held true for online delivery, but there isn't a standard that everyone follows, and some movies get louder than this, around **-3 dB**. People all agree on one thing: you should never hit or go past **0 dB** because that will make the sound foggy.

NOTE

If you have to send to a site with stricter rules, like a TV station, streaming service, or movie theater ad system, you'll have to carefully follow their instructions. Different countries have different standards, but over time, they are likely to require a more complicated way to measure loudness. It's possible to do final editing in FCP, but many high-end processes use a third-party app or tool for that. First, youshould make a workspace that makes working with audio easier. Next, we'll go over the basic controls. Finally, we'll move on to more com-plex dynamic controls.

Creating a custom audio workspace

Since there isn't already an Audio Workspace, making one now is a good way to learn more about them.

1. To start with the **Default** workspace, press **Command-0**.
2. To see the audio meters, go to **Window > Show in Workspace > Audio Meters** or press **shift-command-8**.
3. Drag on the left edge of the audio meters to make them bigger or smaller.
4. To make sure the main window takes up as much room as possible, **option-click** the green window control in the upper left area of the screen.
5. If you double-click the **Inspector's** title bar, that pane will grow to fill the whole window.
6. To open the **Timeline Index**, click the word **Index** to the left of the middle gray bar or press **shift-command-2**.
7. Click **Roles** in the **Timeline Index**.
8. **Window > Workspaces > Save Workspaces** will save the workspace.
9. Give your workspace the name **Audio**.

You should now be able to see your new custom workspace in the **Window > Workspaces** window. To make clip waveforms taller, use the settings in the **Clip Appearance** popup, which is **just to the left of the Effects button. This will focus on audio waveforms while removing or shrinking video thumbnails:**

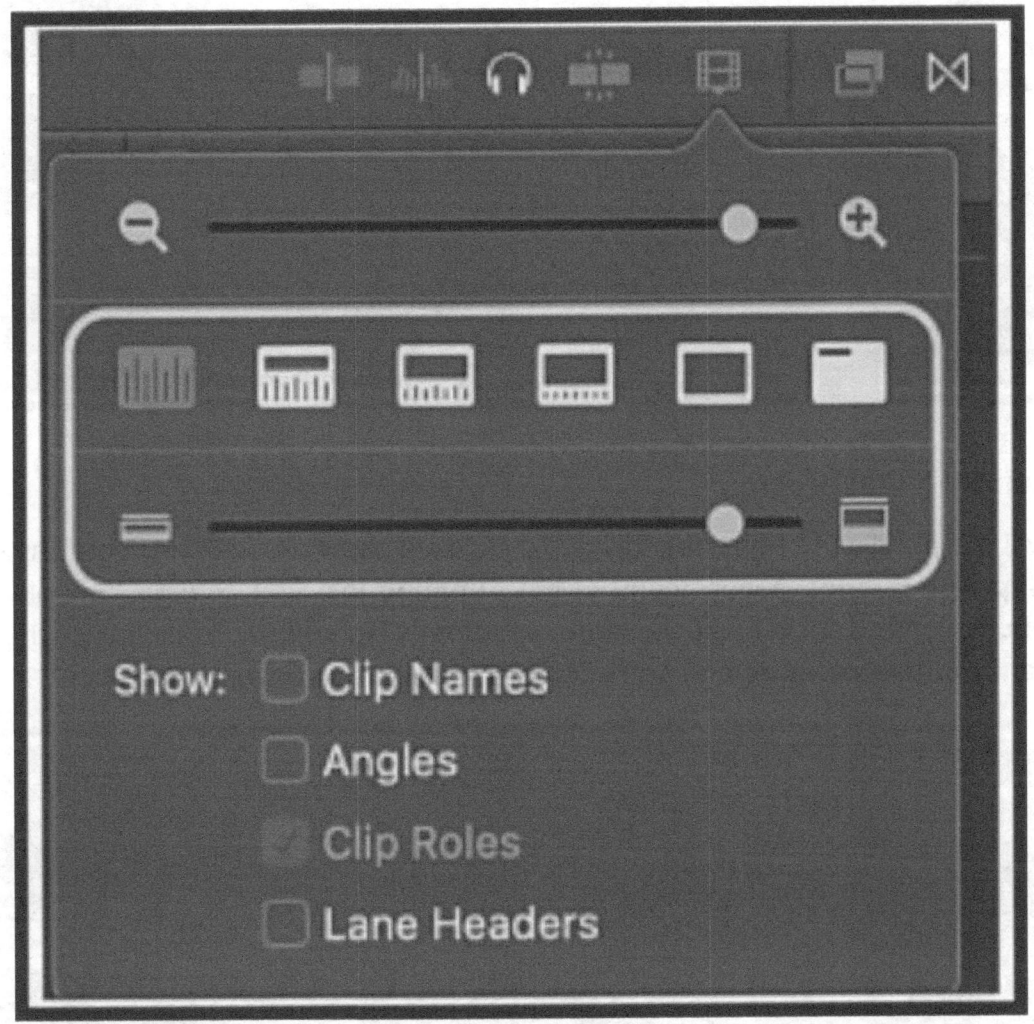

You can also use **shift-command-plus** and **shift-command-minus** to change the height of the clip. Last but not least, you could add **Effects** to this workspace later if you want to.

Here is the new custom workspace:

Understanding waveforms

Just below the clip's title (if it has one), any audio clips will show a waveform. You may remember that the **Clip Appearance** popup menu in the **Timeline** lets you change how big the audio waveform is. You may want to make the audio waveforms bigger now. You can use the computer shortcuts **shift-command-plus** and **shift-command-minus** to ease this process:

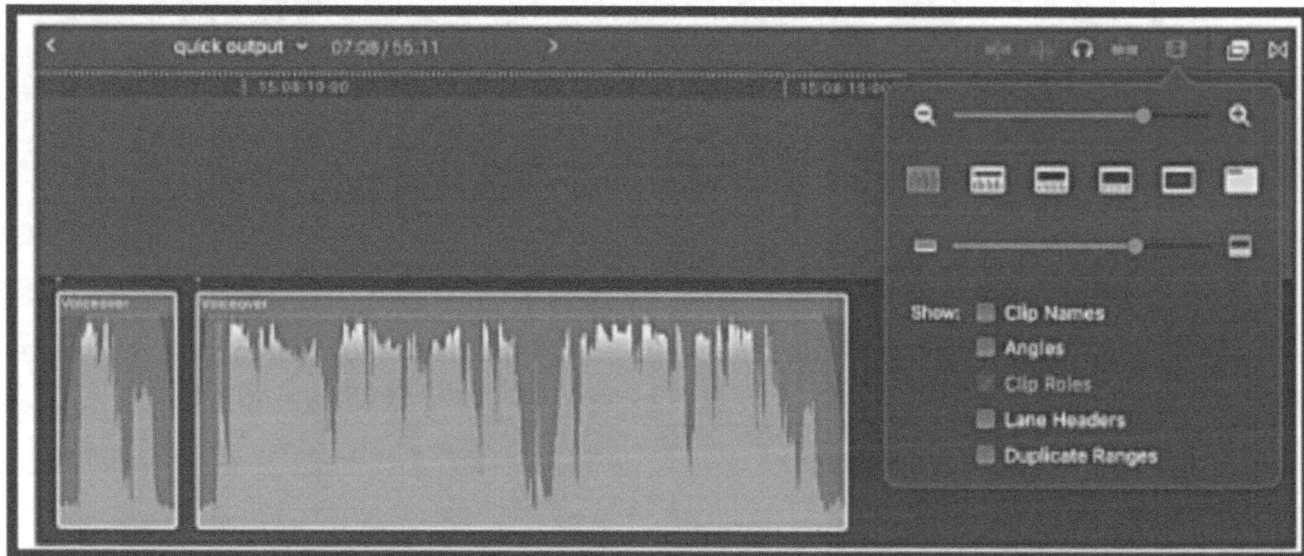

Waveform height tells you how loud a certain piece of audio is. There are clear breaks between words when there is a dip between two peaks. Low-level noise is shown by the dips that never reach the real floor. It's getting louder when the peaks turn yellow, and it's probably too loud when the peaks turn red. Changing the volume levels will change the waves' height, which in turn will change their color.

Changing volume levels

There is a line on top of the audio waveform that turns on and off the volume. There are several options for adjusting the line right on the clip:

- To move the line quickly, **drag it up or down**.
- Hold down the **Cmd key and drag the line up or down**. For more accuracy, move it slowly (gear down).

You can also change one or more clips with keyboard shortcuts. Pick them out and then press one of these:

- Use **Control-plus** to turn up the volume (+1 dB).
- Press "**Control-minus**" to lower the sound (-1 dB).

The Modify > Adjust Volume sub-menu has these two options, along with:

- **Silence (-).**
- **Reset (0 dB).**
- **Absolute (ctrl-option-L).**
- **Relative (ctrl-cmd-L).**

With the **Absolute** and **Relative** Opponents, you can start from scratch to describe a new value (Absolute) or show how the new value changes from the old value (Relative). Each command uses the timecode display below the viewer to show the change that will happen. You **can type a positive or negative number and then click return, just like you would when typing a timecode:**

Lastly, if you'd rather use the **Inspector**, **Volume** is right at the top of the **Audio** tab. It has a scale, a number that you can drag or type, and the well-known keyframe settings. **You'll usually not care about these, though, and instead use the graphic Timeline display:**

The first step is to set the general level of a clip. If one clip is to be the main sound at any given time, the waves should probably peak in yellow and not move to red. If you want to be sure, check the final result because this color can mean different things for mono and stereo clips.

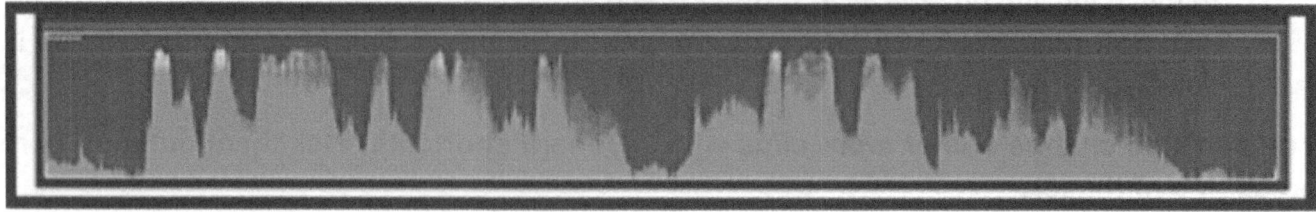

If you're hearing a lot of audio (music, sound effects, etc.) at once, the waveform of a single clip won't give you a good idea of the overall sound. You'll need to look at the **Audio Meters** to see the timeline's overall audio level. The marks are the same color, but the numbers are more important. There will probably be parts of the clip that are loud and parts that are quiet, no matter how you change the volume. This is where you might need to set different volume levels over time.

Changing volume levels over time

The timeline is the best tool for adjusting audio levels across multiple areas. Level changes, which are sometimes called automation, are built on keyframes, and you can use the same keyframe methods:

1. To make a keyframe at a certain point in time, **option-click** on the volume line.
2. If you want to make a keyframe at a different time, **option-click** somewhere else on the volume line.
3. To change the volume at that point, move either keyframe up or down.
4. You can move a keyframe left or right to change where it is in time.

You can get rid of extra keyframes by right-clicking them and selecting "**Delete Keyfame**." That method works when you only need to make two keyframes, like when the music starts out loud and then moves to the background to make room for a speaker. The audio level would have to **be briefly lowered or raised, though, and four keyframes would have to be made. Take the example of music that dips under someone talking, which is known as ducking, and think about where the keyframes would be placed:**

- To mark the beginning of the fade down at the start of the change.
- About a second or two in, to show that the fade down is over.
- Further along, at the same level as the last keyframe at the start of the fade-up.
- About a second or two after the fade up, at the same level as the first keyframe.

If you added four keyframes, this is what you would see:

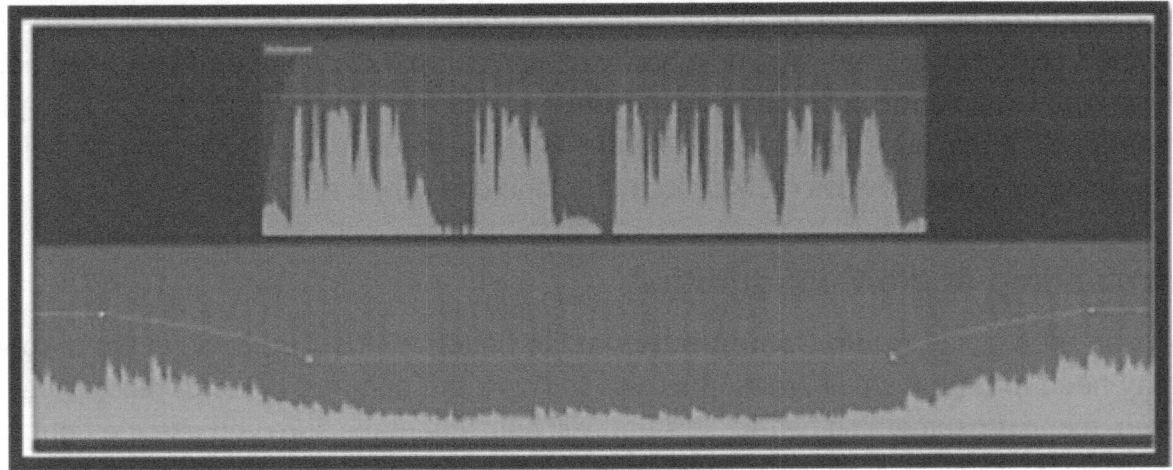

You would have to option-click four times to do this manually with keyframes. You want the keyframes, but there's a much easier way to get the same result with range selection:

1. Pick out the **Range Selection** tool (R).
2. You can pick out a part of a clip by clicking and dragging it.

You can also use I and O to pick out a Primary Storyline clip.

3. In that area, drag the volume line.

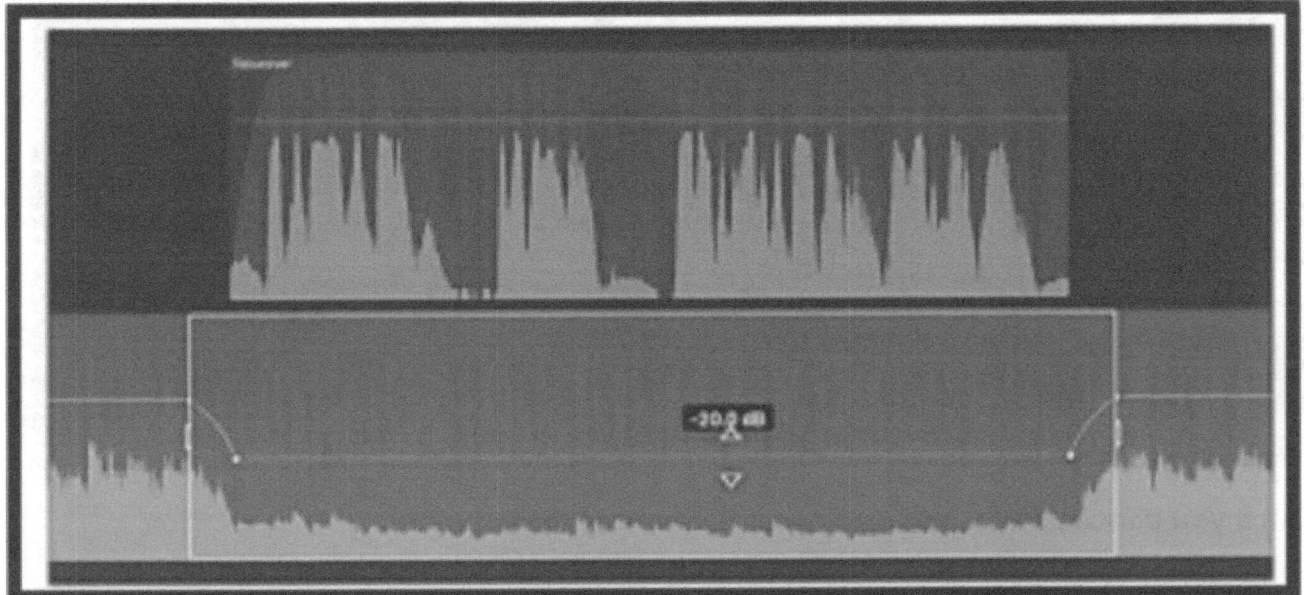

This method works faster and better, and it makes four keyframes that can be changed around as needed. To make the fade less sudden, move the keyframes on the edges outward. To change how low the volume is, move the line between the two keyframes in the middle. If you move the line between two keyframes, you can pick and move them both at the same time. Keep in mind that if you use the shortcuts (**Ctrl-plus** or **Ctrl-minus**) to change the volume by **1 dB**, the keyframes that are already there will be moved up or down. To remove all keyframes and start again, use **Modify > Adjust Volume > Absolute** or **Modify > Adjust Volume > Reset**.
NOTE: Take a deep breath before you start changing the volume all over the place to try to make the volume of a clip the same all the way through. There are effects that can do some of this work for you. Use volume settings to directly duck audio, but don't proceed with small changes

until you've added some common audio effects. You need to know what's going on in a more complicated process now that you know how well you can handle numbers. The good news is that most simple cams will only record two channels, and most of the time, they will be picked up properly. You should pay attention to **Audio Configuration** before you start the full audio process, though, if your devices record more than one channel in each clip.

Understanding Audio Configuration

There is an area called **Audio Configuration** at the bottom of the **Audio** tab in the **Inspector**. You may need to drag a small breakup to see it. There are different types of recordings, such as stereo, mono, or something better. This part will help you make sure you use the right part of your recordings. Panning (audio position in space, in **Stereo** or **Surround**) can be changed later, but first, you must make sure that all of your clips are properly tagged.

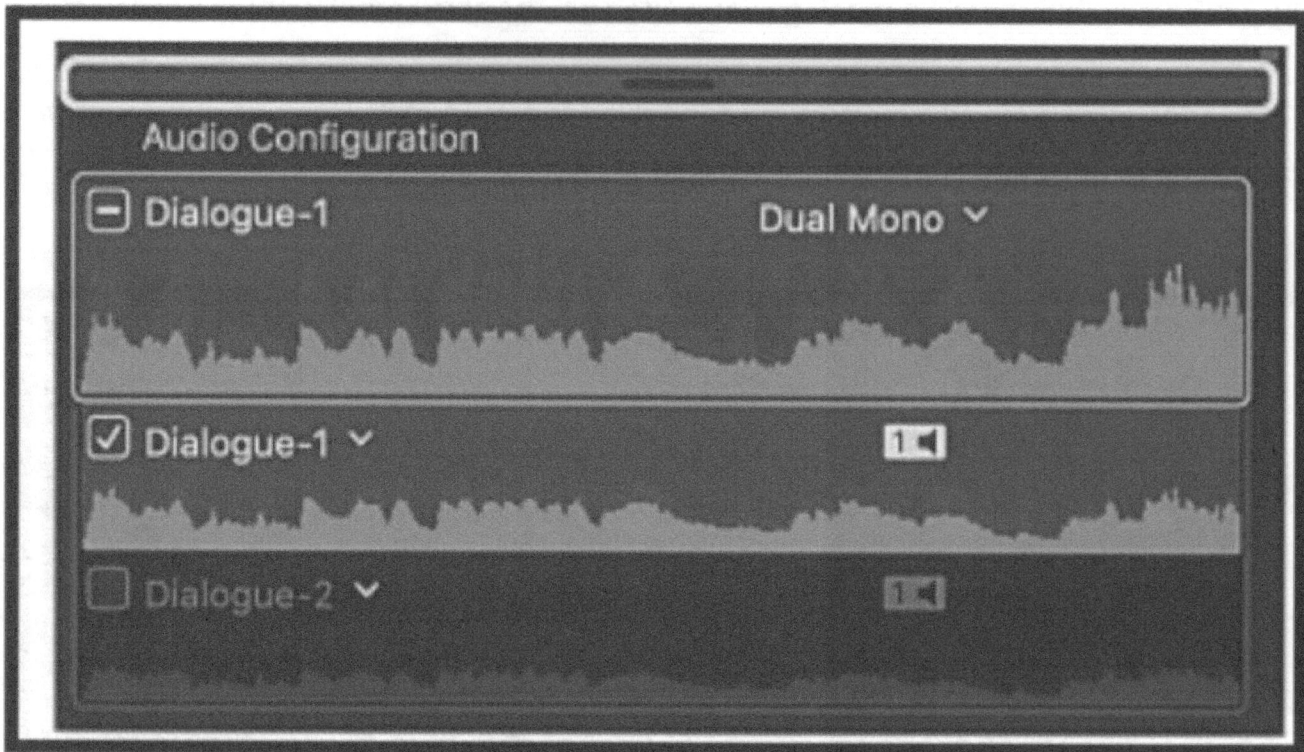

Once you choose a clip, you can see if it is one of these types:

- **Mono** (one channel).
- **Dual mono** (two channels).
- **Stereo** (two channels, left and right).
- **Reverse Stereo** (two channels, right and left).
- **Multitrack** (multiple channels, such as in a multicam clip or from a multitrack recorder).

If the wrong type of source is being used, it can be moved to a different type, and channels can be turned off when they're not needed. Some devices, for instance, record the same single microphone input to two tracks at two different recording levels. One channel is set to a higher level, and the second channel is set to a lower level. If the first channel gets too loud, you can switch back to the second channel to keep the sound from getting distorted. This kind of sound should be understood as **Dual Mono**, and the clean channel with the most volume should be used. You can fix it by directly interpreting it as **Dual Mono** if it was wrongly marked as **Stereo**. Then, use the proper option to turn off the channel you don't need, as shown:

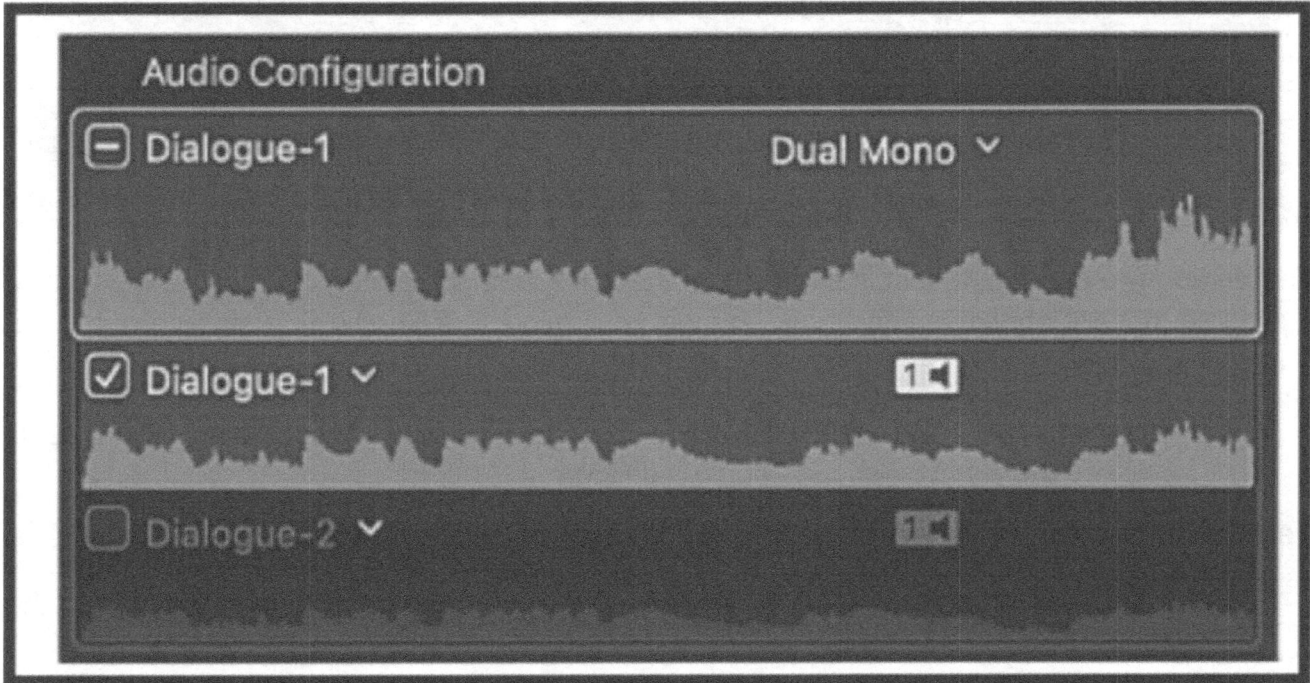

All of the audio will be slightly panned to the left because the first channel would have been louder if this clip had been seen as **stereo** and no components had been removed. A lot of people have this problem online, so make sure you listen to your final output on a sound speaker. Additionally, you can now choose **Reverse Stereo** to fix audio that is stereo but has mies that are reversed (each in the wrong channel). Things will be pretty easy with just one speaker. You may need to do a little more work when multicam audio settings are more complicated, but here's how you can run the process.

Adjusting multiple audio channels

You'll probably only use one channel of audio in the majority of multicam or multitrack records. But what if the chosen microphone breaks down? How do you switch to a different one? What's the best way to actively include audio from multiple sources at the same time, like in a video with more than one person? You can handle audio parts in the timeline in a few different ways. You should remember that double-clicking on an audio waveform makes it bigger, which moves the audio below the video and lets you make split edits. **Another tip for when there is more than one channel:**

- **Option: double-click** on an audio waveform to make the audio parts bigger.

At last, you can see all of the audio parts at once. You can use the volume controls we've already talked about, along with keyframes and other features, to individually manage each channel, or **you can try out another cool trick. Follow these steps while a multi-component clip is on the timeline and all of its audio components are viewable and active:**

1. Pick up the **Range Selection** tool (**R**).
2. Choose part of one of the audio waveforms that you want to enable or disable.

3. To turn that part off, press **V**.

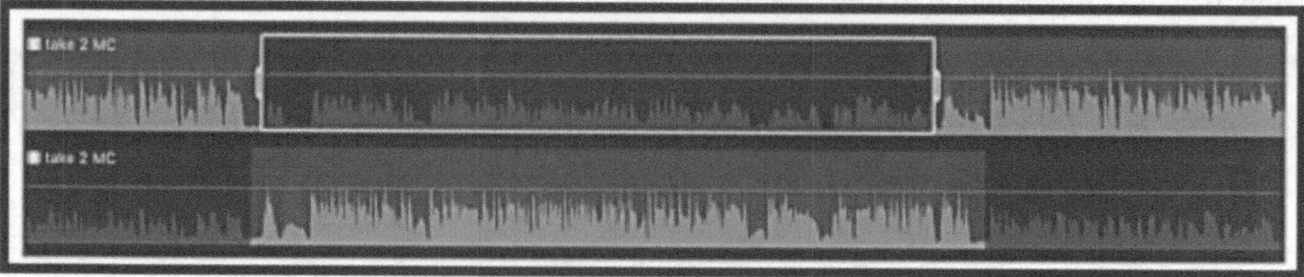

The audio area goes dark, just like it would if the track was completely turned off. Pressing **V** again will make it appear again if you change your mind. We should first smooth out those transitions, though.

4. Move your mouse over the volume line near the edge of the "disabled audio" area until you see the teardrop-shaped audio fade sign.

Yes, the audio changes that show up around the edges of clips also work here.

5. If you want to add an audio fade, move the teardrop-shaped audio fade sign to the allowed area on the side.

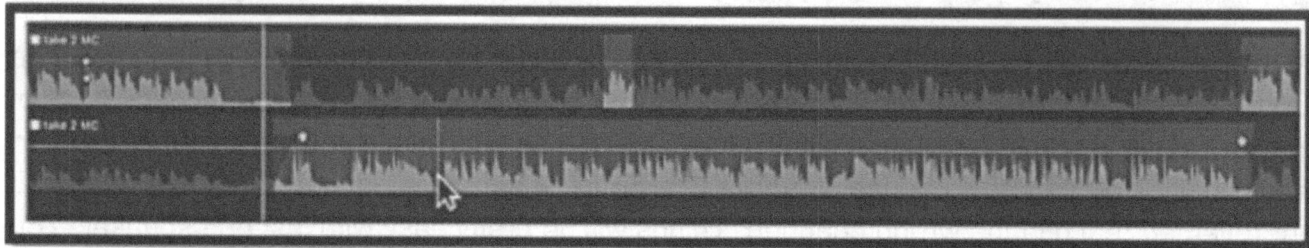

You can roll the edges of any of these areas if they are in the wrong place. The roll cursor will appear when you move your mouse over the edges:

You can switch between active mies or use both at the same time with this method. It lets you record more than one subject at the same time, and you can choose how many tracks to use in the final edit. It's an easier method than simply moving audio and video in a multicam clip because there's no need to cut or remove the audio. There is one small catch, though. When working with more than one channel at once, keep in mind that if you move your mouse over a channel and then press the **space bar**, you'll only hear the channel where thered Skimmer is visible. To hear everything, move your mouse over the timeline bar or a nearby empty spot and let the Skimmer cover all channels:

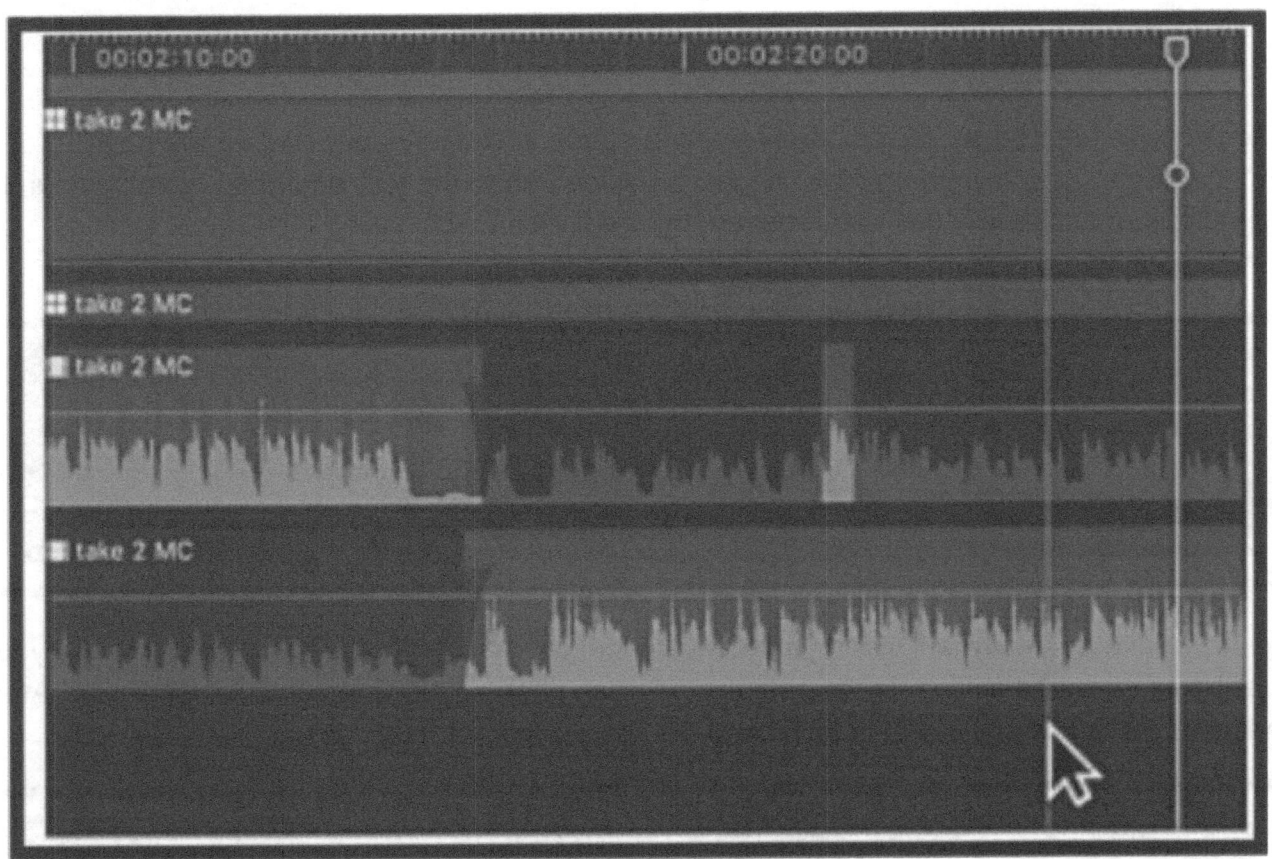

You might also want to put the subjects in a stereo sound field for a more complicated edit where more than one subject can be seen and heard at the same time. That means controlling panning as well as volume, you can do that. Here's how.

Adjusting panning

Stereo sound, which simply involves placing each audio source in a left-to-right, one-dimensional area, is used in the majority of projects. This is usually not taken into account at all: mono speakers are placed in the middle, and stereo background music adds some life to the stereo sound field. You can do more, though, if you put monomies in stereo space. Although most specialized cameras are single and record in the middle by default, some cameras will record stereo audio, which is good for ambient sound (atmosphere). Look for a **Pan** control below the **Audio** improvements in the **Inspector** if you want to have more control over where your subject is in **space. If you need to, set it to show, and then do these steps:**

1. In **Audio Configuration**, select the proper channel setup by selecting **Mono** for one channel or **Dual Mono** for two.
2. In the list of individual channels below, for **Dual Mono** only, click on the channel you want to change.
3. Select **Stereo Left/Right** under **Pan**, and then an **Amount** below that.

Each channel can be set to a different point in space to roughly approximate the position of a sound source. Zero is in the middle, negative values pan to the left, and positive values pan to the right. In most shows, this isn't required, but it's a nice touch. Using the normal settings, you can also keyframe panning to allow moving within a frame:

If you want to get really fancy and your delivery tool can handle it, you might want to send your music to a surround setting. In the settings, you can change your project to 5.1 surround. After that, you can place any clip in both 1D and 2D space all around the viewer:

You can change the level of movement to Basic Surround and then move the puck to where you want it to come from. You can fix things quickly if you don't have time:

- **Dialogue**: Positioned mostly toward the front center.
- **Ambience**: Set up closer to the surround (rear) speakers.
- **Music**: spread out evenly in the surround space.

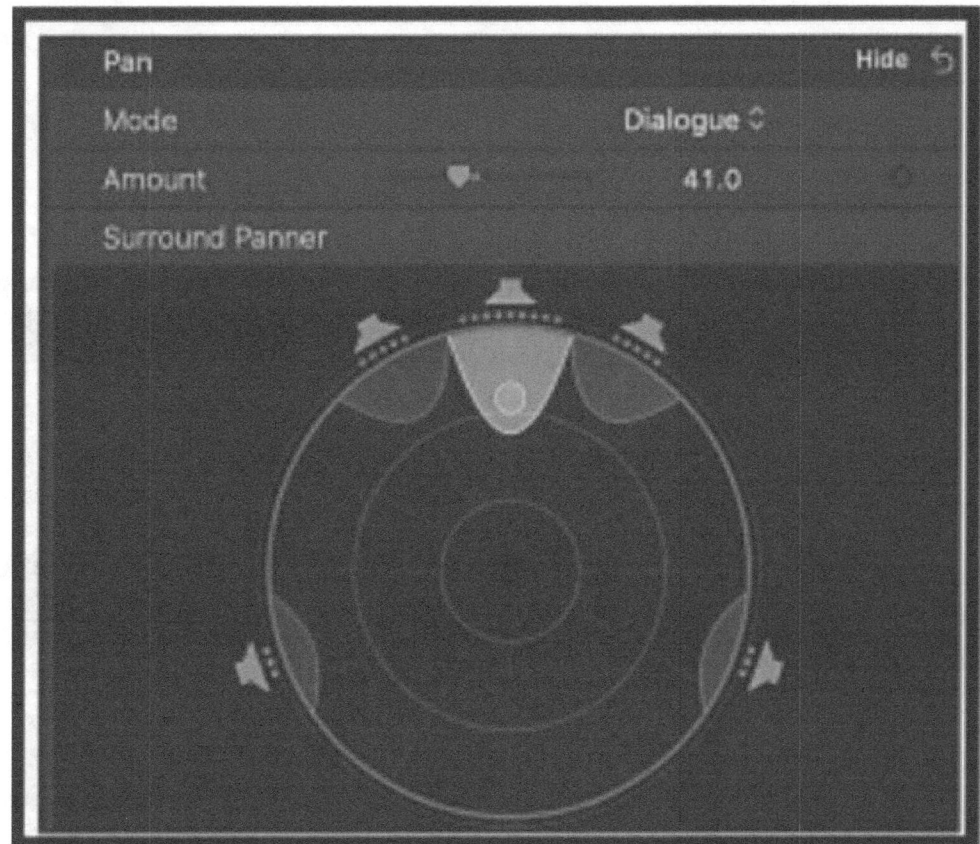

If you are animating a pan, pay more attention to what the amount controls. If you choose one of these options, it might not seem to change anything, but the amount slider acts very differently in each;

- **Basic Surround**: a left and right pan in the surround space.
- **Create Space**: More of a central/front bias; uses more of the surround field at **100**.
- **Dialogue**: **0** means no effect, while **100** is all the way to the front center.
- **Music**: Spread it out evenly; at **100**, use more of the surround field.
- **Ambience**: A value of **100** causes the audio to be pushed to surround only, while a value of **0** puts it back in the center of the room.
- **Circle**: A sound comes from a certain spot in 360° space.
- **Rotate**: Any existing audio position is rotated in 360° space.
- **Back to Front**: Moves the surround space from the back to the front.
- **Left Surround to Right Front**: As a bullet shot, it goes from behind you on the left, flying past you, and in front of you on the right. This is called "left surround to right front."
- **Right Surround to Left Front**: From right behind you on the right to in front of you on the left like a bullet shot cutting through the air.

Even though these options are cool, most people won't be able to hear the surround sound on famous video-sharing sites because it's not possible to do so yet. These ways are only useful for **more fancy deliveries until more options come up, but don't be surprised if sur-round becomes more popular over time.**

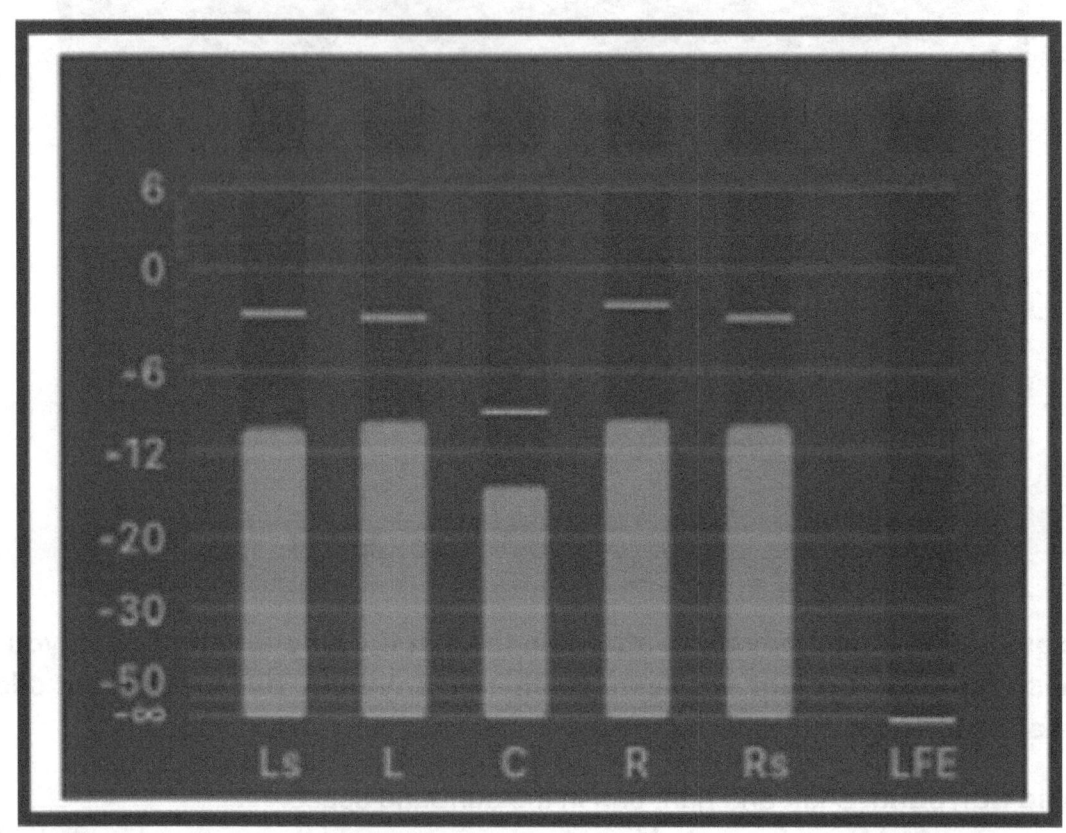

Audio Enhancements

This part talks about some easy ways to improve the sound of audio files using the **Audio Enhancements** area of the **Inspector**. Keep in mind that if an audio clip has more than one part, you might need to click on one of them to pick it up before you can choose from these options. **Equalization**, or EQ, is at the top of the list. **Voice Isolation** (new in 10.6.4 if you have macOS 12.3 or higher) is next, and then **Audio Analysis** with its parts on **Loudness, Noise Removal,** and **Hum Rem Oval**. These are easy and built-in ways to change these things about clips, but they're not the only ones:

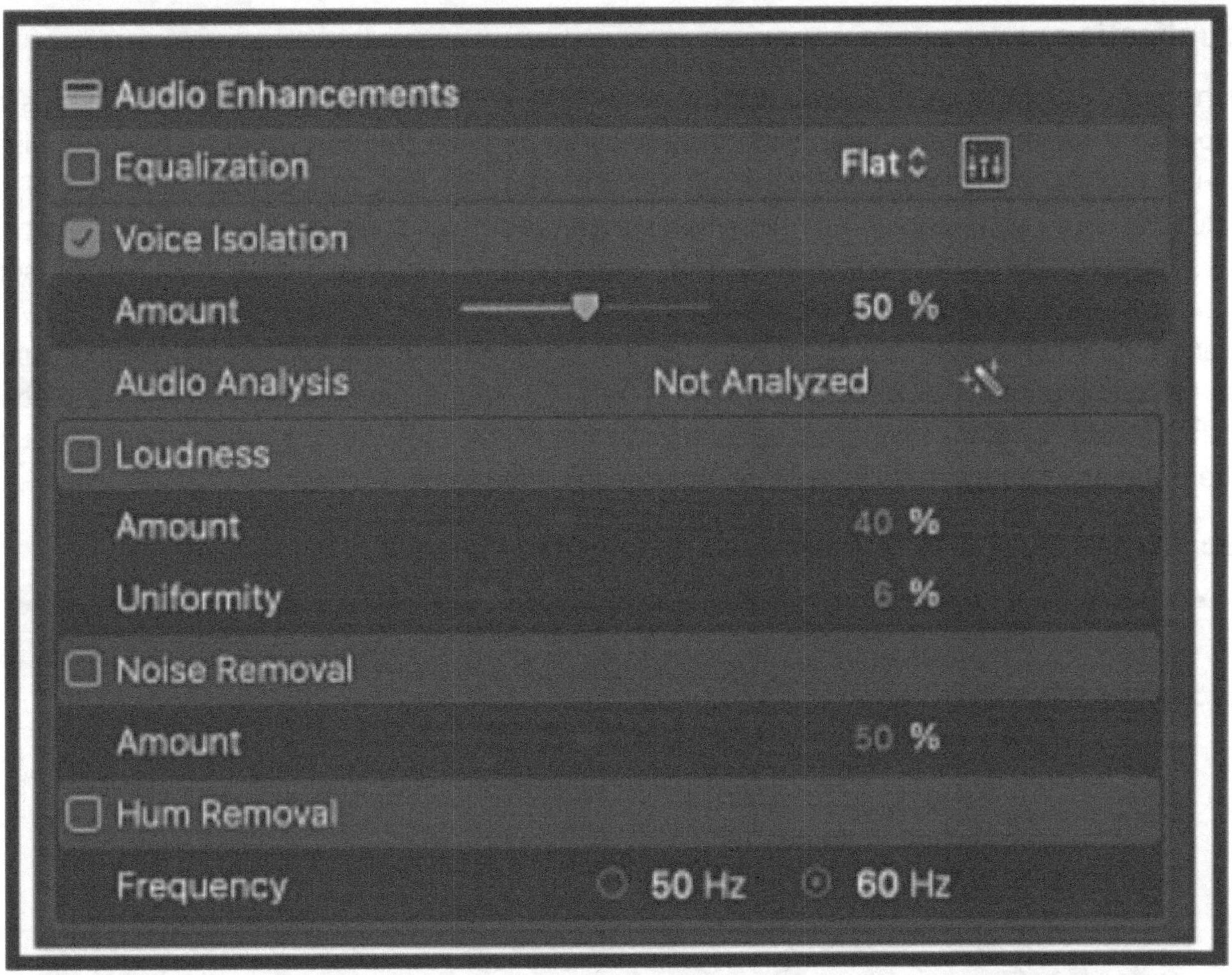

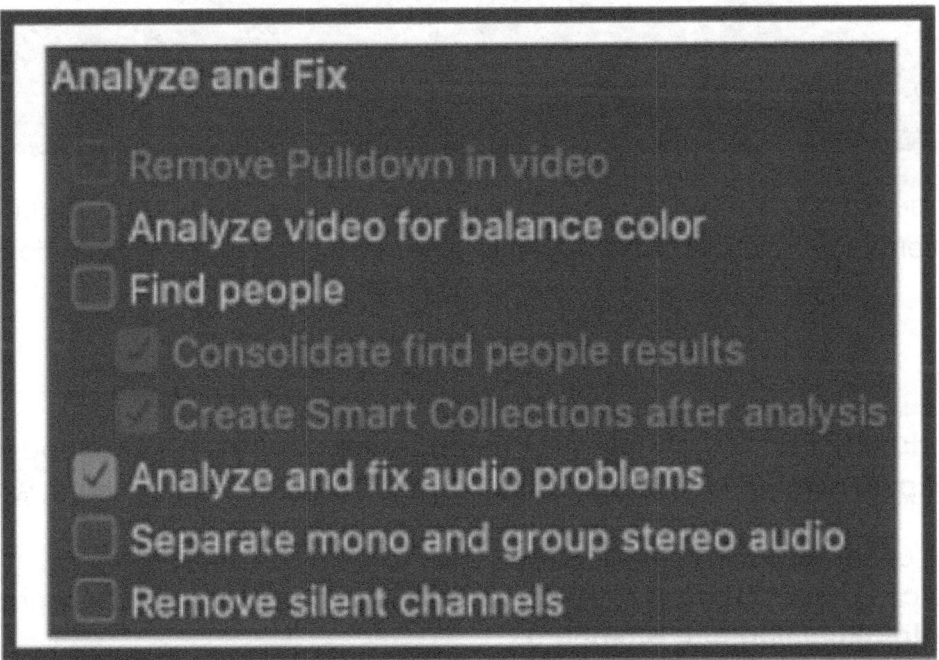

In fact, if you check Analyze and fix audio problems on import, some of these options may already be active. If that's the case, turn them all off to start over:

Remember that these are always the first things that are added to a clip before any other audio effects. As you'll see, this can be a problem sometimes. It's now time to dip into EQ.

Equalization

Each sound is made up of waves that move at different speeds. Low-frequency sounds are deep, like a bassdrum or a tuba. High-frequency sounds, on the other hand, are sharp, like a violin or a child screaming. Many headphones say they can play frequencies between 20 and 20,000 Hz, but most people can't hear that range, and most speakers can't play it either. It's okay, though; there's plenty to work with. **Equalization** lets you boost the level of some frequencies while lowering the volume of others. This lets you make some sounds louder while lowering the volume of others. EQ can be used to do something special, make one clip sound a little more like another, or bring out or hide a part of a sound. If you edit the EQ for a piece of music, you can lower the levels that speech uses. For that reason, talking over that music sounds better, and any change in volume (dubbing) doesn't have to be as clear.

Also, EQ can be used to make voices sound better, like this:

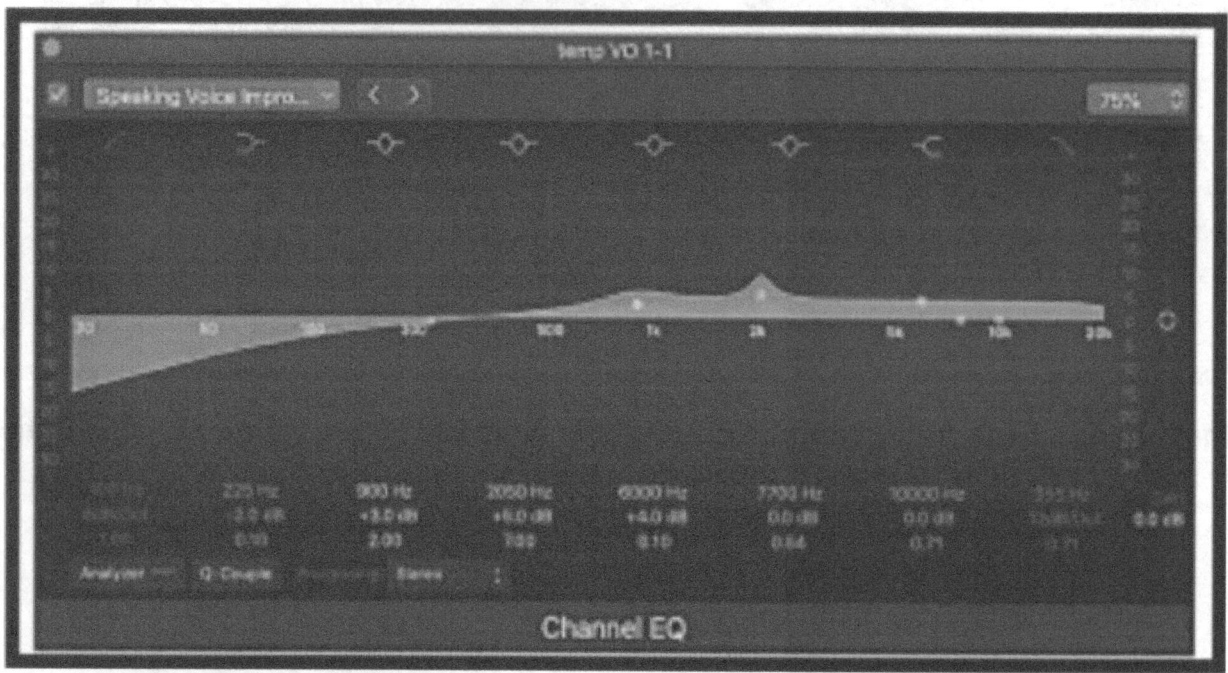

You can choose from a number of presets and have full control over the Equalization part of Audio Enhancements. However, Audio Effects has more complicated EQ options, which we'll review soon.

Manual EQ

Before you add any EQ, you should first listen to the clip. It's also a good idea to focus on just one clip if anything is playing concur-rently. To hear a clip by itself, without music:

1. Pick out a video clip in the timeline.
2. You can press **Option-S** or click the **Solo** button to switch the headphones between **Audio Skimming and Snapping.**

All other audio is grayed out and turned off, leaving only that clip audible. This solo button can be clicked again to bring it back.

3. To start looping, press **Command-L** and go to **View > Playback > Loop Playback**. Make sure that the box next to the menu option is checked.

You can also see a ring around the playback button below the viewer when repeating is on.

4. Press the / (slash) key to play only the clip you choose.

This is the command for **Play Selection.** Make sure you know what the clip sounds like by listening to it a few times. You can cut the clip short by using the **Range Selection (R)** tool to select a range and pressing again. It's now time to try something new. The EQ is flat, which means it is not working right now.

5. Select a number of options from the **Equalization** menu and play the region while you listen to them.

You should be able to tell the difference between settings that are at odds with each other, like **Treble Boost** and **Treble Reduce**, but it's easier to see them, and there's a way to do that.

6. To get to the **Equalization** menu, click the small button next to it.

This opens the window for advanced equalization, which looks like this:

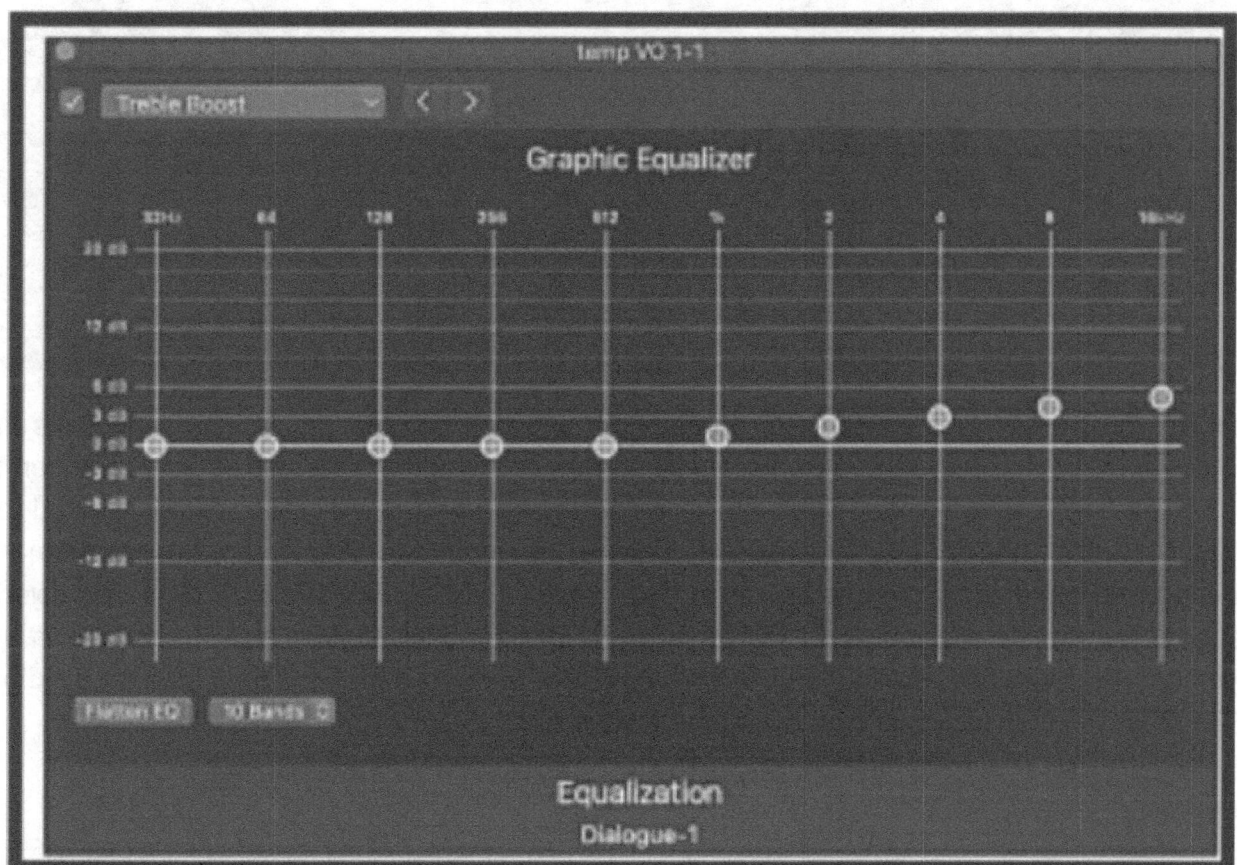

There is a button in the upper left corner of this window that lets you pick the same presets as before. You can change the pucks that match any of these frequencies in the body of the window. Also, you can drag a selection across multiple bands and then change the chosen pucks all at once. But be careful-to pick multiple bands. This way, you need to start dragging on one of the lines, not a puck, and not the empty space between the lines. The best way to set new numbers right away is to **right-click and drag across all the pucks at once**. The **Flatten EQ** button to the right corner of the window restarts the panel, and the pop-up menu lets you **choose between a more exact 31 band option and the previous 10 band option. This lets you pick and choose which frequencies to change, but it may take more work to get the job done since there are more scales to use:**

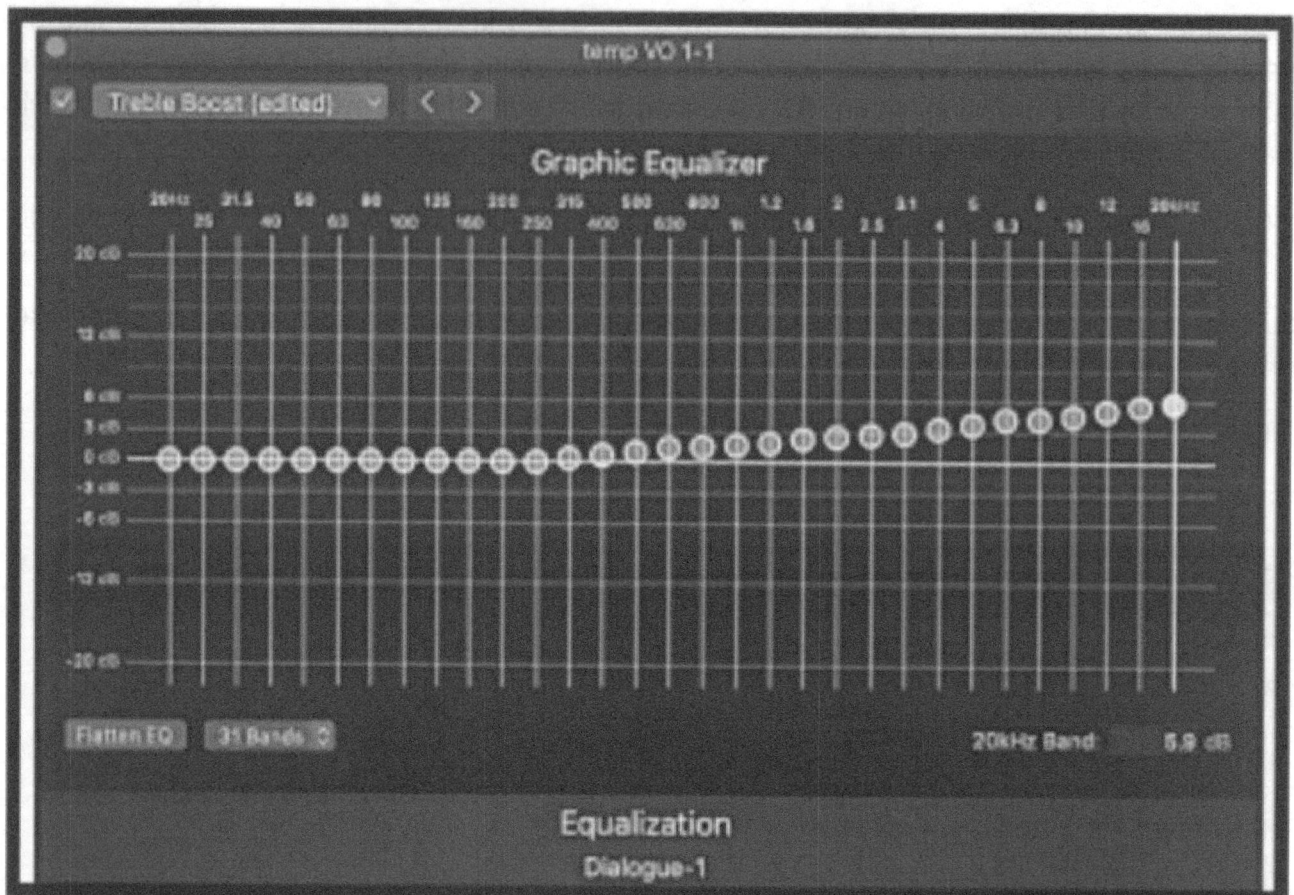

What do you want to do? Try to get rid of things that aren't needed and improve the ones that are. You can move the sliders to lower levels where you think the frequencies are, and then try moving them to different frequencies until you find the problem. If the sound is very limited to a certain frequency, it's not always possible to get rid of it without being heard, but sometimes it works great. This window is a good place to start with EQ, but if you want to make more powerful changes, like seeing a visual representation of the frequencies used in a clip, you should use more complicated audio effects. They will be looked at soon, but for now, let's take a quick look at **Match EQ**, a cool trick that works with the built-in EQ.

MatchEQ

By adding a custom EQ, the Ma tch EQ feature offers a quick way to make two clips sound more alike. Just like the **Match Color** tool, you can't turn it down. But you can turn it off. A target clip and a source clip are the two audio clips you'll need. For the best results, the two records should have some things in common, but not all of them. For example, the same person could be recorded in two different places or by two different devices.

Putting those two clips on a timeline:

1. Pick out the target clip you want to change.
2. To match the sound, go to the EQ menu and select **Match**. To match the sound, go to the **Audio Enhancements** menu and select **Match Audio.**
3. Pick out the source clip and click on it.
4. To apply, click **Apply Match:**

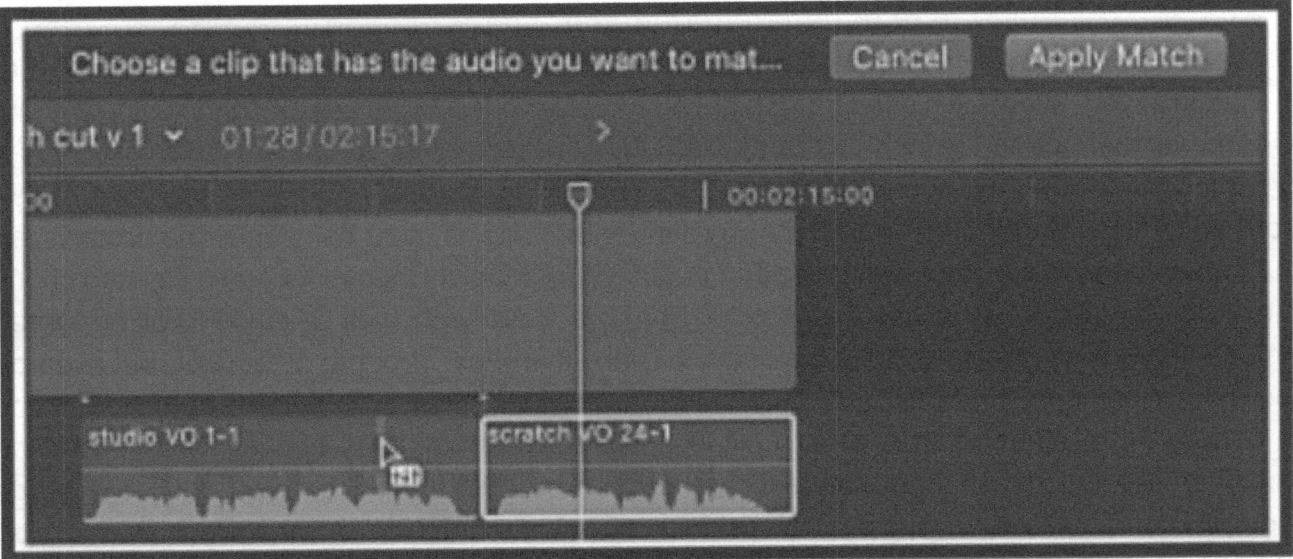

5. Use/to play the chosen clip.

The change should be clear, and you should also be able to hear that the chosen clip now sounds more like the source clip. You can either do the same things again or click the new **microphone icon** to the far right of the Match menu to choose a different source clip. When you click the **button directly next to the Match menu, a new window pops up with the Match EQ effect. This is a more complex change than a simple band-based EQ.**

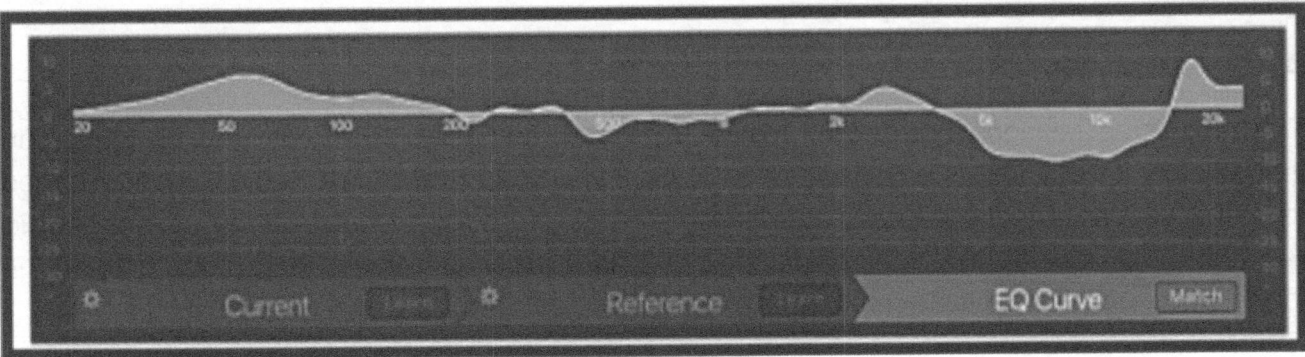

It does a good job for me pretty quickly, and if nothing else, it's helpful as a place to start doing more work. Like with video effects, you can copy a Match EQ from one clip and then go to **Edit > Paste Effects** or **Paste Attributes** to add it to another clip. Voice Isolation is the newest feature here, and you should check it out after EQ. Of all the new features added to the program recently, this is the one that changes how things are done every day the most. Let's start.

Voice Isolation

It's been hard to do well in the past, but human speech is probably the most important part of the audio in your shows. It's been hard to get rid of background noise like air conditioning without a good microphone in the right place and a dedicated recording. Voice Isolation now does a great job of blocking out sounds that aren't people talking, so that's no longer the case. If you don't want hiss, wind, traffic, or even background music, it's all gone early on in the process, so that other changes can start with this clean audio. Wow! Magic! Choose an audio clip and check the **Voice Isolation** box to use this feature. For sure, it will work well because it will be turned on and set to 50%. You can move the scale to make the effect stronger or weaker, but even on the highest settings, it probably won't sound too processed. This built-in noise reduction option is usually more effective than other built-in noise reduction options because it is based on machine learning rather than standard mathematical methods. Note: If you don't see Voice Isolation here, make sure you have at least FCP 10.6.4 and macOS. 12.3 installed. That version of FCP can be used on older macOS, but the Voice Isolat io n tool won't work on them. Were you up to date and still don't see Voice Isolation in the list? Check the Audio Configuration at ion part at the bottom of the Audio Inspector to see if you're working with dual mono or another type of multi-channel audio. You must first choose a single audio channel before you can use voice isolation. It will work with both stereo and single-channel mono audio, but you'll need to click on a single dual mono channel to see the Voice Isolation option. It's below voice isolation. This is where **Audio Analysis** is. You should look at this even if you don't use these settings very often. We'll go through them from most important to least important.

Audio Analysis

The next three sections **Loudness**, **Noise Removal,** and **Hum Removal** can be turned on immediately if the analysis says they need to be. I like to do these fixes manually when I need to, but if you want to try it totally automatically, click the **Magic Wand** button next to **Audio Analysis**. You can do this analysis during the import process if you're in a hurry: that button looks at the clip and plays the next few parts if they're needed.

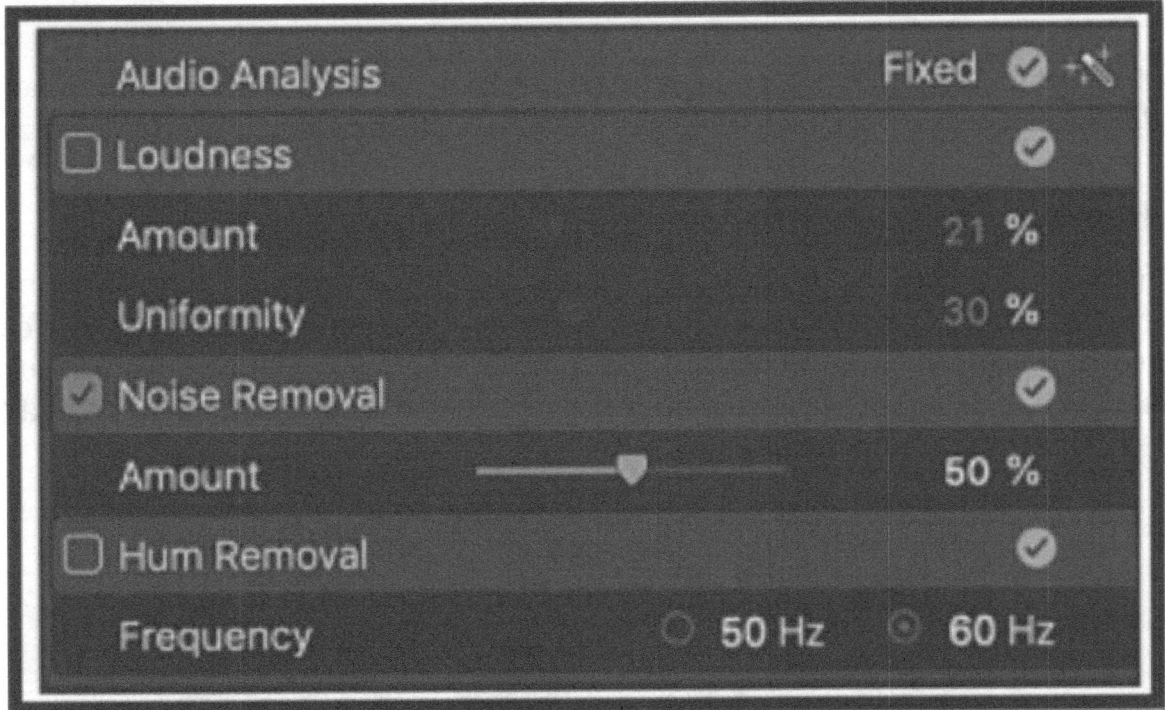

You will now see a yellow or red warning sign next to the area if a problem is found but you choose not to fix it. Just because it's easy to use and handy doesn't mean I like it. Find out more about these changes by reading on.

Loudness

This effect is more complicated than it seems; in order to make the audio level more constant, it compresses the audio and increases the volume of quiet areas. This is a key step in the audio handling process because it lowers the clip's dynamic range. That being said, if your video has any noise, you should get rid of it with Voice Isolation first, if you can. After EQ and Voice Isolation, **loudness** is the first thing that is used. In other words, this function can make it harder to get rid of noise or hiss that is already in your recording. To get more out of your work, you should use audio effects instead of Voice Isolation if you can't.

Noise Removal

Hissing and noise are very common. They can be self-noise (from lower mics) or background noises (from air conditioning, traffic, and other things). This feature does get rid of noise, but it can lower the quality of what's left, leaving effects that can be heard, like a robot talk-ing underwater.

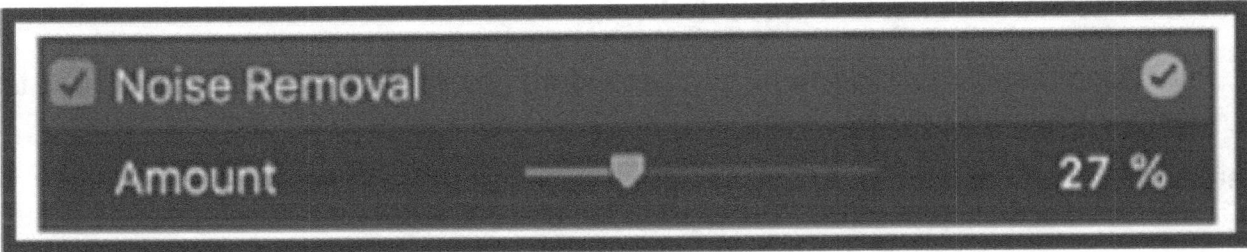

This will be set to 50% by default, and I've found that it can be a problem when it's higher than 30%. Voice Isolation is a more up-to-date tool that I use instead of this **Noise Removal** one.

Hum Removal

If you follow good production rules, you won't need this. The electrical system in your country has a frequency of 50 Hz for PAL territories and 60 Hz for NTSC territories. Sometimes, electrical interference, which can happen near wires, can make a hum that you can hear. Should this **happen to you, picking the right frequency will get rid of it nicely. Keep in mind that there is an EQ option that can be used in the same way:**

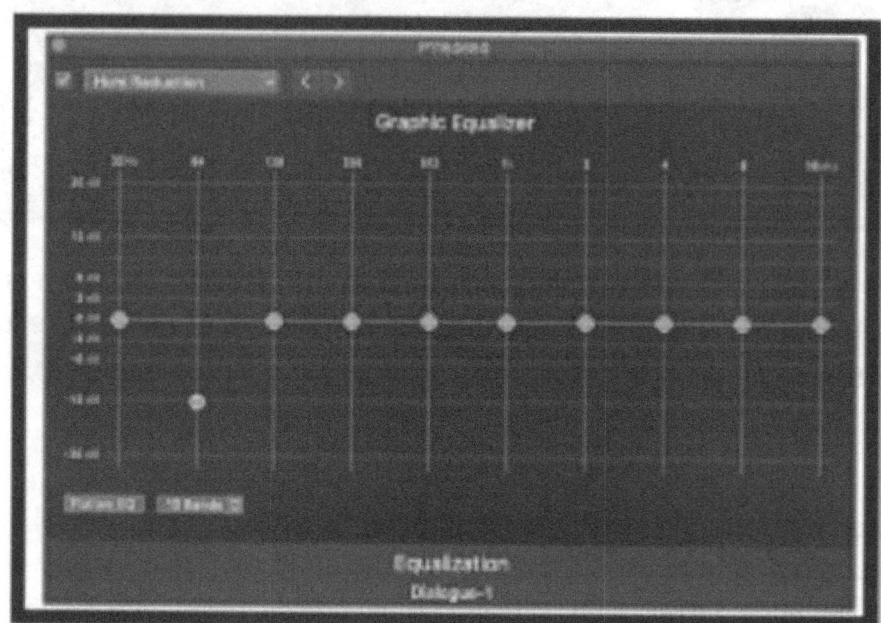

Applying and using audio effects

You can use audio effects to make sounds louder and more robotic, narrow the dynamic range, or warp them in all sorts of crazy ways. This page will tell you about many of them. As you might think, audio effects work a lot like video effects, and you can find them at the bottom of the same **Effects Browser** window. A huge number of effects are included, including many from Apple's Logic Pro. You can also use effects from other programs, so you should be able to handle most jobs.

Adding audio effects

You will need to see the Effects Browser to begin:

- Press **Command-5** or click the button second from the right in the middle gray bar to open the **Effects Browser**.

Remember that the sidebar has AUDIO effects below and VIDEO effects above:

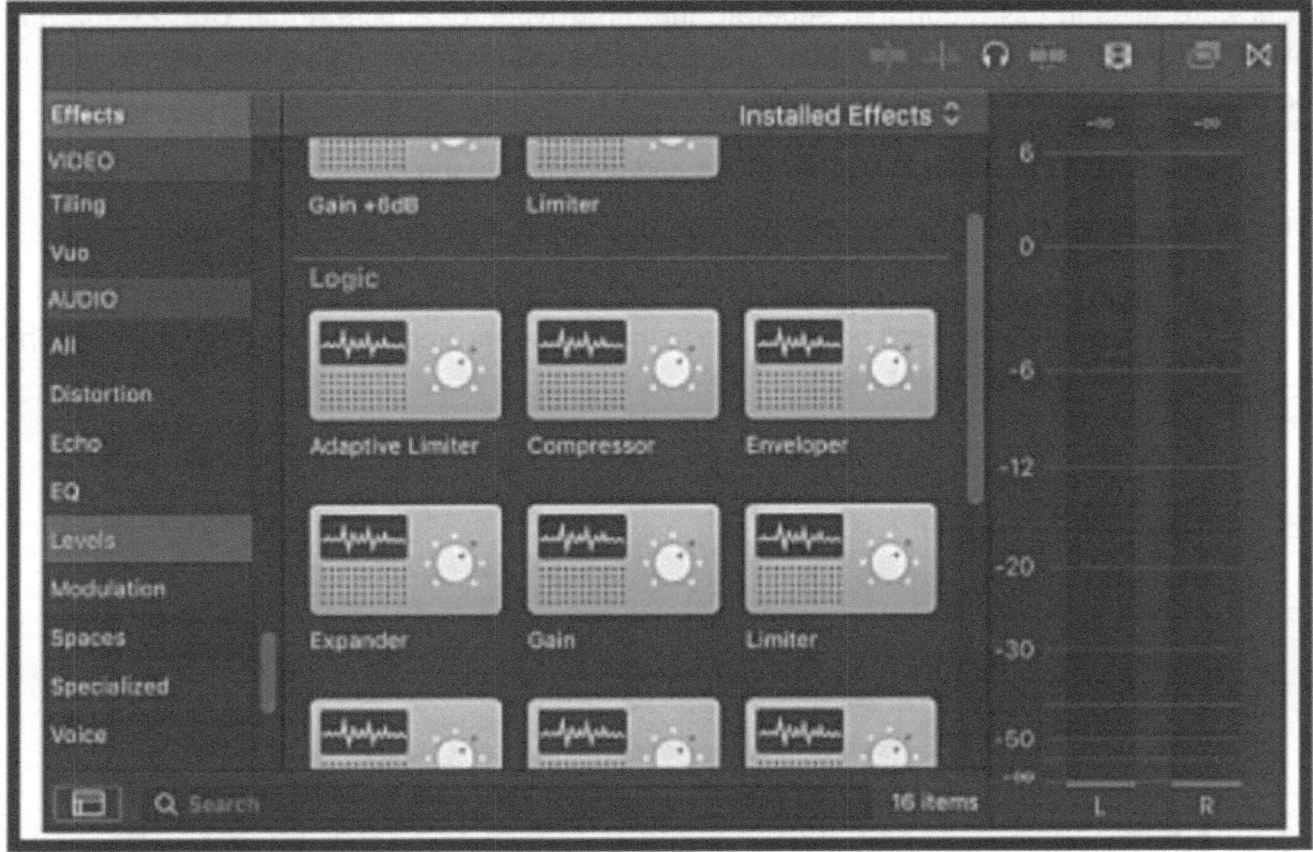

It is easy to look at just audio effects or a certain type of effect:

- Click **All**, which is located right under **AUDIO**. This will show you all of the audio effects.
- When you click on a group name, you'll only see the audio effects that belong to that group.

You can listen to audio effects before you use them, but you have to turn on audio skimming first.

1. Press **Shift-S** to start **Audio Skimming** if it's not already on.

When it's on, the **Audio Skimming** icon will turn blue.

2. Move your mouse over an effect to hear it being used on the clip you've chosen.

Like with video effects, this is just a sneak peek of the default setting of an effect. One of these will work to add an audio sound to a clip:

- Pick out a few clips in the timeline, then double-click an effect to use it.
- Drag an effect to a clip on the timeline.

As always, play the file or skim over it (if audio skimming is still on) to make sure the effect is applied. We'll add some fun effects and mess around with the settings for a short tutorial. There's no problem with using a voice clip you made earlier.

3. Hold down the **option key** and **click** on a clip to pick it up. Then, move the playhead to that spot.
4. For **Echo**, go to the **Effects** pane and click on it.

There are titles in this group that separate the three types of effects: **Final Cut, Logic**, and **macOS**. Even though it doesn't matter where an effect came from, logic-based effects tend to be more complex and have a wider range of interactions. First, let's do something crazy.

5. Choose the **Delay Designer** effect and drag it onto the clip.

This is one of the logic effects, and you can hear what it does.

6. Press / to play the clip again.
7. While playback is still going on, go to the **Inspector** and pick one of the other options from the long **Preset** menu:

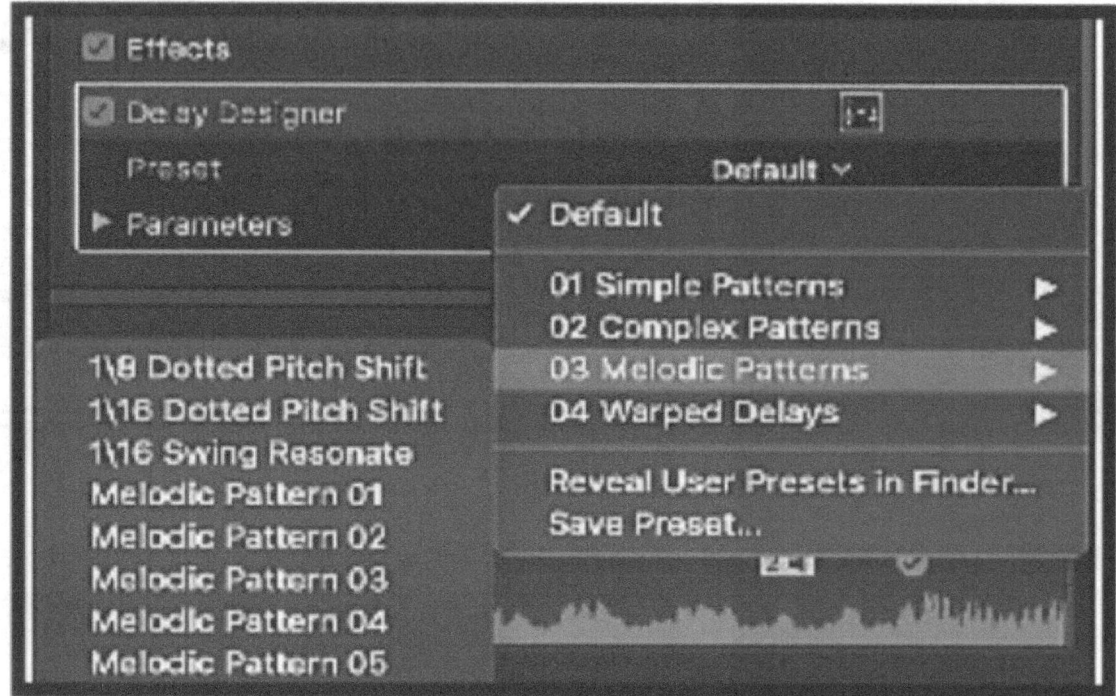

There are enough options here to keep you busy for a short time, and some of them sound really cool.

8. Click the small controller button to the right of **Delay Designer** when you're done.

There will be a lot of knobs, graphs, and settings in the new window.

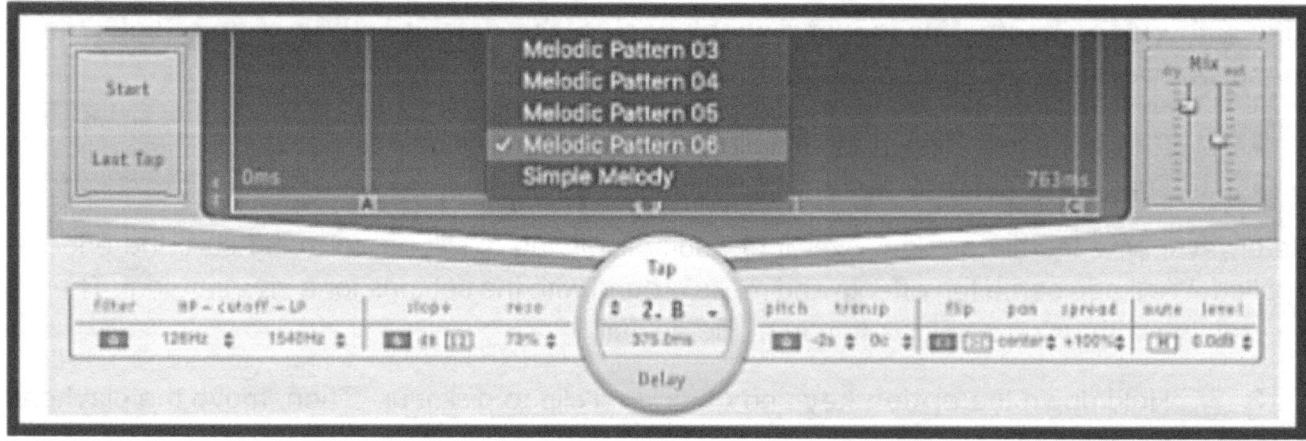

There are a lot of different logic-based effects, but the best way to start is to pick some new presets from the menu in the upper left corner and see what happens.

9. Change the tabs at the top of the window box, click and drag, and look around to see what some of the settings do.

Even though you can change a lot of things, it would take a while to fully understand this one effect. Be wary, as some settings (like theThe **Feedback** option to the right can result in audible provocation. You can save settings that you want to use again if you find them useful.

10. It's in the upper left area. Click on the **Preset** menu and select **Save Preset...**

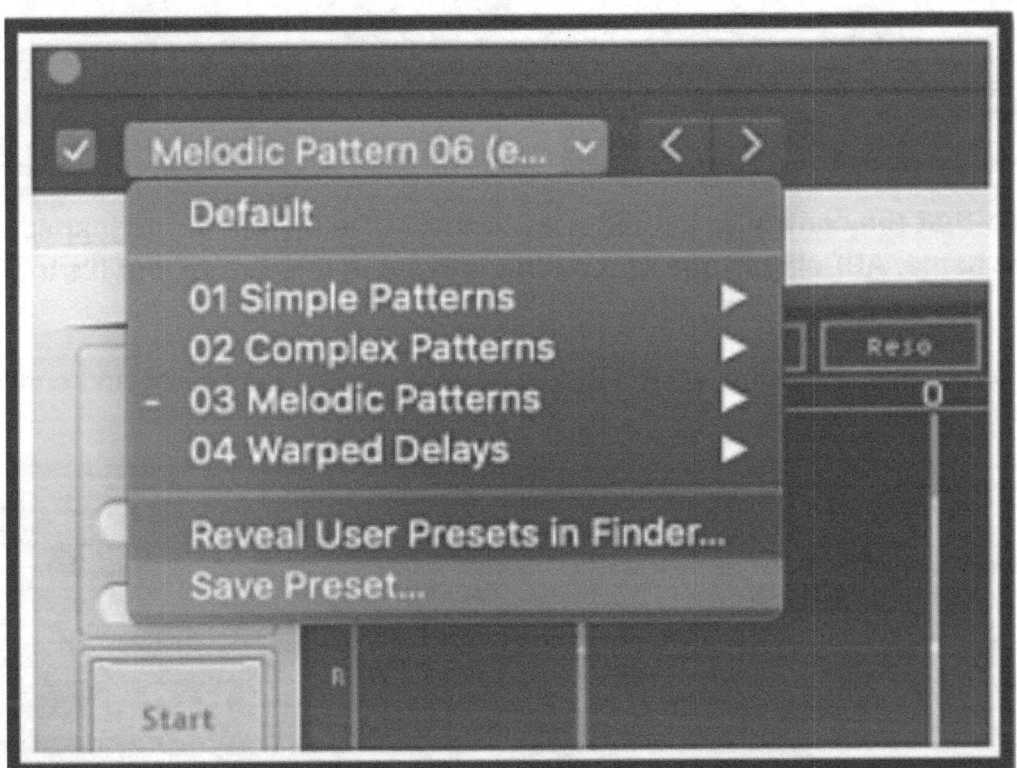

There are different ways that effects can be used. The audio effects in **Logic** and **macOS** each have their own presets, but the effects in **Final Cut** don't. This is because they work a bit like native FCP **Effects Presets**; each one blends one or more separate audio effects to produce a certain result. The different parts can be changed, but the built-in fixed options are the only ones that can be used. There are times when the preset options will change the effects that are occurring.

Follow these steps if you want to learn more about these effects:

1. **Option-click** on another clip to select it and move the playback to that point.
2. For **Echo**, go to the **Effects pane** and click on it.
3. It's easy to add the **Echo Delay** effect to your clip.
4. Press **/** to play the clip again.

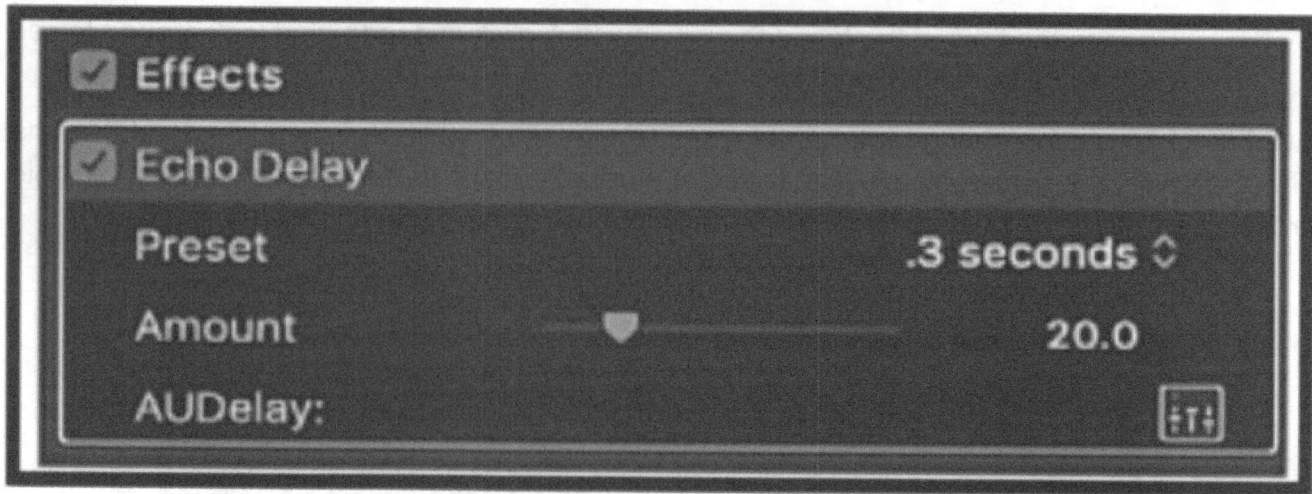

You can see that the controller icon is next to the AUDelay line in the Inspector instead of the effect name. AUDelay is one of the other effects in this group, but it's in the macOS area.

5. For **Metallic PA Echo**, go to the **Preset** menu in the **Inspector** and change it while the track is playing:

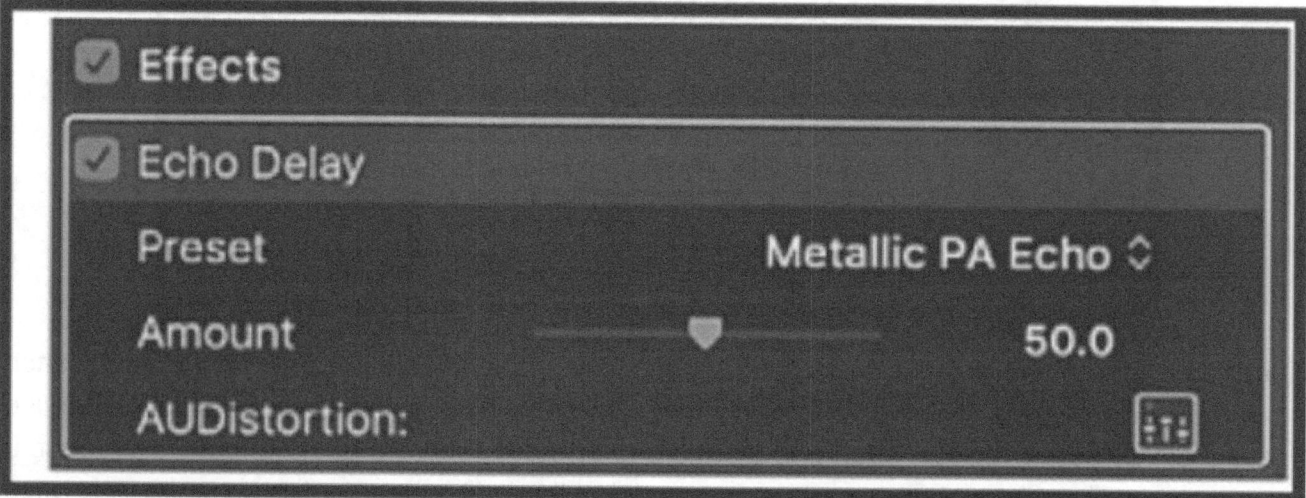

You will now hear something very different, and you will see that the sound has changed to AUDistortion.

6. As it plays, go back to the **Preset** menu in the **Inspector** and change it to **.3 seconds**.
7. To the right of **AUDelay**, click the small icon.
8. **When the window pops up, click and drag the line up and down to change the feedback, and left and right to change the delay.**

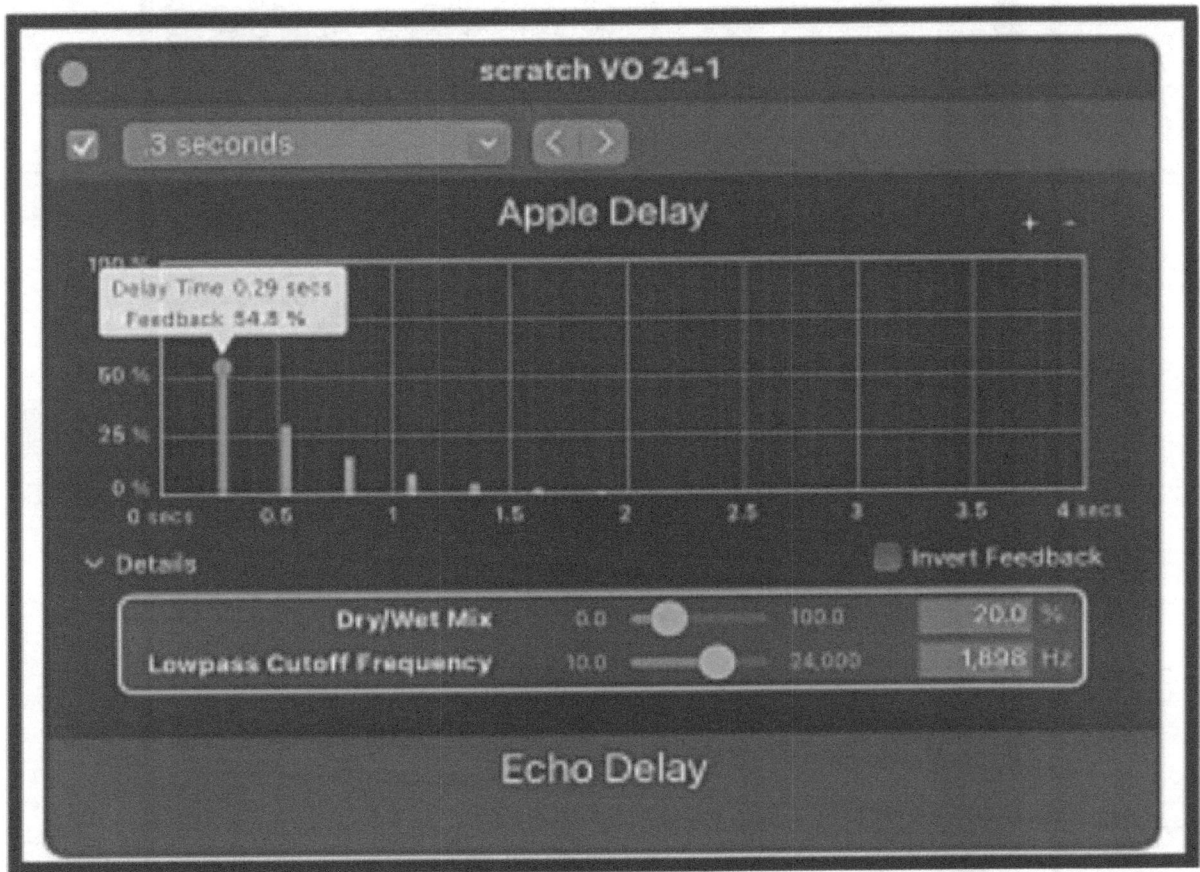

The sliders below give you access to other controls. This is a much easier layout than **Delay Designer**. It's not as powerful, but it's much easier to understand and change. In the upper left **area of this effect, you can find the same Preset menus in the Inspector.**

However, this menu can lead to big changes:

9. Use the **Preset** menu in the floating window to change the sound to **Metallic PA Echo**.

You'll notice that the effect underneath (and the way it looks) changes from **AUDelay** to **Distortion**, which is an effect from a different group that can produce an echo nonetheless. You can try out all of these buttons because there are so many of them. Close the window when you're done. The **Final Cut** group of audio effects does not have a **User Presets** system like most effects do. To get to the presets for the effects inside one of these, like AUDelay or AUDistortion inside Echo Delay, you'll need to find those effects in the **Logic** or **macOS** parts. You can change the custom settings of an effect no matter how you use it, and you can also mix and match different effects to make your effects. Click the **Save Effects Preset** button at the bottom of the Inspector to use the effects from the current clip again, along with all of their current settings.

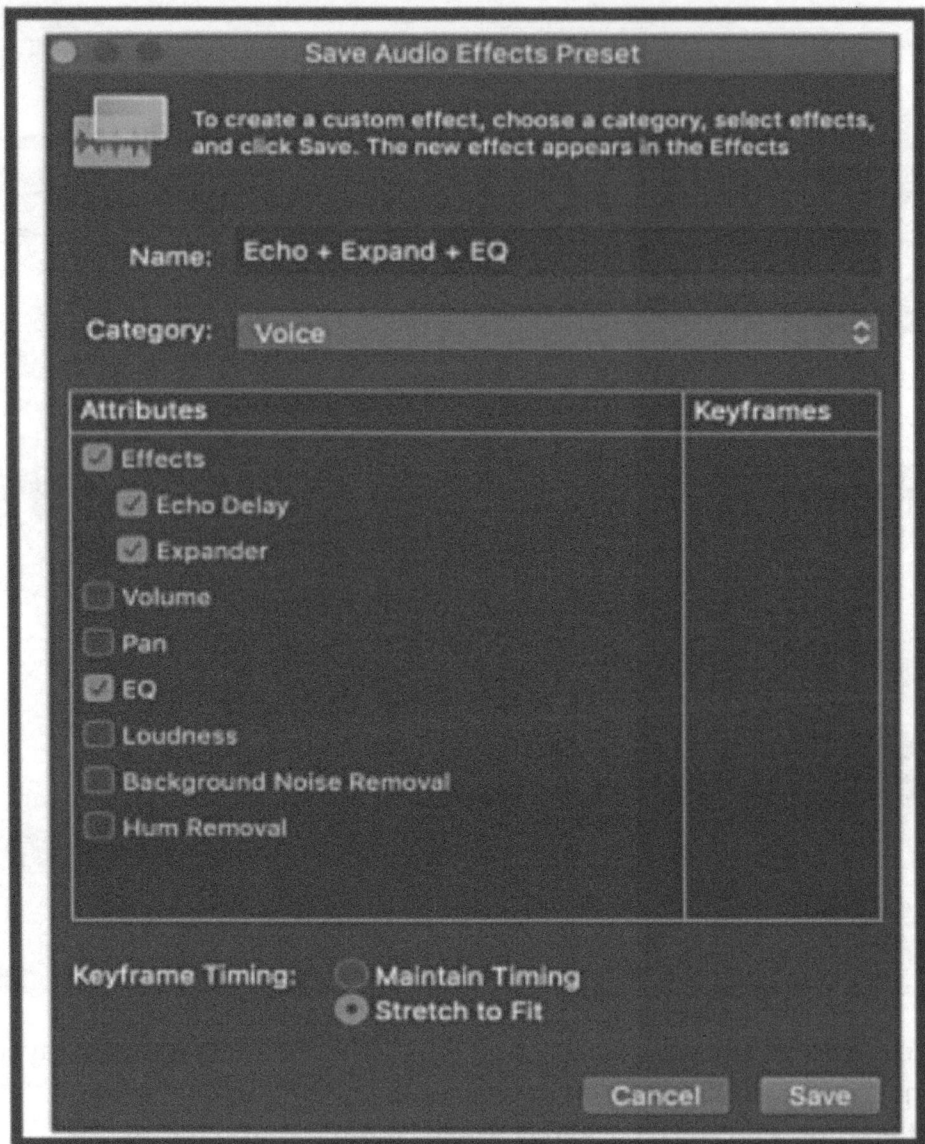

Using Roles with audio

Roles make it easier to understand audio by letting changes and effects be made to a group of sounds, like music or conversation. Roles can also make it easy to send separate audio stems to a different app for more specialized processing, all without the tracks. You will learn how the audio data flows and how to control audio at the role level with compound clips here. By the end, you'll know how to keep the roles you set for your media when you imported it through the creation process.

Understanding signal flow

It doesn't have to be hard to understand how an audio clip gets from the camera to the file, but you should know what's going on to avoid a few problems. If you apply an effect at the wrong point in the chain or to the wrong type of container clip, audio roles may be mixed up, which could be confusing. In a timeline, each clip can have more than one part. Usually, these parts all play the same role, which is **dia-logue**, but that's not always the case. More complicated clips, like **a Compound Clip, might mix different Audio Roles, like music, effects, and** dialogue. An audio clip could also have sound from more than one microphone that is given to different Subroles:

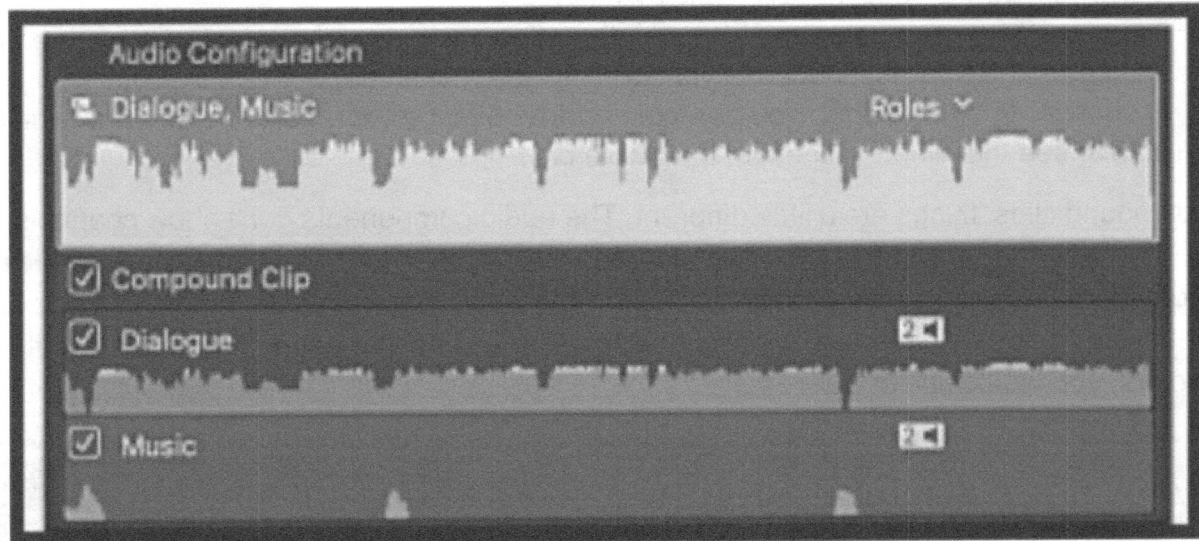

In all of these situations, the different roles or subroles are kept safe apart when the timeline is viewed with **Audio Lanes**, and they can also be exported separately. Any effects you add to a clip that shares roles or subroles, on the other hand, will blur the differences between these roles because the audio parts are mixed before the effects are added. These clips are given a new mixed audio role instead, which is not good. One option is to not use any effects at all and instead have a professional audio engineer do the work. Though that is an option, you don't have to go that far. Instead of applying effects to whole clips when a clip has mixed roles, apply them to audio components. How do you do this? The audio components part of the **Inspector** can be found at the bottom of the **Audio** tab. If you choose **Dual Mono**, there will be two channels below, and in a Multicam clip, there will be a channel for the audio from each camera. In a **simple clip, this will probably show as Mono or Stereo with a single component underneath. Each one can be chosen on its own, and when you add effects to one audio component, they will only be applied to that one:**

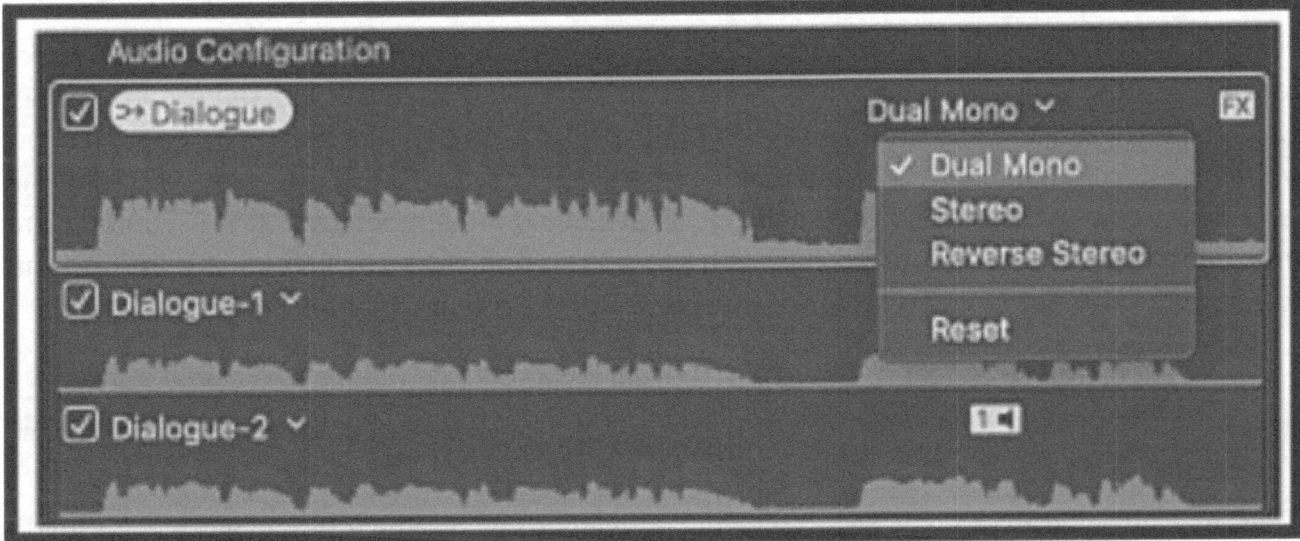

These things are important:

- The above sound will be applied to the whole clip if the first item under **Audio Configuration** is chosen, which it is by default.
- If you choose a component or channel, the effects you see above will only work on that component. Be careful, because youcan only see those effects when that part of the clip is chosen. In other words, you can only add an effect to one part of a clip and won't be able to see that when you select the whole clip.

For compound clips, things are a little different. The audio components don't show channels, but rather the roles that are in this clip. You can choose whether to show **Roles** or **Subroles** as components below using a drop-down choice on the right. If you choose **Roles**, any Subroles will be mixed. If, for instance, you wanted to add various effects to each of the mies of different characters, you would select **Subroles**:

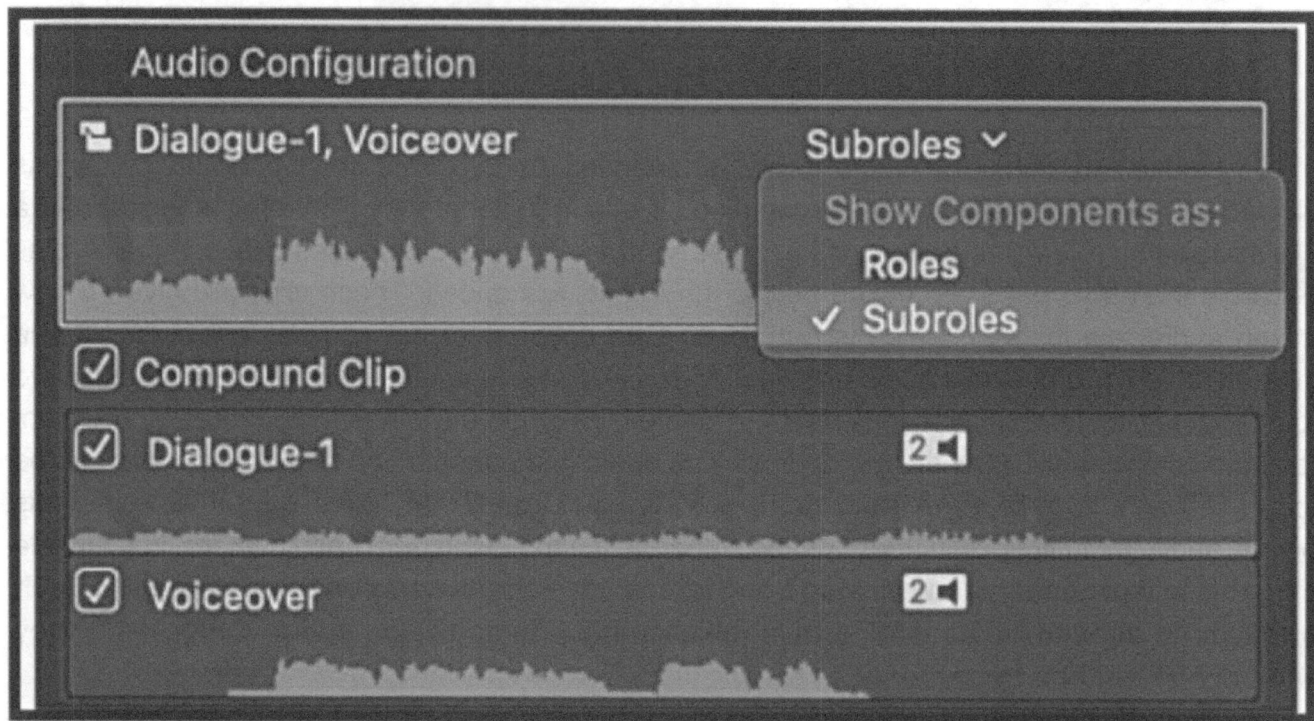

Multicam Clips will send out their role parts based on the angle that is currently selected. Because of how Multicam Clips work, those angles are likely to share the same parent Role. However, each angle could have its own Subrole. When clips are synchronized, they will show two different Role components: the original camera audio, which is usually turned off, and the secondary audio, which is usually turned on. What's going to happen now? And if Subroles are **important, don't apply effects to clips with more than one subrole. If Roles are im-portant, don't apply effects to clips with more than one Role. Do one of these things instead:**

- You can choose a Role or Subrole at the clip level and add effects to a single part.
- To open a Compound Clip, double-click it, and then add effects to separate clips inside the clip.

When the **Timeline Index** is used to mix a full timeline at once, these tips become even more important.

Using Compound Clips for audio mixing

If adding effects to hundreds of separate clips seems like a lot of work, don't. You can instead apply effects to whole roles at once by making your whole project into a compound clip and then using the **Timeline Index** to view individual Roles or Subroles. This will be helpful when exporting, but it's also helpful right now when mixing audio. Before we go any further, it's important to remember that you don't have to do these steps in this order or even at all. For pretty easy jobs, you might only need a few audio clips that are simple enough to handle on their own. As part of some jobs, you may be given audio that has already been processed and doesn't need any work. The audio processing can also be done in more than one step, in any order you choose. Copies of your project should be made before you start the final audio mix in case something goes wrong. For this task, you'll need a project that's almost finished and has some different Audio Roles, as well as any Subroles you want to use.

Get that TV pilot you've been working on or a test project with many audio roles ready, and then follow these steps:

1. To make a duplicate of your project in the **Browser**, click on it and then press **command-D**.
2. Adding "audio mix" to the name of the new duplicate will change it.
3. To edit the new duplicate of the project, right-click on it.
4. To select all of the clips in the **Timeline** pane, click on them and then press **command-A:**

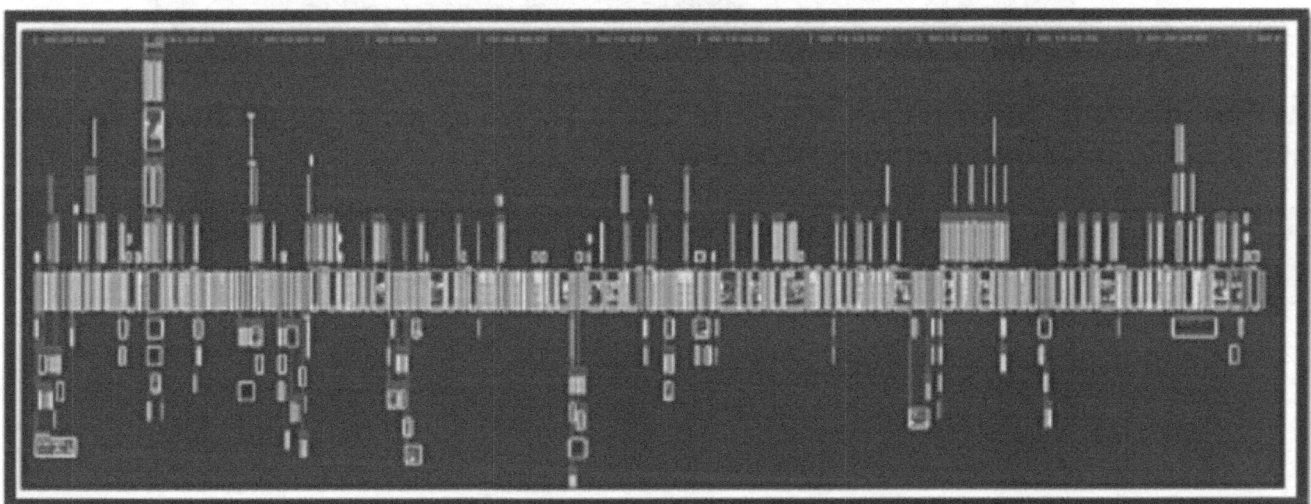

5. To make the whole timeline into a new compound clip, press **Option-G**. In the sheet that comes up, give it a name:
6. Click the index button to the left of the middle gray bar or press **shift-command-2** to bring up the **Timeline Index** if it's not already there.
7. Click Roles at the top of this pane if it isn't already chosen.
8. At the bottom of this window, click Show Audio Lanes.
9. Go to the **Clip Appearance** menu, which is to the right of the middle gray bar. Check **Clip Roles**, then uncheck **Clip Names**:

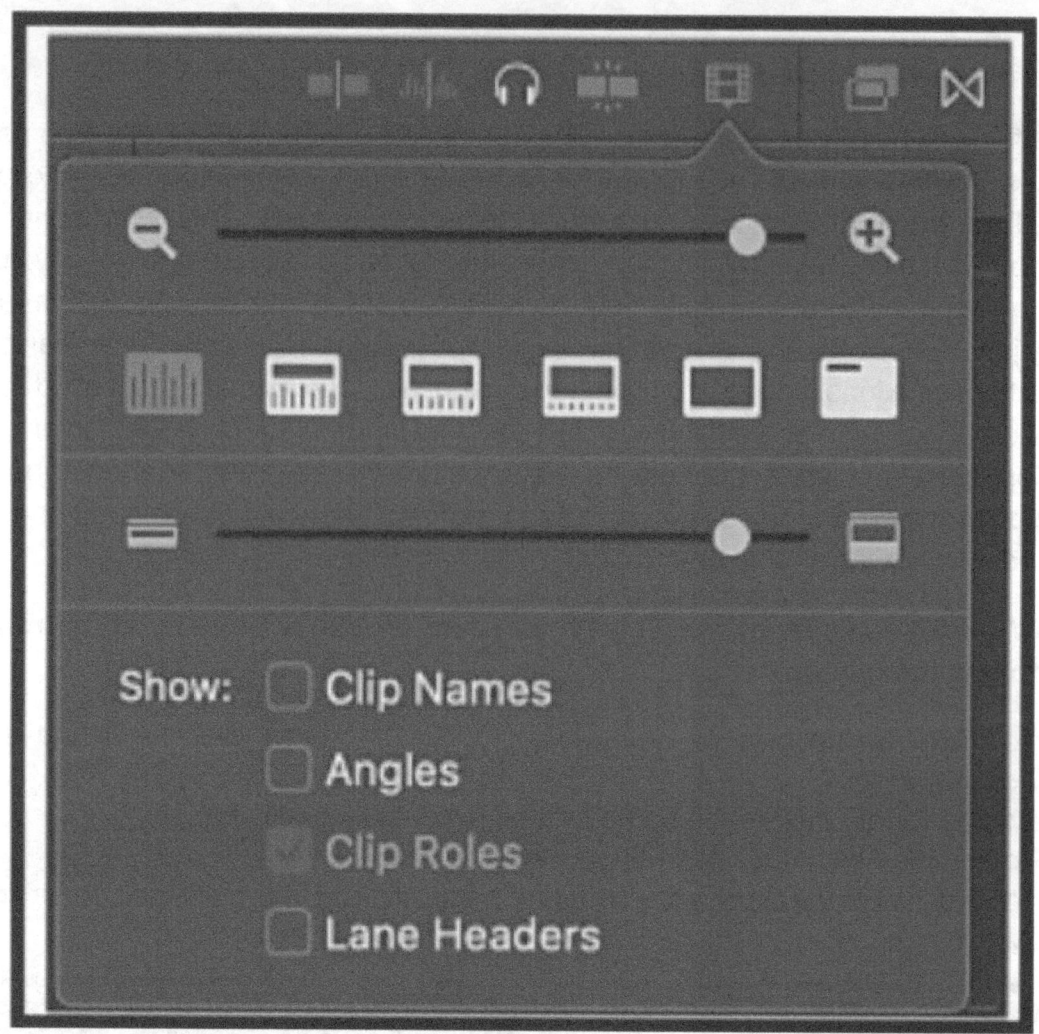

At this point, each Role in the Compound Clip is shown as a clip-length item in its lane, along with a small icon that says "mixdown".

As easily as if it were a single clip, each part can be changed, such as the volume, the audio quality, the panning, and the effects. When you click on a component in the timeline, it automatically opens the **Inspector** and functions just like it does on individual clips.

These steps can help you do the following if you've properly marked your clips with Roles and Subroles:

- Give each voiceover the same Voice over Enhancement effect.
- Give male and female voiceovers different Voice over enhancement effects.
- Give each character speaking different audio effects.

- Change the EQ or compression effects on the dialogue, effects, and music.
- Change the volume of the sound effects, music, and dialogue.
- Give music, effects, and dialogue different surround panning effects.
- Duck (reduce) all sound effects and music while someone is talking.

You can make changes to the Compound Clips as a whole, but you can also make changes to the clips inside them, so don't be afraid to double-click your way in. If you think a certain clip needs something extra, you can add that effect or change the levels. The overall audio mix is usually the last step, or very close to the end of the process. A Compound Clip doesn't have to be a locked-off silo.

Simple methods to increase low-volume

The timeline allows for a maximum of 12 audio levels. There are a few easy ways to make this number greater than +12:

- Select **Loudness** in the Inspector.
- To make a copy of the **Timeline** clip, hold down the Option key and drag down below the clip. That's something you can do many times.
- Use the **Gain** tool, which you can find in the **Levels** panel at the bottom of the **Effects** browser.

It's important to remember that when you turn up the volume of what you want to hear, you also turn up the volume of any background noise and the microphone's internal noise.

Loop playback

It's very helpful to be able to play a piece of audio over and over while you change an effect setting in the inspector. When you hear the same sound over and over, it is much easier to notice a change in the audio quality.

How to do it:

1. Press **Command + L** or and go to **View | Playback | Loop playback**.
2. Choose a part of a clip to play over and over with the **Range** tool.
3. Move the playhead to the part you want to loop, and then press the slash (/) key, which is a shortcut for **Play Selection.**

As you make changes to the sound in the inspector, you will hear the changes right away as the loop keeps playing.

Removing room noise

Room noise has a range of frequencies that often overlap with voice frequencies. Because of this, it is helpful to have a filter that only blocks out background noise when someone is talking and not all frequencies during conversations.

Noise Gate is the filter you need to use. It can be found in the **Effects** tab under **Levels**. Drag it onto the clip, open the panel from the inside, and make the settings look like the image below.

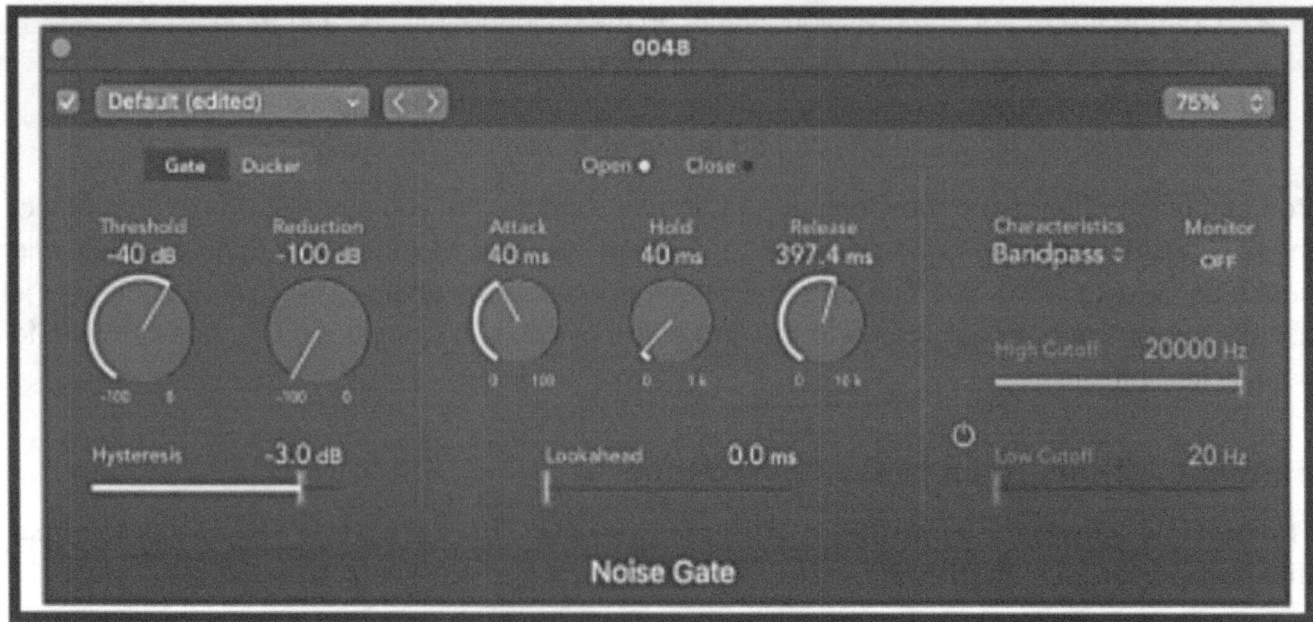

Removing high and low frequencies

Since the human voice doesn't have very high or low sounds, it is possible to take them out of **the audio. When you do this, things that aren't speech will be cut out. When editing movies with conversation, you can use this method:**

1. To get rid of high and low frequencies, add the **Channel EQ** filter to the clip and click the button that looks like a calculator to the right of the screen in the inspector.

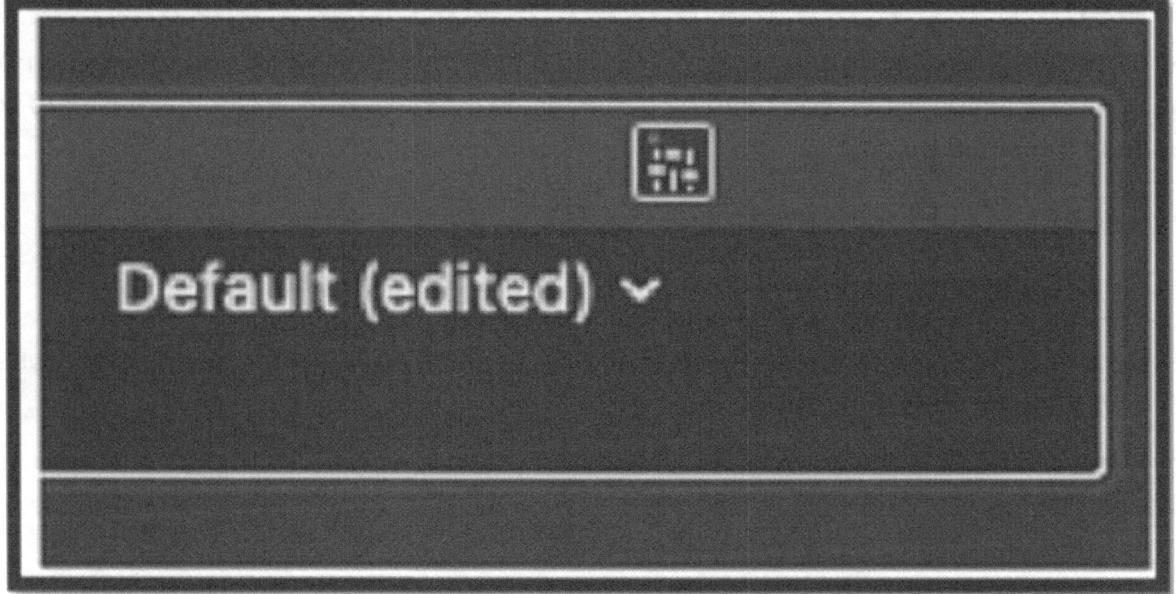

2. Open the **Channel EQ** window, which will show a straight line going through a range of frequencies. As shown below, click on the left side of this line and drag the low frequency to about **100**. Next, move the high frequencies to the right until they reach **5k**. You could also drag down on the center line to soften the sharp peak that can happen at about **1k**. This will get rid of any "**essing**" sounds that might be in voice records. The **DeEsser** filter can also be used to get rid of ess (S) sounds if you have a problem.

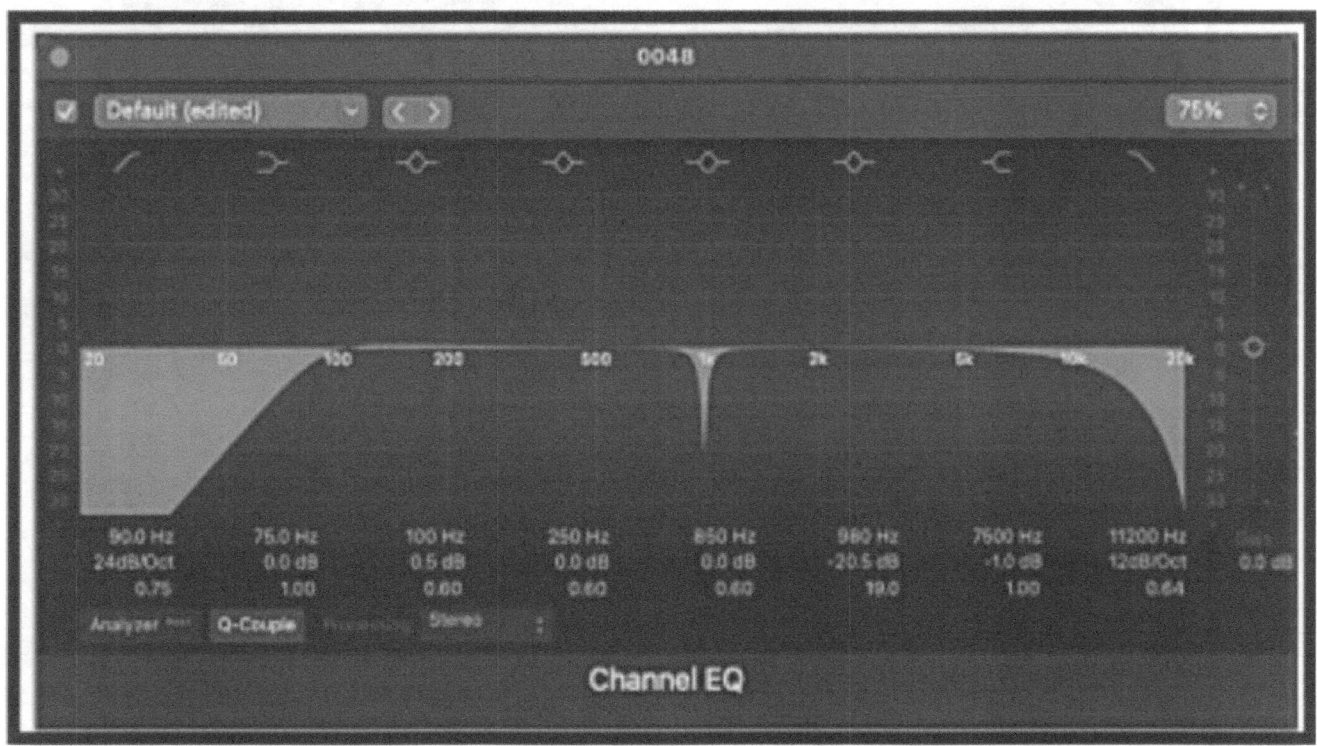

Sweetening male and female voices

Here, the object is to improve the male voice without improving the female. This is what I did with **Channel EQ**. Pick out the settings. Like before, drag **Channel EQ** onto the clip in the timeline. Then, hit the meter button to show the **Channel EQ** meters. The setting can be selected in **Channel EQ** in the inspector. Choose **05 Voice**, and you can pick from three versions for men and two versions for women.

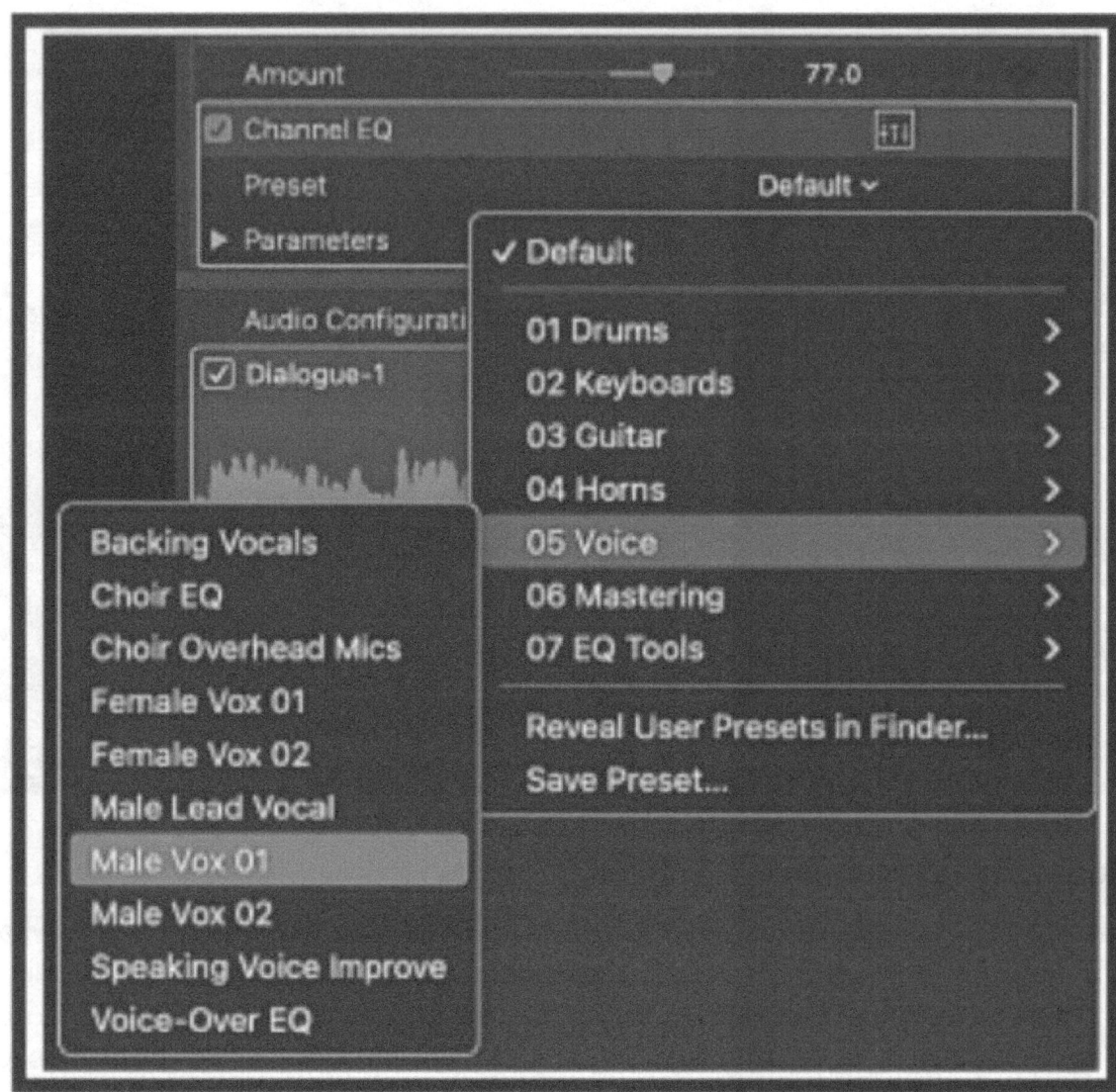

In the screen that comes up, you can change the preset to suit your needs.

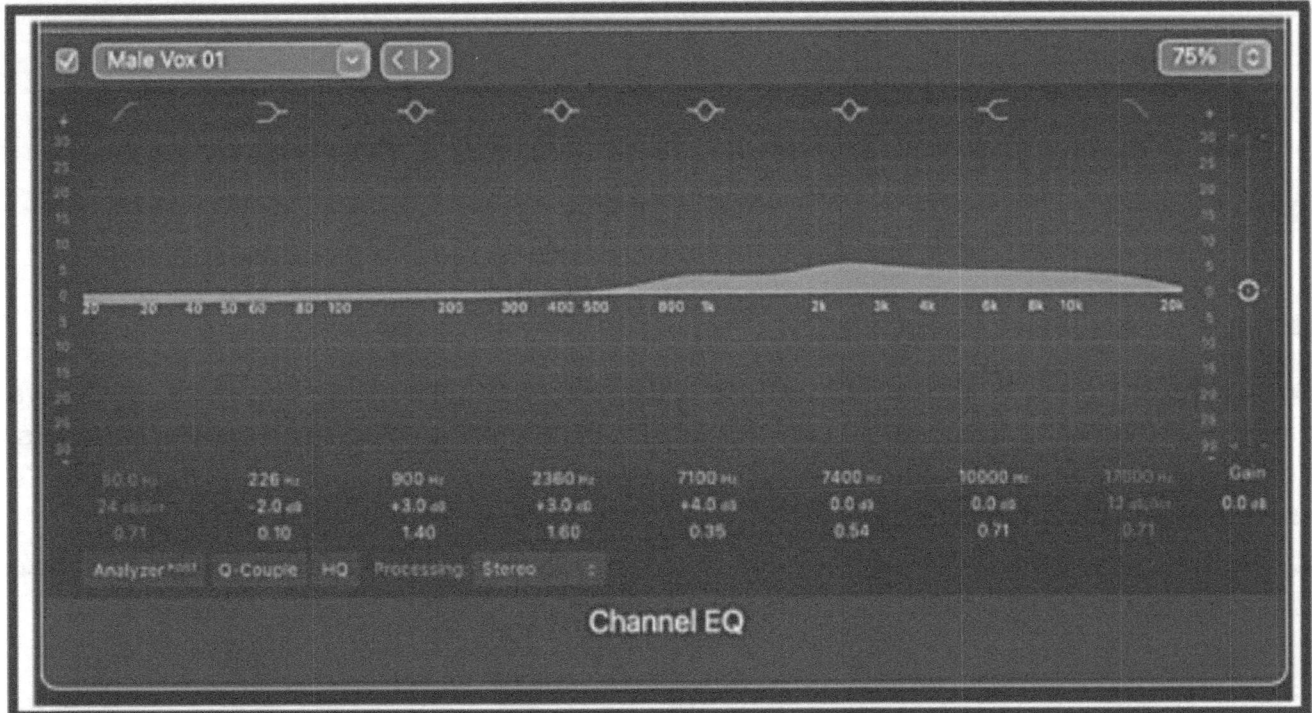

Reducing the music

You can lower the levels in a music track to make the voice stand out, just like we were able to improve the frequencies of human voices. The music will be played at frequencies that the voice **doesn't use. The Channel EQ procedures remains the same as before. The following image shows the new settings that can be used with the music track:**

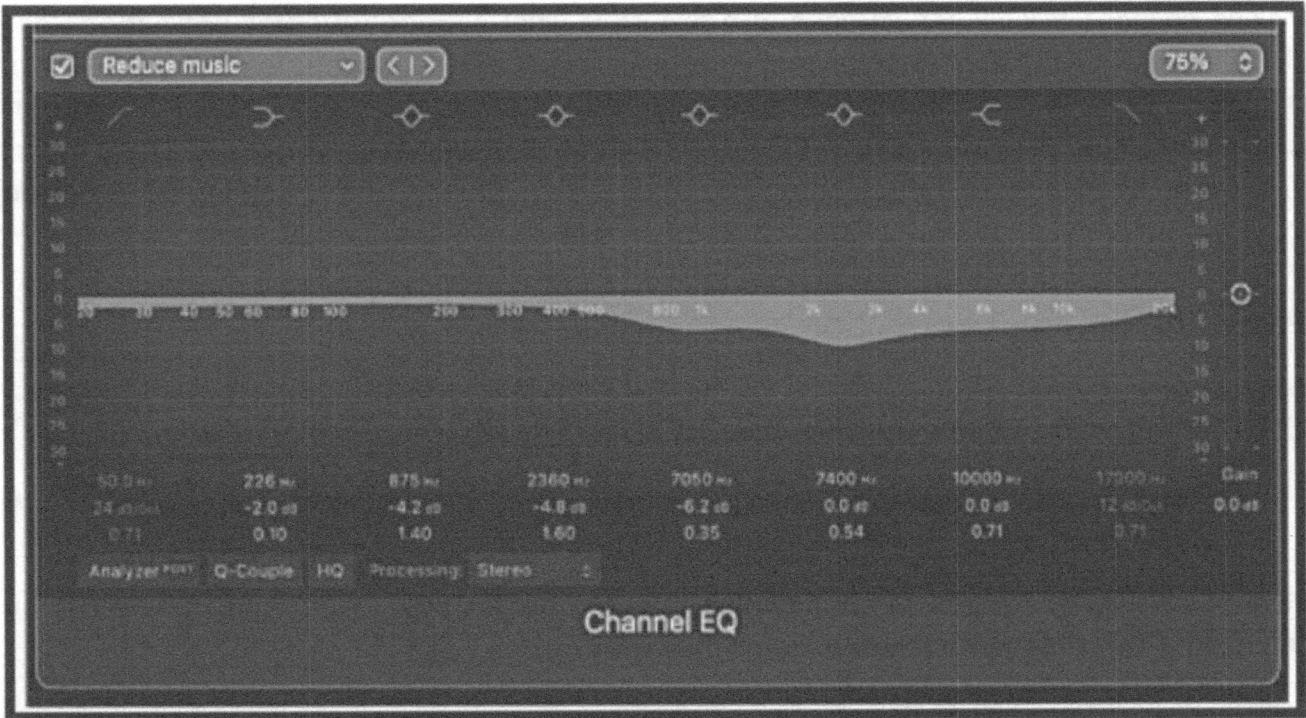

CHAPTER 13: FINE-TUNING WITH COLOR CORRECTION AND GRADING

UNDERSTANDING THE COLOR WORKFLOW

While there are various methods for color correction, the end goal is always the same: to improve the look of the image. Each shot should at least match and look like it belongs to the others. Your subjects shouldn't go back and forth between light and dark or yellow and orange; **it's annoying and not interesting.**

A lot of the time, **primary color correction** means getting the basics of brightness, saturation, and white balance right. You could begin by using an automatic change like **Balance Color** or **Match Color** to make the first few fixes. Then you could add a few human adjustments using the **Color Board, Color Wheels,** and/or **Color Adjustments** (new in 10.6.6).

Making changes to only certain parts of a picture is what **secondary color correction** is all about. One way to change the contrast is to make the highlights brighter on someone's face. Her way is to make the color of an object stronger or the edges of the frame darker. The **Color Curves** and **Hue/Saturation Curves** tools can also be used carefully. Masks are a built-in tool that can be used to make these kinds of changes. Let's make sure we're working correctly and that the right parts of the user interface are visible before we go any further.

Preparing for color correction

Several new interface panes will be useful during a color correction pass, and they can all be turned on or off with specific shortcut keys. For now, here are just two:

- **Video Scopes (command-7, also in the View menu in the Viewer)**
- **Inspector (command-4)**

Most of the interface panes can be found in the **Window > Show in Workspace menu.** You can choose which ones to show or hide on their own:

The **Event Viewer** option (**option-command-3**) opens a second Viewer window just for source clips from the browser, leaving the main Viewer window for the Timeline. You probably don't need this if you're new to editing, but if you're used to working with two viewers in other programs, you can use it while editing. We won't need it right now, though. If you've been following along, you probably won't be adding many new clips right now, so you don't need to see the Browser (**Ctrl-Command-1**) anymore. It's helpful that you can quickly switch to a new **workspace** that has everything you need set up, like this:

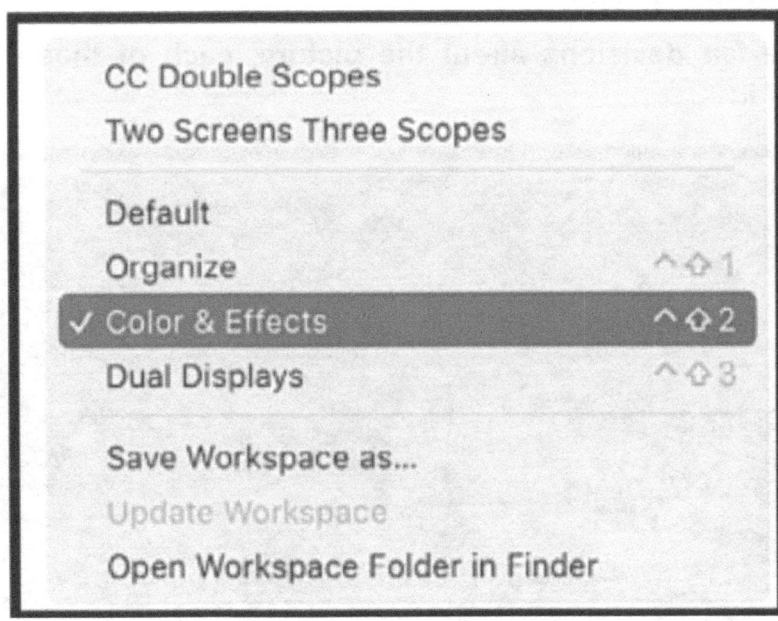

There are some useful defaults here, and you can change them whenever you move from one editing job to another. These are them:

- **Default**, which has the Browser, Timeline, and Inspector for everyday tasks
- **Color & Effects**—hide the browser and show the four-up Video Scopes and Effects
- **Organize**—hide the Timeline when you don't need it.

- **Dual Displays** -the same as **Default**, but the browser is on a second screen.

Once you've looked at a few of these, clear the screen to start color work:

- Click on **Window**, then **Workspaces**, then **Color & Effects**.

Understanding Video Scopes

To help you make fair decisions about the picture, each of these screens shows a different version of it:

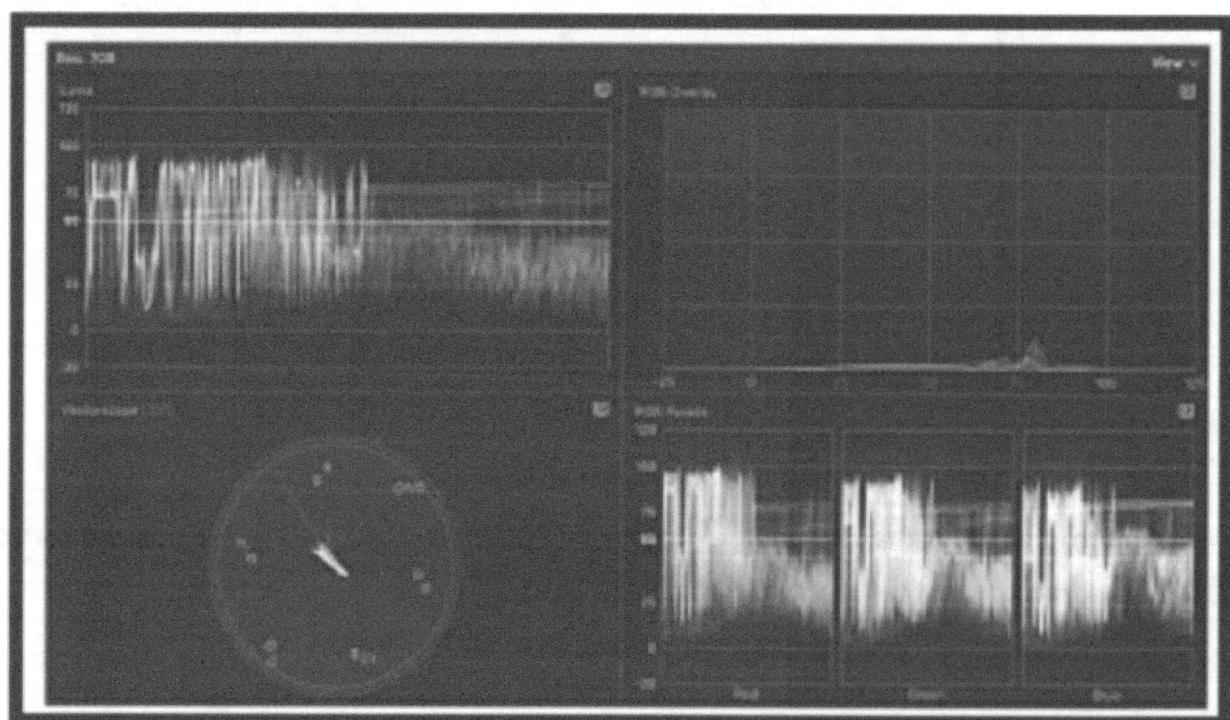

A quick look through a scope can tell you if a picture is too bright or too dark, if skin tones are close to being correct, and if the shot is mostly balanced. There is nothing in your immediate surroundings or how your screen is set that can change the truth of the scope. **Skimming** (S) should be turned on if it isn't already, and then you can quickly learn how scopes work by moving your mouse along your timeline and watching the scopes. The colored lines and dots that change as you move are the **traces**. They show the image's **Luma** (how bright it is) or some **other part of it. By default, the Color Workspace shows the following four Video Scopes:**

- **The histogram,** which is currently shown in the upper right corner with the **RGB Overlay** mode,
- **The vectorscope** is currently displayed in the bottom left corner.
- **The waveform** is currently displayed twice, once in the upper left corner with **Luma** (brightness) and once in the lower right corner as an **RGB Parade.**

A drop-down menu is shown by an icon in the upper-right part of each view. From this menu, you can pick which scope is open in that area and which stations it shows at the moment. There are different options for each type of scope. The **Waveform** scope has the most options, while the **Vectorscope** has the fewest. There is a **View** menu in the upper right area of the Video Scopes pane that lets you change the style of the views that are shown from one to four. You can change the brightness of the traces and switch between a horizontal layout (Video Scopes to the left of the Viewer) and a vertical layout (Video Scopes below the Viewer) from this same menu. Let's stick with the standard four-up view for now and look at each scope type. **You can see an illustration of the histogram in the image below:**

Photographers will know what a histogram is. On a horizontal scale, it shows how much of a picture there is at each number. This is called an area graph, and it's usually used to show color. On that scale, one or more channels are shown. These channels can be Luma, Red, Green, or Blue, or a mix of the last three drawn together (RGB Overlay) or separately for RGB Parade. The scale starts at **IRE**, which stands for "Institute of Radio Engineers." It's kind of like a percentage scale. Luma says that O IRE is black and 100 IRE is white. If a line is higher on the left than the right, there are more dark spots on the Luma or RGB overlay screens. If there is a peak close to 50 IRE, a large part of the picture is in the midtones, which are rooms with middle tones. On the RGB Overlay and RGB Parade screens, the lines should be in the same place in the R, G, and B channels if a part of the picture is supposed to be neutral gray. On the other hand, the histogram only shows the numbers; it doesn't show you where the data is in the picture.

The waveform, on the other hand, does, as you can see:

For most tasks, the waveform is better because it shows you where in the picture the data is. In the viewer, the waveform shows the picture from left to right and shows the brightness (or another channel) of the image vertically. The histogram might say "most of the image is dark," but the waveform can show you exactly which parts of the image are dark or light, as well as the skin tones in the middle or the sky's brighter blues.

This chart has more channels than the histogram. It has RGB Overlay, RGB Parade, Red, Green, Blue, Luma, Chroma, and sometimes Y'CbCr Parade, which looks like this:

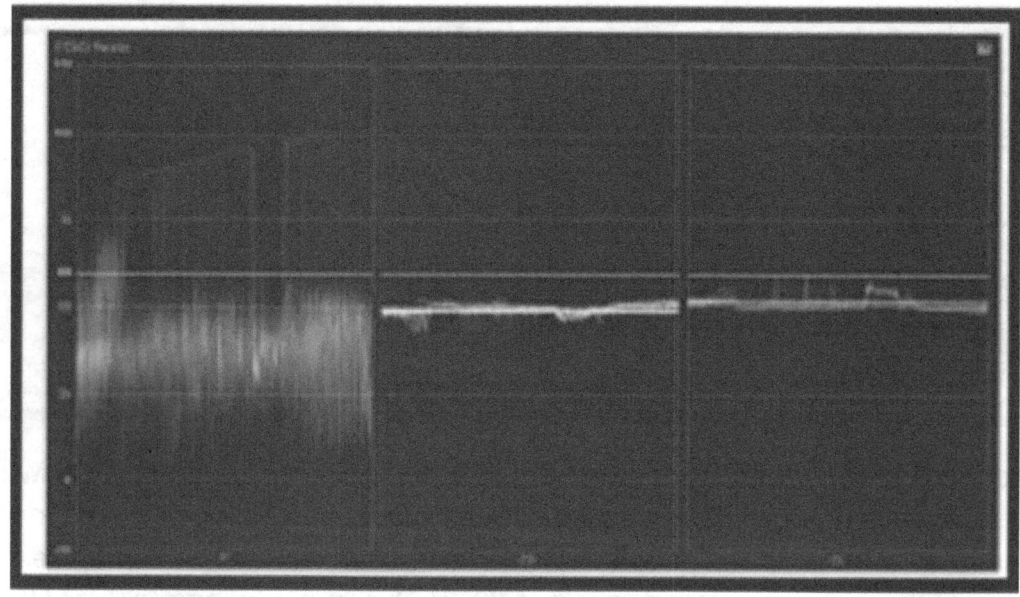

Most of the time, the Luma or RGB Overlay options are easier to read, but techs may find the Y'CbCr Parade useful. But most of the time, people who are interested in color and intensity would rather see that data in a circle than a vertical graph.

The Vectorscope can be seen in the following image:

You can judge color with the round vectorscope, but it doesn't show brightness. From the middle of the graph, the lines go out toward a color, which is shown by the shape of the circle and the six boxes that say Red, Magenta, Blue, Cyan, Green, and Yellow, going clockwise from the top. The lines are more saturated, or bright, the farther they are from the center. If you take a picture of a color chart like the one shown, you can fix it until you see spikes going straight toward each named box. Like the histogram, the image trails only show how much data is at a certain number and not where it is in the picture. This means that you may have to guess which spike is for a person's face and which is for the orange wall behind them. A picture with low brightness will have faint traces, and any dark areas should be right in the middle of the graph.

Understanding Wide Gamut and HDR

Rec. 709 is the normal color space that most projects today will use. It gives you a range of acceptable Luma values between O and 100 IRE. You can, however, use Rec. 2020, a bigger color space that lets you stretch your picture across a wider range of brightness values and colors. This might look better on newer, better screens, but earlier ones won't be able to show the extra color and brightness information. Also, you might need to send different copies of your projects for Rec. 709 and **Rec. 2020** standards, based on the conditions for delivery.

We will use the normal Rec. 709 color space for these examples, but here's what you need to do to try the newer Rec. 2020 space:

1. Go to the **Browser** and choose your **Library**.
2. Go to the **Inspector** and click the **Modify** button.
3. Go to **Wide Gamut HDR** and click on **Change**:

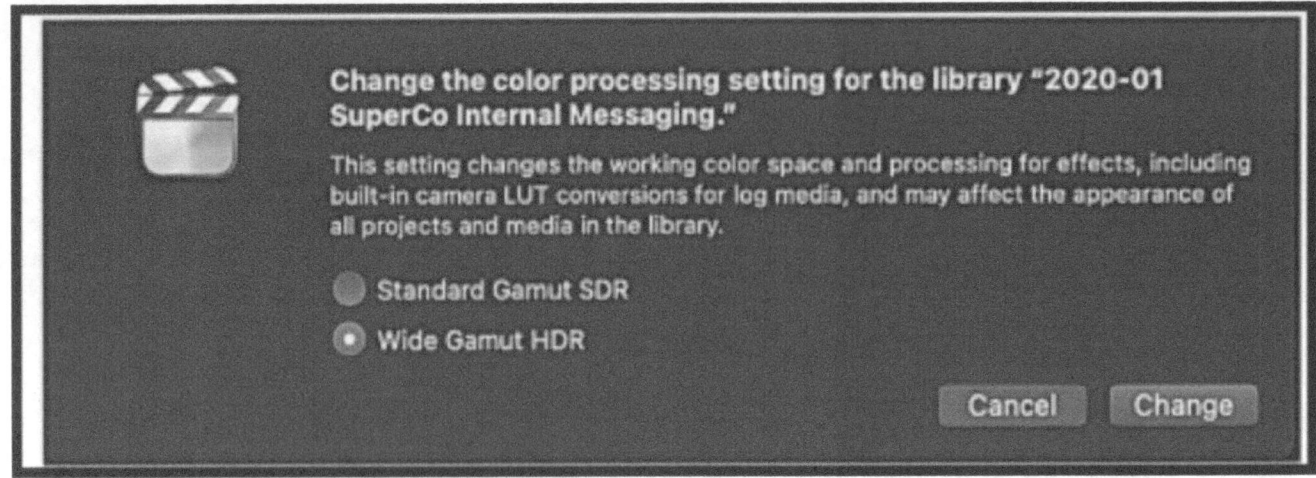

4. Pick a **project** that you want to change to Rec. 2020.
5. Go to the **Inspector** and click the **Modify** button.
6. Pick **Wide Gamut HOR – Rec ... 2020 PQ** from the **Color Space** box, then hit **OK**.

All of the **Wide Gamut** color space options have a bigger range of colors, and **HDR (High Dynamic Range)** options also have a bigger range of brightness values.

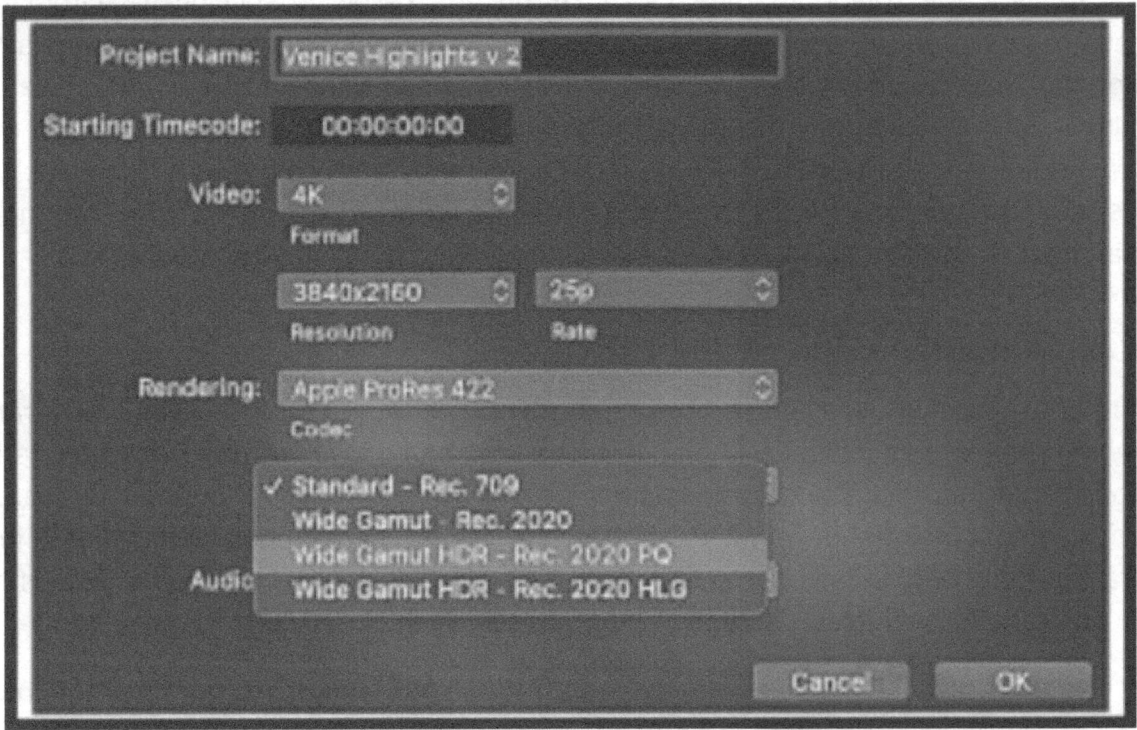

There are a lot of different ways to show a wider range of light levels in HDR standards, and this app supports two of them. There are two types of audio: **PQ (Perceptual Quantizer)** and **HLG (Hybrid Log Gamma)**. PQ is more common right now, but Dolby Vision on new iPhones is an example of HLG. If you choose to use **Wide Gamut HDR**, the brightness will no longer be limited to 100 IRE. Instead, it can go much higher based on the standard you pick. The tools we talk about here for fixing colors will also work a little differently.

Understanding timeline selection subtleties

The Skimmer is great for quickly looking over clips, but there are a few small things you should know to keep things clear:

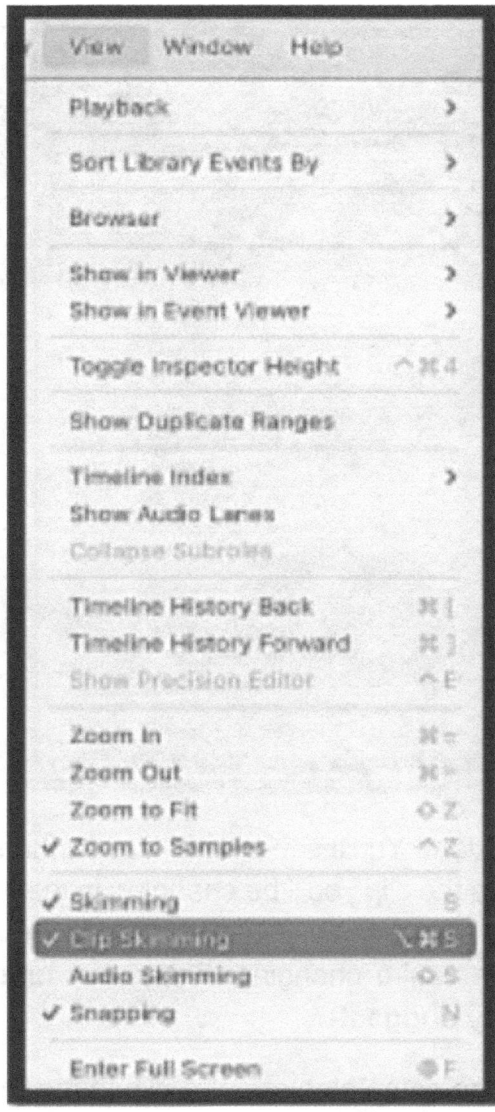

In the **View** menu, there is an option called **Clip Skimming** that changes what you see as you skim. This is the first thing you should know about it. That way, it shows the exact clip that the mouse is on instead of the clip at the top of the timeline stack. This works fine most of the time, but you can turn it off if you'd rather always see the final combined picture. If you want to see the final picture, you can always skip over the clips in the timeline. Also, the Skimmer is great for looking around but not so great for making changes. You'll have to click to place the Playhead if you want to make any changes in the inspector since it goes away when the mouse leaves the Timeline:

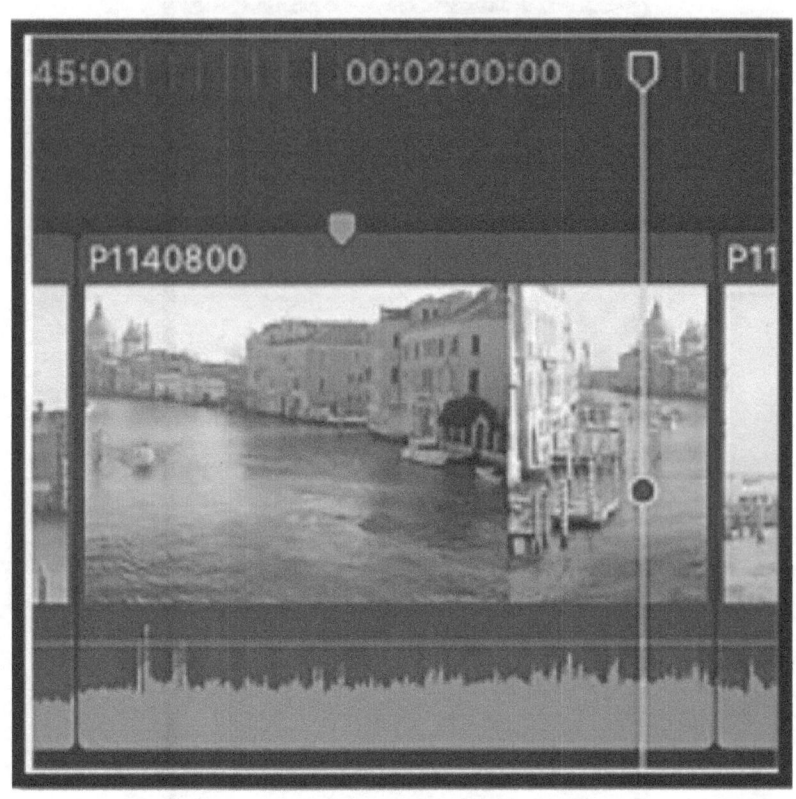

Third, selections are very important. You'll see a small dot on the top clip below the Playhead if you don't select any clips. That's the clip you'll be changing in the inspector. If you only have one layer in your timeline, this works fine, but if you add more layers, you'll need to choose a clip specifically to show which one you're changing. **But don't just click on a clip to pick it! Instead, here's what I strongly suggest:**

- When you want to change something about a clip in the Inspector, always **option-click** on it.

Why is this important? The Playhead stays where it is when you click on a clip to pick it, so you could be looking at a different clip while you make changes to the chosen clip in the Inspector! **Let me give you an example**:

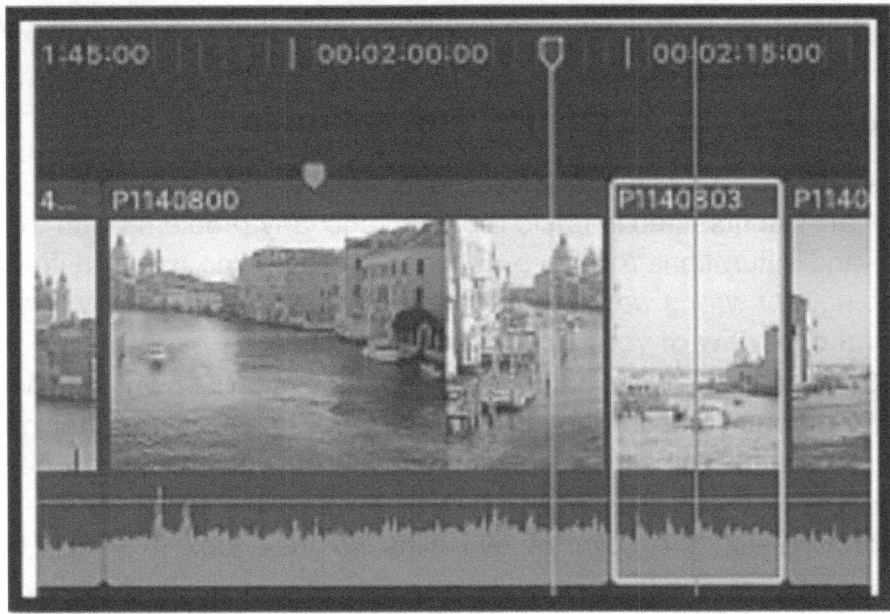

You seldom want to work on a clip that you're not seeing, so keep these things in mind:

- **Always option-click the clip to move the playhead and pick out the clip.**

If you like to use the keyboard a lot, these shortcut keys will help:

- **C** usually chooses the main storyline clip under Playhead or Skimmer. If the Skimmer isn't there and no clip is chosen, a linked clip under the Playhead may be chosen instead.
- **Command-** picks out the clip above the current one.
- **Command-.** picks out the clip below the current one.
- When you press **Command-**, the previous clip in the same role is chosen.
- **Command-** picks the next clip that plays the same role.

You can quickly switch between clips without using the mouse if you press these keys. Finally, if you want to fix B-roll and A-roll clips separately, a rately, it might be easier if you gave B-roll clips a unique role and then used a timeline to quickly go through all the clips you've used.

Correcting white balance, exposure, and saturation

- The next step before you can get artistic is to make your footage look normal. This part is all about that. The first step in basic repair is to fix any problems with the white balance, exposure, and saturation. You have options. Appropriating this in different ways is fine; there is no right or wrong way. **For each clip in your timeline, however, the following is a general overview of your options:**
- **Balance Color** to fix the white balance and brightness on its own. This works sometimes, but the fully automatic option doesn't always work because it eit her goes too far or is fooled by the picture. You can reverse it manually, but you can't turn it down; it's either on or off.
- **Match Color**: Match the color of two clips so they look like they belong together. Otherwise, it's not very useful. This canwork well when two shots have a lot in common.
- **Color Board**: A color board that lets you change the exposure, saturation, and color of different parts of a picture, like the highlights, shadows, midtones, or the whole thing. There is a lot of control, and the process is quick, but it has to be done manually.
- **Color Wheels**: Color wheels that let you change the color, exposure, and saturation of different parts of a picture, as well as the tint, hue, and temperature of the whole image. There are a few small changes between this and the color board, but it does pretty much the same thing.
- **Color Adjustments** (new in 10.6.6): Use a set of knobs instead of pucks or wheels to change the brightness, color, contrast, and tint in certain dark and highlighted areas. This correction works best for people who want surgical controls or who are switching from camera apps that use this kind of correction a lot.

You should use all of these fixes while the video scopes are turned on so you can see what's going on.

Using Balance Color and Match Color

These automatic options are found in the second menu of three to the lower left of the Viewer/Video Scopes area:

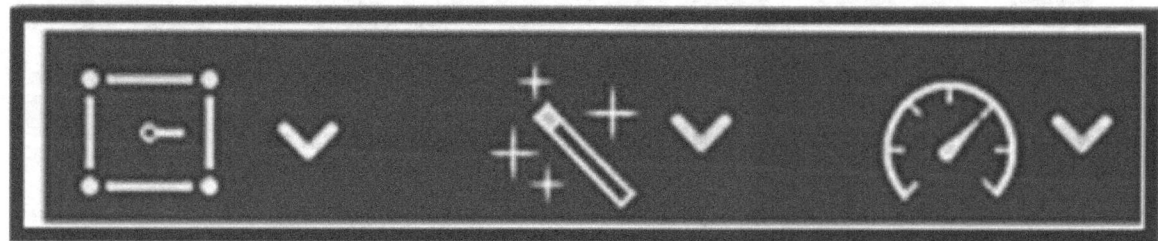

The small magic wand-shaped button for this menu is called Enhancements. To use Balance Color:

1. **Option-click** on a clip to pick it, then move the Playhead to that spot.
2. Press **option-command-B** or choose **Balance Color**. Here's an example of "before" and "after":

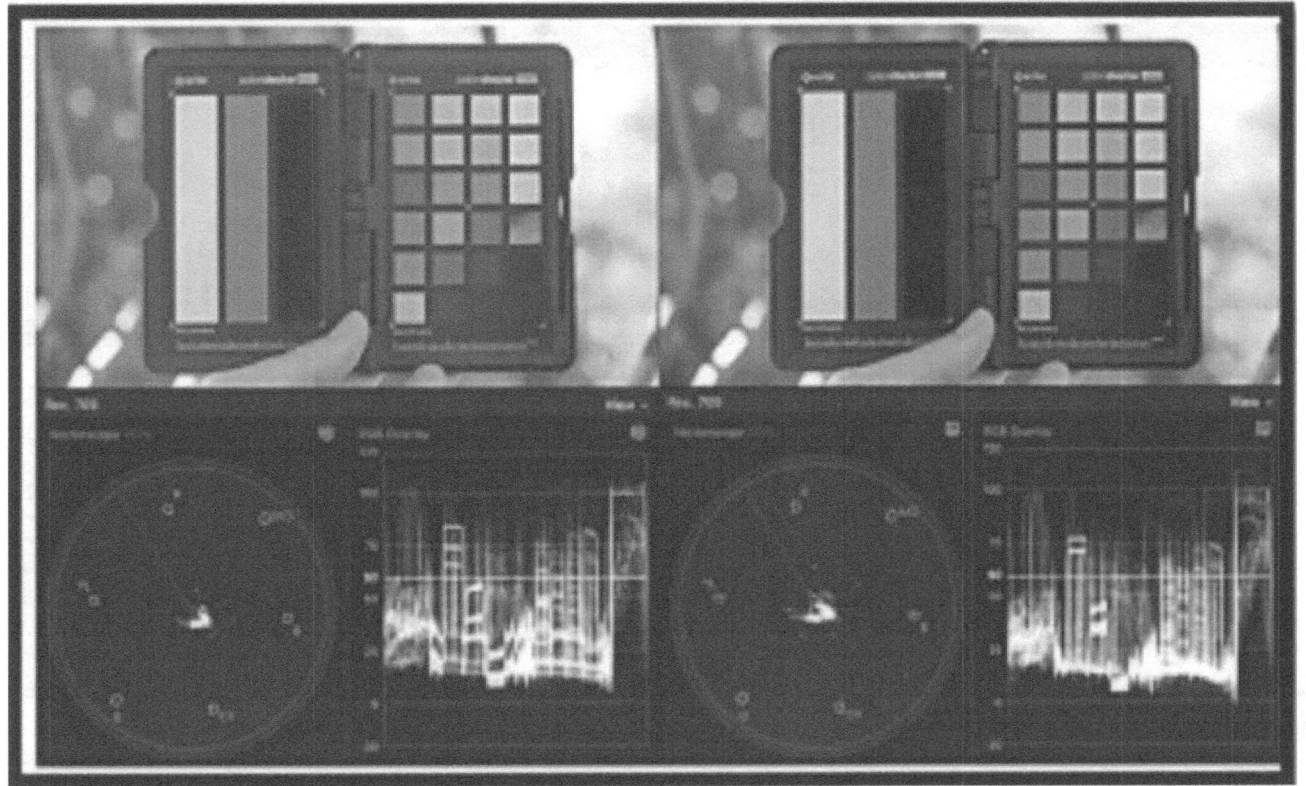

If the Color color process goes wrong, you'll need something gray in the shot to fix it. Any gray will do, but white or black that is too bright or too dark won't work. The procedure is as follows:

1. Go to the **Inspector** and click on the first tab, which says "**Video**."

Most of the tools for correcting colors are in the second tab, called **Color**. However, these first automatic changes can only be found in the **Video** tab.

2. Click on **Method** and switch it from **Automatic** to **White Balance.**

In the Inspector, a small blue-eyedropper icon will become active. In the viewer, a live guide and an eyedropper that moves with the mouse will show up.

3. Click (or drag) over the dark or almost white part of the picture in the **Viewer**.

If the picture had an orange, green, or yellow tint, it should now be gone. The area you click or drag will shift to a neutral gray color. You should also try **Match Color**, which looks like this:

1. **Option-click** on a clip to pick it, then move the Playhead to that spot.
2. To do this, press **option-command-M** or choose **Match Color.**
3. In the timeline, click on a frame in a different clip that has colors you want to copy.

If you don't want to create a strong colored effect, this clip should have the same content as the one you want to change. You'll see these things:

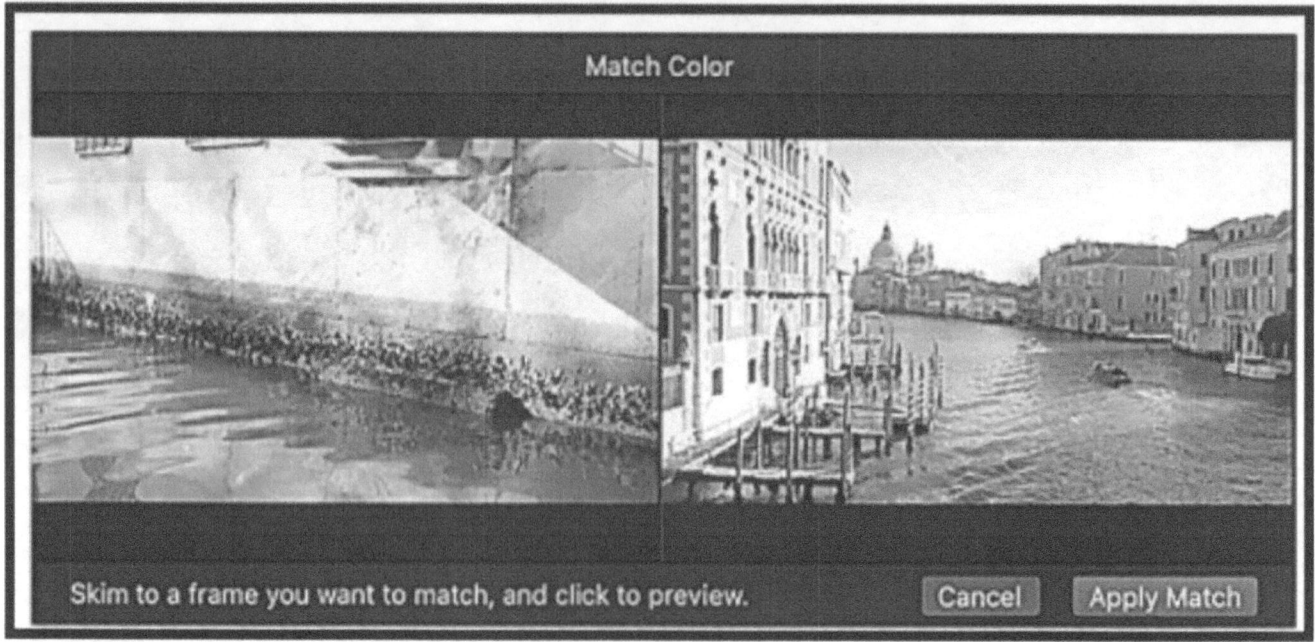

4. Click again, this time on a different frame in the same clip or a different clip altogether.

Keep in mind that you can use Browser clips as a color source, but not when the Browser is closed.

5. To accept the change, click the **Apply Match** button in the bottom-right corner of the **Viewer**, or press **Cancel** if you don't like the results.

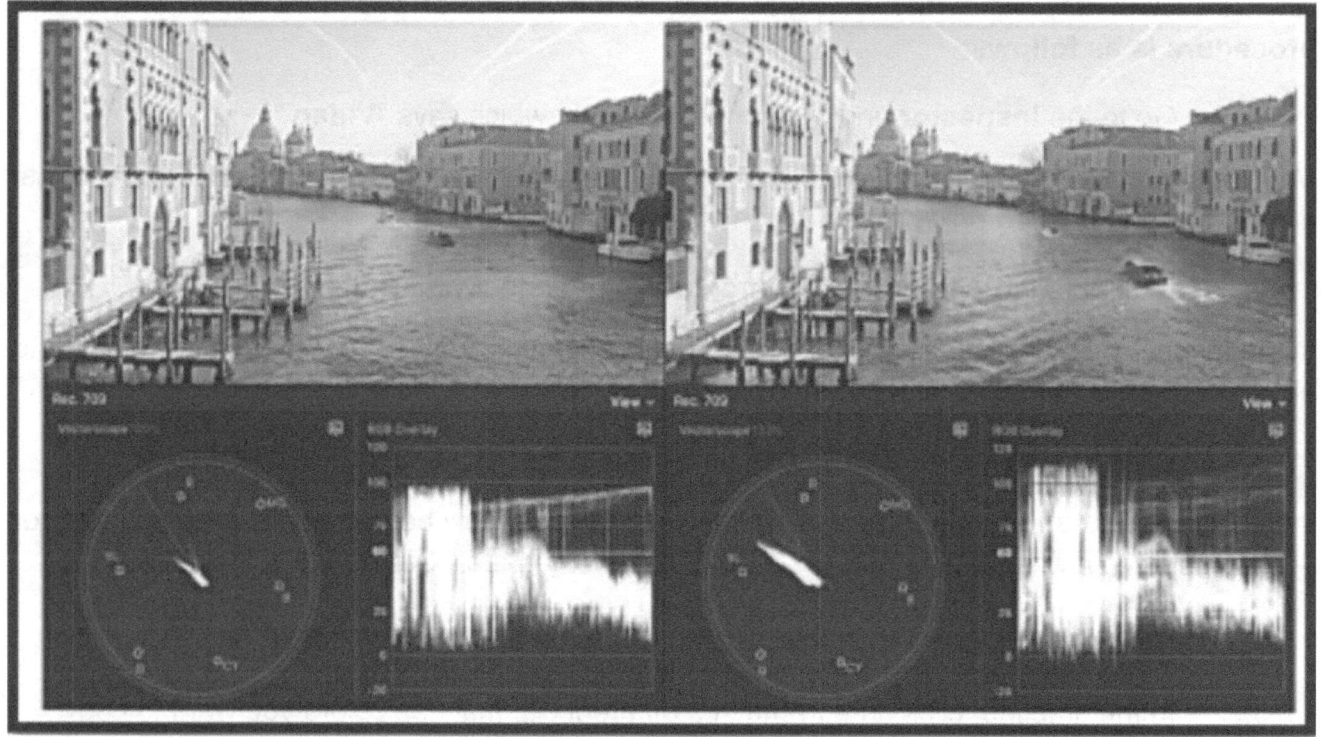

Adjusting Exposure with the Color Board

Most cameras automatically correct images to keep them in the "normal" range, but you'll often want to make them a little brighter or darker. **Before you start, make sure that the color board**

is set as your default:

1. In **Final Cut Pro**, go to **Preferences/Settings** and then **General**.
2. Pick **Color Board** from the **Color Correction** menu:

Most likely, you'll like Color Board or Color Wheels better as your default correction, so let's start easy. When you want to make a change to a clip, you'll follow these steps:

1. **Option-click** on a clip to pick it, then move the Playhead to that spot.
2. Press **command-6** to correct the colors of this clip and make them look better.

The **Color** tab is now open in the Inspector. There isn't a color board added to the clip until one of these settings is changed. What do you think you're seeing? Along the top of the screen are three tabs: **Color, Saturation, and Exposure**. You'll usually work your way from right to left, going down each tab. To start, click on **Exposure**. The four pucks can be moved up and down to change the brightness or darkness of the picture. The four places are:

- **Master**: the whole picture
- **Shadows**: Change the image's darkest parts and keep the brightest parts the same.
- **Midtones**: To change the midtones, lock the highlights and shadows and change the middle parts of the picture.

- **Highlights**: Change the image's lighter parts while keeping the darkest parts.

If your screen is big enough, you'll see the same information below the pucks in the form of numbers:

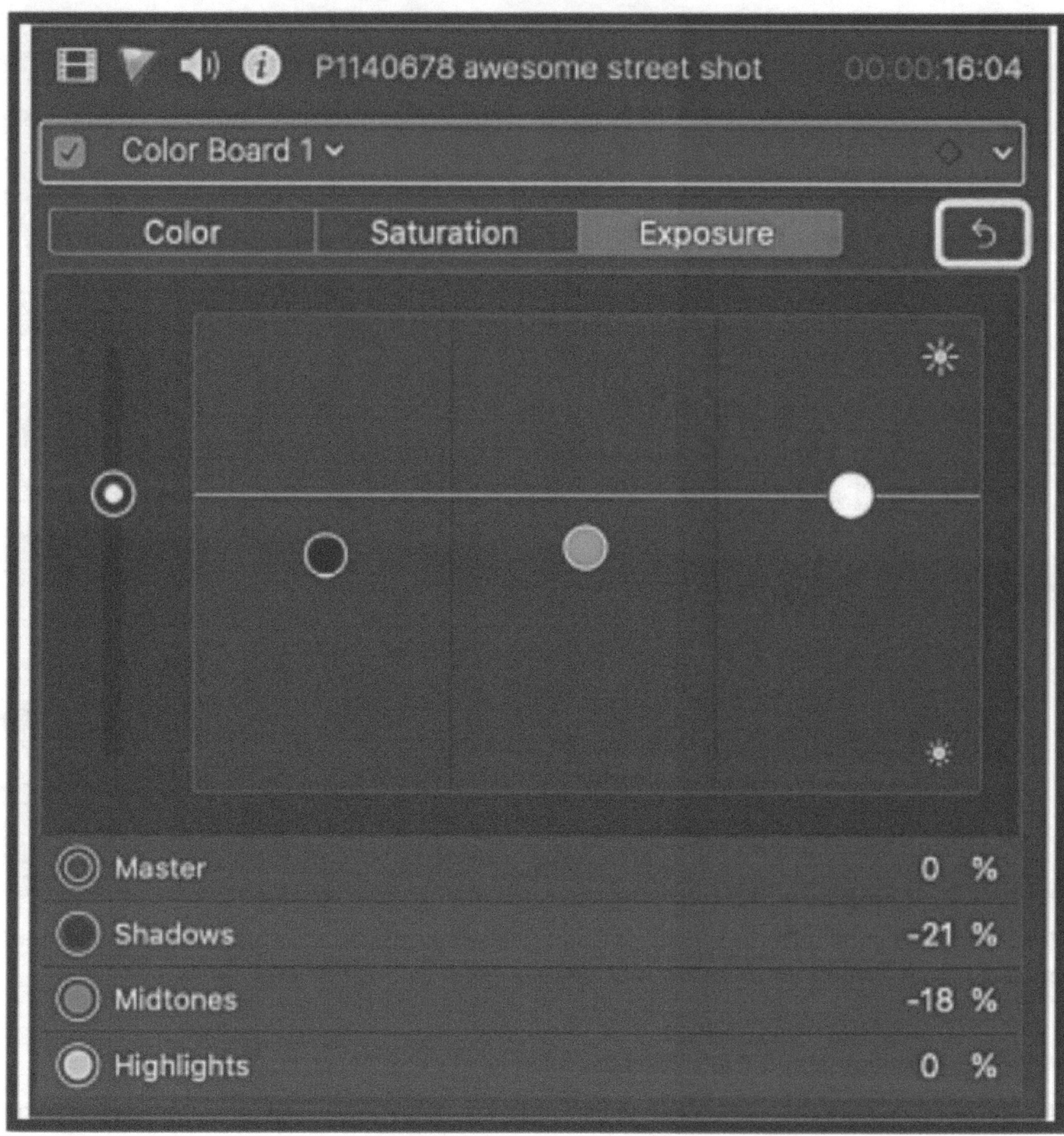

You can change the numbers by dragging them up and down or left and right. If you do this, you can hold down the **option** key to change them faster or the **shift key** to change them more slowly. Also, there is a **hooked arrow** in the upper right corner (shown in bold) that, when clicked, will erase all settings. If you make a mistake, click on it.

Adjusting Saturation with the Color Board

Next, you may need to change the saturation:

1. At the top of the **Color Board**, click on the **Saturation** tab.
2. Move the **Midtones** tool up (or down) until it looks good.
3. If you want, you can move the **Shadows** scale up (or maybe down) until it looks good.

Adjusting white balance with the color board

After you've fixed the exposure and slightly changed the saturation, you should fix any white balance problems that are still there. You'll almost certainly need to fix a yellow, green, blue, or orange tint at some point, no matter how careful the person operating the camera is. Most videos can be changed in some way, but high-quality recording types let you change things in more extreme ways. Because you have more freedom, fixing the color is a little harder than the other changes. **To begin:**

1. Go to the top of the **Color Board** and click on the **Color** tab.

There will be four pucks in front of you. You can move them horizontally to pick a color and vertically to change how strong the movement is. When you move the puck away from blue and toward red, you're doing the same thing. You can skip over the bottom half of the board for now if you want to.

2. Move the **Highlights** puck up and down to move the picture toward or away from a certain color. Move it up and down, like this:

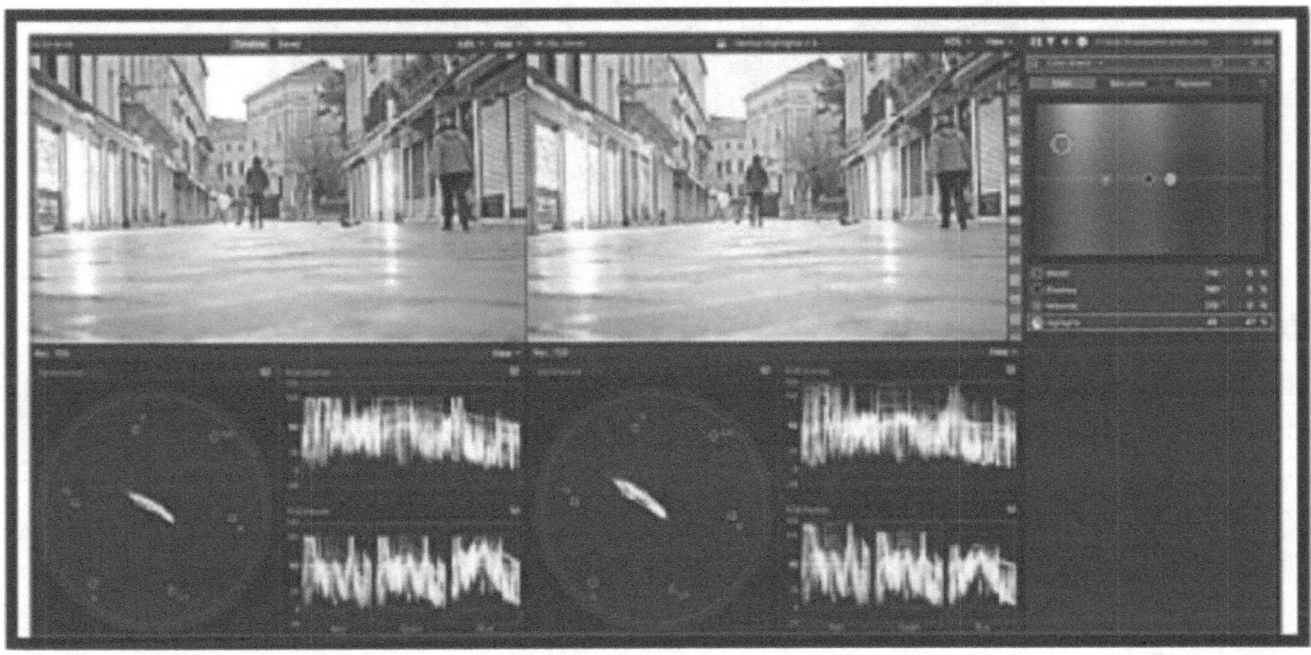

3. For extra control, you can also move the **Midtones** puck up or down to move the picture toward or away from a certain color.

Using color wheels

You can use the color wheels instead of the color board or both of them at the same time. Color Wheels use the same principles and techniques as the Color Board, but there are a few extra **settings that are useful and some small changes as well. Let's start with some steps you already know**:

1. **Option-click** on a clip that hasn't been fixed to pick it and move the Playhead to that spot.
2. Press **command-6** to fix the colors of this clip and make them look better.

That will show the Board for now, but we can change that. There is a message that says "**No Corrections**" at the top of the color board. If you made any changes now, it would show **Color Board 1**. It will be changed to something else.

3. Click on **No Corrections** and pick **+Color Wheels** from the list, as shown:

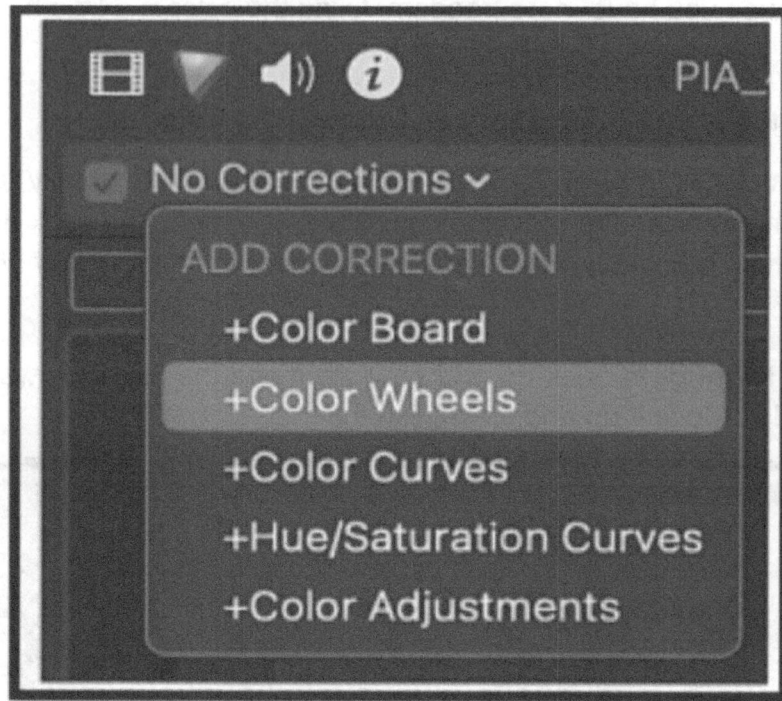

Using Color Adjustments

This is new in 10.6.6 and also available in FCP for iPad. It works like the settings at the top of some photography apps' color correction screens and is very helpful. To begin:

1. **Option-click** on a clip that hasn't been fixed to pick it and move the Playhead to that spot.
2. Press **command-6** to fix the colors of this clip and make them look better.
3. Click on "**No Corrections**" and pick "**+Color Adjustments**" from the list that comes up.

Color curves

- Select "**No Corrections**" and pick "**+Color Curves**" from the drop-down menu:

The picture hasn't changed yet because, like all fixes, it starts blank.

- **To make a new point, click on the white line and pull it up. The picture will get brighter, as shown:**

- **Click on the point you just made and drag it down to make the picture darker:**

- Click on a different part of the line to make a second point. Now move both of them up, down, left, and right to see what happens.

Using the eyedropper to sample the image

For some tasks, it's helpful to mark a point on the curve that fits a place in the picture. This could help you remember which parts of the picture should stay the same color and which parts should change.

The procedure is as follows:

1. Click the eyedropper in the upper right corner of the Luma curve in the **Inspector** to turn it on (blue).
2. Use the eyedropper to click on a part of the picture in the **Viewer**, like this:

Now, the Luma number you clicked on will become a new point on the curve. You can click more than once if you want to.

3. To be sure, click the eyedropper to the top right of the Luma curve in the **Inspector** to turn it off (white).

By moving the new point up, the light will get brighter, and by moving it down, the darkness will grow. If you move it to the left or right, the point will point to a different source of light.

Using the color channel curves

When you use the **Red**, **Green**, or **Blue** curves, you can fix a big problem or give the picture a strong "look." These work like **Luma** curves, but they only change a small part of the picture. It would make the picture greener instead of brighter if you chose green. Blue would have its highlights become bluer and its shadows become more yellow instead of rising in contrast with an S-curve. You can use color contrast to get that look, and an S-curve on the Red channel will give you a "trendy vintage" look right away that's good for social media. **Look at this:**

1. In the **Inspector**, click the eyedropper icon to the upper right of the **Red** curve to turn it on (blue).
2. Click on a part of the picture that isn't red in the **Viewer** to see this:

The color you just clicked on will now show up on the red curve. It could be orange, pink, aqua, or even sea foam. To be thorough, let me say it again:

1. To turn that curve off (white), click the eyedropper to the top right of it in the **Inspector**.
2. To change the color even more, click on the curve's new name. This will bring up a small color choice in the shape of a cir-cle. Turn the circle to choose a different color.

Yes, you can use this color choice instead of the eyedropper right away if you want to:

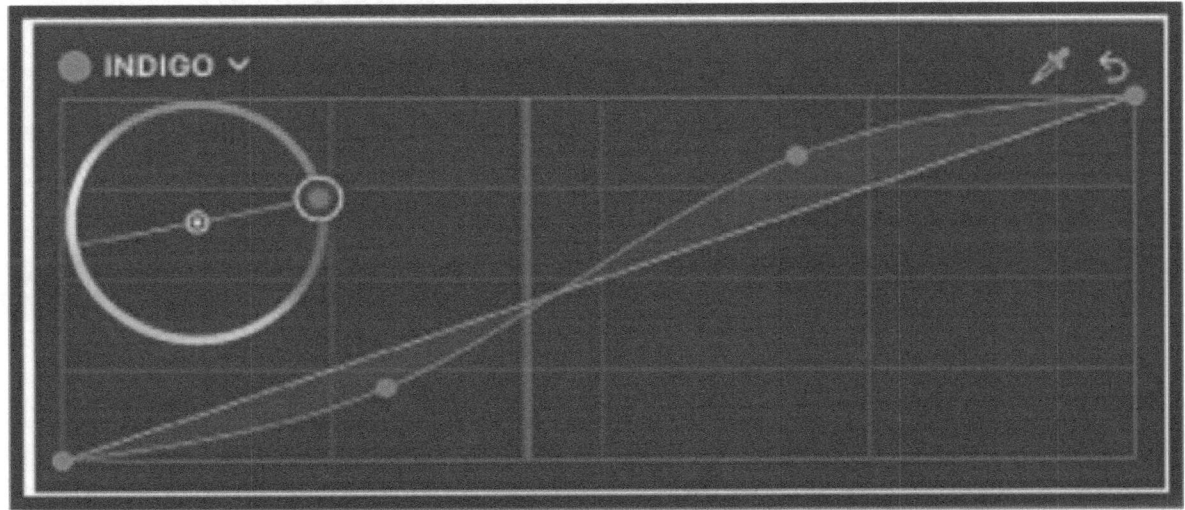

Now you can change only that one color in the picture. You can weaken it by dragging it down, make it stronger by dragging it up, or make the colors around that color stand out more. To "make all orange things dark," this doesn't work. Instead, it "makes things less orange," which is a weird idea. It's possible to switch from "correction" to "grading" this quickly, but it's still something you should try.

Using a color mask to restrict a correction

Any kind of color correction can have masks added to it, as well as any other video effect. Move your pointer over the middle of the title bar to see this.

The following steps will limit the effect of a simple Color Board ins tance. However, the samemethod could be used to limit the effect of a blur, a glitch effect, or extra noise:

1. **Option-click** on a clip to pick it, then move the Playhead to that spot.
2. Press **command-6** to fix the colors of this clip and make them look better.
3. Use the **Master color** puck to make a simple but clear change: move the whole picture toward orange.

Any change will do; just make it clear.

4. Hover your mouse over the color correction's title bar at the top of the **Color** pane, then click the small mask icon (a circle inside a rectangle) and select **Add Color Mask**, as shown in the image below.

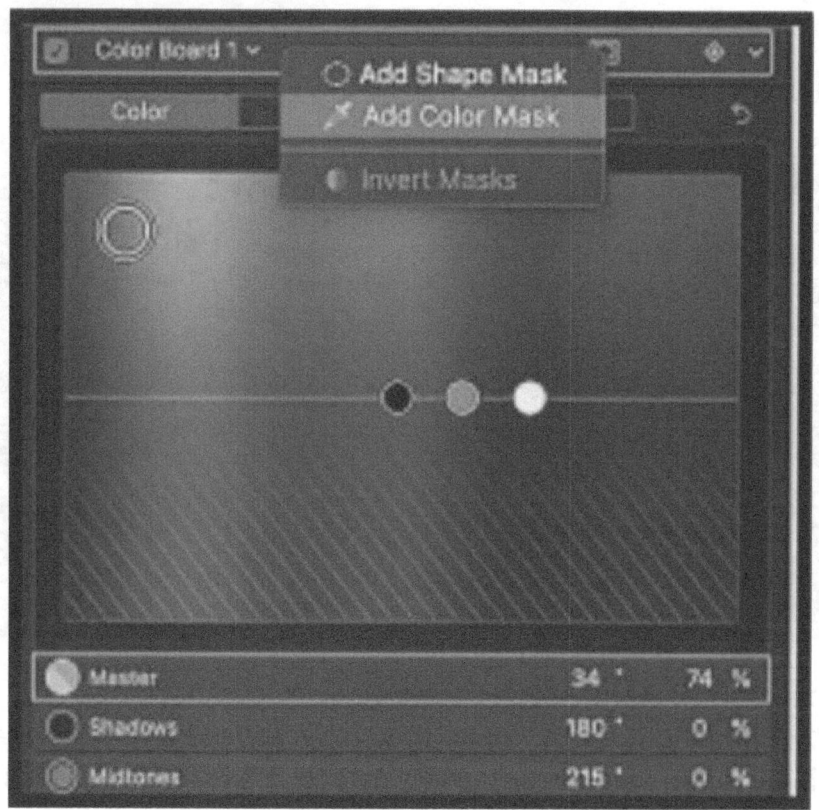

When the mouse moves over the Viewer, an eyedropper now appears.

5. Click and drag on the picture to set a range of colors that can be chosen:

The picture goes from full color to light gray when you start to drag, but as you keep dragging, more and more of it will return to its original color. This shows that the colors you chose have been added to the color mask. The "desaturation" goes away when you let go of the mouse, and you'll see the effects of your earlier changes in any place you selected. Any parts of your picture that are the same color as the ones you dragged will now be moved toward orange.

It's still not likely that the color mask is perfect. To change the Color Mask's color range, do the following:

- Hold down **Shift and drag** the picture to add more colors to the Color Mask.
- **Option-drag** in the picture to get rid of those colors from the Color Mask.
- **Drag** (while holding down any keys) to start the color selection process.

It can be hard to pick the exact right part of a picture with just the eyedropper since dragging the circle over a light area can select all the light areas in the frame:

Advanced color techniques

It's not hard to fix things, but you don't want to start over with every clip. You will learn a few different ways to copy a correction from one clip to another. You will also learn how to use effects presets to get started on correction and how to use a single change to fix whole scenes. Don't skip this, because it will save you a lot of time. Some of these tips are not all clear.

Copying and pasting color adjustments

A lot of clips probably need the same treatment if they were all shot at the same time and place. There are a few ways to make that happen.

Most people know how to copy and paste, and it works pretty well:

1. Apply several kinds of color correction to a clip.
2. Choose that clip, then press **command-C** to go to **Edit > Copy**.

This step copies the clip along with all of its video features, such as color corrections and effects.

3. Pick out a clip or clips that are similar, then press **options-command-V** to go to **Edit > Paste Effects** and add the color fix right away.

One bad thing about **Paste Effects** is that it copies everything onto the target clip(s). Sometimes you don't want to change the volume, the scale, and all the colors at the same time. The step after this is another option.

4. Choose a different clip or clips, then go to **Edit > Paste Attributes**. This will open a window where you can pick which fea-tures to paste:

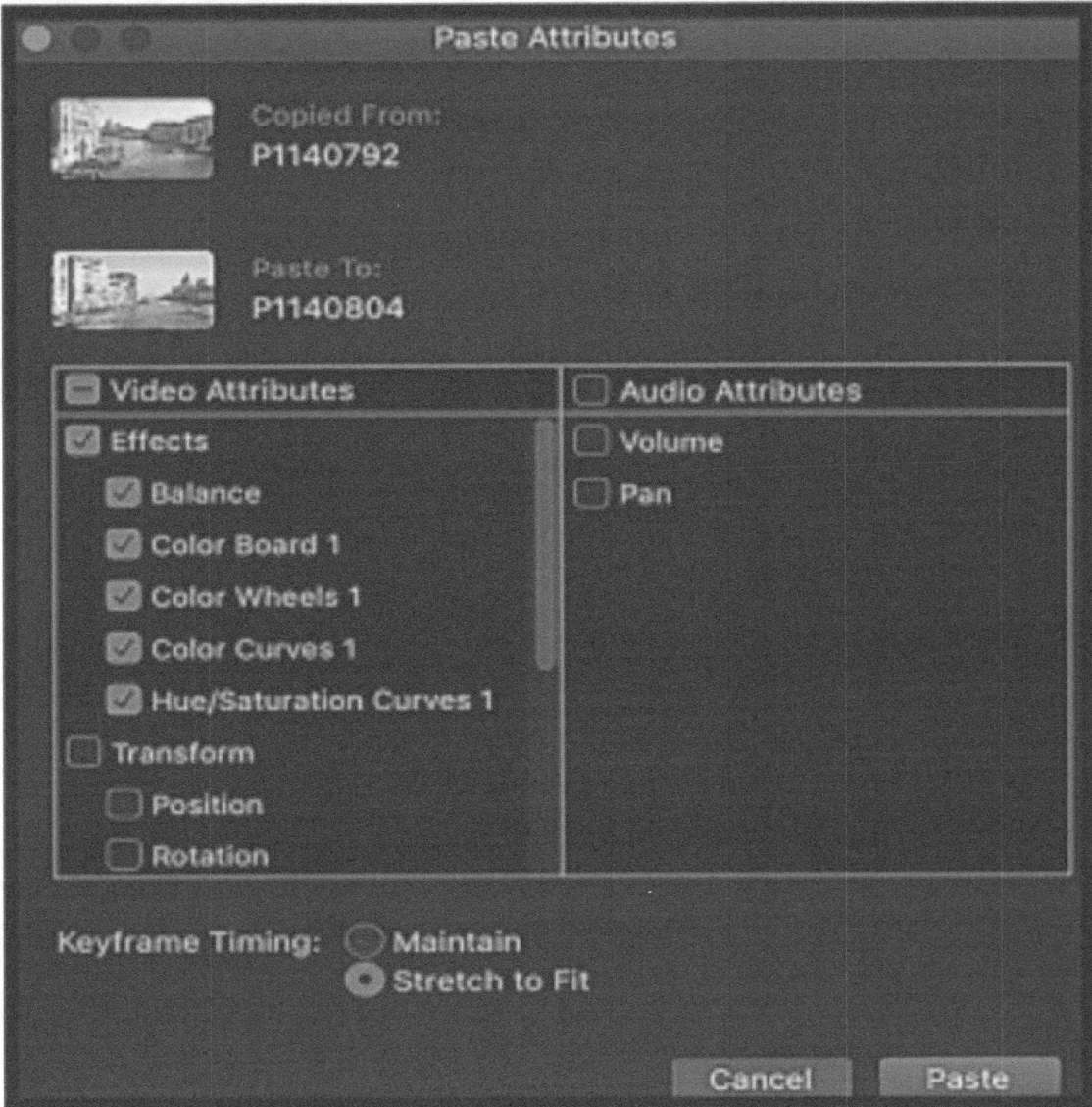

It takes a little longer, but this is much stronger. You can remove things you don't want to paste if you don't want to. To quickly clear out all the boxes, **option-click** on any box. This will clear out all the others as well. This can bedone in either the **Video** or **Audio** columns, so you might need to click a few times. While copying and pasting works, there is still a problem: if the target clip(s) already had any color correc-tions made, the new changes will be added on top of them. It's possible that's not what you want.

For starters, use one of these Edit menu options to get rid of any traits that are already there before you paste:

- **Remove Effects (option-command-X)** to remove all existing properties without asking
- **Remove Attributes (shift-command-X)** brings up a dialogt that lets you selectively remove existing properties.

You could then **Copy** from one clip, **remove effects**, and then **paste effects** back on the target. You will get to know these phrases pretty well because they can be used for more than just color. They can also be used for video and audio features and effects. When you want to fix the color of something, there is a secret trick: there are three hidden words that make it much easier than copying and pasting.

Applying color corrections from nearby clips

Once you're done making changes to your edited timeline, you'll want to use the same color corrections on other clips.

To do this in the best way possible, you'll you'll need to reveal some secret commands:

1. Start **Final Cut Pro** and go to **Commands > Customize**.
2. Look for **color** in the upper right corner.

Below the middle part, you'll see three actions that don't have any shortcuts and aren't in any menu:

- **Apply Color Correction from Previous Clip**
- **Apply Color Correction from Three Clips Back.**
- **Apply Color Correction from Two Clips Back.**

These statements are out of order because of the alphabetical sort (one, three, and two clips back), but they work like magic. It is a secretorders that copy all the fixes from an earlier clip in the timeline and then use those fixes to change any color fixes on the clip that is being chosen. There's no need to delete current fixes because they don't apply on top of them. They also don't change any other video or audio.

qualities or effects. Even better, "color corrections" in this case include all of the things we've looked at so far, such as balance color, match color, and any manual changes you make in the Color tab. This is all you have to do:

3. Put these three orders on three computer keys that aren't being used.
- At the top, pick the modifier keys you want to use, if there are any. Then, drag the commands to keys that aren't being used.
- Pick the command you want to link to the shortcut, and then press the keys on your computer in that order.

I use these enough on an extended keyboard that Iput them on **F17**, **F18**, and **F19**. On a smaller keyboard, I like **shift-7, shift-8, and shift-9**.

These are both of the options:

Apply Color Correction from Previous Clip	F19
Apply Color Correction from Previous Clip	⇧ 9
Apply Color Correction from Three Clips Back	F17
Apply Color Correction from Three Clips Back	⇧ 7
Apply Color Correction from Two Clips Back	F18
Apply Color Correction from Two Clips Back	⇧ 8

4. When you're done, **save** and **close**.

CHAPTER 14: ADJUSTING VIDEO PROPERTIES AND EFFECTS

Adjusting video properties

Your video's features will let you zoom in on or crop a certain part of the frame, make a clip smaller for a picture-in-picture effect, or make one clip interact visually with the clips below it. It's useful to be able to change the way a clip looks in this way, and these settings are easy to use.

- If you want to be sure you're seeing the clip you're editing, **option-click** it first.

Here's the other great rule:

- To change values in the Inspector, you should always dragon the numbers.

Most of these features have sliders or other tools next to the numbers. However, sliders only work in a certain range, while the numbers can often go beyond that range. Now let me show you how to use these numbers:

- To change the numbers, click on them and drag them left and right or up and down.
- Hold down the **shift key** while moving to change numbers faster and make big changes.
- Hold down the **option key** while moving to change numbers more slowly and get better control.

If you simply click rather than dragging, you can:

- Type a new number directly, hitting **return** to complete your entry.
- Use the and keys to change the current value.

There are also on-screen settings for the three most important parts of this page, which can be useful sometimes. As we work from top to bottom, make sure you have a timeline with clips to play with and at least a few clips that are linked at the top.

Compositing

You can choose how a clip is shown to you and how much of it you can see in this area. The easiest thing to understand and change is the opacity slider.

5. One way to pick a linked clip is to **option-click** on it above other clips. This will move the playhead to that place.
6. To change the **Opacity** number, drag it.

The top clip will fade away as the number goes down, showing the clip(s) below it. With regular video, this creates an artistic effect, but when used as a stamp, it's much more useful.

Blend Mode, on the other hand, is both stranger and more useful. It's in the menu just above Opacity. Different blend styles change the method for how to mix clips above and below. To try it out, you should move to a different connected clip.

These are the different blend modes:

- **Normal**: The clip will be shown as normal. You can't see through the clip if opacity is set to 100%.
- **Subtract/Darken/Multiply/Color Burn/Linear Burn**: These use the top clip to make any clips darker. As a "natural-looking-ing" dimming setting, **Multiply** is very useful. All of these take away the bright parts of a clip:

- **Add/Lighten/Screen/ColorDodge/Linear Dodge**: These are all modes that make things lighter, which is the opposite of what was just said about modes that made things darker. **Screen** makes things brighter in a way that looks "natural." All of these will get rid of the darker parts of a clip. Cover the camera on your iPhone, start recording, and then record the screen at the same time. You could then put the screen recording on top of another shot to hide the black.

- **Overlay/Soft Light/Hard Light/Vivid Ligh/Linear Light/Pin Light/Hard Mix** All of these modes mix the first two groups, but you'll need to try them out with different clips. **Overlay** is the simplest to understand because it's a mix of **Screen** on the highlights and **Multiply** on the shadows.

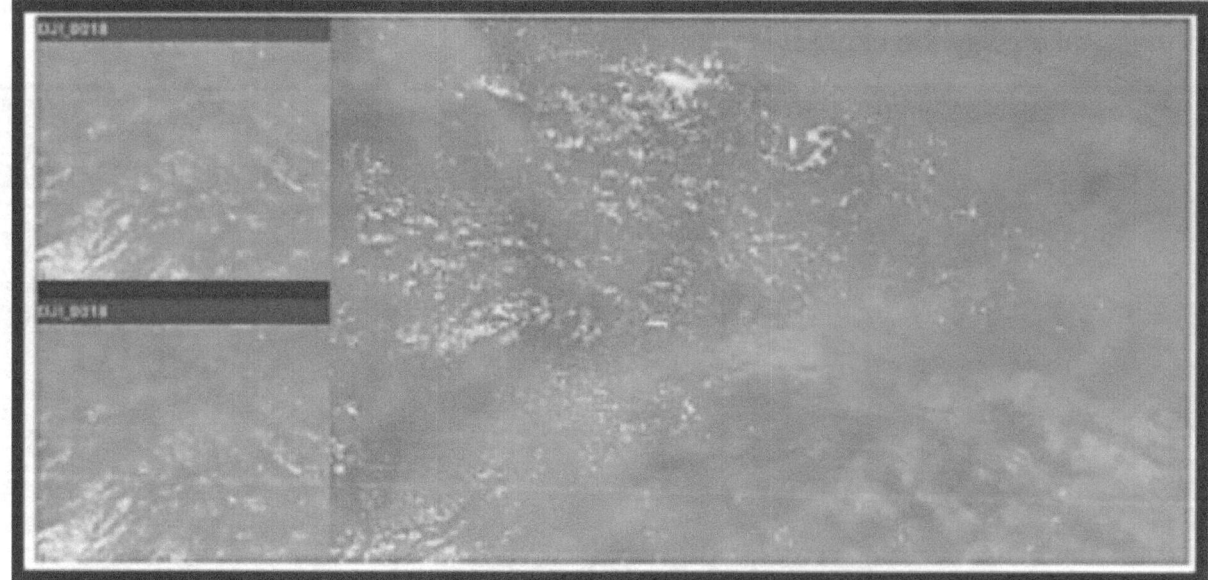

- **Difference/Exclusion**: These are two "opposite" modes that try to get rid of places that are the same color. They work bet-ter for expert tasks than for general editing.

- **Stencil Alpha/Stencil Luma/Silhouette Alpha/Silhouette Luma/Behind**: You can use the Stencil Alpha, Stencil Luma, Silhouette Alpha, Silhouette Luma, and Behind **masking** effects to show (**Stencil**) or hide (**Silhouette**) parts of a clip below based on the brightness (**Luma**) or transparency (**Alpha**) of the clip on top. **Behind** is very sneaky because it moves the clip at the top to the background. This lets you use some unique methods.

- **Alpha Add/Premultiplied Mix**: These let you change information about transparency (alpha). If you're not masking or keying something cool, you probably won't need these.

You can get the most out of Stencil Alpha mode if you want to replace an image with video. Since "alpha" means "transparency," you can use Stencil Alpha to play video inside the logo if your top clip is a clear PNG or another clip with a background that is s completely sethrough. You can play videos outside of the image with Normal, but Silhouette Alpha will hide the parts that aren't visible if you need to. If there isn't any transparency, use Silhouette Luma or Stencil Luma to show lower clips in the darker parts or lighter areas.

But these blend modes cut through all layers, not just the one below the media. How do you put video inside a brand and put it on top of another clip?

To separate the look of a Silhouette or Stencil blend mode, do the following:

1. Pick the top clip and set it to **Stencil Alpha** (or Luma). Do the same for any other clips you want to change.

Do not pick any background clips.

2. Make a new compound clip by going to **File > New > Compound Clip (option-G)** and giving it a name.

Now that the compound clip is there, the stencil mode is contained. Any clips below the name in the timeline will now show up in the space around it:

When blending problems are complicated, compounds can help. But when the problems are simple, like the one shown here, the Behind Blend mode can be used instead. **Instead, we can do the following with the same three clips from the last Stencil Luma example:**

1. Click on the **Position** tool (P).
2. Put the clip in the background at the very top.
3. Change the mode of this top clip to "**Behind**":

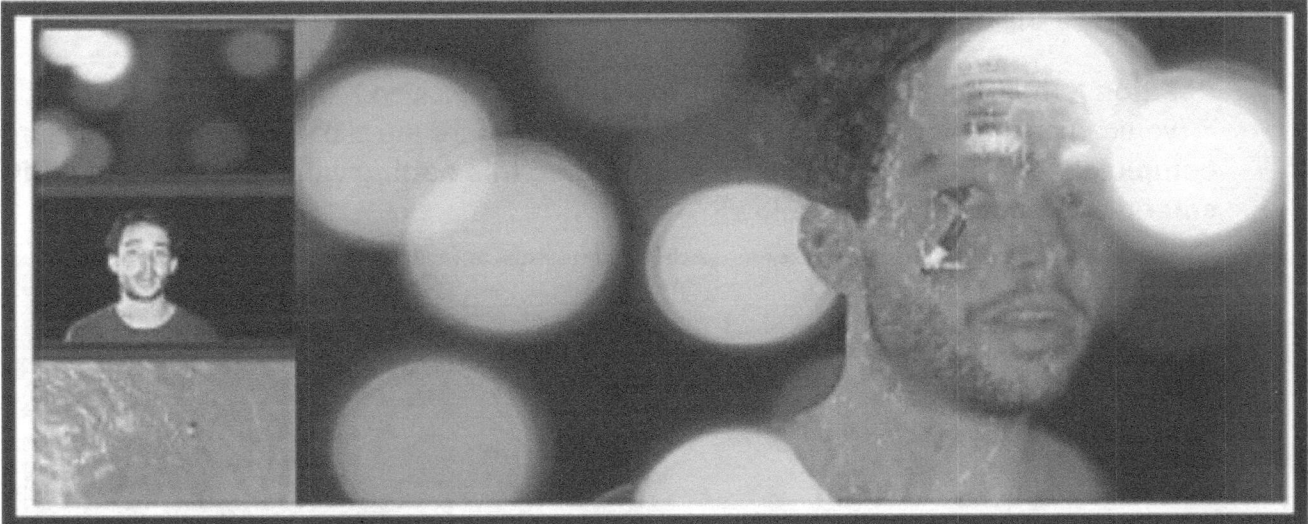

Transform

Change any clip's size, position, and movement in this important part of the inspector. It's simple, but it's useful. When the aspect ratio of both your source clips and project is the same, it's easy. For now, stick with 16:9 widescreen. You'll soon learn that things are a little different when the two aspect ratios aren't the same.

When you use the transform tools, you can:

- **Make a picture-in-picture**: To make a picture-in-picture, shrink and move a clip that is linked to it.

- **Correct a tilted horizon**: Any clip can be rotated and made bigger.
- **Reframe a shot**: Make the sh ot bigger and move it around to change the way it's framed. (Take note that Crop also offers a way to accomplish this.)
- **Punch in for emphasis or disguise a jump cut**: Raise the scale after editing a jump cut.

The Viewer has on-screen tools that you can use to make these changes. The Inspector has sliders, wheels, or (best of all) numbers that you can change. If you can't see the Inspector settings, move your mouse over the word "**Show**" to the right of "Transform" and click it:

The following are the inspector properties:

- **Position X** (horizontal) and **Y** (vertical): In the Viewer, Position X (horizontal) and Position Y (vertical) change the number of pixels that show where the clip's picture is. If a picture **completely covers the screen at first, changing this setting will push some of it off-screen and show any clips below:**

- **Rotation**: This tilts the picture to a certain degree. If you don't make the scale bigger than the frame, you'll get blank spots on the sides.
- **Scale (All):** This changes the frame size so that edges can be hidden or punched in after the previous settings do so. You can get a new shot by scaling up, but don't go too far. It's like using a zoom lens. If you shoot in 1080p and send in 1080p, going over 120% can

produce visible softness because interpolation is required to make up for the missing pixels. People like to shoot in 4K for 1080p delivery because you can zoom in up to 200% before you run out of real pixels. Don't use **Scale X** or **Scale Y** unless you want to make the picture bigger, which you probably don't.

- **Anchor (X and Y):** These change the point around which scaling and turning occur. They're useful for some animation tasks, but not often used for other things.

Clicking on a white icon in two places on the screen will bring up the transform controls:

- In the **Inspector**, to the right of the word "**Transform**."
- Below the **viewer** in the upper left corner, next to a menu that lets you get to on-screen settings for **Transform, Crop,** and **Distort,** If the **Transform** icon is at the top, you can click it to use its on-screen settings. If it's not, you'll need to pick **Transform** from the menu next to it:

If the on-screen tools are turned on, you can move the clip by moving anywhere in the Viewer frame or on the center point. Rotation can be changed by dragging the small handle on the center point, and scale can be changed by dragging any of the corner handles. To keep the image's center in place, keep in mind that the other corner handle will move at the same time. If you hold down the **option key** while you drag, only the corner you drag will move. Also, the edge handles can only change **Scale X** or **Scale Y**, which makes the picture stretch. If you hold down the **option key,** the measurements will be locked in.

Crop

The on-screen controls here are more important, unlike the transform tools. If you want to see the viewer first, click the crop on-screen control button. Then you can use the inspector to switch between the options.

The three crop options are at the bottom of this screen:

- **Trim**: This cuts away part of the frame's edge. It can be used to turn a rectangle into a square for picture-in-picture reactions or to show part of a clip underneath.
- **Crop**: An option to scale, this is a faster way to punch in and let you pick exactly which part of the picture to show.
- **Ken Burns**: This is a visual way to pan or zoom across a frame.

We'll use thet ools on tools on the screen to look atthese in these in more depth. Keep in mind that as you drag these controls you drag these controls, they will only change one side or corner. If you hold down the **option key**, your changes will be balanced be and affect the other side or corner as well. **Trim** gives you easy tools to get rid of pixels from the top, left, right, or bottom edges. I don't use this very often because I think mask effects are faster and give better results, but Trim is simple to understand:

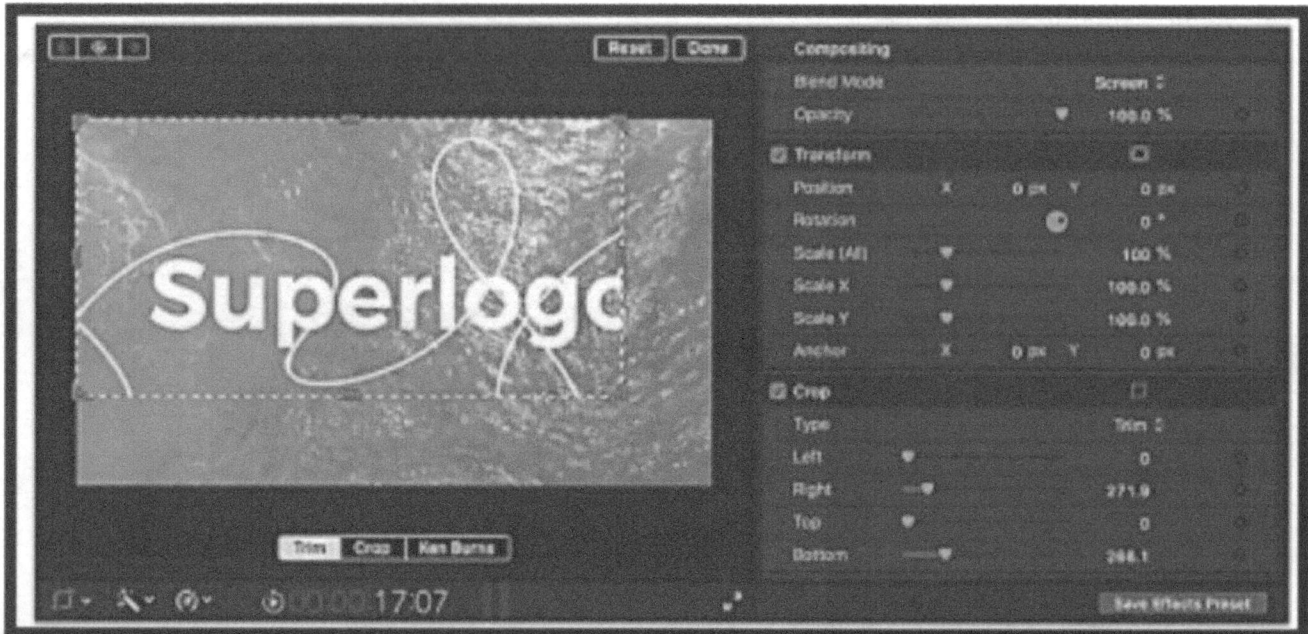

When you're done, click **"Done."**. Here, the aspect ratio will stay the same as the canvas's. This makes it easy to find the best frame for any shot, even ones that are oddly shaped like social media posts or square or vertical. **Ken Burns**, which is named after the signature effect of the documentary director, does an animation automatically between two sets of Start and End crop **boxes. Click on either box to change its size and position, and try a few different settings:**

- A zoom can be produced by putting one box inside the other.
- A tilt is produced by placing one box on top of the other.
- A pan can be produced by placing one box next to the other.
- You can put these together, like putting a smaller box to the lower right of a bigger box.

The button in the upper left corner makes it easy to move the current Start and End boxes around. The button to the right shows a sample of the current effect.

Cinematic Mode

This tool was added to FCP 10.6 and can only be seen when working with shots taken on an iPhone 13 or later in **Cinematic Mode**. You'll also need macOS Ventura or later on your Mac if you have an iPhone running iOS 16 or later. This mode makes fake blur, also called "bokeh," which is usually made by a camera with a small depth of field and a lens with a fast aperture. The iPhone's camera is small, so the picture has a shallow depth of field and is in focus. However, Cinematic Mode can identify items in the frame and add computational noise while the video is being played. If you have an iPhone 13 (or later), you can use the **Import** tool to bring these shots straight into FCP. If you use AirDrop, though, make sure you tap **Options** at the top of the share page and then pick **All Photos Data** from the next page. Each movie has its own folder, which includes sidecar files with depth data. To load a normal movie, you can just drag it into the folder. Don't worry aboutthe pre-rendered movie whose name starts with "**E**." It has already been handled, so you can't change how blurry it is.

Once you have a cinematic clip chosen on the timeline, try these steps to get started:

1. You can use the menu in the lower-left corner of the viewer or click the button to the right of the word "**Cinematic**" to turn on thee on-screen **cinematic** control.
2. If you need to, check the **Cinematic** box in the **Inspector**.
3. To see the Cinematic Editor, right-click on the clip in the timeline and select **Show Cinematic Editor.**

A new area will appear above the clip in the timeline. It will be titled "**Cinematic**." This area has white Automatic Focus Points that show where the camera focused while it was recording and yellow Manual Focus Points that show where you chose to fix after recording on your iPhone or Mac.

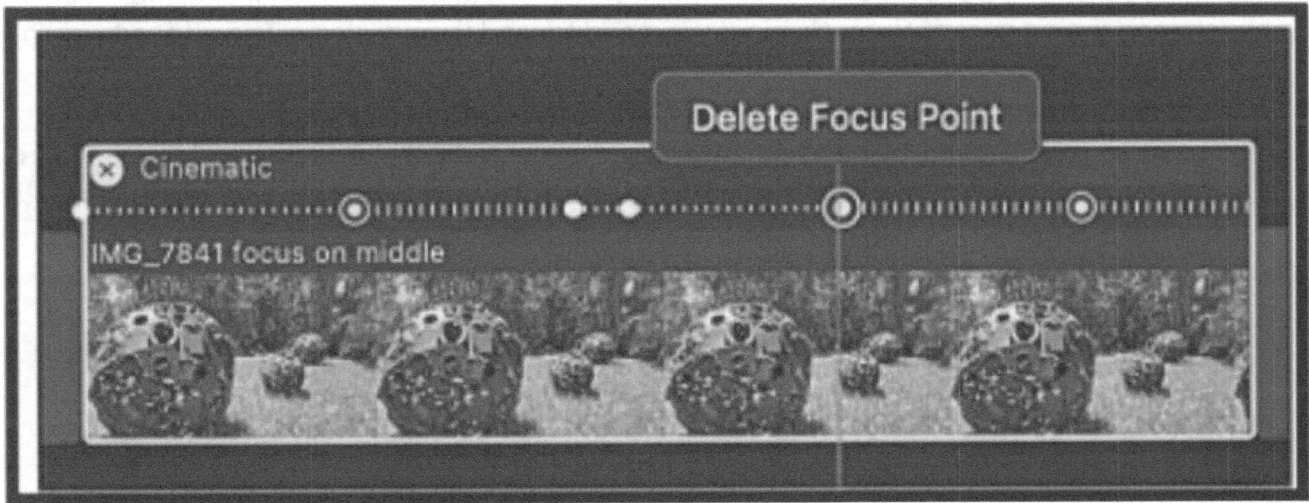

There will also be a yellow focus box that stays in place in the viewer to show you where the focus is right now. To change things:

1. To focus the shot, move the playhead to any point in the clip and then click in the viewer.

2. You can change the blur level by moving the **Depth of Field** slider in the Inspector. The range is from f2.0 (blurry, shallow depth of field) to f1 6 (sharper, deep depth of field).

Stabilization

You might be able to fix the problem by turning on **Stabilization** if your shot is shaky due to shaky hands or shooting while moving. For the first time, play the clip and wait for it to be analyzed. Then, play the clip again to see how it looks.

Depending on the type of shake found, one of two ways will be chosen:

- The best option is **InertiaCam**, but it only works when there isn't a lot of shaking. You can change the amount of **Smooth-ing** if you need to, and there's also a **Tripod Mode** option that stops all movement.
- If the movement is too strong for **InertiaCam, SmoothCam** will be chosen automatically. It can also be chosen by hand if necessary. One of the great things about this option is that you can change the **Translation Smooth, Rotation Smooth,** and **Scale Smooth** buttons separately. However, there is no Tripod mode here.

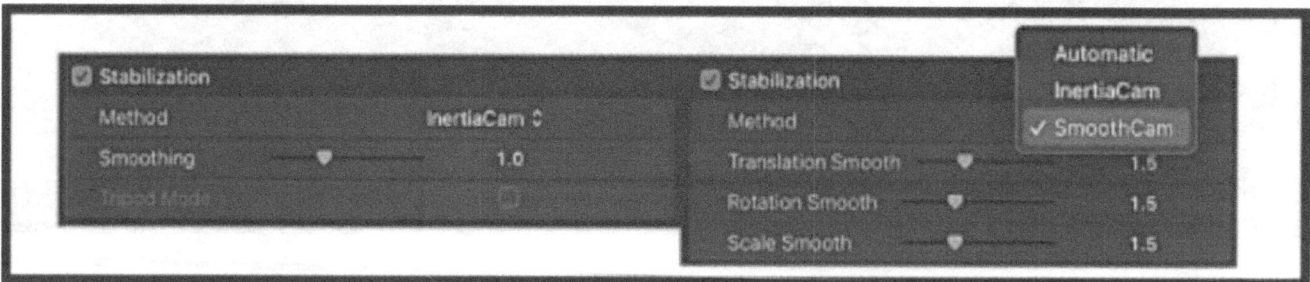

Smoothing in InertiaCam or Translation Smooth in SmoothCam can fix most shake problems. Rot at ion Smooth and Scale Smooth can also help sometimes, but each shot is different, so you'll have to try them all. Should you try all of these options and still not get what you want, you will have to change the shot. For your next shot, use a gimbal for a moving shot and a stand for a still shot.

Rolling Shutter

The sensors in most cameras don't record the whole frame at once; instead, they scan from top to bottom. The picture may be tilted if the camera or its subject is moving quickly:

Rolling Shutter tries to fix this and gives you different levels of correction, but it can be hard to fix the problem, especially when things move quickly. Change the settings here to see what works best, but if this happens with your camera, just pan more slowly.

Spatial Conform

The way your footage is shown will depend on whether it has the same aspect ratio as your timeline or not. **For example, if you're sending to Square for social media, you can choose how your footage is shown:**

- **Fit**: Show the whole frame, but leave the clip's black edges empty.
- **Fill**: This will zoom the clip up to fill the whole frame and crop the clip's edges.
- **None**-Do not change the size at all:

All of these options can use the Crop and Transform features, but **Spatial Conform** is meant to be used first. Moving the scale and then the fill setting will make it zoom in more than you might think. New in the 10.4.9 version is **Smart Conform**, which can be used instead of Spatial Conform. Choose one or more clips, then go to **Modify > Smart Conform** to have your pictures automatically resized and moved to fit what they are.

Rate Conform

It only shows up if the frame rate of your clip doesn't match the frame rate of your text. The options here determine which frames are shown, but if there is a small mismatch, none of the first three options—**Normal (Floor), Nearest Frame, or Frame Blending**—will likely look great. **One of these options should be used if you are into this issue:**

- Change the speed of the clip to match the frame rate of the timeline by going to **Retime > Automatic Speed**.
- When you need to, use the **Optical Flow** method to make smart new frames:

Animating with keyframes and tracking

While tracking refers to following an object's movement, animation simply refers to changing a property's value over time. You might:

- Fade a clip in or out by moving **Opacity**.
- Grow or shrink a clip over time by changing **Scale (All)**.
- Reveal a clip by animating **Crop (Trim)**.
- Brighten a clip over time by animating a color correction:

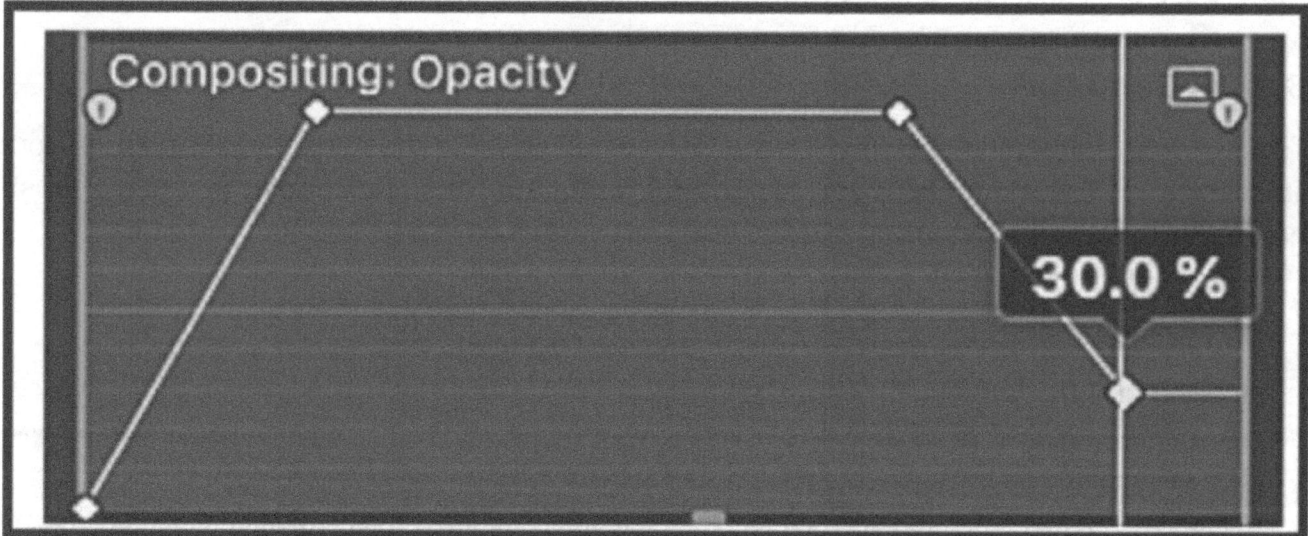

Keyframing is a complete fix that can be used on almost any Inspector property. These examples are just the beginning. We will start with the controls that focus on the Inspector, and then move on to the controls that focus on the Timeline, and finally go back to the controls that focus on the viewer. Another option besides keyframing is the Object Tracker tool, which was added in 10.6 and is useful if you want to keep track of where an object is going. But first, there's the inspector.

Animating in the Inspector

While the Inspector's keyframing system isn't very fancy, it still gives you a clean and easy way to understand and manage any object. For this practice, you'll need two different clips in the timeline, one on top of the other. You'll be working on the clip that was joined before. You'll need to think about not only what the features are but also when their values need to change now that you'll be changing an effect over time. Each keyframe saves a number (what) at a certain point in time (when). They are shown by diamonds. To the left of the **Inspec-tor**, some lines move between keyframes. If there is no keyframe, there is a blank spot. If there is a keyframe, there is a yellow diamond.

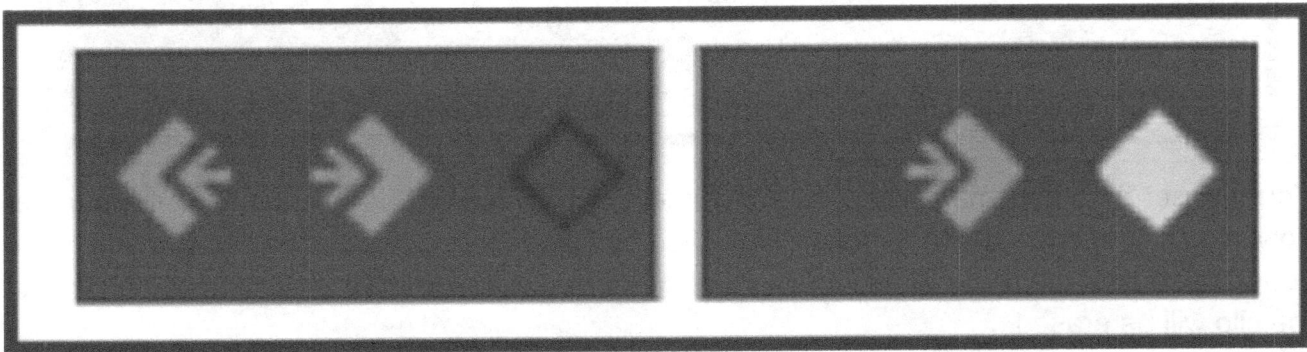

But move the mouse over a clip to see what will happen if you click. The plus and minus signs **only show up when you move the mouse over the spot. There is no keyframe if there is a black diamond with an a + sign around it. You can click to add one, though. Hovering over a keyframe shows a minus, and you can click to delete that keyframe:**

Animating the crop property

The first thing you should do is crop. It's simple, clear, and can look pretty good. This is where you'll move the Left Crop edge from a high number to zero. If you've already changed this clip's **Crop setting, reset it before you begin, and make sure you're on the default trim setting:**

1. **Option-click** on the connected clip, two seconds from its start point, to select it and move the playhead to that point intime.

To move a clip on the screen, start with a keyframe at the end of the animation and lock in the "normal" value first. This makes the process much easier.

2. In the **Inspector**, close to the **Left** property, click the diamond with a plus sign (+) to make a new keyframe:

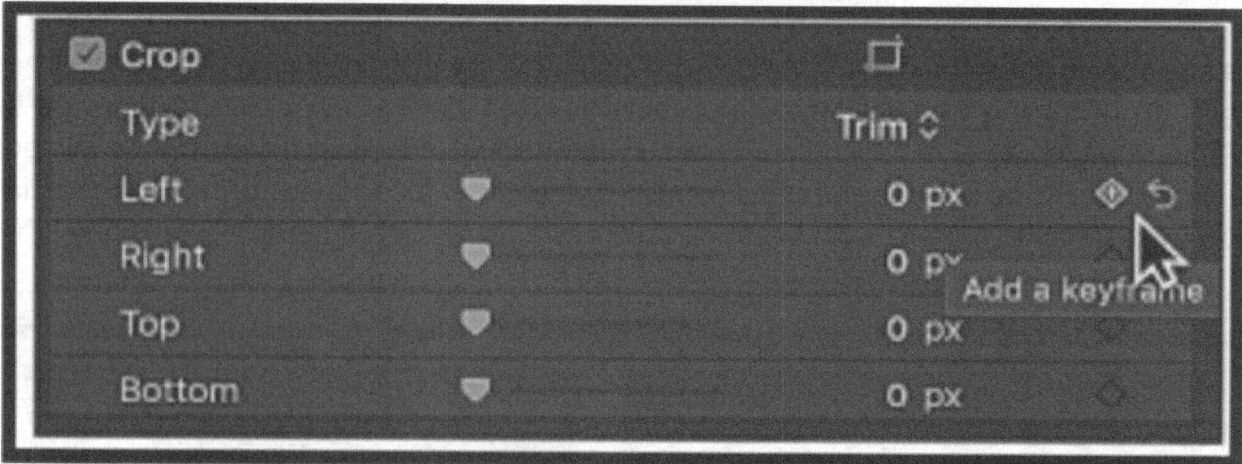

You just set the keyframe to "normal" for this clip, which means it will remember the number now. You can see the keyframe as a yellow diamond if you move the mouse away. If you move your mouse over the same button again, it will now show a-inside the diamond. If you click that, the clip will be erased.

3. Press the key to go back to the beginning of the current clip.

Changing the value of a property at a different point in time will automatically make a new keyframe after the first one has been made.

4. **Move the left number (which starts at 0) around until the clip is gone.**

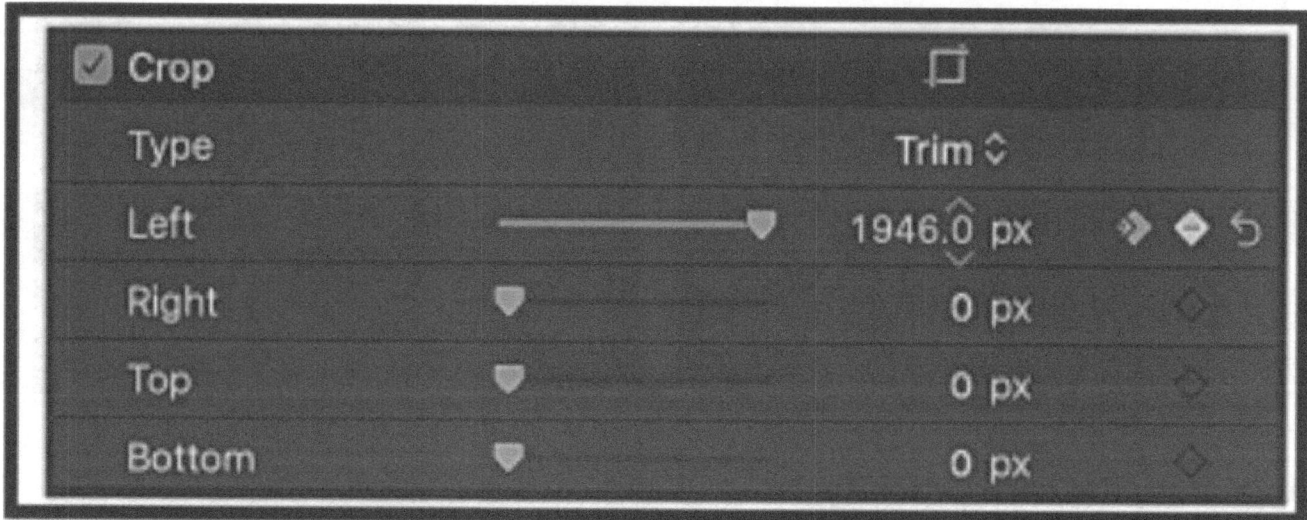

This number needs to be dragged out to at least the width of this clip. Keep in mind that the scale probably won't go all the way to the numbers. Always dragon the numbers directly.

5. Play this clip over and over to see the Crop Left property animate.

Importantly, if you changed any other Crop property, the animation would not start again because each property has its keyframes. For each property, you only need to click the plus sign inside the diamond shape once. However, the first keyframe you click is very important.

Animating a color correction

You can also add animation to color corrections. If the light changes while you're recording, you can fix it by putting in two different expo-sure settings. These will make the darker parts of the shot lighter and the lighter parts of the shot darker.

Any shot will work to learn this trick:

1. Press and hold the **option key** while clicking on a clip to pick it up and move the playhead to that spot.
2. Press **command-6** to fix the colors of this clip and make them look better.
3. To get to the beginning of the clip, use the arrow keys and the JKL key on your keyboard.

You can't accidentally remove the clip if you use the keyboard here. Don't lose your selection if you want to use the mouse instead. Drag in the meas ure bar at the top of the imeline.

4. At this point in the clip, you can correct the **color, saturation,** and **exposure** as you like.
5. To make this correction, move your mouse over the title bar and click the plus sign inside the diamond to make a new keyframe:

At this point, the color correction is set in stone. If you change the exposure settings at a different time, the second and third settings will be locked in.

6. Use the keyboard controls to **move along the clip** for a couple of seconds.
7. Make any changes you want to **color, saturation,** or **exposure**, making the change stand out.
8. **Play through this clip** to see the color correction animate.

If you can add a keyframe to the exact frame where the exposure starts to shift and another to the exact frame where it ends that shift, this method will work in real life. You can always put a cutout on top of this transition to hide it. Now you can start over if you mess up. Just click on the hooked **Reset** arrow or pick **Reset Parameter** from the small menu to the right of the keyframe settings.

Animating a Mask with Tracking

To fix the color with a tracked mask, do the following:

1. To pick a clip on the timeline, press the "**Option**" key and click on it. Move the playhead to that point. (Make sure this frame makes the object you want to track easy to see.)
2. Second, open the **Effects** pane and click on **Color**.
3. Drag a **Color Board** or other color-correcting effect into the viewer and onto an object in the frame that you want to track.

This turns on the new object tracker tool, finds a trackable area in the frame, and makes a shape mask immediately on a new color fix. You could also add a shape mask manually to a color correction that is already there, then use the switch at the top of the viewer to switch from **Shape** to **Tracker**.

4. To better match the position and shape of the object you want to track, use the on-screen settings to adjust the mask's size and shape.
5. Change the color correction settings to make the object you've covered darker, lighter, or a different color.
6. In the upper left corner of the viewer, click the **"Analyze"** button. Then, wait for the study to finish.

This process should work quickly if the area you were trying to track is clear and visible throughout the clip. After tracking, the mask's edge will become much softer. This is a great way to make a face lighter or darker, draw attention to a certain area, or take attention away from another. It's important to note that you can separate the mask shape from the tracker shape. This lets you change the color of one area while tracking a smaller, bigger, or offset area.

7. **Go to Shape and change the mask handles and edge softness:**

Click the arrow next to the word "**Tracker**" and then change the **Behavior** setting from "**Pin**" to "**Tracker**" to " **Offset from Tracker**." This will allow you to move the shape mask away from the tracked area throughout the clip. Everything you do will add to the tracking information. You can keyframe the shape mask if you only want to move this distance for a part of the clip.

Animating a mask with keyframes

Masks can be animated manually by adding keyframes to the shape mask itself. This is useful if tracking wasn't quite good enough or if you need to use an older version of Final Cut Pro. If you've already used Object Tracker to track a mask, you can find its keyframes at the bottom of the Inspector, under **Trackers**. This is a different process. The process of adding keyframes manually from scratch can be time-consuming. Even if you haven't tracked a mask yet, this process is much faster and easier to use to change the distance of Shape Mas k from its tracker.

Here are the steps you need to take to try it:

1. Press and hold the **option key** while clicking on a clip to pick it up and move the playhead to that spot.
2. To add the usual color correction to this clip, press **command-6.** Then, make a clear change, like making the clip darker.
3. Add a **Shape Mask** by clicking on the **Mask** icon at the top of the adjustment.
4. Make the mask's shape and size more or less match where an object is in the frame.

If you want the adjustment to be outside the mask form, you can flip the mask.

5. Move to a point in time where the object starts to move.
6. To make a keyframe, click the plus sign inside the diamond where the mouse is in the lower part of the Inspector, next to **Shape Mask 1.**

Keep in mind that this area is blank until your mouse is close to it if you haven't tracked this mask yet. If you have tracked it already, you'll see a tracking icon here first:

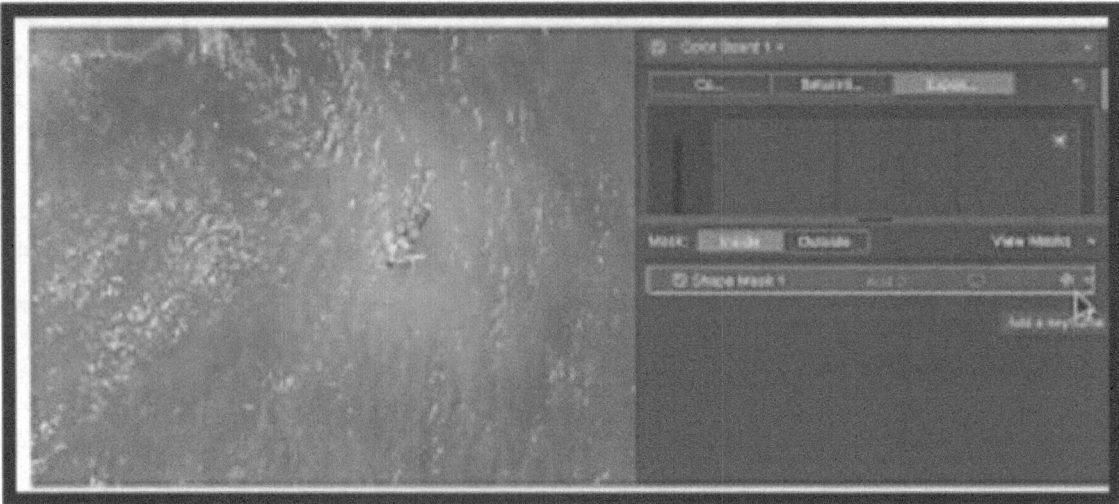

You've now locked in the position, shape, and size of this mask.

1. Use the keyboard to move along the clip, aiming for a spot where the object stops moving.
2. Move the mask to the spot where the object is.
3. Go back and forth in the clip to make sure the mask stays on top of the object the whole time.
4. At any time, you can lock in another keyframe by moving the mask to make it more closely match the position of the object.

You could add a new clip every few seconds or whenever the speed or direction changes, but try to keep the effect smooth. Too many keyframes can make your animation look jerky, so use as few as possible:

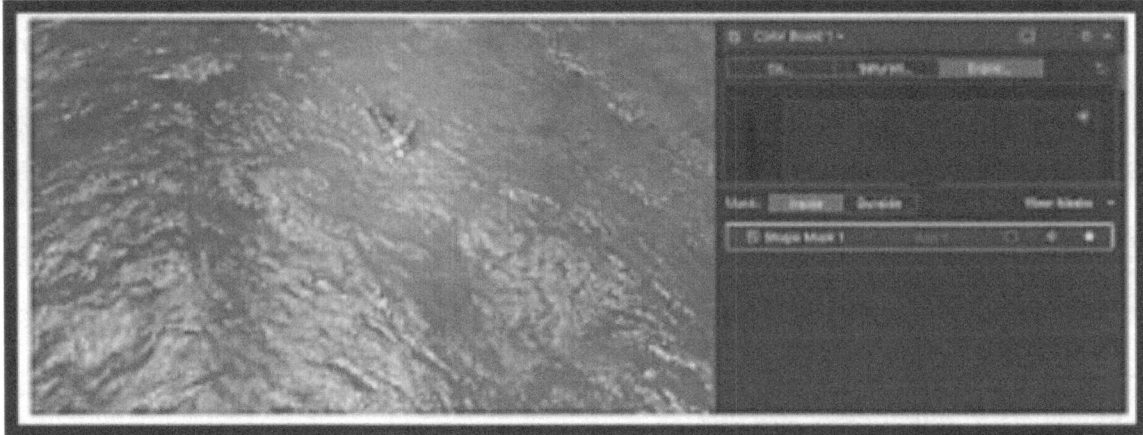

Editing keyframes in the Inspector

When you add keyframes to a property, you may want to go back to the ones that are already there. This lets you remove a keyframe or change the setting that was saved at that time. To get **to existing keyframes, look to the left of the keyframe diamond for a property, and you'll see two more arrows:**

- Click the Previous Keyframe left arrow to go to the previous keyframe.
- Click the Next Keyfram with the left arrow to go to the next frame:

To go over the keyframe diamond one more time, we can do the following:

- While on a keyframe, click the-in the diamond (hover to see the minus sign) to delete it.
- While not on a keyframe, click the + in the diamond to create a new keyframe and record the current value.

If you only need to work with a few keyframes, these tools are fine. But you can also change keyframes on the timeline; keep reading.

Adding video effects

You will need to see the Effects Browser to begin:

- Press **command-5** or click the second-from-right button in the middle graybar to open the **Effects Browser:**

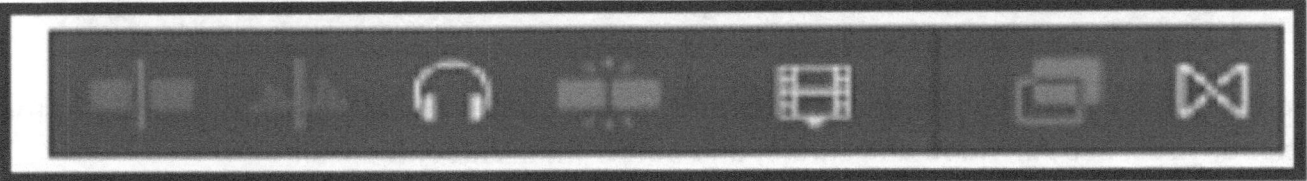

On the left side of the Effects Browser are the categories, and on the right side are the effects in the chosen category:

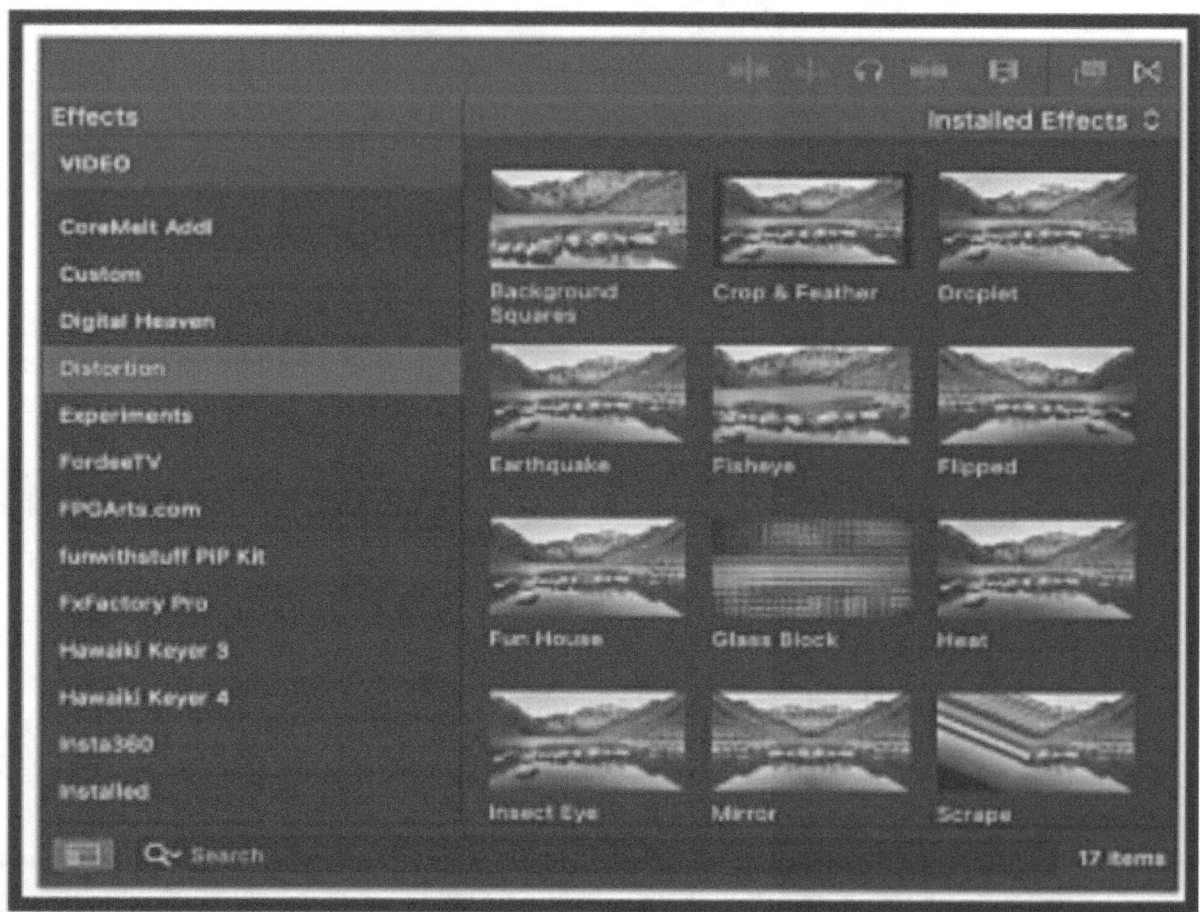

In the sidebar, you'll see video effects on top and audio effects below. At the top of the menu, you'll see All Video and Audio, and below that, Video, then All:

- Click **All**, which is under **Video**. This will show you all the video effects in the right-screen pane.
- Click on **any category name** to see only the effects that belong to that group.

You can see what the video effects will look like on a clip before you apply them:

- Move your mouse over an effect to see it applied to the clip you've chosen:

But keep in mind that you're only seeing a sample of how an effect is set by default because effects can often be changed in a lot of ways. You can get an example that tells you a little more, though:

- Hold down the **option key** and move your mouse over an effect to change its main control.

Most of the time, this primary control changes how strong the effect is. It's a good way to see how an effect will look with a few different settings. After letting go of the **option key**, you can quickly look over the clip to see how the new setting has changed the rest of it.

There are two ways to add a video effect to a clip:

- Pick out a few clips in the timeline, then double-click to use it.
- Drag an effect to a clip in the timeline.

Either of these will work, and either way will show you that the clip has changed: skim over it or play the video.

If you often use a certain effect, you can make it the default by right-clicking on it and selecting "**Make Default Video Effect.**" With **option-E**, you can add that default effect to a clip. On most Macs, most effects work in real-time. However, some complicated effects, like noise reduction, **can be very slow. You can try these things if your Mac isn't fast enough to play back video effects in real-time:**

When you change the **View** menu in the **Viewer** to **Better Performance** (not **Better Quality**),

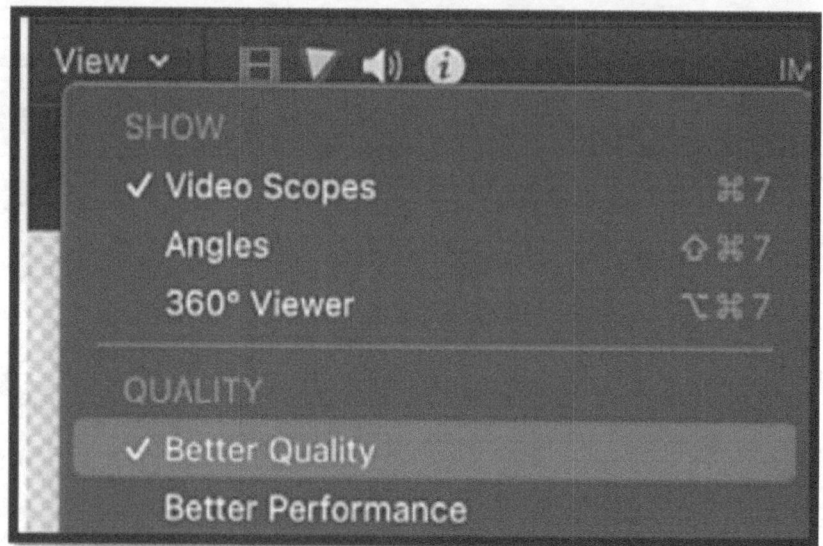

Under **Playback** in **Final Cut Pro > Settings (command-cmoma)**, turn on **Background Render**. When **Background Rendering** is turned on, you'll have to wait a few seconds for your new effect to be calculated. While this is happening, you'll see small dots drop from the timeline's ruler bar.

Adjusting video effects

You should always change the settings for an effect from what they are by default to make sure you're not using the same effect as 90% of other users. The vast majority of titles and effects are applied without any changes. If you want your work to stand out, make it special by moving a scale! The **Video** tab of the Inspector is where you need to go to change settings. That's where **you can change how the effect works after it's been added to the clip. Now let's look at a simple case using the Gaussian Blur filter:**

1. Press and hold the **option key** while clicking on a clip to pick it up and move the playhead to that spot.
2. Go to the **Effects** pane and click on **Blur**.

3. Move your mouse over the **Gaussian** effect to see the preview effect that was added to the clip.
4. Move your mouse over the **Gaussian** effect and hold down the **option key** to see how it looks at different levels of strength.
5. To use the **Gaussian** effect, double-click it. (You could also drag the effect to the clip.)
6. **To see how different strengths look in the Viewer, move the Amount slider up and down in the inspector and lessen the effect overall:**

7. To try a different look, change the other settings in the Inspector (**Horizontal, Vertical, and Blur Boost**).

But you might not want to smooth out a normal shot. Ablur can help make a clip in the background behind a title less noticeable. It can also be useful to move this effect over time to bring a shot back into focus by dulling the noise.

Masking video effects

The process of masking a color fix is very similar to masking a video effect, and the result is the same: the effect is only visible in a partial frame. A color mask would limit the effect to certain colors or lighting levels, while a shape mask would limit it to a certain part of the frame.

1. Give a clip an effect as you normally would.
2. Move your mouse over the effect's title bar and click the **Mask** icon.
3. To change the shape of the effect, select **Add Shape Mask** and move, spin, scale, and shape the mask as needed. Choose **Add Color Mask** instead to limit the effect to a range of colors. Then, click and drag in the Viewer to pick a range of colors, and then tweak that range in the Inspector.

The effect will only go on the inside of the mask for now, but you can invert the mask to make the outside effect too. Masks are shown didirectly beneath the effect to which they are applied, and a choice to the right of the mask's name lets you reset or delete the mask.

What are some times when masking can be useful?

- **Sharpen** to focus attention on the subject.
- **Blur** to de-emphasize the background
- **Comic Looks** to turn only part of the image into a cartoon.
- **A color correction vignette** to darken the extreme corners of the frame
- **Underwater** or **wave**, limited to water, to add ripples to it:

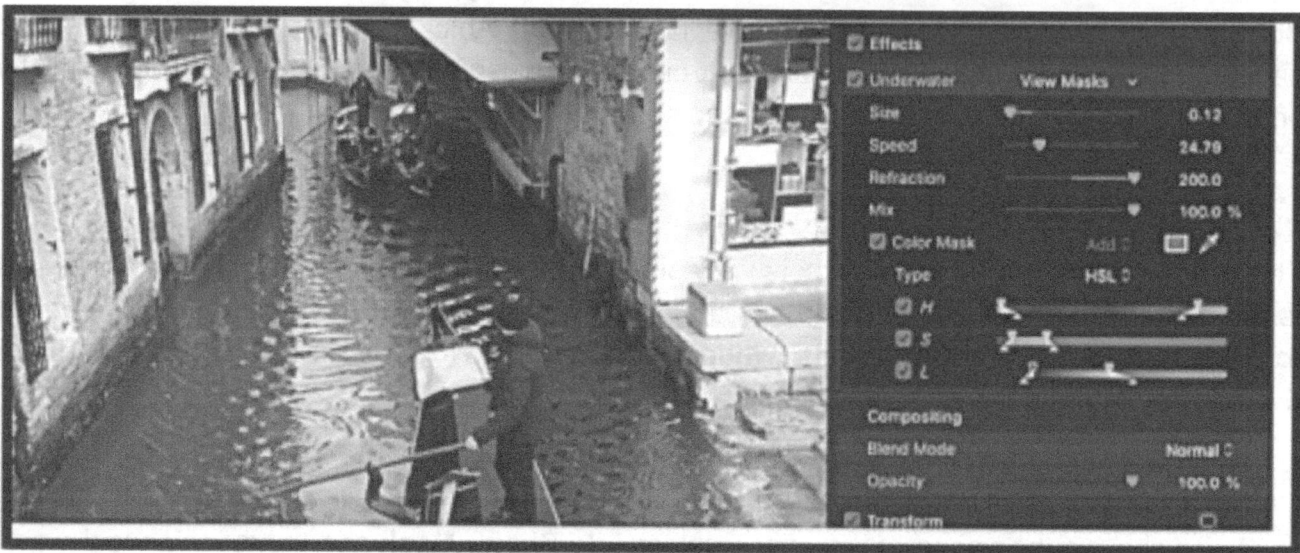

If you're using a Shape Mask, the new Tracking toolin 10.6 has added a **Shape/Tracker** switch at the top of the Viewer. This switch lets you choose between changing and tracking the shape. This tool makes it easy to use tracking if you need to, but there's a better way to do things if you know you'll need to use tracking to move a face.

Animating video effects with tracking

To protect the person's identity, let's use the new Object Tracking tool in 10.6 to track their face automatically as they move around in a shot and pixelate it. When FCP was older, you would have used the **Censor** effect and keyframed the center of it manually.

This is easier:

1. **Option-click** on a person's clip on the timeline to choose them. This will move the playhead to that point in time. (Make sure that the person you want to follow can be seen clearly in this frame.)
2. **Click on Stylize, and then drag Pixellate onto the viewer's face of the person you want to change. If a face is found, the word "Face" should show up:**

3. Modify the shape's sides as necessary to better match the face.
4. Change the **Pixellate** amount in the Inspector to a higher number, like 40, to hide the face even more.
5. Press "**Analyze**" to follow the face through the whole clip.
6. Go to the top and select **Shape**. Then change the softness of the mask's edge.

This will probably look fine most of the time, but there are a few things you can do to fix a track that doesn't quite look right. It's easy to move the shape mask a little away from the tracked area:

1. To make sure you're changing the shape mask, click **Shape** in the Viewer instead of **Tracker**.

2. Click the arrow to the right of the word "**Tracker**" at the top of the Viewer to open the pop-up menu with tracker options.
3. In **Behavior**, switch **Pin** to **Tracker** to **Offset from Tracker.**
4. Change the effect across the whole clip by moving or resizing the Shape Mask:

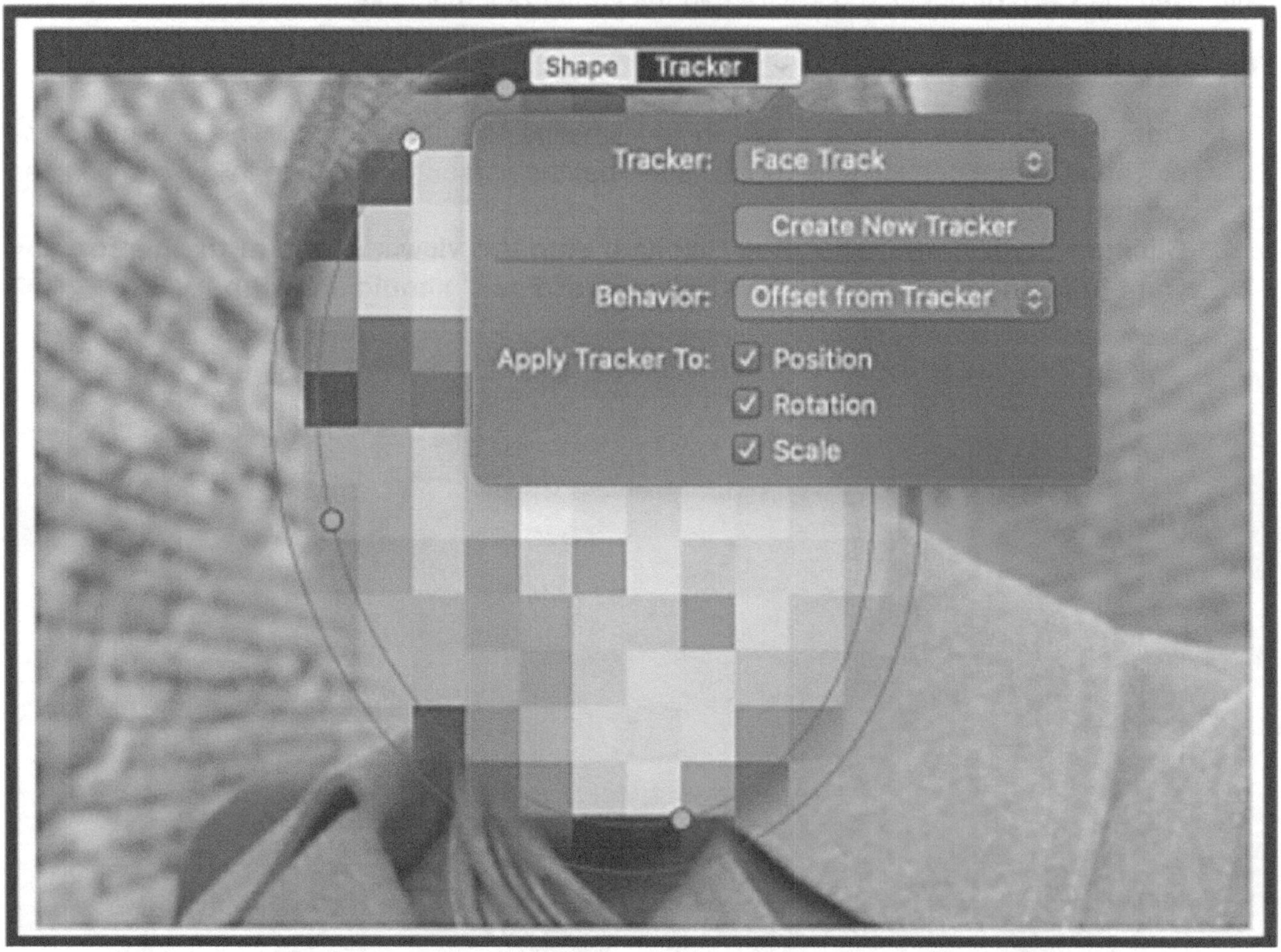

This is the method to use if the pixelated area is just off to the left or right of the face. Re-tracking or adding keyframes to the Shape Mask to remove it from the tracker are the two **options available if the shape begins to drift at a point in the clip. After the previous steps, let's add some keyframes first:**

- Go to the frame in the timeline right before the **Shape Mask** leaves the object.
- **To make a new keyframe, move your mouse over the Tracking icon to the right of the Shape Mask in the Inspector and click the plus sign inside the diamond that appears:**

- To move 10 frames down the timeline or until the Shape Mask is no longer over the place you want it to be, press the **shift key +.**
- Move the Shape Mask around to make a new keyframe.

- Do these steps again and again until the Shape Mask stays with the object throughout the shot.

While adding a few keyframes manually can be a quick fix, re-tracking might be better for bigger problems. Tracking can fail if the area being tracked looks very different, like if a head turns away or if it disappears completely from the frame completely. To fix it manually:

- Get the tracked clip and right-click on it. Then, select **Show Tracking Editor**.
- Click on the spot where the track was lost in the new tracking editing area and drag it to the end of the bad tracking data. In the pop-up window that opens, click "**Delete**" to delete the bad tracking information.
- Move the playhead to any place in the area that was just cleared, and then move and change the size of the tracking mask to cover the face.
- If you want to re-track the area in both ways, you can click "**Analyze**." If you only want to track in one direction, you can click the arrows next to "**Analyze**."

Before you click "**Analyze**," you might want to delete the track and pick a different tracking method (**Combined, Machine Learning, or Point Cloud**) if this still doesn't work.

It's very helpful to use effects with object tracking to hide faces, blue license plates, or add sparkle exactly where it's needed. Not only can you change effects over time, but you can also move, scale, and rotate them. You can change any effect over time with traditional key framing. Here's how to do it.

Animating video effects with keyframes

This page shows some good examples of how to use the keyframing method on Effects, which works just like it does on any other property in the Inspector. Swipe one of an effect's sliders up **and down to quickly see if it will look good when moved. If you like it, you know it will. The method should be easy to understand:**

1. **Option-click** on a clip two seconds from its start point to pick it up and move the playhead to that spot.
2. Choose the **Blur** category, then drag **Gaussian** to the clip (or double-click **Gaussian**).
3. To turn off the effect, set the A**mount** to zero.

We will lock in the second keyframe first, at the end of the animation, just like we did before.

4. To make a new keyframe, click the plus sign plus sign inside the diamond to the right of the **Amount** value in the **Gaussian** part of the Inspector.
5. Press the key to go back to the beginning of the current clip.
6. Make **Amount** a big number, at least **50**.
7. **Watch as the picture comes into focus by playing this clip:**

If tracking isn't working and you need to hide someone's identity, you can use the **Censor** effect. You can keyframe it to hide someone's face as they move. In most cases, tracking will be faster **and easier, but if you want to do things the old-fashioned way, you can do these things:**

1. **Option-click** on a person in a clip to pick them and move the playhead to that spot in the video.
2. Click the **Stylize** button, then drag and then dragor double-click **Censor** to the clip.

We'll use keyframes through this time, starting at the beginning.

3. Press the key to go back to the beginning of the current clip.
4. To put the circle over someone's face, change the **Amount, Radius,** and **Center:**

1. In the **Inspector**, to the right of the **Center** property in the **Censor** section, click the + inside the diamond to create a new keyframe.
2. Press shift+ to go back 10 frames in the timeline.
3. Use the settings on the screen to move the effect's center so that it stays on the face of the person. Even if they haven't moved much, give them a little push to add a new clip.

4. Do this again and again until keyframes are put along the clip.

Create and use effects presets.

Effects presets combine one or more effects or color corrections into a single effect that can be used again and again. They're like having a set of effects already copied out and ready to be put onto as many clips as you want. Some presets come with the program. **Color Board Pre-sets** and Color Grading Presets are two places where you can find Effects Presets:

You may want to use the same color look in different projects if you like it. An Effects preset is a great way to keep things consistent. Because they are easy to use, effects presets are best for **making changes that make something unique, like a scene or a complicated vin-tage look. Here's an example with just one color correction (you could use more if you wanted to):**

1. Press and hold the **option key** while clicking on a clip to pick it up and move the playhead to that spot.
2. Press **command-6** to fix the colors of this clip and make them look better.
3. Make the exposure much darker.
4. The **Masks** menu is at the top of the **Color** pane. Use it to make a new Shape Mask.
5. Make the mask bigger so it's an oval shape with a soft edge.
6. Flip the mask over and change its size so that only the edges are darker.
7. Click on **Save Effects Preset** at the bottom of the Inspector.

When the text box comes up, you can choose to save any effects you've used on the clip as a new preset that you can use with just one click.

8. If there is something that shouldn't be in the preset, remove the features or effects that you don't want to be there:

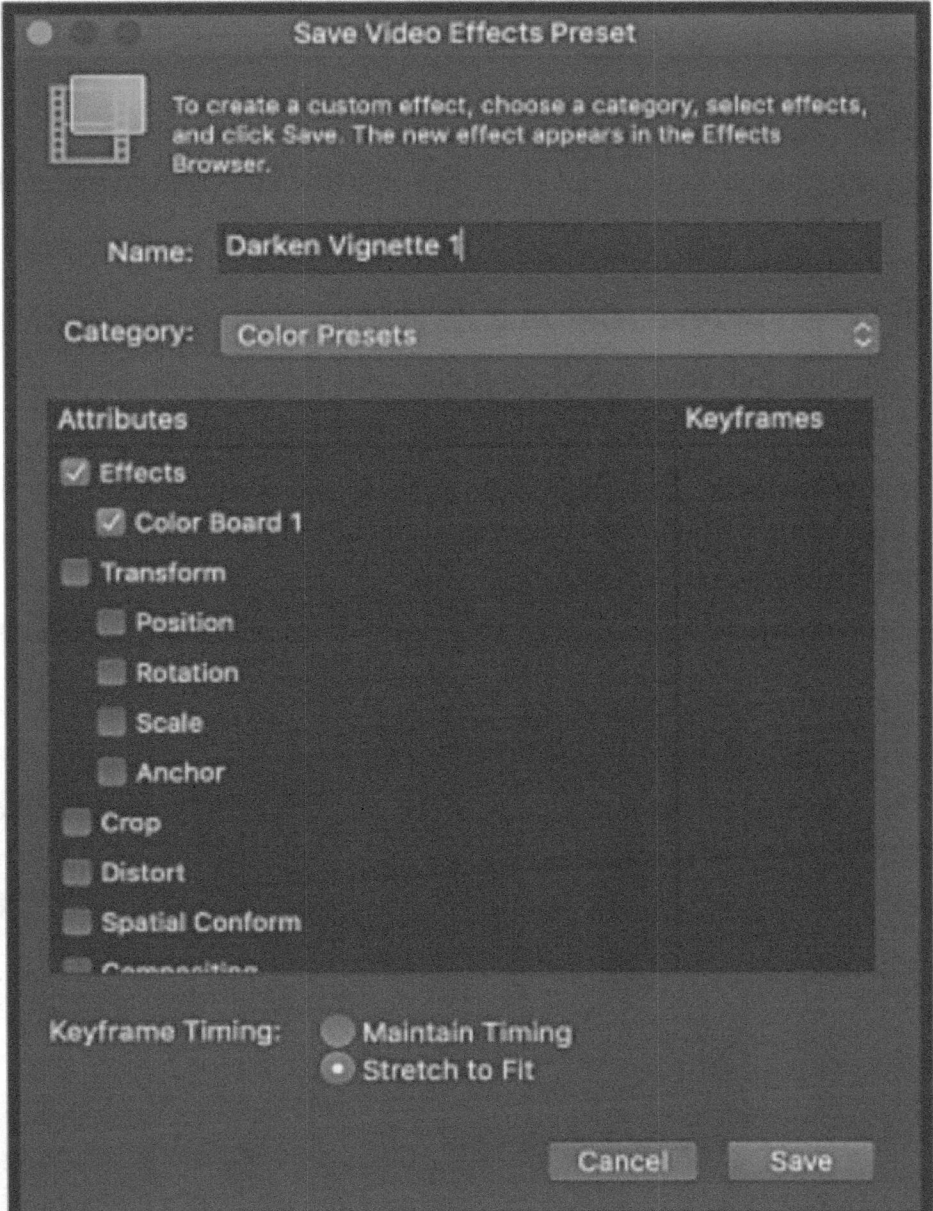

Such as, uncheck the box next to Crop or Scale if it's only supposed to be used on this clip.

9. In the top box, give this effect a new name, like Darken Vignette 1.
10. If the **Color Presets** menu is there, choose it from the **Category** menu. Choose **New Category** at the end of the list to make one if it's notalready there.

When you are done, your new **Effects Preset** will be in the **Effects** pane, in the area you put it in. Hover over it to see a sample. Feel free to try more by putting together a few video effects into one **Effects Preset**, like this:

- **Raindrops** plus **Rain** to add to the weather
- **Film Noir, Projector,** and **Letterbox** for a very "film" look;
- Several color corrections that you want to use together
- Any effect with settings that you can change to suit your tastes.

When you use an Effects Preset, all of the settings are available again, just like when you paste effects after copying. This gives you a lot of options, but you can't deactivate multiple effects at once.

Working with Green Screen (Chroma Keying)

Step 1: In the timeline, put your foreground clip, and then put the green screen shot on top of it.

"Background" in my case is the clip of the buffalo moving, and "foreground" is Darth Vader, which is on top of the background. The image below shows that the Darth Vader clip was shot in front of a green screen.

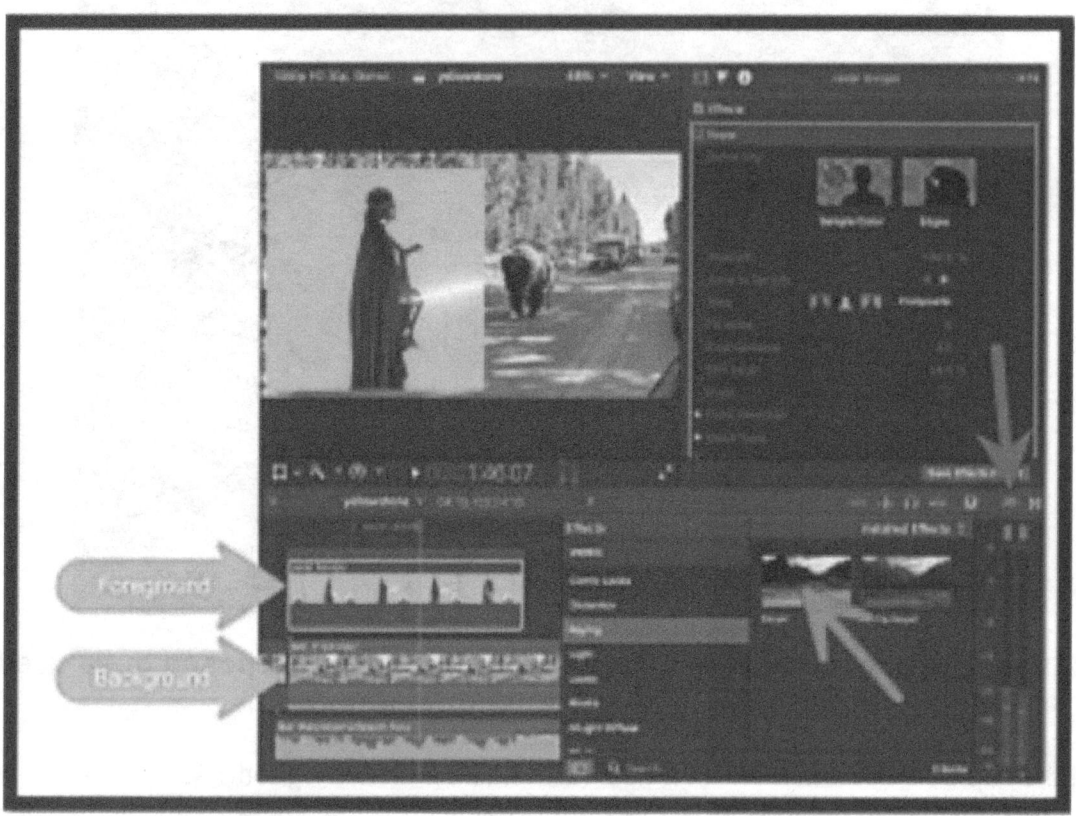

Step 2: Toggle the **Keyer effect** on and off by pressing the purple arrow button in the Effects Browser. This will bring up the **Keyer effect,** which is shown by the red arrow in the image above.

Then move the **Keyer** effect over the Darth Vader clip that is on the green screen. Excellent work. You just put up agreen screen! Most of the time, it will look like the image below, with all the green taken out and a pretty good picture in the center.

But the result can often look like the image below, where the "green" screen is still visible and there is a lot of noise around the edges of the foreground image.

Adjusting the Keyer Settings

Final Cut Pro knows what to do when you drag the Keyer effect into the foreground: it will look for a strong color (green) and get rid of it. But a lot of filmmaking and lighting know-how is needed to make sure that every pixel on a green screen is the same color. That's why Final Cut Pro doesn't always get it right. Not to worry, though. Final Cut Pro has many settings that can help you get it right with a little work. Go to the in-spector while the foreground clip is still **chosen. The Inspector can be turned on or off by hitting the button that the purple arrow is pointing to below.**

More often than not, there are pixels in the "green" screen that area slightly different shade of green, which makes Final Cut Pro confused. This is what happened in the above case. The color that is still there looks more like blue than green in the shot above. The red arrow in the above image leads to the sample color image. If you click there, your cursor will change to a small square. To get rid of the color that's still there, draw a square in any part of your picture and let go. If all goes well, one use of the sample color will be enough. Clicking around your screen a lot will usually get rid of any colors that are still there. To be sure, you may need to move the Playhead around in your clip to see if any movement in the foreground is changing the light and adding new colors that you will need to get rid of with more Sample Color tool hits. More help can be found in Color Selection's settings (see the green arrow). They can help you find the exact colors you need to get rid of.

Making size adjustments

Having taken out the green background, you will probably need to change the size and placement of your subject (Darth Vader) so it fits in with the background (the moving buffalo). To use the transform settings, click on the transform toolicon, which is shown by the purple arrow in the image below. This is the best way to do it.

The Transform tool puts the blue handles (shown above) around your clip and the blue dot close to the middle when it is turned on. The corner handles can be used to zoom in and out of your movie, and simply clicking on your picture will move it anywhere on the screen. Finally, you can turn the picture by clicking on the blue dot in the middle.

The size, placement, and spin of mydancing Darth in the image below are now just right for me after some tweaking:

CHAPTER 15: SEAMLESS TRANSITIONS AND CREATIVE RETIME EDITS

Applying and editing transitions

There are easy and complicated ways to change from one shot to the next. You will learn which ones work best for different tasks, how to change their settings, length, and placement, and why they might not always work here.

Adding transitions

Similar to Effects, you'll launch the Transitions Browser first. Its icon is right next to the Effects Browser button.

1. Press **Ctrl/Command-5** or click the button on the far right of the gray bar in the middle to open the Transitions Browser.

2. Click "**All**" at the top to see all of the transitions in the right pane.
3. Click on the name of any category to see only the transitions in that category.

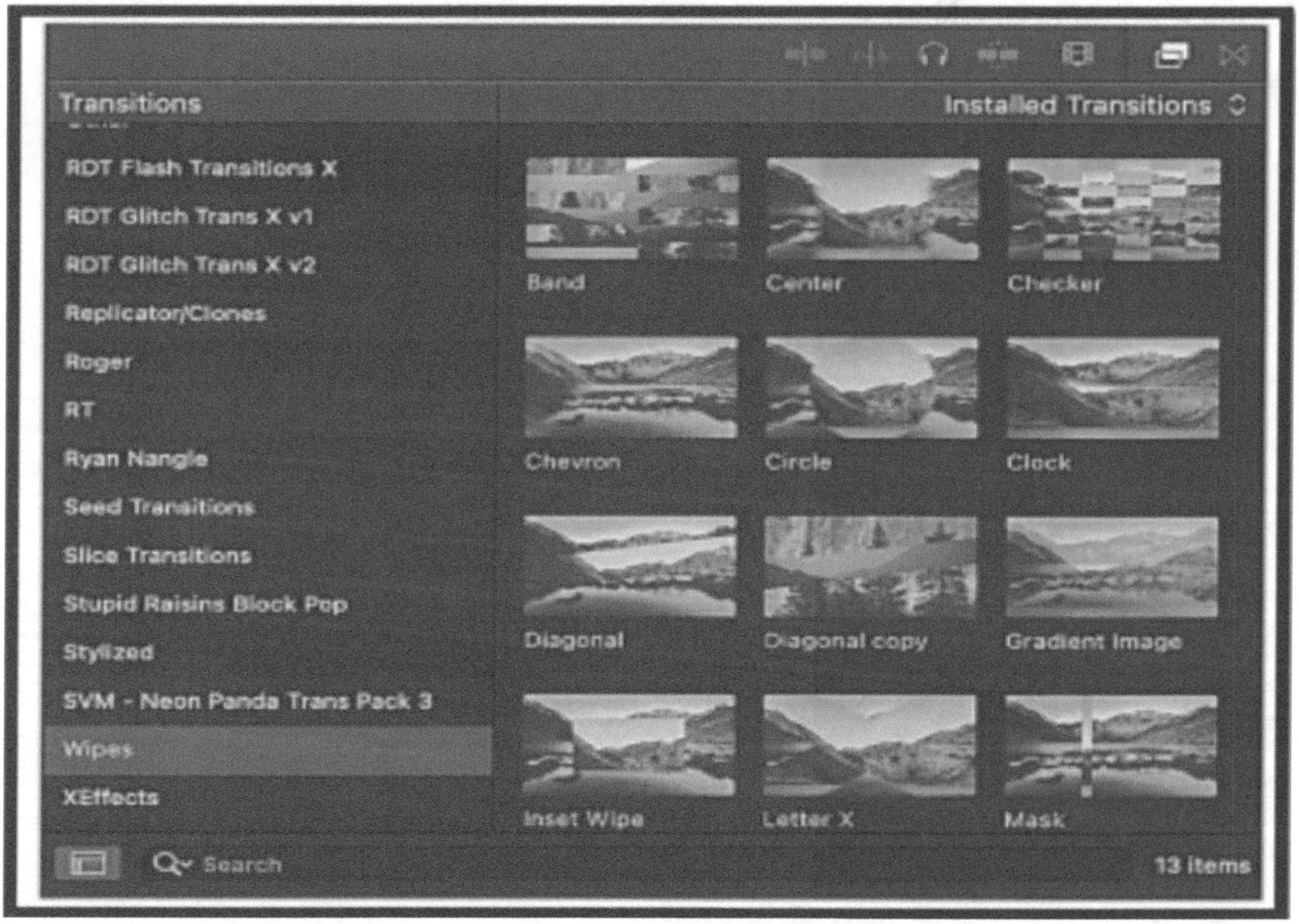

4. Move your mouse over an effect to see a sneak peek of the transition.

Even though a transition might have more options, you can only see the settings and a scene with red trees changing to blue mountains. You'll have to use it for your media to see a transition. **Several options are available in the Transitions Browser to add a video transition to a clip:**

- To add a transition to an edit in the timeline, first select it and then double-click on it.
- Pick out a clip in the timeline. 3. Double-click a transition to make it work on both sides of the clip.
- Pick out several clips or changes in the timeline. Then, double-click a transition to use it on all of them.
- Move an edit in the timeline and drag a transition from the Transitions Browser to it:

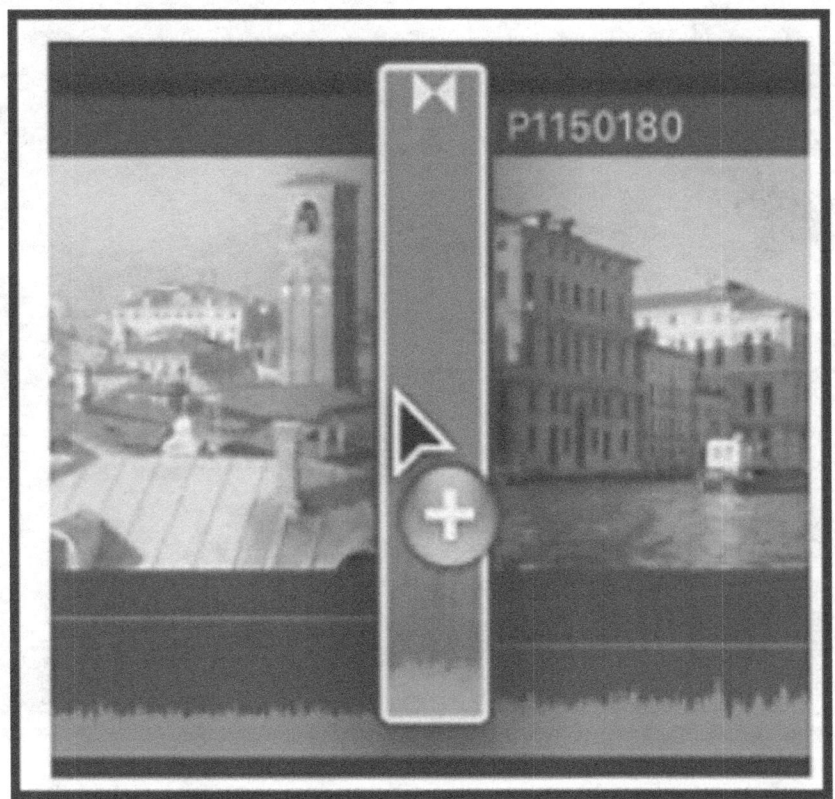

It's helpful that the last "drag" option lets you see how the transition will look before you drop it. You can also drag to move a transition from one edit to another or replace an existing transition while moving it to a different spot.

It also works for copying. You can use a transition you've already added more than once:

- Print out a copy of one transition, then pick out and paste another edit.
- **Option-drag** from one edit to another to make a copy of the transition.

Another option is available if you want to keep things simple. If you choose an edit or clip, then:

- Press **command-T** to add the usual transition, which is a basic Cross Dissolve.

The **Cross Dissolve transition** is something I use a lot in everyday cuts, but I like to keep it short. You can change how long this usual tran-sition lasts in Final Cut Pro > Settings > Editing. I suggest about 0.40 seconds:

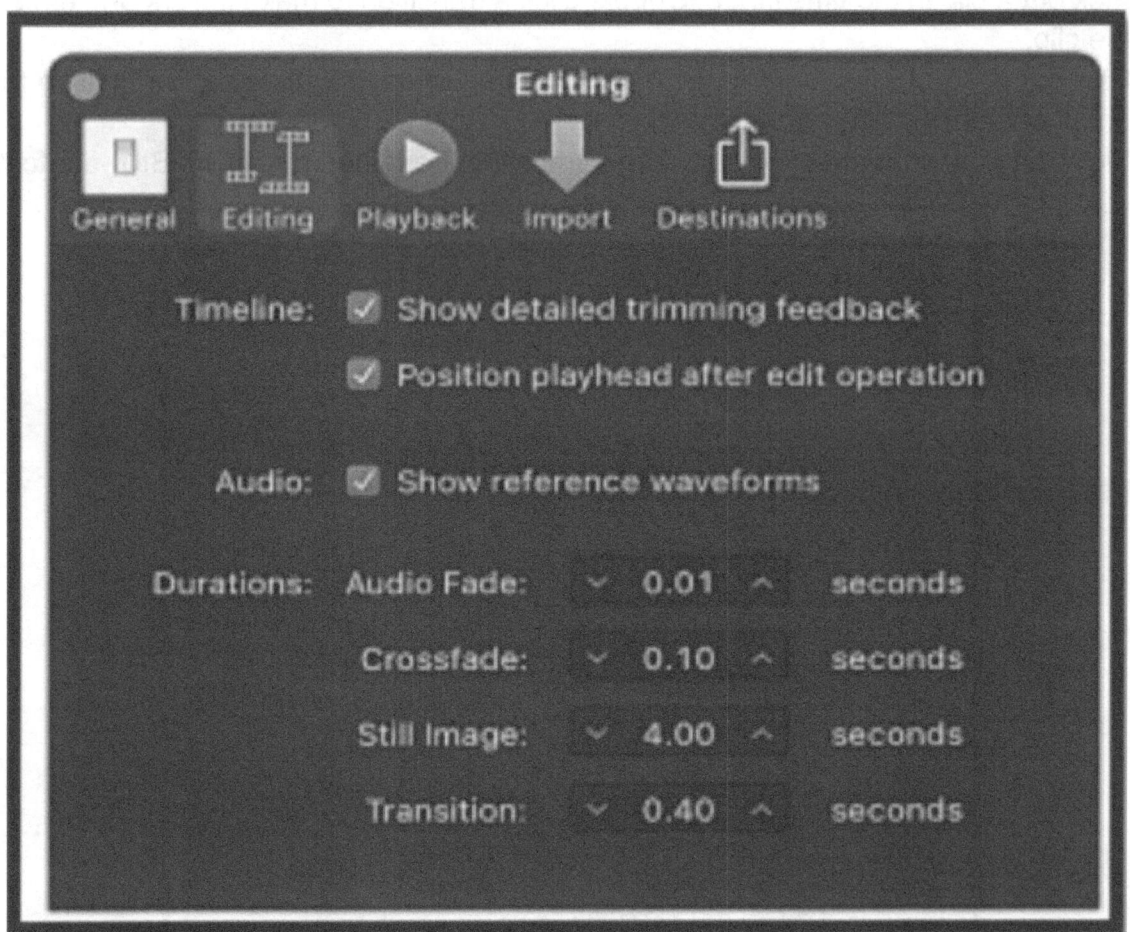

Simple transitions work best when they are short because they get out of the way quickly. More complicated transitions need more time, maybe even a few seconds. But not all changes can support a transition; the source clips need to have extra media, called **handles**, that aren't changed. The **Precision Editor** mode (double-clicks on an edit and press **Escape** to leave) will show you how much media is available if you're not sure. At the end of the clip going out and the beginning of the clip coming in, you'll need extra media to cover the transition on both sides.

There has to be something to show, sin ce you can expect to see a least part of both clips as the transition plays:

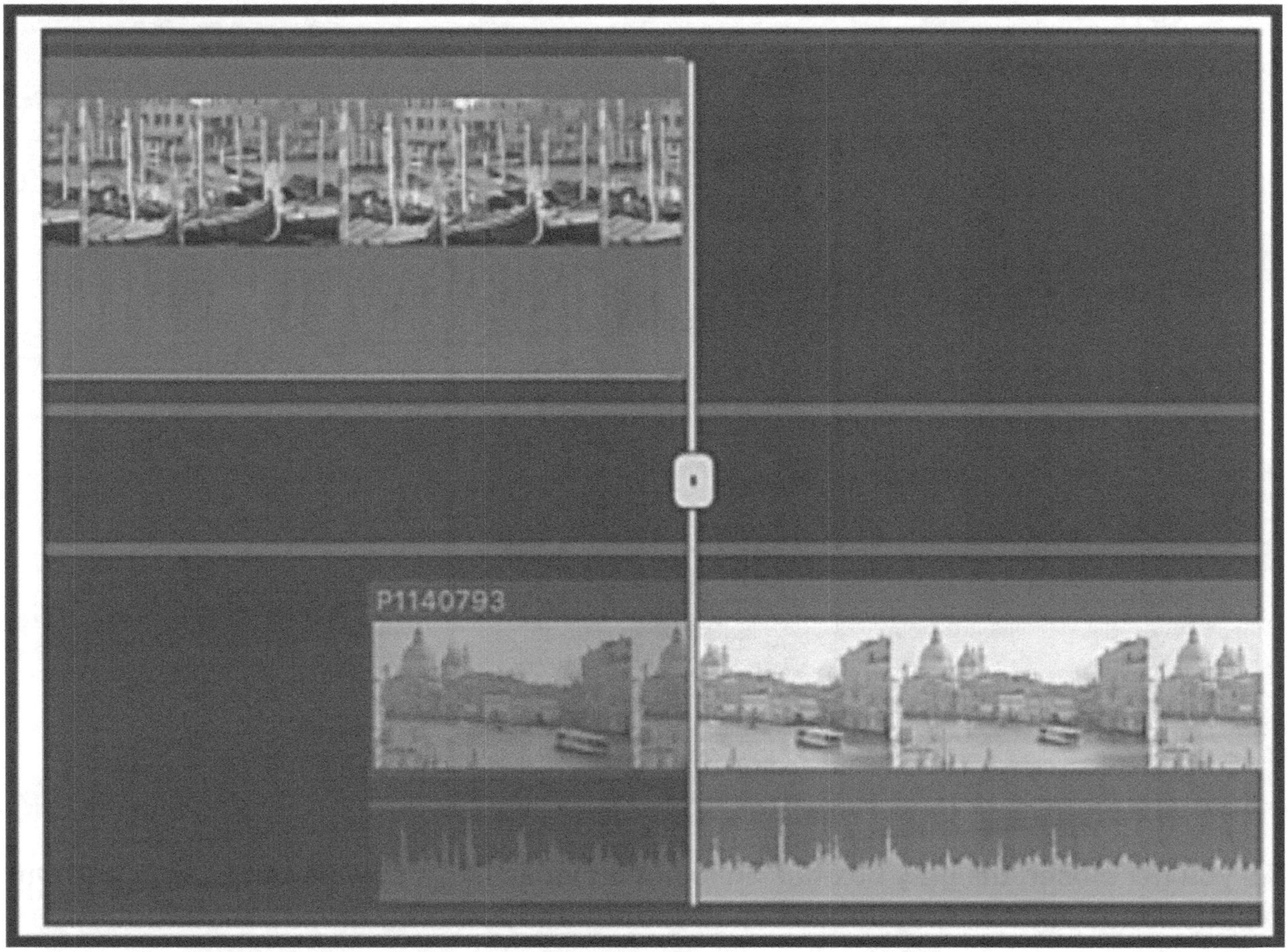

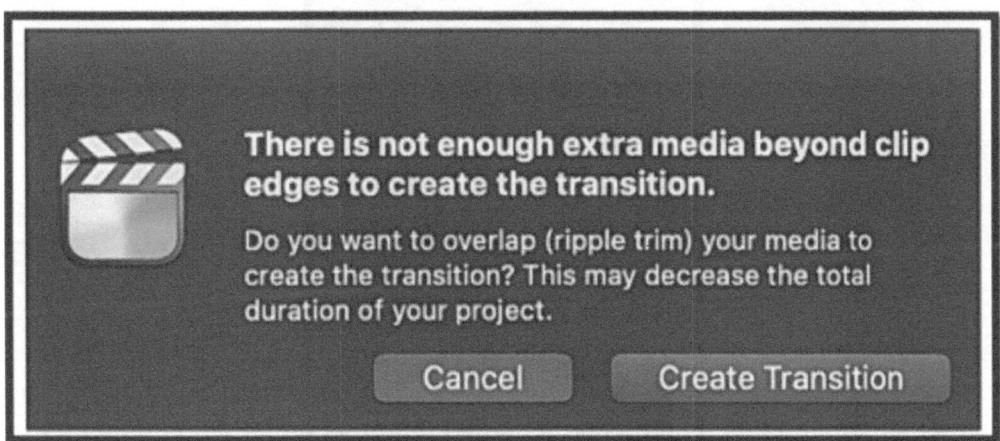

When you try to add a transition and get an error message saying there's not enough media, you know something is wrong:

If you approve the alert, one or both clips will be cut down to get the extra media that the transition needs. If that cutting would mess up the edit, stop it and make changes to make more room. A quick roll edit is enough most of the time, but sometimes you need to use a slip. Keep in mind that if you drag and drop a transition onto an edit that doesn't have enough media, it won't show you a sample of the transition in place. Instead, it will show you the mistake and let you add the transition. You'll see the transition as a new gray box over the edit. Then, based on **how zoomed in your timeline is, you might see one of three different views. You'll see a simple gray**

box when you zoom out all the way:

As you get closer, the gray box has an icon that looks like a bow tie but is an In and Out point:

The bow tie and a two-line handle on each side of the gray box can be seen when you zoom in even more:

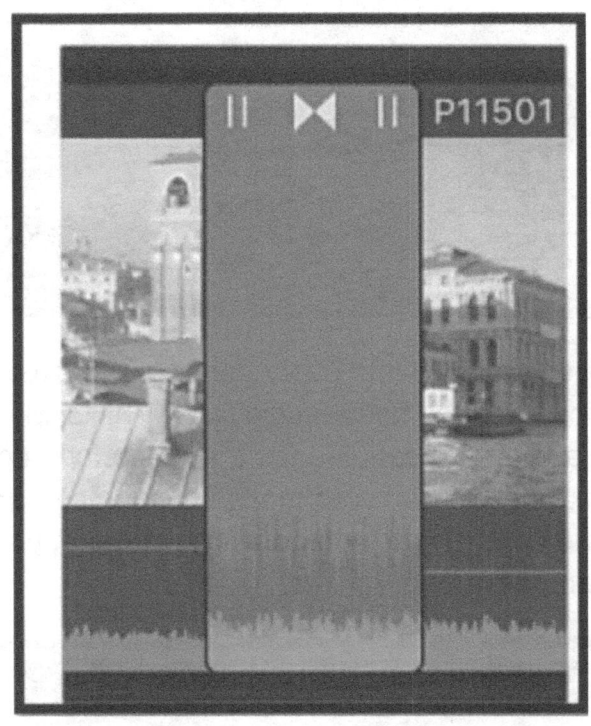

Adjusting a transition

The three things you can change about every transition are any custom settings it provides, its duration, and its position around the edit.

Not all transitions offer customizable settings, but some do, like Dissolve:

- Hold down the option key and click on a cross-dissolve trandsition in the timeline. This will pick the transition and move the play-head to that point.

Keep in mind that you may need to use ← and → to move the playhead to the middle of the transition.

- Try out different options in the **Look** menu in the Inspector. After each choice, press the **"? (shift/)"** key to see the results.

If you want to see the changes between the Film, Additive, and Subtractive options, these are what control how the **Cross Dissolve** looks. There is also an Ease setting and an Ease Amount, but they won't be very useful for a quick transition.

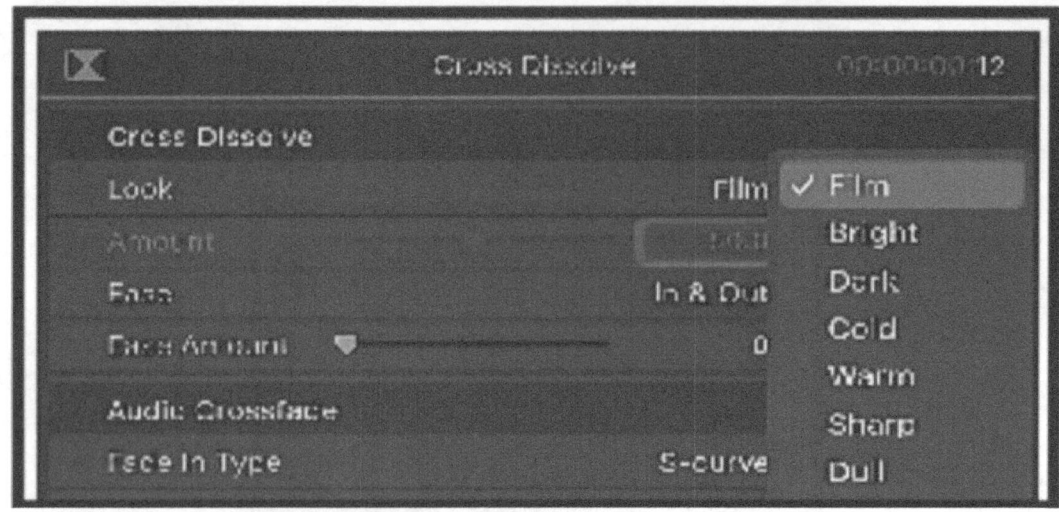

There is also an **Audio Crossfade** built into every transition. If you open the audio on the clips around the transition, you can see the usual audio fade. That's why you don't need to add a separate Crossfade to the audio. You can choose from the standard range of shapes to fade within the Inspector's menu, and you can also make changes by hand. If you move the audio **edges, even by a frame, the default fade will go away. Instead, you can use the audio fade handles to create your transition:**

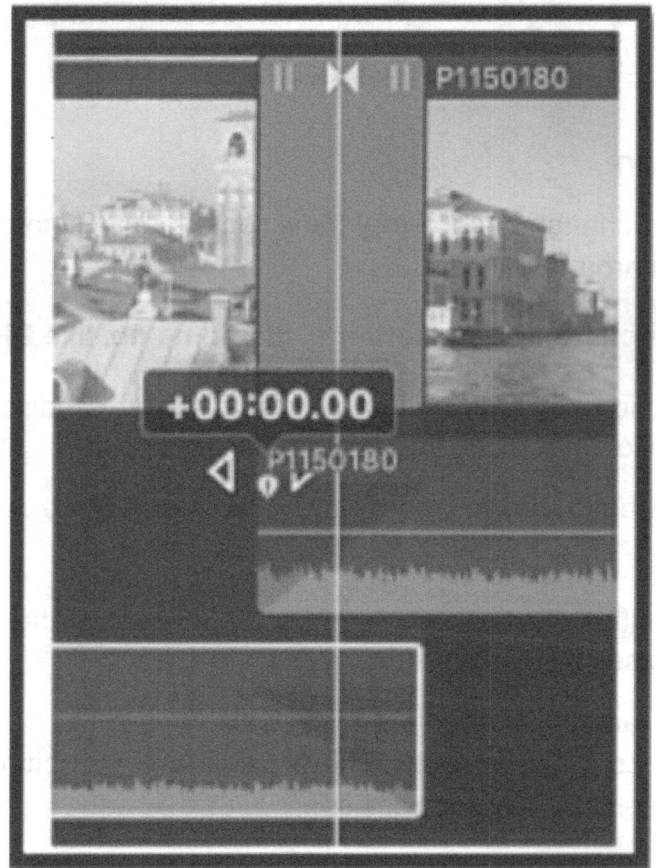

Drag on the transition's left or right edges to change how long it lasts. The change affects both sides at the same time. When you're in the right spot, you'll see the normal trim pointer. **However, there is no filmtrip on the icon because this is not a ripple operation.**

You can move the transition by dragging it when you zoom in to see the bow tie icon. There will be a **Roll icon** to let you know that you're doing a roll action, but you don't need to switch to the Trim tool because it will happen on its own. You can trade one clip for another, and after adding a transition, you might change your mind anyway.

Retiming basics

The menu for retiming is the third button in the lower left corner of the viewer. It has all the important controls. You'll need a timeline with a few clips and, if possible, some fast clips for slow motion to get started. Now is the time to record something moving on your iPhone in **Slo-**

Mo mode. If you want great results, blow a raspberry at the camera, make a splash of water, or dance. If you used your iPhone, don't airdrop it on your Mac. That will lock in a slow-motion effect that you didn't choose. Connect the iPhone to your Mac and import it straight into FCP to get the full source clip. Just import like you normally would from other cameras. It's great if some of your clips are high-speed, but they don't have to be.

Now let's move on:

- Press and hold the **option key** while clicking on a clip to pick it and move the playhead to that spot.
- Choose **Slow > 50%** from the **Retime** menu, then play the video back.

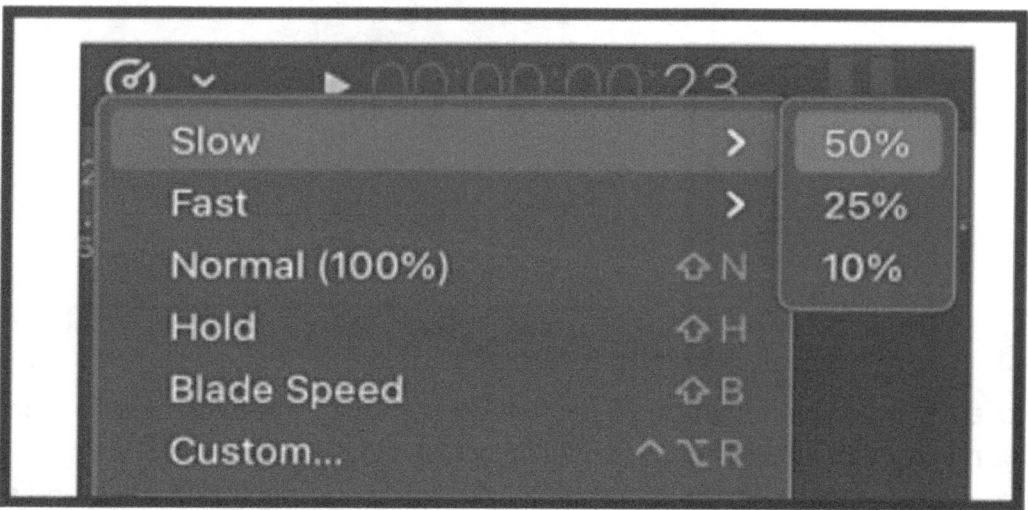

With the same part of the clip as before, this clip will now play for twice as long. There is also a new colored bar above this clip called the Retime Editor that shows the new speed of this clip. **There is also a drop-down menu that has the most important options from the main Retime menu:**

With **command-R**, you can show or hide the **Retime Editor**. Right now, it's orange to show that the video has been slowed down. Blue means the speed is going up, orange means the speed is going down, and green means the speed is normal.

- . Move the single-line handle to the left until the line turns blue. Then, play the video.

The speed at which the clip plays back is set by the handle. If you move it to the left, the clip plays faster and in less time. You can drag the handle to any speed you want, but the menu has some options that will make the slowdown a little smoother: 10/25/50%. You could also use Custom Speed instead.

- . Press **ctrl-option-R** or use the Retime menu to choose **Custom**... The Retime Editor menu on the clip can also be used.

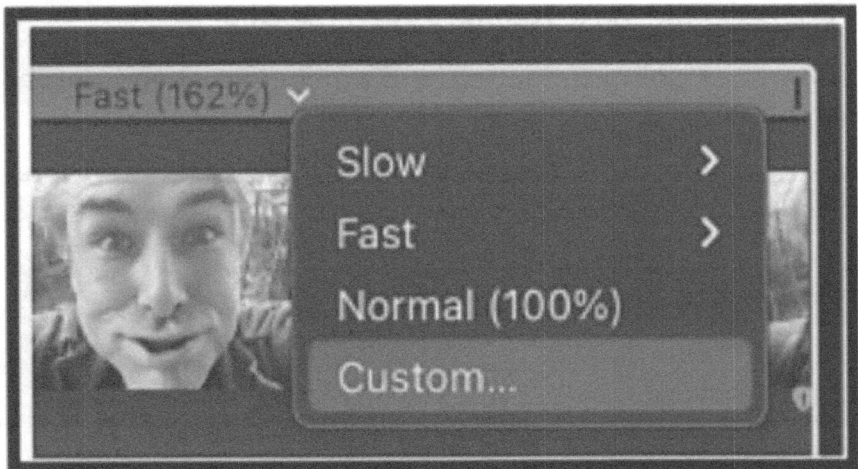

The Custom dialog box has some special features. For example, you can change the clip's speed by setting a new speed as a percentage or a time and playing the clip backward.

- . In the Pop-Up menu, change the **Rate to 20%** and press "**Return**" to apply.

Don't forget to check this important box: Feel it. If you pull the handle or use a pre-defined speed option to change the speed of a main timeline clip, it will change the length of the clip and **send ripples down the timeline. What if you don't want this? You could Lift that clip to make it a connected clip, but sometimes that's not an option either.**

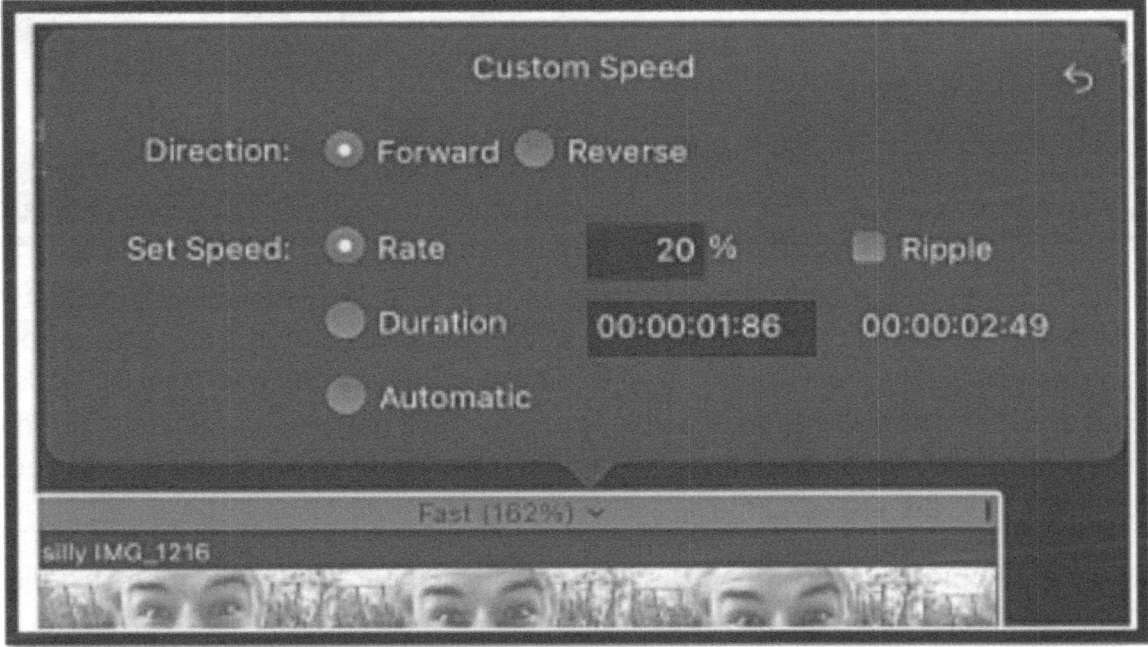

When the Ripple option is turned off, the length of a timeline clip stays the same whether it's linked or in a storyline. By changing the speed, you can see more of the clip. For example, if you set the speed to 200%, you'll see twice as much of the clip, and it will play twice as fast. The in point stays the same, but the out point (of the source clip) will change. It's kind of like a slip, but you change the speed of the original clip instead. If you don't see the best part of the clip, you can switch to the Trim tool (T) and slip the video that comes out of it. (Keep in mind that a break will be made if you speed up a clip but don't have enough media to cover the longer timeline.)

- To play the clip backward, go to **Retime > Reverse Clip**.

In the Retime Editor, lines going to the left and a negative speed percentage show that the track is in reverse:

Understanding slow motion and Automatic Speed

Knowing exactly what's going on is important for getting the most out of slow motion. That's what this part is all about. This lesson will teach you how to use **Automatic Speed** and slow-down video. Frames will be skipped when the video is sped up, as in a time-lapse. This num-ber can **get very, very big. For example, if you record an hour of nonstop video and want to show it as a timelapse over a few seconds, you might use a speed of 2000% or more:**

Moving from 30 frames per second to 25 frames per second is a small difference that will be more visible and is likely to cause the video to stutter. Keep in mind that you should record at the frame rate you want to give, even if you're not going for slow motion. This will work best if you record at a faster frame rate, so you won't have to make any new frames to slow down the **video. Normal-speed video, like 24 fps footage in a 24 fps project, will be put through one of four modes after the speed is slowed down:**

- **Normal (Floor)**: Frames are replayed, getting smaller each time, and there is generally a noticeable stutter.
- **Nearest Frame**: Frames are repeated until they reach the closest frame, which always has a noticeable stutter.

- **Frame Blending**: Frames that are close to each other are typically mixed unnaturally and deceptively.
- **Optical Flow**: This means that close frames are morphed to make new frames. This takes time to process, which can be good for some types of movement but bad for others.

You can get to these options by going to **Retime > Video Quality**. But if you plan, have the right camera, and the source footage was taken at a faster speed, you can use real frames instead of making them up. Your phone may do a better job of this than most professional cameras, though the way it shows the video will bea a little different. By definition, high-speed iPhone footage plays back in "**real-time**," missing a lot of frames. For example, if you shoot at 240 frames per second and then play back only one in ten of those frames at 24 frames per second,

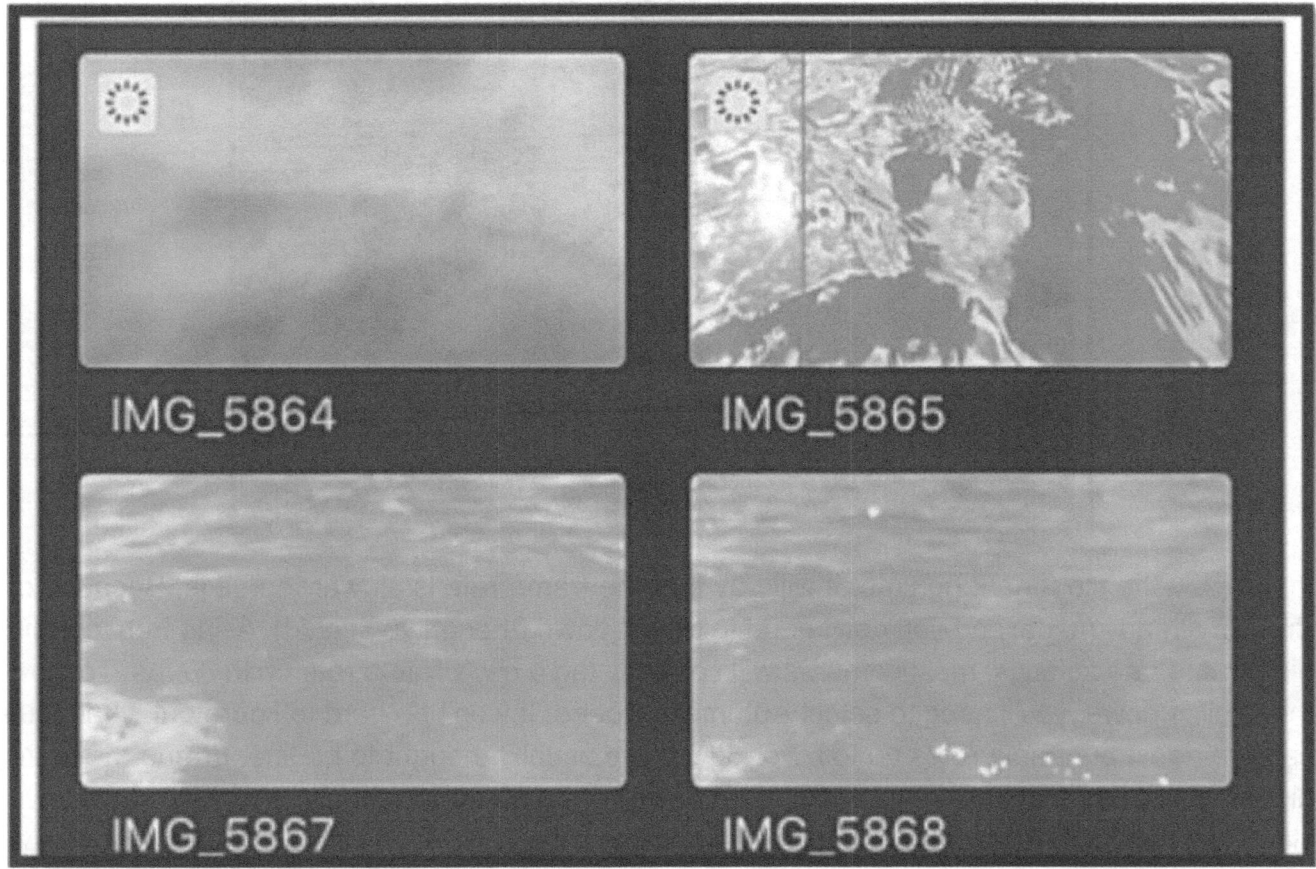

If you slow down the video, more of those frames will show up, and it will look good. To get the most natural, smooth, and slow results, go to **Retime > Automatic Speed** and play each frame at the speed of the timeline.

Automatic Speed is very useful for B-roll clips that aren't quite at the right frame rate. Apply Auto matic Speed to your timeline if it's at 24 or 25 fps, but you were given footage at 30 fps. The clips will play a little slower than normal, making use of all available frames and giving the video a slightly slower, more appealing look. The Retime > Preserve Pitch option, which is enabled by default, will avoid chipmunk noises, but this will also affect audio speed. You won't always have to pick Automatic Speed, though, because many cameras will convert to slow motion for you, at least with the fastest frame rates. "Automatic speed conform" means that many professional cameras that are set to record 180 frames per second will record all of those frames to a file with a "regular" frame rate, which could be anywhere from 24 to 60 frames per second.

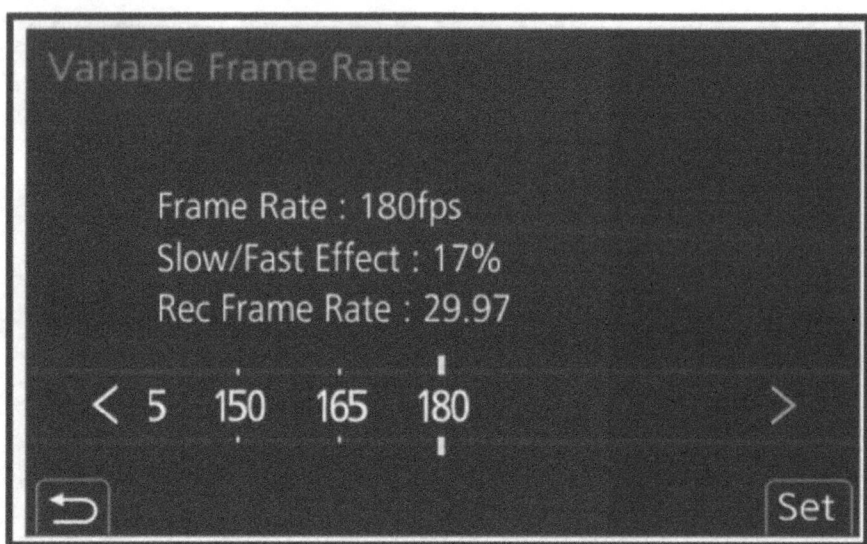

If you play the file for a long time, it will say that the frame rate is slower than it is. Because of this, it's already made, and you don't need to slow it down (though you could). Aside from certain high frame rate settings, most cameras will correctly tag a clip's frame rate up to 60 fps. To slow these clips down, you'll need to select Automatic Speed. It won't be hard to figure out what your camera does, but frame rates up to 50 or 60 fps are usually thought to be fine. Frame rates are higher than those that are likely to be slowed down by the camera. When you want to slow down video, it's helpful to record at twice the regular frame rate, like 50 fps instead of 25 fps or 60 fps instead of 30 fps. That gives you the option to quickly slow down any part of it to 50%, though the shutter speed may have to be adjusted in Pro.

CHAPTER 16: PREPARING AND EXPORTING YOUR FINAL VIDEO

EXPORTING, UPLOADING, AND DISTRIBUTING YOUR VIDEO

You will learn how to finish your timeline and show it to other people here. You should show it to your client first, get their comments, and quickly make the changes they want. If everyone is finally pleased, you should share it on several video-sharing and social media sites. But it all starts with a file, which will be compressed.

Exporting a compressed video

Direct-to-site copies and master files are two easy ways to send a high-quality file, but we'll choose the one that works every time. You should look for a project with captions in either 1080p or 4K quality for the full experience. **The following steps will help you get started:**

- Click twice on the project that you want to send out.

You don't have to do this step because you can export a project that you're not working on at the moment, but it's a good idea to make sure you're sending the right timeline.

- Grab the Range Selection tool (R) and drag a range to choose only a part of the video. You can also press I to start and O to stop the selection.

This step is completely optional; only do it if you only want to share parts of the file.

- **Click on File, then Share, then Computer. or pick Computer... from the menu says "Share" in the upper right corner:**

There is information at the bottom of the text box and three tabs at the top. On the left is a sample of the movie. The resolution, frame rate, and audio type are shown in the bottom left corner. The time is shown on the left, and the file name (container) and expected file size are shown on the right.

- You can change the **Name, Creator, and Tags** boxes if you want to.

This is where the name of the project goes, and it will also be used to make the filename:

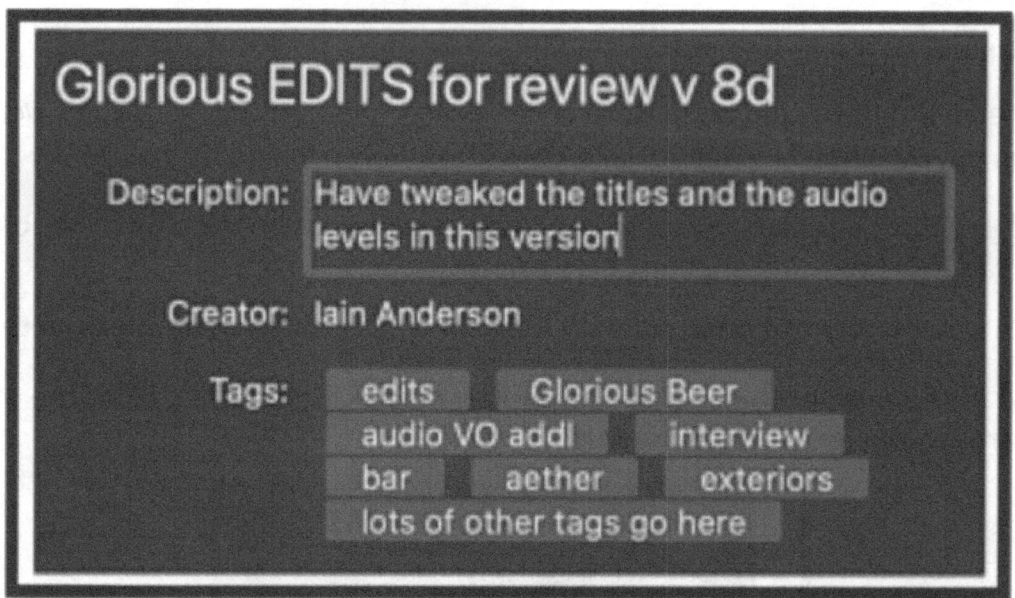

Keep in mind that QuickTime Player will still show this name even if you change the title later, so give it a name that makes sense.

- The options can be seen by clicking on Roles.

If you used comments in this project, this page will give you more options.

- On the bottom of the captions page, check the box that says **Export each SRT language as a separate file**. This will let you export closed captions.

There are some places where style doesn't work, so don't include it when you send SRT captions.

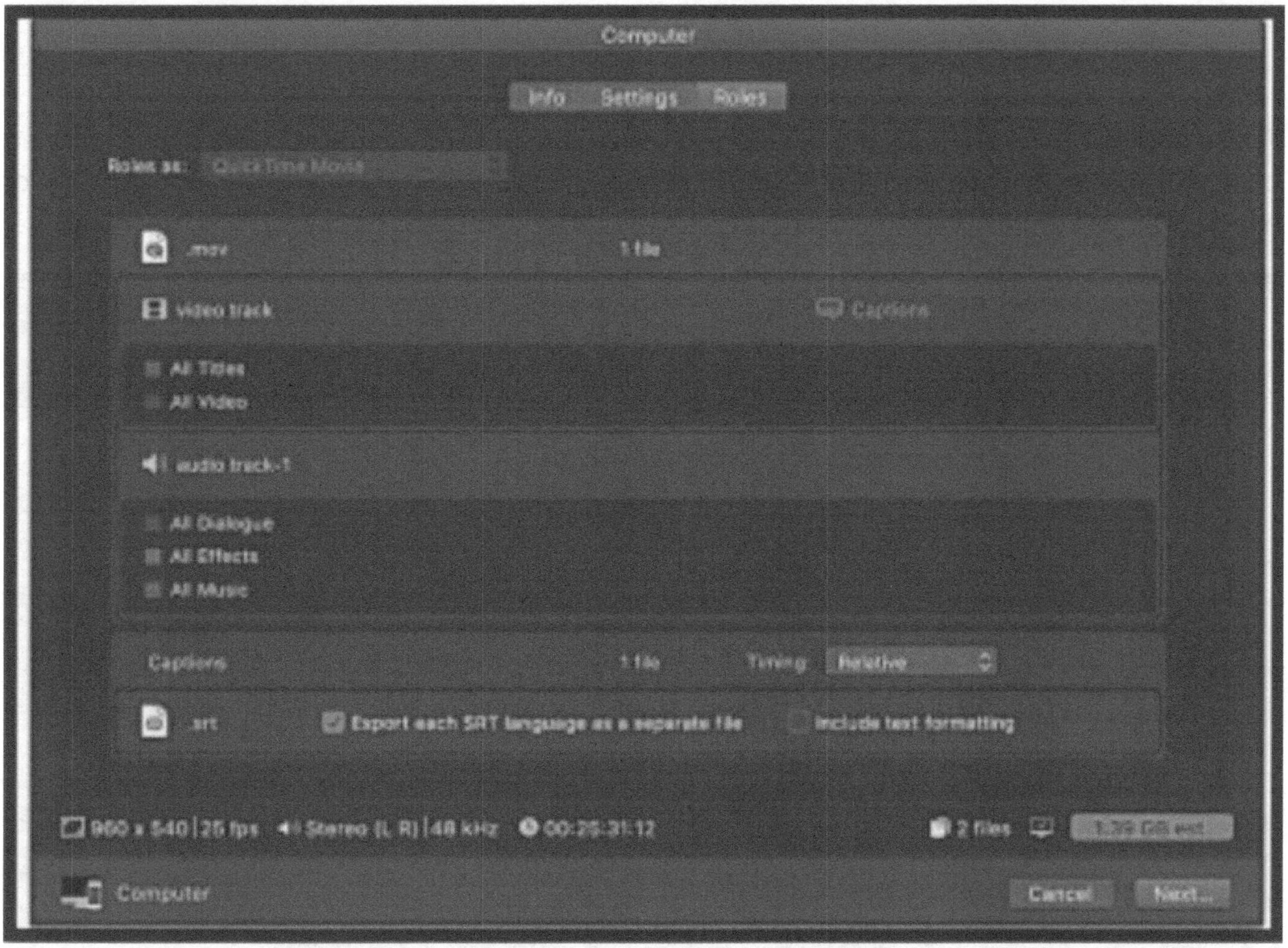

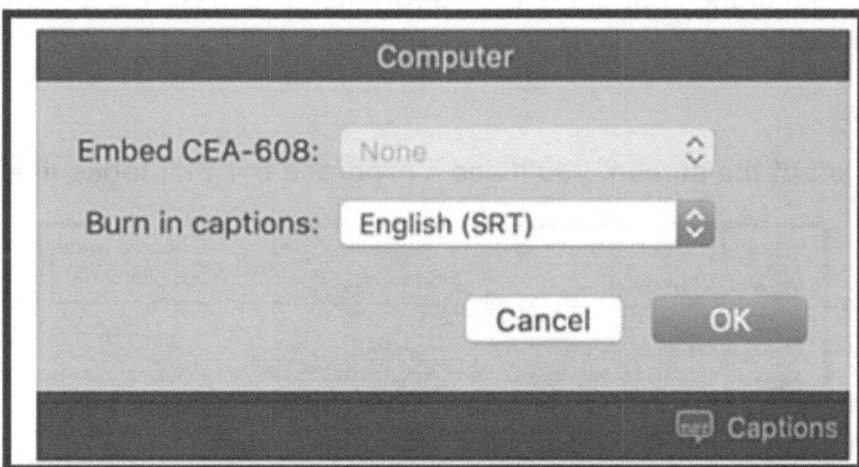

- To download embedded CEA-608 or Open (burned-in) Captions, click the word Captions in the video part above and then choose the right option from the menus.

Keep in mind that you should only use open captions if your delivery method doesn't allow Closed Captions.

There isn't much you can do with burn-in comments here. You'll need to use a third-party app to turn them into titles.

- Before you save, click on **Settings** and make sure the file options are right.

These should be the same as the setting you saved earlier for "Computer." The setting will also change if you make changes here, so don't! Instead, make a new set of presets for each type of export. This is still how it should look:

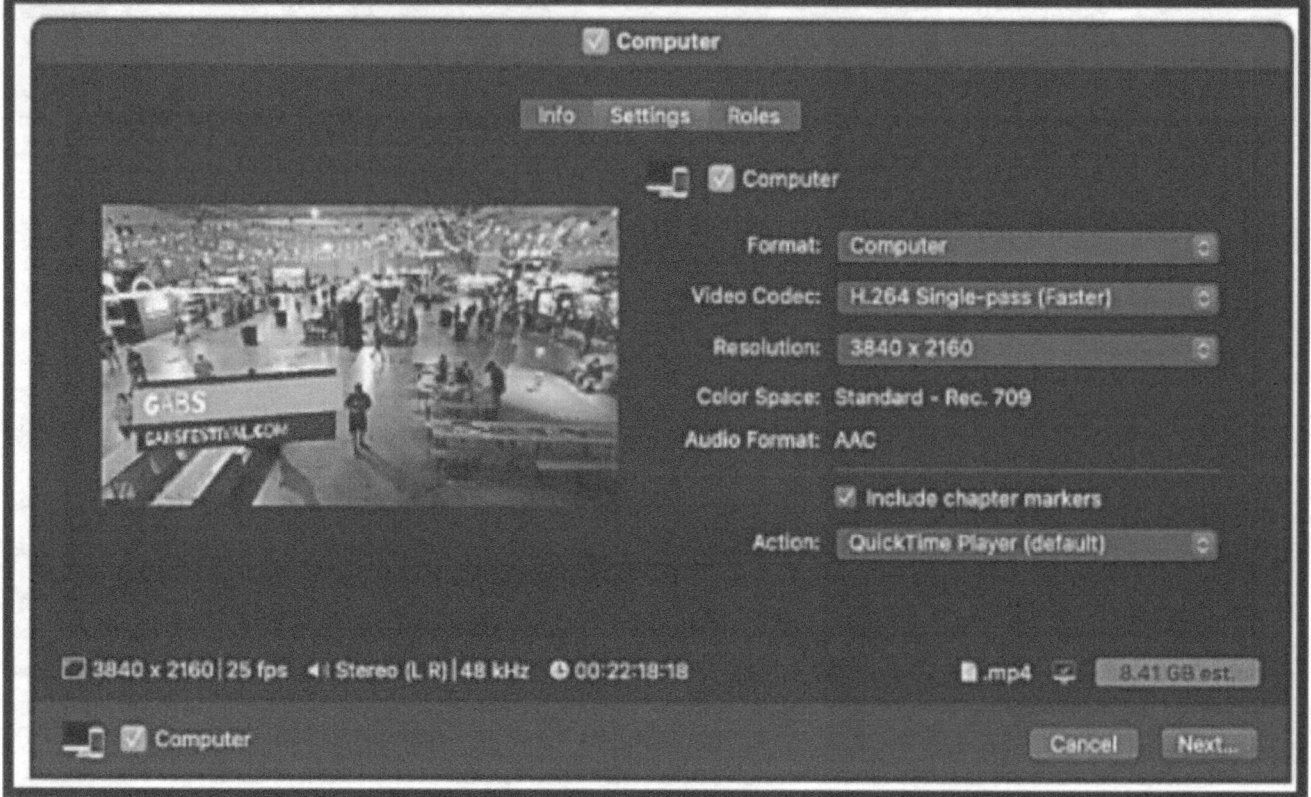

- Pick a place to save the file after clicking **"Next."**

Click the small button to the right of the drop-down menu to make the Save box bigger if you only see a very small one.

- Press **Save**.

Now, at the top left of the screen, you'll see a progress bar that looks like a clock:

- To see the Background Tasks box, click this progress bar.

Any task's progress will be shown in more depth in this optional window:

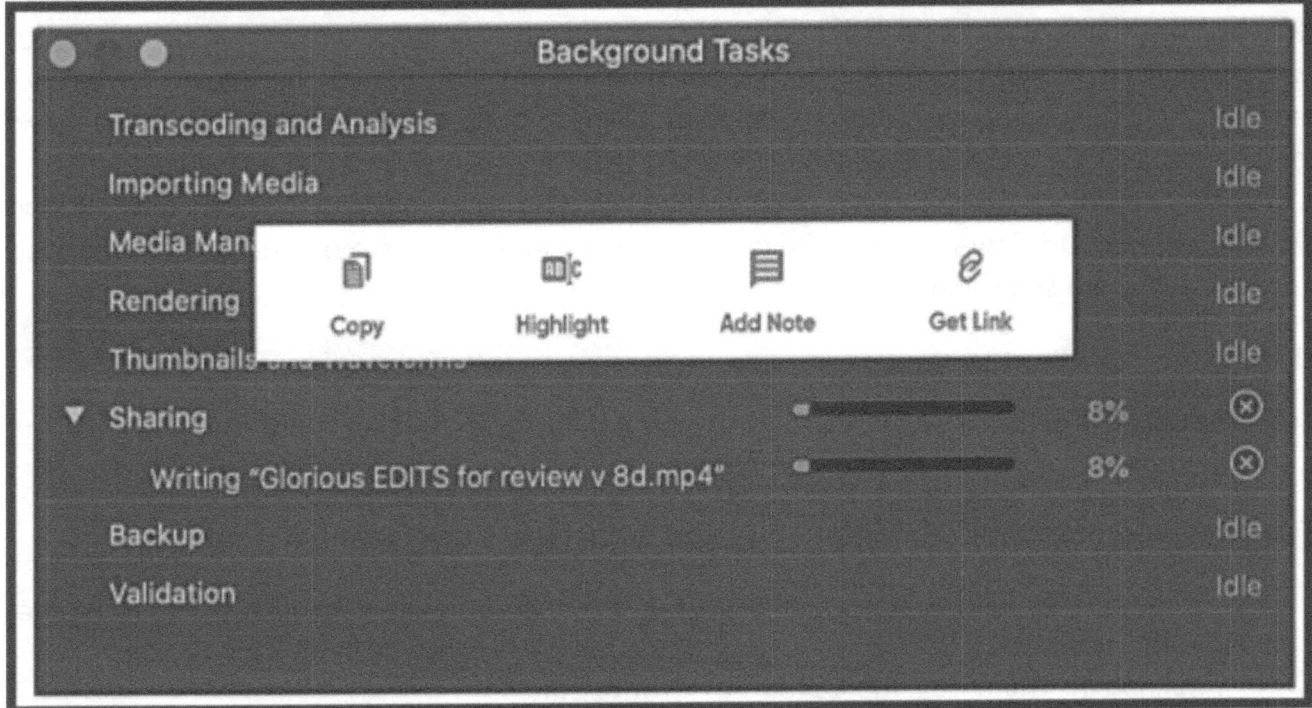

- Play the exported file in QuickTime Player to make sure it's what you want it to be when the timeline is done.
- Make sure the **.srt captions** file is next to the video file if you saved subtitles.

For each upload, all you need to do is make sure the name and text settings are right. It's simple once you know how. The final option is to use File > Export Captions if the closed captions are the only thing that has changed (or if you forgot to include them in the first export!). Importantly, exporting multiple changes is simple.

Don't double-click on them; just pick them all at once in the browser and share them all at once:

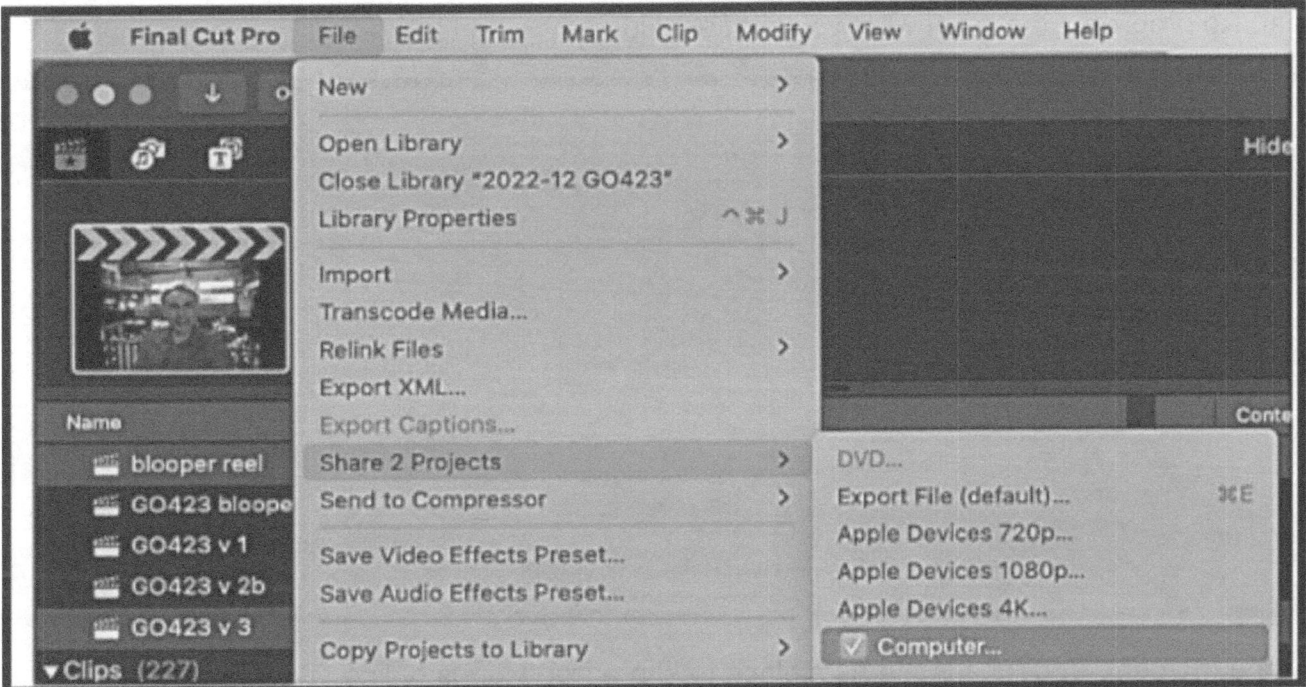

But you can't pick out just a part of a timeline or change the names, descriptions, or settings for each project in a multi-Project file. That's probably not a problem, though, because it saves a lot of time. You can send normal clips or Compound Clips in the same way, but you might not need to. As soon as you have a compressed video and text file, you can post it to any video site using a browser or a dedicated up-loading app. You can also share the file with the client using iCloud Drive, Dropbox, OneDrive, Google Drive, or another service. Let's move on to the next step because there are some fancy options as well.

Uploading for client review

The best option is to use a website through a browser, but you can also share a zipped file using a third-party integrated service or a sharing app.

The basic pro process is as follows if you're uploading a draft using a browser:

- Go to the site where you want to post your movie in a browser (like Safari, Chrome, Firefox, etc.).
- First, log in. Then, click the **Upload or Create** button.
- To play your video file, drag it into the browser.
- Use the privacy settings to keep the movie private for now while it uploads.
- Add your captions.
- Send a link to your client to look over.

Getting comments, making changes, copying your project, and going through all of these steps again will be part of the review loop. The client will have to check the notes before they are sent out, even if they aren't finished until the final version.

Uploading for distribution

You may want to send your video somewhere once the review process is over and everything has been signed off. For a lot of editors, that means putting it online for free. This part is all about that. No problem if that's not what you're after-skip:

At the moment, YouTube is the best place to share free videos online. The website is great; it has a lot of features like auto-captioning and translation, changing captions, comments, making **money, and more. It's very famous, and there are apps for almost every device. It can bring in an audience:**

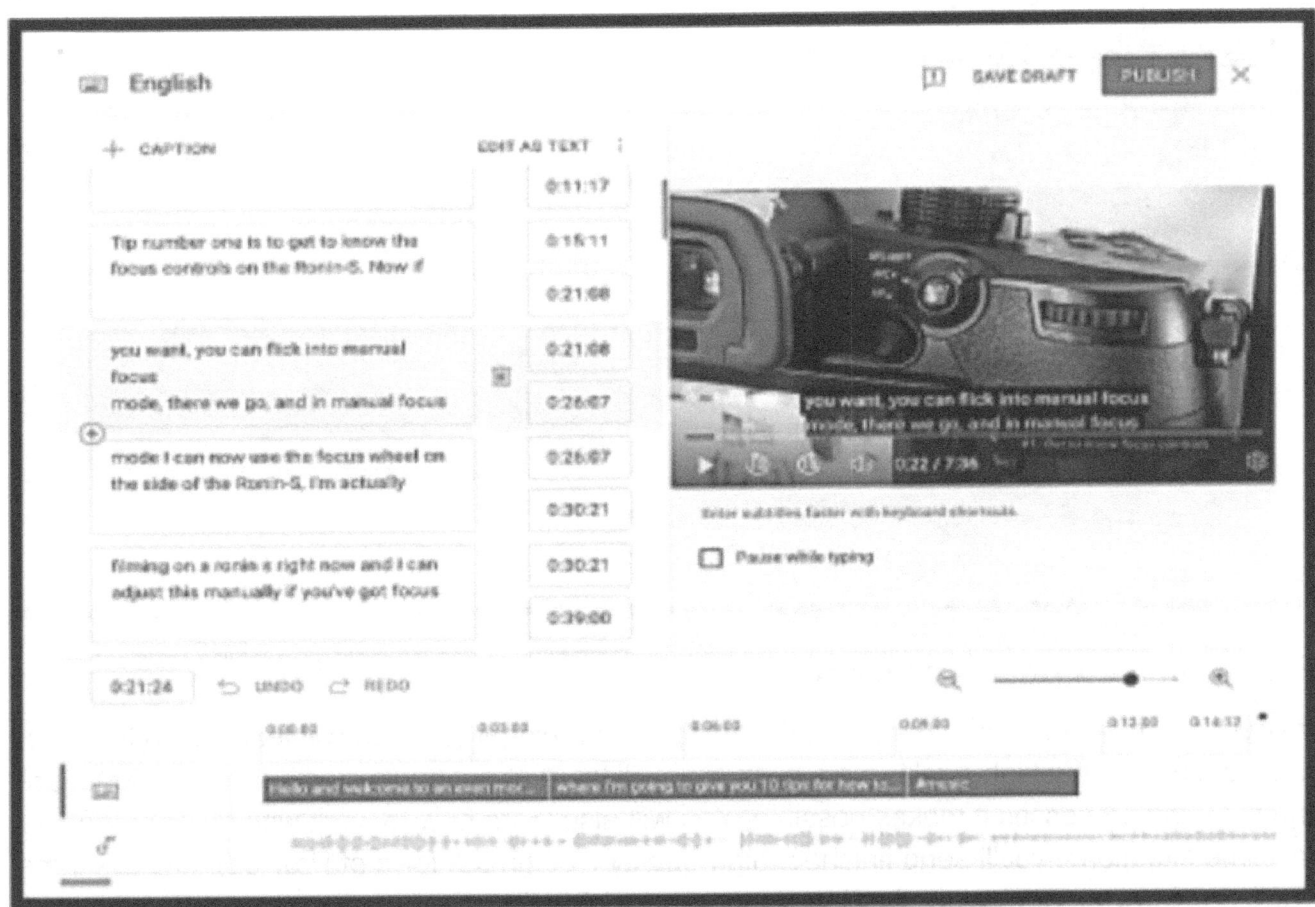

While social media platforms like Twitter, Facebook, Instagram, LinkedIn, and others share short, free videos with millions of people every day, video-focused rivals like Vimeo focus more on paid and embedded sharing. A lot more social media sites are still being built, and by the time you read this, most of them will have failed, so I won't go into too much detail about how you'll finally share your movie. You can use the platform for my website if it has one, but if not, you might need to send the final video file to your phone and share it using a special app. You can easily send files from your Mac to your iPhone or iPad using AirDrop.

To get your video on YouTube, Vimeo, or anothers ite, all you have to do is follow the steps provided in the previous client review. What you'll need:

- The final video file
- The captions file
- Thumbnail images that are intriguing but not annoying
- A full description that appeals to people and algorithms
- A plan for advertising and promotion

Your excellent movie will go unheard and ignored if you undervalue the influence of promotion. It's also important to control expectations. It's bad to have no ideas at all, but having a few can be normal. Remember that most videos are made for a very specific group of people, no matter what niche your clients are trying to reach, and that most videos will never get as many views in a day as a famous music video:

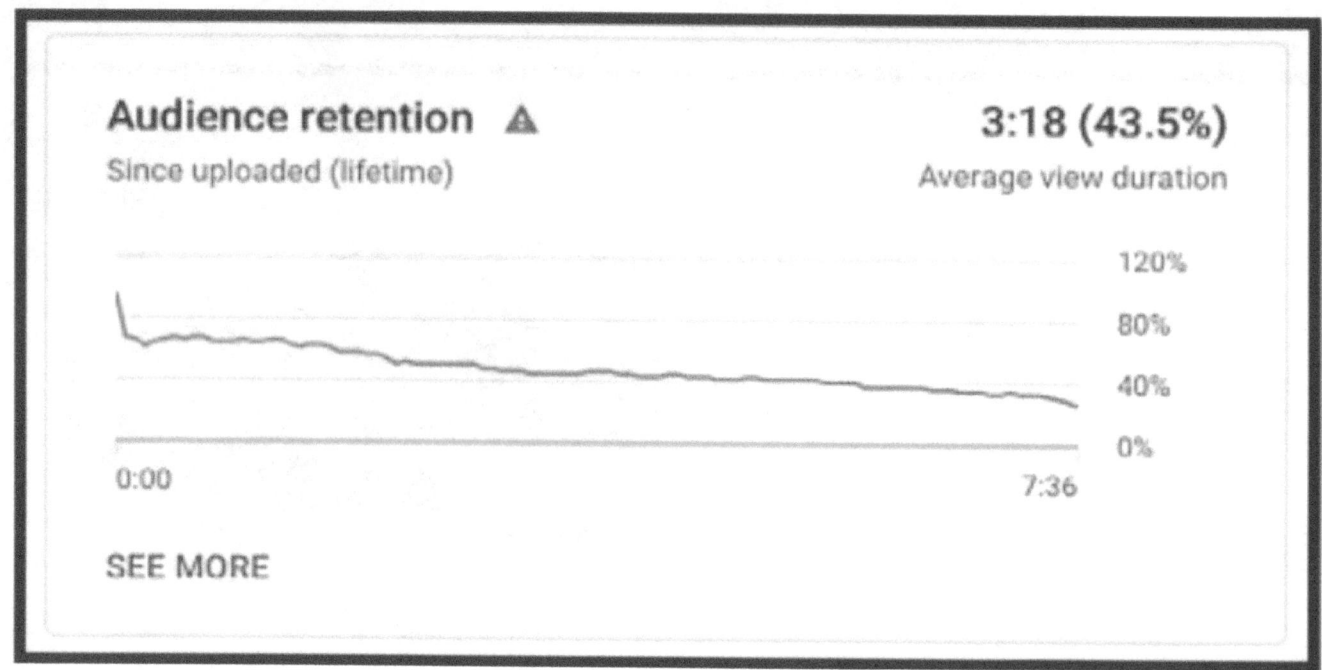

Exporting for further production

If you want to give the final result or just your part of a bigger job, you will learn everything you need to know about high-quality work here. You will learn about audio stems, ProRes, XML, and the amazing processes it makes possible. You will also learn how to work with other producers. In some situations, you'll send finished, high-quality files (in the form of ProRes), and in others, you'll provide your original media files along with an XML file or another compressed version. It's even possible to send a whole Library along with everything in it. Many audio and video programs are used in the creation world as a whole, and if you want to work with other people, you'll need to be able to send them something they can use.

Understanding ProRes

This is a group of intermediate or "mezzanine" formats called ProRes. They are great for exporting high-quality files. Even though it's simple to export to this well-known Apple format, let's talk about why you might want to. You don't have to optimize some compressed files to work with them, but you do have to change them to ProRes 422 first if you can't or don't want to **work with them. Not every file is the same, and not all H.264 files are the same. Some may need to be optimized:**

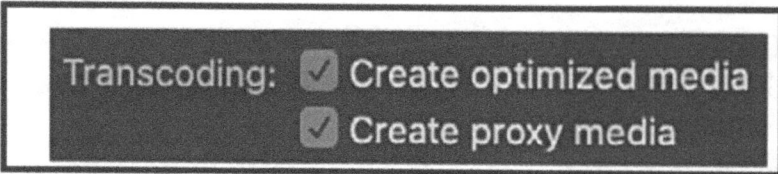

Because ProRes is a standard format in the business, it's a smart choice for sharing high-quality files with other professionals to be edited or produced further. The codec is made to make decoding as fast as possible, even in multicam processes. It can also be repeatedly compressed into the same codec without losing quality. **ProRes is an intra-frame format, which means that each frame is compressed separately. Not all intra-frame codecs are easy to work with, but ProRes is:**

```
Format:         Apple ProRes 4444 XQ (up to 12-bit)
                HD (1-1-1)
                Stereo (L R), Linear PCM, 24 bit little-
                endian signed integer, 48000 Hz
Resolution:     3840 x 2160, 16:9
Encoded FPS:    25
Data Size:      126 MB
Data Rate:      966.65 Mbit/s
Current Size:   3840 x 2160 (Actual Size)
```

When you see **"optimized,"** it always means **"regular" ProRes 422**; however, you can choose to send using another member of the same codec family. Regular ProRes 422 probably won't lose any quality that you can see, but you can use a lower-quality version to save space or a higher-quality version for the most difficult post-production tasks if you'd rather.

Here are your ProRes options, along with the estimated goal data rate for 1080p at 29.97 FPS:

- ProRes 422 Proxy: This codec operates at 45 Mbps and offers low-quality output, often exhibiting visible artifacts. It's not recommended for exporting due to its inferior quality.
- ProRes 422 LT: Operating at 102 Mbps, this codec provides medium-quality output. It may sometimes display visible artifacts and should be used only in situations where storage space or bandwidth is limited.
- ProRes 422: With a bit rate of 147 Mbps, this code delivers high-quality output, suitable for general high-quality exports.
- ProRes 422 HQ: Operating at 220 Mbps, this codec offers very high-quality output, ideal for exporting footage captured by high-end cameras.
- ProRes 4444: This codec operates at 330 Mbps and provides very high-quality output with a 4:4:4 color space and transparency support. It's recommended for high-quality exports, especially when full-color information or transparency is essential.
- ProRes 4444 XQ: With a bit rate of 500 Mbps, this codec delivers extremely high-quality output with a 4:4:4 color space and transparency support. It's the best choice for exporting footage from top-tier cameras when maximum quality, color fidelity, or reliability ransparency is required.

Exporting a ProRes Video

This process is very similar to sending a zipped file, assuming you've already prepared your project for sharing by following the earlier steps.

- Use the **Range Selection** tool or the **I** and **O** keys to pick out a project, a compound clip, a clip, or a part of a project.

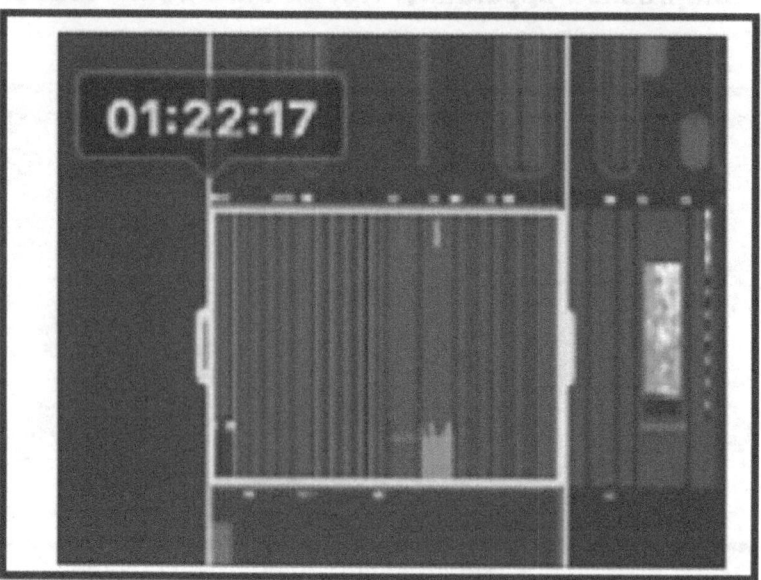

- To get to the master file, go to **File > Share > Master File**, or use the drop-down button in the upper right corner to find it.
- You can change the name, author, and tags if you want to.
- At the top, click **Settings**. Make sure that Format, **Video and Audio** are selected.

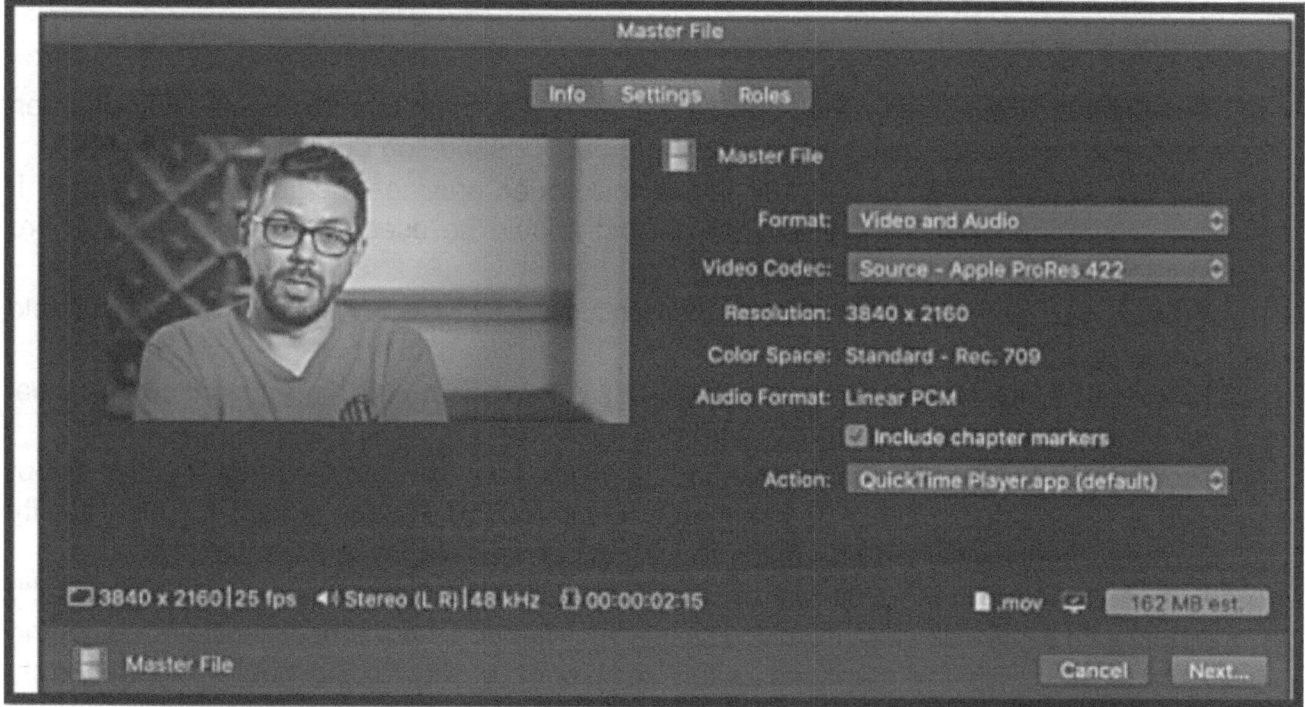

- Under Video Codec, pick the version of ProRes you want, or pick Source to use the default for your project.
- Choose the right options under Roles if you need to send comments.
- Pick a place to save the file, click Next, and then click Save.

Exporting separate elements with roles

Make the project more complicated by adding more titles (using the title role) and different types of audio (Effects and Music).

This will let you share more than one element. Start the export process all over again when you're ready.

- Use the **Range Selection tool**, or I and O, to pick out a project or part of a Project.
- To get to the master file, go to **File > Share > Master File**, or use the drop-down button in the upper right corner to find it.
- There is a **Settings** button at the top. Make sure that the format is set to video and audio.
- Select **Source** from the **Video Codec** menu (other options will also function).
- After clicking on Roles, go to the top left corner and select **Multitrack QuickTime Movie** from the drop-down menu.

There are now more options in the Roles section, and there is one video track and several audio tracks in the main part of this window:

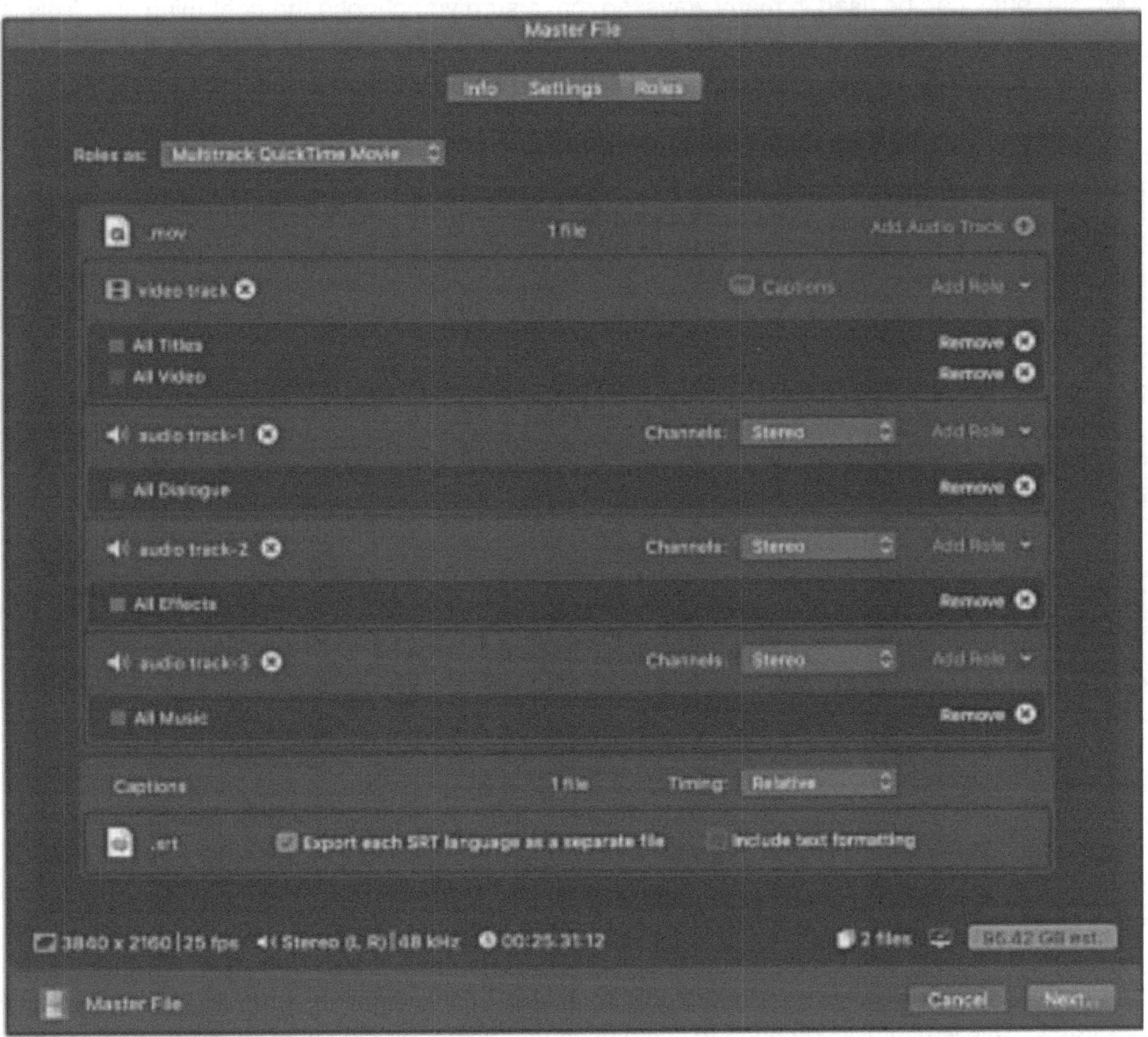

- To turn off one of your video parts, click the "Remove x" button next to it.
- Just find the menu to the right of the video track that says "Add Role." From there, choose the job you want to add back in.

From all the current video parts, only one video track will be produced. Each audio part, on the other hand, will be saved to a different track in the QuickTime movie. This way, someone else can direct each one separately in the future. If you don't want extra parts, you can turn them off.

- Pick out a place to save the file, click Next, and then click Save.

Exporting to XML

You'll often need to send to XML an exchange file that many programs can read to make advanced processes possible. XML stands for "eXtensible Markup Language." It is a text-based language that can be read by humans, but it's not in a set format like JPEG or AIFF. There are different ways for each app to use XML, so it's not enough for an app to support XML in general; it also needs to support the FCP version of XML. In this process, an XML file is exported from Final Cut Pro and then sent to a different app, which changes how it works. It's easy to make an XML file, but it can be used in many ways, so make sure you choose the right thing first. This is because you can export a project, an event, or even a whole library to XML. To find out what you want to export, choose Project, Even, or Library, and then choose File > Ex-port XML.

The name of the file you saved will show you which one you chose:

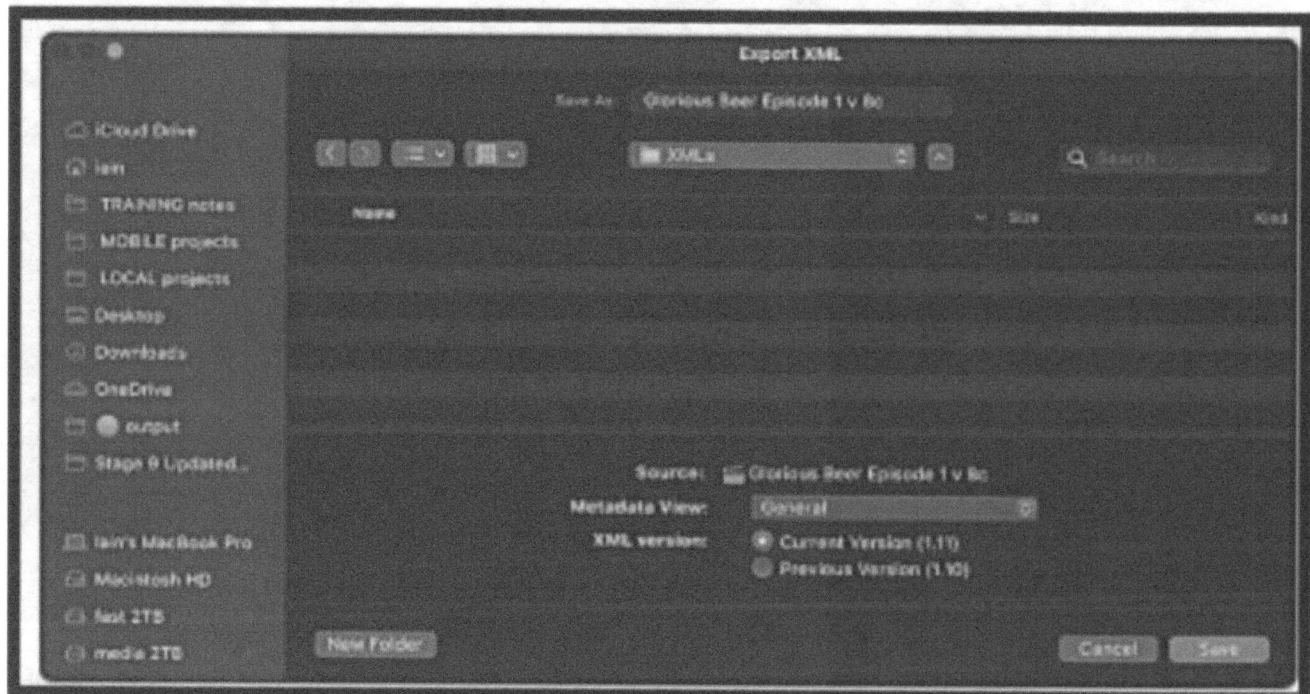

It is important to note that an XML file only explains the files and/or changes; it does not contain any media. You need to provide both the media and the XML file if you're going to use XML. If the audio engineer has the XML and media-ready, a third-party app called **X2Pro** can convert them to AAF. This gives the audio engineer using ProTools full freedom. If you don't have X2Pro, you might be able to use DaVinci Resolve as a conversion tool. It also does a lot of other things. XML lets Resolve and other translation tools send and receive timelines from and to other editing programs. This is useful if you need to finish a job that someone else started. A lot of other apps can also use XML in useful ways. The Producer's Best Friend option is interesting because it can make tables that show the exact lengths of clips, themes, parts, and a lot more. This could be very important if you need to pay for stock video or audio. Most of the time, if you find an outside app that can help you understand the information on a timeline, it probably uses XML:

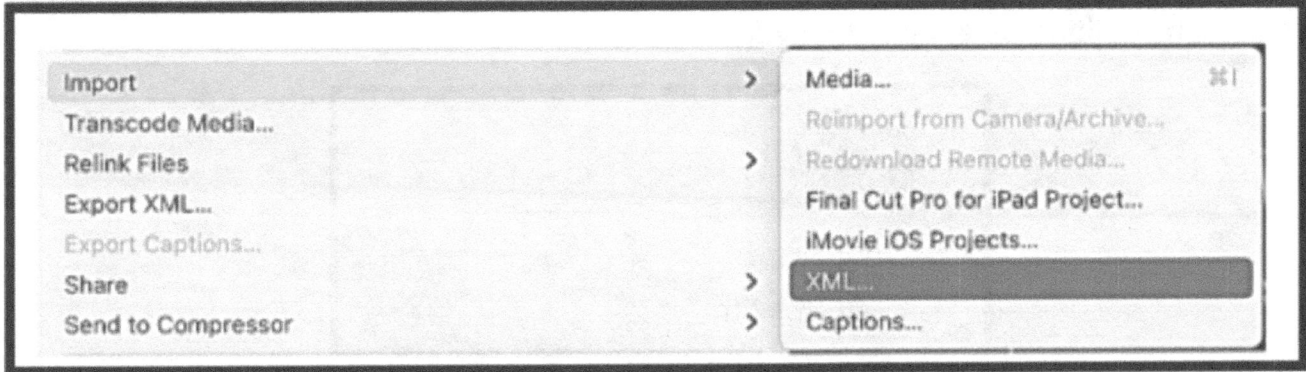

Since you can import an XML file with **File > Import > XML**, you could even occasionally export an XML from your timeline to serve as a backup of sorts. There are, however, some pieces of information that XML doesn't store properly or that aren't read correctly when import-ing and data can be lost. Most of the time, basic changes should work, but some text style and Drop Zone placements may be left in their settings. It's important to make sure that all of the programs that use the. fcpxml file are up-to-date. It's important to note that the FCP 10.6 version changed the XML format to 1.10 and added. fcpxmld, which is a bundle rather than a single file. If you want to add tracking data or make changes in cinematic mode, you'll need this container-based style, just like a library. There's no trouble if XML doesn' t work for you because of its flaws. You should learn more about change libraries.

Working with Final Cut Pro backups

Archiving your work

While the archiving process not be fun, it is very important. If a client comes back to you in six months and needs to quickly and easily re-edit a project you worked on before, you'll get praise. Even though it would be great to have endless storage, you can't keep all of your old jobs in your current storage forever. Video is big, and it can fill up hard drives of any size.

Consolidating media

You can make it easy to copy all the files you need to start working on the same project again in the future by moving them all to one place and consolidating them. If you put your media in a **Library, this is easier because there is only one item to deal with within the Finder. But there are other things to think about as well. Here's what you need to do:**

The first thing you should do is bring a final, finished copy of your movie intothe Library. A ProRes file is best, but an H.264 copy will work in a pinch. Adding the final movie protects against the chance that the library itself will become useless at some point. How can we get a **look inside? To be honest, libraries are just fancy folders.**

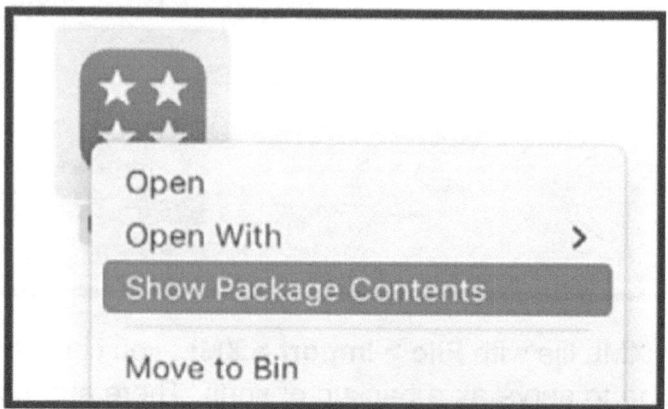

Anyone can open a library and get the movie files inside, even if they don't have Final Cut Pro. To do this, just right-click on the library and pick "**Show Package Contents**." There is a folder inside the box called **Original Media** for each event, and each folder has a name that matches the event. All of the movie files from the Even t are inside. Next, choose whether you want to put your media in the **Library** or somewhere else. Click on your **Library** in the browser's toolbar, then click on **Modify Settings** next to **Storage Locations** in the **Inspector window**. This is where you can make your choice:

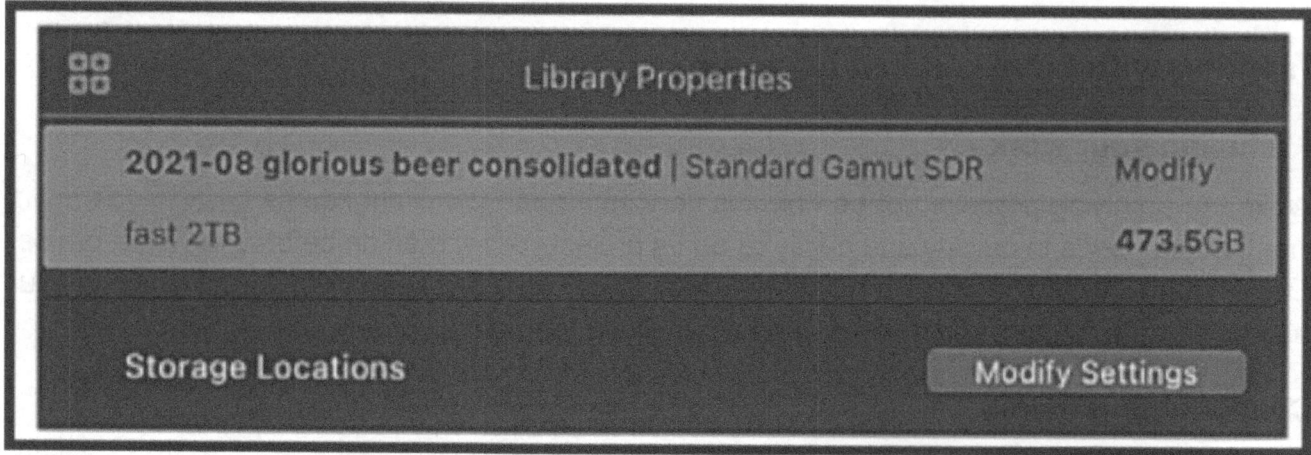

You can stick to the choice you made when you first built the Library, or you can change your mind. As we've already talked about, some advanced processes need external media, but internal media is easier to handle when you're working alone. It can work, but when you finally move this Library to backup storage, you'll need to move two things with external media, **and you might need to rejoin media after reopening:**

But this time, don't put your Motion content in the **Motion Templates** folder on your Mac. Instead, put it in the Library. So, any custom titles, generators, effects, or transitions you've used will be saved in the Library. If you open this Library on a different Mac, they will still be there.

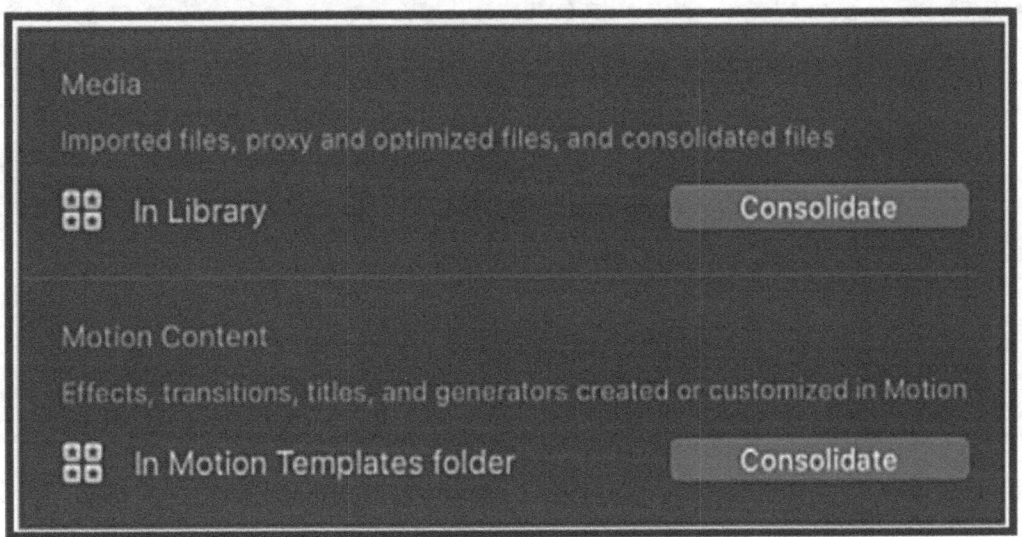

Once you are sure of where everything is, go back to Inspector and click on "**Consolidate**" next to both "**Media**" **and Motion Content.**" This time, make sure you are sure of each one. Now, almost everything you need will be put into the Library, or both the library and the external media place. **What might not be there? Additionally, you'll need the following things to back up manually:**

- **Color LUTs** loaded from your hard drive
- **Non-standard fonts** used in titles

- **Third-party effects, titles, generators, transitions, and other plug-ins that use copy protection**—they'll need to be in-stalled on any other Mac that opens your Library.

The main focus will be on your Library, though. It's going to be big, but you can get some of that room back.

Reducing the size of libraries

To make more room, go to the library. Then, go to **File > Delete Generated Library Files**. (You can also get rid of files that were made for only certain clips.) When the text box comes up, you can delete render files that were made while the Library was open, which could be important. If you want to save room while editing, you can use this command at any time. However, if you have **Background Rendering** turned on in your settings, it will be made again. If the job is complete, you might as well delete not just **Unused** render files but **All** of them.

You can also get rid of any of your **Optimized or Proxy** files. You no longer need them because they were made to speed up the editing process, and you're done with it. Also, that will save a lot of room:

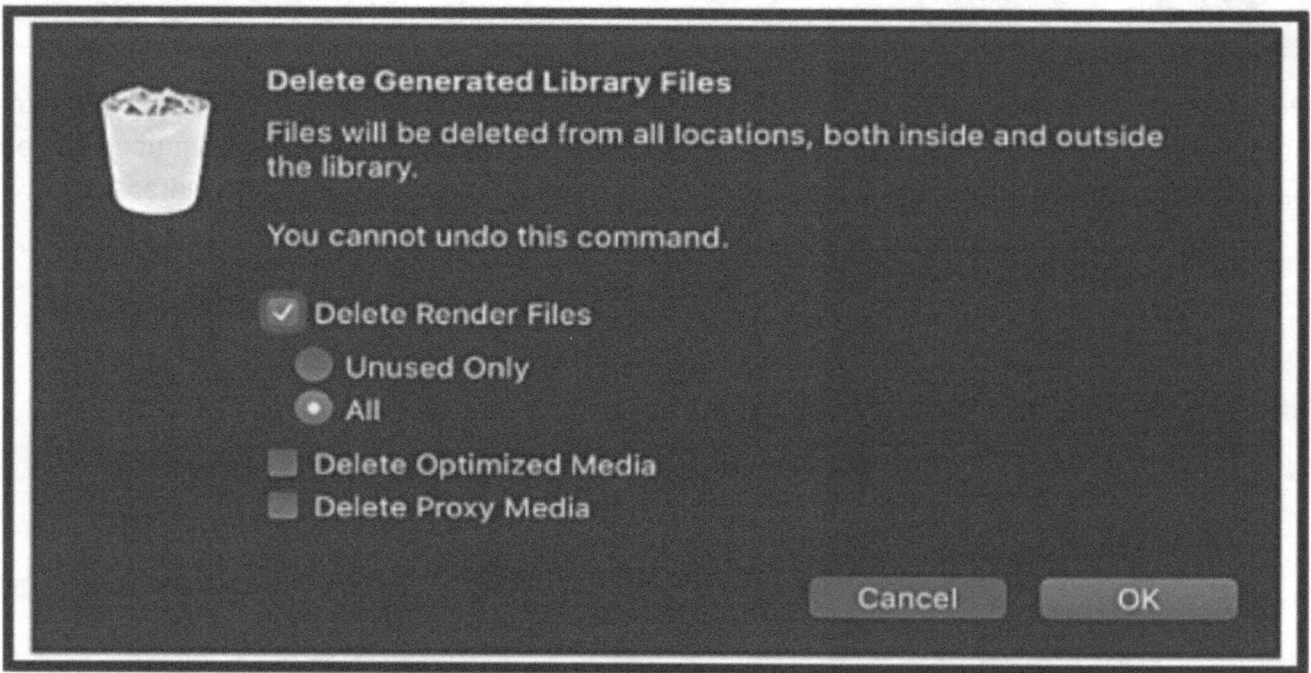

You can still use the original media if you don't have the modified or proxy files. At worst, it will be a little slow. Keep in mind that even the original media can be big, and you can get rid of more if you need to.

Deleting unused media

You can push one more button if your library is still too big. Not everyone will want to take the final step, but it is an option. If some files were never used, you can delete the clips that weren't used and make a new library with only the clips you need.

Here's how the process works:

- Make a new library and give it a new name. Then, set **Motion Content** to "**In Library**."
- From your old full library, drag the final version of any projects you want to keep into the new library.

It only copies the clips that were used in the Project when you copy it to a new Library. Words from clips that were used will come through, but other clips don't make the trip. Don't do this if there are funny behind-the-scenes moments that could be useful later. Also, keep in mind that this method does not trim any media; if you only use 10 frames of an hour-long clip, you will need to keep the whole hour-long clip. It will still leave a lot of room for most jobs, though. Let's get that thing off your main working drive now that you've saved as much room as you can.

Copying to an archive drive

If you're transferring your library to a standard drive without any special requirements, simply utilize the Finder to copy the library (along with your external media folder, if applicable) to a spacious hard drive. Repeat this process with another hard drive for redundancy. It's beneficial to label the drives accordingly to easily identify their contents alongside your main Mac. Additionally, keep a record of the drive names to track the location of your Library. For further **assistance in managing your libraries, consider using a third-party application like Final Cut Library Manager, which offers features such as tracking Library locations and more:**

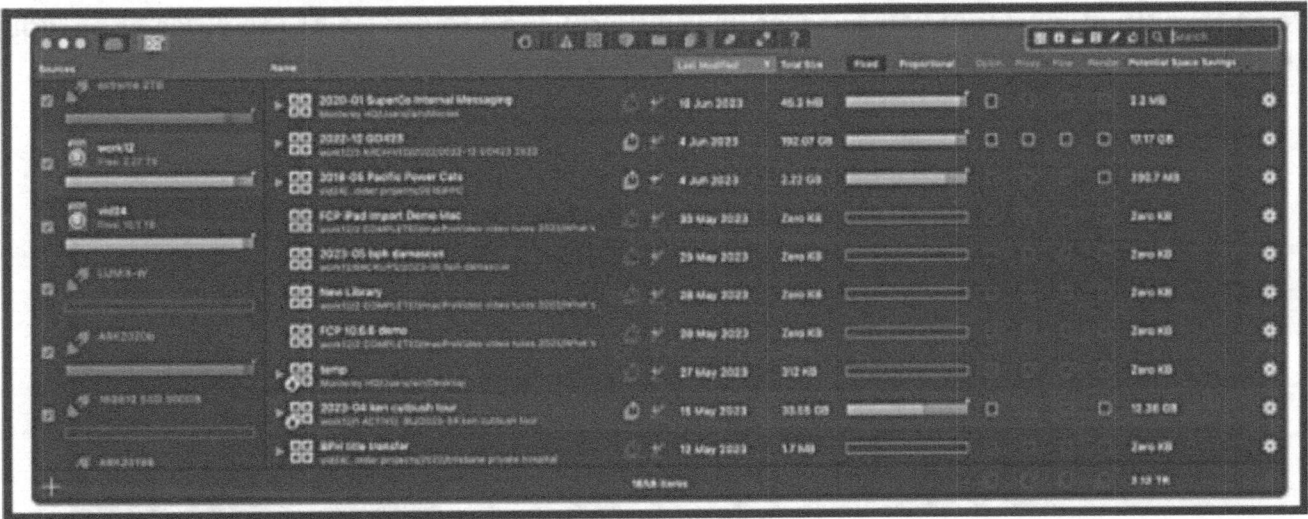

Restoring from a backup

The first step is pretty easy if you want to restore a saved project. You can open the Library, do what you need to do, and then copy it back to your working drive. When you're done, store it again. What if you delete something important by mistake and then close FCP before you can fix it? **That is also usually simple; since FCP regularly saves copies of each library, it opens:**

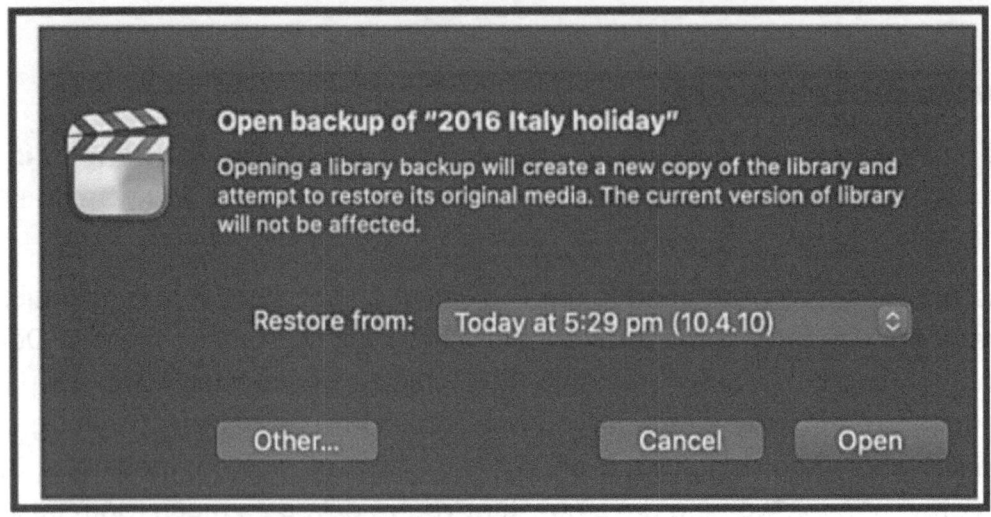

Select **File > Open Library > From Backup** to roll back a library to a previous version of itself. An option to pick older versions of the Library is prese nted in a text box. Pick one, click "**Open**," and it will open with a time stamp in the name. Just close the old Library and open the new one. Then drag any items you need from the old library to the new one. You can still get back even if your Library won't be open at all. You can find your backups by default in your home area, in **Movies**, and in **Final Cut Backups**. Open that folder now. By the way, this isa great place to include if you use cloud backups.) There is a section for every library you've ever worked on, and inside each of those is a group of Libraries that have been given a time stamp. There is no media in any **of these backups, so you'll have to find it in a backup of media, either in a full copy of the library that has media built-in or in an external media folder. Backups don't take up much room without media, but if you need to get rid of the older ones, you should:**

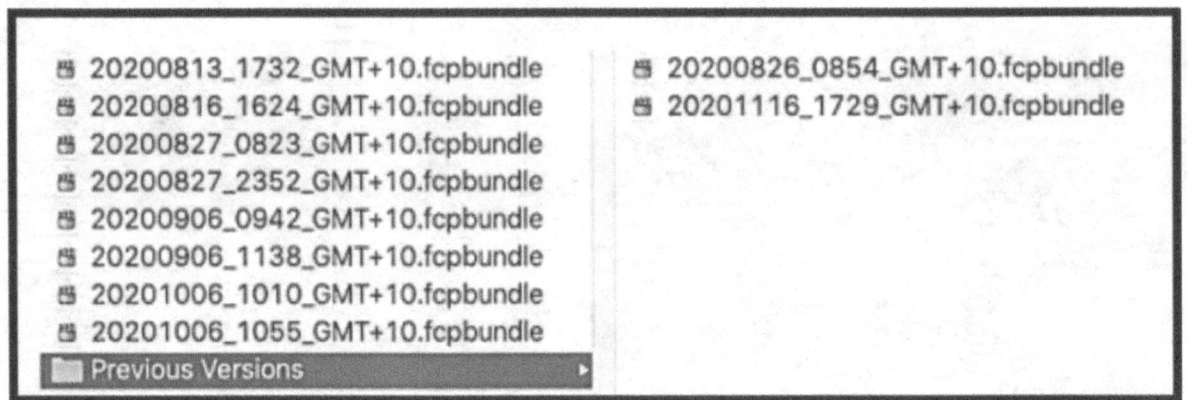

Just double-click on any library to open it, and if you need to, you can join media again. You won't work in that spare library, though. Final Cut Pro should know what you're doing if you open a time-stamped backup library from the backups folder and either move it to the right place or ask you to save it somewhere else. You can give your library a better name without the timestamp when you save it again. All of that works great, but it's not easy to make a backup happen in the first place. It will happen in the background every once in a while, and you can't stop it. You can get this kind of power from a third-party app called **Backups for Final Cut Pro**. We hope you never have to use it.

CHAPTER 17: INTEGRATING WITH OTHER APPLICATIONS AND PLATFORMS

Apple applications that support Final Cut Pro

You can see apps made by Apple that have features that Final Cut Pro producers will find useful in this area.

Motion 5

Motion 5 is a motion graphics program that lets you make titles and transitions in real-time in 2D, 3D, and 360°. All of the effects in Final Cut Pro, both the built-in ones and the ones made by third parties, were made with Motion 5. This shows how well Motion 5 works with Final Cut Pro. Because Motion 5 is so well merged with Final Cut Pro, all of the third-party plug-ins you use with Final Cut Pro are stored in a folder on your hard drive called Motion Templates. You can use third-party plug-ins with this folder, even if you don't own the Motion 5 app. I think you should buy Motion 5. You can make your own digital cartoons that can be used inside or outside of Final Cut Pro by customizing plug-ins and using Pro. If you want to follow along with this part, you will need Motion 5, which doesn't have a sample version like Final Cut Pro. As for the price, I think it's the best deal at $49.00. To be clear, this section will only talk about how Motion 5 works with Final Cut Pro to change plug-ins. We're not going to teach you how to use Motion 5 in any other way besides how to change Final Cut Pro plug-ins.

Modifying default plug-ins

The majority of the plug-ins that come with Final Cut Pro are only capable of changing colors and styles, among other fundamental tasks. Paid plug-ins, on the other hand, let you make a lot more changes. I will use the default Dramatic title plug-in as an example to show you how to change its three text animations to four, along with an alternative-colored background that can be turned off and a fade out of the fourth animated word. You can get to the dramatic title from the Titles tab in the upper left corner of Final Cut Pro, which is next to the **Build In/Out category. The options are shown in the next picture. You can only change the font color and the look of the text.**

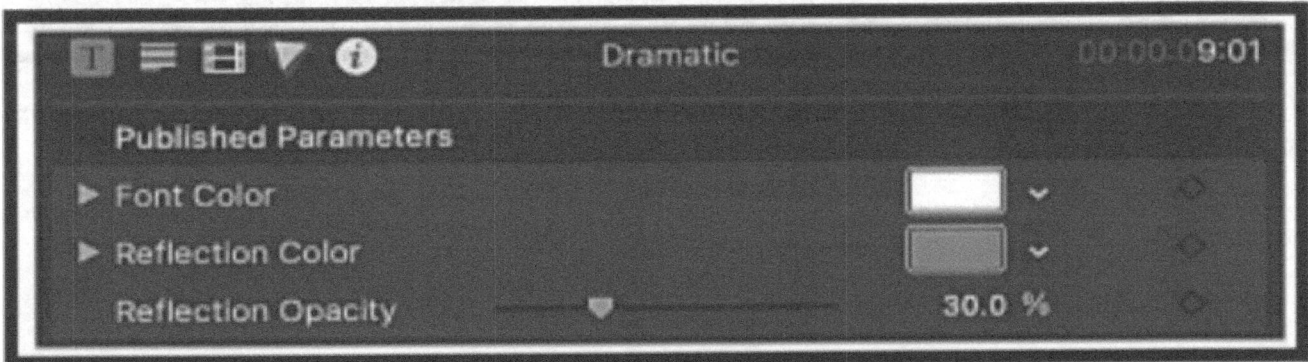

Final Cut Pro locks the default Dramatic title plug-in, so you can't change the settings that are released. You can, however, change a copy. In the browser for the title, the usual title is shown:

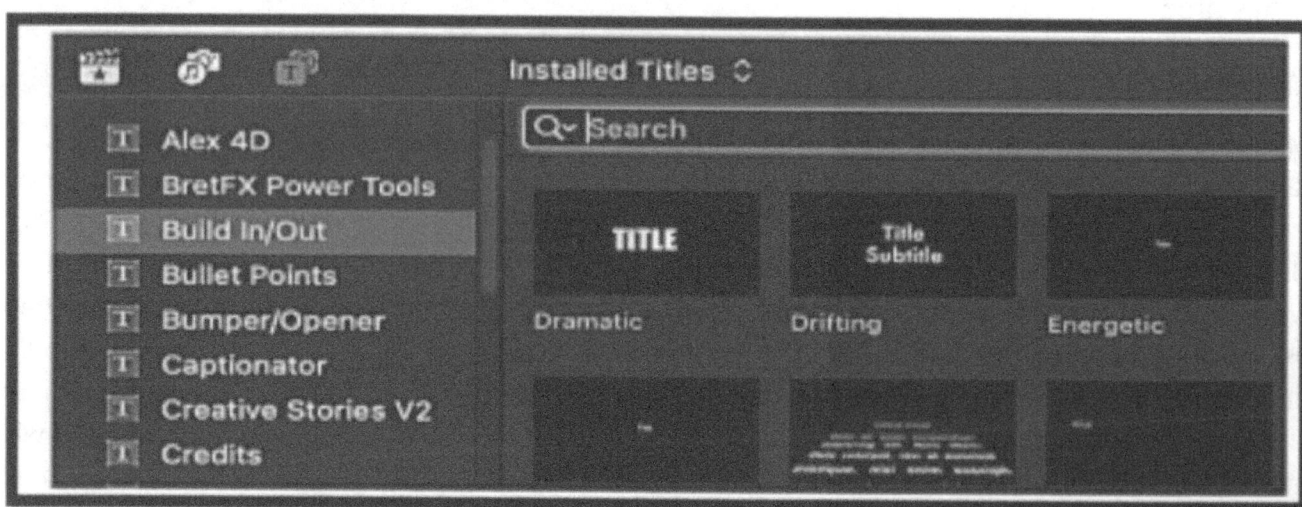

Right-click on the **Dramatic** title in the title browser and choose **"Open a copy in Motion."** This will start the process of changing the title.

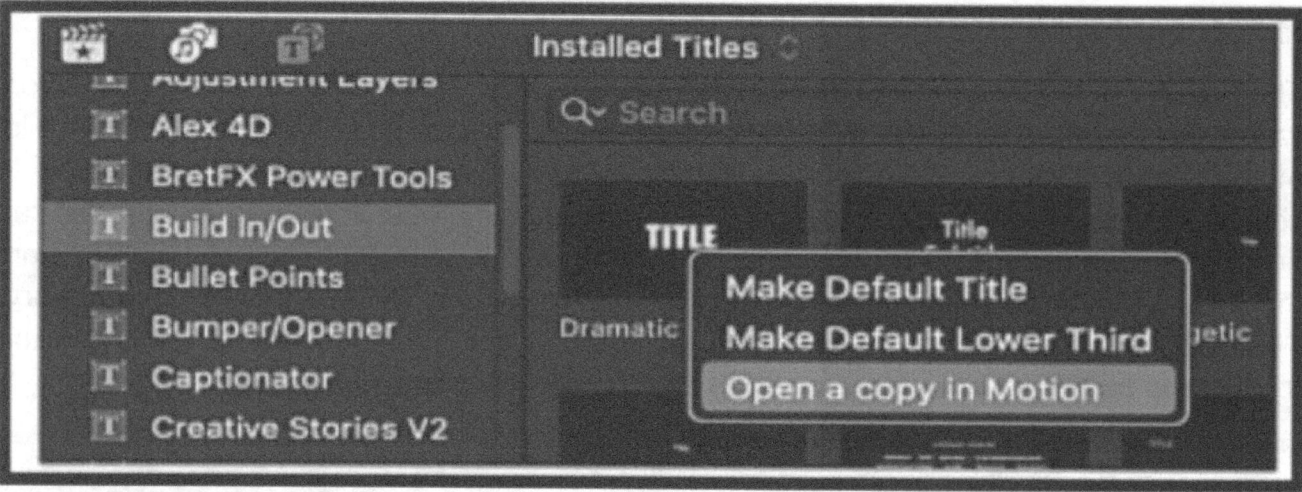

You can now start Motion 5 with the Dramatic title if you have it. It will open in the Project boxon the right:

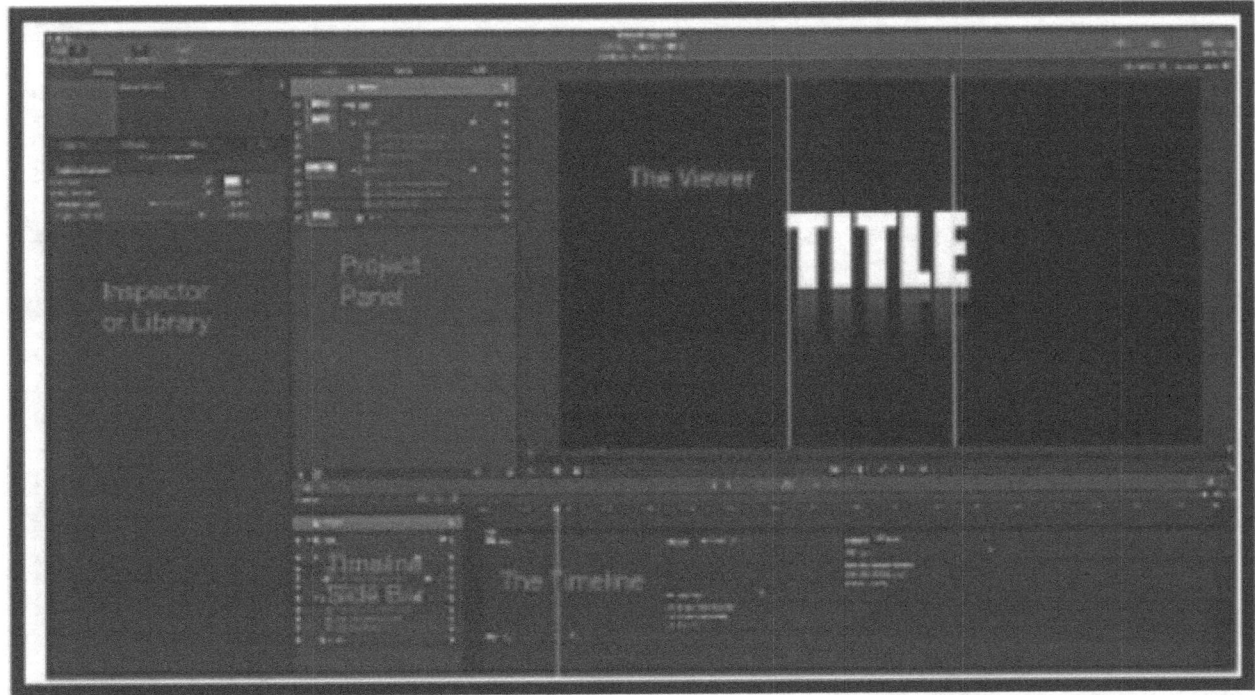

The color scheme in Motion 5 is a lot like the color scheme in Final Cut Pro. In the usual view, there are five screens, which I've marked in red in the graph above:

- **Library and Inspector**: You can use media and items in Motion 5 in the Library panel.
- **Project**: This is where you put the **objects** you pulled from the Library panel or actions you added. You can give things behaviors, which are acts that can be added to them to make them move.
- **Timing**: This panel copies everything in the Project panel so that it's easier to get to when working in the timeline (the panel to theright of the timeline column).
- **Timeline**: The timeline works a lot like the timeline in Final Cut Pro; it's where you can change what's happening.
- **Viewer**: The Viewer works a lot like the Final Cut Pro viewer; when you share, all of your work is shown.

First, let's look at the project panel while the **Dramatic** title is open in Motion 5. You can see that the Dramatic title has three moving words. For this task, we'll add a fourth word that has the same motions as the first three. The idea that allthings are kept in groups is one of the main ideas behind Motion 5. All the things in a group are changed when an action is added to it. When an action is added to a single object, it only changes that object. In some ways, this is like a complex clip in Final Cut Pro. As long as you have at least one object, there has to be at least one group. There is only one group with a dramatic title. A lot of the time, Motion 5 plug-ins have more than one group. As we progress, you will learn how to add more groups.

The name of the group in the Dramatic title is Main. Any object in the Project panel can have its name changed to fit your needs:

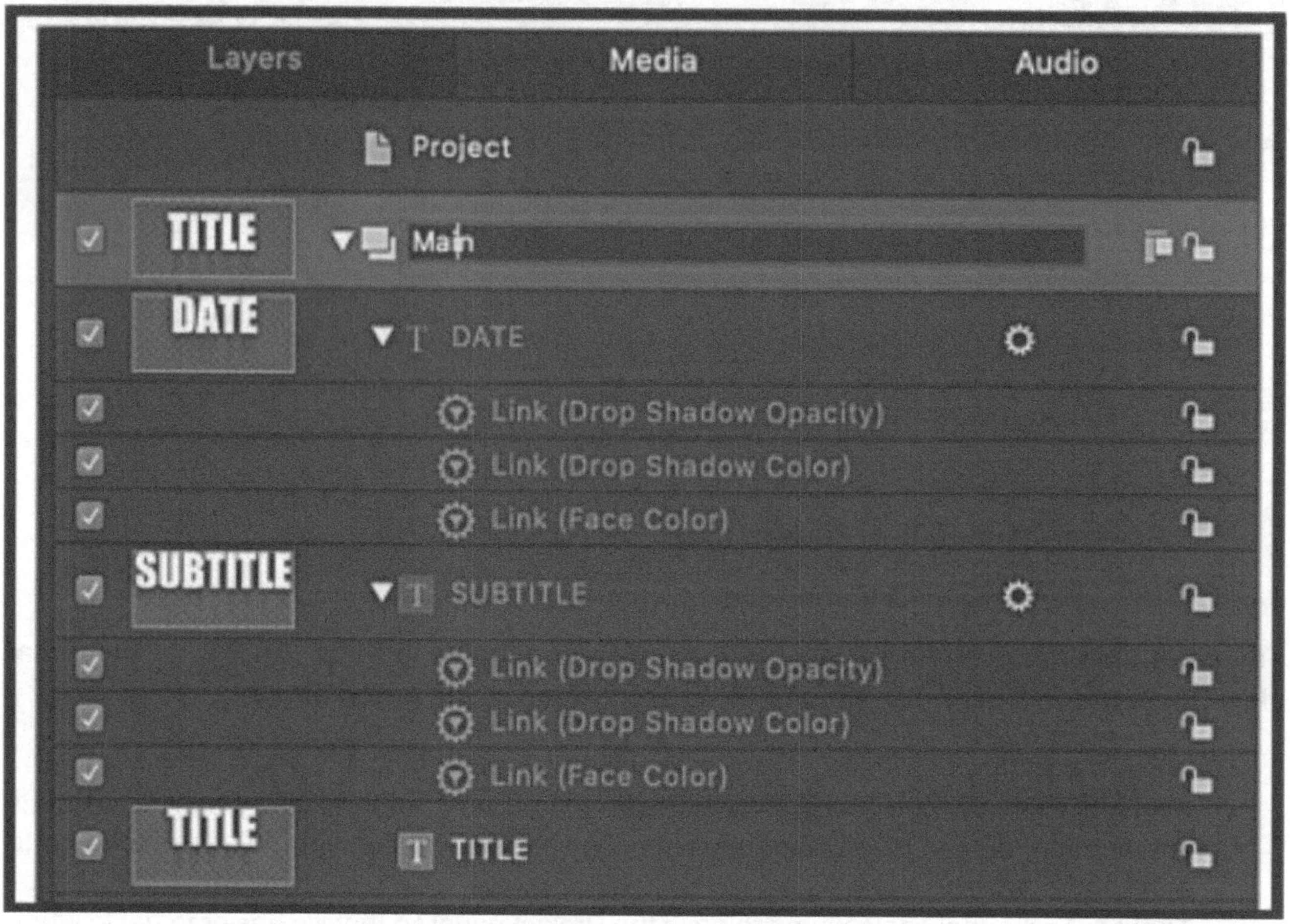

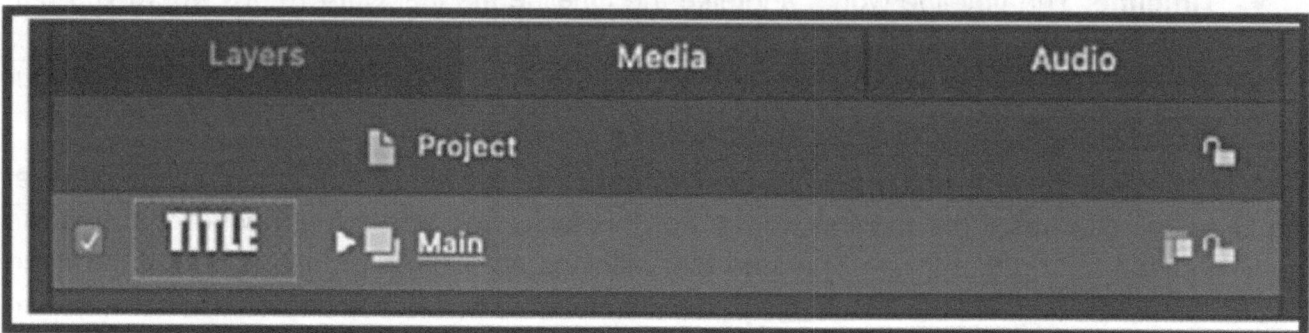

With the arrow, you can open or show groups:

The dramatic title has three words: **DATE, SUBTITLE, and TITLE**. You can change them in the right-hand **Inspector** window or the **Project** box. The word "**DATE**" is chosen in the Project panel **in the figure below. If you select the Text tab at the top of the Inspector window, you can also change it at the bottom left of that window:**

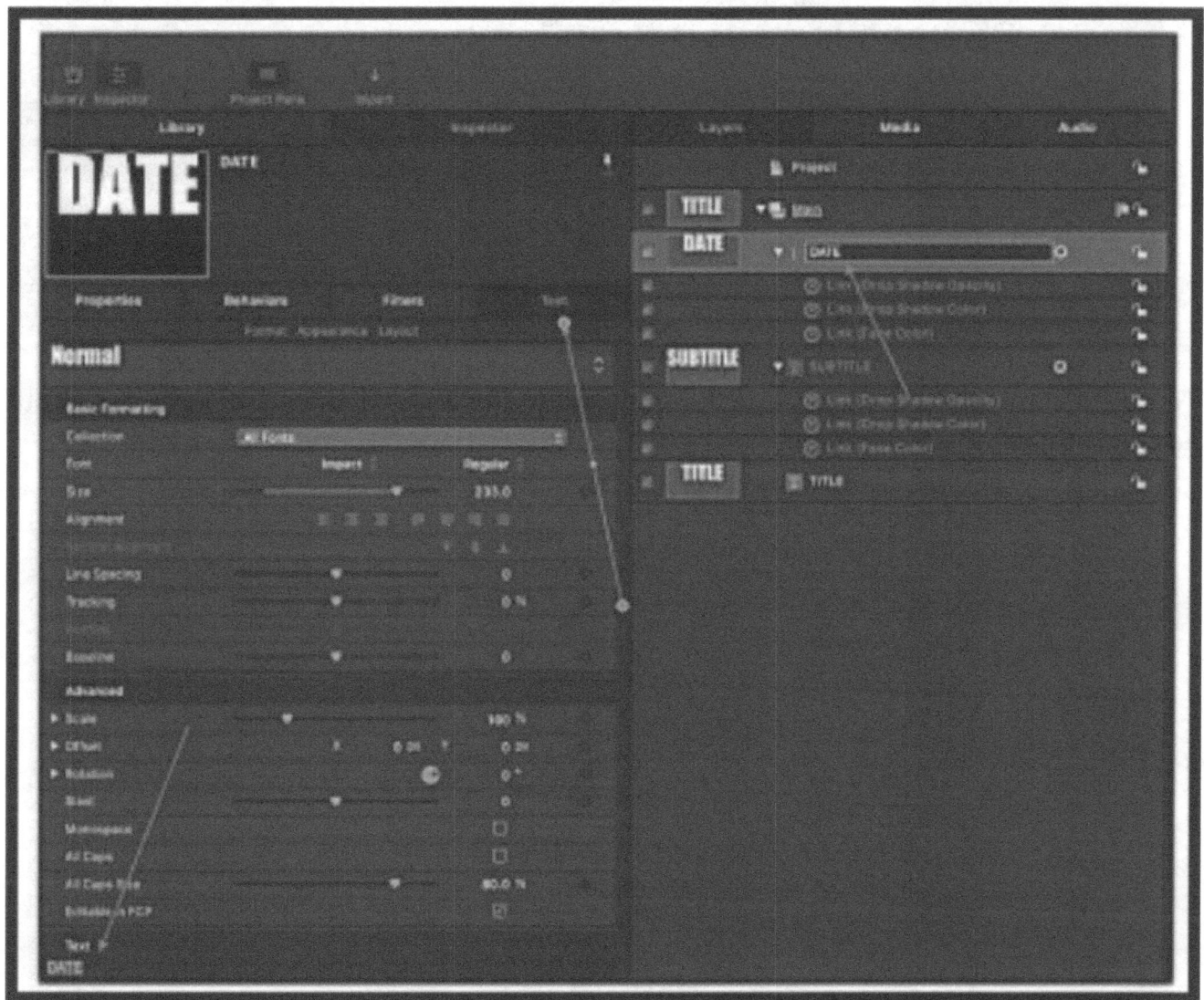

What you change in Motion 5's text properties stays the same when you save the plug-in for Final Cut Pro to use. It's important to remember that if you want to change a Motion 5 plug-in that is being used by Final Cut Pro, you need to publish the option. If you don't, the option will stay the same as it was set in Motion 5, and you won't be able to change it in the Final Cut Pro interface. One thing that doesn't follow that rule is that you can change text in Final Cut Pro. In Motion 5, you can turn off the option to change text, which is on by default. The option to turn it off is shown in the next picture. When **Editable in FCP** is not checked, Final Cut Pro will not let you change text options.

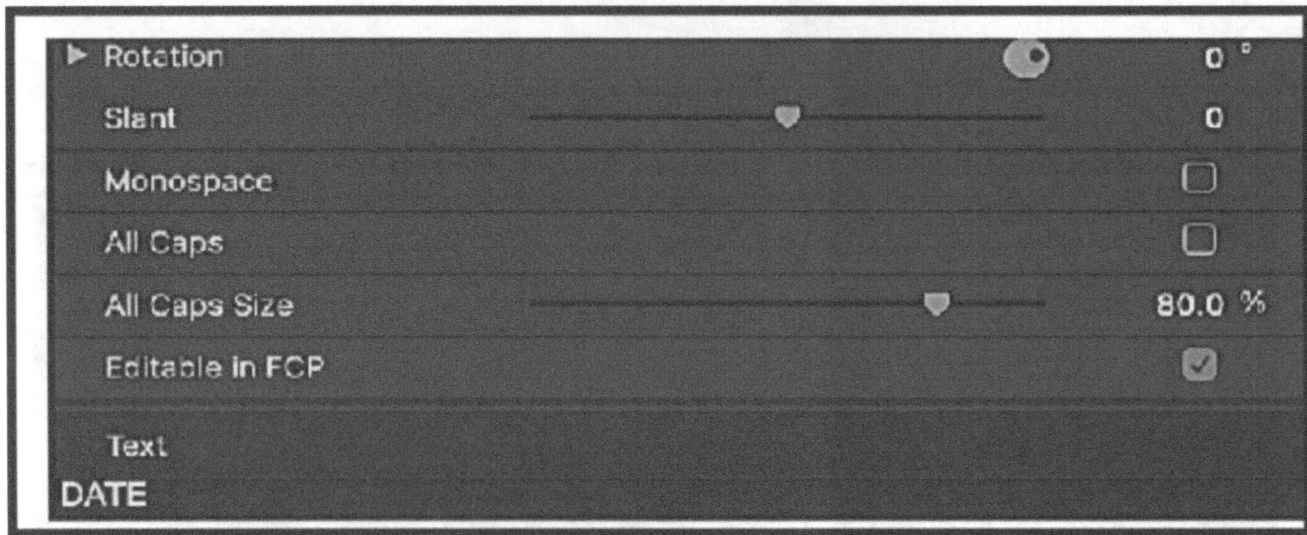

To see the change happen, change the Date text to the 3rd text since this lesson is about adding a fourth text animation:

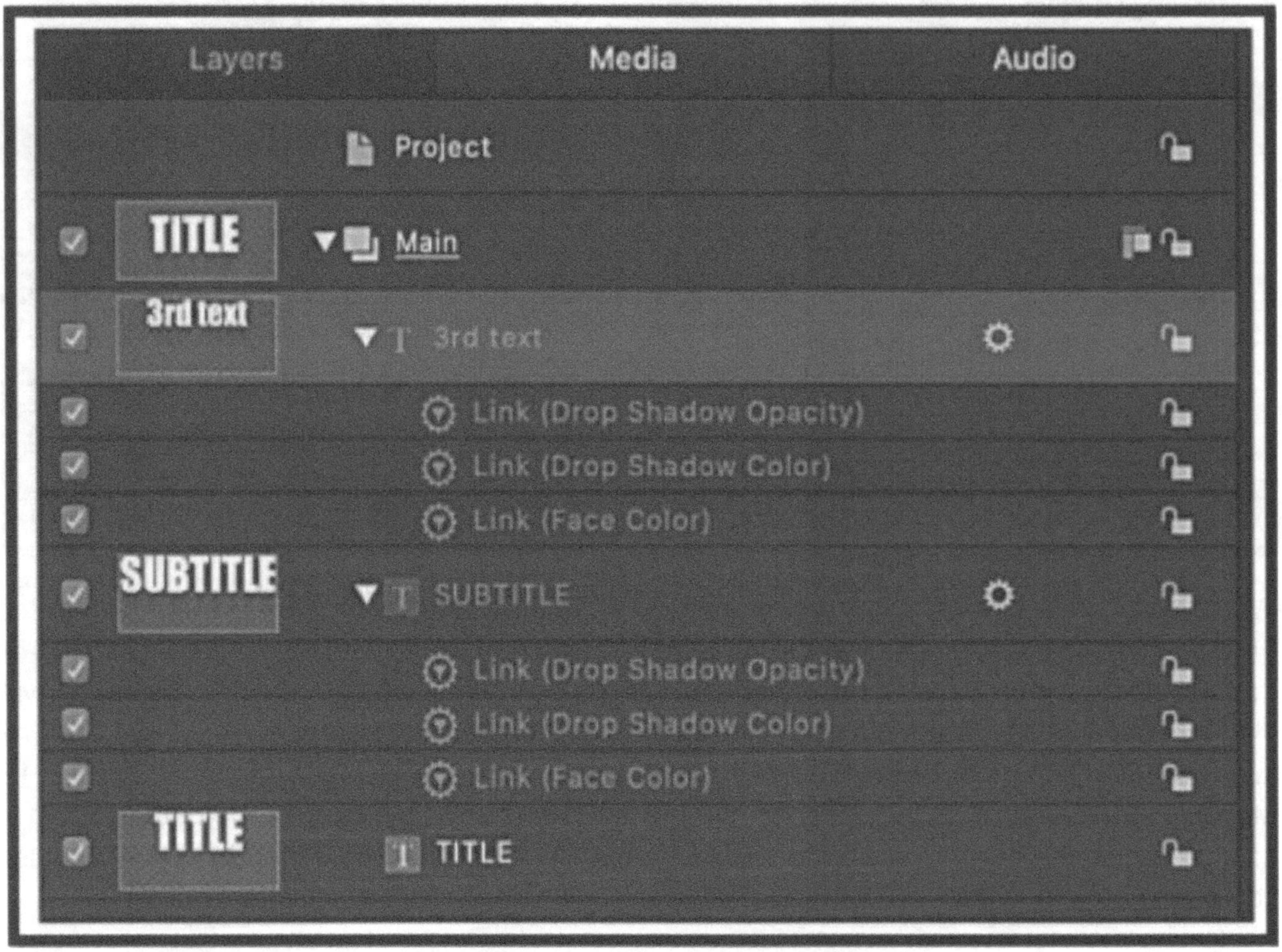

The job needs to go on longer so that there is room for the 4th text animation. It's set to 9 seconds for the **Dramatic** title. Just go to the **Edit menu** and choose **Project Properties** to see that.

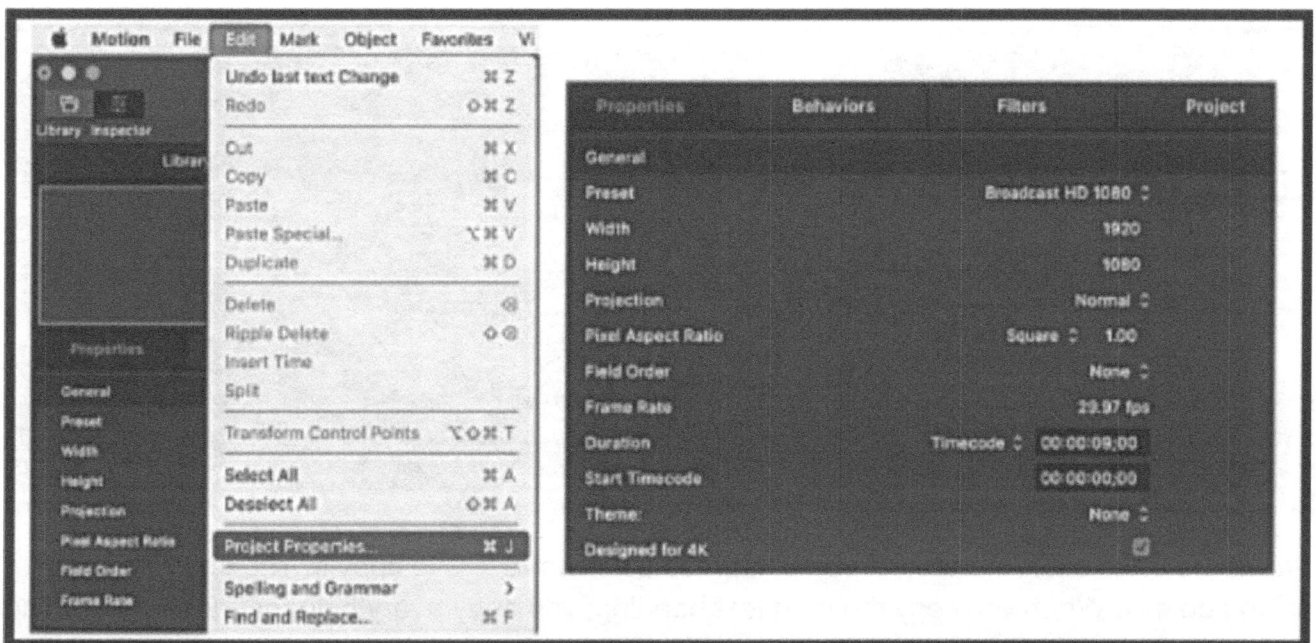

Make the duration 12 seconds. The timecode duration view can be changed to seconds:

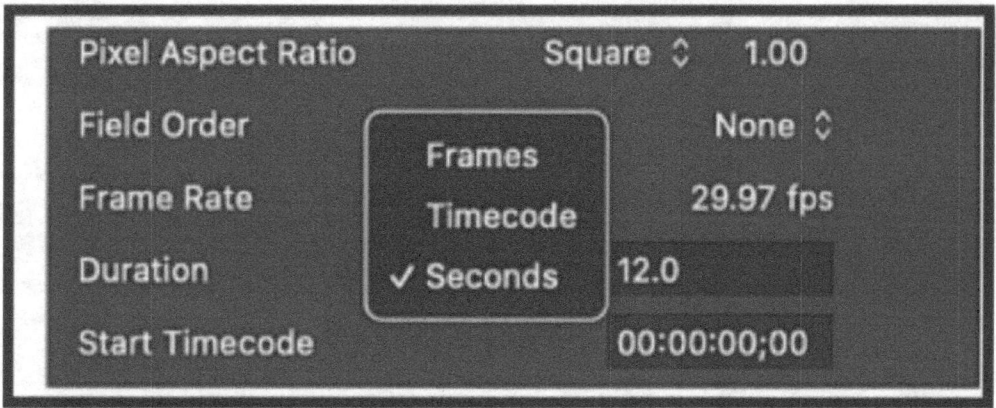

Press **Shift + Z** to make the timeline fit the whole project into the window. This command was also used in Final Cut Pro, as you will re- member. Shorten the length of the **third text** by moving the top **third text** track from the white end triangle at the 12-second mark to the 9-second mark. This will make room for the fourth-text animation. Make sure you don't pull the main track because that will cut the job time in half.

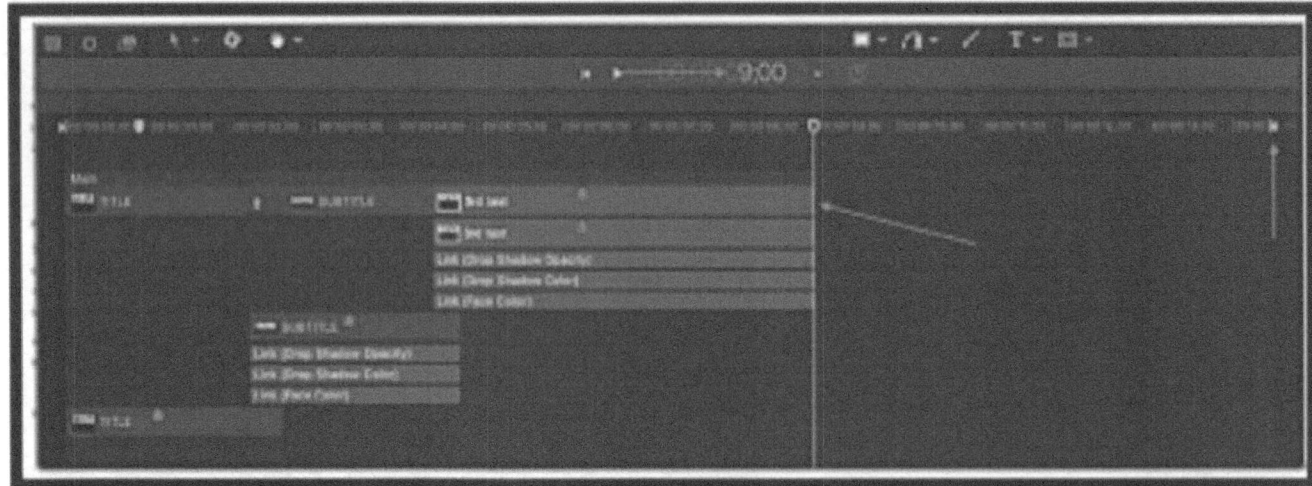

Select the third text in the project box and press **Command + C** to copy it. The text will turn blue as you do this. When you copy the third text heading, you copy everything that goes with it. The gear icon in the heading line can turn on or off all the actions related to that heading. Each line in the project box can be turned on or off by a blue tick.

Select the 8-second mark in the timeline and press Command + V to paste. Both the project title and the inspector box should have the third text copy type changed to the fourth text copy type.

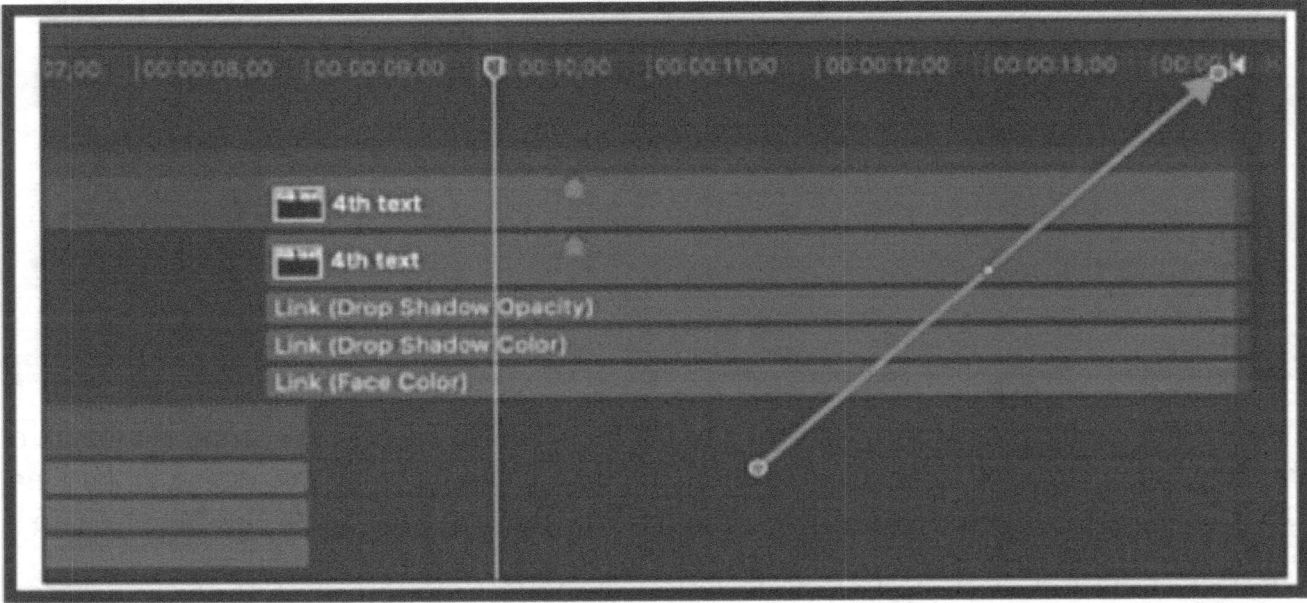

You might need to make the lighter-blue 4th text top track in the timeline longer so that it goes all the way to the white end shape.

Everything you need to do for the fourth motion is done, but let's add a few more things so you can get used to other Motion 5 features. I will add a fade-out on the fourth word of text with a behavior. I will also give the title a background color that can be turned off in Final Cut Pro if needed. Choose the **fourth text** heading, and then click on the behavior gear icon at the top of the screen. Then choose **Basic Motion/Fade In/Fade Out**.

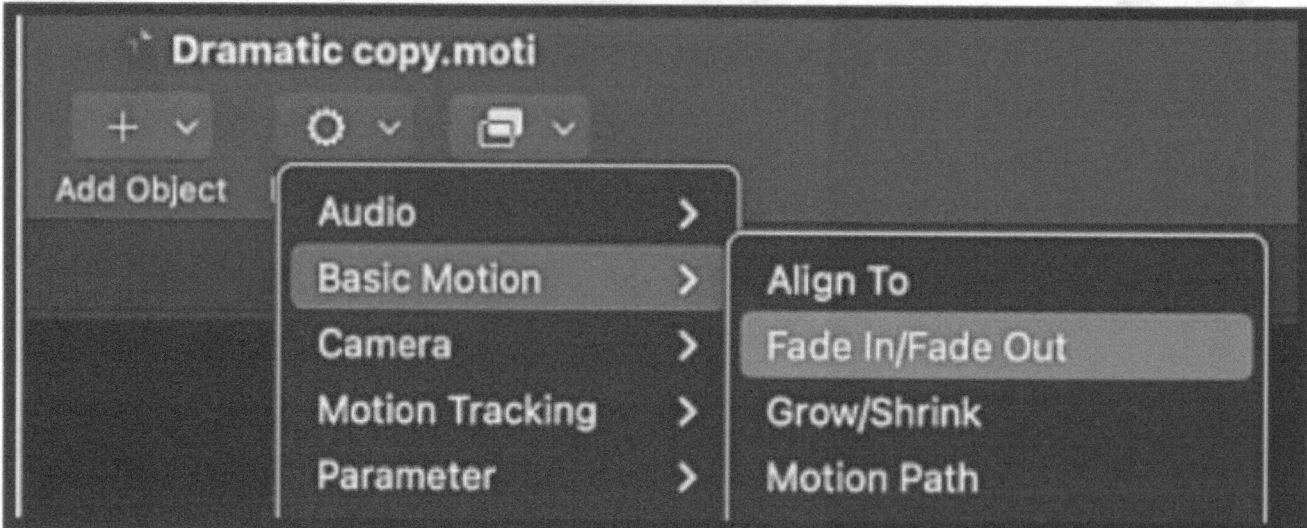

There will be a **Fade In/Fade Out** button added to the **Project** panel. The **Fade In/Fade Out** settings should be on the blue **Behaviors** tab of the **Inspector window** when it opens. Set **Fade Out Time to 12** and **Fade In Time to 0**.

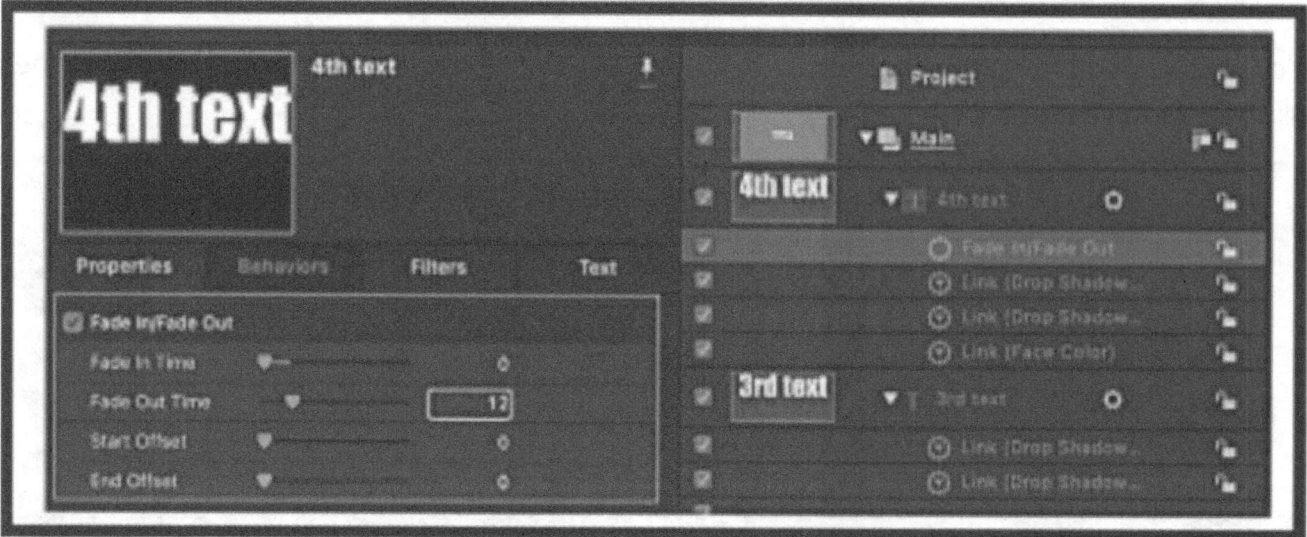

When using the plug-in in Final Cut Pro, it would be helpful to be able to change the length of the fade-out or turn it off. The option to share the settings so that they will appear in the Final Cut Pro Inspector window is provided by Motion 5 Pro. This line says "Fade Out Time." There is a drop-down button to the right of it that shows the "Publish" option when clicked.

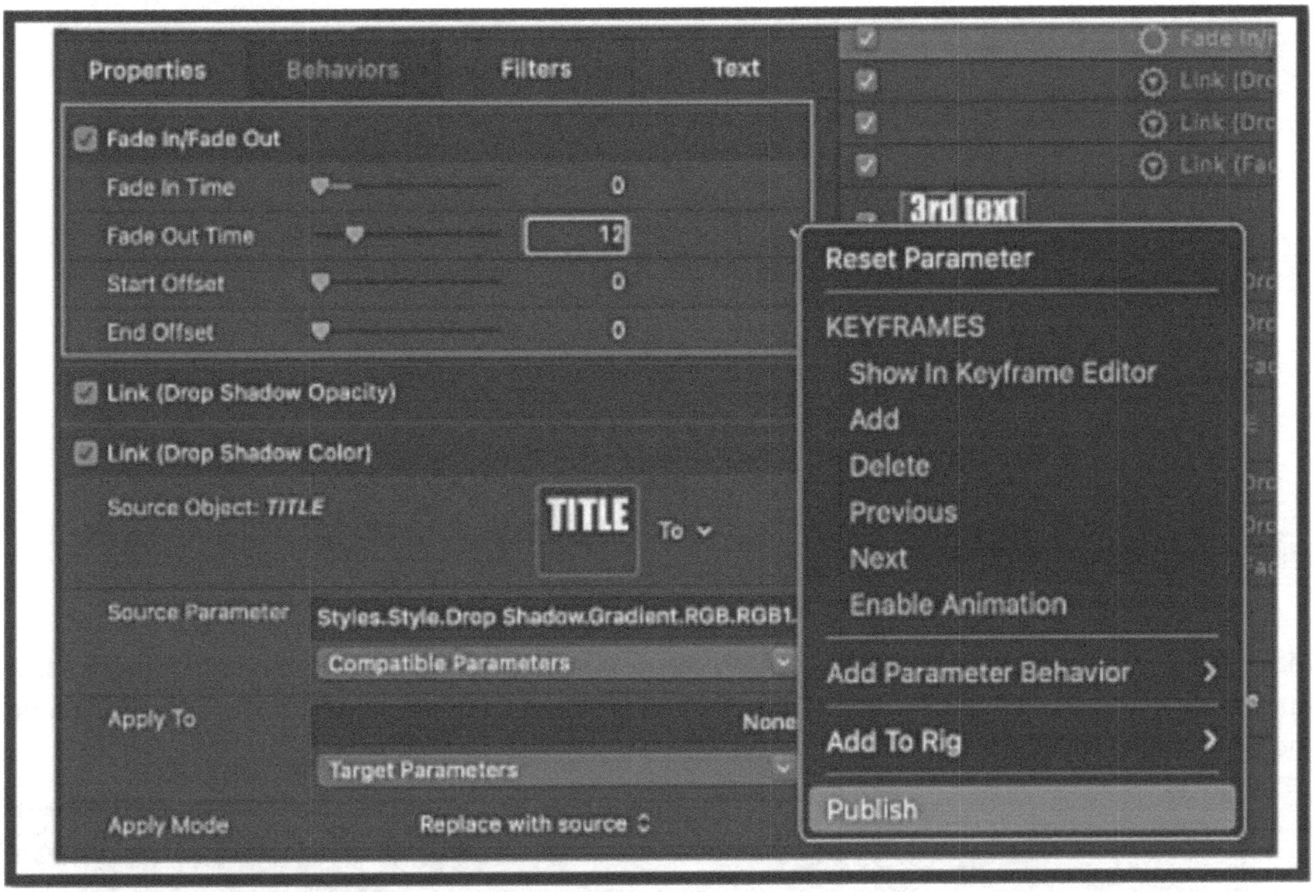

A background that can be turned off in the **Inspector** window of Final Cut Pro is another option for this case. In the timeline, move the playhead to the start of the job. Choose **New Group** from the **Object** menu.

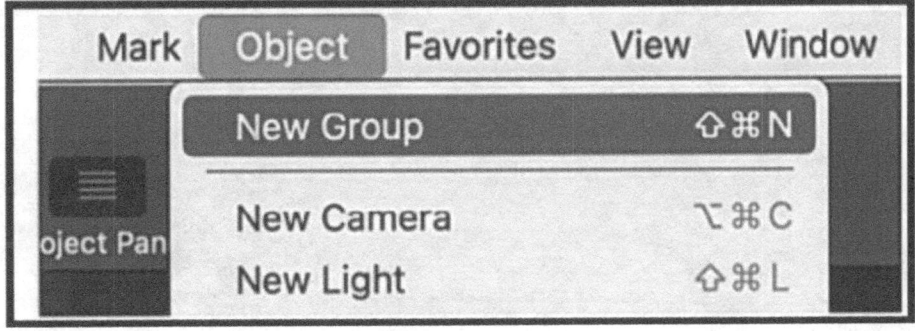

There are new items added at the top of the project panel, next to the word "**Main**." Change the name of the new group to "**background**" and drag it below the title. Choose the **Rectangle** tool in the middle of the screen while the **background** group is selected. The tool button will turn blue when it is chosen.

Make the viewer full by drawing a square. When you pick the Shape tab in the Inspector window and make it stand out in blue, change the Fill Color color. To the right of the word "Fill", click on the button next to "**Hide**" and choose "**Publish**."

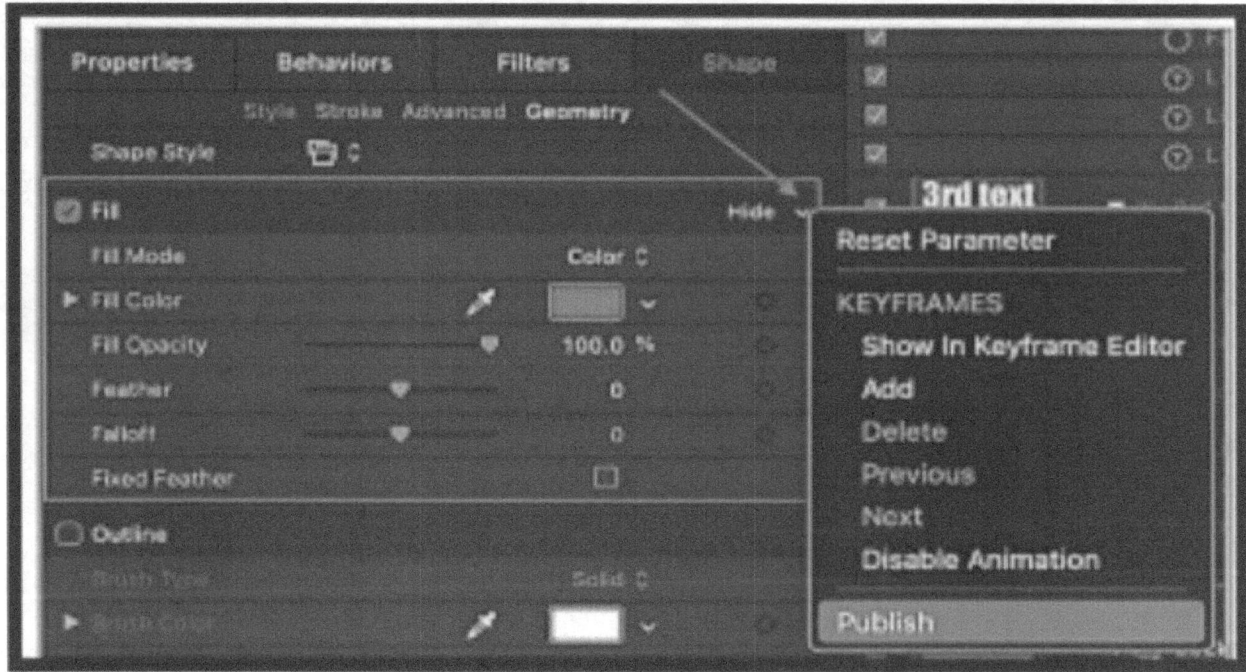

Pick up the arrow that points down to the right of Fill Color and Fill Opacity, then press Publish.

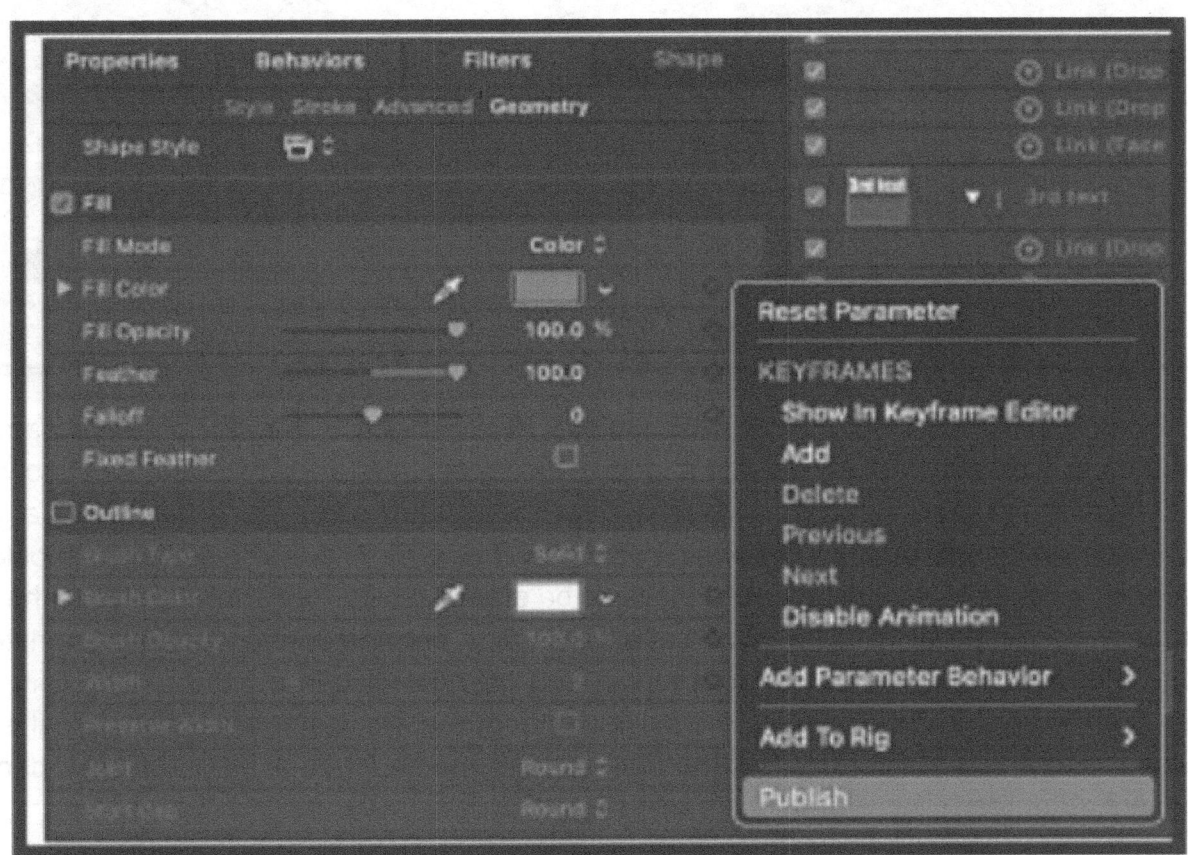

First, you need to make sure that the features you want to see in Final Cut Pro's Inspector window are set. The plug-in is almost ready to save. At the top of the Project panel, click on the word "Project." If you choose the Project tab in the Inspector window, you can see how the settings will look in Final Cut Pro. Choose the arrow to the right to unpublish any controls that you don't want to be in Final Cut Pro. If controls are missing, you will need to go back and make sure that you published them earlier. Take down **Graphics HDR**. You can change the names of the options and move them around. Fade Out Time should be called Fade Out 4th text. Move FillColor to above Filland change fill's name to Fill On/Off.

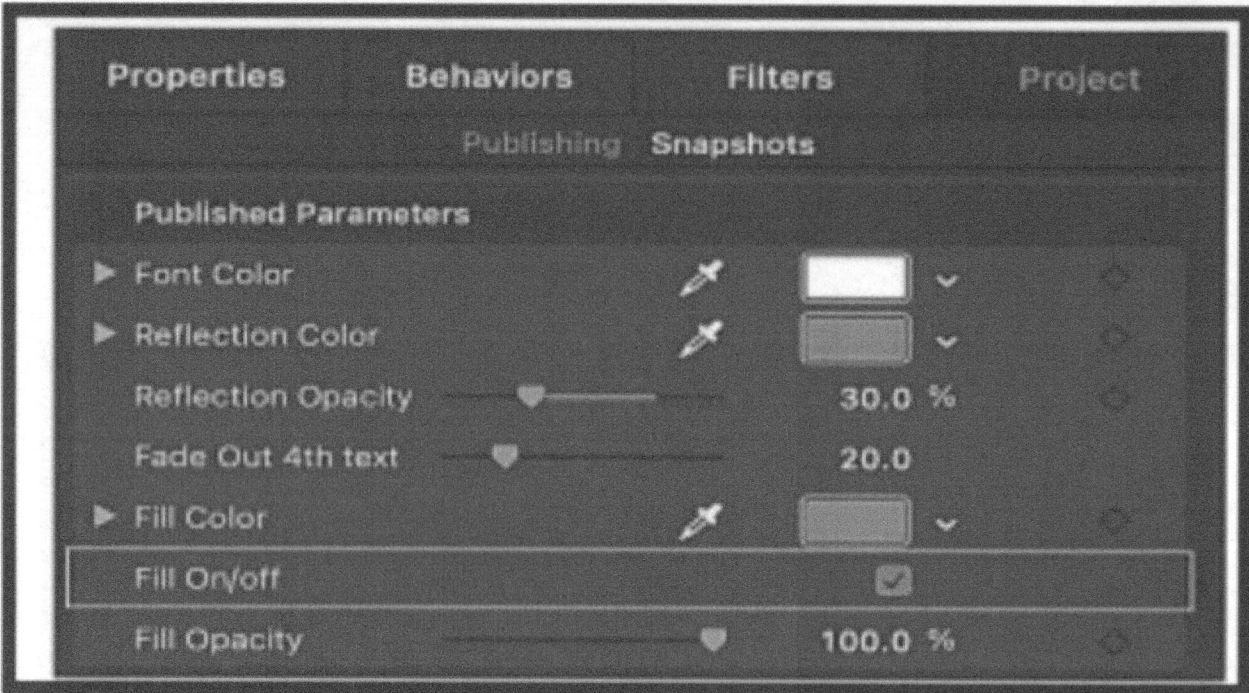

Now the only thing left to do is save the project. You will notice that the project's name is **Dramatic.copy.moti** in the very top and middle of the screen. We already talked about how you can't change the plug-ins that come with Final Cut Pro, so this is a copy. In a way, this is a good thing because it keeps you from overwriting the original plug-in. That being said, you should be careful with third-party plug-insbe-cause they can be erased, as you will see later. Go to the **File** menu and choose **Save**. If you want to save with a different name, choose **Save as** instead. Choose the area where the source was found, and give the plug-in a name under Template Name. Don't worry about the theme. To change a current title, it's best to keep the original name and add the new text at the end. Tick **Include unused media** if you used photos or videos in the project. After that, click "**Publish**."

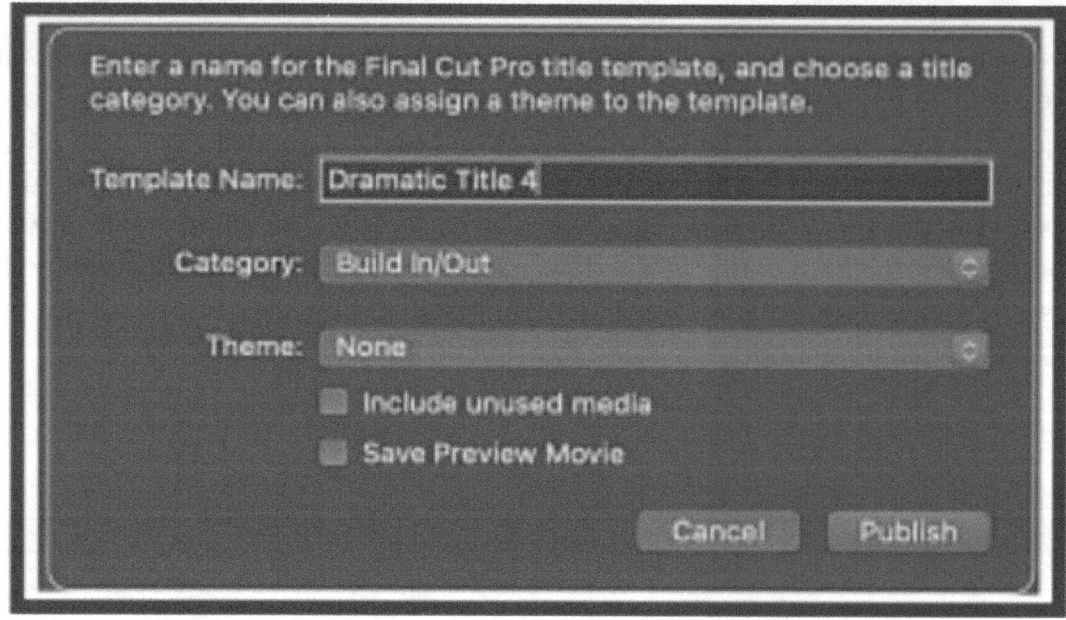

When you open the title category where you saved the changed plug-in in Final Cut Pro, you will see it.

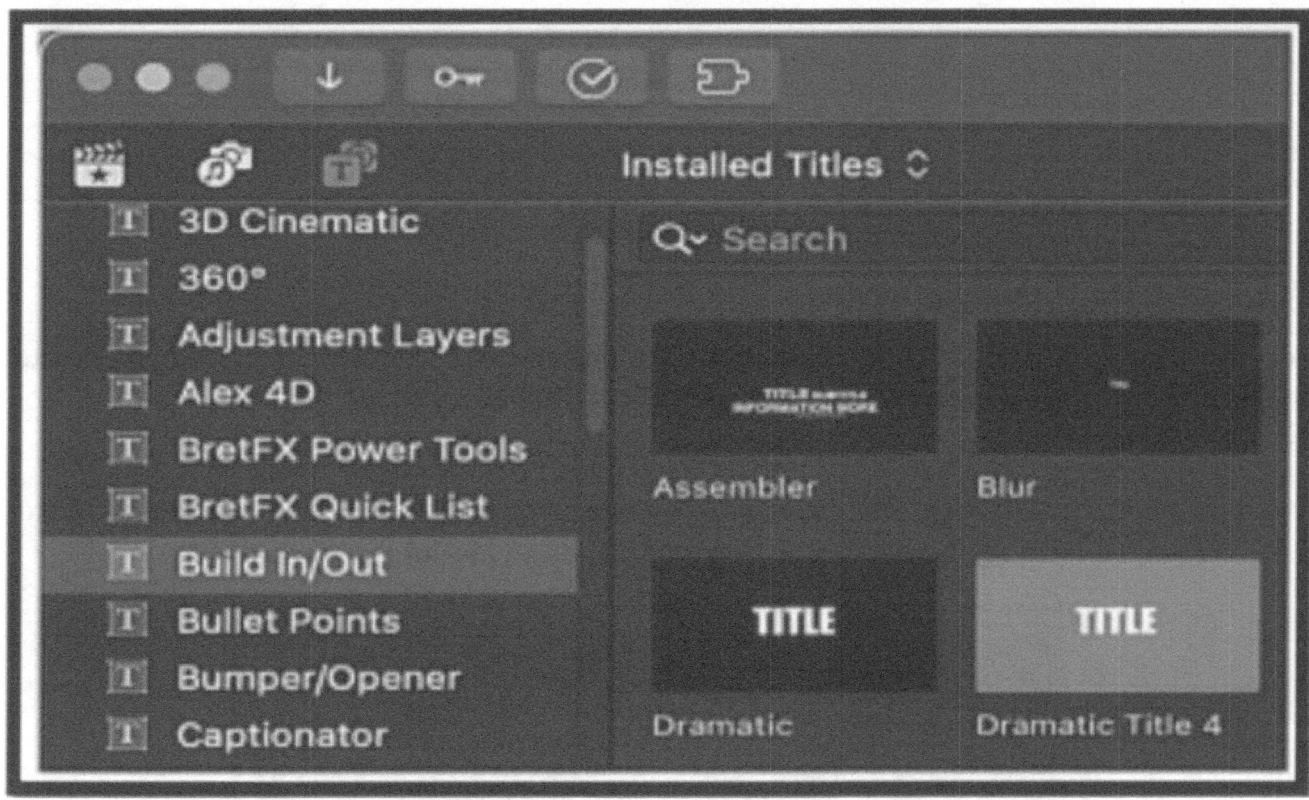

Check out the Inspector window and drag the new title into a timeline. The settings look the same as the ones you put out in Motion 5.

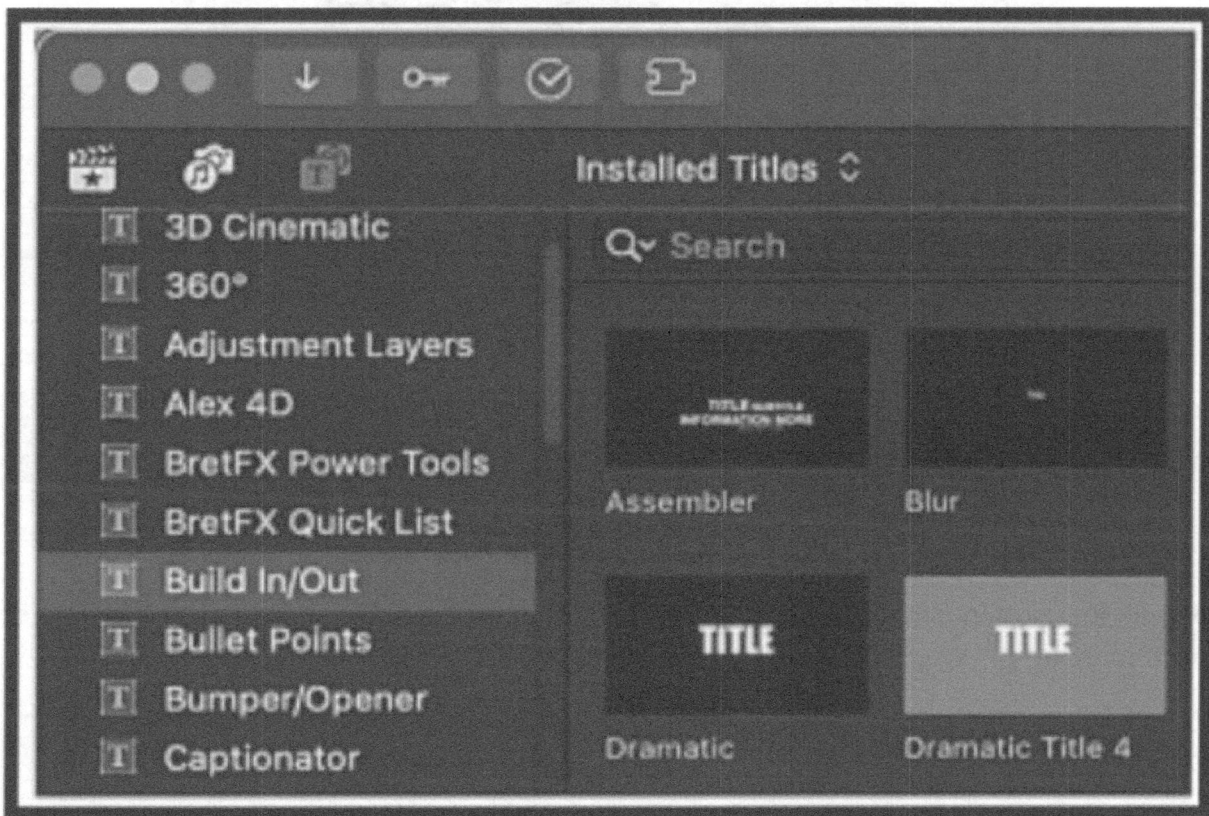

The Dramatic title comes with Final Cut Pro by default. In the next section, we'll look at how to change third-party plug-ins.

Modifying third-party plug-ins

You can get free and paid third-party plug-ins. It's possible to change them just like the default plug-ins, with the small difference that you don't have to make a copy first to change them; you can just overwrite them. Sometimes, when you buy a plug-in, the developer will lock it.

which means you can't change it or even make a copy of it. Before you make changes to a third-party plug-in, you can right-click on it and choose **"Open in Motion."**

As long as the plug-in is not locked, it will open in Motion 5 without showing the **"could not be opened"** message.

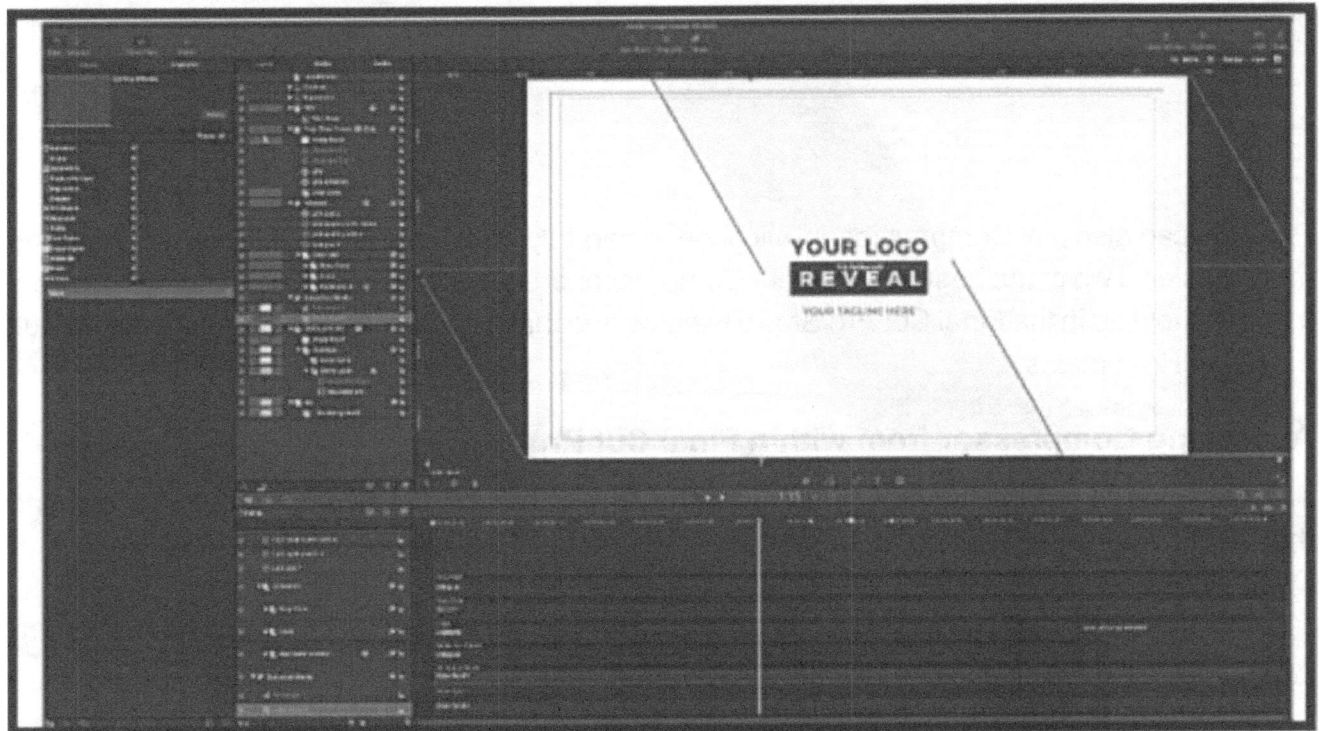

If you make changes to a third-party plug-in and then try to save them, you will see a message that says "**Save as Duplicate**."

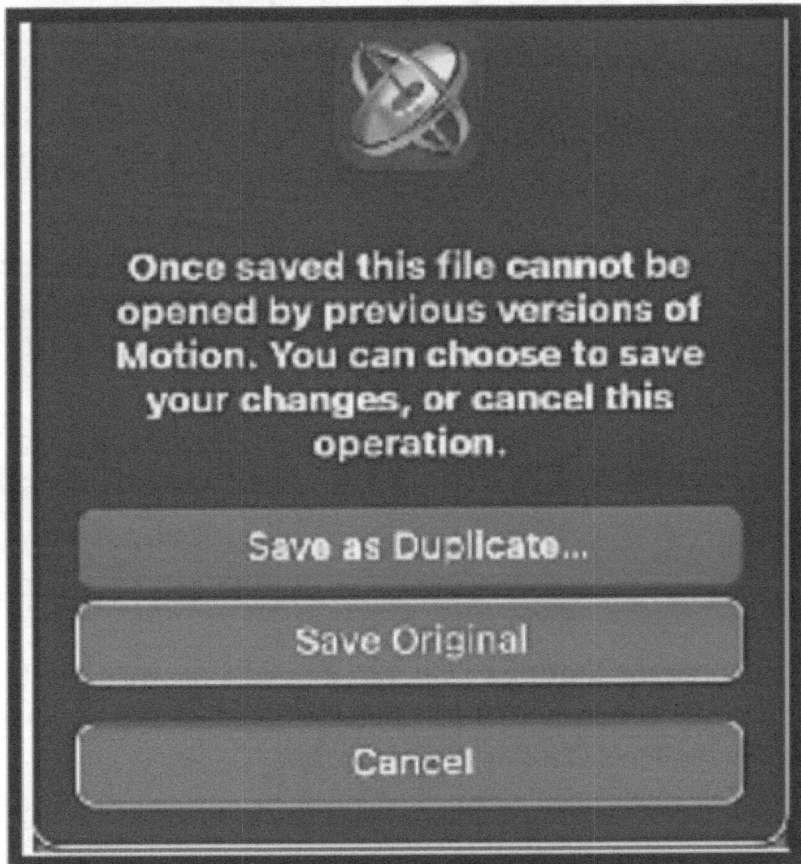

Compressor

You can make custom export modes in Compressor that aren't available by default in Final Cut

Pro. You can also buy Compressor ap-plication separately from Final Cut Pro. It makes exporting much easier. Two of the best things about Compressor are that it lets you make your own presets that will show up in the Final Cut Pro Share window and that it compresses better than the default Final Cut Pro options.

Accessing Compressor from within Final Cut Pro

The best way to get to Compressor in Final Cut Pro is through the **Share** menu. You can find the **"Add Destination"** button at the bottom of the menu. This will open the settings window for Destinations.

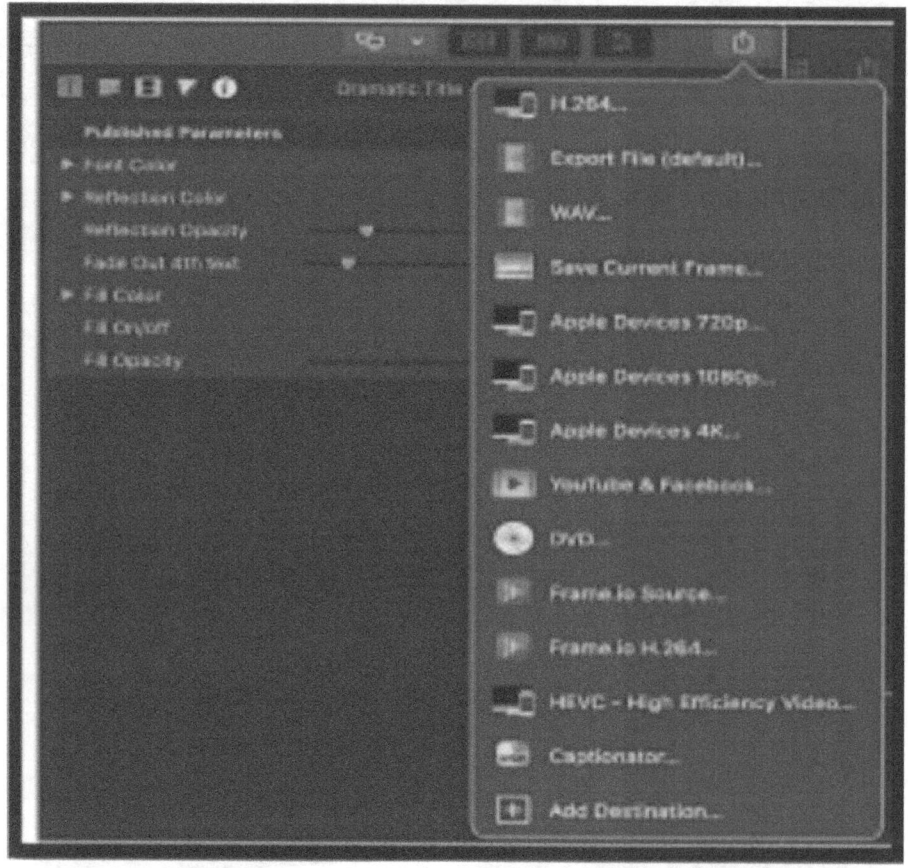

You can drag the **Compressor Settings** icon into the sidebar while the **Destinations tab** is selected in the **Destinations window**. This will open Compressor and let you choose the presets that you can then add to the Final Cut Pro **Share** window.

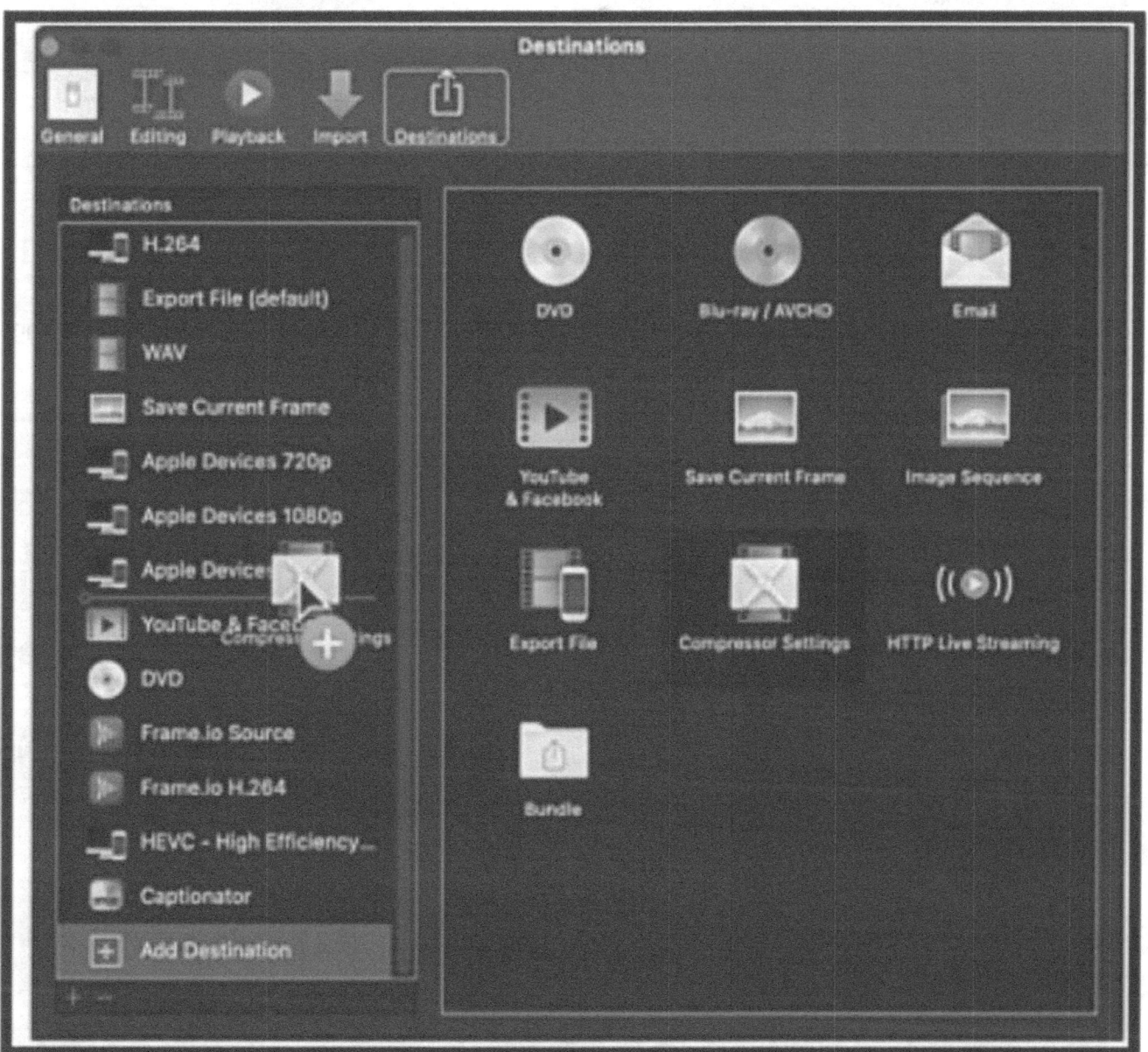

The built-in presets and any that you make yourself in the Custom option will be available to you.

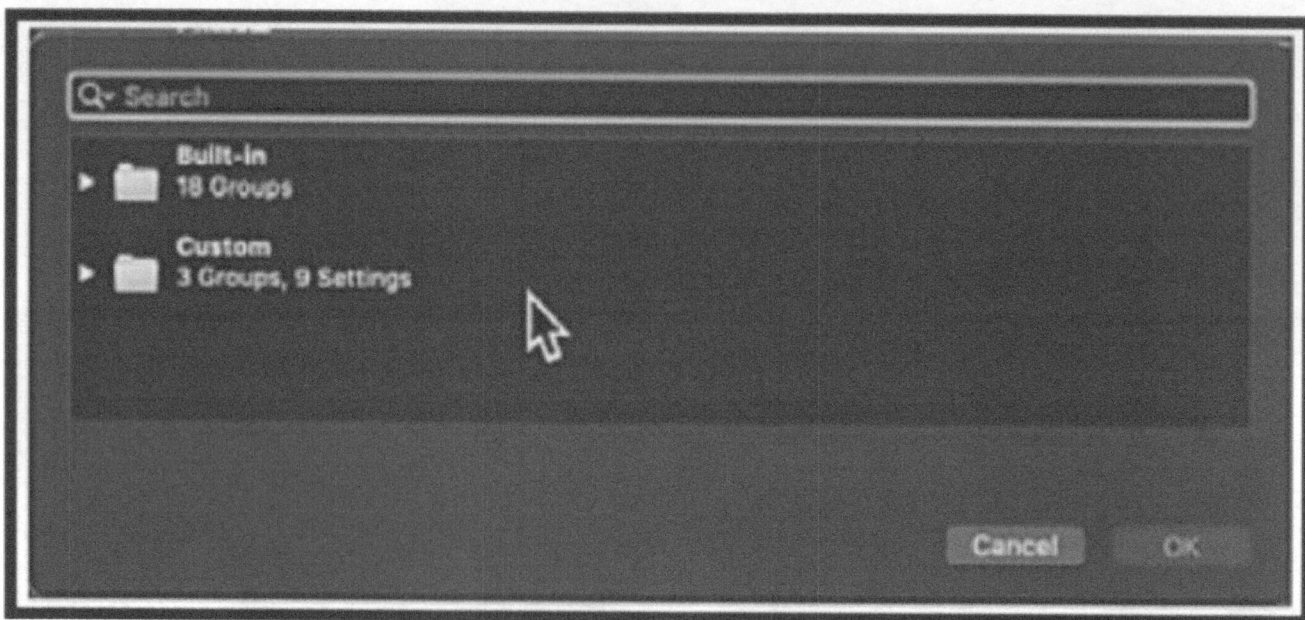

To use a compressor preset, go to the Final Cut Pro settings sidebar and find the new setting. There will be a compressor icon next to it.

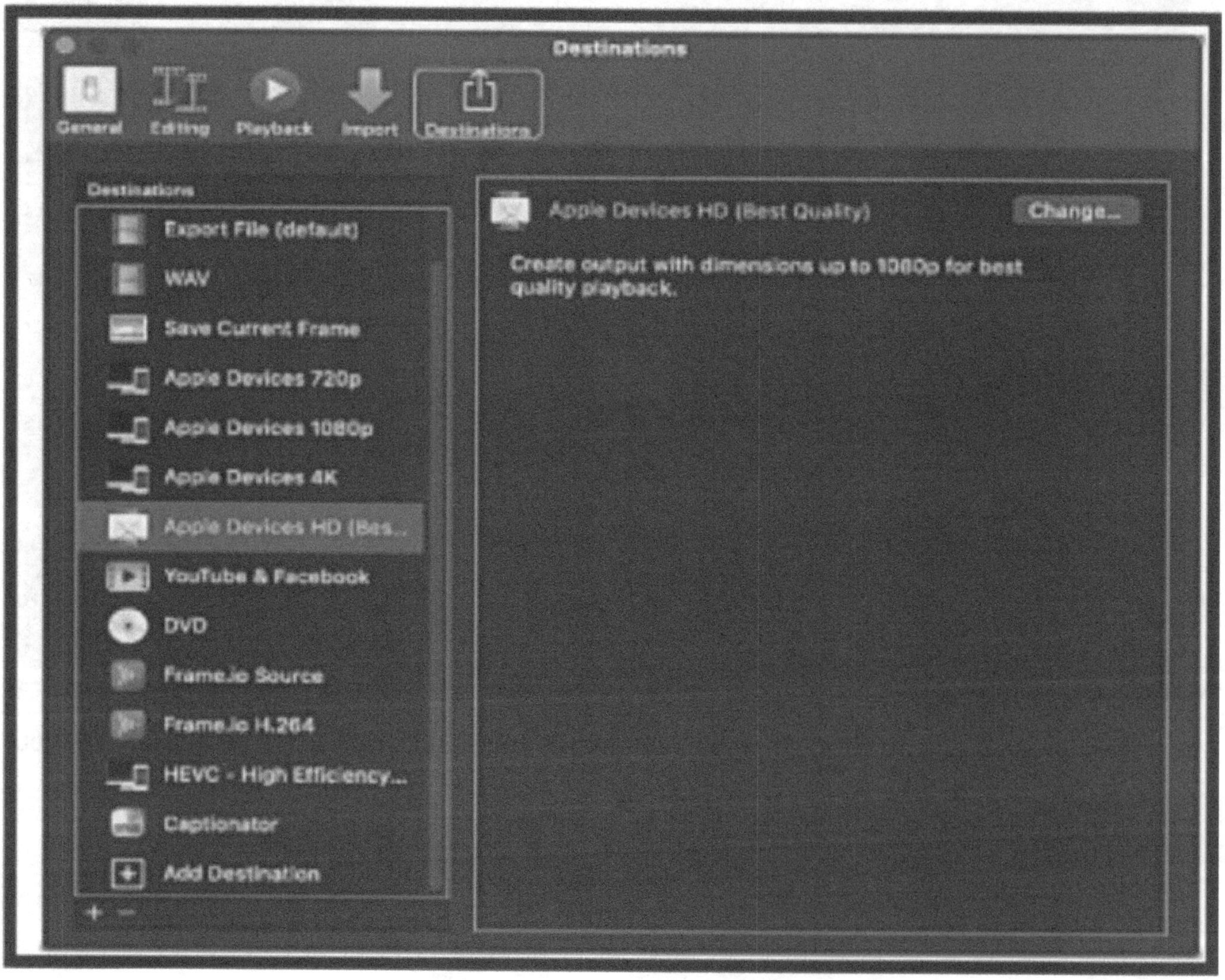

Once the compressor option is set in Destinations, you can get to it from the Share menu at any time. This lets you use any of the Compressor presets. If you choose the compressor option in the Share menu, the Export window will appear. In this window, you can find the Settings button and then the **Change**... button, which will take you to the Compressor application's presets.

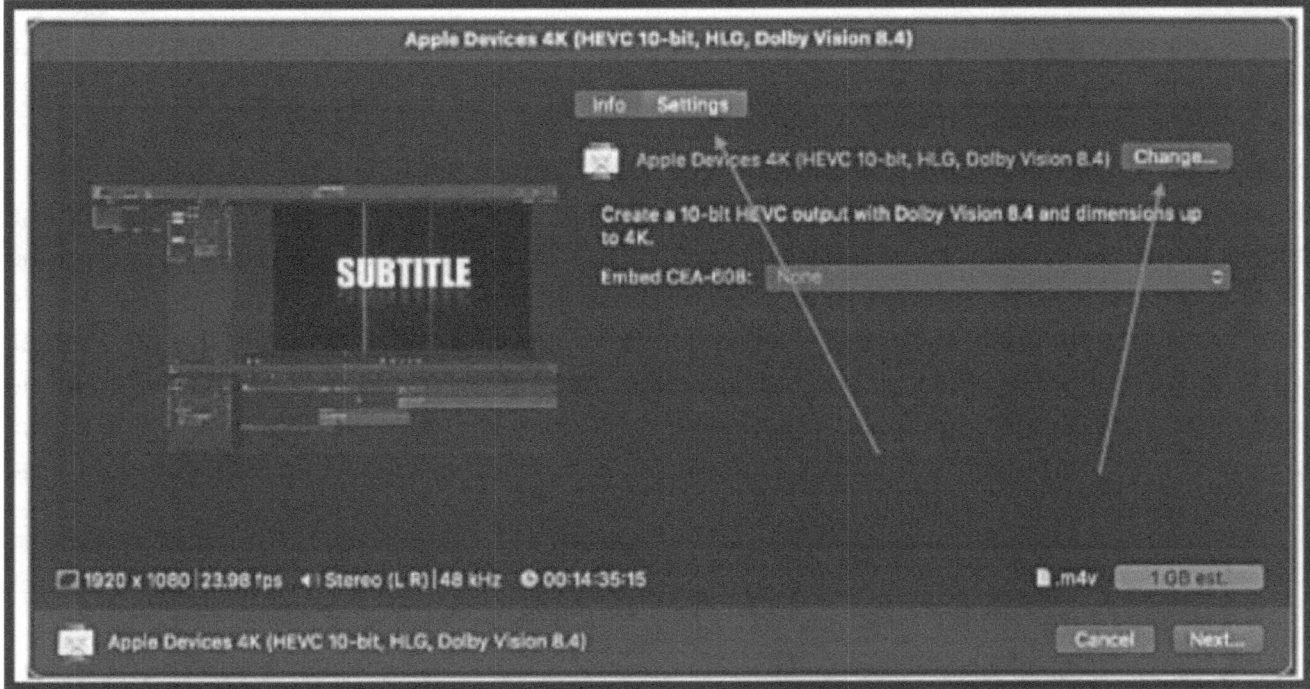

You will only be able to select the default presets when you access the compressor settings; you cannot change the compressor settings. This is a shame because it means you have to open the compressor directly to make changes.

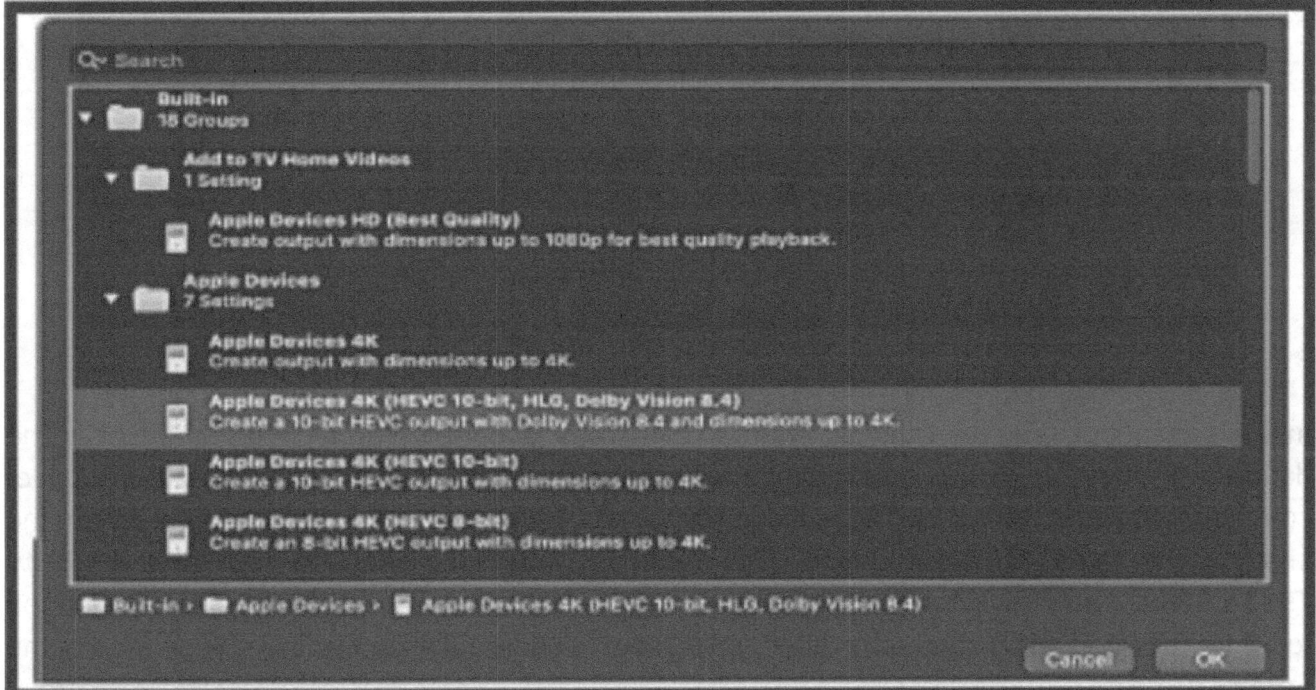

Opening Compressor directly

You will be able to edit the presets and create your own unique presets for use with Final Cut Pro when you open Compressor directly. Pick a basic preset and change it to fit your needs.

This is the best way to make your own presets. The usual presets in Compressor only let you open a copy, so the originals are always unaltered, and only the copy is changed. This makes the process safe for you. There are three tabs at the top of the compressor screen. They are called **Current, Active, and Completed**. When the Current tab is shown, the settings for the presets for accessing Final Cut Pro will be on the left. The **Add File** option is located in the middle panel, which will also display any new videos that need to be compressed. When the video is added, the right side will show information about how it was compressed. If you choose one of the presets in the left panel, more information about it will show up in the right panel, which is called the **inspector**. If you can't see the **inspection** panel, click on the button in the upper right corner of the right panel. The inspector panel has three tabs: **General**, which shows a summary of the preset, and **Video and Audio**, which shows specific information about the video and audio files.

In the main panel, drag the video you want to compress, and then drag a preset on top of it. The details will show up in the Inspector panel, where you can change them to fit the type of compression you want to use. The video in my case is 720p, so the **Automatic** frame size in the image is the same as the video itself. The frame size has been changed from **1280 x 720 to 1920 x 1080**. It now says that the frame size is 1920 x 1080. The frame rate will also be changed to **29.97 fps**. You can change any other setting too, of course. I'm just giving you an idea of the frame size.

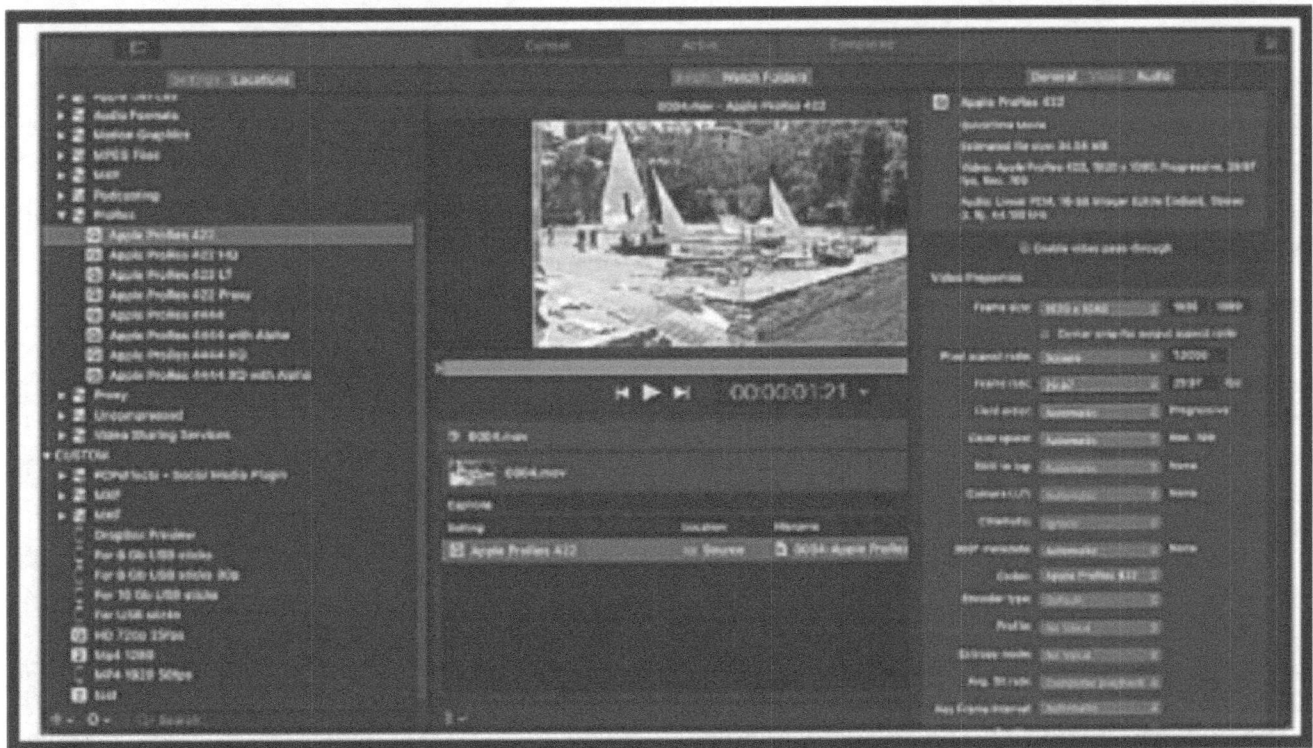

Click the blue button in the upper right corner of the window to close the **Inspector** box after making any necessary settings changes. You can drag the changed preset from the middle panel to the custom area on the left panel, whether the Inspector panel is open or closed. This will make it an alternative preset in Final Cut Pro in the future. In the picture above, the compressor gives the changed setting its own title. Motion 5 has given it the name **Special ProRes** Setting in this case:

Clicking the Start Batch button in the bottom right corner will let you start the compression once the Inspector box is closed. The file's compression process will be shown on the Active tab. When compression is done, the file will show up under **Completed**.

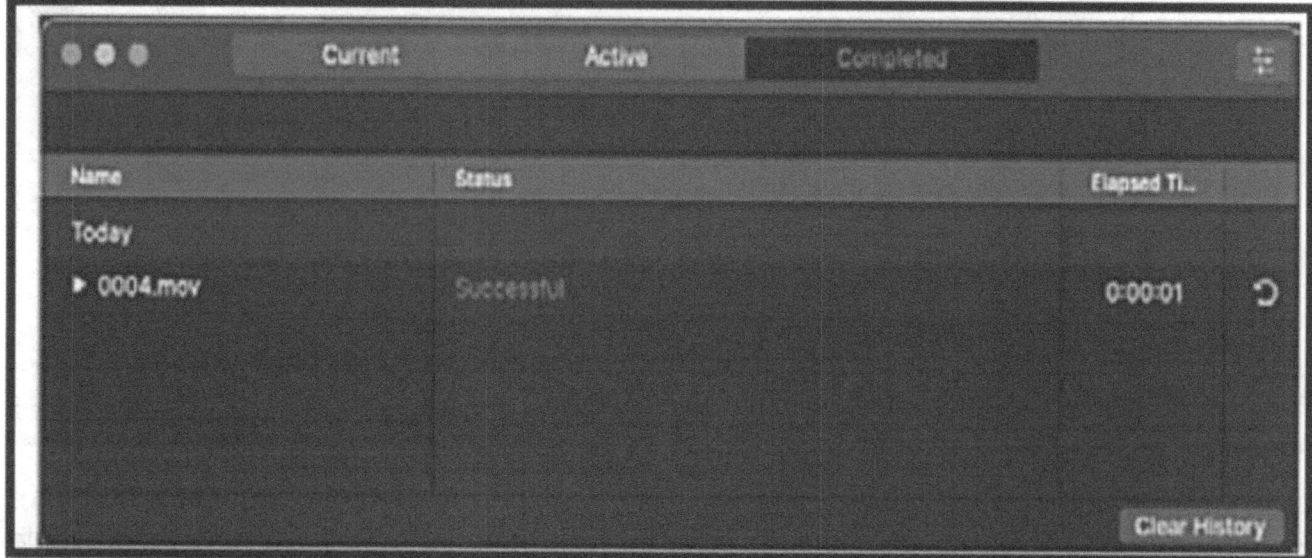

Apple gives Final Cut Pro users a lot of useful apps, and Compressor is just one of them. Next, we'll look at QuickTime, which lets you quickly make basic changes without opening Final Cut Pro. The size of clips saved in the Final Cut Pro library, for instance, can be significantly reduced by cutting long drone videos.

QuickTime

Every Mac comes with QuickTime, which is the third most useful app after Apple's Motion 5 and Compressor. It's easy to trim and combine movies with QuickTime because it's free, and it also has an inspector that lets you quickly see what format and size a video is. Let's look at how to trim QuickTime.

Trimming clips

When only a small part of a clip is to be used in the edit, trimming the clip before loading it into Final Cut Pro will reduce the amount of hard drive space that Final Cut Pro needs to store clips. When you use drone film, trimming is very helpful because the camera is on the whole flight, but you will only use a few seconds of it. When you open QuickTime, you can choose to open a movie from the File menu or by dragging it on top of the QuickTime icon in the Dock. If you choose Trim from the Edit menu, the trim timeline will show up at the bottom of the movie.

To trim a frame, press the play button until you get to it. You can go back and forth with the **J, K, and L** keys. The arrow keys let you move one frame at a time. The timecode will show up when you click the red playhead. Write it down before you drag the yellow edges to it. You can trim the other edge of the clip in the same way.

The clip is quickly mediated when you press the blue trim button. From the **View** menu, choose **Show Clips** if you want to cut out a part of the clip in the middle. The Trim timeline looks like a timeline. With the Split Clip option from the Edit menu, you can cut the timeline in half and delete the part you don't want. You can double-click any part to trim just that selection after you have divided a clip into multiple sections. With a simple editing tool, you can move the separate parts that were made by the Split Clip command around the timeline to change where they are.

The opposite of trimming is combining clips.

Combining clips

In QuickTime, pick out a clip, and then gotothe **Edit** menu, and click **Add Clip at End**. This will bring up the **Finder window**, where you can play another movie.

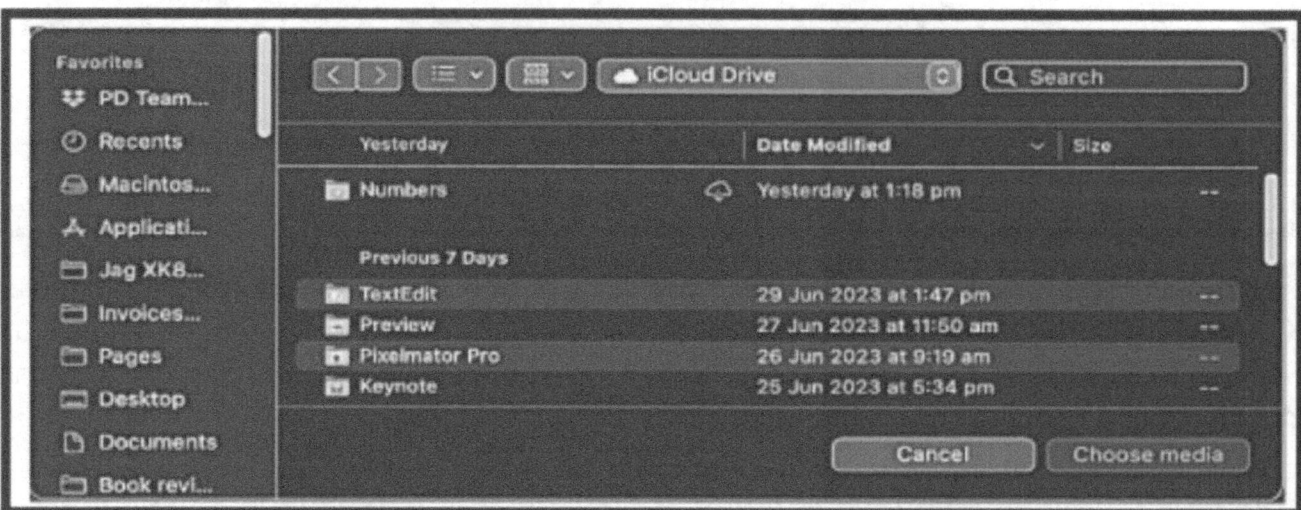

You can drag the new clip anywhere in the timeline, even to a split that has already been made or to a new split. It will be added at the end of the timeline. To make a simple movie, you can add as many extra clips as you want, move them around, split them up, or trim them.

If you open another video and drag a clip from one video into the split spot on another video, you can use the **Insert Clip After Selection** option to add the clip. QuickTime isn't just a tool for editing movies that have already been made; it can also record the screen, audio from the computer or an attached microphone, and video from the built-in webcam or any other connected camera.

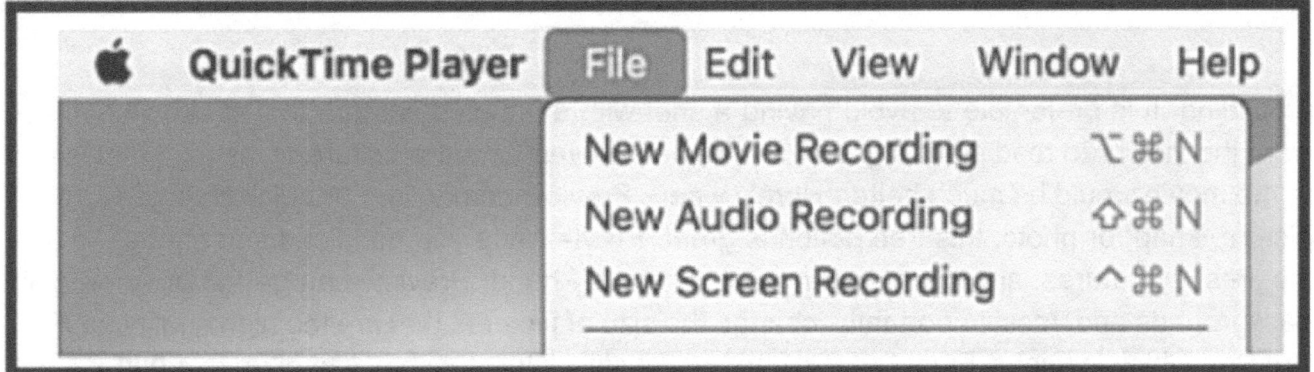

The size and style of a clip can be determined using QuickTime, which is useful for more than just recording or a quick cut or edit. With the QuickTime inspector, you can quickly see how a clip is put together.

The QuickTime inspector

That's easy to check a video file's quality, size, and format before you open it in Final Cut Pro. Just use the QuickTime inspector.

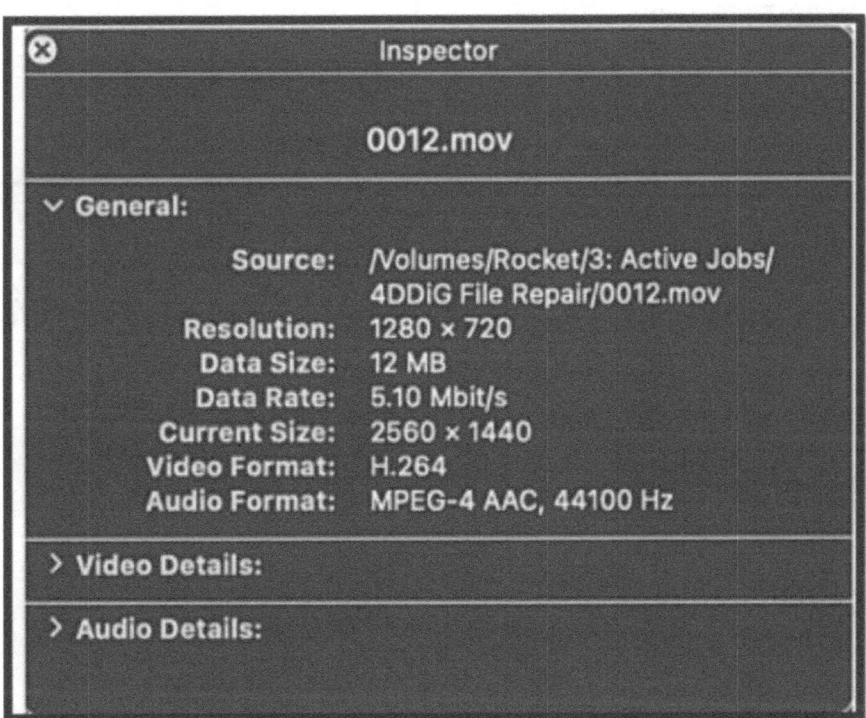

Some types of video files can't be played on the QuickTime app. For that, you will need to think about a different tool. Final Cut Pro will not be able to open the file if QuickTime does not recognize it. There are a few more useful Apple programs that work well with Final Cut Pro. The next part is about Preview, a straight-forward picture viewer, while QuickTime works on video.

Preview

Still, pictures don't always get the care they need when editing videos. You already know that video is just a collection of still images, and a still image is much better than a camera clip when you only need to show an object that doesn't move, like a road sign or a name on the outside of a building. It is preferable to avoid having a shot with a handled camera that shakes when you want the viewer to read static signs. A still frame or, even better, a picture of the sign that is part of the movie would be much better. Here's where Preview comes in. For quick changes to a still picture, snap, or photo, this free option is great. Preview lets you add lines and shapes to text, pictures, signatures, and even drawings you make by hand. Preview can get rid of some plain backgrounds and, most importantly, change the size of pictures that are too high quality for Final Cut Pro, which is useful. Final Cut Pro can handle still pictures with a size of up to **4,000 x 4,000** pixels. Final Cut Pro slows down noticeably as you get close to that size. A high-resolution picture doesn't need to be in the timeline. A picture that is too sharp will take away from the video that is around it. Open **Preview** and go to the **Tool** menu. Then, choose **Adjust Size** to make a picture smaller. Figu re out how many pixels you want to use in the new window that appears. In Preview, set the lowest value of either **Height or Width** to **1920 or 1080**, with **Scale proportionally** selected.

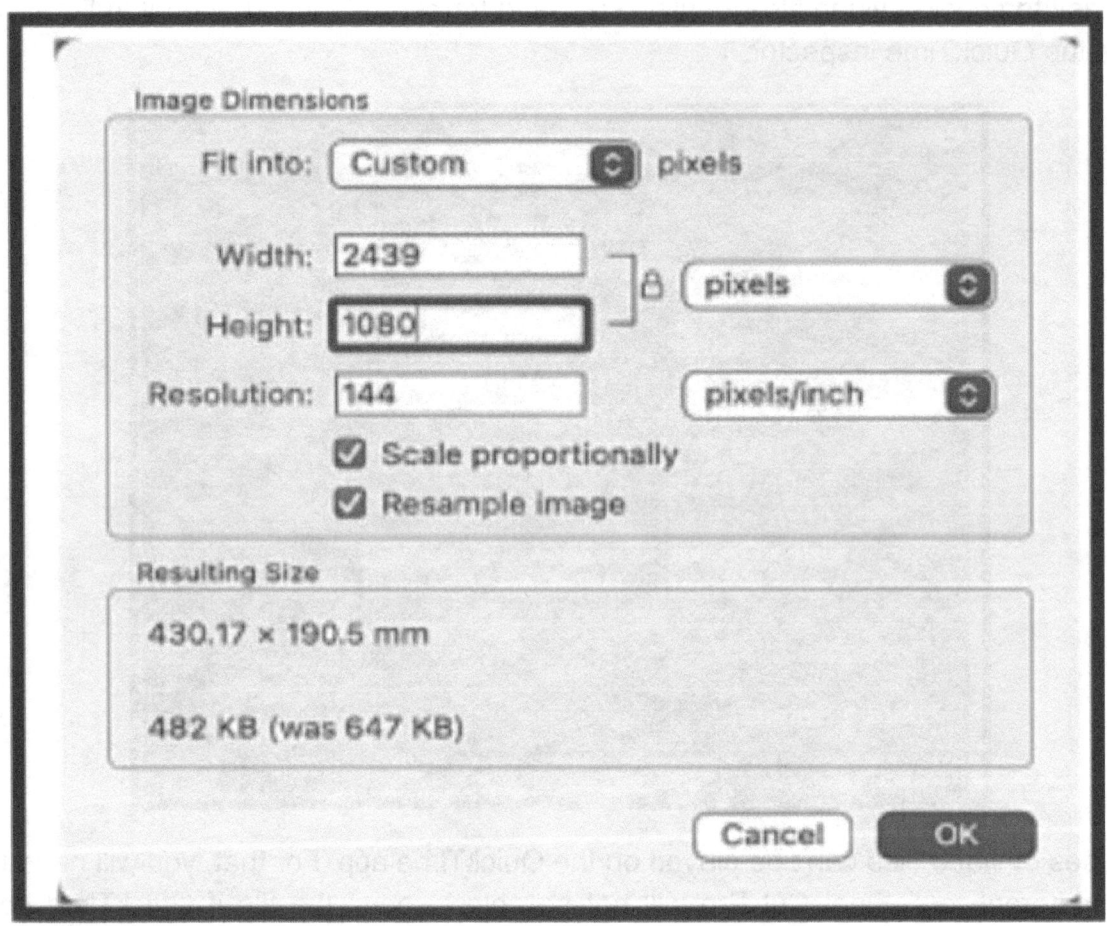

Set the lowest value of either height or width in the Preview window to double the number of pixels in the Final Cut Pro timeline. This will give you more space to see the picture. To use Preview, you need to choose the drawing tools. To do this, click on the A in a circle but ton, which brings up a second menu bar with many options, as shown in the figure below.

To get rid of the background, click the second button from the left on the menu bar, and then drag the mouse over the background until you've removed as much of it as you can.

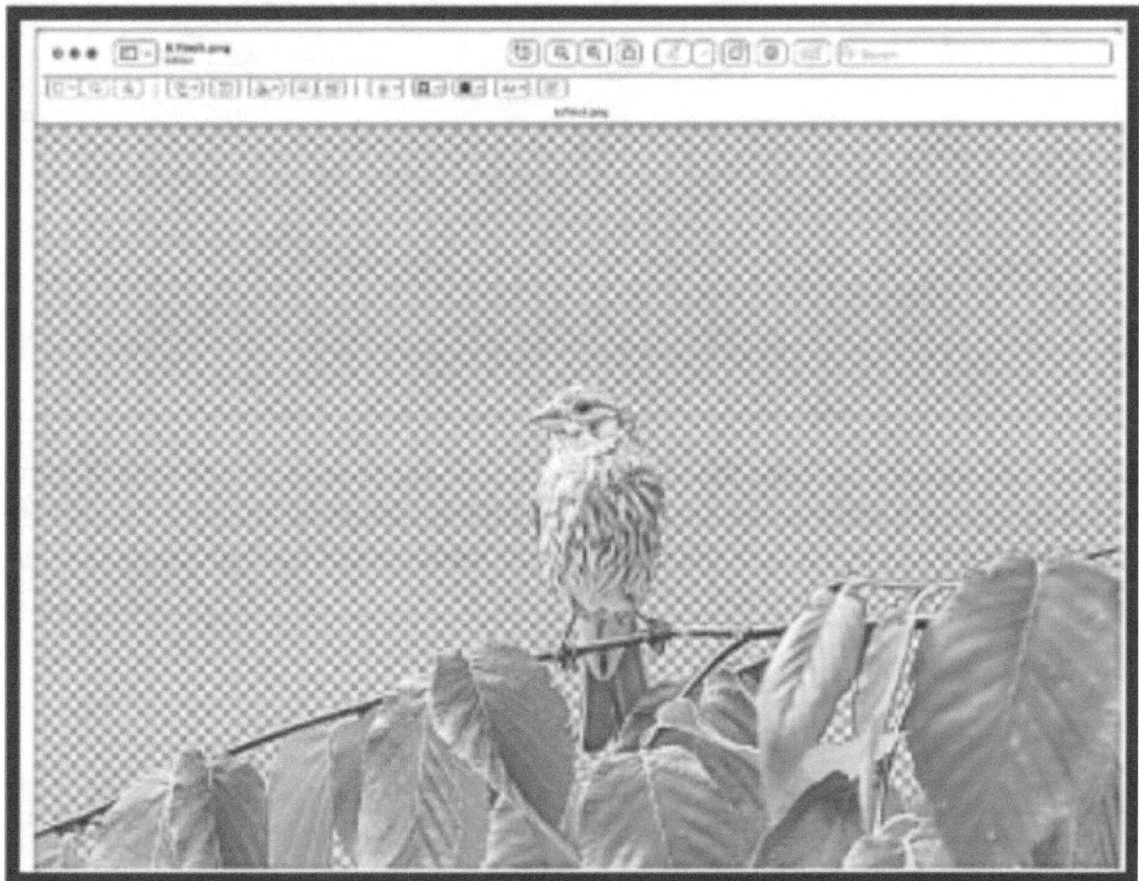

Preview can be used to quickly adjust still images; it's not as sophisticated as industry-standard Photoshop, but it's free with your Mac.

Keynote

You will learn how to save a slideshow in a format that Final Cut Pro can read. From the File menu, choose Export To| Movie... after making your slideshow.

Any file type can be used to save the slideshow, but if you need a picture with a transparent background (maybe you want to see the movie behind the slideshow images), choose **HEVC or Apple ProRes 4444** and make sure the **Export with transparent backgrounds** is checked.

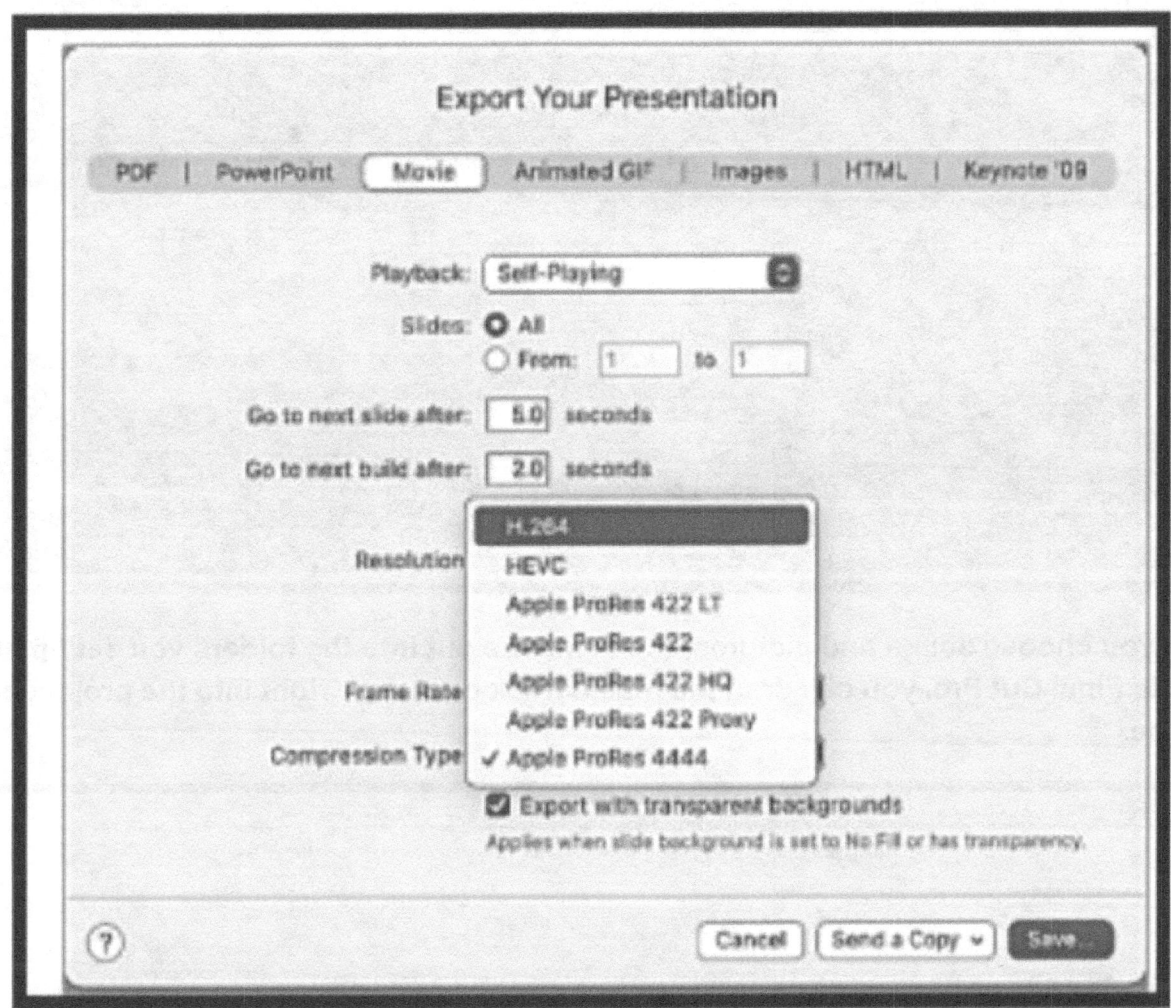

When you bring the movie into Final Cut Pro, you can edit it just like any other camera clip. It is not possible to change the text or objects in the video because they are set in the way they were saved from Keynote. You will have to make changes in Keynote and then send them again to Final Cut Pro if you need to. Because they are built into macOS, the final two Apple apps, Photos and iTunes Music, can be viewed straight from the Final Cut Pro interface.

iTunes and Photos

If you click on the middle tab with the music note icon in the upper left corner of Final Cut Pro, you can get to both iTunes and Photos from the Clip browser.

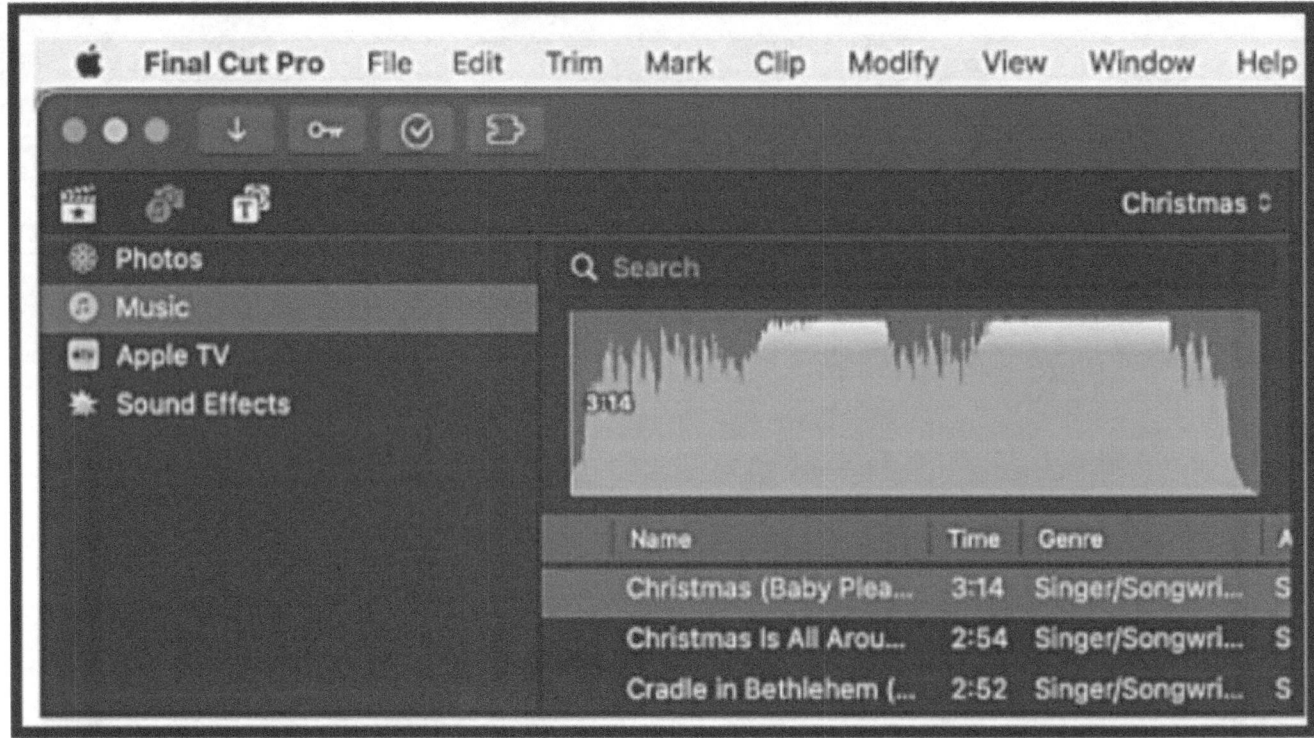

When you choose songs and pictures, the items are put into the folders you set up in the apps. In Final Cut Pro, you can drag the music track or picture right into the project in the timeline.

Non-Apple applications that support Final Cut Pro

These pages will focus on showing the key features of the different apps instead of describing how they work. First, we'll talk about Final Cut Library Manager, an app that was made just for Final Cut Pro. Then, I'll list the other apps in order of how useful I think they are.

Final Cut Library Manager

This app's job is to make it easy to order everything in all of your Final Cut Pro files, even if they're not connected to a computer at the mo-ment. The main goal of Final Cut Library Manager is to minimize library size without missing any media that a Final Cut Pro library needs. Final Cut Library Manager can get rid of **Optimized** and **proxy** media as long as the **original** media is still there. When there is no original media to be found, the Final Cut Library Manager will not get rid of the improved media. Final Cut Library Manager makes sure that the libraries in Final Cut Pro can always be fully edited. It shows every Final Cut Pro library that has been opened on any disk that has been attached to the computer before. You can remove drives from the database that are no longer needed. If you check a disk on the left side of the interface, the main window on the right will only show the resources on that drive. To get rid of **Optimized media, Proxy media, and Flow and Render files**, check the boxes next to each option. Under **Potential Space Savings**, you can see how much space will be saved.

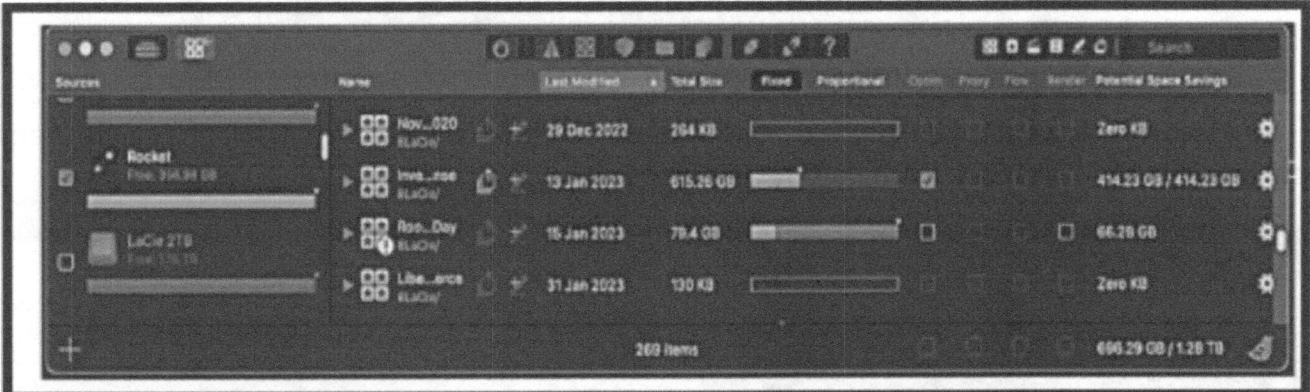

CommandPost

CommandPost is unique to a program. The options only work with Final Cut Pro when it's open. When the Finder is open, the options change to work with it. Being able to use control surfaces like Loupedeck may be the most important change. The free CommandPost app's main goal is to make editing less boring by including features like **Titles to KeyWords,** which turns clip titles into a list of keywords.

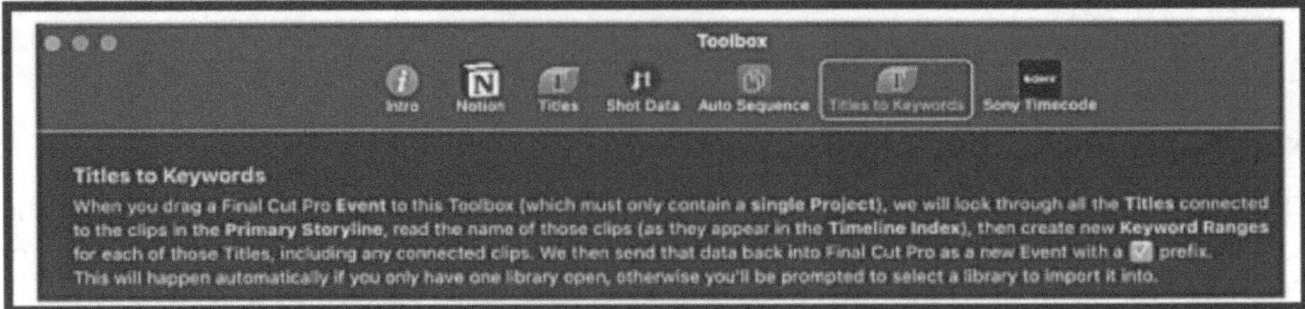

One of the most-used features in CommandPost is the ability to turn the Final Cut Pro timeline into a moving timeline. When the playhead hits the end of the display, the viewable timeline moves to the next point on the timeline. The playhead can always be seen because the timeline moves.

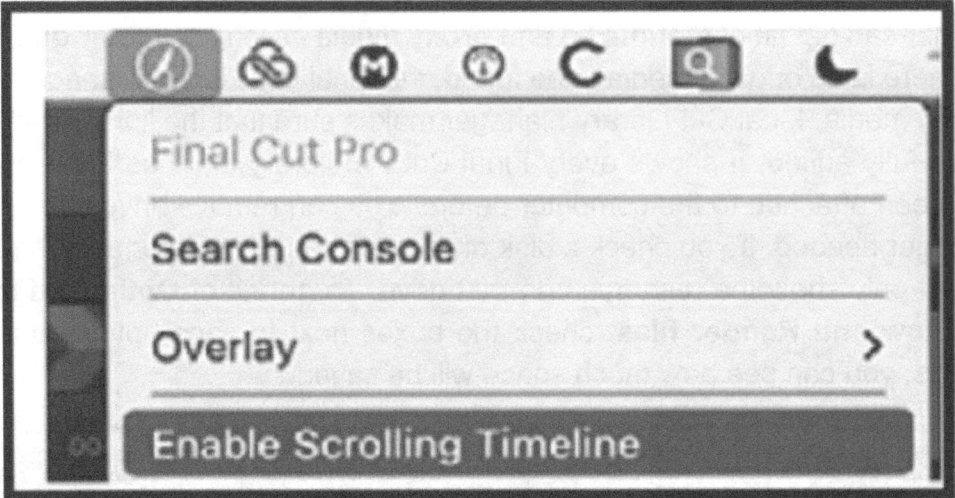

People who make content for social media will love that the Final Cut Pro Index menu lets them make a .csv file, which lets them quickly add timestamps to the titles of YouTube videos.

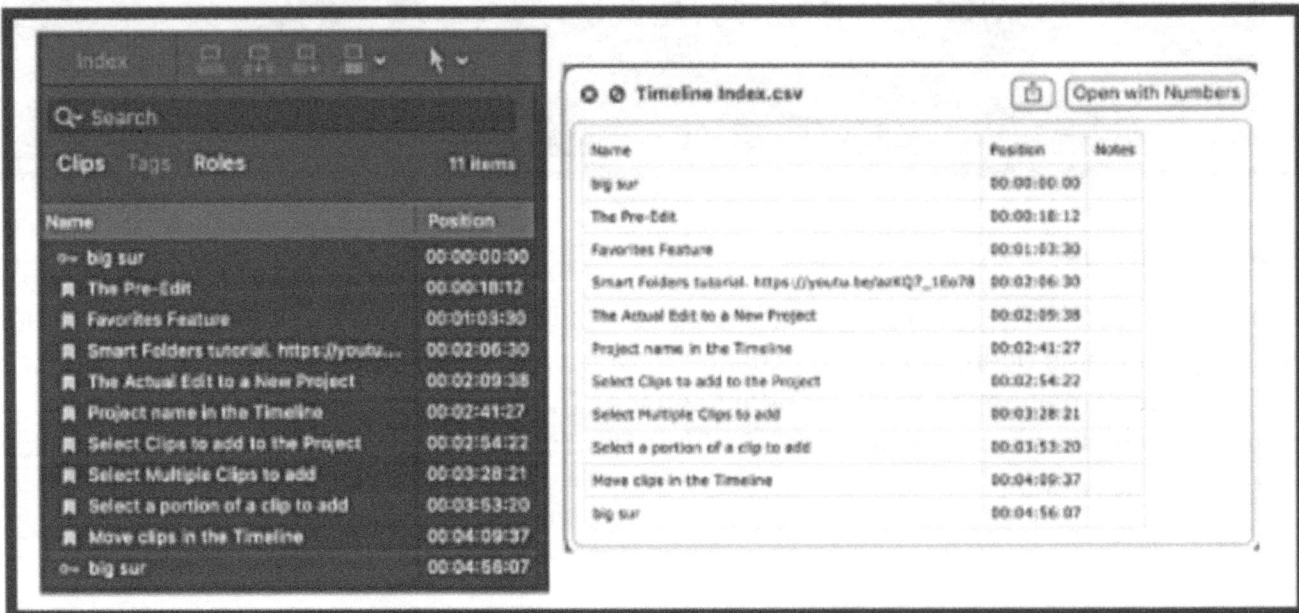

VLC

A file can be converted into a format that is compatible with Final Cut Pro using the free VLC program, which will play any video format.

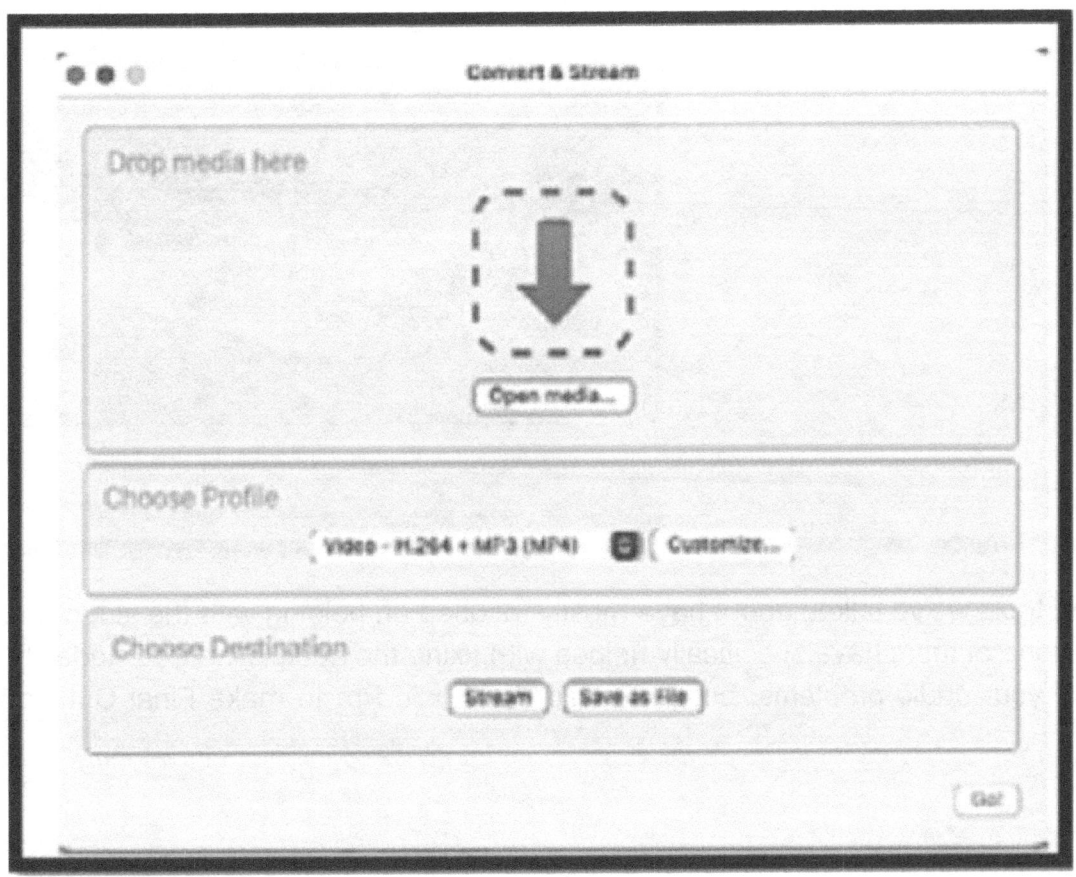

Handbrake

Handbrake has more options for compressing files and changing formats, but it doesn't work with as many types as VLC. Even though Handbrake is easier to use, you will still need VLC for Annodex, Matroska (MKV), Raw Audio: DTS, Raw DV, FLAC, FLV (Flash), and MXF.

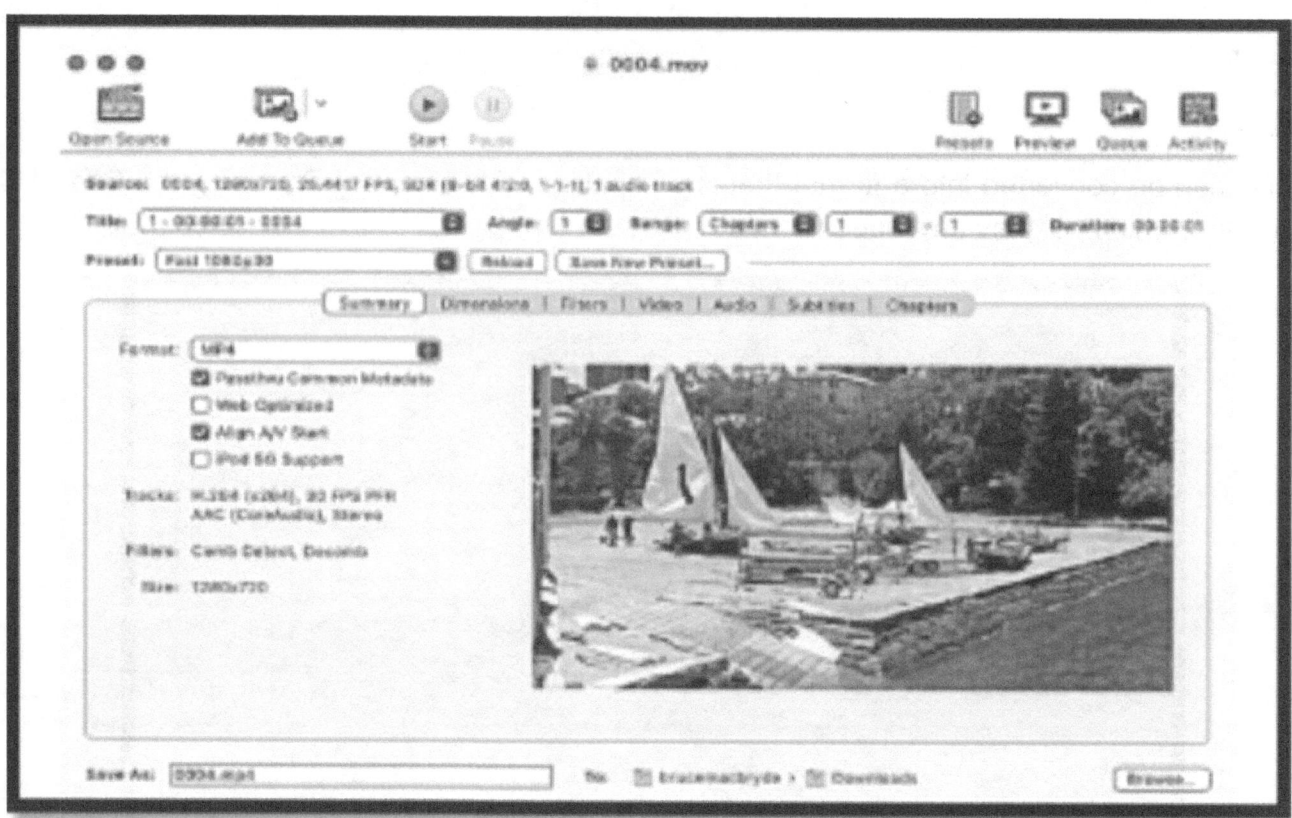

So far, the tools we've talked about have mostly focused on helping with the video part of Final Cut Pro. None of them have specifically helped with fixing the audio. The free Audacity app can fix a lot of your audio problems, but you could use Logic Pro to make Final Cut Pro's sound better.

Audacity

There are built-in audio editing tools in Final Cut Pro, but you will find that you need to do more than what the built-in effects can do. For a free app, Audacity has a huge number of great features. For example, one thing that Final Cut Pro doesn't have is the ability to pick out a noise, like a cough or sniffle, and only use that frequency range in the project's audio. To use **Audacity** with Final Cut Pro, you need to export a WAV file of just the audio from a project and then load it into Audacity. First, you can separate the noise in Audacity's timeline. Next, go to the Effects **menu and choose Noise Reduction and Get Noise Profile, as shown in step 1 of the figure below:**

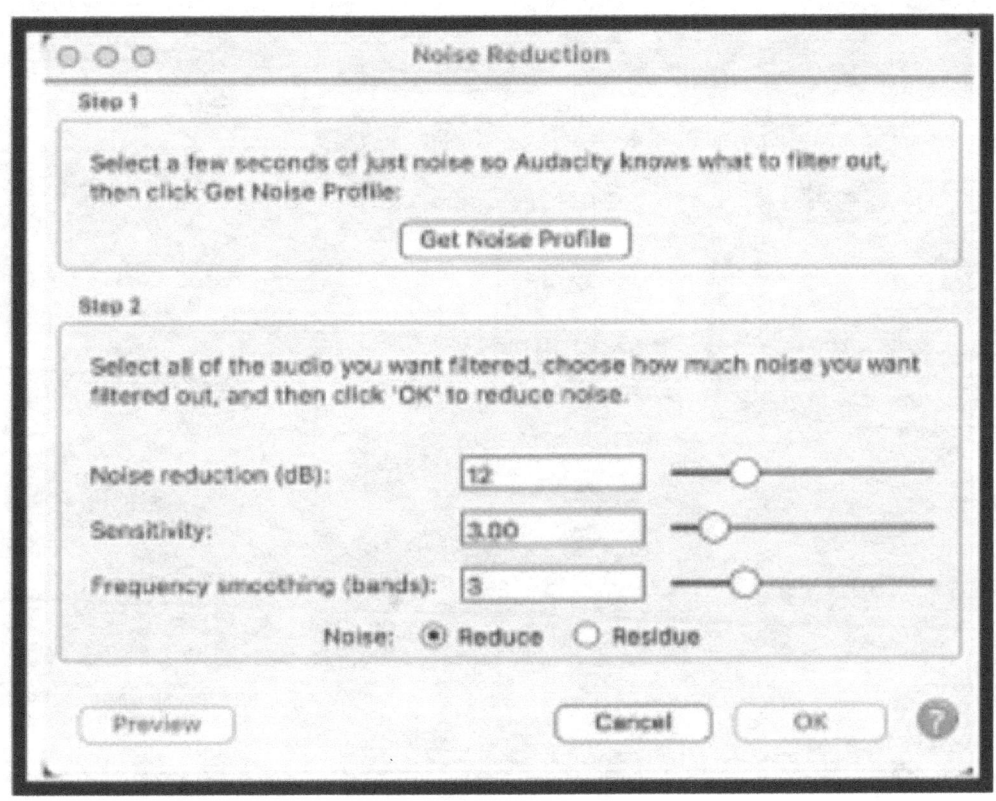

As soon as the profile is saved, you can get the saved noise profile by picking the whole Audacity timeline, going back to the Effects menu, and choosing Noise Reduction again. **Step 2** in the picture above will begin when you press the **OK** button.

Pixelmator Pro

With advanced video support, Pixelmator Pro is a Mac-focused app with many tools that were made with Final Cut Pro in mind. You can edit video right in Pixelmator Pro, add layered graphics, and then round-trip to Final Cut Pro. This means that any changes you make in Pixelmator Pro will also be made in Final Cut Pro.

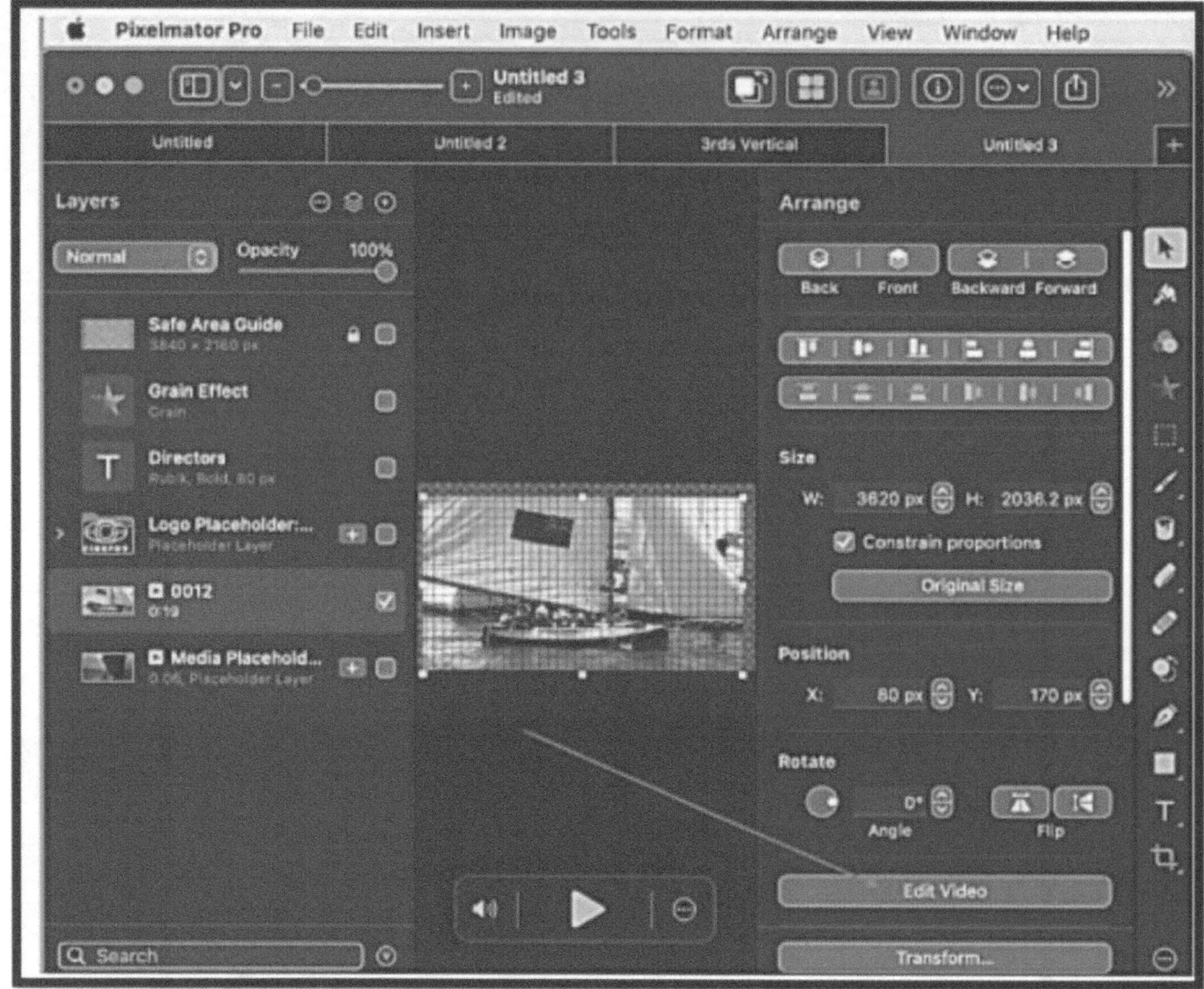

Miscellaneous applications

A lot of other programs can work with Final Cut Pro. The selections here have been made to provide the most crucial assistance. Check out Crumple Pop's free sound app. You can also get Captionator from the Apple App Store to make easy subtitles that can turn spoken words into text.

- **Ulti.Media** helps Final Cut Pro analyze clips and edit them automatically to a beat. To use this feature, drag a song into **BeatMark**, and it will suggest the best places to cut the music. BeatMark will make an FCP XML file for you, which will let you make a new project with the clips cut to the music. Ulti. Media has a lot of other uses as well, such as video tags, which turn media material into keywords.
- **InqScribe** is software that turns audio into text. This is a great idea for video talks where you need to record or take notes with time codes.

You should also look at what Intelligent Assistance has to offer in terms of tools that work with Final Cut Pro. The Final Cut Pro project can be loaded into **Adobe Premiere Pro, Audition, After Effects**, as well as **Avid Media Composer and Pro Tools**, thanks to the **XtoCC** tool, which is also known as **Project X$_2$7**. It does this by using Final Cut Pro's XML. There is also an app called **SendToX** from Intelligent Assistance that can help you move from Premiere to Final Cut Pro. SendToX can also be used to move files from the old Final Cut Pro 7 app to the new Final Cut Pro X app. Live writing and recording are provided by Intelligent Assistance's **Lumberjack** tool pro.

CHAPTER 18: EDITING IMMERSIVE 360° VIDEOS

Adding your clips is the first step in any editing job. You can use the Media Import window or just drag and drop the video like you would with any other video stream. Depending on the settings you choose, imported clips will either be stored in the library, in a place picked by the library, or will be linked to where they are. In the upper left area of each 360° clip, there will be a small **globe (or ball) icon. This icon will be used throughout the app to show features that are linked to 360° footage:**

While the equirectangular view shows the whole shot, it's not a representation of how the viewer will see it. To make it look like a viewer with a smaller field of view, go to the viewer's upper corner and select **View > 360° Viewer. This divides the viewer in two, so you can see both points of view at the same time:**

To make one of these views bigger and the other smaller, just move the line between them left or right. Still, this has a lot of data, so if you have two screens, you might want to put the viewer on the bigger one. When you want to change the frame of the 360° Viewer, just drag on the picture. This will make you pan across to see something else. You can do this even while the video is playing. You can change the **Viewing Angle** tool at the top of the 360° Viewer to make the view of the world look bigger or smaller. Each headset has a fixed field of view, so users can't usually change it. However, it's a great way to get a feel for what the experience might be like. The 360° Viewer does not alter the footage in any way because you cannot control where users look in a 360° timeline. After moving around a bit, you should go to the **360° Viewer's Settings** menu and choose "**Reset Angle**." This will put you back in the middle. This first "straight ahead" view is how everyone will start watching your clips, and a lot of them won't look too far away from it, so it's important to put something interesting here to center the viewer's first experience.

When you need to make a timeline:

- To see this, right-click on one of your 360° clips and selects "**New Project**."

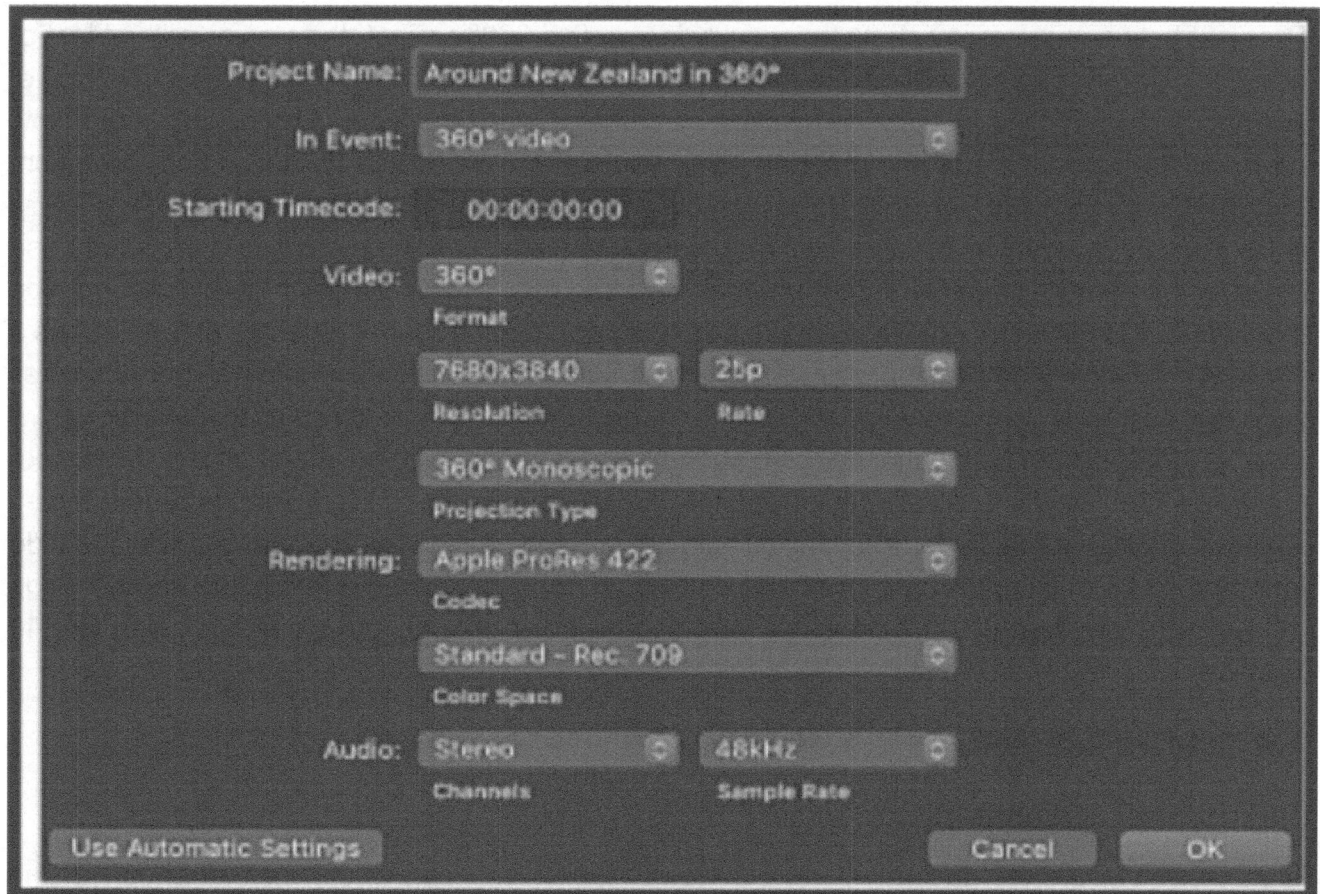

- Next, go to the **Video** menu and click on **Custom**:

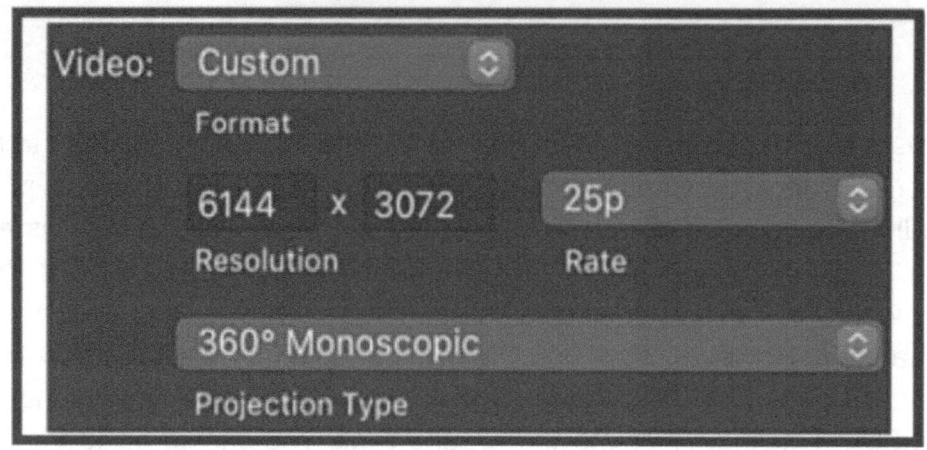

You can see the 6.1K my camera offers above, and this app will make a timeline that will match the quality your camera takes. Keep in mind that if your Mac has trouble, you can use a proxy process or lower the quality to make edits easier. Of course, if you have a binocular 3D 360° camera, you can pick that display type here. I, on the other hand, picked 360° Monoscopic because my cheaper camera only works in 2D.

Editing considerations

If you cut between too many shots too quickly in a native 360° project, the viewer will get lost or feel sick. Still, all of your usual editing tools work the way you'd expect: You can trim, roll, ripple, slip, and slide 360° clips. You can swap clips with others, use Clips, connect clips above or below the main storyline, and edit in almost any way you want. You should try not to edit too much, though. When you move from one place to another, it's best to fade to black (with FadeTo Color), which keeps every viewer at ease. This method is often used in VR movies and games because it makes the camera look like it's not moving. You can also try out different transitions, but you should test themon watchers first to make sure they don't make them sick since everyone has a different tolerance. Another important thing is that you should make your movie shorter overall since not everyone wants to wear VR gear for long periods of time. Once more, everyone will have a different level of patience, but shorter experiences will be more widely accepted, especially if the viewer is borrowing a headset, like at a meeting or a live business presentation. Because of these restrictions, you can still edit, but you will need to think of creative ways to hide your changes. For example, you could use soft-edged masks to blend one clip into another. You can edit in a way that doesn't show, as long as you don't change places with a clear drop to black.

One more thing to think about is which way the video is looking.

Understanding Reorient

Even though you can't decide where the viewer looks, you can direct their attention to the important part. When a video starts, every one will be looking at the same place. This is the center of the equirectangular view, and it's also what you'll see if you go to the Configuration menu and select Reset Angle. This seems like a good place for your first area of study. The new Reorient part in the Inspector lets you spin each of your clips around its center point, which is where the camera is in a virtual sphere. Be careful when using this feature, though. If your camera levels the sky for you, you should probably only change **Pan (Y) and not Tilt (X) or Roll (Z)**. This is because changing **X and Z** can make your viewers sick. You can use these settings to make your shots look more normal if your camera doesn't automatically level the sky for you. The scales, the numbers, or clicking on the numbers and putting in new values can all be used to change these values. If you'd rather work on the picture directly, click the button to the right of the "**Reorient**" section in the **Inspector** or select that icon from the menu in the lower-left corner of the Viewer. A fourth "Reorient" icon will now appear next to the "**Transform,**" "**Crop,"and" Distort**" icons.

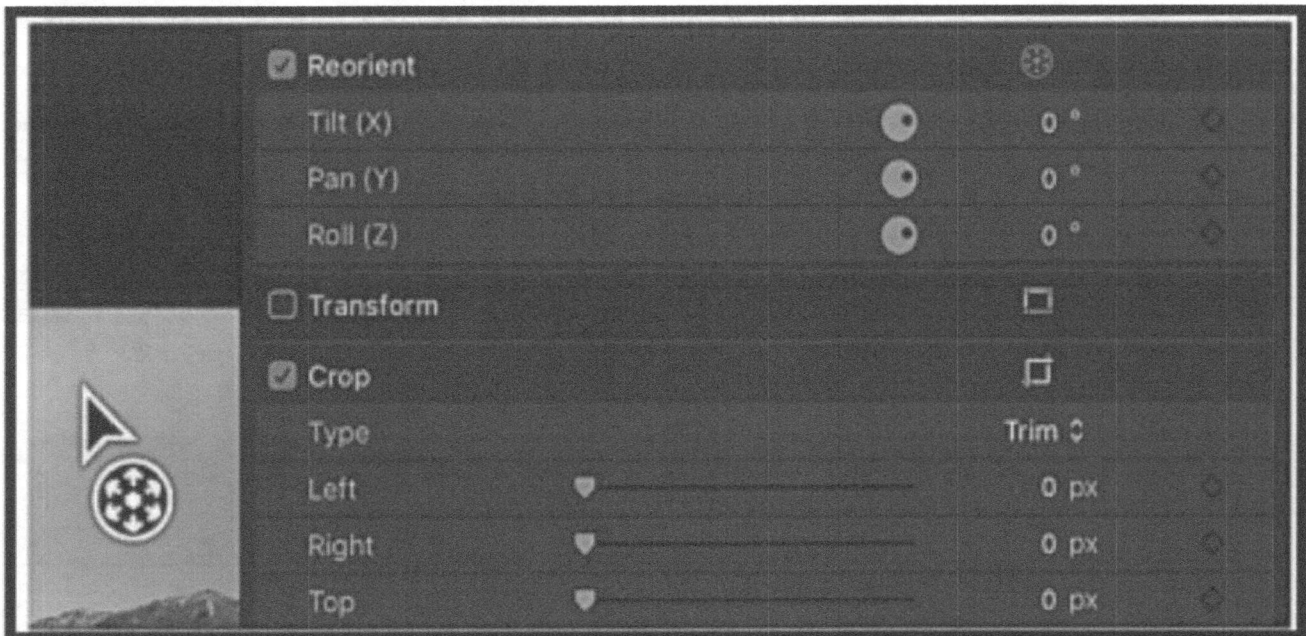

You can change tilt, pan, and roll in this mode by dragging on the equirectangular view instead of the 360° Viewer. If you hold down the **shift** key, you can only change one of these at a time. To change Pan (**Y**), drag horizontally. Try out these options, then go to the top right of the viewer, press **Reset**, and then click **Done**. In the Inspector, you can click on the small menu to the right of the **Reorient** section and choose **Reset Parameter.**

- **Pan (Y)** is always safe, but **Tilt (X) and Roll (Z)** can quickly make things go crazy. It should be used to make sure that the key area stays the same from shot to shot, so the viewer doesn't get lost when the place changes.

For instance, most viewers will follow the person speaking if they start talking to the camera and then walk 90° around the shot to the viewer's right. So that your audience doesn't have to look for what they should be looking at, the area of interest in the next shot should pick up where the area of interest in the last shot left off. To finish, all you have to do is use Pan (Y) to move a shot around until its starting point meets up with the end point of the previous shot's scene. Thus, how can you direct their attention to the most interesting part of the frame? Some of the most obvious ways to lead viewers are probably by moving your subjects around the frame. You could also use sound, titles, or effects. Because that's the fun of the medium, always keep in mind that someone could be looking in any direction. Either put your titles close to where people are looking or leave them up longer than normal. To encourage viewers to spend more time on your subjects, make sure the entire frame is interesting to look at and remove any unnecessary clutter. Your shots are reoriented; what else can you do?

Effects and Transitions in 360°

Be careful with all of your add-ons, like color changes, effects, transitions, titles, and generators, because an equirectangular clip doesn't work like normal video. First, anything that works with regular video means that a clip has edges, which is a pretty safe assumption. But anything that works with an equirectangular frame can cause problems that can be seen at the edges. It's fine to change the colors of the whole picture and to use color masks. You can still fix the sky or the **ground with a graded mask as well. You'll need a flat-shaped Shape Mask that goes through both sides of the frame at the same point to do this, but that's easy to do:**

A shape mask on a color adjustment, on the other hand, can't go past the frame's edges because the impact will stop right there. In effects, even a simple effect like Gaussian blur needs to handle the edges of a 360° project uniquely. Some effects will not work, but a lot of them will. **You can quickly find the ones that don't work by using the 360° Viewer to look at the area around the frame"s edge. Here is an example of both at the same time:**

The best news is that the most popular effects have been changed to work with 360° projects and are now grouped in a 360° area. You can try out 360° Gaussian blur, Aur a, glow, sharpen, noise reduction, and more. So, try them all out and see which ones you like best. One effect stands out: **360° Patch. This effect lets you patch over your camera's monopod or tripod to remove it from the bottom (or nadir) of the frame. How to use this effect:**

- Move the 360° patch effect to a clip that has a stand or shade that you can see.
- Hide the 360° viewer.
- In the Inspector, go to the 360° Patch tab and check the box next to Setup Mode. Now the view moves to the nadir of the frame, where you can see an area around a small green circle (the replacement area) that points to a small red circle.
- Move the green circle to change where the new patch comes from, and move the white sides of the circle to change its size.

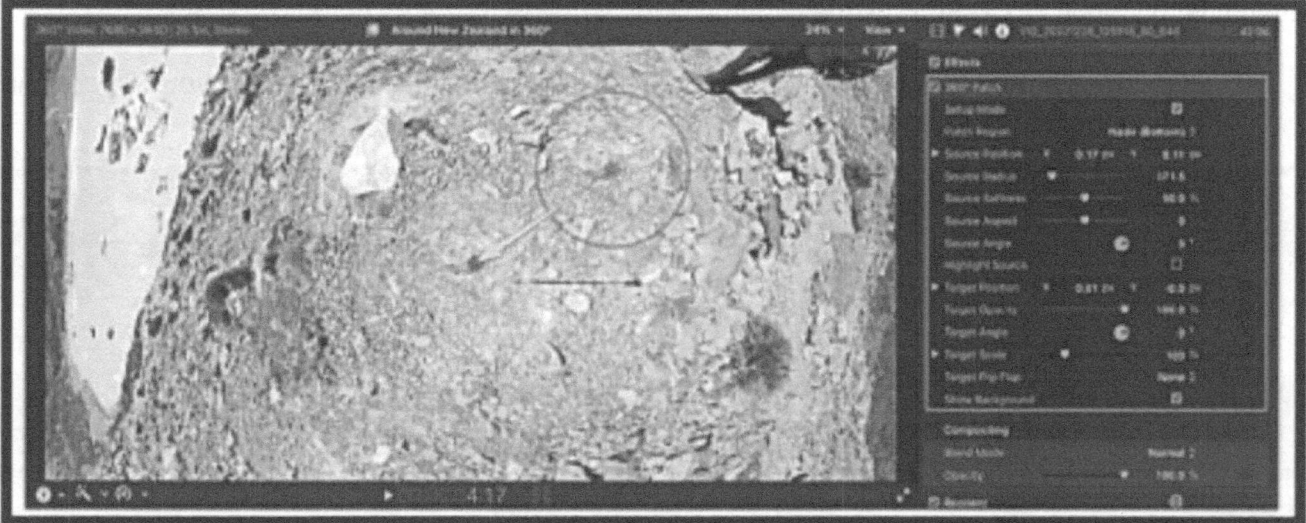

- If the camera support casts a long shadow, you may also need to change the Source Aspect setting to make the replacement area smaller. To hide the edges of the patch, Source Softness and target angle can also be used. Moving the red circle back to the middle may also help.
- **Look over your video to make sure your subject doesn't walk into the fixed areas, and then make any necessary changes:**

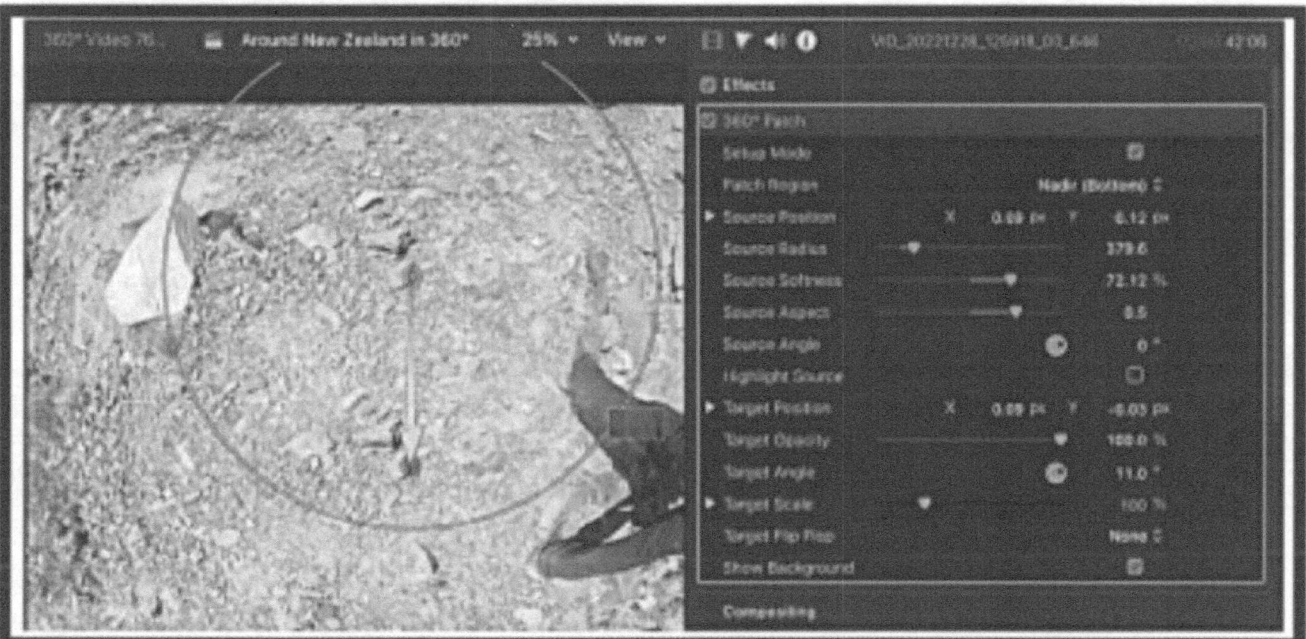

- When you're done, uncheck the box next to **Setup Mode**. Turn on the 360° Viewer again, and then watch the clip again to make sure you can't see the patch.

Do not give up if you cannot find a unique 360° version of the effect you want. Try one of the Comic Looks! It's som et im es acceptable to enjoy the weirdness. A mask can also be used to limit an effect so that it only affects a small part of the frame. But if an effect only changes the picture locally and consistently, and you only see a problem around the frame's edges, there is a way to make the whole thing look smooth. You can use this with other effects if you want to. I used it with Comic Cool. Start with a clip in a 360° timeline that fits your clip's size.

- Give the clip the look you want, such as Comic Cool. In the 360° Viewer, you'll see a line that connects the images.

- Option-drag the clip up to make a copy, but don't move it during the time.
- Go to the inspector and pick the top clip. In the Reorient area, change **Pan (Y) to 180°**. A stitch line will still be there.

- Press Option-G to make this clip joined together into a Compound Clip and give it a name.
- With the top clip still selected, in the **Crop** section of the inspector, set **Left** and **Right** to **500** to trim off the edges.

- Check the box next to the **Transform** part of the Inspector to open it, and then move **Position X** to be exactly half the width of the project's resolution. Suppose the width is 7680 pixels. Set Position X to 3840 pixels. If the width is 6144 pixels, set Position X to 3072 pixels.

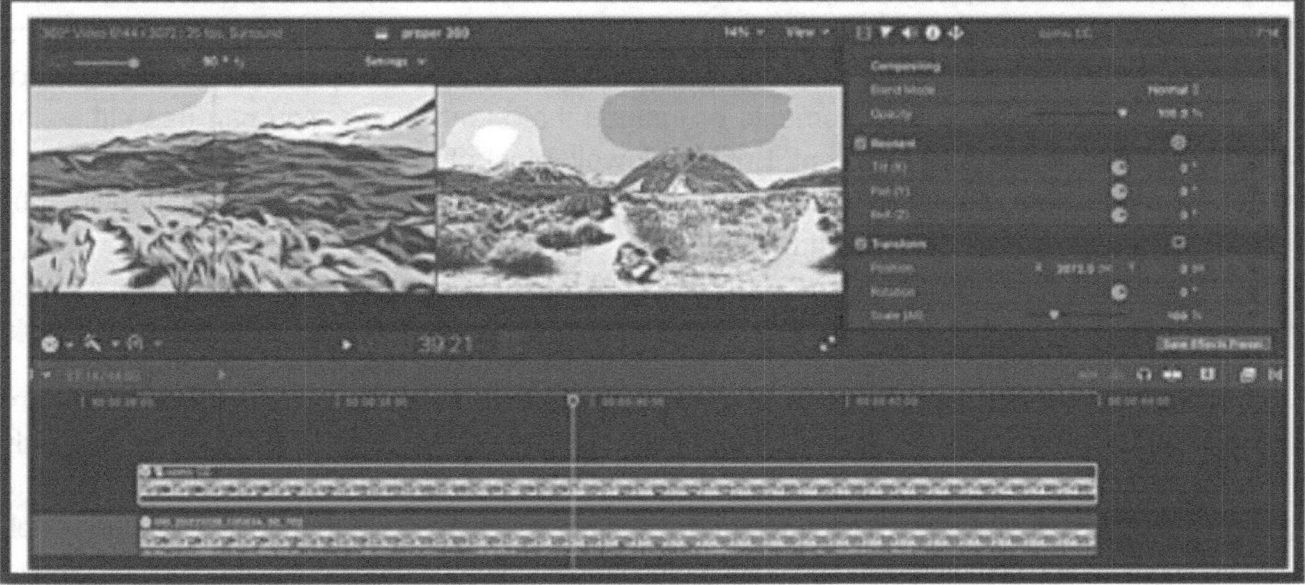

- Optoion-drag this compound clip upward to duplicate it, but do not move it in time.
- On this top clip, change Position X to a negative number that is the same as the current value, like-3840 or -3072.

Now there is no longer any problem around the edges of the equirectangular frame.

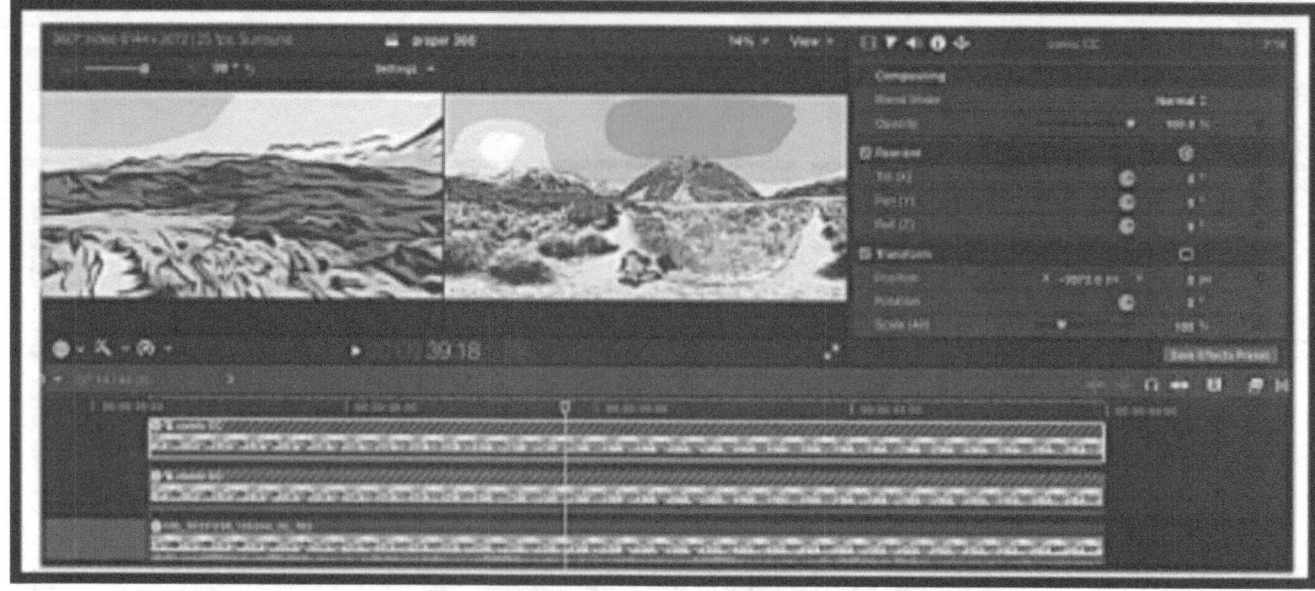

360° Titles and Generators

One problem with regular titles is that some of them expect to move in and out of a normal video frame, which won't work here. Another problem is that regular titles will be skewed. One way to get around this problem is to use one of the 360° titles that are in the 360° group. These titles have straight lines in the 360° viewer or through a headset, which is what you need, but they appear distorted in the equirect-angular view. There are a lot of ways to move text in the 360° Custom 3D title, and there are a lot of other titles in the same area. There are only two generators that work in 360°, but they're the most useful ones because they can be used to add to text or as a background behind keyed elements or images that stand alone. You can use either the 360° Color Solid or the 360° Gradient. Both work well. Most of the other generators won't work for 360° work, so if you need more options, shoot more videos or photos, or make your own 360° content in Motion using a 360° design,

Do you want to deliver in 360°?

Even though it's great to be able to work on 360° projects, delivering a 360° movie is still hard because of the problems with delivery. First, not enough people still use VR glasses. Not only are they out there, but they're also pretty pricey and not very often or for long amounts of time by many people. Second, it's still hard to send VR video at a high enough quality. You can watch it on your computer because you can load a 360° video clip right into your headset. However, many people don't have enough network speed to successfully download even 4K, and 4K isn't even good enough for VR video. Not only is it hard to download higher-quality images like 6K and 8K, but it can also be hard to play back. Third, a lot of watchers don't want to look around, wear a mask, or scroll around in an app that works with VR. It's pretty much the same to export a 360° video as it is to export a regular video. If you want to share your video in full quality on your timeline, make sure to use the Export File option instead of Resize. Pick ProRes as the format for the best quality or H.264 for a smaller file. If you don't want to give 360° footage directly right now, the good news is that you can still include it in a normal, straight timeline with other footage. That's what we'll talk about next.

Editing 360° footage on a regular timeline

Most 360° video today is reframed so that it can be put into a normal timeline. It's always straight, doesn't need to be pointed at the subject, and can be put in strange places and still get the shot. It has many of the same benefits as a 360° camera, but it's much easier to distribute.

This is easy at its core:

1. Import your 360° footage using your standard method.
2. Utilize the 360° Viewer to review your footage.
3. Apply keywords and ratings to your footage as you typically would.
4. Create a standard project, not specifically designated for 360° content. (You can now close the 360° viewer.)
5. Arrange and edit your clips within the project timeline.
6. Utilize the orientation tool to reframe each 360° clip as needed.

We need to focus on that final point, orientation.

Understanding Orientation

The orientation settings are a lot like the Reorient options in a native 360° Project, even down to the icon. However, these settings are more detailed. As with Reorient, the Tilt (X), Pan (Y), and Roll (Z) tools let you change what part of the frame you're seeing. You can also use the on-screen buttons to interact with the scene. (Note that you have to stop the movie before you can use the on-screen tools.) You can push this out to about 132° before you start seeing blacklines at the edge of the frame. A new Field of View control will change how much of the source picture can be seen at once. What a viewer sees will change, but the viewing angle doesn't. This is like the Viewing Angle tool that's above the 360° Viewer. Mapping is the last option here. You can choose between **Normal and Tiny Planet**. With this second option, your frame is turned into a small world surrounded by the sky from the original shot. This is a nice (if skewed) way to show a full 360° frame in a regular movie. But wait a minute.

Set the tilt to 90° and change the field of view to something much smaller than 360°, like 180°. This will give you a very wide-angle shot with a flat horizon:

You can still change Pan and Roll; you'll have a lot more freedom than in Normal view, and the final results will be clearer because you're using more of the pixels from the source. It's a great strategy that works most of the time, but it won't work on all shots.

Working with Final Cut Pro backups

Final Cut Pro backs up your work automatically. You should know the difference between the words "backing up" and "archiving." When you edit, backing up is a temporary process that goes on all the time. Archiving keeps a library's projects in the best possible working state so that they can be opened later without getting the feared red "**Missing File**" message.

Final Cut Pro backs up automatically every few minutes, and the copies are kept in the Users folder on the main disk of the Mac. They don't take up much room on the disk because they don't have any media on them. The back up library only tells you where the media is kept. While this is good because it leaves a small mark, it is also risky because the media needs to be accessible for the backup library to work. If the media is moved, the backup pro will only display the **"Missing File"** message for the relevant clips in the pro library. On your system disk, the **Movies** folder is inside the **Users** folder. This is where you'll find the Final Cut Backups folder. All of the files that can be found for each library that has been opened in Final Cut Pro will be in this folder.

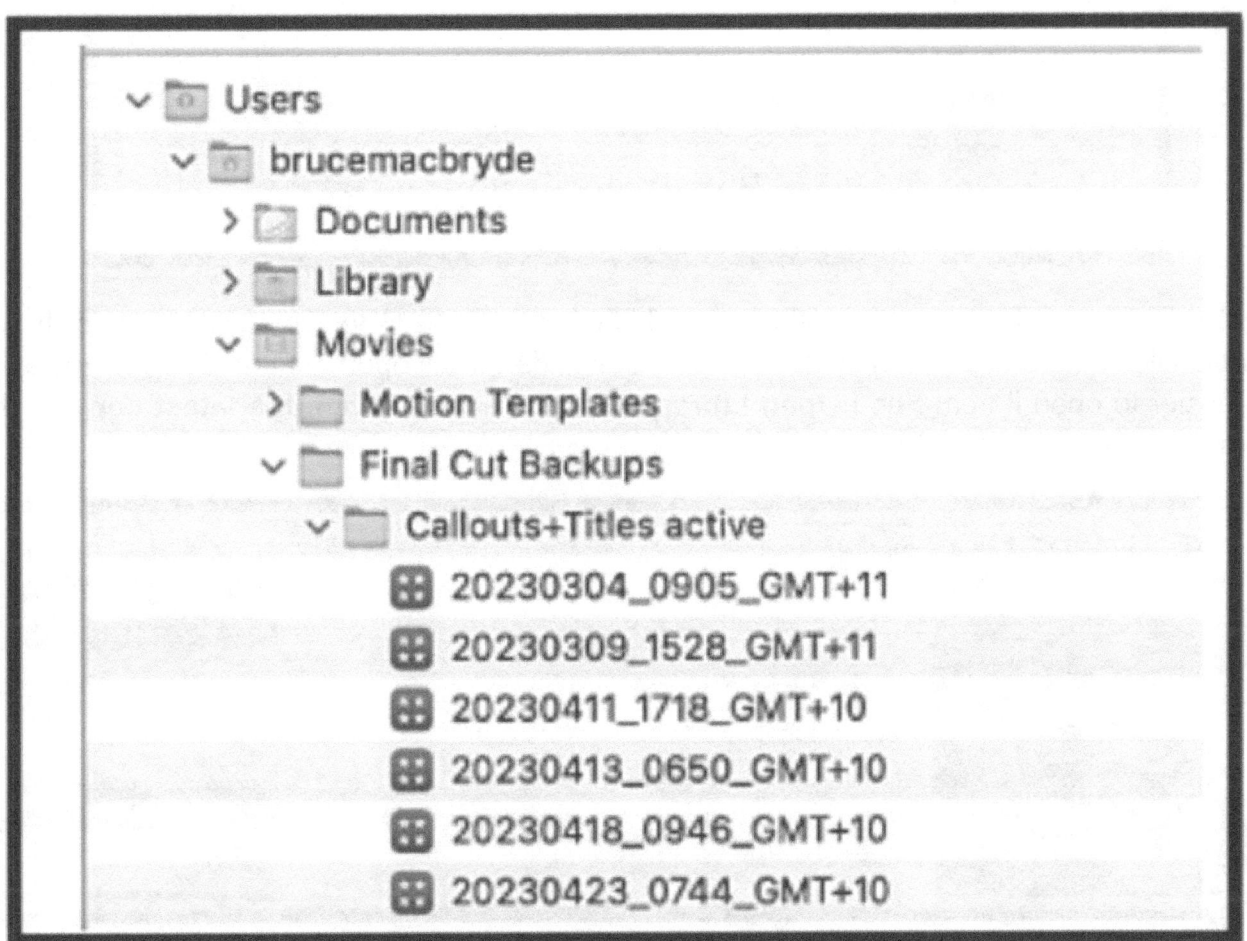

Even though regular copies take up a small amount of room at first, if they are not carefully handled, the storage space can grow a lot over time. When I last looked in my Final Cut files folder, it had 368 files taking up 78 GB of room.

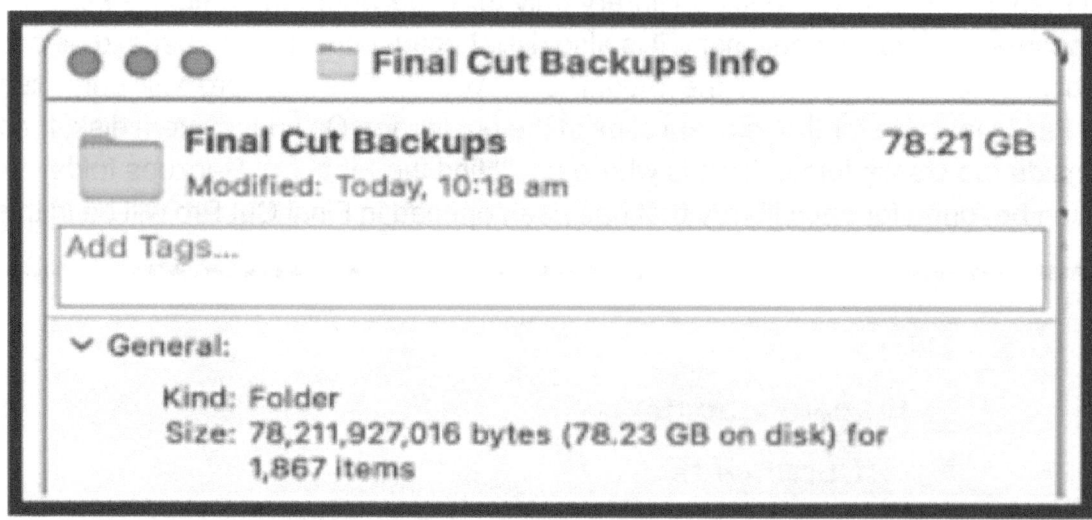

I got rid of saves from three months ago, which freed up 40 GB on my system drive. If you double-click on a backup in the Final Cut Backups folder, it will open in Final CutPro. However, it's easier to open it from **File I Open Library I From Backup. When the latest copy of the library is opened in Final Cut Pro:**

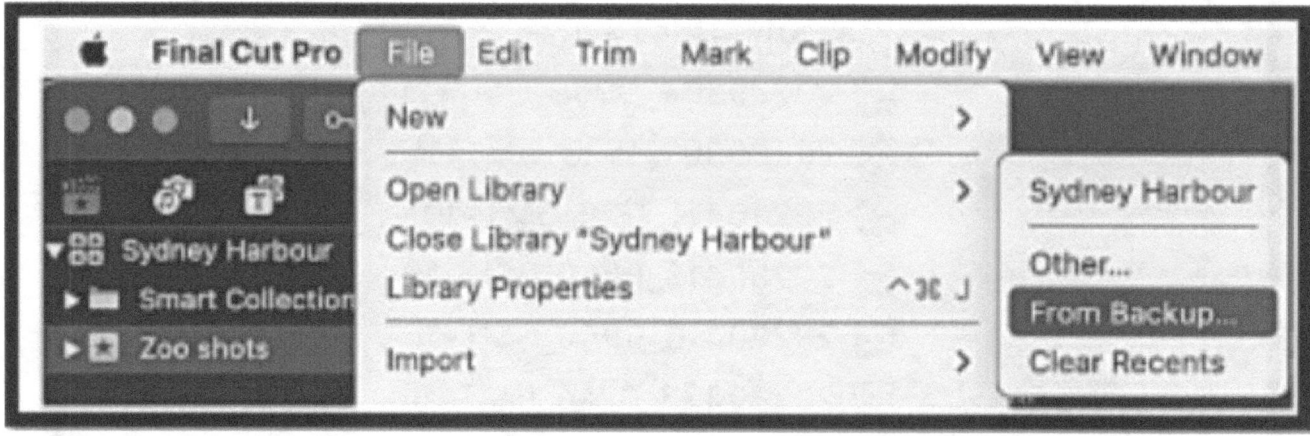

A list of all the files in that library will be shown to you, along with the times they were saved in a manner that you can understand.

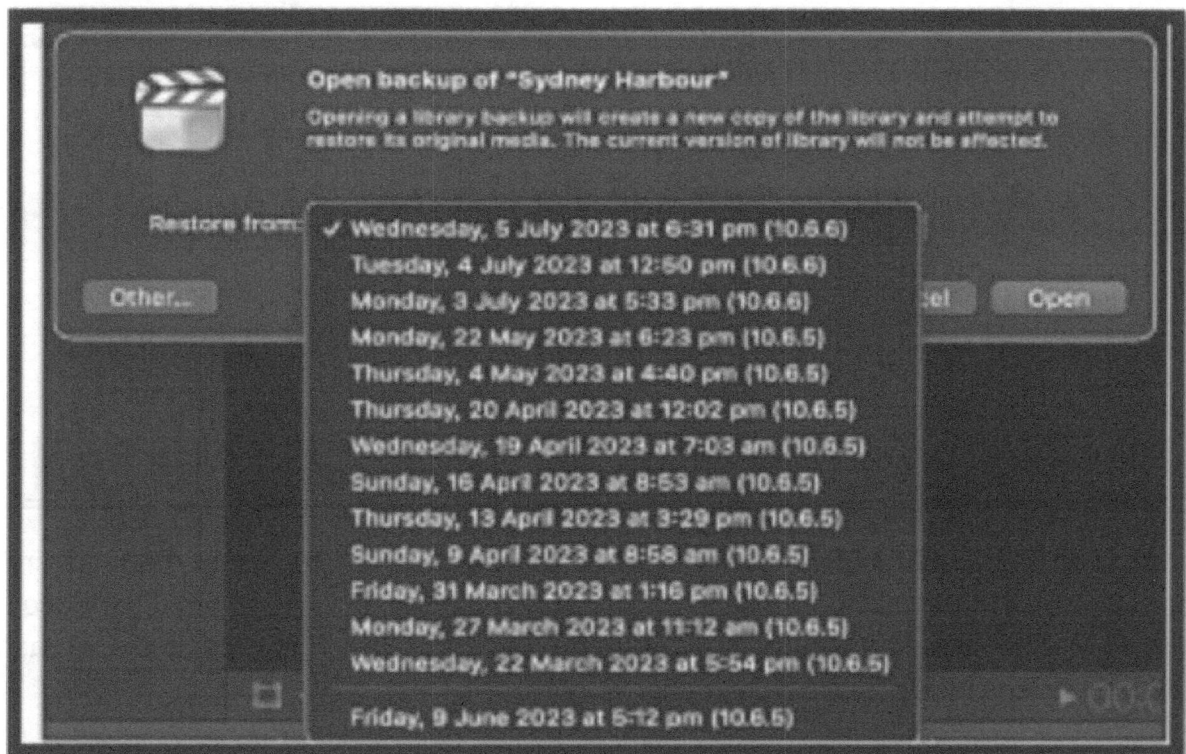

If you look at the list of backups in the Finder window, you will see the times written in a coded way next to each library's folder. There are four digits for the year, two digits for the month, and two digits for the date. The time is shown as **+/- GMT**. The same coded style is shown when the backup library is opened in Final Cut Pro's browser tab.

When you open a backup library, Final Cut Pro will back up that backed-up library in a folder with the original name, including the date code:

To avoid confusion, I recommend promptly renaming the backed-up version of the library with the date format. This will ensure that when it's backed up again, it will automatically acquire a meaningful name, such as **"Version2 recovered from Backup."** This proactive approach will help maintain clarity and organization in your workflow.

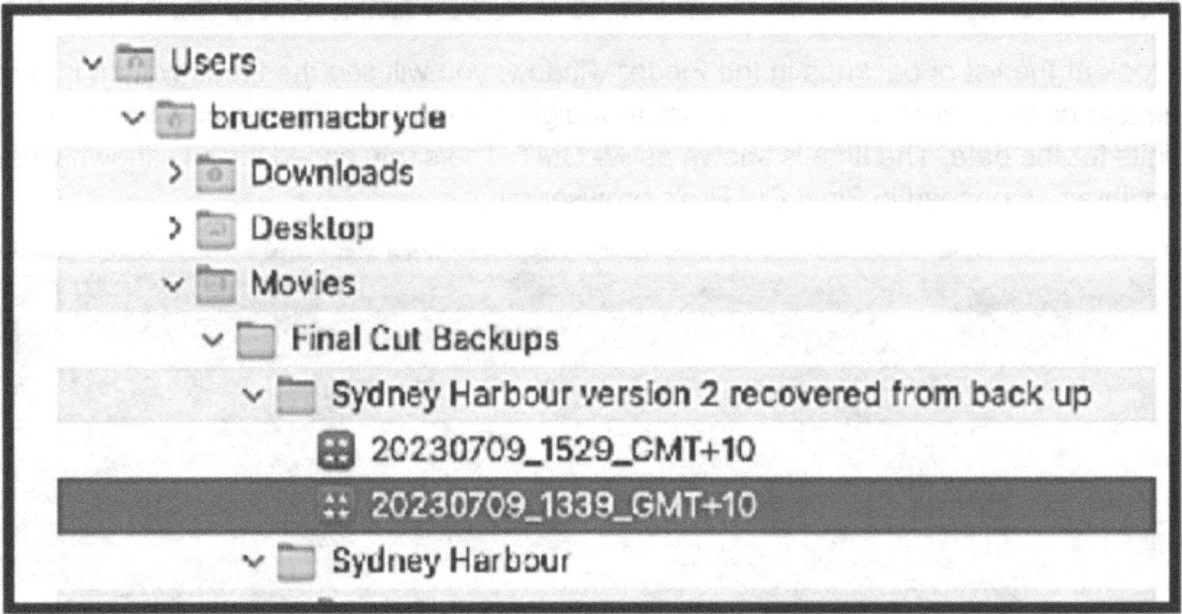

The automatic backups are for recovery purposes and are not intended to be used for archiving completed projects for posterity.

CHAPTER 19: TROUBLESHOOTING AND PROBLEM SOLVING

UPDATING MACOS AND FINAL CUT PRO

Older versions of Final Cut Pro will not be able to open an updated library that has been updated with a newer version of the program. A message will appear if you try to open an older library.

Note: If you are working with other editors, make sure that everyone changes at the same time. Editors who are still using an older version of Final Cut Pro will not be able to open libraries that have been updated. From the **Final Cut Pro** menu, choose **About Final Cut Pro** to see what version of Final Cut Pro you have. The version number will then show on the flash screen.

You can keep a copy of the old version of Final Cut Pro before updating if you want to be safe. To do that, right-click on the app in **Finder**, make a copy of it, and then shrink the copy.

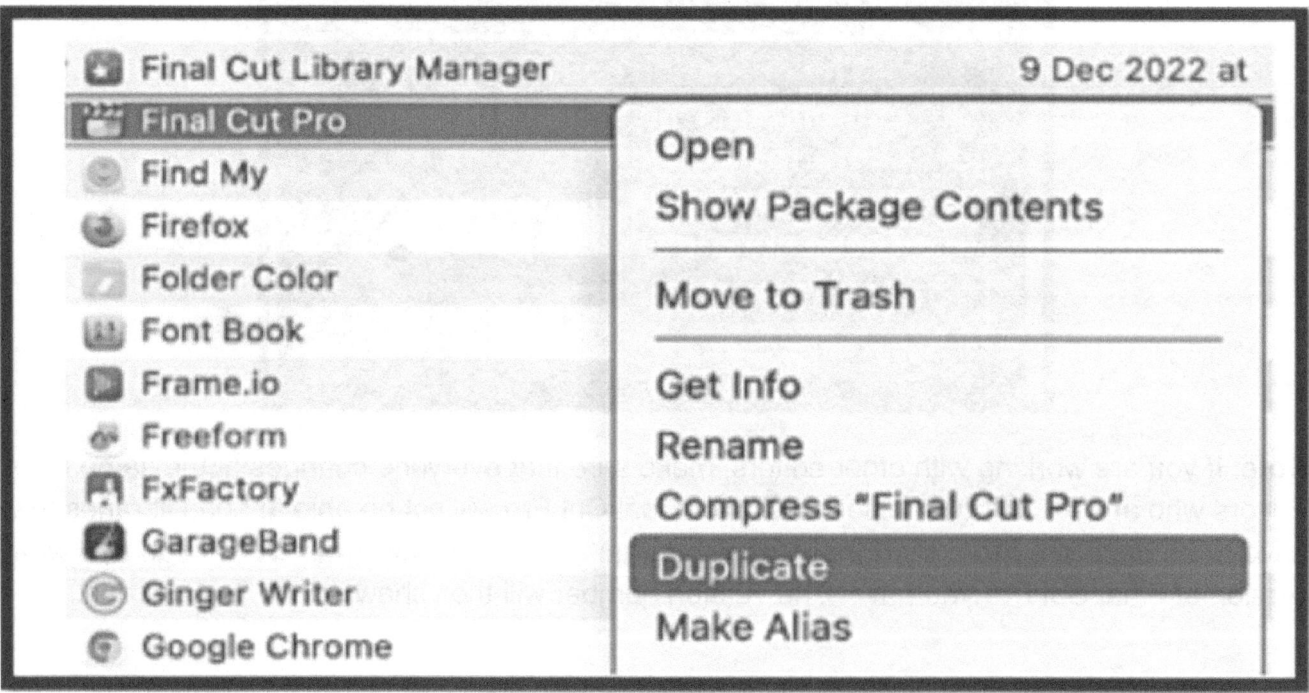

If you experience problems after an update, a compact copy will allow you to rollback to an earlier version.

Note: If you are working with other people, don't make any changes until the lead editor tells you to.

If you follow the rule that the OS version and the Final Cut Pro version should match, and if you wait to update until it's safe to do so, you should have fewer problems. But that doesn't mean there won't be problems like crashes and file mistakes that will test your patience and make things hard. The spinning beach ball is a sign that will help you figure out when something is wrong.

The spinning beach ball

Once in a while, the beach ball will spin because Final Cut Pro is having trouble getting enough speed from your disk. Of course, you need an SSD for your media and Final Cut Pro library. If you do anything else, the beach ball will start spinning. Slow disks aren't the only ones that will make the beach ball spin. It could also mean that your computer is too slow or that you have too many programs open at once. It could even mean that your internet link is too slow. I think you should close all programs that don't need to be open while you are working in Final Cut Pro if you see the spinning beach ball a lot. Making improved media or even proxy media for more options with 4K videos is an easy way to speed up a computer that is running slowly. It's not the beach ball that will cause transfer mistakes.

Fixing problems

It is known that the best way to fix problems with Final Cut Pro is to start with the easiest fixes and work your way up to the more difficult ones. It's possible to see the feared red warning message or a vague "**can't export**" message.

It's even more scary when you seeframe or render problem messages. What does it all mean?

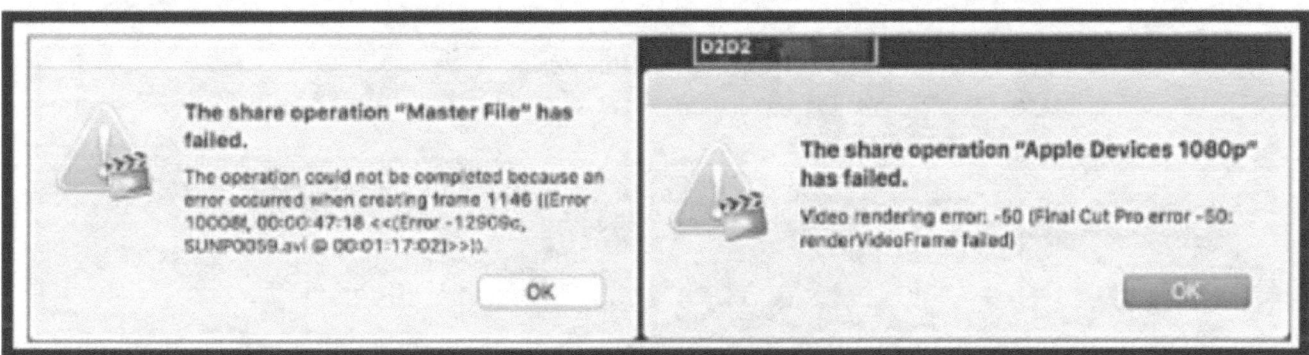

When Final Cut Pro crashes, it shows a message like this:

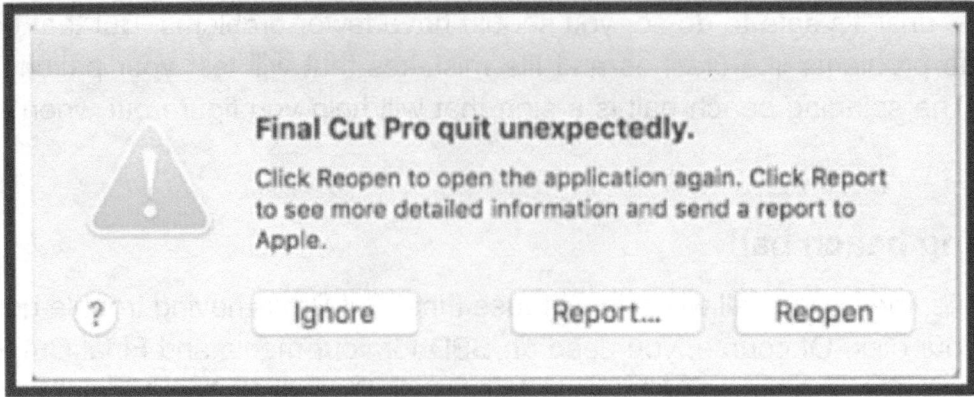

The easy fixes

Most of the time, these fixes only need one or two clicks of the mouse. In general, the problem is most likely to be fixed by doing something simple.

Quitting Final Cut Pro and restarting the computer

It is amazing how many problems can be fixed by just turning the computer off and on again. Most of the time, Iquit Final Cut Pro shuts down the machine and then restarts it after about a minute.

Deleting the render files

This is about as easy as things get. In the **Browser's** menu, choose the library. Choose **Delete Generated Library Files** from the File menu. There will be a box with options for you. I want to tell you one last time that this process will not cause you to lose any original media or work on projects. It is completely safe. Indeed, Final Cut Pro will never delete the source media from your disk.

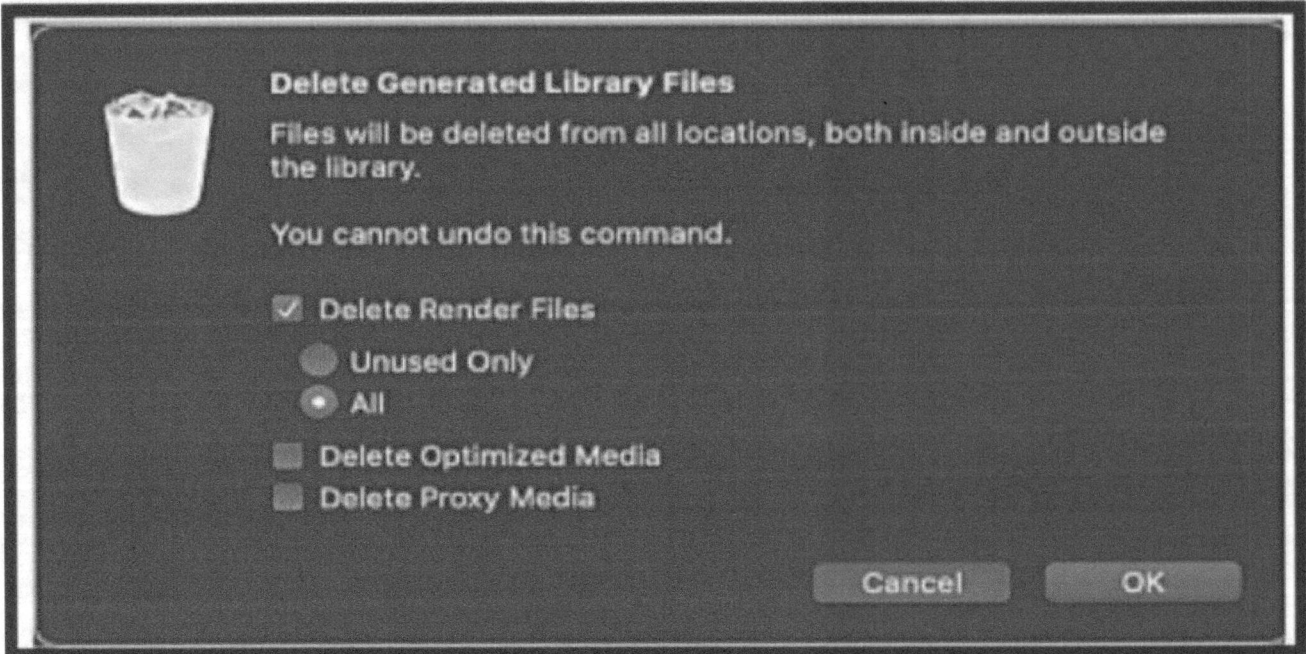

Final Cut Pro render files to speed up exporting and make the editing process faster. Even without them, the editing will go on, and Final Cut Pro will make new ones because it needs them to send. Render files can get damaged and take up space on your machine. Final Cut Pro makes copies of them in case they are needed again. You could delete only the render files that aren't being used, but I would choose all of them because any of them could be broken. There are a few reasons for this. One is that you will have to wait for render files to be rebuilt if you delete them all. Also, get rid of any customized or substitute media you have. If exports are giving you trouble, try again. If that doesn't work, close Final Cut Pro and restart your computer. Then try again. Since I already said that macOS and Final Cut Pro are connected, restarting will reset both of them.

Background rendering

Background rendering is a useful process that aids in rendering by automatically generating render files when Final Cut Pro is idle (such as when you're on the phone or taking a coffee break). While enabling background rendering offers several advantages, it also comes with its drawbacks. You can keep an eye on the process running in the background by hitting **Command + 9** to open the **Background Task** window. When render files are made, the export process goes faster because there is no need to wait for rendering to finish when it's time to export. Also, rendered clips play more smoothly in the timeline, which means that computers that aren't as fast can gain a lot from rendering clips. There are some problems with this method. Rendering clips take up more room on your computer and slow it down a bit, even if you set it to run in the background. In the **Settings** menu of **Final Cut Pro**, you can change how the background is rendered.

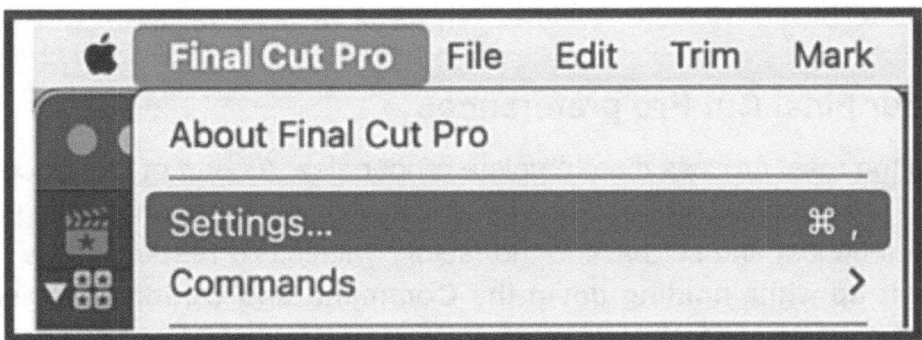

There will be five tabs in the new window. Click on the **Playback tab**. As it stands, the Start after option should be set to a few seconds, since **Background Render** turns on after only one second of inaction. So Final Cut Pro would keep on and off switching background render-ing on and off. Having it turn on after a longer period of idleness is best.

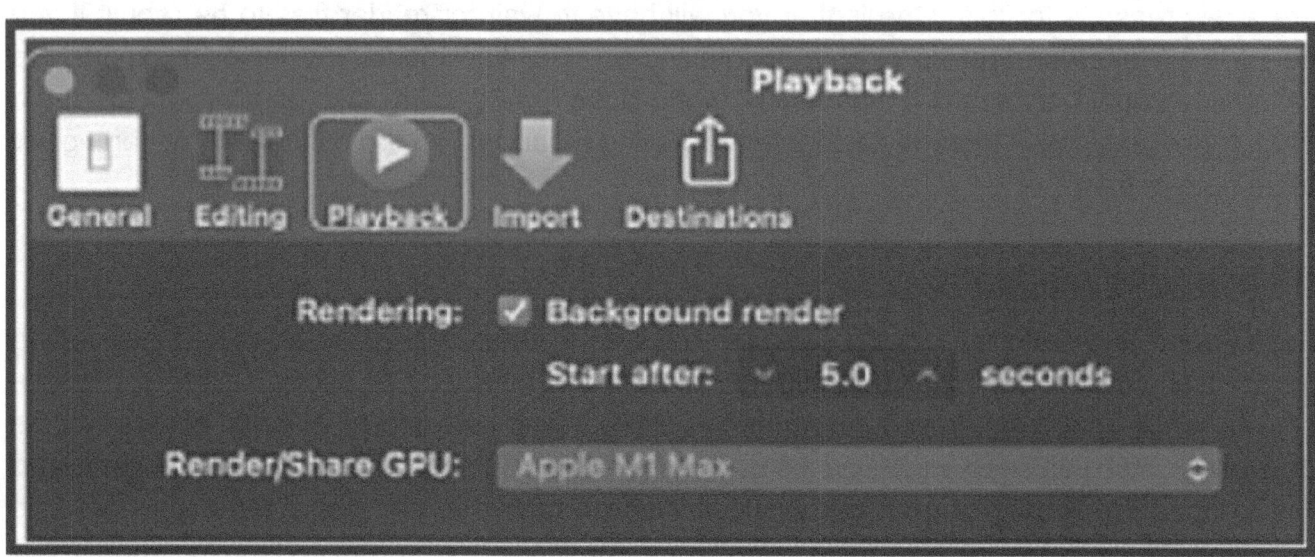

If you have a new computer, I think you should uncheck the **Background Render**. You should try both options to see which one works best for you before deciding. As for the extra room that render files take up, you should always get rid of them when the library is ready to be stored. Even if you turn off background render, processes like **Optical Flow and Multicam** will still render files on their own. The next step is to restart your Final Cut Pro settings if your export still fails after the render files have been deleted.

Resetting your Final Cut Pro preferences

It's easier to do the reset process than to delete render files. As part of the process, temporary files related to Fin-al-Cut Pro are also deleted. However, this time, any settings you made in Final Cut Pro will be lost and set back to the factory values. **To restart, close Final Cut Pro and then start it up while holding down the Command and Option keys. You will see a window that says:**

If you delete the preferences, you will see what's **New in Final Cut Pro** splash screen that showed when you first launched Final Cut Pro.

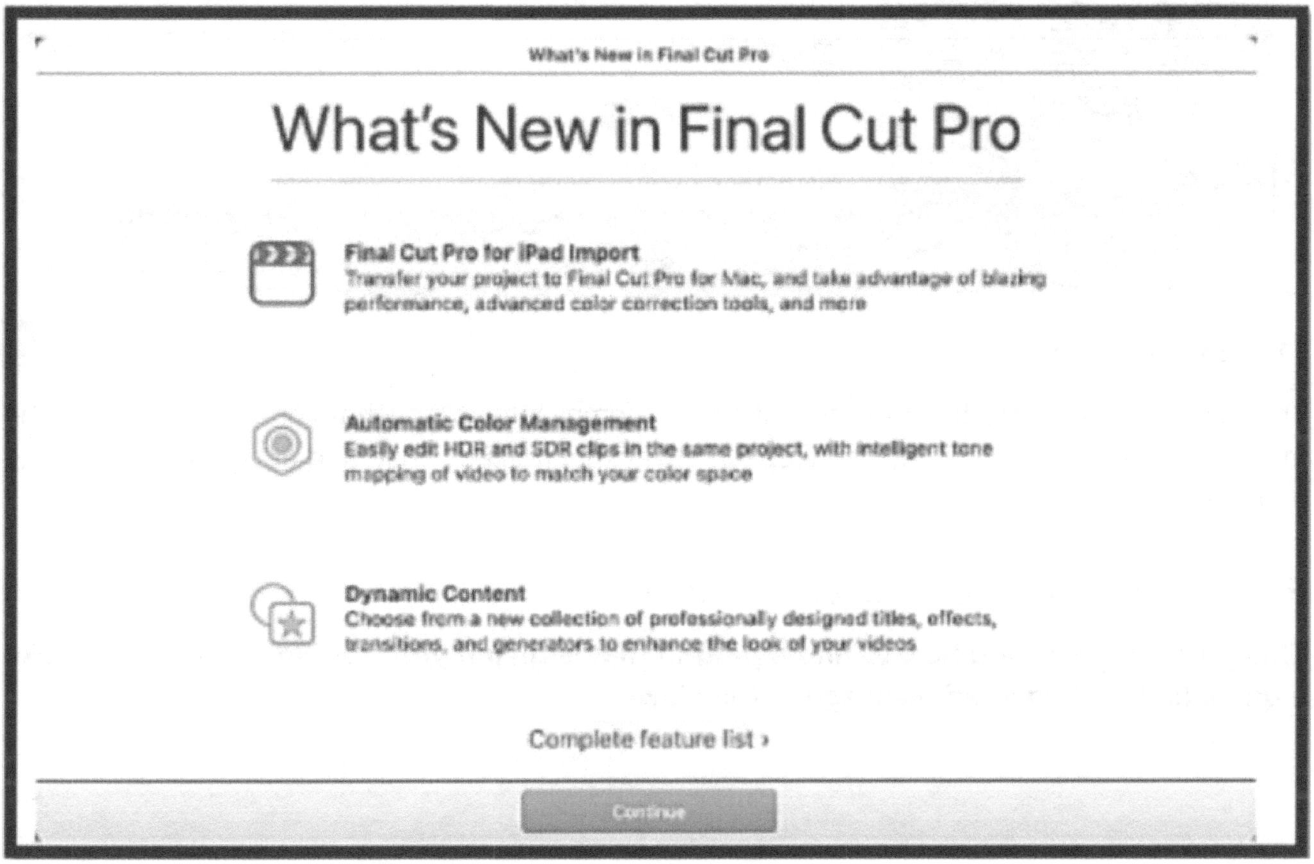

Copying to a new project

This is another easy fix that often fixes problems that stop files from working and doesn't change any changes that have already been done. Find the project that won't export and right-click on it. Then, click on **Snapshot Project**. Change the name of the image. To keep track of which project was the original, it's helpful to put **"Fix Error"** or something similar before the original name. To save the **Fix Error** project, try to export it. If it doesn't export, make a new project, copy everything from the **Fix Error** project, and paste it all into the new project. To copy something to a new project that doesn't work, you can export the XML and then load it into a new library.

The harder fixes

This will take some time to fix because it's more complicated than what you've tried so far. The most important thing is to follow the steps in a way that makes sense and not get upset with the process.

Fixing a faulty effect, transition, or title

This part will show you how to find a plug-in that is giving you trouble. It might only take a quick look to find a red message in the viewer:

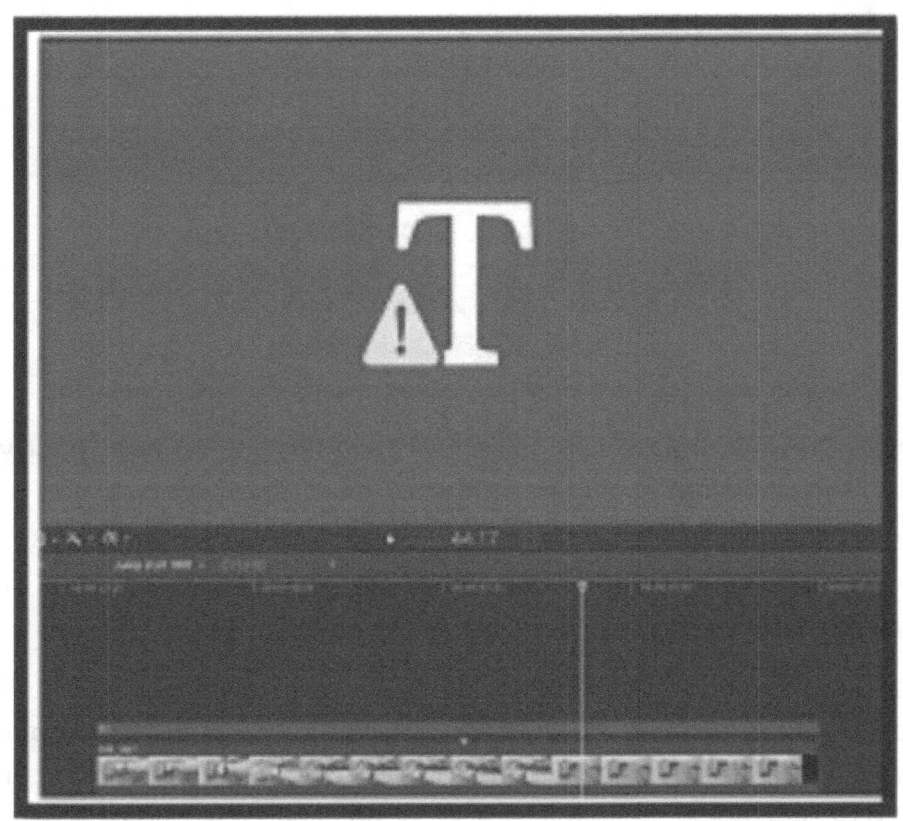

Then you can press the Delet e key to get rid of the plug-in or the Control + V key to cut to turn it off in the timeline.

Deleting plug-ins from your computer

As a quick reminder, the path to the Titles plug-ins folder is as follows:

Change **Username** to your name. On the way, change the **Titles to Effects, Transitions, or Generators** to get to them. To get rid of the **"New Template"** title, all you have to do is drag it to the trash:

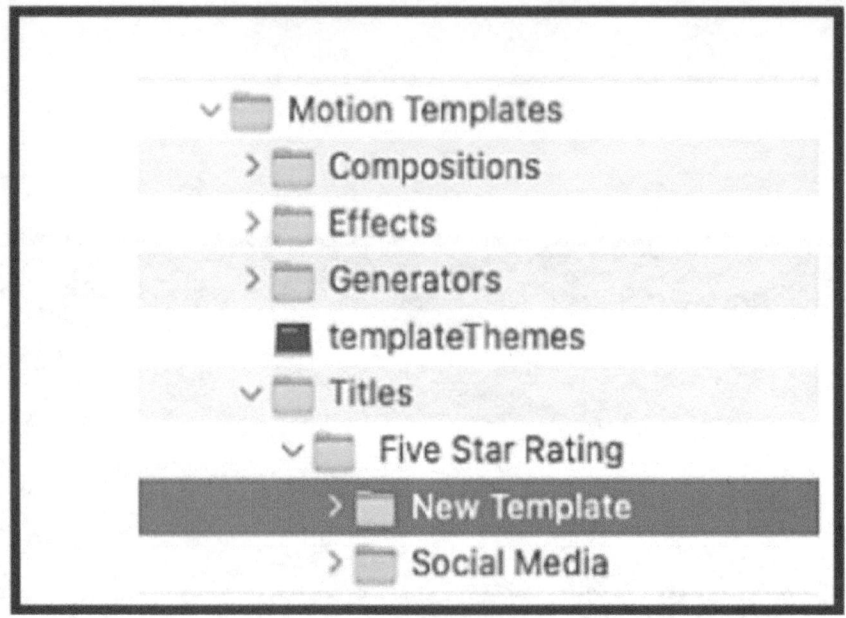

Be careful; the title "**New Template**" will still show up in the title browser after you close Final Cut Pro. Once you've ruled out a plug-in as the cause of the problem, you'll need to find a problem with the project itself.

Locating a corruption

Many things can lead to corruption. First, make sure you haven't used the **Flow** transition, **Optical Flow** to slow down a clip in the time line, or even the **Stabilization** command. **Optical Flow** and the **Flow Transition** should be tried first because they can mess up an export. In the timeline, open the project index, make sure the **Clip** tab is chosen, and type **flow**:

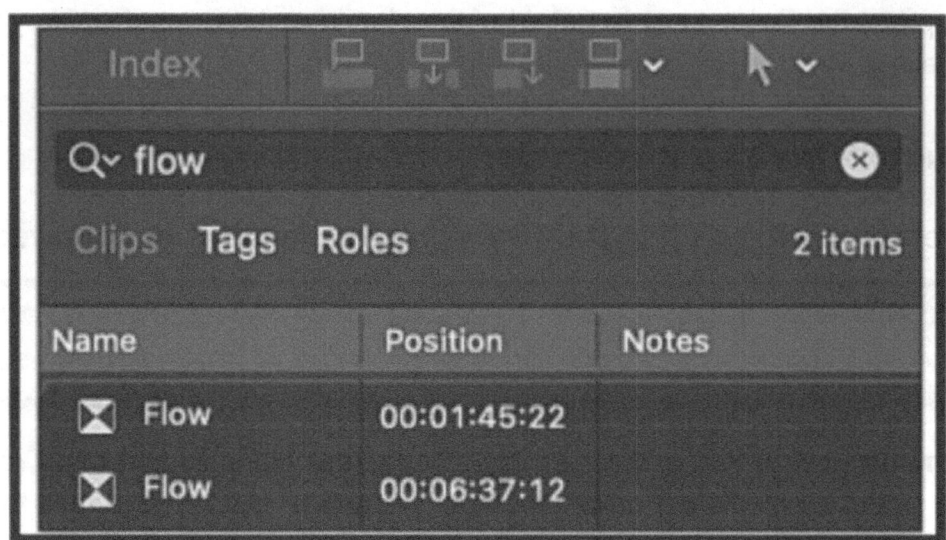

You could delete all of the **Flow** transitions at once, or you could delete them one by one. After that, try to export. In my experience, all I have to do to fix the problem is select the **Flow** transitions in the timeline. This will make the transition work again. It's a lot harder to find the clips that have **Optical Flow and Stabilization**. When you upload from Final Cut Pro, it often shows you a "**Stabilization**" message. Check the clips you think have extra Optical Flow and Stabilization. There is no other way to do it. You can test the whole project if you're not sure if you've used either of them.

Checking for Optical Flow

Press **Command + A** and click in the timeline to look for Optical Flow. This will make a yellow line around all of the clips. To see if any clips have been slowed down, press **Command + R**. Clips that are playing normally will show up in green, and clips that have been slowed down will show up in orange:

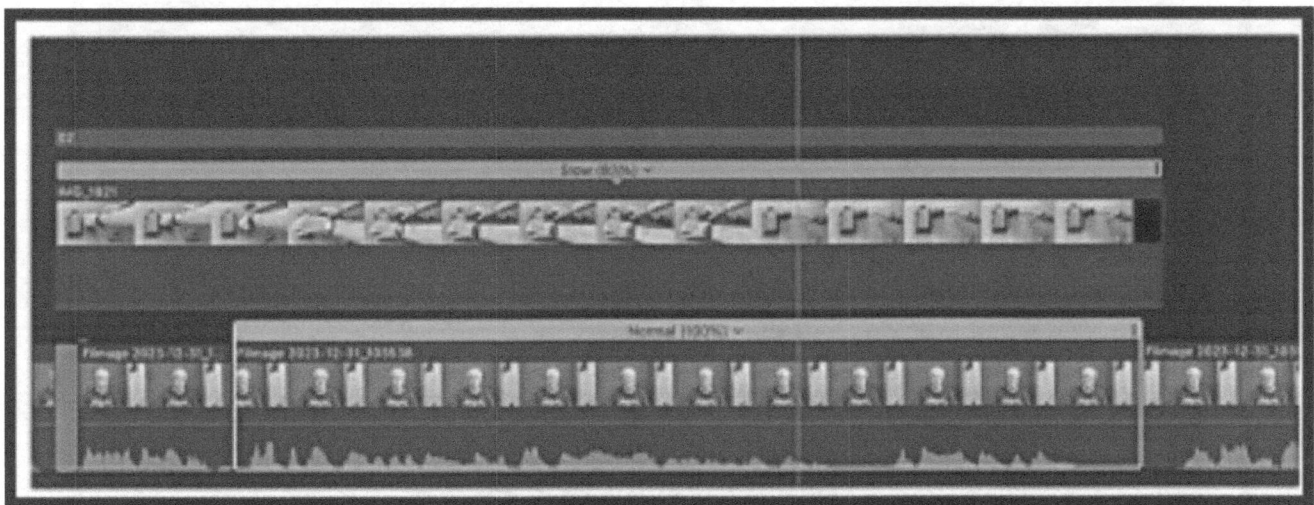

Check the **Video Quality I Optical Flow** for each of the orange clips that you've chosen. You could try Frame Blending in the worst case, but I've found that just choosing the clip with Optical Flow turned on will restart any delayed render for Optical Flow, just like it does for the Flow transition.

Checking for Stabilization

The inspector will show you which video clips have **Stabilization** turned on. You need to group all of the video clips and leave out the still pictures, titles, generators, and transitions. In the inspector, choose the **Filmstrip** tab and scroll down until you see **Stabilization**. Then, select a group of video clips. The box will show a dash if any clips have been fixed.

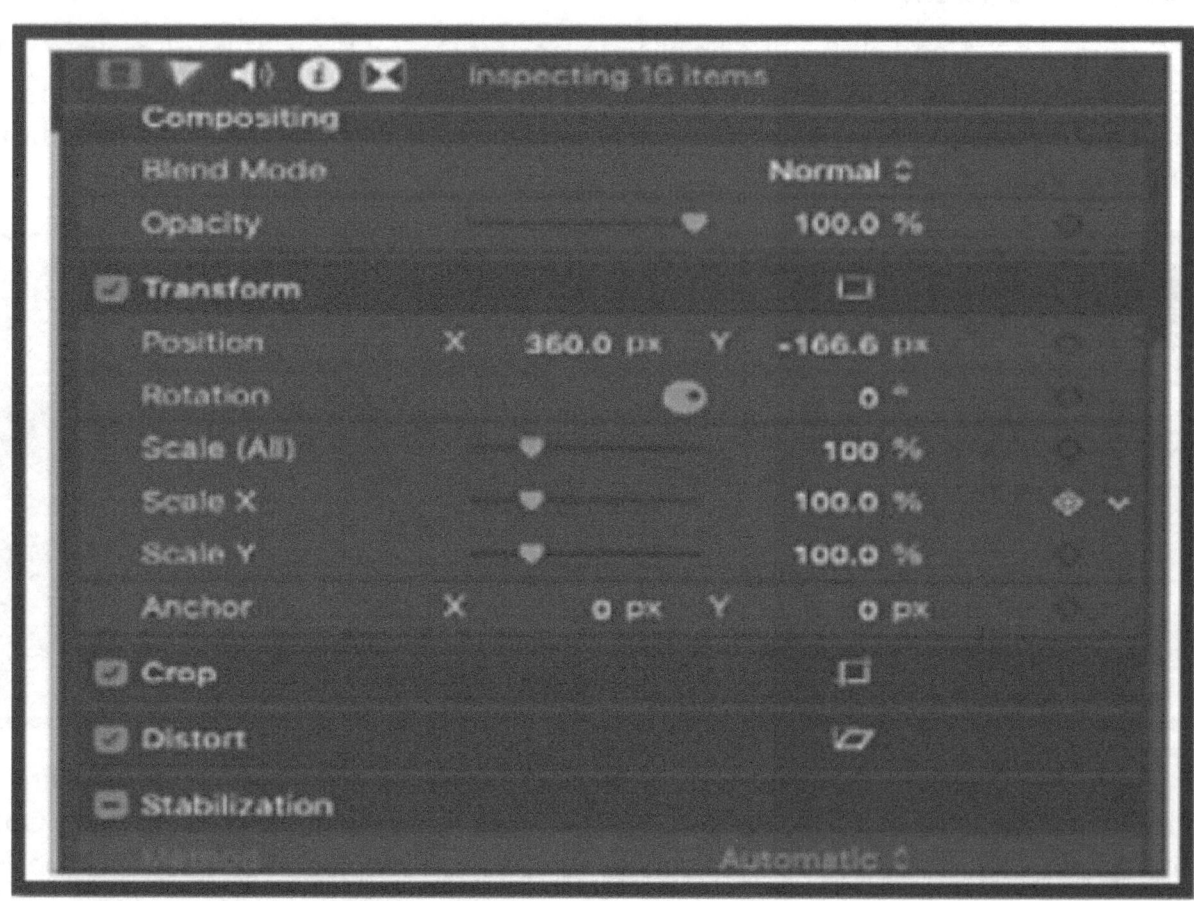

If you select the clips that you think have both **Optical Flow and Stabilization**, then choose **Remove Attributes** from the **Edit** menu, and you can get rid of both of them at the same time. Check that only **Retiming and Compositing** are checked, then click **Remove**.

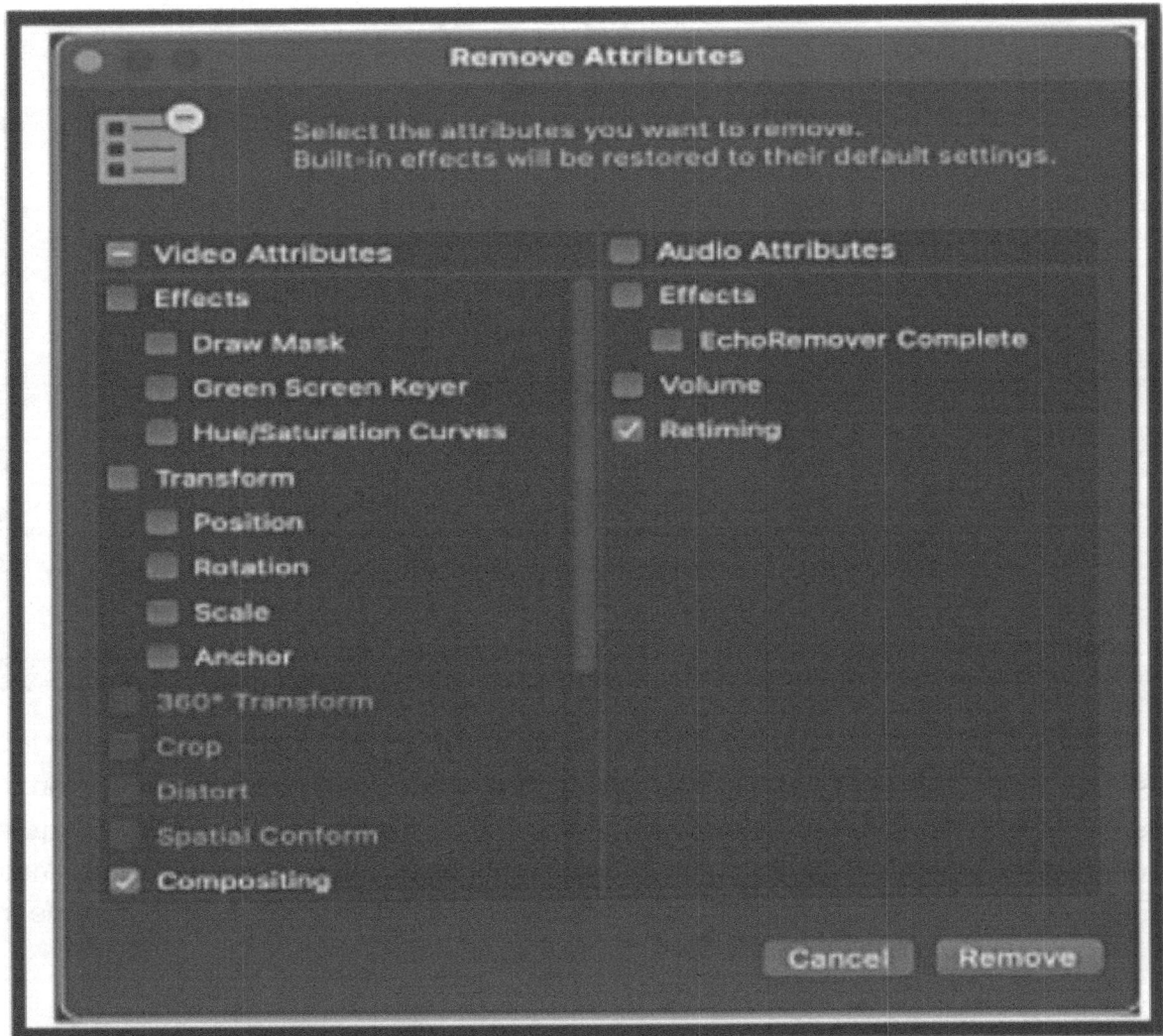

If a project doesn't send, you may also get an error message.

Clearing export error messages

Different error numbers and messages that don't make sense will show up in export error messages. This part will help you figure out those codes.

It's not useful to try to remember all the different problem codes they stand for. It's better to have a process that will help clear up all flaws because mistakes don't happen very often. Error messages come in two different types. If you get an error message like "**Render frame error failed**", it means that something went wrong with a render file that Final Cut already made. A frame number is shown by the second type of mistake. That means it's a broken frame in the timeline. It's the same process, so let's look at the first routine.

Render frame error message

This is a similar process to what you saw when you selected **Delete Generated Library Files**. If you didn't delete the library render files already, open the project in your browser and go to the File menu. From there, choose **Delete Generated Project Files**. I all render files. Press **OK**, and then try the export again. If you keep getting the same error message, close Final Cut Pro and start your computer up again. You should make a new library and copy the project from the old library to the new library if you have already done all the steps shown here.

Copying the project to a new library

For the broken project, select it in the browser. It will then have a yellow circle around it. Choose either **Copy Project to Library** or **Move Project to Library** from the **File** menu.

Then choose New Library.

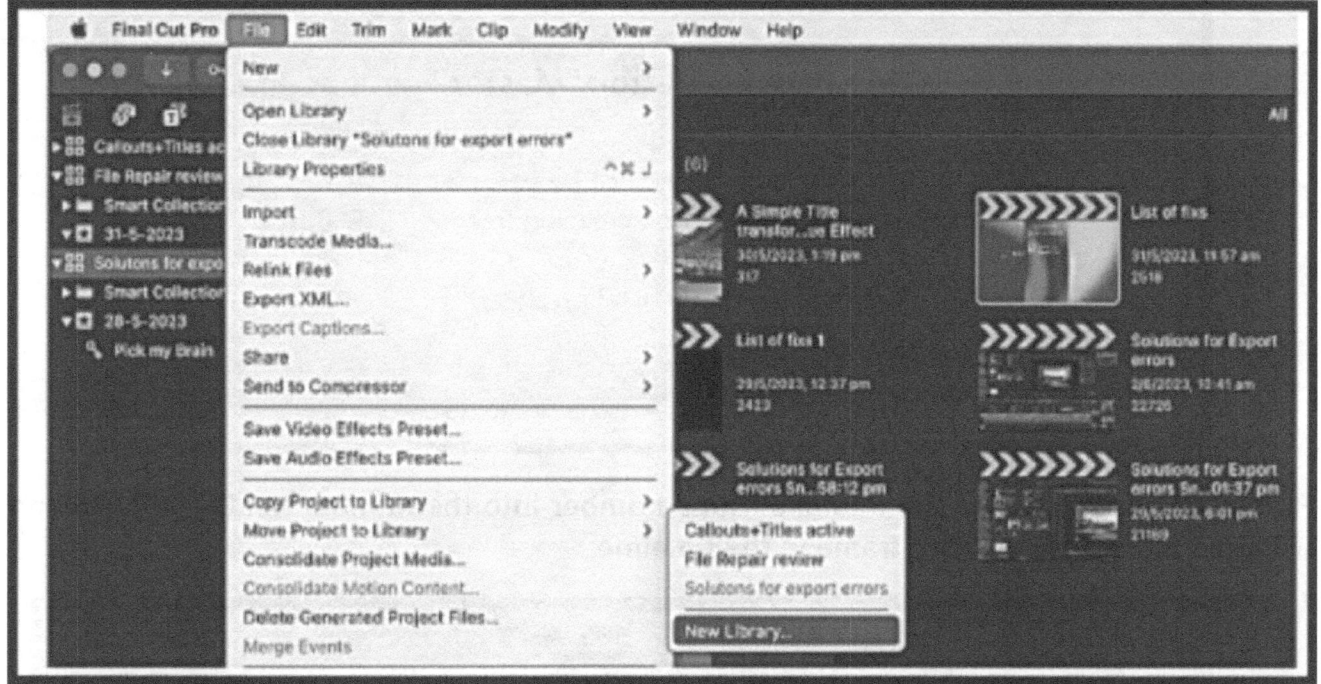

Final Cut Pro may be broken if you still can't download it. Try a different user account or a different computer from now on. Render errors are one of the two types of export error messages; the other is a **Frame error** message.

Frame number error message

Check the problem message for a frame number. If it is there, go to Final Cut Pro settings and change **Time Display to Frames** in the General tab.

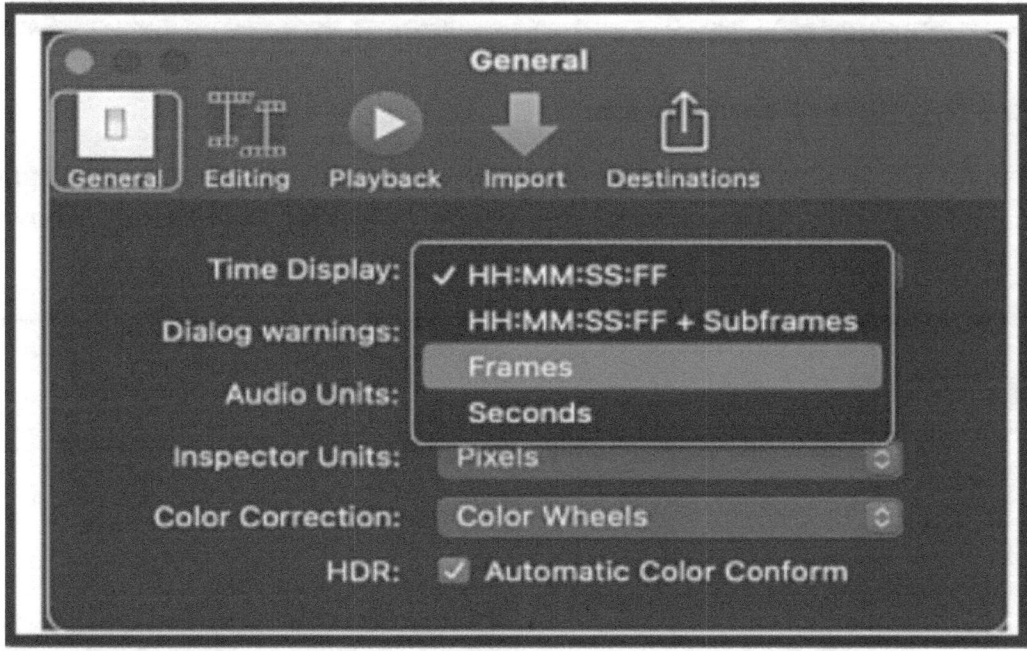

You need to go to the frame number in the mistake message in the timeline. The best place to type the number is between the viewer and the timeline, where the timecode is.

The frame number in the following error message is 1146, as an example:

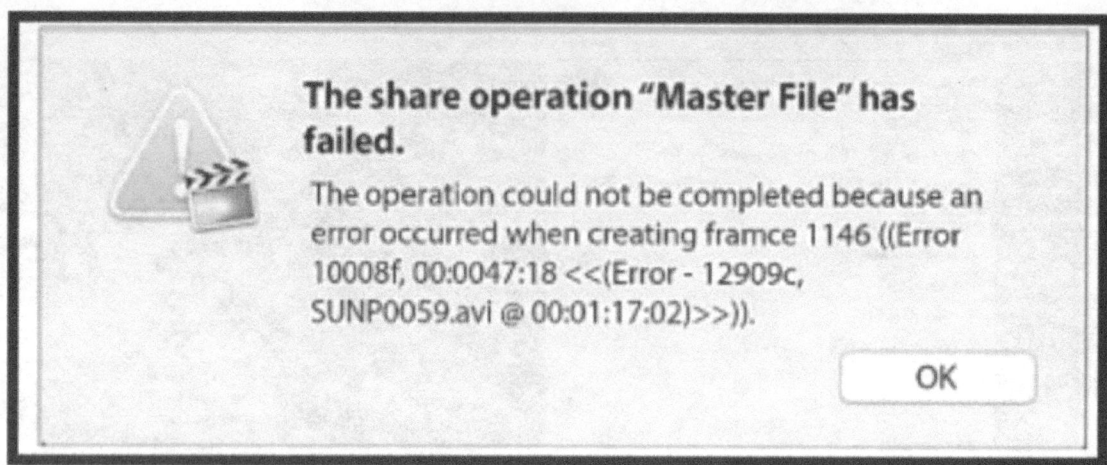

Press "Return" and type the mistake frame number into the number field. The playhead will then move to that video frame in the timeline.

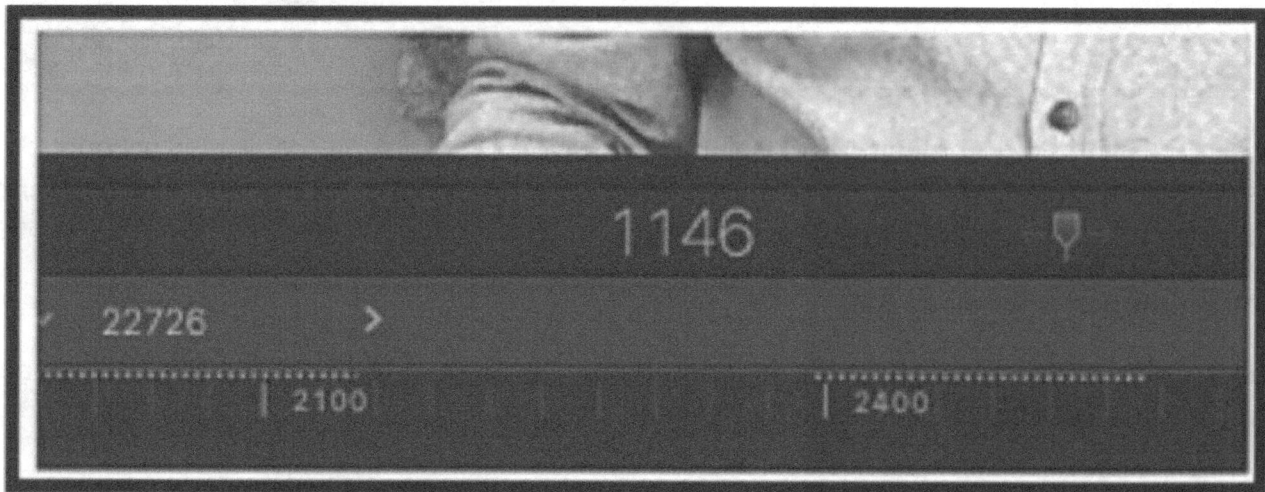

A Final Cut Pro library won't open.

If you try to open a library, you might not feel anything. It's pretty usual for this to happen, but it's easy to fix: just right-click on the purple library icon in **Finder** and choose **Show Package Contents**.

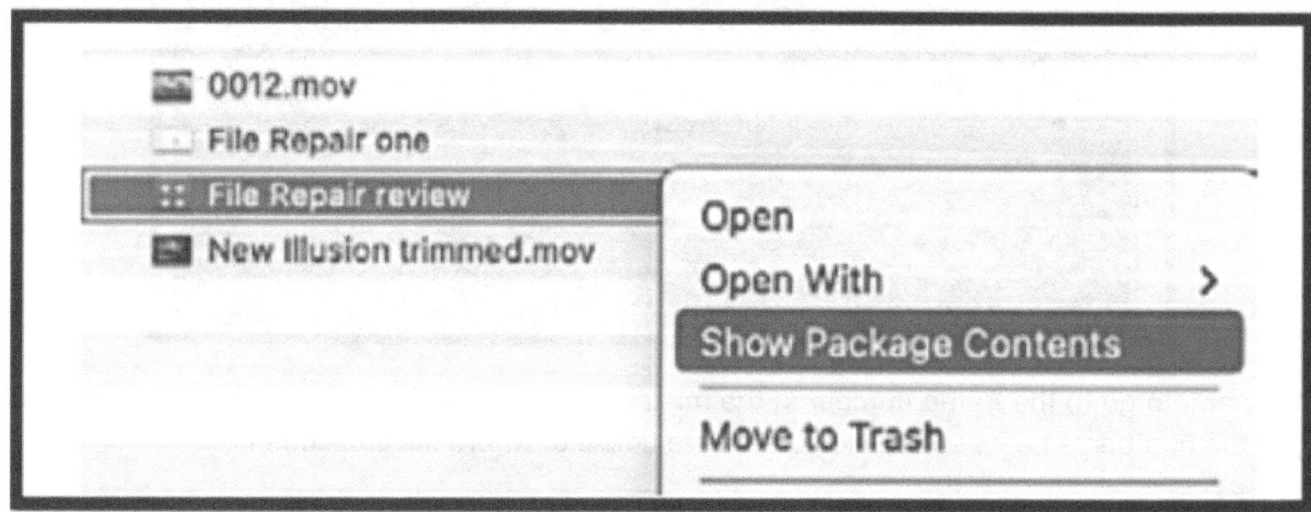

You can delete **CurrentVersion.flexolibrary** and **Settings.plist** without harm. Then try to start the library again. This fix works almost all the time.

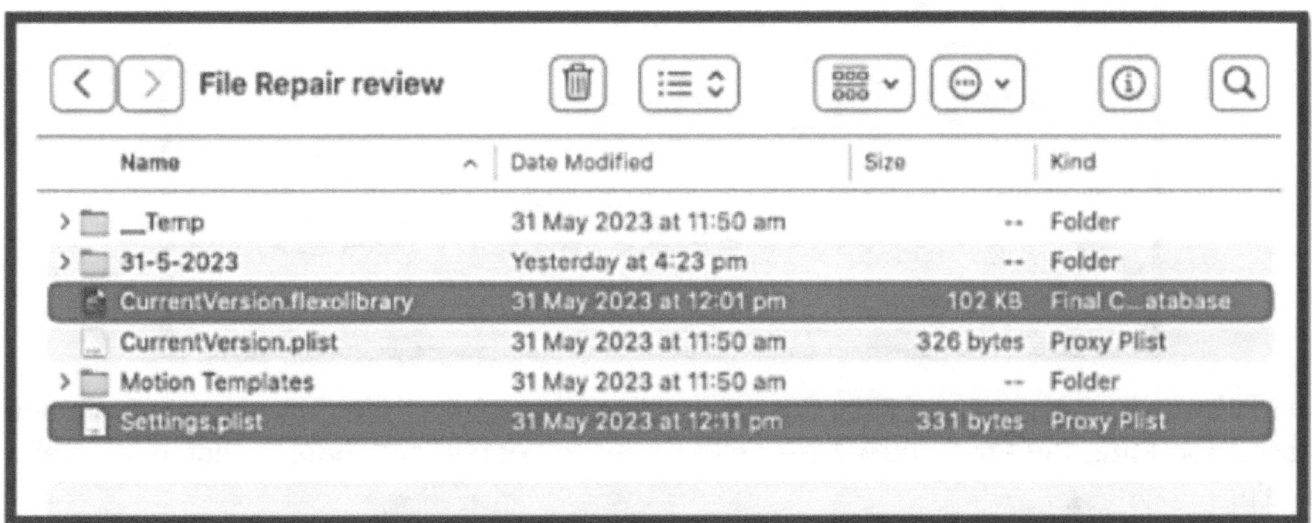

The following message will show up when you open the library again.

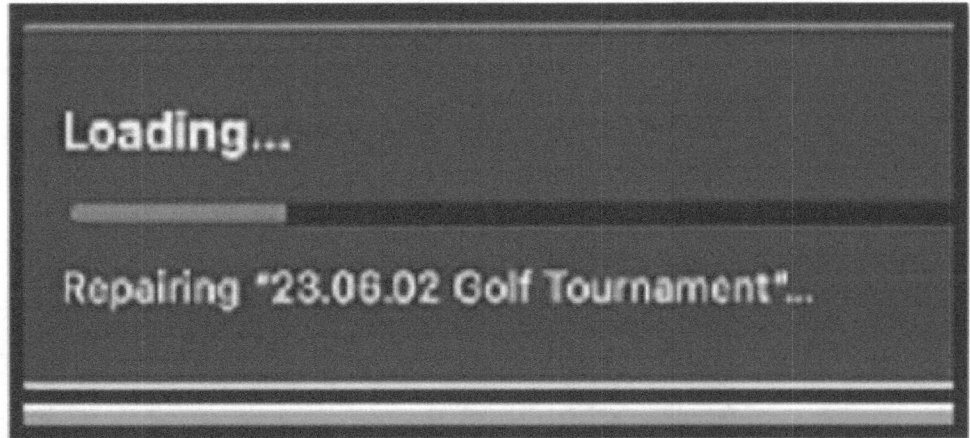

Reinstalling Final Cut Pro

This is not a very bad idea, but don't jump into it without giving it some thought. You will not lose any work or videos that are saved in your files. Depending on how fast your internet is, the longest time you will have to wait is while the app downloads. You should close Final Cut Pro and start it up again before you do anything else. After a new copy of Final Cut Pro has been loaded, **there is no reason to keep the old settings. Pick up Final Cut Pro from the Applications folder on your hard drive, then right-click to shrink the program.**

Throw away the full version of Final Cut Pro, but keep the ZIP file. Now go to the App Store and search for "**Final Cut Pro**." You will see options tions to "**install**" and "**open**." After that, install it again.

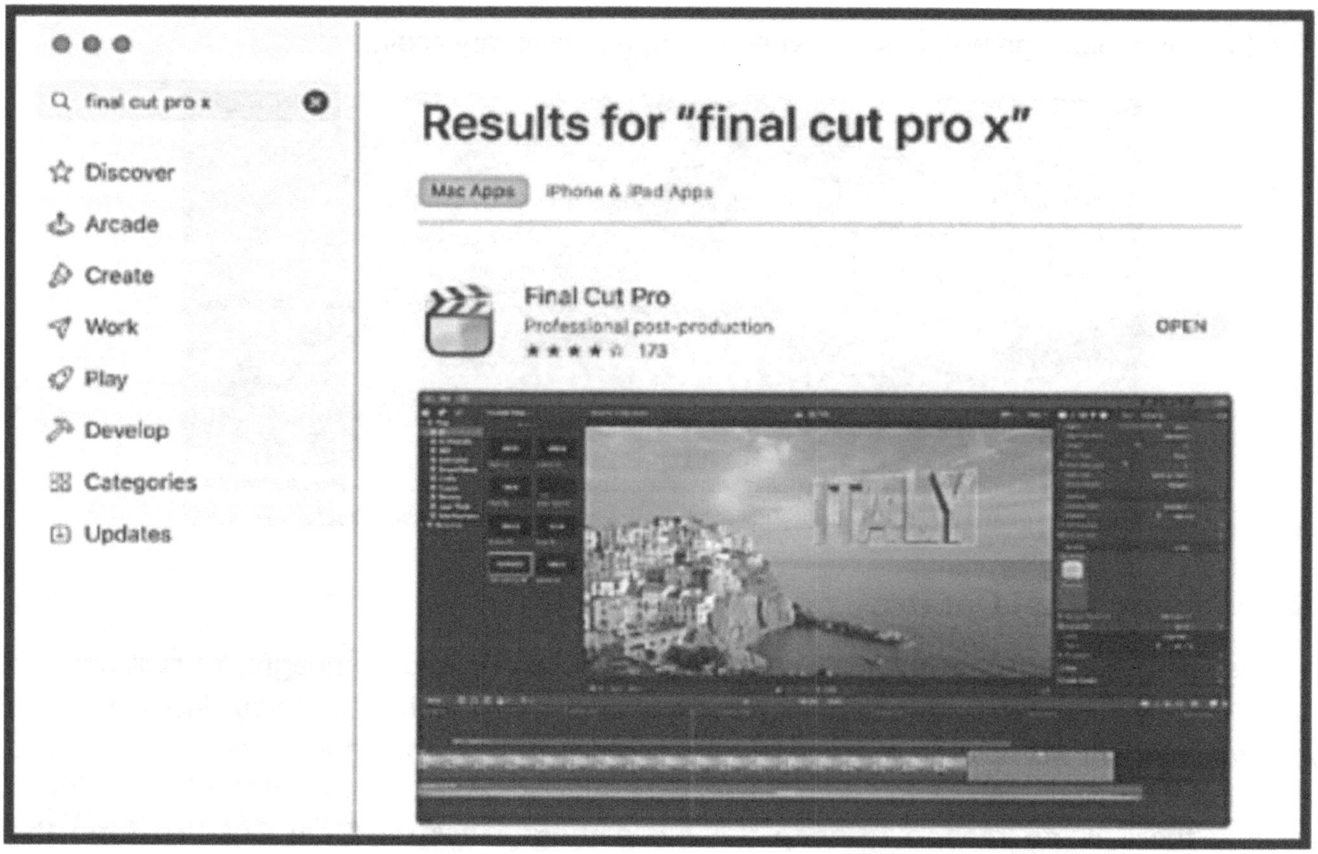

All of your work will be open. Then you can delete the Final Cut Pro ZIP file from the Applications area after making sure everything is all right. You will still have the saved copy of your old version of Final Cut Pro if things don't go as planned. If Final Cut Pro is already open, close it and delete the copy you just downloaded. Then open the ZIP file. After getting to the Apple App Store, you will be back to the same version of Final Cut Pro that you had before. If the problem was still there after the restart, it might be with macOS. Let us talk about how to check macOS and restart it by starting up in recovery mode.

Booting into recovery mode

It depends on whether you have an Intel or a Silicon M-series Mac as to how you can get into recovery mode. With an Intel processor, rest the computer and hold down Command + R until a white bar shows across the screen. When the window opens, follow the on-screen instructions. Silicon M-series Macs: Hold down the power button until you see the HDD and gear icons. To continue, click the gear and then **Continue**. You will be asked to enter a password and pick a master user. In the next box, choose **Disk Utility**. On both copies of **Macintosh HD**, run **First Aid**. There may be one or two **Macintosh HD** in st an ces, depending on the OS you are using. If you have two, run **first Aid** on both of them.

Restart the computer after **First Aid** is done. You will need to talk to *Apple help* if the problems are still there.

Relinking missing media

The first thing you should know about the red "**Missing File**" message is that it's not as big of a deal as it seems at first. For relinking files, Final Cut Proworks works well as long as you tell it where the files are. There is a way to have Sirisearch your whole disk, but it might take a while if the files haven't been organized in a while. Given that you have a rough idea of where the lost files are, it is best to point Final Cut Pro in that direction. It will then find them for you. After finding one file, it will be able to relink others at that spot. To avoid choosing too many files at once to relink, I suggest that you start with just one or two.

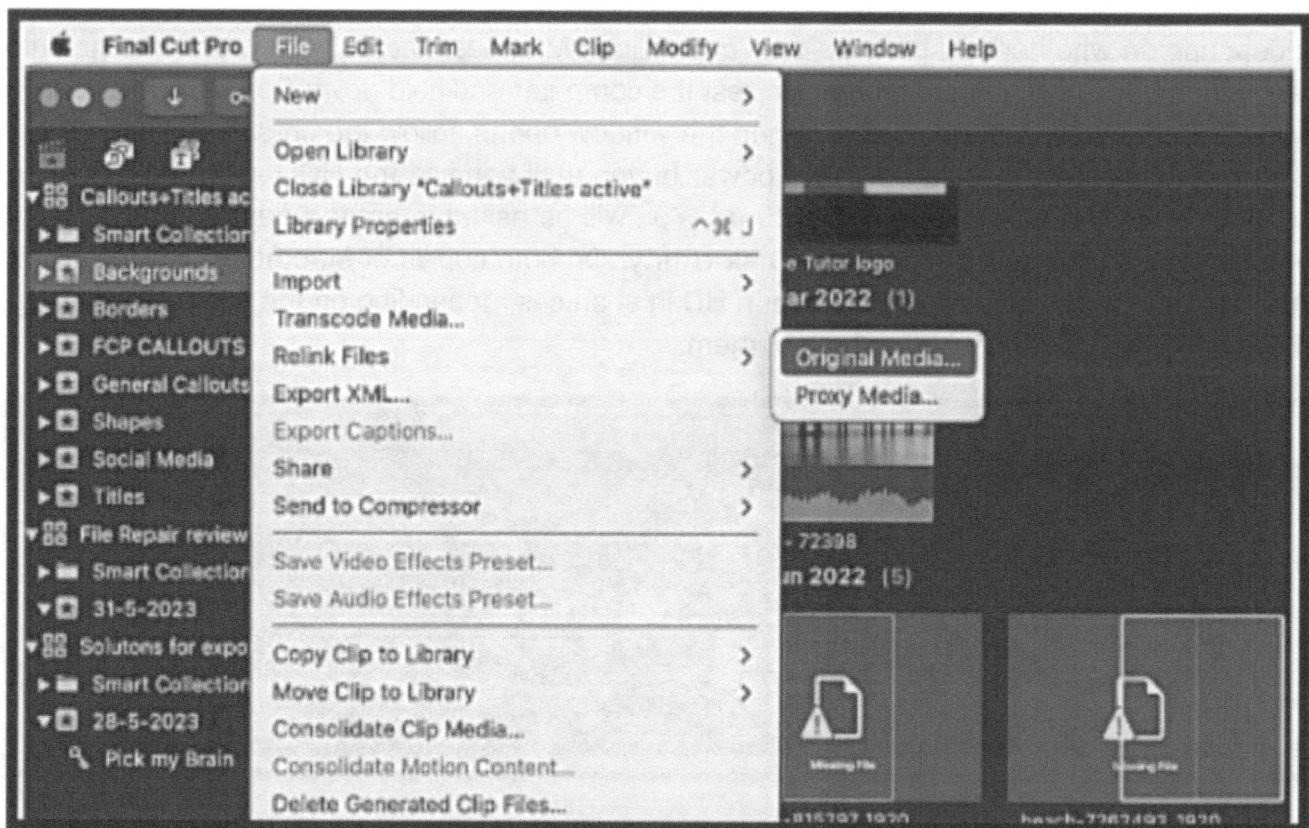

The procedure is to select the media that is missing in the browser, then choose **Relink Files I Original Media** from the **File** menu. You can choose to relink only the lost media or all of the files, whether the media is absent or not. If you choose the second option, "**All**," you can connect to different copies of media in different places than the media that was originally chosen. The only thing that should be different about the files is where they are stored. Pick either the **Missing or All** option and click on **Locate All**. If you only chose media, that is miss-ing in the browser.

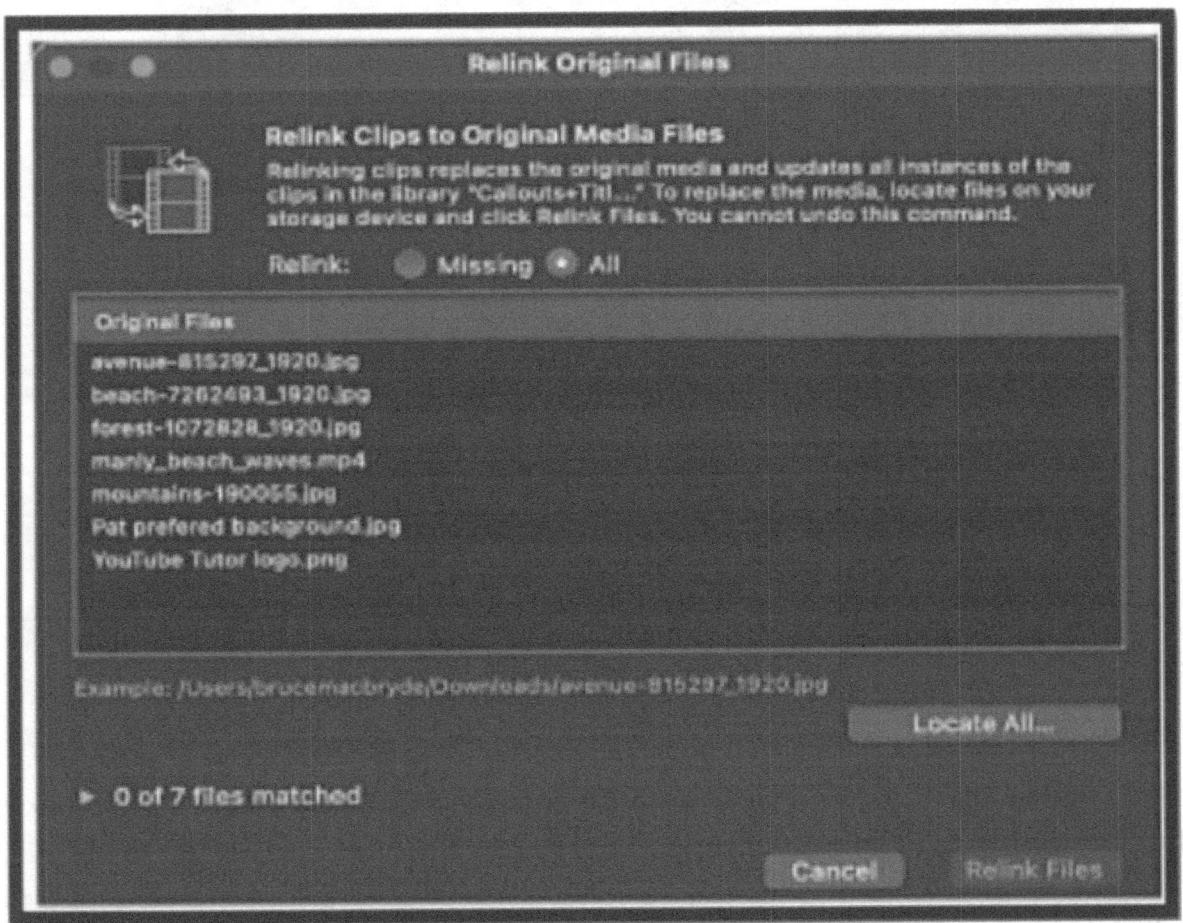

If you think the missing media is somewhere on your disk, you can search that area. You don't have to go to the actual lost file, but don't make the search too narrow either. If you want to relink, don't choose the top level of a disk that has many terabytes of space. It will probably find the file, but the search could take a long time. Once Final Cut Pro finds the lost files, they will be **taken off the list, and you will see how many files have been matched. In the following figure, you can see that 7 out of 7 files matched:**

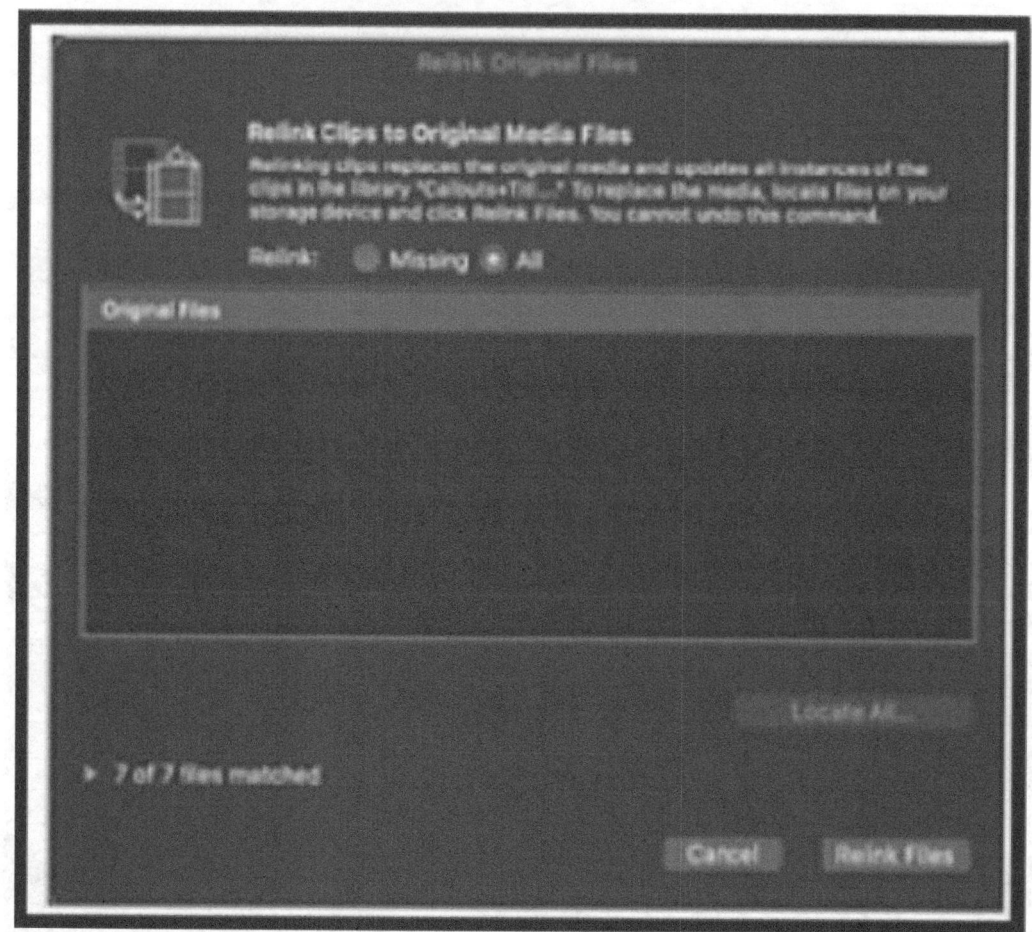

After you click **"Relink Files**," they will show up in the browser without any alerts. It does make you feel **"heart in your mouth"** when you see the red lost word for the first time! If the files are still on your disks, trust relinking to find them. Putting media together after you're done with a library will help you avoid getting the **"missing file"** message.

Consolidating media

If you use the "**In Library**" option in your import settings process, you should consolidate. If you use In Library, your library will take up more space on your hard drive because of the media files. However, the library is fully movable and can be moved as a single unit with all of its contents. You should combine every time you're done working on a library, even at the end of each session. To do this, select the library in the browser sidebar and choose **Combine Library Media** from the File menu. Pick whether you want **Original, optimized, or proxy** media. If you are saving, I recommend that you only choose **Original media**. The other two can be made later if needed, but you will see the red lost file message once the original is gone.

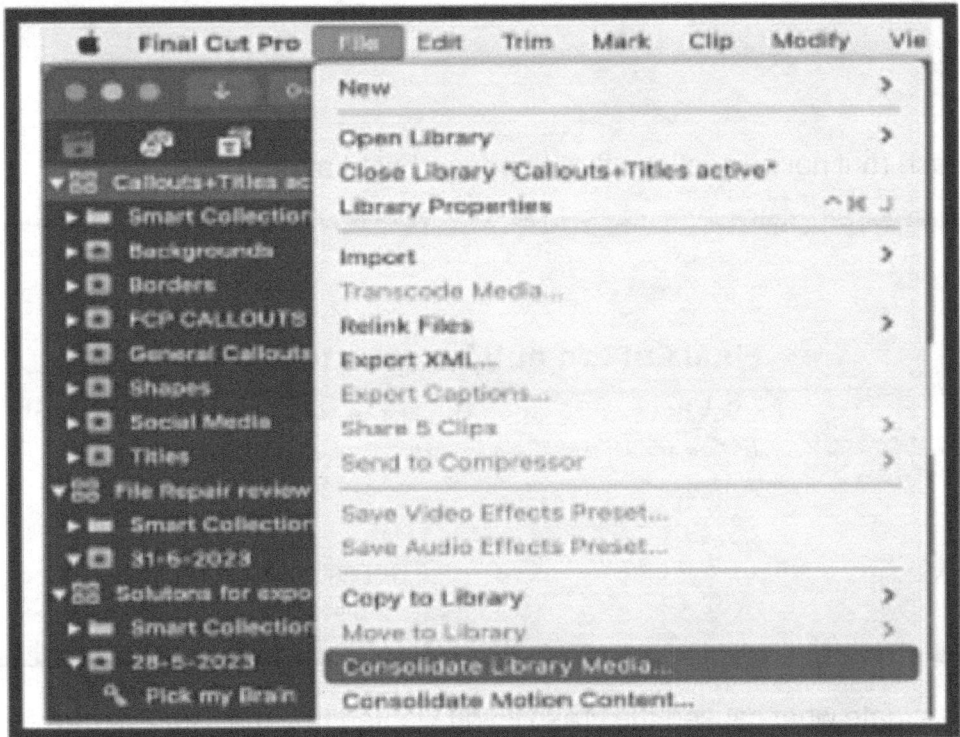

Again and again, click on **Consolidate Library Media** until you see **there are no files to consolidate:**

After this, you can be sure that all the files will be there when you move the library to your backup disk.

Final Cut Pro quitting unexpectedly.

A sudden decision to quit without warning is called a crash. While it can be annoying, the way that an unexpected quit happens does protect you. Normally, your software will quickly save everything you do. This way, if it crashes, all of your work will be saved, even the action that caused the crash (but not any actions that happened right after that).

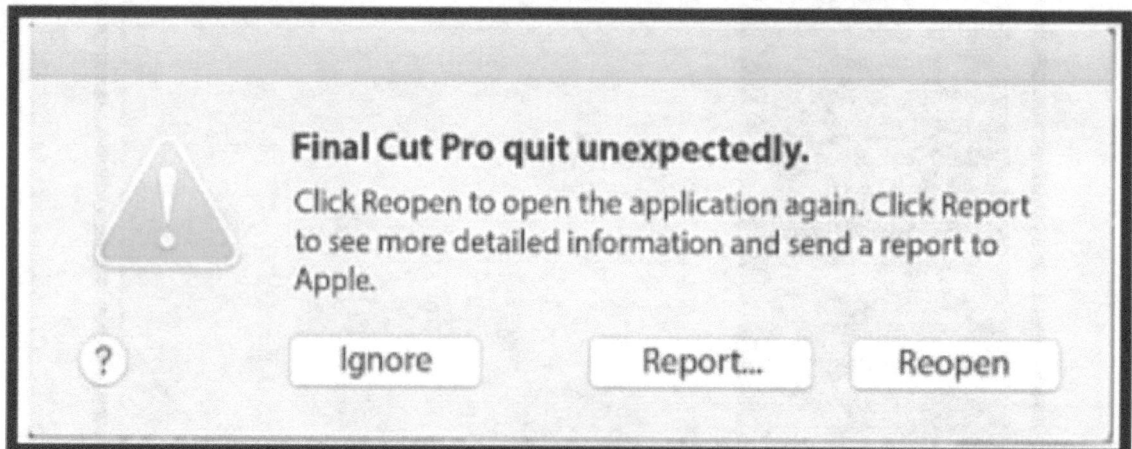

You could investigate what caused the crash if you wanted to. Final Cut Pro makes a report with the technical information and the Mac system's current state. If you choose **"Reope**," you can send the report to Apple so they can look into it. Do not worry-the report does not contain any private information.

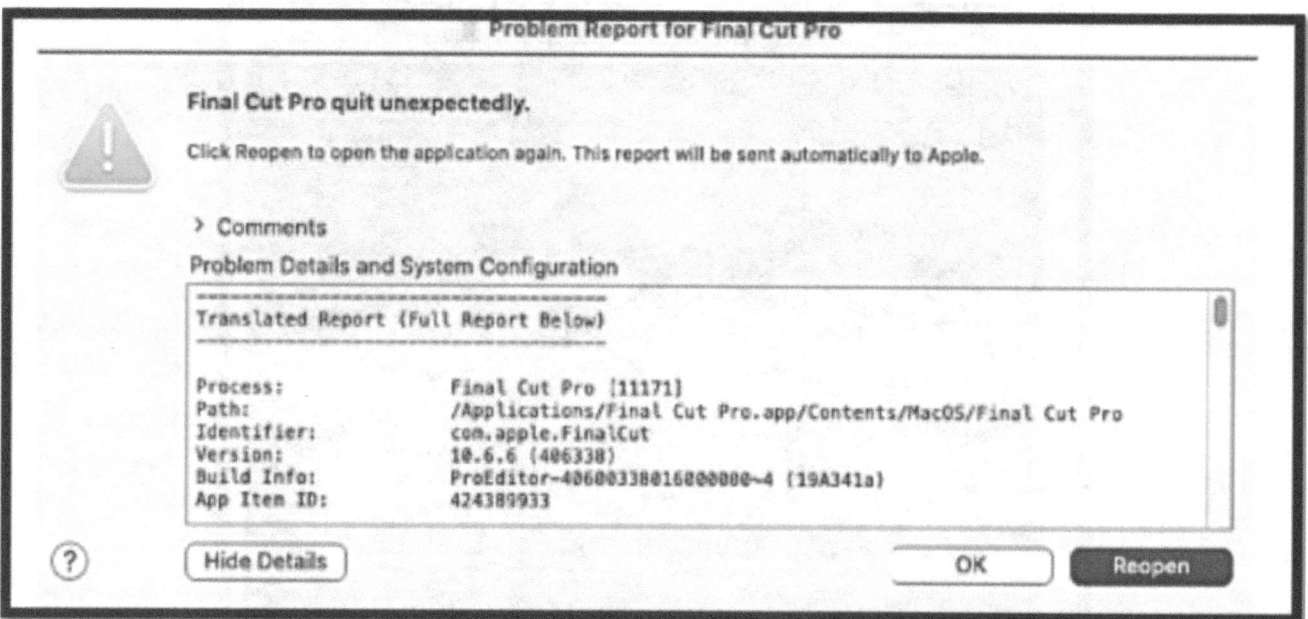

You could send the report, or you could just press OK to start Final Cut Pro again in the same state it was in before it crashed. Even though the playhead is in the same place in the timeline as before, the same files will be opened.

CONCLUSION

As you reach the end of this guide, you've traveled a transformative journey through the world of video editing, unlocking a wide range of tools, techniques, and insights to elevate your creative process. What once might have seemed daunting has become a landscape of possibilities, where every frame, cut, and transition is an opportunity to tell a story or convey a vision. You've learned not just the mechanics of editing but also the mindset of a storyteller, and this marks a significant step in your creative growth.

Video editing is more than a technical skill—it's a craft that combines artistry, precision, and problem-solving. The power to shape raw footage into cohesive and compelling content lies in your hands, and with the knowledge gained, you're now equipped to approach projects with confidence and clarity. Whether you're crafting simple projects, exploring artistic experiments, or tackling professional assignments, the skills you've developed here are a foundation upon which you can continue to build.

The process of editing mirrors storytelling itself: it has a beginning, middle, and end. From setting up a project and organizing your media to refining each edit and adding polish through effects, audio, and color grading, every stage plays a critical role in the final outcome. Each decision along the way reflects your creative intent, guiding the audience's experience and shaping their perception of your work.

The journey doesn't end with mastering the basics. One of the most exciting aspects of video editing is that there's always more to learn. Even experienced editors find new techniques, explore fresh workflows, and experiment with emerging trends. The field is constantly evolving, and your creativity evolves with it. With each project, you'll refine your skills, discover new approaches, and gain a deeper understanding of the medium.

Through this guide, you've explored not only the foundational tools and techniques but also the advanced capabilities that elevate your editing to the next level. You've delved into organizing media efficiently, managing timelines with precision, and employing creative enhancements such as titles, transitions, and effects. You've also embraced the technical artistry of color grading, audio refinement, and advanced editing tools that cater to complex projects.

Equally important is the emphasis on workflow and efficiency. Professional editing isn't just about making each cut perfect—it's about working smarter, saving time, and ensuring your creative process remains fluid and stress-free. You've learned how to navigate challenges, troubleshoot issues, and stay organized, all of which are essential for maintaining momentum and focus during any project.

One of the most rewarding aspects of video editing is the moment when your project comes together—the satisfaction of seeing scattered clips transform into a polished, coherent piece of art. It's in these moments that the effort, planning, and creative decisions come to fruition. Yet, the real reward is the ability to share your vision with others, to connect with audiences and inspire them through your work.

As you continue on your editing journey, remember that creativity thrives on experimentation. Don't be afraid to take risks, try new techniques, and push the boundaries of what you can achieve. Mistakes are a natural part of learning, and every challenge you encounter is an opportunity to grow. The more you experiment, the more you'll discover the unique style and voice that define your work.

Video editing is an ever-expanding field, with new trends, technologies, and formats shaping the way we tell stories. From immersive 360° videos to seamless integration with other applications and platforms, the tools at your disposal are designed to keep pace with the demands of modern media. Staying curious and open to innovation will ensure you remain at the forefront of this exciting and dynamic industry.

As you reflect on the progress you've made, take pride in the dedication and effort you've invested in mastering the art of editing. The skills you've developed extend far beyond the technical—they encompass creativity, critical thinking, and a deep understanding of storytelling. These qualities will serve you well, not only in video editing but in any creative endeavor you pursue.

Moving forward, consider every project an opportunity to refine your craft and expand your horizons. The knowledge you've gained provides a strong foundation, but your growth as an editor is a lifelong journey. With each project, you'll gain new insights, discover fresh perspectives, and build upon the techniques you've learned. Embrace challenges, celebrate successes, and stay curious about the possibilities of what you can create.

Editing is not just about the final product; it's about the process. It's about the decisions you make, the problems you solve, and the creativity you bring to each frame. The journey of crafting a video is as rewarding as the outcome itself, and it's in this process that you'll find fulfillment and inspiration.

As you continue to explore the world of video editing, remember that your voice matters. Every decision you make as an editor shapes how your story is told and how your message is received. Whether you're creating content for entertainment, education, marketing, or personal expression, your unique perspective adds value to every project you undertake. Stay true to your vision, and let your creativity shine.

The knowledge and skills you've acquired are tools for expression and innovation. Use them to push boundaries, break conventions, and create work that resonates with audiences. Video editing is a powerful medium, capable of inspiring change, evoking emotion, and connecting people across cultures and experiences. By mastering this craft, you've joined a community of storytellers who shape the way we see the world.

In closing, this journey has equipped you with the tools, techniques, and mindset to approach any editing challenge with confidence. It has prepared you to take raw ideas and transform them into polished, meaningful content. More importantly, it has instilled in you the understanding that creativity knows no limits. Every project is a canvas, and every edit is a brushstroke in the masterpiece of your storytelling.

Made in United States
Cleveland, OH
03 May 2025